murach's
ADO.NET 3.5
LINQ and the
Entity Framework
with VB 2008

Anne Boehm

MIKE MURACH & ASSOCIATES, INC.

1-800-221-5528 • (559) 440-9071 • Fax: (559) 440-0963
murachbooks@murach.com • www.murach.com

Author:	Anne Boehm
Editor:	Mike Murach
Cover Design:	Zylka Design
Production:	Cynthia Vasquez

Books for .NET 3.5 developers

Murach's Visual Basic 2008

Murach's ADO.NET 3.5, LINQ, and the Entity Framework with VB 2008

Murach's ASP.NET 3.5 Web Programming with VB 2008

Murach's C# 2008

Murach's ADO.NET 3.5, LINQ, and the Entity Framework with C# 2008

Murach's ASP.NET 3.5 Web Programming with C# 2008

Books for application developers using SQL

Murach's SQL Server 2008 for Developers

Murach's Oracle SQL and PL/SQL

Books for Java developers

Murach's Java SE 6

Murach's Java Servlets and JSP (Second Edition)

Four books for every IBM mainframe programmer

Murach's OS/390 and z/OS JCL

Murach's Mainframe COBOL

Murach's CICS for the COBOL Programmer

DB2 for the COBOL Programmer, Part 1

For more on Murach books, please visit us at www.murach.com

Printed in the United States of America

10 9 8 7 6 5 4 3 2 1

ISBN-13: 978-1-890774-52-3

Contents

Expanded contents

Section 2 How to use data sources and datasets for Rapid Application Development

Chapter 5   How to use the Dataset Designer

Section 3   Three-layer Windows Forms applications

Chapter 6   How to work with connections, commands, and data readers

Chapter 7　How to work with parameters and stored procedures

Chapter 8　How to work with transactions

Chapter 9　How to work with object data sources

Section 4 How to use LINQ

Chapter 11 An introduction to LINQ

Chapter 12 How to use LINQ to DataSet

Chapter 13 How to use LINQ to SQL (part 1)

Section 5   How to use the Entity Framework

Chapter 17   How to create an Entity Data Model

Chapter 18   How to use LINQ to Entities

Chapter 19   How to use Entity SQL

Chapter 20   How to use Entity data source controls with web applications

Appendix A How to install and use the software and files for this book

Introduction

Today, most of the critical applications in any company are database applications. Those are the applications that store, retrieve, and update the data in a database like a Microsoft SQL Server or Oracle database. That's why you can't get far as a Visual Basic programmer unless you know how to write serious database applications.

That, of course, is where this book comes in. Its goal is to show you how to use Visual Studio 2008, ADO.NET 3.5, and the new LINQ and Entity Framework features to develop database applications the way the best professionals develop them.

Although this book assumes that you already know the basics of Visual Basic programming, you don't need any database programming experience. But if you do have some experience, you'll move more quickly through this book, and this book will take you to new levels of expertise.

What this book does

To present the database programming skills in a manageable progression, this book is divided into five sections.

- Section 1 presents the background concepts and skills that you need for database programming with ADO.NET 3.5. If you're new to database programming, this section is essential to getting started right. But if you already have database experience, you can skim this section.

- Section 2 shows you how to use data sources and datasets for prototyping and Rapid Application Development (RAD). These are essential skills that will help you develop working versions of database applications at a rapid rate.

- In contrast to section 2, section 3 shows you how to develop 3-layer applications that use presentation, business, and database classes. This is the way professionals develop serious database applications because it gives them complete control over the database operations. However, you'll also learn how to use ADO.NET's object data sources because they can make this approach to application development even more effective.

- In section 4, you'll learn how to use the new Language Integrated Query (LINQ) feature. This feature provides new Visual Basic language that lets you access data in collections like arrays and generic lists. It also provides new ADO.NET classes and services that let you access data in datasets and access and update data in SQL Server databases. And it provides a new XML API that makes it easy to work with XML data.

- Finally, in section 5, you'll learn how to use the new Entity Framework feature. This feature lets you create an Entity Data Model that defines a conceptual model for the business objects used by an application, a storage model for the objects in a database, and mappings that relate the two. Then, you can use LINQ or a special form of SQL to retrieve data into the business objects. You can work with the business objects using code that's generated when you create the Entity Data Model. And if you update the data in the business objects, you can save the data to the database using code that's generated based on the Entity Data Model.

Why you'll learn faster and better with this book

Like all our books, this one has features that you won't find in competing books. That's why we believe you'll learn faster and better with our book than with any other. Here are just a few of those features.

- This book presents everything you need to know to develop ADO.NET, LINQ, and Entity Framework applications. That sounds simple. But to get all of this information from other sources would take you 3 or 4 other books …and you'd still have to figure out how it all worked together!

- At the end of most of the chapters, you'll find exercises that guide you through the development and enhancement of the book applications. That will help you become familiar with Visual Studio and ADO.NET. After you do those exercises, you should be able to apply what you've learned without any further guidance.

- To show you how all of the pieces of a database application interact, this book presents 23 complete applications ranging from the simple to the complex. As we see it, the only way to master database programming is to study the code in applications like these. And yet, you won't find anything like this in other books.

- If you page through this book, you'll see that all of the information is presented in "paired pages," with the essential syntax, guidelines, and examples on the right page and the perspective and extra explanation on the left page. This helps you learn faster by reading less...and this is the ideal reference format when you need to refresh your memory about how to do something.

Four companion books that will enhance your skills

As you read this book, you may discover that your Visual Basic skills aren't as strong as they ought to be. In that case, we recommend that you get a copy of *Murach's Visual Basic 2008*. It will get you up-to-speed with the language. It will show you how to work with the most useful .NET classes. And it will show you how to use business classes, which is essential when you develop 3-layer database applications.

Two other books that we recommend for database programmers are *Murach's SQL Server 2008 for Developers* and *Murach's Oracle SQL and PL/SQL*. To start, these books show you how to write SQL statements in all their variations so you can code the right statements for your ADO.NET command objects. This often gives you the option of having SQL Server or Oracle Database do more so your ADO.NET applications can do less. Beyond that, these books show you how to design and implement databases and how to use advanced features like stored procedures, triggers, and functions.

If you need to learn how to develop web applications with Visual Basic, *Murach's ASP.NET 3.5 with Visual Basic 2008* is the fourth companion. By the time you finish the first four chapters, you'll know how to develop and test multi-form web applications. By the time you finish the book, you'll be able to develop commercial web applications at a professional level. And that's especially true if you have the database skills that you'll learn in this book.

What software you need

To develop Windows and web applications with Visual Basic 2008, you can use any of the full editions of Visual Studio 2008, including the Standard Edition, Professional Edition, or Team System. All of these come with everything you need to develop the applications presented in this book, including Visual Studio, version 3.5 of the Microsoft .NET Framework, Visual Basic 2008, a built-in web server, and a scaled-back version of SQL Server called SQL Server 2005 Express Edition.

However, you can also use Visual Basic 2008 Express Edition to develop Windows applications. You can use Visual Web Developer 2008 Express Edition to develop ASP.NET 3.5 applications. And you can use SQL Server 2008 Express Edition to develop database applications. Together, these products provide everything you need for developing both Windows and web applications. And all three can be downloaded from Microsoft's web site for free!

If you use Visual Basic 2008 Express Edition with this book, you should be aware that this edition has a few minor differences from the Professional edition. The good news is that all of the skills and applications that you develop with the Express edition will also work with any of the full editions.

How our downloadable files can help you learn

If you go to our web site at www.murach.com, you can download all the files that you need for getting the most from this book. These files include:

- all of the applications presented in this book

- the starting points for all of the exercises

- the database and files that are used by the applications and exercises

The code for the book applications is especially valuable because it lets you run the applications on your own PC, view all of the source code, experiment with the code, and copy and paste any of the source code into your own applications.

Support materials for trainers and instructors

If you're a corporate trainer or a college instructor who would like to use this book for a course, we offer an Instructor's CD that includes: (1) a complete set of PowerPoint slides that you can use to review and reinforce the content of the book; (2) instructional objectives that describe the skills a student should have upon completion of each chapter; (3) test banks that measure mastery of those skills; (4) the solutions to the exercises in this book; (5) projects that the students start from scratch; (6) solutions to those projects; and (7) the source code and database for the book applications.

To learn more about this Instructor's CD and to find out how to get it, please go to our web site at www.murach.com and click on the Trainers link or the Instructors link. Or, if you prefer, you can call Kelly at 1-800-221-5528 or send an email to kelly@murach.com.

Please let us know how this book works for you

In 2003, we published our first ADO.NET book for version 1.0. Our goal at that time was to teach you how to become a professional database programmer in just a few weeks. Next, with version 2.0, ADO.NET offered some new features that made RAD easier, and we improved our book accordingly.

Now, with version 3.5, the new LINQ and Entity Framework features offer another set of programming improvements. So once again, we've reorganized and improved our book to help you take advantage of these features. But our goal is still to teach you how to become a professional database programmer as quickly and easily as possible.

Now, if you have any comments about this book, we would appreciate hearing from you at murachbooks@murach.com. We thank you for buying this book. We hope you enjoy reading it. And we wish you great success with your database programming.

Anne Boehm, Author

Mike Murach, Publisher

Section 1

An introduction to ADO.NET programming

Before you can learn the details of developing database applications with ADO.NET 3.5, you need to understand the background concepts and terms. That's why chapter 1 introduces you to the basics of using relational databases and SQL. Then, chapter 2 introduces you to the ADO.NET classes that you'll use for developing database applications as well as the two basic approaches that you'll use for developing those applications.

1

An introduction to database programming

This chapter introduces you to the basic concepts and terms that apply to database applications. In particular, it explains what a relational database is and how you work with it using SQL, the industry-standard language for accessing data in relational databases.

If you have much experience with database programming, you can just review the figures in this chapter to make sure that you understand everything. Otherwise, this chapter will give you the background that you need for learning how to develop ADO.NET applications.

To illustrate the required concepts and terms, this chapter presents examples that use *Microsoft SQL Server 2008 Express* as the database management system. Please note, however, that any application that you develop with SQL Server Express will also run on any of the professional editions of *Microsoft SQL Server 2008*. Similarly, because SQL is a standard language, the underlying concepts and terms also apply to database management systems like Oracle or MySQL.

An introduction to client/server systems

In case you aren't familiar with client/server systems, this topic introduces you to their essential hardware and software components. Then, the rest of this chapter presents additional information on these components and on how you can use them in database applications.

The hardware components of a client/server system

Figure 1-1 presents the three hardware components of a *client/server system*: the clients, the network, and the server. The *clients* are usually the PCs that are already available on the desktops throughout a company. And the *network* is made up of the cabling, communication lines, network interface cards, hubs, routers, and other components that connect the clients and the server.

The *server*, commonly referred to as a *database server*, is a computer that has enough processor speed, internal memory (RAM), and disk storage to store the files and databases of the system and to provide services to the clients of the system. This computer is often a high-powered PC, but it can also be a midrange system like an IBM iSeries or a Unix system, or even a mainframe system. When a system consists of networks, midrange systems, and mainframe systems, often spread throughout the country or world, it is commonly referred to as an *enterprise system*.

To back up the files of a client/server system, a server usually has a tape drive or some other form of offline storage. It often has one or more printers or specialized devices that can be shared by the users of the system. And it can provide programs or services like email that can be accessed by all the users of the system. In larger networks, however, features such as backup, printing, and email are provided by separate servers. That way, the database server can be dedicated to the task of handling database requests.

In a simple client/server system, the clients and the server are part of a *local area network* (*LAN*). However, two or more LANs that reside at separate geographical locations can be connected as part of a larger network such as a *wide area network* (*WAN*). In addition, individual systems or networks can be connected over the Internet.

A simple client/server system

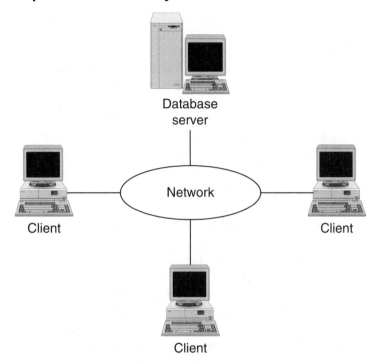

The three hardware components of a client/server system

- The *clients* are the PCs, Macintoshes, or workstations of the system.
- The *server* is a computer that stores the files and databases of the system and provides services to the clients. When it stores databases, it's often referred to as a *database server*.
- The *network* consists of the cabling, communication lines, and other components that connect the clients and the servers of the system.

Client/server system implementations

- In a simple *client/server system* like the one shown above, the server is typically a high-powered PC that communicates with the clients over a *local area network* (*LAN*).
- The server can also be a midrange system, like an IBM iSeries or a Unix system, or it can be a mainframe system. Then, special hardware and software components are required to make it possible for the clients to communicate with the midrange and mainframe systems.
- A client/server system can also consist of one or more PC-based systems, one or more midrange systems, and a mainframe system in dispersed geographical locations. This type of system is commonly referred to as an *enterprise system*.
- Individual systems and LANs can be connected and share data over larger private networks, such as a *wide area network* (*WAN*) or a public network like the Internet.

Figure 1-1   The hardware components of a client/server system

The software components of a client/server system

Figure 1-2 presents the software components of a typical client/server system. In addition to a *network operating system* that manages the functions of the network, the server requires a *database management system* (*DBMS*) like Microsoft SQL Server, Oracle, or MySQL. This DBMS manages the databases that are stored on the server.

In contrast to a server, each client requires *application software* to perform useful work. This can be a purchased software package like a financial accounting package, or it can be custom software that's developed for a specific application. This book, of course, shows you how to use Visual Basic for developing custom software for database applications.

Although the application software is run on the client, it uses data that's stored on the server. To make this communication between the client and the data source possible for a Visual Basic application, the client accesses the database via a *data access API* such as ADO.NET 3.5.

Once the software for both client and server is installed, the client communicates with the server by passing *SQL queries* (or just *queries*) to the DBMS through the data access API. These queries are written in a standard language called *Structured Query Language* (*SQL*). SQL lets any application communicate with any DBMS. After the client sends a query to the DBMS, the DBMS interprets the query and sends the results back to the client. (In conversation, SQL is pronounced as either *S-Q-L* or *sequel*.)

As you can see in this figure, the processing done by a client/server system is divided between the clients and the server. In this case, the DBMS on the server is processing requests made by the application running on the client. Theoretically, at least, this balances the workload between the clients and the server so the system works more efficiently. In contrast, in a file-handling system, the clients do all of the work because the server is used only to store the files that are used by the clients.

Client software, server software, and the SQL interface

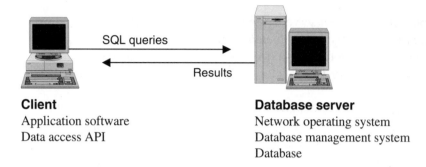

Client
Application software
Data access API

Database server
Network operating system
Database management system
Database

Server software

- To manage the network, the server runs a *network operating system* such as Windows Server 2008.

- To store and manage the databases of the client/server system, each server requires a *database management system* (*DBMS*) such as Microsoft SQL Server.

- The processing that's done by the DBMS is typically referred to as *back-end processing*, and the database server is referred to as the *back end*.

Client software

- The *application software* does the work that the user wants to do. This type of software can be purchased or developed.

- The *data access API* (*application programming interface*) provides the interface between the application program and the DBMS. The newest data access API is ADO.NET 3.5, which is a part of Microsoft's .NET Framework.

- The processing that's done by the client software is typically referred to as *front-end processing*, and the client is typically referred to as the *front end*.

The SQL interface

- The application software communicates with the DBMS by sending *SQL queries* through the data access API. When the DBMS receives a query, it provides a service like returning the requested data (the *query results*) to the client.

- *SQL,* which stands for *Structured Query Language*, is the standard language for working with a relational database.

Client/server versus file-handling systems

- In a client/server system, the processing done by an application is typically divided between the client and the server.

- In a file-handling system, all of the processing is done on the clients. Although the clients may access data that's stored in files on the server, none of the processing is done by the server. As a result, a file-handling system isn't a client/server system.

Figure 1-2   The software components of a client/server system

Other client/server system architectures

In its simplest form, a client/server system consists of a single database server and one or more clients. Many client/server systems today, though, include additional servers. In figure 1-3, for example, you can see two client/server systems that include an additional server between the clients and the database server.

The first illustration is for a Windows-based system. With this system, only the user interface for an application runs on the client. The rest of the processing that's done by the application is stored in one or more *classes* on the *application server*. Then, the client sends requests to the application server for processing. If the request involves accessing data in a database, the application server formulates the appropriate query and passes it on to the database server. The results of the query are then sent back to the application server, which processes the results and sends the appropriate response back to the client.

As you can see in this illustration, two types of classes can be stored on an application server. *Business classes* can represent business entities used by an application. For example, an application that accepts invoices for a vendor might use business classes that represent vendors, invoices, and invoice line items. In addition, business classes can implement business rules.

An application server can also be used to store *database classes*. These classes provide the code that's needed to process the database requests, such as retrieving data from the database and storing data in the database. Because these classes work directly with the database, they are sometimes stored on the database server instead of the application server.

Web-based applications use a similar type of architecture, as illustrated by the second example in this figure. In a web application, a *web browser* running on the client is used to send requests to a *web application* running on a *web server* somewhere on the Internet. The web application, in turn, can use *web services* to perform some of its processing. Then, the web application or web service can pass requests for data on to the database server.

Although this figure gives you an idea of how client/server systems can be configured, you should realize that they can be much more complicated than what's shown here. In a Windows-based system, for example, business classes and database classes can be distributed over any number of application servers, and those classes can communicate with databases on any number of database servers. Similarly, the web applications and services in a web-based system can be distributed over numerous web servers that access numerous database servers.

A Windows-based system that uses an application server

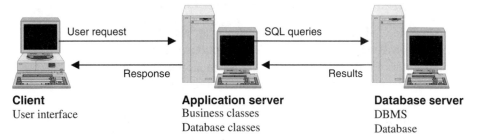

Client
User interface

Application server
Business classes
Database classes

Database server
DBMS
Database

A simple web-based system

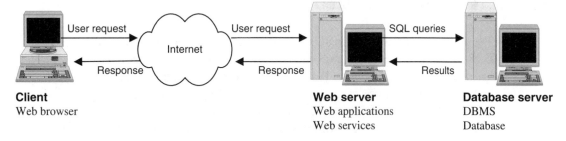

Client
Web browser

Web server
Web applications
Web services

Database server
DBMS
Database

Description

- In addition to a database server and clients, a client/server system can include additional servers, such as *application servers* and *web servers*.

- Application servers are typically used to store *business classes*. Business classes can represent business entities, such as vendors or invoices, or they can implement business rules, such as discount or credit policies.

- An application server can also be used to store *database classes*, which handle all of the application's data processing. These classes can also be stored on the database server.

- Web servers are typically used to store *web applications* and *web services*. Web applications are applications that are designed to run on a web server. Web services are like business components, except that, like web applications, they are designed to run on a web server.

- In a web-based system, a *web browser* running on a client sends a request to a web server over the Internet. Then, the web server processes the request and passes any requests for data on to the database server.

- More complex system architectures can include two or more application servers, web servers, and database servers.

Figure 1-3   Other client/server system architectures

An introduction to relational databases

In 1970, Dr. E. F. Codd developed a model for what was then a new and revolutionary type of database called a *relational database*. This type of database eliminated some of the problems that were associated with standard files and other database designs. By using the relational model, you can reduce data redundancy, which saves disk storage and leads to efficient data retrieval. You can also view and manipulate data in a way that is both intuitive and efficient. Today, relational databases are the de facto standard for database applications.

How a table is organized

The model for a relational database states that data is stored in one or more *tables*. It also states that each table can be viewed as a two-dimensional matrix consisting of *rows* and *columns*. This is illustrated by the relational table in figure 1-4. Each row in this table contains information about a single vendor.

In practice, the rows and columns of a relational database table are sometimes referred to by the more traditional terms, *records* and *fields*. In fact, some software packages use one set of terms, some use the other, and some use a combination.

If a table contains one or more columns that uniquely identify each row in the table, you can define these columns as the *primary key* of the table. For instance, the primary key of the Vendors table in this figure is the VendorID column.

In this example, the primary key consists of a single column. However, a primary key can also consist of two or more columns, in which case it's called a *composite primary key*.

In addition to primary keys, some database management systems let you define additional keys that uniquely identify each row in a table, called *non-primary keys*. In SQL Server, these keys are also called *unique keys*, and they're implemented by defining *unique key constraints* (also known simply as *unique constraints*). The main difference between a unique key and a primary key is that a unique key can be null and a primary key can't. Each column of a unique key can have only one null value, however.

Indexes provide an efficient way to access the rows in a table based on the values in one or more columns. Because applications typically access the rows in a table by referring to their key values, an index is automatically created for each key you define. However, you can define indexes for other columns as well. If, for example, you frequently need to sort the rows in the Vendors table by zip code, you can set up an index for that column. Like a key, an index can include one or more columns.

The Vendors table in a Payables database

Primary key   Columns

VendorID	Name	Address1	Address2
1	US Postal Service	Attn: Supt. Window Services	PO Box 7005
2	National Information Data Ctr	PO Box 96621	*NULL*
3	Register of Copyrights	Library Of Congress	*NULL*
4	Jobtrak	1990 Westwood Blvd Ste 260	*NULL*
5	Newbrige Book Clubs	3000 Cindel Drive	*NULL*
6	California Chamber Of Commerce	3255 Ramos Cir	*NULL*
7	Towne Advertiser's Mailing Svcs	Kevin Minder	3441 W Macarthur Blvd
8	BFI Industries	PO Box 9369	*NULL*
9	Pacific Gas & Electric	Box 52001	*NULL*
10	Robbins Mobile Lock And Key	4669 N Fresno	*NULL*
11	Bill Marvin Electric Inc	4583 E Home	*NULL*
12	City Of Fresno	PO Box 2069	*NULL*
13	Golden Eagle Insurance Co	PO Box 85826	*NULL*
14	Expedata Inc	4420 N. First Street, Suite 108	*NULL*
15	ASC Signs	1528 N Sierra Vista	*NULL*
16	Internal Revenue Service	*NULL*	*NULL*

Rows

Concepts

- A *relational database* uses *tables* to store and manipulate data. Each table consists of one or more *records*, or *rows*, that contain the data for a single entry. Each row contains one or more *fields*, or *columns*, with each column representing a single item of data.

- Most tables contain a *primary key* that uniquely identifies each row in the table. The primary key often consists of a single column, but it can also consist of two or more columns. If a primary key uses two or more columns, it's called a *composite primary key*.

- In addition to primary keys, some database management systems let you define one or more *non-primary keys*. In SQL Server, these keys are called *unique keys*, and they're implemented using *unique key constraints*. Like a primary key, a non-primary key uniquely identifies each row in the table.

- A table can also be defined with one or more *indexes*. An index provides an efficient way to access data from a table based on the values in specific columns. An index is automatically created for a table's primary and non-primary keys.

Figure 1-4   How a table is organized

How the tables in a database are related

The tables in a relational database can be related to other tables by values in specific columns. The two tables shown in figure 1-5 illustrate this concept. Here, each row in the Vendors table is related to one or more rows in an Invoices table. This is called a *one-to-many relationship*.

Typically, relationships exist between the primary key in one table and the *foreign key* in another table. The foreign key is simply one or more columns in a table that refer to a primary key in another table. In SQL Server, relationships can also exist between a unique key in one table and a foreign key in another table. For simplicity, though, you can assume that the relationships are between primary keys and foreign keys.

One-to-many relationships are the most common type of database relationship. However, two tables can also have a one-to-one or many-to-many relationship. If a table has a *one-to-one relationship* with another table, the data in the two tables could be stored in a single table. Because of that, one-to-one relationships are used infrequently.

In contrast, a *many-to-many relationship* is usually implemented by using an intermediate table, called a *linking table*, that has a one-to-many relationship with the two tables in the many-to-many relationship. In other words, a many-to-many relationship can usually be broken down into two one-to-many relationships.

The relationship between the Vendors and Invoices tables in the database

Primary key

VendorID	Name	Address1	Address2	City
114	Postmaster	Postage Due Technician	1900 E Street	Fresno
115	Roadway Package System, Inc	Dept La 21095	NULL	Pasadena
116	State of California	Employment Development Dept	PO Box 826276	Sacramento
117	Suburban Propane	2874 S Cherry Ave	NULL	Fresno
118	Unocal	P.O. Box 860070	NULL	Pasadena
119	Yesmed, Inc	PO Box 2061	NULL	Fresno
120	Dataforms/West	1617 W. Shaw Avenue	Suite F	Fresno
121	Zylka Design	3467 W Shaw Ave #103	NULL	Fresno
122	United Parcel Service	P.O. Box 505820	NULL	Reno
123	Federal Express Corporation	P.O. Box 1140	Dept A	Memphis

InvoiceID	VendorID	InvoiceNumber	InvoiceDate	InvoiceTotal
29	108	121897	7/19/2008	450.0000
30	123	1-200-5164	7/20/2008	63.4000
31	104	P02-3772	7/21/2008	7125.3400
32	121	97/486	7/21/2008	953.1000
33	105	94007005	7/23/2008	220.0000
34	123	963253232	7/23/2008	127.7500
35	107	RTR-72-3662-X	7/25/2008	1600.0000
36	121	97/465	7/25/2008	565.1500
37	123	963253260	7/25/2008	36.0000
38	123	963253272	7/26/2008	61.5000

Foreign key

Concepts

- The tables in a relational database are related to each other through their key columns. For example, the VendorID column is used to relate the Vendors and Invoices tables above. The VendorID column in the Invoices table is called a *foreign key* because it identifies a related row in the Vendors table.

- Usually, a foreign key corresponds to the primary key in the related table. In SQL Server, however, a foreign key can also correspond to a unique key in the related table.

- When two tables are related via a foreign key, the table with the foreign key is referred to as the *foreign key table* and the table with the primary key is referred to as the *primary key table*.

- The relationships between the tables in a database correspond to the relationships between the entities they represent. The most common type of relationship is a *one-to-many relationship* as illustrated by the Vendors and Invoices table. A table can also have a *one-to-one relationship* or a *many-to-many relationship* with another table.

Figure 1-5   How the tables in a database are related

How to enforce referential integrity

Although the primary keys and foreign keys indicate how the tables in a database are related, those relationships aren't enforced automatically. To enforce relationships, you use *referential integrity* features like the ones described in figure 1-6. Although the features covered here are for SQL Server 2008, most database systems have similar features.

To understand why referential integrity is important, consider what would happen if you deleted a row from the Vendors table and referential integrity wasn't in effect. Then, if the Invoices table contained any rows for that vendor, those rows would be *orphaned*. Similar problems could occur if you inserted a row into the foreign key table or updated a primary key or foreign key value.

To avoid these problems and to maintain the referential integrity of the tables, you can use one of two features: foreign key constraints or triggers. A *foreign key constraint* defines how referential integrity should be enforced when a row in a primary key table is updated or deleted. The most common options are to raise an error if the primary key row has corresponding rows in the foreign key table or to *cascade* the update or delete operation to the foreign key table.

For example, suppose a user attempts to delete a vendor that has invoices in the Invoices table. In that case, the foreign key constraint can be configured to either raise an error or automatically delete the vendor's invoices along with the vendor. Which option is best depends on the requirements of the application.

Triggers are special procedures that can be executed automatically when an insert, update, or delete operation is executed on a table. A trigger can determine whether an operation will violate referential integrity. If so, the trigger can either cancel the operation or perform additional actions to ensure that referential integrity is maintained.

Although most database servers provide for foreign key constraints, triggers, or both, not all databases take advantage of these features. In that case, it's up to the application programmer to enforce referential integrity. For example, before deleting a vendor, your application would have to query the Invoices table to make sure the vendor has no invoices. Whenever you develop an application that modifies database information, you need to find out what the application's referential integrity requirements are, whether those requirements are implemented in the database by constraints or triggers, and which referential integrity requirements must be implemented in the application's code.

The dialog boxes for defining foreign key constraints in SQL Server 2008

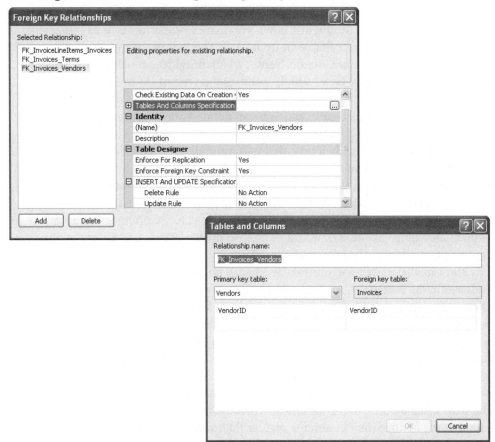

Description

- *Referential integrity* means that the relationships between tables are maintained correctly. That means that the foreign key values in a table with a foreign key must have matching primary key values in the related table.

- In SQL Server 2008, you can enforce referential integrity by using foreign key constraints or triggers.

- A *foreign key constraint* tells SQL Server what to do when a row in a primary key table is updated or deleted and a foreign key table has related rows. The two most common options are to return an error (No Action) or to *cascade* the update or delete operation to all related rows in the foreign key table.

- A *trigger* is a SQL procedure that's defined in the database and executed automatically whenever an insert, update, or delete operation is performed on a table. A trigger can determine if a referential integrity violation has occurred and then handle it accordingly.

- If referential integrity isn't enforced and a row is deleted from the primary key table that has related rows in the foreign key table, the rows in the foreign key table are said to be *orphaned*.

Figure 1-6   How SQL Server enforces referential integrity

How the columns in a table are defined

When you define a column in a table, you assign properties to it as indicated by the design of the Invoices table in figure 1-7. The two most important properties for a column are Column Name, which provides an identifying name for the column, and Data Type, which specifies the type of information that can be stored in the column. With SQL Server, you can choose from *system data types* like the ones in this figure, and you can define your own data types that are based on the system data types. As you define each column in a table, you generally try to assign the data type that will minimize the use of disk storage because that will improve the performance of the queries later.

In addition to a data type, you must identify whether the column can be *null*. Null represents a value that's unknown, unavailable, or not applicable. It isn't the same as an empty string or a zero numeric value. Columns that allow nulls often require additional programming, so many database designers avoid columns that allow nulls unless they're absolutely necessary.

You can also assign a *default value* to each column. Then, that value is assigned to the column if another value isn't provided. If a column doesn't allow nulls and doesn't have a default value, you must supply a value for the column when you add a new row to the table. Otherwise, an error will occur.

Each table can also contain a numeric column whose value is generated automatically by the DBMS. In SQL Server, a column like this is called an *identity column*. Identity columns are often used as the primary key for a table.

A *check constraint* defines the acceptable values for a column. For example, you can define a check constraint for the Invoices table in this figure to make sure that the InvoiceTotal column is greater than zero. A check constraint like this can be defined at the column level because it refers only to the column it constrains. If the check constraint for a column needs to refer to other columns in the table, however, it can be defined at the table level.

After you define the constraints for a database, they're managed by the DBMS. If, for example, a user tries to add a row with data that violates a constraint, the DBMS sends an appropriate error code back to the application without adding the row to the database. The application can then respond to the error code.

An alternative to using constraints is to validate the data that is going to be added to a database before the program tries to add it. That way, the constraints shouldn't be needed and the program should run more efficiently. In many cases, both data validation and constraints are used. That way, the programs run more efficiently if the data validation routines work, but the constraints are there in case the data validation routines don't work or aren't coded.

The Server Explorer design view window for the Invoices table

Column Name	Data Type	Allow Nulls
▶⬤ InvoiceID	int	☐
VendorID	int	☐
InvoiceNumber	varchar(50)	☐
InvoiceDate	date	☐
InvoiceTotal	money	☐

Column Properties

☐ (General)	
(Name)	InvoiceID
Allow Nulls	No
Data Type	int
Default Value or Binding	
☐ Table Designer	
Collation	<database default>
⊞ Computed Column Specification	

(General)

Common SQL Server data types

Type	Description
bit	A value of 1 or 0 that represents a True or False value.
char, varchar, text	Any combination of letters, symbols, and numbers.
date, time, datetime, smalldatetime	Alphanumeric data that represents a date, a time, or both a date and time. Various formats are acceptable.
decimal, numeric	Numeric data that is accurate to the least significant digit. The data can contain an integer and a fractional portion.
float, real	Floating-point values that contain an approximation of a decimal value.
bigint, int, smallint, tinyint	Numeric data that contains only an integer portion.
money, smallmoney	Monetary values that are accurate to four decimal places.

Description

- The *data type* that's assigned to a column determines the type of information that can be stored in the column. Depending on the data type, the column definition can also include its length, precision, and scale.

- Each column definition also indicates whether or not the column can contain *null values*. A null value indicates that the value of the column is not known.

- A column can be defined with a *default value*. Then, that value is used for the column if another value isn't provided when a row is added to the table.

- A column can also be defined as an *identity column*. An identity column is a numeric column whose value is generated automatically when a row is added to the table.

- To restrict the values that a column can hold, you define *check constraints*. Check constraints can be defined at either the column level or the table level.

Figure 1-7   How the columns in a table are defined

The design of the Payables database

Now that you've seen how the basic elements of a relational database work, figure 1-8 shows the design of the Payables database that we'll use in the programming examples throughout this book. Although this database may seem complicated, its design is actually much simpler than most databases you'll encounter when you work on actual database applications.

The purpose of the Payables database is to track vendors and their invoices for the payables department of a small business. The top-level table in this database is the Vendors table, which contains one row for each of the vendors the company purchases from. For each vendor, this table records the vendor's name, address, phone number, and other information. The primary key for the Vendors table is the VendorID column. This column is an identity column, so SQL Server automatically generates its value whenever a new vendor is created.

Information for each invoice received from a vendor is stored in the Invoices table. Like the Vendors table, the primary key for this table, InvoiceID, is an identity column. To relate each invoice to a vendor, the Invoices table includes a VendorID column. A foreign key constraint is used to enforce this relationship. That way, an invoice can't be added for a vendor that doesn't exist, and vendors with outstanding invoices can't be deleted.

The InvoiceLineItems table contains the line item details for each invoice. The primary key for this table is a combination of the InvoiceID and InvoiceSequence columns. The InvoiceID column relates each line item to an invoice, and a foreign key constraint that cascades updates and deletes from the Invoices table is defined to enforce this relationship. The InvoiceSequence column gives each line item a unique primary key value. Note, however, that this column is not an identity column. As a result, the application programs that create line items must calculate appropriate values for this column.

The other three tables in the Payables database—States, Terms, and GLAccounts—provide reference information for the Vendors, Invoices, and InvoiceLineItems tables. The States table has a row for each state in the U.S. The primary key for this table is StateCode. Each Vendor has a State column that relates the vendor to a row in the States table.

The Terms table records invoice terms, such as "Net Due 10 Days" or "Net Due 90 Days." The primary key of this table is TermsID, which is an identity column. Each invoice also has a TermsID column that relates the invoice to a row in the Terms table. In addition, each Vendor has a DefaultTermsID column that provides the default terms for new invoices for that vendor.

Finally, the GLAccounts table provides general-ledger account information for the Payables database. The primary key of this table is AccountNo. Each line item also includes an AccountNo column that specifies which account the purchase should be charged to, and each Vendor has a DefaulAccountNo column that provides a default account number for new invoices. The foreign key constraints that enforce the relationships between the GLAccounts table and the Vendors and InvoiceLineItems tables are defined so that updates are cascaded to those tables. That way, if an account number changes, that change is reflected in the related vendors and invoices.

The tables that make up the Payables database

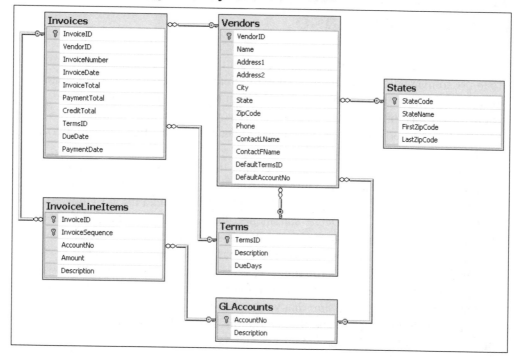

Description

- The Vendors table contains one row for each vendor. Its primary key is VendorID, which is an identity column that's generated automatically by SQL Server whenever a new vendor is added.

- The Invoices table contains one row for each invoice. Its primary key is InvoiceID, which is an identity column that's generated automatically whenever a new invoice is added. VendorID is a foreign key that relates each invoice to a vendor. TermsID is a foreign key that relates each invoice to a row in the Terms table.

- The InvoiceLineItems table contains one row for each line item of each invoice. Its primary key is a combination of InvoiceID and InvoiceSequence. InvoiceID is also a foreign key that relates the line item to an invoice.

- States, Terms, and GLAccounts are simple reference tables that are related to the Vendors, Invoices, and InvoiceLineItems tables by foreign keys.

- The relationships between the tables in this diagram appear as links, where the endpoints indicate the type of relationship. A key indicates the "one" side of a relationship, and the infinity symbol (∞) indicates the "many" side.

Figure 1-8   The design of the Payables database

How to use SQL to work with a relational database

In the topics that follow, you'll learn about the four SQL statements that you can use to manipulate the data in a database: Select, Insert, Update, and Delete. As you'll learn later in this book, you can often let Visual Studio generate the SQL statements for you based on the selections you make. To master the material in this book, however, you need to understand what these statements do and how they're coded.

Although you'll learn the basics of coding these statements in the topics that follow, you may want to know more than what's presented here. In that case, we recommend *Murach's SQL Server 2008 for Developers*. In addition to the Select, Insert, Update, and Delete statements, this book teaches you how to code the statements that you use to define the data in a database, and it teaches you how to use the other features of SQL Server that the top professionals use.

Although SQL is a standard language, each DBMS is likely to have its own *SQL dialect*, which includes extensions to the standard language. So when you use SQL, you need to make sure that you're using the dialect that's supported by your DBMS. In this chapter and throughout this book, all of the SQL examples are for Microsoft SQL Server's dialect, which is called *Transact-SQL*.

How to query a single table

Figure 1-9 shows how to use a Select statement to query a single table in a database. In the syntax summary, you can see that the Select clause names the columns to be retrieved and the From clause names the table that contains the columns. You can also code a Where clause that gives criteria for the rows to be selected. And you can code an Order By clause that names one or more columns that the results should be sorted by and indicates whether each column should be sorted in ascending or descending sequence.

If you study the Select statement below the syntax summary, you can see how this works. Here, the Select statement retrieves columns from the Invoices table. It selects a row only if the row has a balance due that's greater than zero. And it sorts the returned rows by invoice date in ascending sequence (the default).

Please note in this Select statement that the last column in the query, BalanceDue, is calculated by subtracting PaymentTotal and CreditTotal from InvoiceTotal. In other words, a column by the name of BalanceDue doesn't actually exist in the database. This type of column is called a *calculated column*, and it exists only in the results of the query.

This figure also shows the *result table*, or *result set*, that's returned by the Select statement. A result set is a logical table that's created temporarily within the database. When an application requests data from a database, it receives a result set.

Simplified syntax of the Select statement

```
SELECT column-1 [, column-2]...
FROM table-1
[WHERE selection-criteria]
[ORDER BY column-1 [ASC|DESC] [, column-2 [ASC|DESC]]...]
```

A Select statement that retrieves and sorts selected columns and rows from the Invoices table

```
SELECT InvoiceNumber, InvoiceDate, InvoiceTotal,
    PaymentTotal, CreditTotal,
    InvoiceTotal - PaymentTotal - CreditTotal AS BalanceDue
FROM Invoices
WHERE InvoiceTotal - PaymentTotal - CreditTotal > 0
ORDER BY InvoiceDate
```

The result set defined by the Select statement

	InvoiceNumber	InvoiceDate	InvoiceTotal	PaymentTotal	CreditTotal	BalanceDue
1	39104	2008-09-10	85.31	0.00	0.00	85.31
2	963253264	2008-09-18	52.25	0.00	0.00	52.25
3	31361833	2008-09-21	579.42	0.00	0.00	579.42
4	263253268	2008-09-21	59.97	0.00	0.00	59.97
5	263253270	2008-09-22	67.92	0.00	0.00	67.92
6	263253273	2008-09-22	30.75	0.00	0.00	30.75
7	P-0608	2008-09-23	20551.18	0.00	1200.00	19351.18
8	9982771	2008-09-24	503.20	0.00	0.00	503.20
9	134116	2008-09-28	90.36	0.00	0.00	90.36
10	0-2436	2008-09-30	10976.06	0.00	0.00	10976.06
11	547480102	2008-10-01	224.00	0.00	0.00	224.00

Concepts

- The result of a Select statement is a *result table*, or *result set*, like the one shown above. A result set is a logical set of rows that consists of all of the columns and rows requested by the Select statement.

- The Select clause lists the columns to be included in the result set. This list can include *calculated columns* that are calculated from other columns in the table and columns that use SQL Server *functions*.

- The From clause names the table that the data will be retrieved from.

- The Where clause provides a condition that specifies which rows should be retrieved. To retrieve all rows from a table, omit the Where clause.

- The Order By clause lists the columns that the results are sorted by and indicates whether each column is sorted in ascending or descending sequence.

- To select all of the columns in a table, you can code an asterisk (*) in place of the column names. For example, this statement will select all of the columns from the Invoices table:

```
Select * From Invoices
```

Figure 1-9   How to query a single table

How to join data from two or more tables

Figure 1-10 presents the syntax of the Select statement for retrieving data from two tables. This type of operation is called a *join* because the data from the two tables is joined together into a single result set. For example, the Select statement in this figure joins data from the Invoices and Vendors table into a single result set.

An *inner join* is the most common type of join. When you use an inner join, rows from the two tables in the join are included in the result set only if their related columns match. These matching columns are specified in the From clause of the Select statement. In the Select statement in this figure, for example, rows from the Invoices and Vendors tables are included only if the value of the VendorID column in the Vendors table matches the value of the VendorID column in one or more rows in the Invoices table. If there aren't any invoices for a particular vendor, that vendor won't be included in the result set.

Although this figure shows how to join data from two tables, you should know that you can extend this syntax to join data from additional tables. If, for example, you want to include data from the InvoiceLineItems table in the results shown in this figure, you can code the From clause of the Select statement like this:

```
From Vendors
    Join Invoices
        On Vendors.VendorID = Invoices.VendorID
    Join InvoiceLineItems
        On Invoices.InvoiceID = InvoiceLineItems.InvoiceID
```

Then, in the column list of the Select statement, you can include any of the columns in the InvoiceLineItems table.

The syntax of the Select statement for joining two tables

```
SELECT column-list
FROM table-1
    [INNER] JOIN table-2
    ON table-1.column-1 {=|<|>|<=|>=|<>} table-2.column-2
[WHERE selection-criteria]
[ORDER BY column-list]
```

A Select statement that joins data from the Vendors and Invoices tables

```
SELECT Name, InvoiceNumber, InvoiceDate, InvoiceTotal
FROM Vendors JOIN Invoices
    ON Vendors.VendorID = Invoices.VendorID
WHERE InvoiceTotal >= 500
ORDER BY Name, InvoiceTotal DESC
```

The result set defined by the Select statement

	Name	InvoiceNumber	InvoiceDate	InvoiceTotal
11	IBM	Q545443	2008-08-09	1083.58
12	Ingram	31359783	2008-08-03	1575.00
13	Ingram	31361833	2008-09-21	579.42
14	Malloy Lithographing Inc	0-2058	2008-07-28	37966.19
15	Malloy Lithographing Inc	P-0259	2008-09-19	26881.40
16	Malloy Lithographing Inc	0-2060	2008-09-24	23517.58
17	Malloy Lithographing Inc	P-0608	2008-09-23	20551.18
18	Malloy Lithographing Inc	0-2436	2008-09-30	10976.06
19	Pollstar	77290	2008-07-13	1750.00
20	Reiter's Scientific & Pro Books	C73-24	2008-09-19	600.00
21	United Parcel Service	989319-457	2008-06-08	3813.33
22	United Parcel Service	989319-447	2008-09-24	3689.99

Concepts

- A *join* lets you combine data from two or more tables into a single result set.
- The most common type of join is an *inner join*. This type of join returns rows from both tables only if their related columns match.

Figure 1-10   How to join data from two or more tables

How to add, update, and delete data in a table

Figure 1-11 presents the basic syntax of the SQL Insert, Update, and Delete statements. You use the Insert statement to insert one or more rows into a table. As you can see, the syntax of this statement is different depending on whether you're adding a single row or selected rows.

To add a single row to a table, you specify the name of the table you want to add the row to, the names of the columns you're supplying data for, and the values for those columns. The example in this figure adds a row to the Terms table. Because the value of the TermsID column is generated automatically, though, it's not included in the Insert statement. If you're going to supply values for all the columns in a table, you can omit the column names, but then you must be sure to specify the values in the same order as the columns appear in the table.

Note that you typically use single quotes to identify strings. For example, the string for the Description column is enclosed in single quotes. However, if a string value contains a single quote, you'll need to replace the single quote with two single quotes.

To add selected rows to a table, you include a Select statement within the Insert statement. Then, the Select statement retrieves data from one or more tables based on the conditions you specify, and the Insert statement adds rows with that data to another table. In the example in this figure, the Select statement selects all the columns from the rows in the Invoices table that have been paid in full and inserts them into a table named InvoiceArchive.

To change the values of one or more columns in a table, you use the Update statement. On this statement, you specify the name of the table you want to update, the names of the columns you want to change and expressions that indicate how you want to change them, and a condition that identifies the rows you want to change. In the example in this figure, the Update statement changes the TermsID value to 4 for each row in the Invoices table that has a TermsID value of 1.

To delete rows from a table, you use the Delete statement. On this statement, you specify the table you want to delete rows from and a condition that indicates the rows you want to delete. The Delete statement in this figure deletes all the rows from the Invoices table that have been paid in full.

How to add a single row

The syntax of the Insert statement for adding a single row

```
INSERT [INTO] table-name [(column-list)]
    VALUES (value-list)
```

A statement that adds a single row to a table

```
INSERT INTO Terms (Description, DueDays)
    VALUES ('Net due 90 days', 90)
```

How to add selected rows

The syntax of the Insert statement for adding selected rows

```
INSERT [INTO] table-name [(column-list)]
    Select-statement
```

A statement that adds selected rows from one table to another table

```
INSERT INTO InvoiceArchive
    SELECT * FROM Invoices
    WHERE InvoiceTotal - PaymentTotal - CreditTotal = 0
```

How to update rows

The syntax of the Update statement

```
UPDATE table-name
    SET column-1 = expression-1 [, column-2 = expression-2]...
    [WHERE selection-criteria]
```

A statement that changes the value of the TermsID column for selected rows

```
UPDATE Invoices
    SET TermsID = 4
    WHERE TermsID = 1
```

How to delete rows

The syntax of the Delete statement

```
DELETE [FROM] table-name
    [WHERE selection-criteria]
```

A statement that deletes all paid invoices

```
DELETE FROM Invoices
    WHERE InvoiceTotal - PaymentTotal - CreditTotal = 0
```

Description

- You can use the Insert statement to insert a single row or selected rows into a database table.

- You can use the Update statement to change the values of one or more columns in one or more rows of a database table.

- You can use the Delete statement to delete one or more rows from a database table.

Figure 1-11   How to add, update, and delete data in a table

How to work with other database objects and functions

In addition to the tables you've already learned about, relational databases can contain other database objects like views, stored procedures, and triggers. You can also use functions to work with the data in a database. In the topics that follow, you'll be introduced to these objects and functions.

How to work with views

A *view* is a predefined query that's stored in a database. To create a view, you use the Create View statement as shown in figure 1-12. This statement causes the Select statement you specify to be stored with the database. In this case, the Create View statement creates a view named VendorsMin that retrieves three columns from the Vendors table.

To access a view, you issue a Select statement that refers to the view. This causes a *virtual table*—a temporary table that's created on the server—to be created from the Select statement in the view. Then, the Select statement that referred to the view is executed on this virtual table to create the result set.

Although views can be quite useful, they require some additional overhead. That's because every time an application refers to a view, the view has to be created from scratch. If that's a problem, an alternative is to use stored procedures.

A Create View statement for a view named VendorsMin

```
CREATE VIEW VendorsMin AS
    SELECT Name, State, Phone
    FROM Vendors
```

A Select statement that uses the VendorsMin view

```
SELECT * FROM VendorsMin
WHERE State = 'CA'
ORDER BY Name
```

The virtual table that's created when the Select statement that uses the view is executed

	Name	State	Phone
1	US Postal Service	WI	8005551205
2	National Information Data Ctr	DC	3015558950
3	Register of Copyrights	DC	NULL
4	Jobtrak	CA	8005558725
5	Newbrige Book Clubs	NJ	8005559980
6	California Chamber Of Commerce	CA	9165556670
7	Towne Advertiser's Mailing Svcs	CA	NULL
8	BFI Industries	CA	5595551551
9	Pacific Gas & Electric	CA	8005556081

The result set that's created from the view

	Name	State	Phone
1	Abbey Office Furnishings	CA	5595558300
2	American Express	CA	8005553344
3	ASC Signs	CA	NULL
4	Aztek Label	CA	7145559000
5	Bertelsmann Industry Svcs. Inc.	CA	8055550584
6	BFI Industries	CA	5595551551
7	Bill Jones	CA	NULL
8	Bill Marvin Electric Inc	CA	5595555106
9	Blanchard & Johnson Associates	CA	2145553647

Description

- A *view* consists of a Select statement that's stored with the database. Because views are stored as part of the database, they can be managed independently of the applications that use them.

- When you refer to a view, a *virtual table* is created on the server that represents the view. Then, the result set is extracted from this virtual table. For this reason, a view is also called a *viewed table*.

- Views can be used to restrict the data that a user is allowed to access or to present data in a form that's easy for the user to understand. In some databases, users may be allowed to access data only through views.

Figure 1-12   How to work with views

How to work with stored procedures and triggers

A *stored procedure* is a set of one or more SQL statements that are stored together in a database. To create a stored procedure, you use the Create Procedure statement as shown in figure 1-13. Here, the stored procedure contains a single Select statement. To use the stored procedure, you send a request for it to be executed.

When the server receives the request, it executes the stored procedure. If the stored procedure contains a Select statement like the one in this figure, the result set is sent back to the calling program. If the stored procedure contains Insert, Update, or Delete statements, the appropriate processing is performed.

Notice that the stored procedure in this figure accepts an *input parameter* named @State from the calling program. The value of this parameter is then substituted for the parameter in the Where clause so only vendors in the specified state are included in the result set.

When it's done with its processing, a stored procedure can also pass *output parameters* back to the calling program. In addition, stored procedures can include *control-of-flow language* that determines the processing that's done based on specific conditions.

A *trigger* is a special type of stored procedure that's executed automatically when an insert, update, or delete operation is performed on a table. Triggers are used most often to validate data before a row is added or updated, but they can also be used to maintain the relationships between tables. Although you don't work with triggers directly from an application program, you need to know what triggers exist for the tables in a database and what operations they perform. That way, you'll know what processing an application needs to do before it updates the table.

A Create Procedure statement for a procedure named spVendorsByState

```
CREATE PROCEDURE spVendorsByState @State char AS
    SELECT Name, State, Phone
    FROM Vendors
    WHERE State = @State
    ORDER BY Name
```

The result set that's created when the stored procedure is executed with the @State variable set to 'CA'

	Name	State	Phone
1	Abbey Office Furnishings	CA	5595558300
2	American Express	CA	8005553344
3	ASC Signs	CA	NULL
4	Aztek Label	CA	7145559000
5	Bertelsmann Industry Svcs. Inc.	CA	8055550584
6	BFI Industries	CA	5595551551
7	Bill Jones	CA	NULL
8	Bill Marvin Electric Inc	CA	5595555106
9	Blanchard & Johnson Associates	CA	2145553647

Concepts

- A *stored procedure* consists of one or more SQL statements that have been compiled and stored with the database. A stored procedure can be started by application code on the client.

- Stored procedures can improve database performance because the SQL statements in each procedure are only compiled and optimized the first time they're executed. In contrast, SQL statements that are sent from a client to the server have to be compiled and optimized every time they're executed.

- In addition to Select statements, a stored procedure can contain other SQL statements such as Insert, Update, and Delete statements. It can also contain *control-of-flow language*, which lets you perform conditional processing within the stored procedure.

- A *trigger* is a special type of procedure that's executed when rows are inserted, updated, or deleted from a table. Triggers are typically used to check the validity of the data in a row that's being updated or added to a table.

Figure 1-13   How to work with stored procedures and triggers

How to work with functions

Figure 1-14 introduces you to three types of *functions* that you can use when you code SQL statements. Here, each table lists just a few of the functions that are available in each category. But please note that all functions return a single value.

To illustrate, the first coding example in this figure is a Select statement that uses three *scalar functions*. These are functions that can operate on the data in a single row. Here, the GETDATE function is used to get the current date, which is displayed in the first column of the result set. Then, the GETDATE function is used as a parameter for the DATEDIFF function, which returns the number of days between the date in the InvoiceDate column and the current date.

In contrast, the second coding example is a SELECT statement that uses two *aggregate functions*. These are functions that can operate on the data in two or more rows. In this case, the COUNT function returns the number of rows selected by the query, and the SUM function returns the sum of the values in the InvoiceTotal column of the selected rows.

The third table in this figure presents two of the *system functions* that are available with SQL Server, and each database management system has its own system functions. In this table, both functions return the last value that was generated for an identity column. As you may remember from figure 1-7, an identity column is a numeric column whose value is generated automatically when a row is added to a table. As a result, you can use one of these functions to find out what the generated number is after you add a row to a table.

Besides these three types of functions, you can create *user-defined functions* that are stored with the database. These functions are most often written and used by SQL programmers within the stored procedures and triggers that they write. Although user-defined functions can also be used by application programmers, there are no examples of their use in this book.

Some of the SQL Server scalar functions

Function name	Description
LTRIM(string)	Returns the string with any leading spaces removed.
LEFT(string,length)	Returns the specified number of characters from the beginning of the string.
GETDATE()	Returns the current system date and time.
DATEDIFF(datepart,startdate,enddate)	Returns the number of datepart units between the specified start and end dates.

Some of the SQL Server aggregate functions

Function name	Description
AVG([ALL|DISTINCT] expression)	The average of the non-null values in the expression.
SUM([ALL|DISTINCT] expression)	The total of the non-null values in the expression.
COUNT(*)	The number of rows selected by the query.

Some of the SQL Server system functions

Function name	Description
@@IDENTITY	Returns the last value generated for an identity column on the server. Returns Null if no identity value was generated.
IDENT_CURRENT('tablename')	Returns the last identity value that was generated for a specified table.

A Select statement that includes three scalar functions

```
SELECT InvoiceDate, GETDATE() AS 'Today''s Date',
    DATEDIFF(day, InvoiceDate, GETDATE()) AS Age
FROM Invoices
```

	InvoiceDate	Today's Date	Age
1	2008-06-08	2008-08-19 11:03:52.653	72
2	2008-06-10	2008-08-19 11:03:52.653	70
3	2008-06-13	2008-08-19 11:03:52.653	67

A Select statement that includes two aggregate functions

```
SELECT COUNT(*) AS NumberOfInvoices, SUM(InvoiceTotal) AS
    TotalInvoiceAmount
FROM Invoices
WHERE InvoiceDate > '2008-01-01'
```

	NumberOfInvoices	TotalInvoiceAmount
1	114	214290.51

Description

- A *function* performs an operation and returns a single value. A *scalar function* operates on one or more values in a single row and returns a single value. An *aggregate function* operates on values in two or more rows and returns a summarizing value. And a *system function* returns information about SQL Server values, objects, and settings.

Figure 1-14   How to work with functions

Perspective

In this chapter, you've learned the basic concepts and terms that relate to client/server programming, relational databases, and SQL. Although you don't need to be an expert in database design or SQL programming to develop database applications with Visual Basic, you at least need to be familiar with those concepts and terms. There's a lot more to learn, though, and for that we recommend *Murach's SQL Server 2008 for Developers*.

Terms

SQL Server 2008 Express	table	Transact-SQL
SQL Server 2008	record	result table
client/server system	row	result set
client	field	calculated column
server	column	join
network	primary key	inner join
database server	composite primary key	view
enterprise system	non-primary key	virtual table
local area network (LAN)	unique key	viewed table
wide area network (WAN)	unique key constraint	stored procedure
network operating system	index	input parameter
database management	foreign key	output parameter
system (DBMS)	foreign key table	control-of-flow language
back-end processing	primary key table	trigger
back end	one-to-many	function
application software	relationship	scalar function
data access API	one-to-one	aggregate function
application programming	relationship	system function
interface (API)	many-to-many	user-defined function
front-end processing	relationship	
front end	linking table	
SQL query	referential integrity	
query	foreign key constraint	
Structured Query	cascade update	
Language (SQL)	cascade delete	
query results	trigger	
application server	orphaned row	
business class	data type	
database class	system data type	
web browser	null value	
web application	default value	
web server	identity column	
web service	check constraint	
relational database	SQL dialect	

2

An introduction to ADO.NET 3.5

ADO.NET consists of a set of classes defined by the .NET Framework that you can use to access the data in a database. The current version of ADO.NET is ADO.NET 3.5, and that's the version you'll learn about in this book.

This chapter introduces you the primary ADO.NET classes that you'll use as you develop database applications with Visual Basic. This chapter also introduces you to the two basic ways that you can develop database applications with ADO.NET.

If you've used ADO.NET 2.0, you'll see that the classes that are included in ADO.NET 3.5 and the basic features Visual Studio provides for developing database applications using ADO.NET 3.5 have changed very little. If you haven't used ADO.NET 2.0, though, you'll see that the Visual Studio features have changed a lot. In addition, you should know that ADO.NET 3.5 includes two major new features: LINQ and the Entity Framework. You'll learn how to use these features later in this book.

An overview of ADO.NET

ADO.NET (*ActiveX Data Objects .NET*) is the primary data access API for the .NET Framework. It provides the classes that you use as you develop database applications with Visual Basic as well as the other .NET languages. In the topics that follow, you'll learn the two basic ways that you can use the ADO.NET classes for accessing and updating the data in a database.

How to use ADO.NET with datasets

One way to develop database applications with ADO.NET is to use datasets. With this approach, your application gets data from a database and stores it in a *dataset* that is kept in cache memory on disk. Then, your application can add, update, or delete rows in the dataset, and it can later save those changes from the dataset to the database.

When you use this approach, your application uses the ADO.NET objects shown in figure 2-1. To load data into a *data table* within a dataset, you use a *data adapter*. Its main function is to manage the flow of data between a dataset and a database. To do that, it uses *commands* that define the SQL statements to be issued. The command for retrieving data, for example, typically defines a Select statement. Then, the command connects to the database using a *connection* and passes the Select statement to the database. After the Select statement is executed, the result set it produces is sent back to the data adapter, which stores the results in the data table.

To update the data in a database, the data adapter determines which rows in the data table have been inserted, updated, or deleted. Then, it uses commands that define Insert, Update, and Delete statements for the data table to update the associated rows in the database. Like the command that retrieves data from the database, the commands that update the database use a connection to connect to the database and perform the requested operation.

Note that the data in a dataset is independent of the database that the data was retrieved from. In fact, the connection to the database is typically closed after the data is retrieved from the database. Then, the connection is opened again when it's needed. Because of that, the application must work with the copy of the data that's stored in the dataset. The architecture that's used to implement this type of data processing is referred to as a *disconnected data architecture*.

Although this approach is more complicated than a connected architecture, it has several advantages. One advantage is that using a disconnected data architecture can improve system performance due to the use of fewer system resources for maintaining connections. Another advantage is that it makes ADO.NET compatible with ASP.NET web applications, which are inherently disconnected.

Basic ADO.NET objects

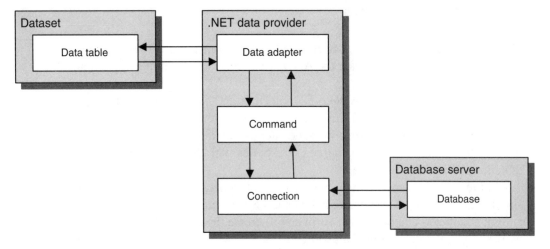

Description

- A *.NET data provider* provides the classes that let you create the objects that you use to retrieve data from a database and to store data in a database.

- One way to work with a database when you use ADO.NET is to retrieve data from a database into a dataset and to store data from the dataset to the database.

- A *dataset* contains one or more *data tables* that store the data retrieved from the database. Then, the application can work with the data in the data tables, and it can insert, update, and delete rows in the data tables.

- To retrieve data from a database and store it in a data table, a *data adapter* object issues a Select statement that's stored in a *command* object. Next, the command object uses a *connection* object to connect to the database and retrieve the data. Then, the data is passed back to the data adapter, which stores the data in the dataset.

- To update the data in a database based on the data in a data table, the data adapter object issues an Insert, Update, or Delete statement that's stored in a command object. Then, the command object uses a connection to connect to the database and update the data.

- When you use a data adapter to work with the data in a database, the data provider remains connected to the database only long enough to retrieve or update the specified data. Then, it disconnects from the database and the application works with the data via the dataset object. This is referred to as a *disconnected data architecture.*

- The disconnected data architecture offers improved system performance due to the use of fewer system resources for maintaining connections.

Figure 2-1   How to use ADO.NET with datasets

Two ways to create the ADO.NET objects for working with datasets

When you use datasets in your database applications, there are two basic techniques you can use to create the ADO.NET objects that you need. Both are illustrated in figure 2-2.

First, you can create the ADO.NET objects from a *data source* that's shown in the *Data Sources window*. Data sources are a feature of .NET 3.5 that makes it easy to create forms that work with the data in a data source such as a database. In this example, the data source corresponds with the data in the Terms table in the Payables database.

In the next chapter, you'll learn how to create a data source. For now, you should know that once you create a data source, you can drag it onto a form to automatically add controls to the form and to create the ADO.NET objects for working with the data in the data source.

In this figure, for example, you can see the controls and objects that are generated when you drag the Terms table onto the form. Here, a DataGridView control has been added to the form to display the terms in the Terms table, and a toolbar has been added that lets you work with this data.

In addition, five objects have been added to the *Component Designer tray* below the form. Three of these are ADO.NET objects. The first one, named PayablesDataSet, defines the dataset for the form. Then, an object named TermsTableAdapter defines the table adapter for the Terms table. A *table adapter* is an object that's generated by the designer. It includes a data adapter, a connection object, and one or more command objects. In essence, then, it combines the three classes of a .NET data provider that you saw in the previous figure. You'll learn more about table adapters in the next chapter.

Finally, an object named TableAdapterManager makes sure that if two or more related tables are updated by the form, referential integrity is maintained. This is a new feature of Visual Studio 2008, and it's available by default.

The other two objects in the Component Designer tray are used to bind the controls on the form to the data source. The first object, named TermsBindingSource, identifies the Terms table as the data source for the controls. The second object, named TermsBindingNavigator, defines the toolbar that's displayed across the top of the form.

Although you don't usually need to change the properties of the objects in the Component Designer tray, you should know that you can do that using the same technique you use to change the properties of a control on a form. That is, you just select an object to display its properties in the Properties window and then work with them from there.

The second technique for creating ADO.NET objects is to write the code yourself. In this figure, for example, you can see the code that creates four objects: a connection, a command named selectCommand that contains a Select statement, a data adapter named termsDataAdapter, and a dataset named termsDataSet. Because you're most likely to use data sources to work with datasets, I won't present this coding technique in this book.

Using the Data Sources window to create ADO.NET objects

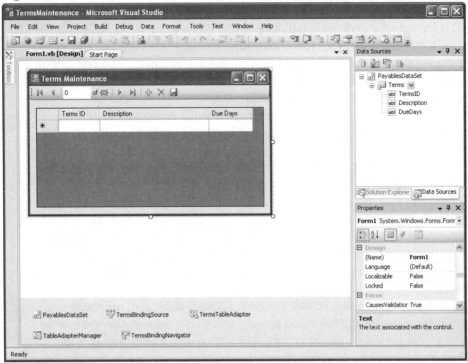

Visual Basic code that creates ADO.NET objects

```
Dim connectionString As String _
    = "Data Source=localhost\SqlExpress;Initial Catalog=Payables;" _
    & "Integrated Security=True"
Dim connection As New SqlConnection(connectionString)

Dim selectStatement As String = "SELECT * FROM Terms"
Dim selectCommand As New SqlCommand(selectStatement, connection)

Dim termsDataAdapter As New SqlDataAdapter(selectCommand)

Dim termsDataSet As New DataSet
```

Description

- You can use the *Data Sources window* in Visual Studio to create a *data source*. Then, you can drag the data source onto the form to automatically generate a table adapter object and a dataset object.

- A *table adapter* is like a data adapter, but it has a built-in connection object, and it can contain more than one query. You'll learn how to work with table adapters in chapter 3.

- To create ADO.NET objects in code, you write declarations that identify the class each object is created from.

Figure 2-2   Two ways to create the ADO.NET objects for working with datasets

How to use ADO.NET without using datasets

The second way to develop database applications using ADO.NET is to work with the database directly, without using datasets. This approach is illustrated in figure 2-3. As you can see, you still use command and connection objects to access the database. But instead of using a data adapter to execute the commands, you execute the commands directly.

When you work this way, you have to provide the code that handles the result of each command. If you issue a command that contains an Insert, Update, or Delete statement, for example, the result is an integer that indicates the number of rows that were affected by the operation. You can use that information to determine if the operation was successful.

The code example in this figure illustrates how this works. Here, a command that inserts a row into the Terms table is created. In this case, the Insert statement uses parameters to identify the column values that must be supplied. Then, values are assigned to these parameters before the command is executed. Finally, the connection is opened, the command is executed, and the connection is closed.

If you execute a command that contains a Select statement, the result is a result set that contains the rows you requested. To read through the rows in the result set, you use a *data reader* object. Although a data reader provides an efficient way of reading the rows in a result set, you can't use it to modify those rows. In addition, it only lets you read rows in a forward direction, so once you read the next row, the previous row is unavailable. Because of that, you typically use a data reader either to retrieve rows that are displayed in a control such as a combo box, or to retrieve and work with a single database row at a time.

ADO.NET components for accessing a database directly

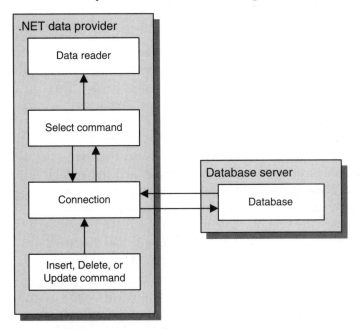

Code that creates and executes a command that inserts a row

```
Dim insertStatement As String _
    = "INSERT Terms (Description, DueDays) " _
    & "VALUES (@Description, @DueDays)"
Dim insertCommand As New SqlCommand(insertStatement, connection)
insertCommand.Parameters.AddWithValue("@Description", terms.Description)
insertCommand.Parameters.AddWithValue("@UnitPrice", terms.DueDays)
connection.Open()
Dim count As Integer = insertCommand.ExecuteNonQuery
connection.Close()
```

Description

- Instead of executing the commands associated with a data adapter to manage the flow of data between a dataset and a database, you can execute those commands directly. When you do that, you create and work with the ADO.NET objects through code.

- To retrieve data from a database, you execute a command object that contains a Select statement. Then, the command object uses a connection to connect to the database and retrieve the data. You can then read the results one row at a time using a *data reader* object.

- To insert, update, or delete data in a database, you execute a command object that contains an Insert, Update, or Delete statement. Then, the command object uses a connection to connect to the database and update the data. You can then check the value that's returned to determine if the operation was successful.

Figure 2-3   How to use ADO.NET without using datasets

Concurrency and the disconnected data architecture

Although the disconnected data architecture has advantages, it also has some disadvantages. One of those is the conflict that can occur when two or more users retrieve and then try to update data in the same row of a table. This is called a *concurrency* problem. This is possible because once a program retrieves data from a database, the connection to that database is dropped. As a result, the database management system can't manage the update process.

To illustrate, consider the situation shown in figure 2-4. Here, two users have retrieved the Vendors table from a database, so a copy of the Vendors table is stored on each user's PC. These users could be using the same program or two different programs. Now, suppose that user 1 modifies the address in the row for vendor 123 and updates the Vendors table in the database. And suppose that user 2 modifies the phone number in the row for vendor 123 and then tries to update the Vendors table in the database. What will happen? That will depend on the *concurrency control* that's used by the programs.

When you use ADO.NET, you have two choices for concurrency control. First, you can use *optimistic concurrency*, which checks whether a row has been changed since it was retrieved. If it has, the update or deletion will be refused and a *concurrency exception* will be thrown. Then, the program should handle the error. For example, it could display an error message that tells the user that the row could not be updated and then retrieve the updated row so the user can make the change again.

In contrast, the *"last in wins"* technique works the way its name implies. Since no checking is done with this technique, the row that's updated by the last user overwrites any changes made to the row by a previous user. For the example above, the row updated by user 2 will overwrite changes made by user 1, which means that the phone number will be right but the address will be wrong. Since errors like this corrupt the data in a database, optimistic concurrency is used by most programs, which means that your programs have to handle the concurrency exceptions that are thrown.

If you know that concurrency will be a problem, you can use a couple of programming techniques to limit concurrency exceptions. If a program uses a dataset, one technique is to update the database frequently so other programs can retrieve the current data. The program should also refresh its dataset frequently so it contains the recent changes made by other programs.

Another way to avoid concurrency exceptions is to retrieve and work with just one row at a time. That way, it's less likely that two programs will update the same row at the same time. In contrast, if two programs retrieve the same table, they will of course retrieve the same rows. Then, if they both update the same row in the table, even though it may not be at the same time, a concurrency exception will occur when they try to update the database.

Of course, you will understand and appreciate this more as you learn how to develop your own database applications. As you develop them, though, keep in mind that most applications are multi-user applications. That's why you have to be aware of concurrency problems.

Two users who are working with copies of the same data

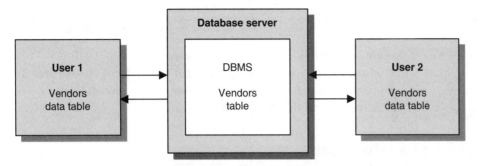

What happens when two users try to update the same row

- When two or more users retrieve the data in the same row of a database table at the same time, it is called *concurrency*. Because ADO.NET uses a disconnected data architecture, the database management system can't prevent this from happening.

- If two users try to update the same row in a database table at the same time, the second user's changes could overwrite the changes made by the first user. Whether or not that happens, though, depends on the *concurrency control* that the programs use.

- By default, ADO.NET uses *optimistic concurrency*. This means that the program checks to see whether the database row that's going to be updated or deleted has been changed since it was retrieved. If it has, a *concurrency exception* occurs and the update or deletion is refused. Then, the program should handle the exception.

- If optimistic concurrency isn't in effect, the program doesn't check to see whether a row has been changed before an update or deletion takes place. Instead, the operation proceeds without throwing an exception. This is referred to as "*last in wins*" because the last update overwrites any previous update. And this leads to errors in the database.

How to avoid concurrency errors

- For many applications, concurrency errors rarely occur. As a result, optimistic concurrency is adequate because the users will rarely have to resubmit an update or deletion that is refused.

- If concurrency is likely to be a problem, a program that uses a dataset can be designed so it updates the database and refreshes the dataset frequently. That way, concurrency errors are less likely to occur.

- Another way to avoid concurrency errors is to design a program so it retrieves and updates just one row at a time. That way, there's less chance that two users will retrieve and update the same row at the same time.

Figure 2-4   Concurrency and the disconnected data architecture

The ADO.NET data providers and their classes

The *.NET data providers* provide the ADO.NET classes that you use for connecting to and working directly with a database. That's why these classes are sometimes called the *connected classes*. In the topics that follow, you'll learn more about the data providers and the classes that they provide.

The .NET data providers

All .NET data providers include the core classes for creating the four types of objects listed in the first table in figure 2-5. You've already learned the basic functions of these classes, and you'll learn more about these classes throughout this book.

The second table in this figure lists the four data providers that come with the .NET Framework. The SQL Server data provider is designed to provide efficient access to a Microsoft SQL Server database. The OLE DB data provider is a generic data provider that can access any database that supports the industry standard OLE DB interface. The ODBC provider lets you access any database that can work with ODBC, another industry standard database interface. And the Oracle provider lets you access data that's stored in Oracle databases. Although you can use the OLE DB data provider to access a SQL Server database, you shouldn't do that unless you plan on migrating the data to another database since the SQL Server data provider is optimized for accessing SQL Server data.

Besides the providers that come with the .NET Framework, several database vendors have developed .NET data providers that are optimized for use with their databases. For example, .NET data providers are available for the popular MySQL and Sybase databases as well as for a variety of other databases. Before you develop an application using the OLE DB provider, then, you should check with your database vendor to see if a specialized .NET data provider is available.

The third table in this figure lists the names of the classes you use to create objects using the SQL Server, OLE DB, ODBC, and Oracle providers. Notice that these classes use prefixes ("Sql," "OleDb," "Odbc," and "Oracle") to indicate which provider each class belongs to.

When you develop a Visual Basic application that uses ADO.NET, you'll want to add an Imports statement for the namespace that contains the data provider classes at the beginning of each source file that uses those classes. That way, you won't have to qualify the references to these classes. These namespaces are listed in the second table in this figure.

Now that you're familiar with the core classes of the four .NET data providers that come with the .NET Framework, the next four topics describe the classes of the SQL Server data provider in more detail. You should realize, though, that the information presented in these topics applies to the classes of the other data providers as well.

.NET data provider core objects

Object	Description
Connection	Establishes a connection to a database.
Command	Represents an individual SQL statement or stored procedure that can be executed against the database.
Data reader	Provides read-only, forward-only access to the data in a database.
Data adapter	Provides the link between the command and connection objects and a dataset object.

Data providers included with the .NET framework

Provider	Namespace	Description
SQL Server	System.Data.SqlClient	Lets you access SQL Server databases.
OLE DB	System.Data.OleDb	Lets you access any database that supports OLE DB.
ODBC	System.Data.Odbc	Lets you access any database that supports ODBC.
Oracle	System.Data.OracleClient	Lets you access Oracle databases.

Class names for the data providers

Object	SQL Server	OLE DB	ODBC	Oracle
Connection	SqlConnection	OleDbConnection	OdbcConnection	OracleConnection
Command	SqlCommand	OleDbCommand	OdbcCommand	OracleCommand
Data reader	SqlDataReader	OleDbDataReader	OdbcDataReader	OracleDataReader
Data adapter	SqlDataAdapter	OleDbDataAdapter	OdbcDataAdapter	OracleDataAdapter

An Imports statement for the SQL Server data provider namespace

```
Imports System.Data.SqlClient
```

Description

- The *.NET data providers* provide the ADO.NET classes that are responsible for working directly with a database. In addition to the core classes shown above, classes are provided for other functions such as passing parameters to commands and working with transactions.

- To use a .NET data provider in an application, you should add an Imports statement for the appropriate namespace at the beginning of the source file. Otherwise, you'll have to qualify each class you refer to with the SqlClient, OleDb, Odbc, or OracleClient namespace since these namespaces aren't included as references by default.

- Other .NET data providers are available to provide efficient access to non-Microsoft databases such as MySQL, Sybase, PostgreSQL, and IBM DB2.

- All of the ADO.NET objects are implemented by classes in the System.Data namespace of the .NET Framework. However, the specific classes used to implement the connection, command, data reader, and data adapter objects depend on the .NET data provider you use.

Figure 2-5   The .NET data providers

The SqlConnection class

Before you can access the data in a database, you have to create a connection object that defines the connection to the database. To do that, you use the SqlConnection class presented in figure 2-6.

The most important property of the SqlConnection class is ConnectionString. A *connection string* is a text string that provides the information necessary to establish a connection to a database. That means it includes information such as the name of the database you want to access and the database server that contains it. It can also contain authentication information such as a user ID and password.

The two methods of the SqlConnection class shown in this figure let you open and close the connection. In general, you should leave a connection open only while data is being retrieved or updated. That's why when you use a data adapter, the connection is opened and closed for you. In that case, you don't need to use the Open and Close methods.

The SqlCommand class

To execute a SQL statement against a SQL Server database, you create a SqlCommand object that contains the statement. Figure 2-6 presents the SqlCommand class you use to create this object. Notice that the Connection property of this class associates the command with a SqlConnection object, and the CommandText property contains the SQL statement to be executed.

The CommandType property indicates how the command object should interpret the value of the CommandText property. Instead of specifying a SQL statement for the CommandText property, for example, you can specify the name of a stored procedure. If you specify a SQL statement, you set the value of the CommandType property to CommandType.Text. If you specify the name of a stored procedure, you set it to CommandType.StoredProcedure.

Earlier in this chapter, you learned that you can use a data adapter to execute command objects. In addition, you can execute a command object directly using one of the three Execute methods shown in this figure. If the command contains a Select statement, for example, you can execute it using either ExecuteReader or ExecuteScalar. If you use ExecuteReader, the results are returned as a DataReader object. If you use ExecuteScalar, only the value in the first column and row of the query results is returned. You're most likely to use this method with a Select statement that returns a single summary value or the value of an identity column for a row that was just inserted into the database.

If the command contains an Insert, Update, or Delete statement, you'll use the ExecuteNonQuery method to execute it. This method returns an integer value that indicates the number of rows that were affected by the command. For example, if the command deletes a single row, the ExecuteNonQuery method returns 1.

Common properties and methods of the SqlConnection class

Property	Description
ConnectionString	Contains information that lets you connect to a SQL Server database. The connection string includes information such as the name of the server, the name of the database, and login information.

Method	Description
Open	Opens a connection to a database.
Close	Closes a connection to a database.

Common properties and methods of the SqlCommand class

Property	Description
Connection	The SqlConnection object that's used by the command to connect to the database.
CommandText	The text of the SQL command or the name of a stored procedure.
CommandType	A constant in the CommandType enumeration that indicates whether the CommandText property contains a SQL statement (Text) or the name of a stored procedure (StoredProcedure).
Parameters	The collection of parameters used by the command.

Method	Description
ExecuteReader	Executes a query and returns the result as a SqlDataReader object.
ExecuteNonQuery	Executes the command and returns an integer representing the number of rows affected.
ExecuteScalar	Executes a query and returns the first column of the first row returned by the query.

Description

- Each command object is associated with a connection object through the command's Connection property. When a command is executed, the information in the ConnectionString property of the connection object is used to connect to the database.

- When you use a data adapter to work with a database, the connection is opened and closed automatically. If that's not what you want, you can use the Open and Close methods of the connection object to open and close the connection.

- You can use the three Execute methods of a command object to execute the SQL statement it contains. You can also execute the SQL statement in a command object using methods of the data adapter. See figure 2-7 for more information.

Figure 2-6   The SqlConnection and SqlCommand classes

The SqlDataAdapter class

As you have learned, the job of a data adapter is to provide a link between a database and a dataset. The four properties of the SqlDataAdapter class listed in figure 2-7, for example, identify the four SQL commands that the data adapter uses to transfer data from the database to the dataset and vice versa. The SelectCommand property identifies the command object that's used to retrieve data from the database. And the DeleteCommand, InsertCommand, and UpdateCommand properties identify the commands that are used to update the database based on changes made to the data in the dataset.

To execute the command identified by the SelectCommand property and place the data that's retrieved in a dataset, you use the Fill method. Then, the application can work with the data in the dataset without affecting the data in the database. If the application makes changes to the data in the dataset, it can use the data adapter's Update method to execute the commands identified by the DeleteCommand, InsertCommand, and UpdateCommand properties and post the changes back to the database.

The SqlDataReader class

A data reader provides an efficient way to read the rows in a result set returned by a database query. In fact, when you use a data adapter to retrieve data, the data adapter uses a data reader to read through the rows in the result set and store them in a dataset.

A data reader is similar to other types of readers you may have encountered in the .NET Framework, such as a TextReader, a StreamReader, or an XmlReader. Like these other readers, a data reader lets you read rows but not modify them. In other words, a data reader is read-only. In addition, it only lets you read rows in a forward direction. Once you read the next row, the previous row is unavailable.

Figure 2-7 lists the most important properties and methods of the SqlDataReader class. You use the Read method to read the next row of data in the result set. In most cases, you'll code the Read method in a loop that reads and processes rows until the end of the data reader is reached.

To access a column of data from the current row of a data reader, you use the Item property. To identify the column, you can use either its index value like this:

```
drVendors.Item(0)
```

or its name like this:

```
drVendors.Item("Name")
```

Since Item is the default property, you can also omit it like this:

```
drVendors("Name")
```

Common properties and methods of the SqlDataAdapter class

Property	Description
SelectCommand	A SqlCommand object representing the Select statement or stored procedure used to query the database.
DeleteCommand	A SqlCommand object representing the Delete statement or stored procedure used to delete a row from the database.
InsertCommand	A SqlCommand object representing the Insert statement or stored procedure used to add a row to the database.
UpdateCommand	A SqlCommand object representing the Update statement or stored procedure used to update a row in the database.

Method	Description
Fill	Executes the command identified by the SelectCommand property and loads the result into a dataset object.
Update	Executes the commands identified by the DeleteCommand, InsertCommand, and UpdateCommand properties for each row in the dataset that was deleted, added, or updated.

Common properties and methods of the SqlDataReader class

Property	Description
Item	Accesses the column with the specified index or name from the current row.
FieldCount	The number of columns in the current row.

Method	Description
Read	Reads the next row. Returns True if there are more rows. Otherwise, returns False.
Close	Closes the data reader.

Description

- When the Fill method of a data adapter is used to retrieve data from a database, the data adapter uses a data reader to load the results into a dataset. If you don't use a dataset, you can work with a data reader directly.

- A data reader provides read-only, forward-only access to the data in a database. Because it doesn't require the overhead of a dataset, it's more efficient than using a data adapter. However, it can't be used to update data. To do that, you have to use other techniques.

Figure 2-7   The SqlDataAdapter and SqlDataReader classes

ADO.NET datasets

Unlike the .NET data providers that provide the connected classes for accessing the data in a database, an ADO.NET dataset provides the *disconnected classes* for working with the data in a database. In the next two topics, you'll learn how a dataset is organized, and you'll get an overview of the classes you use to define dataset objects.

How a dataset is organized

Figure 2-8 illustrates the basic organization of an ADO.NET dataset. The first thing you should notice in this figure is that a dataset is structured much like a relational database. It can contain one or more tables, and each table can contain one or more columns and rows. In addition, each table can contain one or more constraints that can define a unique key within the table or a foreign key of another table in the dataset. If a dataset contains two or more tables, the dataset can also define the relationships between those tables.

Although a dataset is structured much like a relational database, it's important to realize that each table in a dataset corresponds to the result set that's returned from a Select statement, not necessarily to an actual table in a database. For example, a Select statement may join data from several tables in a database to produce a single result set. In this case, the table in the dataset would represent data from each of the tables involved in the join.

You should also know that each group of objects in the diagram in this figure is stored in a collection. All of the columns in a table, for example, are stored in a collection of columns, and all of the rows are stored in a collection of rows. You'll learn more about these collections in the next figure and in later chapters.

The basic dataset object hierarchy

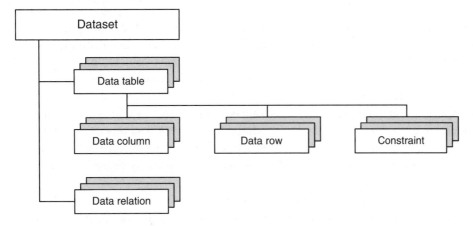

Description

- A dataset object consists of a hierarchy of one or more data table and *data relation* objects.

- A data table object consists of one or more *data column* objects and one or more *data row* objects. The data column objects define the data in each column of the table, including its name, data type, and so on, and the data row objects contain the data for each row in the table.

- A data table can also contain one or more *constraint* objects that are used to maintain the integrity of the data in the table. A unique key constraint ensures that the values in a column, such as the primary key column, are unique. And a foreign key constraint determines how the rows in one table are affected when corresponding rows in a related table are updated or deleted.

- The data relation objects define how the tables in the dataset are related. They are used to manage constraints and to simplify the navigation between related tables.

- All of the objects in a dataset are stored in collections. For example, the data table objects are stored in a data table collection, and the data row objects are stored in a data row collection. You can refer to these collections through the properties of the containing objects.

Figure 2-8   How a dataset is organized

The dataset classes

Figure 2-9 presents some of the properties and methods of the four main classes that you use to work with a dataset: DataSet, DataTable, DataColumn, and DataRow. As you saw in the previous figure, the objects you create from these classes form a hierarchy where each dataset can contain one or more tables and each table can contain one or more rows and one or more columns.

Because of that, a dataset contains a Tables property that provides access to the collection of tables in the dataset. Similarly, a data table contains a Columns property and a Rows property that provide access to the collections of columns and rows in the table. These are the properties you're most likely to use as you work with these objects.

Although they're not shown in this figure, the collections you refer to through the Tables property of a dataset and the Columns and Rows properties of a data table have properties and methods of their own. For instance, each collection has a Count property that you can use to determine how many items are in the collection. To get the number of tables in a dataset named payablesDataSet, for example, you can use code like this:

```
payablesDataSet.Tables.Count()
```

To access a specific item in a collection, you use the Item property. On that property, you specify the index value or name of the item you want to access. To access the Vendors table in payablesDataSet, for example, you can use code like this:

```
payablesDataSet.Tables.Item("Vendors")
```

Since Item is the default property of the collection class, however, you typically omit it like this:

```
payablesDataSet.Tables("Vendors")
```

The code in this figure shows how you can use a For Each...Next statement to loop through the items in a collection. Here, the statement loops through the rows in the Vendors table. To do that, it uses a variable that's declared as a DataRow object. Then, the For Each...Next statement uses this variable to retrieve the value of the Name column in each row. You can use similar code to loop through the columns in a table or the tables in a dataset.

Common properties of the DataSet class

Property	Description
DataSetName	The name of the dataset.
Tables	A collection of the DataTable objects contained in the dataset.
Relations	A collection of the DataRelation objects contained in the dataset.

Common properties and methods of the DataTable class

Property	Description
TableName	The name of the table.
Columns	A collection of the DataColumn objects contained in the data table.
Rows	A collection of the DataRow objects contained in the data table.
Constraints	A collection of the Constraint objects contained in the data table.

Method	Description
NewRow	Creates a new row in the table.

Common properties of the DataColumn class

Property	Description
ColumnName	The name of the column.
AllowDBNull	Indicates whether the column allows null values.
AutoIncrement	Indicates whether the column is an auto-increment column, which is similar to an identity column in SQL Server.

Common properties and methods of the DataRow class

Property	Description
Item	Accesses the specified column of the row.

Method	Description
Delete	Deletes a row.
IsNull	Indicates whether the specified column contains a null value.

Code that refers to the rows collection in the tables collection of a dataset

```
Dim message As String
For Each dr As DataRow In vendorsDataSet.Tables("Vendors").Rows
    message &= dr.Item("Name") & vbCrLf
Next
MessageBox.Show(message)
```

Description

- You'll use the properties and methods of the dataset classes most often when you work with ADO.NET objects through code.

- Each collection of objects has properties and methods that you can use to work with the collection.

Figure 2-9   The DataSet, DataTable, DataColumn, and DataRow classes

How ADO.NET applications are structured

As you saw earlier in this chapter, you can use two basic techniques to retrieve and work with the data in a database. With the first technique, you use a data adapter (or a table adapter that contains a data adapter) to retrieve the data and store it in a dataset and to update the database with changes made to the dataset. With the second technique, you work with the database by executing command objects directly, and you work with result sets using a data reader. In the next two topics, you'll see how the structures of applications that use these two techniques differ.

How an application that uses datasets is structured

When you develop an application that uses datasets, it typically consists of the two layers shown in figure 2-10. The first layer, called the *presentation layer*, consists of the form classes that display the user interface, plus the dataset classes used by the application. When you use a data source as shown in figure 2-2, for example, the application includes a dataset class that defines the tables and columns in the data source. Then, you can use the objects that are created when you drag the data source to a form for working with the data in the dataset that's created.

The second layer, called the *database layer*, always includes the database itself. In addition, this layer can include database classes that provide the data access required by the application. These classes typically include methods that connect to the database and retrieve, insert, add, and delete information from the database. Then, the presentation layer can call these methods to access the database, leaving the details of database access to the database classes.

Please note, however, that you can't use database classes when you develop an application by using a data source. That's because the table adapter object that you use to work with the database is generated for you when you drag a date source to a form. As a result, all of the code in an application like this is typically stored in the presentation layer.

The primary benefit of using data sources and datasets is rapid application development. This is especially useful for developing small, relatively simple applications and for prototyping larger applications. As an application gets more complicated, though, so does the use of data sources and datasets. So at some point, it often makes sense to use a three-layer architecture with business classes as shown in the next figure.

In case you aren't familiar with the term *prototyping*, it refers to quickly developing a working model of an application that can be reviewed by the intended users. Then, the users can point out what's wrong with the prototype or what they want changed, and the prototype can be changed accordingly. When the users agree that the prototype does or will do everything that they want, the application can be completely rewritten, often with a three-layer architecture.

The standard architecture of an application that uses datasets

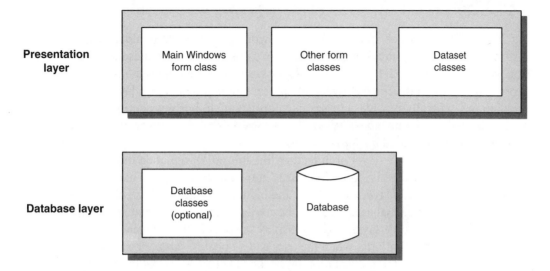

Description

- When you use a dataset to store the data that's retrieved from a database, the application is typically separated into two layers: the presentation layer and the database layer.

- The *presentation layer* consists of the forms that provide the application's user interface. In addition, this layer contains the dataset classes that define the data that the forms can use.

- The *database layer* consists of the database itself, and it can also include database classes that provide the methods for retrieving and updating the database for the application.

- If you create ADO.NET objects using a data source, you won't be able to use database classes in the database layer. If you create ADO.NET objects through code, you will be able to use database classes in the database layer, although that isn't a common practice.

- You can also store the dataset classes in a layer between the presentation layer and the database layer. Since data sources and datasets are typically used for rapid application development, however, this isn't a common technique.

Figure 2-10   How an application that uses datasets is structured

How an application that uses business classes is structured

If you use commands and data readers to work with the data in a database instead of using data sources and datasets, you can structure a database application as shown in figure 2-11. This *three-layer architecture* includes a *middle layer* that acts as an interface between the presentation and database layers. The middle layer typically includes classes that correspond to business entities (for example, vendors and invoices). When the classes represent *business objects*, they are commonly called *business classes*.

When you use a three-layer architecture like this, all of the code that's related to database access is stored in classes in the database layer. Then, a form class in the presentation layer can (1) call the methods of the database classes to retrieve data from the database, (2) store the retrieved data in the related business objects in the middle layer, and (3) display the data in these business objects on the form. Similarly, when the user adds, updates, or deletes data in a form, the form class in the presentation layer can (1) change the data in the related business objects, and (2) call the methods of a database class to save the changes to the database.

Although this approach to application development may seem complicated, using an architecture like this has some distinct advantages. First, it is usually easier to debug and maintain a three-layer application because you have complete control over the code. In contrast, you are forced to rely on a large amount of generated code when you use data sources and data sets.

Second, a three-layer architecture allows classes to be shared among applications. In particular, the classes that make up the database and middle layers can be placed in *class libraries* that can be used by more than one project.

Third, a three-layer architecture allows application development to be spread among members of a development team. For instance, one group of developers can work on the database layer, another group on the middle layer, and a third group on the presentation layer.

Fourth, you can run different layers of an application on different servers to improve performance. In that case, a three-layer architecture is often referred to as a *three-tier architecture*. But often, these terms are used interchangeably without implying how the layers are implemented in terms of hardware.

Finally, using a three-layer architecture makes it possible to use object data sources. As you will see in chapter 9, object data sources let you use database classes to get the data you need for an application, store that data in business objects, and still get some of the benefits that are associated with the use of data sources.

The architecture of an application that uses business classes

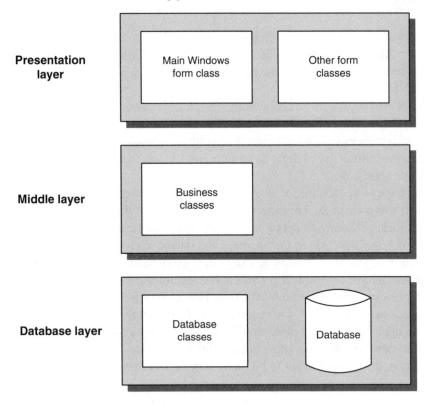

Description

- To simplify development and maintenance, many applications that use business classes use a *three-layer architecture* that includes a middle layer.

- The classes in the *middle layer*, sometimes called the *business rules layer*, act as an interface between the classes in the presentation and database layers. These classes can represent business entities, such as vendors or invoices, or they can implement business rules, such as discount or credit policies.

- When the classes in the middle layer represent business entities, the classes can be referred to as *business classes*, and the objects that are created from these classes can be referred to as *business objects*.

- When you use business classes, you don't use datasets. Instead, you use commands and data readers to work directly with the database, and the data you retrieve from the database is stored in business objects.

- Often, the classes that make up the database layer and the middle layer are implemented in *class libraries* that can be shared among applications.

Figure 2-11   How an application that uses business classes is structured

Perspective

One of the goals of this chapter was to introduce you to the two basic ways that you can develop ADO.NET applications: with datasets and without datasets. The other goal was to introduce you to some of the classes that you'll be using as you develop ADO.NET applications.

With that as background, the three chapters in section 2 will show you how to build significant database applications by using data sources and datasets. As you will see, this approach is especially useful for developing simple applications or prototyping larger applications. By chapter 5, though, you'll start to see some of the limitations of this approach.

Then, the five chapters in section 3 will show you how to build database applications without using datasets. This approach lets you use the three-layer architecture, which makes it easier to debug and maintain a complicated application and also lets you reuse the code in the business and database classes. By the time you finish section 3, you'll know how to use both approaches to application development, and you'll have a good feel for when you should use each approach.

Keep in mind, however, that these aren't the only two approaches for developing database applications. In section 4, for example, you'll learn how to use LINQ to develop database applications. And in section 5, you'll learn how to use the Entity Framework to develop database applications. Before you decide how to develop an application, then, you'll want to be familiar with all of these techniques.

Terms

ADO.NET	.NET data provider
ActiveX Data Objects	connected classes
dataset	connection string
data table	disconnected class
data adapter	data relation
command	data column
connection	data row
disconnected data architecture	constraint
data source	presentation layer
Data Sources window	database layer
Component Designer tray	prototyping
table adapter	three-layer architecture
data reader	middle layer
concurrency	business rules layer
concurrency control	business class
optimistic concurrency	business object
concurrency exception	class library
"last in wins"	three-tier architecture

Section 2

How to use data sources and datasets for Rapid Application Development

Now that you're familiar with the basic concepts and terms related to database programming, you're ready to learn the details of developing database applications. In this section, you'll learn how to use Visual Studio's data sources feature that you were introduced to in chapter 2. This is the quickest and easiest way to develop database applications.

In chapter 3, you'll learn the basic skills for working with data sources and datasets. Then, in chapter 4, you'll learn some additional skills for working with bound controls, and you'll learn one way to create queries that use parameters. Finally, in chapter 5, you'll learn how to use the Dataset Designer to work with the schema for a dataset. When you complete this section, you'll be able to develop significant database applications on your own.

3

How to work with data sources and datasets

In this chapter, you'll learn how to use data sources and datasets to develop database applications. This makes it easier than ever to generate Windows forms that work with the data that's in the data sources. And this is especially useful for developing simple applications or prototyping larger applications.

How to create a data source

As its name implies, a *data source* specifies the source of the data for an application. Since most applications get their data from a database, the figures that follow show how to create a data source that gets data from a database.

How to use the Data Sources window

The data sources that are available to a project are listed in the Data Sources window as shown in figure 3-1. Here, the second screen shows a data source for the Terms table that's available from the Payables database that's described in figure 1-8 of chapter 1. As you can see, this data source includes three columns from the Terms table named TermsID, Description, and DueDays.

If no data sources are available to a project, the Data Sources window will display an Add New Data Source link as shown in the first screen. Then, you can click on this link to start the Data Source Configuration Wizard described in figures 3-2 through 3-6. This wizard lets you add a new data source to the project. When you're done, you can drag the data source onto a form to create bound controls as described later in this chapter.

An empty Data Sources window

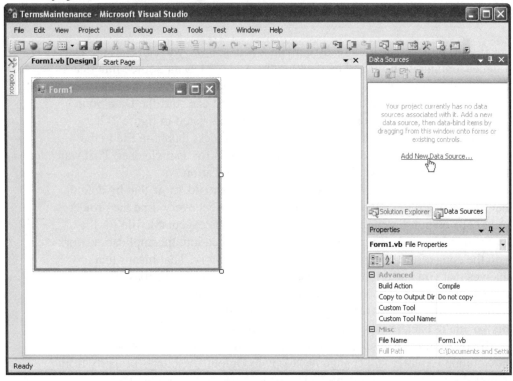

A Data Sources window after a data source has been added

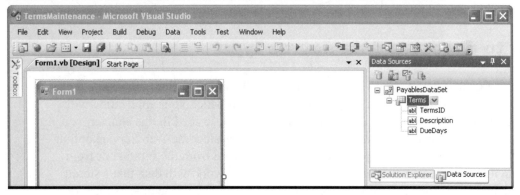

Description

- A *data source* shows all the tables and columns in the dataset that are available to your application.

- You can display the Data Sources window by clicking on the Data Sources tab that's usually grouped with the Solution Explorer at the right edge of the Visual Studio window or by selecting the Show Data Sources command from the Data menu.

- To create a data source, you can click the Add New Data Source link. Then, you can drag the data source to a form to create controls that are bound to the data source.

Figure 3-1   How to use the Data Sources window

How to start the Data Source Configuration Wizard

If your project doesn't already contain a data source, you can start the Data Source Configuration Wizard by clicking the Add New Data Source link that's shown in the previous figure. However, if your project already contains a data source, this link won't be available. In that case, you can start the Data Source Configuration Wizard by using one of the techniques listed in figure 3-2.

The last technique is to add a SQL Server or Access database file to the project. You may want to do that if the application is for a single user. That way, the database can easily be distributed with the application.

If you add a database file to your project, you should know that by default, that file is copied to the output directory for the project every time the project is built. (The output directory is the directory where the executable file for the application is stored.) Then, when you run the application, the application works with the copy of the database file in the output directory. That means that any changes that you make to the database aren't applied to the database file in the project directory. And each time you rebuild the application, the database in the output directory is overwritten by the unchanged database in the project directory so you're back to the original version of the database.

If you want to change the way this works, you can select the database file in the Solution Explorer and change its "Copy to Output Directory" property from "Copy always" to "Copy if newer." Then, the database file in the output directory won't be overwritten unless the database file in the project directory contains more current data.

How to choose a data source type

Figure 3-2 also shows the first step of the Data Source Configuration Wizard. This step lets you specify the source from which your application will get its data. To work with data from a database as described in this chapter, you select the Database option. However, you can also select the Web Service option to work with data from a web service that's available from the Internet or from an intranet. Or, you can select the Object option to work with data that's stored in a business object. This option lets you take advantage of the objects that are available from the middle layer of an application as described in chapter 9. It also lets you take advantage of the objects that are available from an object model that you create with LINQ to SQL as described in chapter 13. And it lets you take advantage of the objects that are available from an Entity Data Model that you create with the Entity Framework as described in chapter 18.

The first step of the Data Source Configuration Wizard

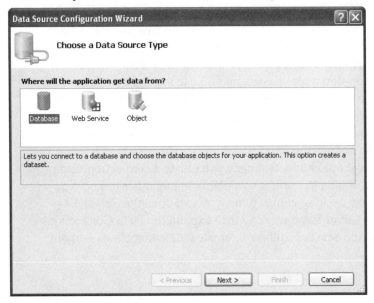

How to start the Data Source Configuration Wizard

- Click on the Add New Data Source link that's available from the Data Sources window when a project doesn't contain any data sources.
- Click on the Add New Data Source button at the top of the Data Sources window.
- Select the Add New Data Source command from Visual Studio's Data menu.
- Add a SQL Server (.mdf) or Access (.mdb) data file to the project using the Project→Add→Existing Item command. Then, the wizard will skip to the step shown in figure 3-6 that lets you choose the database objects you want to include.

How to choose a data source type

- To get your data from a database, select the Database option. This option lets you create applications like the ones described in this chapter.
- To get your data from a web service, select the Web Service option. This option lets you browse the web to select a web service that will supply data to your application.
- To get your data from a business object, select the Object option. This option lets you create applications like the ones described in chapter 9. You can also use this option with applications that use LINQ to SQL or the Entity Framework as described in chapters 13 and 18.

Note

- Before you start this procedure, you need to install your database server software on your own PC or on a network server, and you need to attach your database to it. For more information, please refer to appendix A.

Figure 3-2   How to start the Data Source Configuration Wizard and choose a data source type

How to choose the connection for a data source

The second step of the Data Source Configuration Wizard, shown in figure 3-3, lets you choose the data connection you want to use to connect to the database. If you've previously defined a data connection, you can choose that connection from the drop-down list. To be sure you use the right connection, you can click the button with the plus sign on it to display the connection string.

If the connection you want to use hasn't already been defined, you can click the New Connection button. Then, you can use the dialog boxes shown in the next figure to create the connection.

Before I go on, you should know that once you create a connection using the Data Source Configuration Wizard, it's available to any other project you create. To see a list of the existing connections, you can open the Server Explorer window (View→Server Explorer) and then expand the Data Connections node. You can also use the Server Explorer to create data connections without creating a data source.

The second step of the Data Source Configuration Wizard

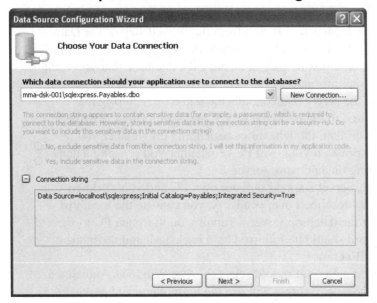

Description

- When you click the Next button in the first step of the Data Source Configuration Wizard, the Choose Your Data Connection step shown above is displayed.

- If you've already established a connection to the database you want to use, you can choose that connection. Otherwise, you can click the New Connection button to display the Add Connection dialog box shown in the next figure.

- To see the connection string for an existing connection, click the button with the plus sign on it.

Figure 3-3   How to choose the connection for a data source

How to create a connection to a database

If you click the New Connection button from the second step of the Data Source Configuration Wizard, the Add Connection dialog box shown in figure 3-4 is displayed. This dialog box helps you identify the database that you want to access and provides the information you need to access it. That includes specifying the name of the server that contains the database, entering the information that's required to log on to the server, and specifying the name of the database. How you do that, though, varies depending on whether you're running SQL Server Express on your own PC or whether you're using a database server that's running on a network server.

If you're using SQL Server Express on your own PC and you've downloaded and installed it as described in appendix A, you can use the localhost keyword to specify that the database server is running on the same PC as the application. This keyword should be followed by a backslash and the name of the database server: SqlExpress.

For the logon information, you should select the Use Windows Authentication option. Then, SQL Server Express will use the login name and password that you use to log in to Windows as the name and password for the database server too. As a result, you won't need to provide a separate user name and password in this dialog box.

Last, you enter or select the name of the database that you want to connect to. In this figure, for example, the connection is for the Payables database that's used throughout this book. When you're done supplying the information for the connection, you can click the Test Connection button to be sure that the connection works.

In contrast, if you need to connect to a database that's running on a database server that's available through a network, you need to get the connection information from the network or database administrator. This information will include the name of the database server, logon information, and the name of the database. Once you establish a connection to the database, you can use that connection for all of the other applications that use that database.

By default, Visual Studio assumes you want to access a SQL Server database as shown here. This works for SQL Server 7, 2000, 2005, and 2008 databases including SQL Server Express databases. If you want to access a different type of database, though, you can click the Change button to display the Change Data Source dialog box. Then, you can select the data source and data provider you want to use to access that data source. If you want to access an Oracle database, for example, you can select the Oracle Database item in the Data Source list. Then, you can choose the data provider for Oracle or the data provider for OLE DB from the Data Provider drop-down list.

The Add Connection and Change Data Source dialog boxes

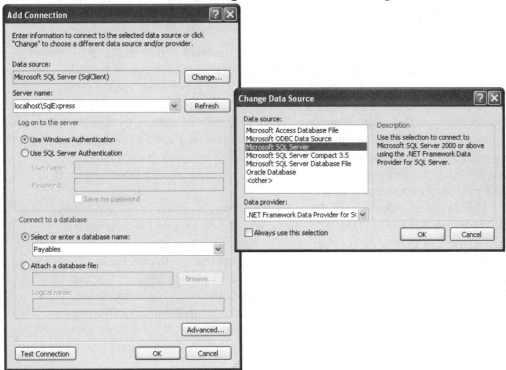

Description

- By default, a connection uses the SQL Server data provider. If that's not what you want, you can click the Change button in the Add Connection dialog box to display the Change Data Source dialog box. Then, you can choose the data source and data provider you want to use.

- To create a connection, specify the name of the server that contains the database, enter the information that's required to log on to the server, and specify the name of the database you want to connect to.

- To be sure that the connection is configured properly, you can click the Test Connection button in the Add Connection dialog box.

Express Edition differences

- The Change Data Source dialog box provides only three options: Microsoft Access Database File, Microsoft SQL Server Compact 3.5, and Microsoft SQL Server Database File. The default is Microsoft SQL Server Compact 3.5, which probably isn't what you want.

- The Add Connection dialog box is simpler, and it includes a Database File Name text box that you use to specify the database. To do that, you click the Browse button to the right of the text box and use the resulting dialog box to point to the data file for the database.

Figure 3-4   How to create a connection to a database

How to save a connection string in the app.config file

After you select or create a data connection, the third step of the Data Source Configuration Wizard is displayed. This step, shown in figure 3-5, asks whether you want to save the connection string in the application configuration file (app.config). In most cases, that's what you'll want to do. Then, any table adapter that uses the connection can refer to the connection string by name. That way, if the connection information changes, you only need to change it in the app.config file. Otherwise, the connection string is stored in each table adapter that uses the connection, and you'll have to change each table adapter if the connection information changes.

This figure also shows how the connection string is stored in the app.config file. Although this file contains XML data, you should be able to understand it even if you don't know XML. Here, for example, you can see that the connectionStrings element contains an add element that contains three attributes. The first attribute, name, specifies the name of the connection string, in this case, PayablesConnectionString. The second attribute, connectionString, contains the actual connection string. And the third attribute, providerName, identifies the data provider, in this case, SqlClient.

The third step of the Data Source Configuration Wizard

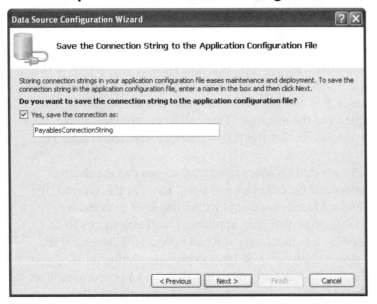

The information that's stored in the app.config file

```
<connectionStrings>
    <add name="TermsMaintenance.My.MySettings.PayablesConnectionString"
        connectionString="Data Source=localhost\sqlexpress;
                          Initial Catalog=Payables;
                          Integrated Security=True"
        providerName="System.Data.SqlClient" />
</connectionStrings>
```

Description

- By default, the connection string is saved in the application configuration file (app.config). If that's not what you want, you can remove the check mark from the Yes option in the third step of the Data Source Configuration Wizard shown above.

- If you don't save the connection string in the app.config file, the string is specified for the connection of each table adapter you create from the data source. Because of that, we recommend you always save the connection string in the app.config file. Then, only the name of the connection string is stored in the connection for each table adapter.

- You can also enter the name you want to use for the connection string in this dialog box. By default, the connection string is given a name that consists of the database name appended with "ConnectionString".

Figure 3-5   How to save a connection string in the app.config file

How to choose database objects for a data source

Figure 3-6 shows how you can use the last step of the Data Source Configuration Wizard to choose the database objects for a data source. This step lets you choose any tables, views, stored procedures, or functions that are available from the database. In some cases, you can just select the table you need from the list of tables that are available from the database. Then, all of the columns in the table are included in the dataset. In this figure, for example, the Terms table is selected.

If you want to include selected columns from a table, you can expand the node for the table and select just the columns you want. Later in this chapter, for example, you'll see a Vendor Maintenance application that uses selected columns from the Vendors table. Note that if an application will allow rows to be added to a table, you can omit a column only if it can have a null value or if it's defined with a default value. Otherwise, you have to provide a value for it.

If you include a column with a default value in a dataset, you need to realize that this value isn't assigned to the column in the dataset, even though the dataset enforces the constraints for that column. Instead, the column will be defined with a default value of null, even though null values aren't allowed in columns with default values. As a result, an exception will be thrown whenever a new row is added to the dataset and a value other than null isn't provided for that column.

This means that either the user or the application must provide an acceptable value for the column. One way to do that is to provide a way for the user to enter a value for the column. Another way is to use the Dataset Designer to set the DefaultValue property for this column as described in this figure. You'll learn more about working with the Dataset Designer later in this chapter.

In a larger project, you might want to include several tables in the dataset. Then, the dataset will maintain the relationships between those tables whenever that's appropriate. Or, you might want to use views, stored procedures, or functions to work with the data in the database. If you have experience working with these database objects, you shouldn't have any trouble understanding how this works. Otherwise, you can refer to *Murach's SQL Server 2008 for Developers* for more information.

If you're using Visual Studio 2008 Service Pack 1, this step of the wizard also lets you select whether you want to store any of the data in a local database cache. If you select this option, another wizard step is displayed that lets you choose which tables you want to store in the cache and how you want the data in each table to be synchronized with the data in the database. Then, when you complete the wizard, a local database is added to your application. This database is then used to populate the associated tables in the dataset. After that, the local database is updated only if the data in the database on the server changes.

A local database cache can be useful if the data in the database changes infrequently. To use this feature, however, you have to add code that starts the synchronization process. For more information on how to do that, please refer to the Visual Studio documentation.

The last step of the Data Source Configuration Wizard

Description

- In the last step of the Data Source Configuration Wizard, you can choose the database objects that you want to include in the dataset for your project.

- In this step, you can choose from any tables, views, stored procedures, or functions that are available from the database. In addition, you can expand the node for any table, view, stored procedure, or function and choose just the columns you want to include in the data source.

- You can also enter the name you want to use for the dataset in this dialog box. By default, the name is the name of the database appended with "DataSet".

- If you select the Enable Local Database Caching option, another wizard step is displayed that lets you choose which tables you want to cache and how you want those tables synchronized with the tables in the database. For more information, see the Visual Studio documentation.

How to work with columns that have default values

- If a column in a database has a default value, that value isn't included in the column definition in the dataset. Because of that, you may want to omit columns with default values from the dataset unless they're needed by the application. Then, when a row is added to the table, the default value is taken from the database.

- If you include a column that's defined with a default value, you must provide a value for that column whenever a row is added to the dataset. One way to do that is to let the user enter a value. Another way is to display the Dataset Designer as described in figure 3-16, click on the column, and use the Properties window to set the DefaultValue property.

Figure 3-6   How to choose database objects for a data source

The schema file created by the Data Source Configuration Wizard

After you complete the Data Source Configuration Wizard, the new data source is displayed in the Data Sources window you saw in figure 3-1. In addition to this data source, Visual Studio generates a file that contains the *schema* for the dataset class. This file defines the structure of the dataset, including the tables it contains, the columns that are included in each table, the data types of each column, and the constraints that are defined for each table.

This schema file is listed in the Solution Explorer window and is given the name you specified for the dataset in the last step of the Data Source Configuration Wizard with a file extension of *xsd*. In figure 3-7, for example, you can see the schema file named PayablesDataSet.xsd. As you'll learn later in this chapter, you can view a graphic representation of this schema by double-clicking on this file.

Beneath the schema file, the Solution Explorer displays the file that contains the generated code for the dataset class. In this figure, this code is stored in the PayablesDataSet.Designer.vb file. When you create bound controls from the data source as shown in this chapter, the code in this class is used to define the dataset object that the controls are bound to. Although you may want to view this code to see how it works, you shouldn't change it. If you do, the dataset may not work correctly.

By the way, you should know that a dataset that's created from a dataset class like the one shown here is called a *typed dataset*. The code in the dataset class makes it possible for you to refer to the tables, rows, and columns in the typed dataset using the simplified syntax you'll see in this chapter and the next chapter.

A project with a dataset defined by a data source

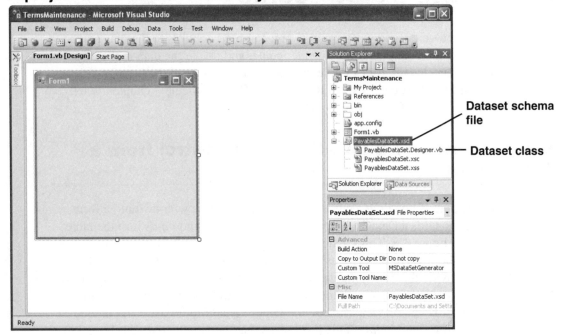

Dataset schema file

Dataset class

Description

- After you create a data source, it's displayed in the Data Sources window. Then, you can use it to create bound controls as shown in this chapter.

- Visual Studio also generates a file that contains the *schema* for the dataset defined by the data source. This file appears in the Solution Explorer and has a file extension of *xsd*. It defines the structure of the dataset, including the tables it contains, the columns in each table, the data types of each column, and the constraints for each table.

- Subordinate to the schema file is a file that contains the generated code for the dataset class. Visual Studio uses this class to create a dataset object when you add the data source to a form.

Notes

- The schema that's generated for a dataset also includes classes that define the table adapter and table adapter manager classes that provide for working with the database. You'll learn about the objects created from these classes in the next figure.

- To see the files that are subordinate to the schema file, click the Show All Files button at the top of the Solution Explorer. Then, expand the node for the schema file.

Figure 3-7   The schema file created by the Data Source Configuration Wizard

How to use a data source

Once you've created a data source, you can bind controls to the data source and then use the bound controls to add, update, and delete the data in the data source. In this chapter, for example, you'll learn how to bind the DataGridView control and TextBox controls to a data source. Then, in the next chapter, you'll learn how to bind a ComboBox control to a data source.

How to generate a DataGridView control from a data source

By default, if you drag a table from the Data Sources window onto a form, Visual Studio adds a DataGridView control to the form and *binds* it to the table as shown in figure 3-8. This creates a DataGridView control that lets you browse all the rows in the table as well as add, update, and delete rows in the table. To provide this functionality, Visual Studio adds a toolbar to the top of the form that provides navigation buttons along with Add, Delete, and Save buttons.

To bind a DataGridView control to a table, Visual Studio uses a technique called *complex data binding*. This just means that the *bound control* is bound to more than one data element. The DataGridView control in this figure, for example, is bound to all the rows and columns in the Terms table.

When you generate a DataGridView control from a data source, Visual Studio also adds five additional objects to the Component Designer tray at the bottom of the Form Designer. First, the DataSet object defines the dataset that contains the Terms table. Second, the TableAdapter object provides commands that can be used to work with the Terms table in the database. Third, the TableAdapterManager object provides for writing the data in two or more related tables to the database so that referential integrity is maintained. Fourth, the BindingSource object specifies the data source (the Terms table) that the controls are bound to, and it provides functionality for working with the data source. Finally, the BindingNavigator defines the toolbar that contains the controls for working with the data source.

Before I go on, I want to point out that in addition to commands, the TableAdapter object provides a built-in connection and a data adapter object that manages the flow of data between the database and the dataset. As you'll see in chapter 4, it can also contain more than one command that retrieves data from the database. A TableAdapter object can only be created by using Visual Studio design tools like the Data Source Configuration Wizard.

I also want to mention that, in general, you shouldn't have any trouble figuring out how to use the binding navigator toolbar. However, you may want to know that if you click the Add button to add a new row and then decide you don't want to do that, you can click the Delete button to delete the new row. However, there's no way to cancel out of an edit operation. Because of that, you may want to add a button to the toolbar that provides this function. You'll learn how to do that in the next chapter.

A form after the Terms table has been dragged onto it

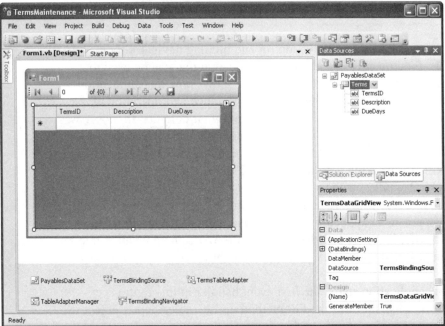

The controls and objects that are created when you drag a data source to a form

Control/object	Description
DataGridView control	Displays the data from the data source in a grid.
BindingNavigator control	Defines the toolbar that can be used to navigate, add, update, and delete rows in the DataGridView control.
BindingSource object	Identifies the data source that the controls on the form are bound to and provides functionality for working with the data source.
DataSet object	Provides access to all of the tables, views, stored procedures, and functions that are available to the project.
TableAdapter object	Provides a data adapter, a connection, and commands for reading data from and writing data to the specified table in the database.
TableAdapterManager object	Provides for writing data in related tables to the database while maintaining referential integrity.

Description

- To *bind* a DataGridView control to a table in a dataset, just drag the table from the Data Sources window onto the form. Then, Visual Studio automatically adds a DataGridView control to the form along with the other controls and objects it needs to work properly. Because the DataGridView control is bound to the table, it can be referred to as a *bound control*.

- To bind a DataGridView control to a data table, Visual Studio uses a technique called *complex data binding*. This means that the control is bound to more than one data element, in this case, all the rows and columns in the table.

Figure 3-8   How to generate a DataGridView control from a data source

A Terms Maintenance application that uses a DataGridView control

At this point, the DataGridView control and binding navigator toolbar provide all the functionality needed for an application that can be used to maintain the data in the Terms table. Figure 3-9 shows how this application appears to the user at runtime. Note that the appearance and operation of the DataGridView control haven't been changed from their defaults. In most cases, however, you'll want to at least make some minor changes in the appearance of this control. You'll learn how to do that in the next chapter when I present some additional skills for working with the DataGridView control.

This figure also presents the code that Visual Studio generates when you create this application, which includes everything needed to make it work. As a result, you can create an application like this one without having to write a single line of code. If you've ever had to manually write an application that provides similar functionality, you can appreciate how much work this saves you.

When this application starts, the first event handler in this figure is executed. This event handler uses the Fill method of the TableAdapter object to load data into the DataSet object. In this example, the data in the Terms table of the Payables database is loaded into the Terms table of the dataset. Then, because the DataGridView control is bound to this table, the data is displayed in this control and the user can use it to modify the data in the table by adding, updating, or deleting rows.

When the user changes the data in the DataGridView control, those changes are saved to the dataset. However, the changes aren't saved to the database until the user clicks the Save button in the toolbar. Then, the second event handler in this figure is executed. This event handler starts by calling the Validate method of the form, which causes the Validating and Validated events of the control that's losing focus to be fired. Although you probably won't use the Validated event, you may use the Validating event to validate a row that's being added or modified. However, I've found that this event doesn't work well with the binding navigator toolbar, so you won't see it used in this book.

Next, the EndEdit method of the BindingSource object applies any pending changes to the dataset. That's necessary because when you add or update a row, the new or modified row isn't saved until you move to another row.

Finally, the UpdateAll method of the TableAdapterManager object saves the data in the DataSet object to the Payables database. When this method is called, it checks each row in each table of the dataset to determine if it's a new row, a modified row, or a row that should be deleted. Then, it causes the appropriate SQL Insert, Update, and Delete statements to be executed for these rows. As a result, the Update method works efficiently since it only updates the rows that need to be updated. In addition, the Insert, Update, and Delete statements are executed in a sequence that maintains referential integrity.

Now that you understand this code, you should notice that it doesn't provide for any exceptions that may occur during this processing. Because of that, you need to add the appropriate exception handling code for any production applications that you develop so that they won't crash. You'll learn how to do that later in this chapter.

The user interface for the Terms Maintenance application

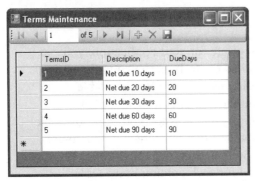

The code that's generated by Visual Studio

```
Private Sub Form1_Load(ByVal sender As System.Object, _
        ByVal e As System.EventArgs) Handles MyBase.Load
    'TODO: This line of code loads data into the 'PayablesDataSet.Terms'
    'table. You can move, or remove it, as needed.
    Me.TermsTableAdapter.Fill(Me.PayablesDataSet.Terms)
End Sub

Private Sub TermsBindingNavigatorSaveItem_Click( _
        ByVal sender As System.Object, ByVal e As System.EventArgs) _
        Handles TermsBindingNavigatorSaveItem.Click
    Me.Validate()
    Me.TermsBindingSource.EndEdit()
    Me.TableAdapterManager.UpdateAll(Me.PayablesDataSet)
End Sub
```

The syntax of the Fill method

```
TableAdapter.Fill(DataSet.TableName)
```

The syntax of the UpdateAll method

```
TableAdapterManager.UpdateAll(DataSet)
```

Description

- Visual Studio automatically generates the code shown above and places it in the source code file when you drag a data source onto a form. If necessary, you can edit this code.
- The generated code uses the Fill method of the TableAdapter object that's generated for the table to read data from the database, and it uses the UpdateAll method of the TableAdapterManager object that's generated for the dataset to write data to the database. It also uses the EndEdit method of the BindingSource object to save any changes that have been made to the current row to the dataset.
- The Validate method causes the Validating and Validated events of the control that is losing the focus to be fired. You can use the Validating event to perform any required data validation for the form.
- Users of a DataGridView control can sort the rows by clicking on a column heading and can size columns by dragging the column separators to the left or right.

Figure 3-9   A Terms Maintenance application that uses a DataGridView control

How to change the controls associated with a data source

If the DataGridView control isn't appropriate for your application, you can bind the columns of a data source to individual controls as shown in figure 3-10. Here, the data source consists of several columns from the Vendors table.

To associate the columns in a table with individual controls, you select the Details option from the drop-down list that's available when you select the table in the Data Sources window. This is illustrated in the first screen in this figure. Then, if you drag that table from the Data Sources window onto a form, Visual Studio generates a label and a bound control for each column in the table.

For most string and numeric columns, Visual Studio generates a TextBox control. That's the case for the Vendors table, as you'll see in the next figure. If you want to change the type of control that's associated with a column, though, you can select the column in the Data Sources window and then use the drop-down list that's displayed to select a different type of control. You can see the list of controls that are available in the second screen in this figure.

How to change the default control for a data table

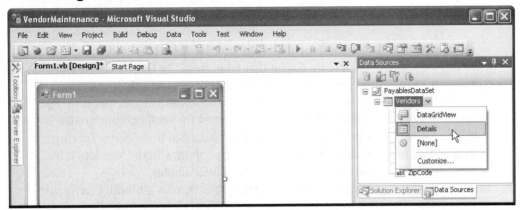

How to change the default control for a column in a data table

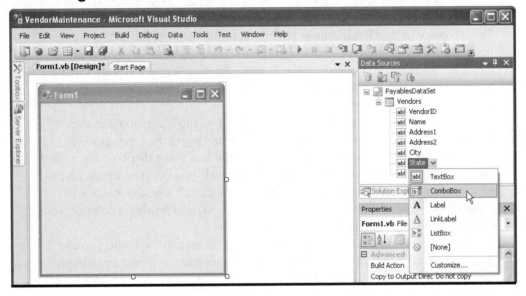

Description

- By default, a data table is associated with a DataGridView control. To change this default so that each column in the table is displayed in a separate control, select the Details option from the drop-down list for the table.

- By default, most string and numeric columns within a data table are associated with the TextBox control. To change this default, select the type of control you want to use from the drop-down list for the column.

Figure 3-10   How to change the controls associated with a data source

How to generate detail controls from a data source

If you change the control type that's associated with a table from DataGridView to Details and then drag that table from the Data Sources window onto a form, Visual Studio will add the appropriate controls to the form as shown in figure 3-11. In addition, it will bind those controls to the appropriate columns in the table, and it will add a Label control for each column to identify it. In this figure, for example, you can see that Visual Studio added a TextBox control and a Label control for each of the seven columns in the Vendors table. In addition, it added DataSet, BindingSource, TableAdapter, TableAdapterManager, and BindingNavigator objects, plus a binding navigator toolbar, just as it does when you generate a DataGridView control.

Notice that when you use text boxes to work with the data in a table, only one row of the table is displayed at a time. Then, Visual Studio uses *simple data binding* to bind each text box to a single column value. To do that, it sets the Text property in the DataBindings collection to the name of the data column that the control is bound to. In this figure, for example, you can see the drop-down list for the Text property of the DataBindings collection. It shows that the Vendor ID text box is bound to the VendorID column of the VendorsBindingSource object.

Once the labels and text boxes are displayed on the form, you can use standard skills for editing the labels and text boxes to get the form to work correctly. For example, if you want to change the text that's displayed in a label, you can select the label and edit its Text property. If you don't want the user to be able to enter data for a particular column, you can change the ReadOnly property of the text box to True. Or, if you don't want to display a column, you can delete the label and text box for that column.

Alternatively, instead of dragging the entire table onto the form, you can drag just the columns you want. In addition, if you want to create a read-only form, you can edit the BindingNavigator toolbar to remove its Add, Delete, and Save buttons. You'll learn how to do that in the next chapter.

A form after the Vendors table has been dragged onto it

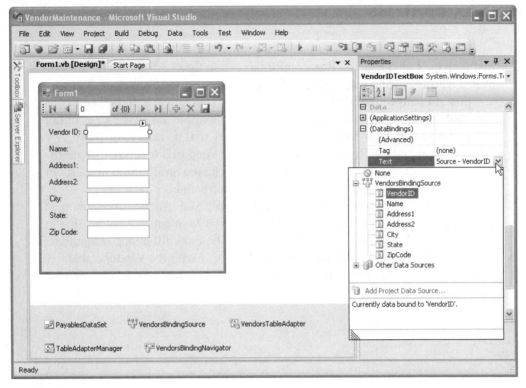

Description

- When you drag a table whose columns are associated with individual controls to a form, Visual Studio automatically adds the controls along with labels that identify the columns. It also adds a binding navigator toolbar and the objects for working with the bound data just as it does for a DataGridView control.
- To display the value of a column in a text box, Visual Studio sets the Text property in the DataBindings collection to the name of the data column. This is known as *simple data binding* because the control is bound to a single column value. To change the binding, you can use the drop-down list for the Text property as shown above.

Note

- When you drag individual controls to a form, don't drop them at the top of the form. If you do, the toolbar will overlay the first label and text box and make them difficult to move.

Figure 3-11   How to generate detail controls from a data source

A Vendor Maintenance application that uses TextBox controls

Figure 3-12 shows the user interface for a Vendor Maintenance application that uses the Label and TextBox controls shown in the previous figure. However, I rearranged and made several changes to those controls.

First, I changed the label for the Address1 text box to "Address:" and I removed the label from the Address2 text box. Next, I changed the sizes of the text boxes so they're appropriate for the data they will be used to display. Finally, I changed the ReadOnly property of the VendorID text box to True so the user can't enter data into this control, and I change the TabStop property of this text box to False so it isn't included in the tab sequence.

This figure also shows the code for the Vendor Maintenance application. If you compare this code with the code for the Terms Maintenance application in figure 3-9, you'll see that it's almost identical. The only difference is that the code for the Vendor Maintenance application works with the Vendors table, table adapter, and binding source instead of the Terms table, table adapter, and binding source.

The user interface for the Vendor Maintenance application

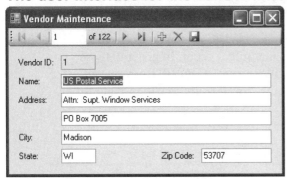

The code for the application

```
Public Class Form1

    Private Sub Form1_Load(ByVal sender As System.Object, _
            ByVal e As System.EventArgs) Handles MyBase.Load
        'TODO: This line of code loads data into the
        'PayablesDataSet.Vendors' table.
        'You can move, or remove it, as needed.
        Me.VendorsTableAdapter.Fill(Me.PayablesDataSet.Vendors)
    End Sub

    Private Sub VendorsBindingNavigatorSaveItem_Click( _
            ByVal sender As System.Object, ByVal e As System.EventArgs) _
            Handles VendorsBindingNavigatorSaveItem.Click
        Me.Validate()
        Me.VendorsBindingSource.EndEdit()
        Me.TableAdapterManager.UpdateAll(Me.PayablesDataSet)
    End Sub

End Class
```

Figure 3-12   A Vendor Maintenance application that uses TextBox controls

How to handle data errors

When you develop an application that uses a data source, you'll want to provide code that handles any data errors that might occur. In general, those errors fall into three categories: data provider errors, ADO.NET errors, and errors that the DataGridView control detects. You'll learn how to provide for these errors in the topics that follow.

How to handle data provider errors

When you access a database, there is always the possibility that an unrecoverable error might occur. For example, the database server might be shut down when you try to access it, or the network connection to the database server might be broken. Either way, your applications should usually anticipate such problems by catching any database exceptions that might occur.

Figure 3-13 shows the exceptions thrown by the .NET data providers when an unrecoverable error occurs. You can refer to these errors as *data provider errors*. As you can see, each data provider has its own exception class. So, if you're using the SQL Server data provider, you should catch exceptions of the SqlException class. If you're using the Oracle data provider, you should catch exceptions of the OracleException class. And so on.

The code example in this figure shows how you can catch a SqlException that might occur when attempting to fill a dataset using a table adapter. Here, the shaded lines show the code that has been added to the generated code. This code will display an error message when a SqlException occurs, and it uses the Number and Message properties of the SqlException class to display details about the exception. It also uses the GetType method to indicate the type of exception that occurred.

Although it's uncommon, more than one server error can occur as the result of a single database operation. In that case, an error object is created for each error. These objects are stored in a collection that you can access through the Errors property of the exception object. Each error object contains a Number and Message property just like the exception object. However, because the Number and Message properties of the exception object are set to the Number and Message properties of the first error in the Errors collection, you don't usually need to work with the individual error objects.

.NET data provider exception classes

Name	Description
SqlException	Thrown if a server error occurs when accessing a SQL Server database.
OracleException	Thrown if a server error occurs when accessing an Oracle database.
OdbcException	Thrown if a server error occurs when accessing an ODBC database.
OleDbException	Thrown if a server error occurs when accessing an OLE DB database.

Common members of the .NET data provider exception classes

Property	Description
Number	An error number that identifies the type of error.
Message	A message that describes the error.
Source	The name of the provider that generated the error.
Errors	A collection of error objects that contain information about the errors that occurred during a database operation.

Method	Description
GetType()	Gets the type of the current exception.

Code that catches a SQL exception

```
Private Sub Form1_Load(ByVal sender As System.Object, _
        ByVal e As System.EventArgs) Handles MyBase.Load
    Try
        Me.VendorsTableAdapter.Fill(Me.PayablesDataSet.Vendors)
    Catch ex As SqlException
        MessageBox.Show("SQL Server error # " & ex.Number _
            & ": " & ex.Message, ex.GetType.ToString)
    End Try
End Sub
```

Description

- Whenever the data provider (SQL Server, Oracle, ODBC, or OLE DB) encounters a situation it can't handle, a data provider exception is thrown. You can handle these types of exceptions by catching them and displaying appropriate error messages.

- The Number and Message properties pinpoint the specific server error that caused the data provider exception to be thrown.

- The SqlException class is stored in the System.Data.SqlClient namespace.

Figure 3-13   How to handle data provider errors

How to handle ADO.NET errors

When you work with bound controls, *ADO.NET errors* can occur when the data in those controls is saved to the dataset (not the database), or when an Insert, Update, or Delete statement can't be executed against the database. Figure 3-14 presents some of the most common of those errors.

Here, ConstraintException and NoNullAllowedException are subclasses of the DataException class, so you can catch either of these errors by catching DataException errors. In contrast, DBConcurrencyException isn't a subclass of the DataException class, so you must catch DBConcurrencyException errors separately. All of the ADO.NET exception classes are members of the System.Data namespace.

The error-handling code in this figure catches errors caused by the EndEdit method of a binding source and the UpdateAll method of a table adapter manager. The first exception, DBConcurrencyException, occurs if the number of rows that are affected by an insert, update, or delete operation is zero, which typically indicates that concurrency errors have occurred. Then, a message box is used to display an error message, and the Fill method of the table adapter is used to retrieve the current data from the database and load it into the Vendors data table. That will help prevent further concurrency errors from occurring.

Although you might think that a concurrency error would be generated by the database rather than ADO.NET, that's not the case. To understand why, you need to realize that the Update and Delete statements that are generated for a table adapter contain code that checks that a row hasn't changed since it was retrieved. But if the row has changed, the row with the specified criteria won't be found and the SQL statement won't be executed. When the table adapter discovers that the row wasn't updated or deleted, however, it realizes there was a concurrency error and throws an exception.

Like other exception classes provided by the .NET Framework, each ADO.NET exception class has a Message property and a GetType method that you can use to display information about the error. You can see how this property and method are used in the second Catch block in this figure, which catches any other ADO.NET exceptions that may occur. This Catch block displays a dialog box that uses the Message property and the GetType method of the DataException object to describe the error. Then, it uses the CancelEdit method of the binding source to cancel the current edit operation.

Incidentally, to test your handling of concurrency exceptions, you can start two instances of Visual Studio and run the same application from both of them. Then, you can access and update the same row from both instances.

Common ADO.NET exception classes

Class	Description
DBConcurrencyException	The exception that's thrown by the data adapter if the number of rows affected by an insert, update, or delete operation is zero. This exception is typically caused by a concurrency violation.
DataException	The general exception that's thrown when an ADO.NET error occurs.
ConstraintException	The exception that's thrown if an operation violates a constraint. This is a subclass of the DataException class.
NoNullAllowedException	The exception that's thrown when an add or update operation attempts to save a null value in a column that doesn't allow nulls. This is a subclass of the DataException class.

Common members of the ADO.NET exception classes

Property	Description
`Message`	A message that describes the exception.

Method	Description
`GetType()`	Gets the type of the current exception.

Code that handles ADO.NET errors

```
Try
    Me.VendorsBindingSource.EndEdit()
    Me.TableAdapterManager.UpdateAll(Me.PayablesDataSet)
Catch ex As DBConcurrencyException
    MessageBox.Show("A concurrency error occurred. " _
        & "The row was not updated.", "Concurrency Exception")
    Me.VendorsTableAdapter.Fill(Me.PayablesDataSet.Vendors)
Catch ex As DataException
    MessageBox.Show(ex.Message, ex.GetType.ToString)
    VendorsBindingSource.CancelEdit()
Catch ex As SqlException
    MessageBox.Show("SQL Server error # " & ex.Number _
        & ": " & ex.Message, ex.GetType.ToString)
End Try
```

Description

- An ADO.NET exception is an exception that occurs on any ADO.NET object. All of these exceptions are members of the System.Data namespace.

- In most cases, you'll catch specific types of exceptions if you want to perform special processing when those exceptions occur. Then, you can use the DataException class to catch other ADO.NET exceptions that are represented by its subclasses.

Figure 3-14   How to handle ADO.NET errors

How to handle data errors for a DataGridView control

Because the DataGridView control was designed to work with data sources, it can detect some types of data entry errors before they're saved to the dataset. If, for example, a user doesn't enter a value for a column that's required by the data source, or if a user tries to add a new row with a primary key that already exists, the DataGridView control will raise the DataError event. Then, you can code an event handler for this event as shown in figure 3-15.

The second parameter that's received by this event handler has properties you can use to display information about the error. The one you'll use most often is the Exception property, which provides access to the exception object that was thrown as a result of the error. Like any other exception object, this object has a Message property that provides a description of the error. You can also use the RowIndex and ColumnIndex properties of the second parameter to identify the row and column that caused the data error.

An event of the DataGridView control

Event	Description
DataError	Raised when the DataGridView control detects a data error such as a value that isn't in the correct format or a null value where a null value isn't valid.

Three properties of the DataGridViewDataErrorEventArgs class

Property	Description
Exception	The exception that was thrown as a result of the error. You can use the Message property of this object to get additional information about the exception.
RowIndex	The index for the row where the error occurred.
ColumnIndex	The index for the column where the error occurred.

Code that handles a data error for a DataGridView control

```
Private Sub TermsDataGridView_DataError(ByVal sender As System.Object, _
        ByVal e As System.Windows.Forms.DataGridViewDataErrorEventArgs) _
        Handles TermsDataGridView.DataError
    Dim row As Integer = e.RowIndex + 1
    Dim errorMessage As String = "A data error occurred." & vbCrLf _
        & "Row: " & row & vbCrLf _
        & "Error: " & e.Exception.Message
    MessageBox.Show(errorMessage, "Data Error")
End Sub
```

Description

- You can code an event handler for the DataError event of the DataGridView control to handle any data errors that occur when working with the DataGridView control.

- You can use the Exception, RowIndex, and ColumnIndex properties of the second parameter of the event handler to display a meaningful error message.

Figure 3-15   How to handle data errors for a DataGridView control

How to use the Dataset Designer

The *Dataset Designer* lets you work with a dataset schema using a graphic interface. In the topics that follow, you'll learn three basic skills for working with the Dataset Designer. Then, in chapter 5, you'll learn some additional skills for using this designer.

How to view the schema for a dataset

To learn more about a dataset, you can display its schema in the Dataset Designer. In figure 3-16, for example, you can see the schema for the Payables dataset used by the Vendor Maintenance application. For this simple application, this dataset contains just the Vendors table since this is the only table used by the application. The key icon in this table indicates that the VendorID column is the primary key for the table.

For each table in a dataset, the dataset schema also includes a table adapter that lists the queries that can be used with the table. Each table adapter includes at least a *main query* named Fill that determines the columns that are used when you drag the table from the Data Sources window. This query is also used to generate the Insert, Update, and Delete statements for the table. In addition, the table adapter includes any other queries you've defined for the table. You'll learn more about defining additional queries in the next two chapters.

If you click on a table adapter in the Dataset Designer, you'll see that its properties in the Properties window include the ADO.NET objects that the table adapter defines. That includes a Connection object, as well as SelectCommand, InsertCommand, UpdateCommand, and DeleteCommand objects. If you expand any of these command objects, you can look at the CommandText property that defines the SQL statement it executes. In this figure, for example, you can see the beginning of the Select statement for the SelectCommand object that's used by the Fill query of the table adapter for the Vendors table. If you click on the ellipsis button for this property, you can work with the query using the Query Builder that's described in chapter 5.

Note that the Dataset Designer also makes it easy to set the properties for a column in a table that's in the dataset. To do that, just select a column and use the Properties window. For instance, you can use this technique to set the DefaultValue property for a column in the dataset, which is something that you often have to do.

The schema displayed in the Dataset Designer

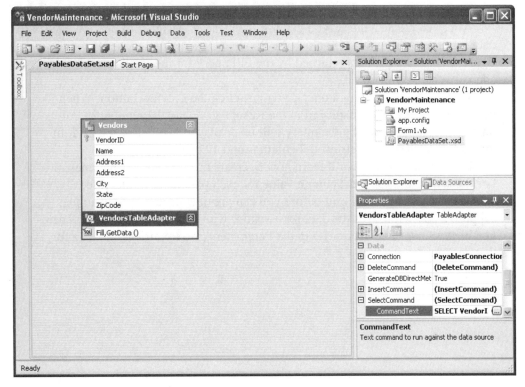

Description

- To view the schema for the dataset of a data source, double-click on the schema file for the dataset (.xsd) in the Solution Explorer, or select the schema file and click the View Designer button at the top of the Solution Explorer. The schema is displayed in the *Dataset Designer.*

- To view the properties for a table adapter in the Properties window, select the table adapter in the Dataset Designer. These properties include the Connection object that's used to connect to the database, and the SelectCommand, InsertCommand, UpdateCommand, and DeleteCommand objects that are used to work with the data in the database.

- For each table adapter, the query named Fill is the *main query.* This query determines the columns that are used when you drag a table from the Data Sources window onto a form. The Insert, Update, and Delete statements for the table are also based on this query.

- To view the properties for a query, select the query in the Dataset Designer.

- To work with the SQL statement in a CommandText property, you can click on the ellipsis button that appears when that property is selected. This displays the statement in the Query Builder, which you'll learn about in chapter 5.

- To view and set the properties for a column in a table, select the column. This is an easy way to set the DefaultValue property for a column.

Figure 3-16   How to view the schema for a dataset

How to preview the data for a query

After you create a query, you can use the Dataset Designer to preview the data it retrieves. To do that, you use the Preview Data dialog box as shown in figure 3-17. Here, the data returned by the Fill query for the Vendors table adapter is being previewed.

To preview the data for a query, you just click the Preview button. When you do, the data will be displayed in the Results grid, and the number of columns and rows returned by the query will be displayed just below the grid. In this example, the query retrieved 7 columns and 122 rows.

In the next chapter, you'll learn how to create queries that use parameters. For those queries, you must enter a value for each parameter in the Value column of the Parameters grid before you can preview its data. For example, suppose a query retrieves the data for a vendor with a specific vendor ID. Then, you have to enter that vendor ID in the Parameters grid to retrieve the data for that vendor.

The Preview Data dialog box

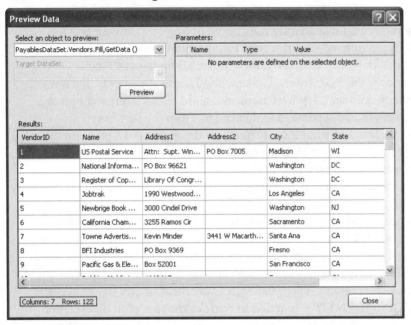

Description

- To display the Preview Data dialog box for a query, right-click on the query in the Dataset Designer and select the Preview Data command, or select the query and then use the Data➔Preview Data command.

- To preview the data, click the Preview button. When you do, the data will be displayed in the Results grid, and the number of columns and rows returned by the query will be displayed just below the Results grid.

- If a query requires parameters, you must enter a value for each parameter in the Value column of the Parameters grid. See chapter 4 for more information on query parameters.

Figure 3-17   How to preview the data for a query

How to interpret the generated SQL statements

The Fill method of a table adapter uses the SQL Select statement that's stored in the SelectCommand object for the Fill query of the table adapter to retrieve data from a database. Similarly, the UpdateAll method of a table adapter manager uses the SQL Insert, Update, and Delete statements that are stored in the InsertCommand, UpdateCommand, and DeleteCommand objects of the table adapters to add, update, and delete data from the database.

To help you understand what these statements do, figure 3-18 presents the Select statement for the Vendor Maintenance form and the Insert and Update statements that were generated from this statement. Although these statements may look complicated, the information presented here will give you a good idea of how they work.

To start, notice that the Insert statement is followed by a Select statement that retrieves the row that was just added to the database. That may be necessary in cases where the database generates some of the data for the new row. When a vendor row is added to the database, for example, the database generates the value of the VendorID column. Then, the Select statement in this figure uses the SQL Server SCOPE_IDENTITY function to retrieve the row with this ID. For now, just realize that if the database doesn't generate or calculate any of the column values, this Select statement, as well as the one after the Update statement, aren't needed.

Also notice that the Update statement uses optimistic concurrency. (Although the Delete statement isn't shown here, it uses optimistic concurrency as well.) Because of that, code is added to the Where clause of this statement to check whether any of the column values have changed since they were retrieved from the database. This code compares the current value of each column in the database against the original value of the column, which is stored in the dataset. If one or more columns can contain a null value, it also checks if both the original value and the current value of those columns are null. That's the case for the Address2 column in the Vendors table. This is necessary because one null value isn't considered equal to another null value. Then, if none of the values have changed, the operation is performed. Otherwise, it's not.

Finally, notice that most of the statements in this figure use one or more parameters. For example, parameters are used in the Values clause of the Insert statement and the Set clause of the Update statement to refer to the current values of the columns in the dataset. Parameters are also used in the Where clause of the Update statement to refer to the original values of the columns in the dataset. The wizard inserts these parameters when it creates the command objects for a table adapter. Then, before each statement is executed, Visual Studio substitutes the appropriate value for each variable.

This should give you more perspective on how the dataset is refreshed and how optimistic concurrency is provided when you use ADO.NET. Because of the disconnected data architecture, these features can't be provided by the database management system or by ADO.NET. Instead, they are provided by the SQL statements that are generated by the Data Source Configuration Wizard.

SQL that retrieves vendor rows

```
SELECT      VendorID, Name, Address1, Address2, City, State, ZipCode
FROM        Vendors
```

SQL that inserts a vendor row and refreshes the dataset

```
INSERT INTO Vendors
            (Name, Address1, Address2, City, State, ZipCode)
VALUES      (@Name,@Address1,@Address2,@City,@State,@ZipCode);

SELECT      VendorID, Name, Address1, Address2, City, State, ZipCode
FROM        Vendors
WHERE       (VendorID = SCOPE_IDENTITY())
```

SQL that updates a vendor row and refreshes the dataset

```
UPDATE      Vendors
SET         Name = @Name, Address1 = @Address1, Address2 = @Address2,
            City = @City, State = @State, ZipCode = @ZipCode
WHERE       ((VendorID = @Original_VendorID) AND
            (Name = @Original_Name) AND (Address1 = @Original_Address1) AND
            (@IsNull_Address2 = 1) AND (Address2 IS NULL) AND
            (City = @Original_City) AND (State = @Original_State) AND
            (ZipCode = @Original_ZipCode)
            OR
            (VendorID = @Original_VendorID) AND
            (Name = @Original_Name) AND (Address1 = @Original_Address1) AND
            (Address2 = @Original_Address2) AND (City = @Original_City) AND
            (State = @Original_State) AND (ZipCode = @Original_ZipCode));

SELECT      VendorID, Name, Address1, Address2, City, State, ZipCode
FROM        Vendors
WHERE       (VendorID = @VendorID)
```

Description

- By default, the Data Source Configuration Wizard adds code to the Where clause of the Update and Delete statements that checks that the data hasn't changed since it was retrieved. (Although the Delete statement isn't shown here, its Where clause is identical to the Where clause of the Update statement.)

- By default, the Data Source Configuration Wizard adds a Select statement after the Insert and Update statements to refresh the new or modified row in the dataset.

- If a column can contain a null value, code is added to the Where clause of the Update and Delete statements that checks if both the original column value and the current value of the column in the database are null. That's necessary because two null values aren't considered equal.

- The SQL statements use parameters to identify the new values for an insert or update operation. Parameters are also used for the original column values, which are used to check that a row hasn't changed for an update or delete operation. And one is used in the Where clause of the Select statement after the Update statement to refer to the current row. The values for these parameters are stored in and retrieved from the dataset.

Figure 3-18   How to interpret the generated SQL statements

Perspective

Now that you've completed this chapter, you should be able to use a data source to create simple applications that let you view and maintain the data in one table of a database. That should give you some idea of how quickly and easily you can create applications when you use the data source feature. And in the next two chapters, you'll learn how you can use data sources and datasets to build more complex applications.

Terms

data source
schema
typed dataset
binding a control
bound control
complex data binding

simple data binding
data provider error
ADO.NET error
Dataset Designer
main query

Before you do any of the exercises...

Before you do any of the exercises in this book, you need to download the directories and files for this book from our web site and install them on your PC. When you do, a directory named ADO.NET 3.5 VB will be created on your C drive. This directory will contain the subdirectories and files you need to do the exercises. For example, you can build the applications for this chapter in the C:\ADO.NET 3.5 VB\Chapter 03 directory. You also need to install SQL Server Express and attach the Payables database that you've downloaded as explained in appendix A.

Exercise 3-1   Build a DataGridView application

In this exercise, you'll build the application shown in figure 3-9. That will show you how to build a simple application with data sources, a dataset, and a DataGridView control.

Build the form and test it with valid data

1. Start a new application named TermsMaintenance in your chapter 3 directory, and use the techniques in figures 3-1 through 3-8 to create the data source and drag it onto the form. Then, adjust the size of the form and the DataGridView control as needed, but don't change anything else.

2. Test the application with valid data in three phases. First, sort the rows by clicking on a column header, and size one of the columns by dragging its column separator. Second, change the data in one column of a row, and move

to another row to see that the data is changed in the dataset. Third, add a new row with valid data in all columns, and move to another row to see that the row has been added. At this point, the changes have been made to the dataset only, not the database. Now, click the Save button in the toolbar to save the changes to the database.

Test the form with invalid data and provide exception handling

3. Test the application with invalid data by deleting the data in the Description column of a row and moving to another row. This should cause a NoNullAllowedException that's automatically handled by the DataGridView control so the application doesn't crash.

4. Add an exception handler for the DataError event of the DataGridView control as shown in figure 3-15. To start the code for that handler, click on the control, click on the Events button in the Properties window, and double-click on the DataError event. Then, write the code for the event, and redo the testing of step 3 to see how your code works.

5. When you're through experimenting, end the application and close the project.

Exercise 3-2   Build an application with text boxes

In this exercise, you'll build the application shown in figure 3-12. That will show you how to use data sources with controls like text boxes.

Build the form and test it with valid data

1. Start a new application named VendorMaintenance in your chapter 3 directory, and create a data source for the fields in the Vendor table that are used by the form in figure 3-12. Then, use the techniques in figures 3-10 and 3-11 to drag the data source fields onto the form as text boxes. At this point, the form should look like the one in figure 3-11.

2. Test the application with valid data in three phases. First, use the toolbar to navigate through the rows. Second, change the data in one column of a row, move to another row, and return to the first row to see that the data has been changed in the dataset. Third, add a new row with valid data in all columns, move to another row, and return to the added row to see that the row has been added to the dataset. Now, click the Save button to save the dataset to the database.

Test the form with invalid data and provide exception handling

3. Add a new row to the dataset, but don't enter anything into the City field. Then, click on the Save button. This should cause a NoNullAllowedException, since City is a required field.

4. Add exception handling code for an ADO.NET DataException as shown in figure 3-14 to catch this type of error. Then, run the application and redo the testing of step 3 to see how this error is handled now.

5. Delete the data in the Name column of a row, which means that the column contains an empty string. Next, move to another row, and return to the first row to see that the row has been accepted into the dataset. Then, click on the Save button and discover that this doesn't throw an exception because an empty string isn't the same as a null value. This indicates that data validation is required because an empty string isn't an acceptable value in the database. In the next chapter, you'll learn one way to provide data validation.

6. Adjust the controls on the form and any related properties so the form looks like the one in figure 3-12. This should take just a minute or two.

Use the Dataset Designer

7. Use one of the techniques in figure 3-16 to view the schema for the dataset in the Dataset Designer.

8. Click on the table adapter in the Dataset Designer and review its properties in the Properties window. Then, look at the Select statement that's used for getting the data into the dataset. To do that, click on the plus sign in front of SelectCommand, and click on the ellipsis button for CommandText. This opens up the Query Builder, which you'll learn about in chapter 5, and there you can see the Select statement that's used for getting the data into the dataset. Now, close the Query Builder.

9. Right-click on the query in the Dataset Designer, and preview the data that will be retrieved by that query as shown in figure 3-17.

10. When you're through experimenting, close the project.

4

How to work with bound controls and parameterized queries

In the last chapter, you learned the basic skills for developing applications by using data sources and datasets. Now, you'll learn some additional skills for building database applications that way. Specifically, you'll learn how to work with bound controls, how to use parameterized queries, how to customize the generated toolbars, and how to work with a DataGridView control.

How to work with bound text boxes and combo boxes

The topics that follow show you how to work with bound text boxes and combo boxes. First, you'll learn how to format the data that's displayed in text boxes. Second, you'll learn how to bind data to a combo box. And third, you'll learn how to work with the BindingSource object to make sure that the data and controls are synchronized.

How to format the data displayed in a text box

In the last chapter, you learned how to use bound text boxes to work with the data in a Vendors table. However, because the columns of that table contain string data, it wasn't necessary to format the data when it was displayed. In many cases, though, you'll want to format the data so it's displayed properly.

Figure 4-1 shows how you can apply standard formatting to the data that's displayed in a bound text box. To do that, you use the Formatting and Advanced Binding dialog box. From this dialog box, you can select the format you want to apply from the Format Type list. Then, you can enter appropriate values for the options that are displayed to the right of this list. In this figure, for example, a Date Time format is being applied to the text box that's bound to the InvoiceDate column of the Invoices table.

The dialog box that you can use to apply formatting to a column

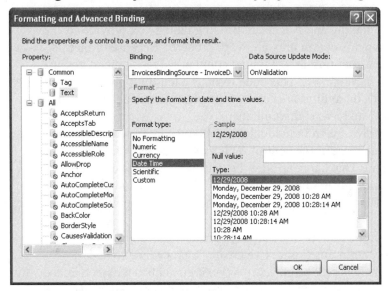

Description

- To display the Formatting and Advanced Binding dialog box, select the text box whose data you want to format, expand the DataBindings group in the Properties window, and then click the ellipsis button that appears when you select the Advanced option.

- To apply a format, select the format you want to use from the Format Type list and enter any additional options that appear to the right of the list. Numeric, Currency, and Scientific let you enter the number of decimal places to be displayed. Date Time lets you select from a number of date and time formats. And Custom lets you enter a custom format.

- Each format also lets you enter the value you want to display in place of a null value. The default is an empty string.

- If you select the Custom format, a note is displayed indicating that the format may not be applied and that you should use the Format or Parse event of the Binding object to apply it instead. See figure 4-2 for more information.

Figure 4-1   How to format the data displayed in a text box

How to use custom formatting

Although the Formatting and Advanced Binding dialog box provides a Custom format option, this option may not work properly. Because of that, if you need to apply a custom format to a bound column, we recommend you use code like that shown in figure 4-2. This code formats a ten-digit phone number so it's displayed with a three-digit area code, followed by a period, a three-digit prefix, another period, and a four-digit number.

To format bound data for an individual control, you can provide an event handler for the Format event of the control. This event is raised when the control is bound to the column. That happens after the data to be displayed by the control has been retrieved from the data source, but before it's assigned to the control. As a result, the event handler for the Format event can modify the data before it's displayed.

The first step to formatting bound data is to create a procedure that can handle the Format event. In this figure, I've created a procedure named FormatPhoneNumber. This procedure accepts two arguments: an object named sender and a ConvertEventArgs object named e. Within this procedure, you can use the Value property of the e argument to work with the column value. Because this property returns an object, the method starts by using the GetType method to verify that the value of the object is a string. Since the phone numbers are stored as character data in the database, they should be stored as strings in the dataset. This code is included just to be sure that's the case.

If the value of the object is a string, the procedure converts the object to a string and stores it in a string variable. Then, it checks that the string contains numeric data and that it has ten digits. In other words, it checks that it contains a standard 10-digit phone number. If so, it formats the variable and assigns the result to the Value property.

Once you've created a procedure to serve as the event handler, the next step is to wire the procedure to the Format event. To understand how this wiring works, you need to realize that the Format event is not raised directly by a control. Instead, this event is raised by the Binding object that's created for each bound property of the control. To wire an event handler to the Format event, then, you must first retrieve the Binding object for the bound property of the control. Then, you can add your event handler to the binding object's Format event.

The second code example in this figure shows the two lines of code needed to do that. The first line declares a Binding variable and assigns the binding object for the Text property of the PhoneTextBox to it. This code accesses the Binding object through the control's DataBindings property. This property returns a collection of all the data bindings for the control, indexed by the name of the property each binding refers to.

The second line in this example associates the Format event of the Binding object with the event handler. To do that, it uses an AddHandler statement. Note in this statement that the AddressOf operator is used to implicitly create an instance of the FormatPhoneNumber event handler at runtime.

Code that you can use to apply formatting to a column

A procedure that formats a phone number that's stored as a string

```
Private Sub FormatPhoneNumber(ByVal sender As Object, _
        ByVal e As ConvertEventArgs)
    If e.Value.GetType.ToString = "System.String" Then
        Dim s As String = e.Value.ToString
        If IsNumeric(s) Then
            If s.Length = 10 Then
                e.Value = s.Substring(0, 3) _
                        & "." _
                        & s.Substring(3, 3) _
                        & "." _
                        & s.Substring(6, 4)
            End If
        End If
    End If
End Sub
```

Code that wires the procedure to the Format event of a text box

```
Dim b As Binding = PhoneTextBox.DataBindings("Text")
AddHandler b.Format, AddressOf FormatPhoneNumber
```

Description

- To apply formatting to a column using code, you can wire an event handler to the Format event of the Binding object for the control. The Format event is raised when the control is bound to the column.

- In the Format event handler, you can use the Value property of the ConvertEventArgs argument to retrieve and format the value of the data to be bound to the control. Because the Value property returns an object, you'll want to check the type of this property to be sure it's what you expect. Then, you can convert the value to the appropriate type.

- To wire the Format event handler, you start by getting the Binding object for the control. To do that, you use the control's DataBindings property with the name of the bound property as an index. Then, you use the AddHandler statement to associate the Format event of the Binding object with the event handler.

- You can also use the Parse event of the Binding object for a control to apply formatting to a column. This event occurs whenever the value of the bound control changes.

Figure 4-2   How to use custom formatting

How to bind a combo box to a data source

Figure 4-3 shows how to bind a combo box so it displays all of the rows in one table and updates a column in another table. In the Vendor Maintenance form shown in this figure, for example, the combo box is bound to the States table and is used to update the State column in the Vendors table. The easiest way to create a combo box like this is to use the Data Sources window to change the control that's associated with the column in the main table to a combo box before you drag the table to the form. Then, you can use the combo box's smart tag menu to set the binding properties.

To start, you'll need to select the Use Data Bound Items check box to display the binding properties as shown here. Then, you can set these properties.

In this figure, the DataSource property of the State combo box is set to StatesBindingSource (which points to the States table), the DisplayMember property is set to the StateName column (which provides the full name of the state), and the ValueMember property is set to the StateCode column (which provides the two-letter code for the state). That way, this combo box will list the full name of each state in the visible portion of the combo box.

Finally, the SelectedValue property is used to bind the ValueMember property to a column in another data source. In this case, the SelectedValue property is set to the State column of the VendorsBindingSource. That way, the StateCode column of the States table is bound to the State column of the Vendors table. Then, when the data for a vendor is displayed, the state that's selected in the combo box is determined by the State column of the Vendors table. Also, if the user selects a different item from the combo box list, the States column in the Vendors table is changed to the value selected by the user.

In addition to the four properties in the smart tag menu, you may also need to set a couple of other properties when you bind a combo box. In particular, you can set the DropDownStyle property to DropDownList to prevent the user from entering text into the text portion of the combo box. Then, you can set the Text property in the DataBindings group to None so the application doesn't bind the value stored in this property to the data source. *If this property isn't set correctly, the combo box won't work properly.*

Although you've learned only how to bind combo boxes in this topic, you should realize that you can use similar skills to work with other types of controls. In particular, you can use most of these skills to work with list boxes. If you experiment with this on your own, you shouldn't have any trouble figuring out how it works.

A combo box that's bound to a data source

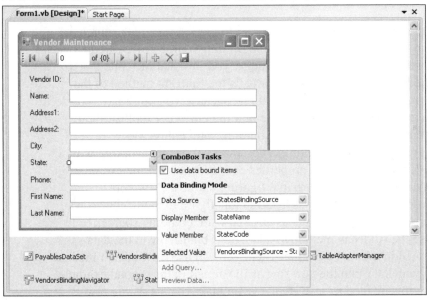

Combo box properties for binding

Property	Description
DataSource	The name of the data table that contains the data displayed in the list.
DisplayMember	The name of the data column whose data is displayed in the list.
ValueMember	The name of the data column whose value is stored in the list. This value is returned by the SelectedValue property of the control.
SelectedValue	Gets the value of the currently selected item. You can use this property to bind the ValueMember property to a column in another data source.

Description

- To access the most common properties for binding a combo box, you can display the smart tag menu for the combo box and select the Use Data Bound Items check box. This will display the properties shown above.

- To set the DataSource property, display the drop-down list; expand the Other Data Sources node, the Project Data Sources node, and the node for the dataset; and select the table you want to use as the data source. This adds BindingSource and TableAdapter objects for the table to the form. Then, you can set the DisplayMember and ValueMember properties to columns in this table.

- The SelectedValue property is typically bound to a column in the main table. That way, if you select a different item from the combo box, the value of the bound column is set to the value of the ValueMember property for the selected item.

- When you bind a combo box to a data source, you'll typically set the DropDownStyle property of the combo box to DropDownList so the user can only select a value from the list. You'll also want to change the (DataBindings) - Text property to None to remove the binding from the text box portion of the combo box.

Figure 4-3   How to bind a combo box to a data source

How to use code to work with a binding source

When you use the binding navigator toolbar to work with a data source, it works by using properties and methods of the BindingSource object. In the two applications presented in chapter 3, for example, you saw that the code that's generated for the Save button of this toolbar calls the EndEdit method of the binding source to end the current edit operation. Because you don't have control over most of the code that's executed by the binding navigator toolbar, though, you may sometimes want to work with the binding source directly.

Figure 4-4 presents some of the properties and methods for working with a binding source. If you review these properties and methods and the examples in this figure, you shouldn't have any trouble figuring out how they work.

You can use the first four methods listed in this figure to modify the rows that are stored in the data source that's associated with a binding source. To start, you can use the AddNew method to add a new, blank row to the data source as illustrated in the first example. Then, you can use the EndEdit method to save the data you enter into the new row as illustrated in the second example. You can also use this method to save changes you make to an existing row.

If an error occurs when you try to save changes to a row, or if the user decides to cancel an edit operation, you can use the CancelEdit method to cancel the changes as illustrated in the third example. Note, however, that you don't have to explicitly start an edit operation. The binding source takes care of that automatically when you make changes to a row. Finally, you can use the RemoveCurrent method to remove the current row from the data source as illustrated in the fourth example.

You can use the last four methods in this figure to move to the first, previous, next, or last row in a data source. You can also use the Position property to get or set the index of the current row. And you can use the Count property to get the number of rows in the data source.

To illustrate how you might use these properties and methods, the last example in this figure presents an event handler that responds to the Click event of a button. This event handler uses the MoveNext method to move to the next row in the data source. Then, it uses the Position property to get the index of the current row, and it adds one to the result since the index is zero-based. Finally, it uses the Count property to get the total number of rows in the data source, and it displays the position and count in a text box. This is similar to the display that's included in the binding navigator toolbar.

Common properties and methods of the BindingSource class

Property	Description
Position	The index of the current row in the data source.
Count	The number of rows in the data source.

Method	Description
AddNew()	Adds a new, blank row to the data source.
EndEdit()	Saves changes to the current row.
CancelEdit()	Cancels changes to the current row.
RemoveCurrent()	Removes the current row from the data source.
MoveFirst()	Moves to the first row in the data source.
MovePrevious()	Moves to the previous row in the data source, if there is one.
MoveNext()	Moves to the next row in the data source, if there is one.
MoveLast()	Moves to the last row in the data source.

A statement that adds a new row to a data source

```
Me.VendorsBindingSource.AddNew()
```

A statement that saves the changes to the current row and ends the edit

```
Me.VendorsBindingSource.EndEdit()
```

A statement that cancels the changes to the current row

```
Me.VendorsBindingSource.CancelEdit()
```

A statement that removes the current row from a data source

```
Me.VendorsBindingSource.RemoveCurrent()
```

Code that moves to the next row and displays the position and count

```
Private Sub btnNext_Click(ByVal sender As System.Object, _
        ByVal e As System.EventArgs) Handles btnNext.Click
    Me.VendorsBindingSource.MoveNext()
    Dim position As Integer = VendorsBindingSource.Position + 1
    txtPosition.Text = position & " of " & VendorsBindingSource.Count
End Sub
```

Description

- The binding source ensures that all controls that are bound to the same data table are synchronized. That way, when you move to another row, the data-bound controls will display the values in that row.
- If a form provides for updating the rows in a data table, moving from one row to another causes any changes made to the current row to be saved to the data table.
- When you add a new row using the AddNew method, the Position property of the binding source is set to one more than the position of the last row in the data table.
- You can use the EndEdit and CancelEdit methods to save or cancel the changes to an existing row or a new row that was added using the AddNew method.

Figure 4-4   How to use code to work with a binding source

How to work with parameterized queries

In the last chapter, you learned how the Data Source Configuration Wizard uses parameters in the SQL statements it generates. A query like this that contains parameters is called a *parameterized query*. In the topics that follow, you'll learn one way to create parameterized queries for your forms.

How to create a parameterized query

For some applications, such as the Terms Maintenance application presented in the previous chapter, it's acceptable (or even preferable) to fill the table in the dataset with every row in the database table. However, if a database table contains many columns and rows, this can have a negative impact on the performance of your application. In addition, for some types of applications, you will only want to allow the user to retrieve certain rows from a table. In either case, the solution is to use a parameterized query.

Fortunately, Visual Studio provides an easy way to create a parameterized query, as shown in figure 4-5. When you use this technique, Visual Studio generates a toolbar that lets the user enter the parameters for the query. It also generates the code that fills the table in the dataset with the results of the query.

To create a parameterized query, you can begin by displaying the smart tag menu for any control that's bound to the data source. Then, you can select the Add Query command from this menu. When you do, Visual Studio will display a Search Criteria Builder dialog box like the one shown here. This dialog box lets you enter the name and parameters for the query.

By default, a query is named FillBy, but you can change it to anything you want. I recommend that you name a query based on the function it performs. In this figure, for example, the query has been named FillByVendorID because it will be used to retrieve a vendor row based on the vendor ID.

After you enter the query name, you can modify the Where clause of the query so it includes one or more parameters. In SQL Server, you specify a parameter by coding an @ sign in front of the parameter name. In this figure, for example, the query will return all rows where the value in the VendorID column equals the value of the @VendorID parameter that's entered by the user.

When you finish specifying the query in the Search Criteria Builder dialog box, Visual Studio automatically adds a toolbar to your form. This toolbar contains one or more text boxes that let the user enter the parameters that are needed by the query and a button that lets the user execute the query. You can see this toolbar in the Vendor Maintenance form shown in this figure.

Using this toolbar, the user can retrieve a single row that contains the vendor's data by entering the ID for the vendor and then clicking the FillByVendorID button. In this figure, for example, the user has displayed the row for the vendor with an ID of 34. That's why the binding navigator toolbar shows that only one row exists in the Vendors data table.

The dialog box for creating a parameterized query

The Vendor Maintenance form with a toolbar for the query

Description

- You can add a *parameterized query* to a data table using the Search Criteria Builder dialog box. To display this dialog box, display the smart tag menu for a control that's bound to the data table and then select the Add Query command.

- When you finish specifying the query in the Search Criteria Builder dialog box, Visual Studio automatically adds a toolbar to your form. This toolbar contains the text boxes that let the user enter the parameters that are needed by the query, and it contains a button that lets the user execute the query.

- You can add more than one parameterized query to a data table using the Search Criteria Builder. Each query you add is displayed in its own toolbar. Because of that, you may want to modify one of the toolbars so that it provides for all the queries.

Figure 4-5   How to create a parameterized query

Although the parameterized query in this example retrieves a single row from the Vendors table, all of the rows are still retrieved when the form loads. If that's not what you want, you can delete the statement that fills the Vendors table from the Load event handler for the form. Then, when the form is first displayed, the Vendors table won't contain any rows.

How to use code to work with a parameterized query

As I mentioned, when you create a parameterized query using the Search Criteria Builder dialog box, Visual Studio automatically generates code to fill the data table using the query. This code is shown at the top of figure 4-6. It calls a method of the TableAdapter object to fill the appropriate table in the dataset based on the values the user enters for the parameters when the user clicks the button in the toolbar. In this example, the code fills the Vendors table with the row for the vendor with the vendor ID value the user entered.

If you review the generated code, you'll see that it's a little unwieldy. First, it uses the CType function to convert the value of the VendorID parameter from a String type to an Integer type. Second, it qualifies references to the Exception class and the MessageBox class even though that isn't necessary within the context of this form.

To make this code easier to read, you can clean it up as shown in the second example in this figure. Here, the CType function has been replaced with the more concise Convert.ToInt32 method and all the unnecessary qualification has been removed. In addition, to enhance the error handling provided by this code, the Catch block that catches a generic exception has been replaced by two Catch blocks. The first one catches the exception that occurs if the user enters anything other than an integer for the vendor ID. And the second one catches any SQL Server exception that occurs when the FillByVendorID method of the table adapter is executed.

As you can see, the method that fills the dataset is given the same name as the query, and it works similarly to the Fill method of the TableAdapter object that you learned about in the previous chapter. The difference is that the method for a parameterized query lets you specify the parameter or parameters that are required by the query. In this figure, for example, the FillByVendorID method of the VendorsTableAdapter object requires a single parameter of the Integer type. To get this parameter, the code gets the string that's entered by the user into the text box on the toolbar, and it converts this string to an Integer type.

Note that the FillByVendorID method of the table adapter fills the Vendors table of the dataset with only one row. Then, if the user makes any changes to that row, he or she must click the Save button to save those changes to the database. If the user retrieves another row instead, that row fills the dataset and the changes are lost. Similarly, the user must click the Save button to save a deletion before moving to another row. Although this user interface works, it isn't very intuitive. As a result, you'll typically want to modify interfaces like this one.

The generated code for a parameterized query

```
Private Sub FillByVendorIDToolStripButton_Click( _
        ByVal sender As System.Object, ByVal e As System.EventArgs) _
        Handles FillByVendorIDToolStripButton.Click

    Try
        Me.VendorsTableAdapter.FillByVendorID( _
            Me.PayablesDataSet.Vendors, _
            CType(VendorIDToolStripTextBox.Text, Integer))
    Catch ex As System.Exception
        System.Windows.Forms.MessageBox.Show(ex.Message)
    End Try

End Sub
```

The same code after it has been cleaned up and enhanced

```
Private Sub FillByVendorIDToolStripButton_Click( _
        ByVal sender As System.Object, ByVal e As System.EventArgs) _
        Handles FillByVendorIDToolStripButton.Click

    Try
        Dim vendorID As Integer _
            = Convert.ToInt32(VendorIDToolStripTextBox.Text)
        Me.VendorsTableAdapter.FillByVendorID( _
            Me.PayablesDataSet.Vendors, vendorID)
    Catch ex As FormatException
        MessageBox.Show("Vendor ID must be an integer.", "Entry Error")
    Catch ex As SqlException
        MessageBox.Show("SQL Server error # " & ex.Number _
            & ": " & ex.Message, ex.GetType.ToString)
    End Try

End Sub
```

The syntax of the method for filling a table using a parameterized query

```
TableAdapter.QueryName(DataSet.TableName, param1 [,param2]...)
```

Description

- When you finish specifying a query in the Search Criteria Builder dialog box, Visual Studio automatically generates the code that uses the appropriate method to fill the table in the dataset when the user clicks the button in the toolbar.

- If necessary, you can modify the generated code to make it easier to read or to change the way it works.

Figure 4-6   How to use code to work with a parameterized query

How to work with a ToolStrip control

When you create a parameterized query, Visual Studio automatically generates a ToolStrip control that lets the user enter the parameter for the query. Although this ToolStrip control works well for simple applications, you may want to modify it as your applications become more complex. For example, you may want to change the text on the button that executes the query. Or, you may want to add additional text boxes and buttons that work with other queries. Fortunately, the ToolStrip control is easy to customize.

Before I go on, you should know that the binding navigator toolbar that gets generated when you drag a data source onto a form is a customized ToolStrip control. As a result, you can work with this toolbar just as you would any other ToolStrip control. If, for example, a form won't provide for inserts, updates, and deletes, you can remove the Add, Delete, and Save buttons from this toolbar. You can also add controls that perform customized functions.

How to use the Items Collection Editor

To work with the items on a ToolStrip control, you use the Items Collection Editor shown in figure 4-7. To start, you can add an item by selecting the type of control you want to add from the combo box in the upper left corner and clicking the Add button. This adds the item to the bottom of the Members list. Then, if necessary, you can move the item using the up and down arrow buttons to the right of the Members list.

You can also use the Items Collection Editor to set the properties for a new or existing item. To do that, just select the item in the Members list and use the Properties list at the right side of the dialog box to set the properties. The table in this figure lists the four properties you're most likely to change. Note that when you add a new Button control, the DisplayStyle property is set to Image by default. If you want to display the text that you specify for the Text property instead of an image, then, you need to change the DisplayStyle property to Text.

Finally, you can use the Items Collection Editor to delete an existing item. To do that, just select the item and click the Delete button to the right of the Members list.

The Items Collection Editor for an enhanced ToolStrip control

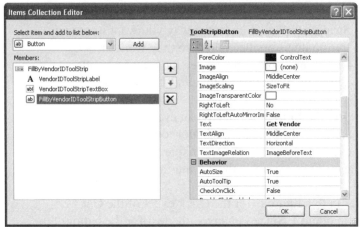

Common properties of ToolStrip items

Property	Description
DisplayStyle	Indicates whether a button displays an image, text, or both an image and text.
Image	The image that's displayed on a button if you select Image or ImageAndText for the DisplayStyle property.
Text	The text that's displayed on a button if you select Text or ImageAndText for the DisplayStyle property.
Width	The width of the item.

Description

- To display the Items Collection Editor dialog box, display the smart tag menu for the ToolStrip and select the Edit Items command.

- To add an item, select the type of control you want to add from the combo box and click the Add button. To add a separator bar, choose Separator. You can also add an item by using the drop-down list that's displayed when the ToolStrip is selected in the Form Designer.

- To move an item, select the item in the Members list and click the up and down arrows to the right of the list.

- To delete an item, select it in the Members list and click the Delete button to the right of the list.

- To set the properties for an item, select the item in the Members list and use the Properties list on the right side of the dialog box to set the properties. You can also set the properties of an item by selecting it in the Form Designer and then using the Properties window.

Note

- Because the BindingNavigator control is a ToolStrip control, you can also use the Items Collection Editor to work with the BindingNavigator control.

Figure 4-7   How to use the Items Collection Editor for a ToolStrip control

How to code an event handler for a ToolStrip item

After you modify a ToolStrip control so it looks the way you want it to, you need to code event handlers for the items on the control so they work the way you want them to. In figure 4-8, for example, you can see the top of a Vendor Maintenance form that uses a binding navigator toolbar and the ToolStrip control that was defined in figure 4-7.

For this application to work, the form must include an event handler for the Cancel button that has been added to the binding navigator toolbar. To generate the code for the start of that event, you can use the technique that's summarized in this figure. In this case, the event just cancels the editing that has been started.

The second event handler in this figure is for the Click event of the Get Vendor button on the ToolStrip control. Since I changed the text for the button but not its name, the button is still named FillByVendorIDToolStripButton. In this case, I just enhanced the code that was generated for that button. First, I cleaned up the generated code, and then I added code for catching errors.

How to code a custom event handler for a control on a binding navigator toolbar

In the last chapter, you learned that when a binding navigator toolbar is added to a form, an event handler is added for the Click event of the toolbar's Save button. That way, you can modify this event handler if you need to. In some cases, you'll want to modify the code that's executed for one of the other controls on the toolbar. For example, you may want to display a confirmation dialog box before a row is deleted. Since the event handler for the Click event of the Delete button isn't exposed by the toolbar, however, you can't modify it directly. Fortunately, there is a way to use a custom event handler with an item on a binding navigator toolbar.

To start, you need to keep the code that's built into the toolbar for an item from being executed. To do that, you can use the properties that are listed in the Items group of the Properties window for the toolbar. These properties associate an action with the toolbar item that initiates the action. For example, the DeleteItem property identifies the toolbar item that initiates the delete action, and the AddItem property identifies the toolbar item that initiates the add action.

To remove the association between an action and a toolbar item so that the default code isn't executed for that item, you change the appropriate Item property to "(none)". For example, to stop the RemoveCurrent method of the binding source from being executed when the Delete button is clicked, you change the DeleteItem property to "(none)". Then, you can code your own custom event handler for the Click event of this button. Note that this code must execute the RemoveCurrent method since it's no longer executed by default. You can use a similar technique to use custom event handlers for the other controls on a binding navigator toolbar. In most cases, though, the built-in code is sufficient.

Customized toolbars for a Vendor Maintenance application

The event handler for the Cancel button on the BindingNavigator Toolstrip control

```
Private Sub BindingNavigatorCancelItem_Click( _
        ByVal sender As System.Object, ByVal e As System.EventArgs) _
        Handles BindingNavigatorCancelItem.Click

    VendorsBindingSource.CancelEdit()

End Sub
```

The event handler for the Get Vendor button on the FillByVendorID ToolStrip control

```
Private Sub FillByVendorIDToolStripButton_Click( _
        ByVal sender As System.Object, ByVal e As System.EventArgs) _
        Handles FillByVendorIDToolStripButton.Click

    Try
        Dim vendorID As Integer _
        = Convert.ToInt32(VendorIDToolStripTextBox.Text)
            Me.VendorsTableAdapter.FillByVendorID( _
            Me.PayablesDataSet.Vendors, vendorID)
    Catch ex As FormatException
        MessageBox.Show("Vendor ID must be an integer.", "Entry Error")
    Catch ex As SqlException
        MessageBox.Show("SQL Server error # " & ex.Number _
                & ": " & ex.Message, ex.GetType.ToString)
    End Try

End Sub
```

Description

- To code an event handler for a ToolStrip item, display the form in the Form Designer, click on the item to select it, and click on the Events button of the Properties window to display the list of events for the item. Then, you can use standard techniques to generate or select an event handler for a specified event.

- The BindingNavigator ToolStrip control includes properties that identify the ToolStrip items that are associated with specific actions. For example, The DeleteItem property identifies the item that causes a row to be deleted, and the AddItem property identifies the item that causes a row to be added.

- You can code a custom event handler for any of the items on a BindingNavigator ToolStrip control. To do that, change the appropriate Item property to "(none)" so that no action is associated with that item. Then, add your own custom event handler for the item.

Figure 4-8   How to code an event handler for a ToolStrip item

An enhanced Vendor Maintenance application

To illustrate some of the new skills you've learned so far in this chapter, I'll now present an enhanced version of the Vendor Maintenance application that you saw in the last chapter.

The user interface

Figure 4-9 presents the user interface for the Vendor Maintenance application. This time, the application uses a parameterized query to retrieve a row from the Vendors table based on its vendor ID, and the form uses a combo box that lets the user select a state. In addition, this form formats the phone number, and its generated toolbars have been modified.

The code

Figure 4-9 also presents the code for the Vendor Maintenance application. Since you've already seen most of this code, you shouldn't have any trouble understanding how it works. So I'll just point out two highlights.

First, the procedure for the Click event of the Cancel button contains a single statement that cancels the current edit operation. Since this operation can't cause any exceptions, you don't have to use a Try…Catch statement with it.

Second, the event handler for the Click event of the Save button starts by calling a function named IsValidData. This procedure checks that the user has entered a value into each control on the form that requires a value. This is necessary for the combo box to be sure that a value is selected for a new row. And it's necessary for the text boxes because if the user deletes the data in a text box, its value becomes an empty string. Then, if the user saves the row to the database, an empty string is saved in the table. This works even if the column doesn't allow nulls, which probably isn't what you want.

To check that each control contains a value, the IsValidData function calls another function named IsPresent. If the control doesn't contain a value, this function displays an error message and moves the focus to the appropriate control. Then, the IsValidData function returns a value of False. Otherwise, if all the controls contain values, this function returns a value of True. This is just one way that you can validate the controls on a form.

Incidentally, if you have any problems understanding the data validation code or any of the other code that isn't related to ADO.NET, we recommend that you get a copy of *Murach's Visual Basic 2008*. It is a terrific reference that lets you quickly learn or refresh your memory about how some aspect of Visual Basic works. And this book assumes that you already know what's in our Visual Basic 2008 book.

The user interface for the Vendor Maintenance application

The code for the application   **Page 1**

```vb
Imports System.Data.SqlClient

Public Class Form1

    Private Sub Form1_Load(ByVal sender As System.Object, _
            ByVal e As System.EventArgs) Handles MyBase.Load

        Dim b As Binding = PhoneTextBox.DataBindings("Text")
        AddHandler b.Format, AddressOf FormatPhoneNumber

        Try
            Me.StatesTableAdapter.Fill(Me.PayablesDataSet.States)
            Me.VendorsTableAdapter.Fill(Me.PayablesDataSet.Vendors)

        Catch ex As SqlException
            MessageBox.Show("SQL Server error # " & ex.Number _
                & ": " & ex.Message, ex.GetType.ToString)
        End Try
    End Sub

    Private Sub FormatPhoneNumber(ByVal sender As Object, _
            ByVal e As ConvertEventArgs)
        If e.Value.GetType.ToString = "System.String" Then
            Dim s As String = e.Value.ToString
            If IsNumeric(s) Then
                If s.Length = 10 Then
                    e.Value = s.Substring(0, 3) & "." _
                            & s.Substring(3, 3) & "." _
                            & s.Substring(6, 4)
                End If
            End If
        End If
    End Sub
```

Figure 4-9   An enhanced Vendor Maintenance application (part 1 of 3)

The code for the application

```vb
Private Sub FillByVendorIDToolStripButton_Click( _
        ByVal sender As System.Object, ByVal e As System.EventArgs) _
        Handles FillByVendorIDToolStripButton.Click
    Try
        Dim vendorID As Integer _
            = Convert.ToInt32(VendorIDToolStripTextBox.Text)
        Me.VendorsTableAdapter.FillByVendorID( _
            Me.PayablesDataSet.Vendors, vendorID)
    Catch ex As FormatException
        MessageBox.Show("Vendor ID must be an integer.", "Entry Error")
    Catch ex As SqlException
        MessageBox.Show("SQL Server error # " & ex.Number _
            & ": " & ex.Message, ex.GetType.ToString)
    End Try
End Sub

Private Sub BindingNavigatorCancelItem_Click( _
        ByVal sender As System.Object, ByVal e As System.EventArgs) _
        Handles BindingNavigatorCancelItem.Click
    VendorsBindingSource.CancelEdit()
End Sub

Private Sub VendorsBindingNavigatorSaveItem_Click( _
        ByVal sender As System.Object, ByVal e As System.EventArgs) _
        Handles VendorsBindingNavigatorSaveItem.Click
    If IsValidData() Then
        Try
            Me.VendorsBindingSource.EndEdit()
            Me.TableAdapterManager.UpdateAll(Me.PayablesDataSet)
        Catch ex As ArgumentException
            ' This block catches exceptions such as a value that's beyond
            ' the maximum length for a column in a dataset.
            MessageBox.Show(ex.Message, "Argument Exception")
            VendorsBindingSource.CancelEdit()
        Catch ex As DBConcurrencyException
            MessageBox.Show("A concurrency error occurred. " _
                & "The row was not updated.", "Concurrency Exception")
            Me.VendorsTableAdapter.Fill(Me.PayablesDataSet.Vendors)
        Catch ex As DataException
            MessageBox.Show(ex.Message, ex.GetType.ToString)
            VendorsBindingSource.CancelEdit()
        Catch ex As SqlException
            MessageBox.Show("SQL Server error # " & ex.Number _
                & ": " & ex.Message, ex.GetType.ToString)
        End Try
    End If
End Sub
```

Figure 4-9   An enhanced Vendor Maintenance application (part 2 of 3)

The code for the application   **Page 3**

```
Private Function IsValidData() As Boolean
    Return _
        IsPresent(NameTextBox, "Name") AndAlso _
        IsPresent(Address1TextBox, "Address1") AndAlso _
        IsPresent(CityTextBox, "City") AndAlso _
        IsPresent(StateComboBox, "State") AndAlso _
        IsPresent(ZipCodeTextBox, "Zip code")
End Function

Private Function IsPresent(ByVal control As Control, _
        ByVal name As String) As Boolean
    If control.GetType.ToString = "System.Windows.Forms.TextBox" Then
        Dim textBox As TextBox = CType(control, TextBox)
        If textBox.Text = "" Then
            MessageBox.Show(name & " is a required field.", "Entry Error")
            textBox.Select()
            Return False
        Else
            Return True
        End If
    ElseIf control.GetType.ToString = "System.Windows.Forms.ComboBox" Then
        Dim comboBox As ComboBox = CType(control, ComboBox)
        If comboBox.SelectedIndex = -1 Then
            MessageBox.Show(name & " is a required field.", "Entry Error")
            comboBox.Select()
            Return False
        Else
            Return True
        End If
    End If
End Function

End Class
```

Figure 4-9   An enhanced Vendor Maintenance application (part 3 of 3)

How to work with a DataGridView control

In chapter 3, you saw how easy it is to use a DataGridView control to work with the data in a table of a dataset. Now, you'll learn how to modify a DataGridView control so it looks and functions the way you want. In addition, you'll learn how to work with a DataGridView control in code.

How to modify the properties of a DataGridView control

When you generate a DataGridView control from a data source, Visual Studio sets many of the properties of this control and the other objects it creates the way you want them. However, if you want to modify any of these properties, you can do that just as you would for any other type of object. In particular, you'll probably want to edit the properties of the DataGridView control to change its appearance and function.

For the examples in the next five topics, I'll use a DataGridView control that displays data from the Invoices table. This control will let the user modify selected columns of the invoices. It won't let the user add or delete invoices. As you'll see, the data source that's used to generate the DataGridView control includes all the columns from the Invoices table except for the TermsID column.

To change the most common properties of a DataGridView control, you can use its smart tag menu as shown in figure 4-10. From this menu, you can create a read-only data grid by removing the check marks from the Enable Adding, Enable Editing, and Enable Deleting check boxes. Or, you can let a user reorder the columns in the grid by checking the Enable Column Reordering check box. In this example, you can see that I removed the check marks from the Enable Adding and Enable Deleting check boxes so the grid won't provide for these functions.

In addition to editing the properties for the grid, you may want to edit the properties for the columns of the grid. For example, you may want to apply currency formatting to a column, or you may want to change the column headings or widths. To do that, you can select the Edit Columns command to display the Edit Columns dialog box shown in the next figure.

By default, when you run an application that uses a DataGridView control, you can sort the rows in a column by clicking in the header at the top of the column. The first time you do this, the rows are sorted in ascending sequence by the values in the column; the next time, in descending sequence. Similarly, you can drag the column separators to change the widths of the columns. Last, if the Enable Column Reordering option is checked, you can reorder the columns by dragging them. These features let the user customize the presentation of the data.

The smart tag menu for a DataGridView control

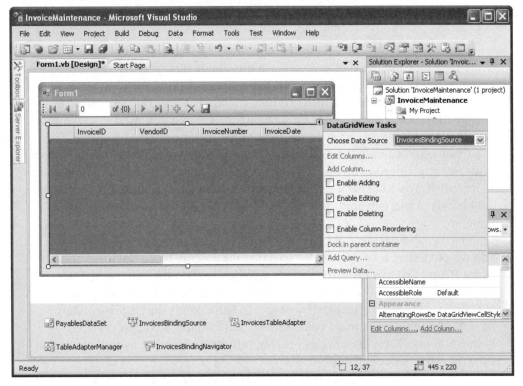

Description

- You can use the smart tag menu of a DataGridView control to edit its most commonly used properties.

- To edit the columns, select the Edit Columns command to display the Edit Columns dialog box. Then, you can edit the columns as described in the next figure.

- To prevent a user from adding, updating, or deleting data that's displayed in the DataGridView control, uncheck the Enable Adding, Enable Editing, or Enable Deleting check boxes.

- To allow a user to reorder the columns in a DataGridView control by dragging them, check the Enable Column Reordering check box.

- You can edit other properties of a DataGridView control by using the Properties window for the control.

Figure 4-10   How to modify the properties of a DataGridView control

How to edit the columns of a DataGridView control

Figure 4-11 shows how to edit the columns of a DataGridView control using the Edit Columns dialog box. From this dialog box, you can remove columns from the grid by selecting the column and clicking the Remove button. That's what I did for the VendorID column in the Invoices grid. You can also change the order of the columns by selecting the column you want to move and clicking the up or down arrow to the right of the list of columns.

Finally, you can use the Add button in this dialog box to add a column to the grid. You might need to do that if you delete a column and then decide you want to include it. You can also use the dialog box that's displayed when you click the Add button to add unbound columns to the grid. You'll learn how to do that in a minute.

Once you've got the right columns displayed in the correct order, you can edit the properties for a column by selecting the column to display its properties in the Bound Column Properties window. When you see the Invoice Maintenance form later in this chapter, for example, you'll see that I changed the Visible property for the InvoiceID column to False so it's not displayed. Although you might think that I could remove this column, I couldn't. That's because, as you'll see later in this chapter, this column is used by the application even though it isn't displayed.

I also changed the HeaderText property for each of the visible columns by adding a space between the two words in each column name, and I changed the Width property of each column as appropriate. I also changed the ReadOnly property of the InvoiceNumber, InvoiceDate, and InvoiceTotal columns to True so that these columns can't be modified. Finally, I used the DefaultCellStyle property to apply a date format to the InvoiceDate, DueDate, and PaymentDate columns and numeric formatting and right alignment to the InvoiceTotal, PaymentTotal, and CreditTotal columns. You'll see the dialog boxes for doing that in the next figure.

The dialog box for editing the columns of a DataGridView control

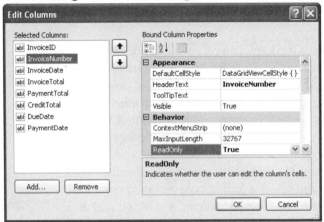

Common properties of a column

Property	Description
HeaderText	The text that's displayed in the column header.
Width	The number of pixels that are used for the width of the column.
DefaultCellStyle	The style that's applied to the cell. You can use the dialog boxes shown in figure 4-12 to set style elements such as color, format, and alignment.
Visible	Determines if the column is visible in the control.
ReadOnly	Determines if the data in the column can be modified.
SortMode	Determines if the data in the grid can be sorted by the values in the column and how the sorting is performed. The default option is Automatic, which uses the built-in sorting mechanism. To provide for custom sorting, select the Programmatic option. To turn off sorting, select the NotSortable option.

Description

- You can use the Edit Columns dialog box to control which columns are displayed in the grid and to edit the properties of those columns. To display this dialog box, choose the Edit Columns command from the smart tag menu for the control.

- To remove columns from the grid, select the column and click the Remove button.

- To add a column to the grid, click the Add button and then complete the dialog box that's displayed. This dialog box lets you add both bound and unbound columns. See figure 4-13 for more information on adding unbound columns.

- To change the order of the columns, select the column you want to move and click the up or down arrow to the right of the list of columns.

- To edit the properties for a column, select the column and use the Bound Column Properties window to edit the properties.

Figure 4-11   How to edit the columns of a DataGridView control

How to format the data in the columns of a DataGridView control

To format the columns of a DataGridView control, you can use the two dialog boxes shown in figure 4-12. The CellStyle Builder dialog box lets you specify the general appearance of a column including the font and colors it uses. You can also use this dialog box to specify the value you want displayed in place of a null value (the default is an empty string) and the layout of the column. In this figure, for example, you can see that the Alignment property has been set to MiddleRight.

To format the data that's displayed in a column, you use the Format String dialog box. From this dialog box, you select a format type and then enter any other available options. In this figure, the Numeric format is selected and the default number of decimal places (2) is used. When you accept this format, the format code is assigned to the Format property in the CellStyle Builder dialog box as shown here. Of course, if you already know the format code you want to use, you can enter it directly into the CellStyle Builder dialog box.

The dialog boxes for formatting the columns of a DataGridView control

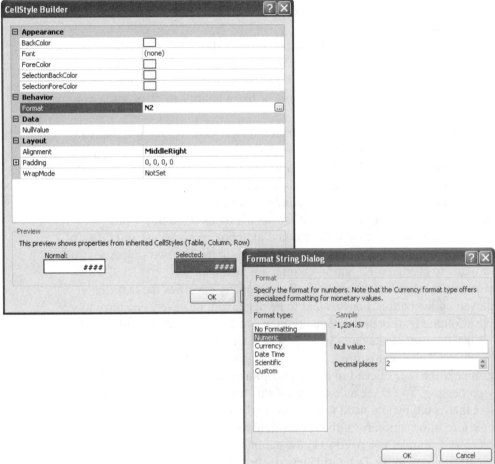

Description

- To display the CellStyle Builder dialog box, click the ellipsis button that appears when you select the DefaultCellStyle property in the Edit Columns dialog box.

- To apply a format to a column, select the Format property and then click the ellipsis button to display the Format String dialog box. Select the format you want to use from the Format Type list and enter any options that appear to the right of the list.

Figure 4-12   How to format the data in the columns of a DataGridView control

How to add an unbound column to a DataGridView control

In addition to the bound columns that are added to a DataGridView control by default, you may occasionally want to add an unbound column. In figure 4-13, for example, you can see that I added a column of buttons to the Invoices DataGridView control. You can click one of these buttons to display the line items for the invoice in that row.

To add an unbound column to a DataGridView control, you use the Add Column dialog box shown in this figure. This dialog box lets you specify a name for the column, the type of column you want to create, and the header text for the column. Although you can create columns that contain a variety of controls, including buttons, check boxes, and combo boxes, you're most likely to create columns that contain buttons. So that's what I'll focus on in this topic.

After you complete the Add Column dialog box, you can use the Edit Columns dialog box to set other properties of the column. The two properties you're most likely to change for a button column are Text and UseColumnTextForButtonValue. The Text property specifies the text that's displayed on the button. For this text to be displayed, however, you have to set the UseColumnTextForButtonValue property to True since its default is False.

When the user clicks on any cell in a DataGridView control, the CellContentClick event is fired. You can code an event handler for this event to determine if the user clicked in a button column and, if so, to perform the necessary processing. You'll see an example of this later in this chapter. For now, just realize that you typically need to determine which button was clicked so that you can retrieve information from the appropriate row. To display the line items for an invoice, for example, you need to know the invoice ID. That's why I included the InvoiceID column in the DataGridView control even though it's not visible.

The Add Column dialog box

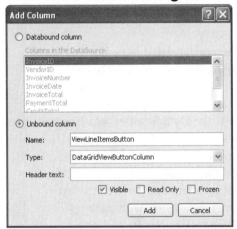

Common properties for button columns

Property	Description
`Text`	The text that's displayed on a button cell if the UseColumnTextForButtonValue property is set to True.
`UseColumnTextForButtonValue`	Determines whether the value of the Text property is displayed on button cells. The default is False.

A DataGridView control with an unbound button column

Invoice Number	Invoice Date	Invoice Total	Payment Total	Credit Total	Due Date	Payment Date	
963253239	9/8/2008	$147.25	$147.25	$0.00	10/7/2008	10/11/2008	View Line Items
39104	9/10/2008	$85.31	$0.00	$0.00	10/9/2008		View Line Items
963253252	9/12/2008	$38.75	$38.75	$0.00	10/11/2008	10/11/2008	View Line Items
111-92R-10095	9/15/2008	$32.70	$32.70	$0.00	10/4/2008	10/6/2008	View Line Items
111897	9/15/2008	$16.62	$16.62	$0.00	10/14/2008	10/14/2008	View Line Items

Description

- To add an unbound column to a DataGridView control, display the Edit Columns dialog box and click the Add button to display the Add Column dialog box. Then, select the Unbound Column option, enter a name for the column, select a column type, and enter the optional header text.

- You can create unbound columns that contain a variety of controls. However, you're most likely to use columns that contain buttons.

- When you create an unbound button column, you usually leave the header text blank. Then, you can use the Text and UseColumnTextForButtonValue properties to display text on the buttons in the column.

- To respond to the user clicking on a button column, you use the CellContentClick event. Within that event handler, you can use the second argument that's passed to it to get the index of the row and column that was clicked.

Figure 4-13   How to add an unbound column to a DataGridView control

How to use a DataGridView control to create a Master/Detail form

A form that displays the data from a main table and a related table is commonly referred to as a *Master/Detail form*. Figure 4-14 shows how to use a DataGridView control to create a Master/Detail form. In this example, the main table is the Vendors table, and the related table is the Invoices table.

The first thing you should notice in this figure is the Data Sources window. Although you would expect the data source for this form to include both the Vendors and Invoices tables, the Invoices table shows up twice in the Data Sources window. First, it shows up separately from the Vendors table. Second, it shows up subordinate to the Vendors table. This subordinate entry indicates that the Vendors and Invoices tables have a one-to-many relationship with each other. It's this relationship, which is based on the VendorID column in each table, that Visual Studio uses to generate a DataGridView control that displays the appropriate data.

To create a DataGridView control that displays data from a table that's related to the main table for a form, you simply drag the subordinate table to the form. When you do, Visual Studio generates the DataGridView control along with the appropriate BindingSource and TableAdapter objects. In addition, it sets the properties of the BindingSource object so the data from the related table will be displayed.

To understand how this works, this figure also presents the properties of the BindingSource object that accomplish the binding for the DataGridView control. First, instead of naming a dataset, the DataSource property names the binding source for the main table. Second, instead of naming a data table, the DataMember property names the foreign key that relates the two tables. In this figure, for example, the DataSource property of the InvoicesBindingSource object is set to VendorsBindingSource, and the DataMember property is set to a foreign key named FK_Invoices_Vendors.

Of course, you can also set the DataSource and DataMember properties of a binding source manually to create a Master/Detail form. That's what I did for the Invoice Maintenance form shown here because I added the DataGridView control before I added the controls that display the Vendor data.

When you create a Master/Detail form, you should realize that you must retrieve all of the rows you want to be able to display from the detail table. For example, because the Invoice Maintenance form shown here lets the user display all the invoices for any vendor, the invoices for all vendors must be retrieved when the form is loaded. If the Invoices table contains a large number of rows, that may not be what you want. In that case, you can create a parameterized query to retrieve the invoices just for the vendor the user selects. You'll see an example of that when I present a complete Invoice Maintenance application later in this chapter.

A form that uses a DataGridView control to display data from a related table

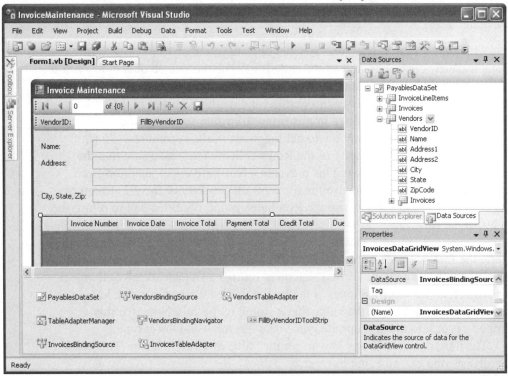

Two BindingSource properties for displaying data from a related table

Property	Description
DataSource	The source of the data for the BindingSource object. To display data from a table that's related to the main table for the form, this property should be set to the BindingSource object for the main table.
DataMember	A sub-list of the data source for the BindingSource object. To display data from a table that's related to the main table for the form, this property should be set to the foreign key that relates the two tables.

The property settings for the InvoicesBindingSource object

Property	Setting
DataSource	VendorsBindingSource
DataMember	FK_Invoices_Vendors

Description

- If a table has a one-to-many relationship with another table, that table will appear subordinate to the main table in the Data Sources window. Then, you can drag the subordinate table to a form to create a DataGridView control that displays the rows in the subordinate table that are related to the current row in the main table.

Figure 4-14   How to use a DataGridView control to create a Master/Detail form

How to work with the values in a DataGridView control

Although Visual Studio generates the objects you need to work with a DataGridView control as well as the code for filling the related data table, you'll frequently need to write additional code to work with the values in the grid. To do that, you can use the classes, properties, and methods shown in the table in figure 4-15. The code examples in this figure illustrate some common uses.

The first example shows how to get the index of the current row. To start, you can use the Count property of the Rows collection to make sure that the grid contains at least one row. This prevents a NullReferenceException from being thrown. Then, you can use the CurrentCell property of the grid to return the current cell, and you can use the RowIndex property of that cell to return the index of the row.

The second example shows how to get the value that's stored within a cell. Here, the first statement returns a DataGridViewRow object for the row at the specified index. Then, the second statement returns a DataGridViewCell object for the cell at the specified index. Finally, the third statement uses the Value property of the cell to get the value that's stored in the cell. Note that this property is cast to the appropriate type since it returns an Object type.

The third example shows how to set the value of a cell in a row. This works like the second example, but in reverse.

The fourth example shows how to use a For Each...Next statement to loop through all of the rows in a grid. Within the loop, the first two statements get the value that's stored in the fourth cell (in this case, the invoice total), and the third statement adds that value to a grand total.

The fifth example shows how to refresh the grid so it reflects any changes that have been made to it. Most of the time, the DataGridView control refreshes itself automatically. But if it doesn't, you can use the Refresh method as shown in this example.

The sixth example shows an event handler for the CellDoubleClick event of a DataGridView control. You'll code an event handler like this if you want to allow the user to select a row in the grid by double-clicking on it. Then, you can use the RowIndex property of the second argument that's passed to this event handler to determine which row the user clicked.

How to delete a row from a DataGridView control

The last example in figure 4-15 shows how to delete a row from a DataGridView control. To do that, you use the Rows property to get the collection of rows and then use the RemoveAt method of that collection to remove the row at the specified index. Note that if the DataGridView control is bound to a data table, this also marks the row as deleted in that table. Then, if the table adapter manager is later used to update the database, the row is deleted from the database.

Important properties and methods for working with a DataGridView control

Class	Property/Method	Description
DataGridView	Rows	Gets a collection of DataGridViewRow objects.
DataGridView	CurrentCell	Gets a DataGridViewCell object for the current cell.
DataGridView	Refresh	Refreshes the grid so it shows any changes that have been made to the underlying data source.
DataGridViewRow	Cells	Gets a collection of DataGridViewCell objects.
DataGridViewCell	Value	Gets or sets the value that's stored in the cell.
DataGridViewCell	RowIndex	Gets the index for the row that contains the cell.

How to get the index of the currently selected row

```
If InvoicesDataGridView.Rows.Count > 0 Then
    Dim rowIndex As Integer = InvoicesDataGridView.CurrentCell.RowIndex
End If
```

How to get the value of the first cell in the selected row

```
Dim row As DataGridViewRow = InvoicesDataGridView.Rows(rowIndex)
Dim cell As DataGridViewCell = row.Cells(0)
Dim invoiceID As Integer = CInt(cell.Value)
```

How to set the value of the first cell in the selected row

```
Dim invoiceID As Integer = 10
Dim row As DataGridViewRow = InvoicesDataGridView.Rows(rowIndex)
row.Cells(0).Value = invoiceID
```

How to loop through all rows in the grid

```
Dim grandTotal As Decimal = 0
For Each row As DataGridViewRow In InvoicesDataGridView.Rows
    Dim cell As DataGridViewCell = row.Cells(3)
    Dim invoiceTotal As Decimal = CDec(cell.Value)
    grandTotal += invoiceTotal
Next
```

How to refresh the grid

```
InvoicesDataGridView.Refresh()
```

A method that handles the CellDoubleClick event

```
Private Sub InvoicesDataGridView_CellDoubleClick( _
        ByVal sender As System.Object, _
        ByVal e As System.Windows.Forms.DataGridViewCellEventArgs) _
        Handles InvoicesDataGridView.CellDoubleClick
    Dim rowIndex As Integer = e.RowIndex
    Me.DisplayLineItems(rowIndex)
End Sub
```

How to delete a row

```
InvoicesDataGridView.Rows.RemoveAt(rowIndex)
```

Figure 4-15   How to work with the values and delete a row in a DataGridView control

An Invoice Maintenance application

Now that you've learned some additional skills for working with a DataGridView control, you're ready to see an Invoice Maintenance application that uses some of those skills.

The user interface

Figure 4-16 presents the user interface for the Invoice Maintenance application. As you can see, this application consists of two forms. The Invoice Maintenance form lets the user retrieve the data for a vendor by entering a vendor ID into the toolbar and then clicking the Get Vendor button. The data for the vendor is then displayed in the text boxes on the form, and the invoices for the vendor are displayed in the DataGridView control. At that point, the user can modify the data in the Payment Total, Credit Total, Due Date, and Payment Date columns of any invoice.

To save any changes made to the invoices to the database, the user must click the Update Database button. Although I could have used the Save button in the binding navigator toolbar for the DataGridView control for this purpose, none of the other controls in the toolbar were needed for this application. So I chose to delete the toolbar and use a standard button instead.

In addition to modifying the data in the DataGridView control, the user can click the View Line Items button for any invoice to display the Line Items form. This form retrieves the line items for the selected invoice and displays them in a DataGridView control.

Before I go on, you should realize that this isn't a realistic application for a couple of reasons. First, you probably wouldn't use a DataGridView control to let the user modify invoice data. Instead, you would let the user modify the data for one invoice at a time. Second, if the user forgets to click the Update Database button after entering some invoice changes, the changes won't be saved when the user selects the next vendor. For the purposes of illustrating the skills presented in this chapter, though, the Invoice Maintenance application is sufficient.

The Invoice Maintenance form

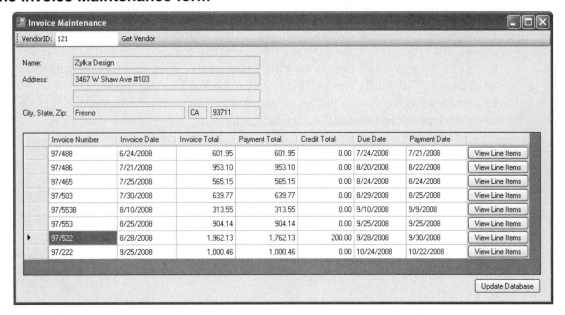

The Line Items form

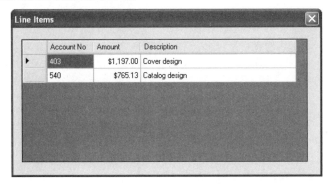

Description

- The Invoice Maintenance form displays the Invoices for a selected vendor and lets the user modify the data in the Payment Total, Credit Total, Due Date, and Payment Date columns.

- The user can also display the line items for an invoice by clicking the View Line Items button for that invoice.

- Because this application doesn't let the user add or delete invoices, the binding navigator toolbar has been omitted from the Invoice Maintenance form and an Update Database button has been added to the form. This button performs the same function as the Save button in the binding navigator toolbar.

Figure 4-16   The user interface for the Invoice Maintenance application

The dataset schema

Figure 4-17 shows the dataset schema for this application. As you would expect, this schema includes the three tables used by the application. The most important thing to notice here is the FillBy query that's been created for each table adapter. The FillByVendorID queries for the Vendors and Invoices table adapters are used to display the appropriate data on the Invoice Maintenance form. And the FillByInvoiceID query for the InvoiceLineItems table adapter is used to display the appropriate data on the Line Items form.

Please note, however, that you don't need the FillByVendorID query for the Invoices table when you use a Master/Detail form that relates the Vendors and Invoices tables. For this application, this FillByVendorID query will be used just to make the application more efficient. You'll see how this query is used in the code that follows. And you can get some hands-on experience with this by doing exercise 4-2 at the end of this chapter.

The dataset schema

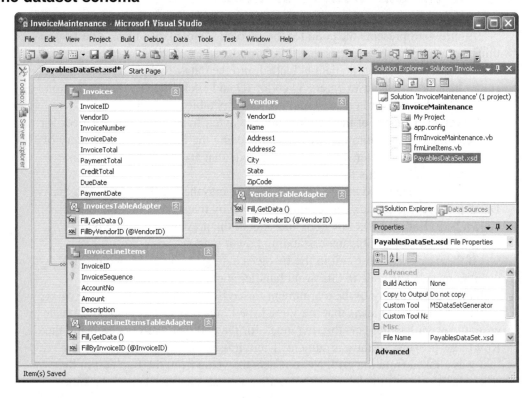

Description

- The Payables dataset defines the three tables used by this application: Vendors, Invoices, and InvoiceLineItems.

- The FillByVendorID query for the Vendors table adapter is used to retrieve the vendor data that's displayed on the Invoice Maintenance form. This query is based on the vendor ID the user enters into the toolbar on the form.

- The FillByVendorID query for the Invoices table adapter is used to retrieve the invoice data that's displayed on the Invoice Maintenance form. This query is also based on the vendor ID the user enters into the toolbar on the form.

- The FillByInvoiceID query for the InvoiceLineItems table adapter is used to retrieve the line item data that's displayed on the Line Items form. This query is based on the InvoiceID of the invoice whose View Line Items button is clicked on the Invoice Maintenance form.

Figure 4-17   The dataset schema for the Invoice Maintenance application

The code for the Invoice Maintenance form

Figure 4-18 presents the code for the Invoice Maintenance form. The first thing you should notice here is that this form doesn't include a Load event handler. Because of that, no data is loaded into the dataset when the application starts. Instead, when a user enters a vendor ID and clicks the Get Vendor button, the row for that vendor is loaded into the Vendors table using the FillByVendorID query of the Vendors table adapter. In addition, any invoices for the vendor are loaded into the Invoices table using the FillByVendorID query of the Invoices table adapter. You can see the code that accomplishes this in the first event handler in this figure.

If an error occurs when the user enters data into the Invoices data grid, the DataError event is raised. This event is handled by the second event handler shown here. Because you saw code like this in the previous chapter, you shouldn't have any trouble understanding how it works.

If the user clicks on a cell in the Invoices data grid, the CellContentClick event is raised. The code in this event handler starts by checking the ColumnIndex property of the e argument to see if the column index of the cell is equal to 8. If it is, it means that the View Line Items button was clicked. In that case, the event handler gets the row index for the cell that was clicked using the RowIndex property of the e argument. Then, it uses that index to get the row that was clicked from the grid. Next, it gets the value from the first cell in that row, which contains the invoice ID. Finally, it creates an instance of the Line Items form, assigns the invoice ID to the form's Tag property so the form will have access to that value, and displays the form as a dialog box.

The code for the Invoice Maintenance form   **Page 1**

```vb
Imports System.Data.SqlClient

Public Class frmInvoiceMaintenance

    Private Sub FillByVendorIDToolStripButton_Click( _
            ByVal sender As System.Object, ByVal e As System.EventArgs) _
            Handles FillByVendorIDToolStripButton.Click
        Try
            Dim vendorID As Integer _
                = Convert.ToInt32(VendorIDToolStripTextBox.Text)
            Me.VendorsTableAdapter.FillByVendorID( _
                Me.PayablesDataSet.Vendors, vendorID)
            Me.InvoicesTableAdapter.FillByVendorID( _
                Me.PayablesDataSet.Invoices, vendorID)
        Catch ex As FormatException
            MessageBox.Show("Vendor ID must be an integer.", "Entry Error")
        Catch ex As SqlException
            MessageBox.Show("SQL Server error # " & ex.Number _
                & ": " & ex.Message, ex.GetType.ToString)
        End Try
    End Sub

    Private Sub InvoicesDataGridView_DataError( _
            ByVal sender As System.Object, _
            ByVal e As System.Windows.Forms.DataGridViewDataErrorEventArgs) _
            Handles InvoicesDataGridView.DataError
        Dim row As Integer = e.RowIndex + 1
        Dim errorMessage As String = "A data error occurred." & vbCrLf _
            & "Row: " & row & vbCrLf _
            & "Error: " & e.Exception.Message
        MessageBox.Show(errorMessage, "Data Error")
    End Sub

    Private Sub InvoicesDataGridView_CellContentClick( _
            ByVal sender As System.Object, _
            ByVal e As System.Windows.Forms.DataGridViewCellEventArgs) _
            Handles InvoicesDataGridView.CellContentClick
        If e.ColumnIndex = 8 Then ' View Line Items button clicked
            ' Get the ID of the selected invoice
            Dim i As Integer = e.RowIndex
            Dim row As DataGridViewRow = InvoicesDataGridView.Rows(i)
            Dim cell As DataGridViewCell = row.Cells(0)
            Dim invoiceID As Integer = CInt(cell.Value)

            ' Display the Line Items form
            Dim lineItemsForm As New frmLineItems
            lineItemsForm.Tag = invoiceID
            lineItemsForm.ShowDialog()
        End If
    End Sub
```

Figure 4-18   The code for the Invoice Maintenance application (part 1 of 2)

The last event handler for the Invoice Maintenance form is the one that handles the Click event of the Update Database button. It works much like the code you saw earlier in this chapter for the Click event of the Save button in the Vendor Maintenance application. The main difference is that this event handler doesn't start by validating the data. That's not necessary because the only four columns the user can modify contain either decimal or date time data. And if the user enters data that can't be converted to these data types, the error will be handled by the event handler for the DataError event of the data grid.

The code for the Line Items form

Figure 4-18 also presents the code for the Line Items form. This form consists of a single event handler for the Load event of the form. To start, this event handler retrieves the invoice ID that was stored in the Tag property of the form. Then, it uses this value in the FillByInvoiceID query of the Invoice Line Items table adapter to retrieve the line items for the invoice.

The code for the Invoice Maintenance form   **Page 2**

```vbnet
Private Sub btnUpdate_Click(ByVal sender As System.Object, _
        ByVal e As System.EventArgs) Handles btnUpdate.Click
    Try
        Me.InvoicesBindingSource.EndEdit()
        Me.TableAdapterManager.UpdateAll(Me.PayablesDataSet)
    Catch ex As DBConcurrencyException
        MessageBox.Show("A concurrency error occurred.", _
            "Concurrency Error")
        Me.InvoicesTableAdapter.Fill(Me.PayablesDataSet.Invoices)
    Catch ex As DataException
        MessageBox.Show(ex.Message, ex.GetType.ToString)
        Me.InvoicesBindingSource.CancelEdit()
    Catch ex As SqlException
        MessageBox.Show("Database error # " & ex.Number _
            & ": " & ex.Message, ex.GetType.ToString)
    End Try
End Sub

End Class
```

The code for the Line Items form

```vbnet
Imports System.Data.SqlClient

Public Class frmLineItems

    Private Sub frmLineItems_Load(ByVal sender As System.Object, _
            ByVal e As System.EventArgs) Handles MyBase.Load
        Try
            ' Get the invoice ID
            Dim invoiceID As Integer = CInt(Me.Tag)
            ' Fill the InvoiceLineItems table
            Me.InvoiceLineItemsTableAdapter.FillByInvoiceID( _
                Me.PayablesDataSet.InvoiceLineItems, invoiceID)
        Catch ex As InvalidCastException
            MessageBox.Show("Invoice ID not an integer.", "Property Error")
        Catch ex As SqlException
            MessageBox.Show("SQL Server error # " & ex.Number _
                & ": " & ex.Message, ex.GetType.ToString)
        End Try
    End Sub

End Class
```

Figure 4-18   The code for the Invoice Maintenance application (part 2 of 2)

Perspective

Now that you've completed this chapter, you should be able to use data sources and datasets to develop substantial database applications. You should also realize how quickly you can prototype these applications. But if you do the exercises that follow, which guide you through the development of the chapter applications from scratch, you should start to see that using data sources isn't quite as easy as it may at first appear.

As I said earlier, if you have any trouble following some of the non-ADO.NET code in this book, we recommend that you get a copy of *Murach's Visual Basic 2008*. It is a terrific reference that will help you quickly learn or refresh your memory about how some aspect of Visual Basic works.

Terms

parameterized query
Master/Detail form

Exercise 4-1   Build the Vendor Maintenance application

This exercise will guide you through the development of the application in figure 4-9. You'll learn a lot by doing that.

Build the user interface

1. Start a new project named VendorMaintenance in your chapter 4 directory. Then, create a data source for the columns in the Vendors table that are used by the form in figure 4-9, plus the StateCode and StateName columns in the States table.

2. Drag the first five data source columns in the Vendors table onto the form as text boxes, but leave enough room at the top for two toolbars. Next, drag the State column onto the form as a combo box, and the ZipCode column as a text box. Then, rearrange the controls and change any required properties so those controls look like the ones in figure 4-9.

3. Drag a GroupBox control onto the form, adjust its size, and drag the last three Vendor columns from the Data Source window into the group box as text boxes. Then, rearrange them and change any required properties as shown in figure 4-9.

4. Use the procedure in figure 4-3 to bind the State combo box on the form to the States table in the data source. Then, set the DropDownStyle property for the combo box to DropDownList, and set its (DataBindings) – Text property to None.

5. Test the application to see how this user interface works. Use the combo box to change one of the State entries. End the application, and review the code that has been generated for the form.

Add a parameterized query

6. Use the procedure in figure 4-5 to add a parameterized query named FillByVendorID that finds the Vendor row for a specific vendor ID. Then, note the toolbar that has been added to the form. Now, review the code that has been added to the application, and review the schema for the application.

7. Test the application to see how it works. First, use the binding navigator toolbar to move through the rows. Then, enter a vendor ID of 8 in the second toolbar and click the FillByVendorID button. Now, go back to the binding navigator toolbar, and you'll discover that you can't use it to go through the rows any more because the dataset contains only one row.

8. With the application still running, use the second toolbar to go to row 10, and select a new state from the combo box, but don't click the Save button. Then, go to row 20, select a new state, and click the Save button. Now, go to row 10 to see that the state has reverted to what it was originally, and go to row 20 to see that the state has been changed. This shows that you must click the Save button after each change if you want the changes to be made to the database. That's because the dataset consists of only one row at a time.

9. Add a valid row to the dataset and click the Save button. Then, note that the binding navigator toolbar lets you navigate between the previous row and the one you just added because two rows are now in the dataset. As soon as you use the second toolbar to go to a different row, though, the first toolbar shows only one row in the dataset.

10. Delete the row that you added in step 9 by going to that row and clicking the Delete button, which makes the row disappear. Then, click the Save button to apply the deletion to the database. If you don't do that, the row won't be deleted. When you're done, end the application.

Modify the toolbars

11. Use the procedure in figure 4-7 to add a Cancel button to the binding navigator toolbar and to change the text on the FillByVendorID button in the second toolbar to Get Vendor. Then, use the procedure in figure 4-8 to start the event handler for the Cancel button, and add the one line of code that it requires.

12. Test these changes to see how they work. At this point, the application should work like the one in figure 4-9. You just need to enhance the code so it provides for formatting and data validation.

Enhance the code

13. Add the FormatPhoneNumber procedure in figure 4-9 to the form. Then, in the Load event handler for the form, add the code for wiring the Format event of the Phone text box to the FormatPhoneNumber procedure. Now, test this enhancement to make sure the phone number is formatted correctly.

14. Comment out the code for filling the Vendors table in the Load event handler, and run the application. As you'll see, only the State combo box has a value when the application starts because no vendor has been selected. To fix that, use this statement to set the index for the State combo box to -1:

```
StateComboBox.SelectedIndex = -1
```

Then, test this change.

15. At this point, you have a prototype of the application. Although you could add the data validation and error handling code that's shown in figure 4-9, that isn't always necessary for a prototype. Just experiment more if you want to, and then end the application.

Add another parameterized query to the form

16. Add a parameterized query named FillByState that gets all the vendor rows for a specific state based on the state code. Next, run the application and use the third toolbar to get all of the rows for a specific state code like CA. Note that the binding navigator toolbar lets you navigate through these rows.

17. Add a separator at the right of the controls on the FillByVendorID ToolStrip, followed by a label, text box, and button that look like the three controls on the FillByState ToolStrip. Then, delete the FillByState ToolStrip.

18. Modify the code for the form so the FillByState button in the FillByVendorID ToolStrip gets the vendor rows by state. Then, test this enhancement. When you've got it working right, close the project.

Exercise 4-2   Build the Invoice Maintenance application

This exercise will guide you through the development of the application in figure 4-16. Here again, you'll learn a lot by doing that. But you may find that this takes a lot longer than you thought.

Build the user interface for the Invoice Maintenance form

1. Start a new project named InvoiceMaintenance in your chapter 4 directory. Then, create a data source for the tables and columns shown in the schema in figure 4-17.

2. Drag the columns in the Vendors table onto the form as text boxes, and adjust them as shown in figure 4-16. Then, drag the Invoices table that's subordinate to the Vendors table onto the form as a DataGridView control.

3. Run the application and use the binding navigator toolbar to scroll through the vendor rows. When you come to a row that has related Invoice rows, like the row for VendorID 34, you'll see that the invoice rows are displayed. Now, close the application, and review the code that has been generated for it.

4. Delete the binding navigator toolbar, and comment out the code in the Load event handler for the form that fills the Vendors table. Next, use the procedure in figure 4-5 to create a parameterized query named FillByVendorID that gets the Vendor data for a specific VendorID. Then, run the form and use VendorIDs like 34 and 121 to see how the Vendor and Invoice data is displayed.

5. Use the procedures in figures 4-10 and 4-11 to disable adding and deleting rows in the DataGridView control, to turn off the Visible property of the InvoiceID column, to delete the VendorID column, to set the header text widths of the visible columns as appropriate, to format the date columns, and to set the ReadOnly property for the InvoiceNumber, InvoiceDate, and Invoice Total columns to True. Then, set the formatting for the three total columns to Numeric with 2 decimal places, and set their Alignment properties to MiddleRight. Now, run the form to make sure that you've got everything right.

6. Use the procedure in figure 4-13 to add an unbound DataGridViewButtonColumn named ViewLineItemsButton to the DataGridView control. Then, set the Text property for this column to "View Line Items" and set the UseColumnTextForButtonValue property to True. Now, run the form to make sure this is working right. (Warning: If the columns in the DataGridView control move around as you edit the columns and test their appearance, that's due to bugs in Visual Studio. So you just have to keep trying it until it works right.)

Build the user interface for the Line Items form

7. Add a new form to the project. Next, drag the InvoiceLineItems table onto the form. Then, create a parameterized query named FillByInvoiceID that gets the InvoiceLineItems rows for a specific InvoiceID.

8. Delete the toolbars that were generated by the queries, and set the properties of the DataGridView control so the form looks like the one in figure 4-16.

9. Add the code for the CellContentClick event of the DataGridView control on the Invoice Maintenance form, as shown in figure 4-18. This code starts by checking whether column 8 (counting from 0) was clicked, which should be the column that the View Line Items buttons are in. If so, it gets the invoice ID from the row that was clicked, saves it as the Tag property of a new Line Items form, and displays a new Line Items form.

10. Modify the code for the Load event of the Line Items form, as shown in figure 4-18. This code starts by getting the invoice ID from the Tag property of the new form. Then, it fills the InvoiceLineItems table in the dataset. For this statement, you can just copy and modify the statement that was generated for the event handler for the Click event of the FillByInvoiceID ToolStrip button. Now, delete the code for the other event handlers for this form.

11. Test the application to make sure that the Line Items form is displayed when you click on a View Line Items button for an invoice.

Change the way the application gets the invoice data

12. Review the code for the Load event handler for the Invoice Maintenance form. There, you can see that all the rows in the Invoices table are loaded into the dataset when the form is loaded. Then, the dataset rows for a specific VendorID are displayed in the DataGridView control each time the VendorID changes. For some applications, that may be okay, but if there are thousands of invoice rows in the dataset that may be inefficient.

13. To change the way that works, create a parameterized query named FillByVendorID for the DataGridView control that gets the Invoice rows for a specific VendorID, and delete the ToolStrip that gets generated. Then, modify the code in the event handler for the Click event of the FillByVendorIDToolStripButton so it looks like the code in figure 4-18 (but don't bother with the error handling code).

14. Delete the Load event handler for this form. Then, test the application again. It should work the same as it did before, but now only the invoice rows for the selected vendor are in the Invoices table in the dataset.

Complete the application

15. At this point, you have a prototype of the application, and you should have learned a lot about how building applications with data sources and datasets works. Now, if you want to finish this application, you just need to: (1) add an Update Database button to the bottom of the Invoice Maintenance form as shown in figure 4-16; (2) code the event handler for this button's Click event; (3) add the error handling code for both forms; and (4) make sure all of the properties for both forms and all of the controls on both forms are set right.

5

How to use the Dataset Designer

In chapter 3, you learned how to use the Dataset Designer to view the schema of a dataset and to preview the data in a query. Now, in this chapter, you'll learn how to use the Dataset Designer to work with queries and schema. You'll also learn the basic skills for using code to work with a dataset.

Then, you'll see how these techniques can be applied to another application. This application will give you a good idea of how powerful these techniques are. But it will also show you some of the limitations of working with data sources and datasets.

How to work with an existing dataset schema

When you use the Data Source Configuration Wizard to create one or more data sources as described in chapter 3, a dataset schema is created for you. Then, you can use the skills in the topics that follow to work with that schema.

Basic skills for using the Dataset Designer

Figure 5-1 presents some basic skills for using the Dataset Designer. To start, you can display the properties for an object in the Properties window by clicking on the object in the Designer window. To display the properties for a column, for example, just click on the column. Then, you can change the properties for the column.

In particular, if you'll be adding rows to a table that contain columns that are defined with default values in the database (which aren't automatically set by the dataset), you can change the DefaultValue properties of those columns so you don't have to specify values for them in the rows that you add.

You can also display the properties for the dataset by clicking on any empty area in the designer window. Then, you can change the properties as necessary. In particular, you may want to set the Hierarchical Update property to False so that a table adapter manager isn't generated for the dataset. That makes sense if an application doesn't provide for updates or it only provides for updating a single table. It also makes sense if an application inserts rows into two or more tables that are related by identity columns. You'll see an example of this in the Invoice Entry application that's presented later in this chapter. If a table adapter manager isn't generated for the dataset, you can use the table adapters to perform update operations instead as you'll see in figure 5-13.

The Dataset Designer is most useful for working with queries. To start, you can use it to preview the data in a query as you saw in chapter 3. You can also use it to add new queries and edit existing queries. For example, suppose you want to add a query to the Invoice Maintenance application of the last chapter that lets you select vendors based on the Name column. If you use the technique presented in the last chapter to do that, a separate toolbar would be created for the query, which probably isn't what you want. Instead, you can create the query using the Dataset Designer and then add it to the existing toolbar. You can also create more complex queries using the Dataset Designer.

To add a new query, just select the table adapter you want to add the query to. Then, right-click on the table adapter and select the Add Query command. This will start the TableAdapter Query Configuration Wizard, which you'll see in the next figure. To edit an existing query, right-click on the query and select the Configure command. This, too, starts the TableAdapter Query Configuration Wizard.

The Dataset Designer

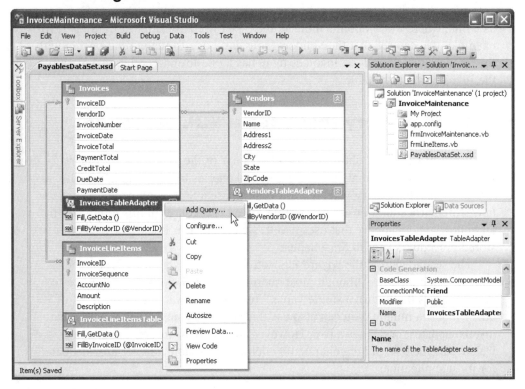

Description

- To display the Dataset Designer for a dataset, double-click the dataset class in the Solution Explorer. Or, select the dataset class and then click the View Designer button at the top of the Solution Explorer.

- To view the properties for a table, column, table adapter, or query, click the object in the Dataset Designer. To view the properties for the dataset, click in an empty area of the designer.

- To delete a column from a table, right-click the column in the Dataset Designer and select the Delete command. This will update the Select, Insert, Update, and Delete statements that are used by the table adapter for the table. It will also delete the column from the data source.

- To add a query, select the table adapter you want to add the query to, and then right-click on the table adapter and select the Add Query command. Then, use the wizard shown in figure 5-2 to define the query.

- To edit a query, right-click on the query and select the Configure command. Then, use the wizard steps shown in part 2 of figure 5-2 to edit the query.

- To preview the data that's returned by a query, right-click on the query and select the Preview Data command. Then, use the Preview Data dialog box that you saw in figure 3-17 of chapter 3 to preview the data.

Figure 5-1   Basic skills for using the Dataset Designer

By the way, when you add two related tables to a dataset, a data relation is automatically added for those tables. A relation appears in the Dataset Designer as a link, where the endpoints indicate the type of relationship. In figure 5-1, for example, you can see that the Vendors table has a one-to-many relationship with the Invoices tables, and the Invoices table has a one-to-many relationship with the InvoiceLineItems table.

How to add a query that uses a SQL statement

Part 1 of figure 5-2 shows the first two steps of the TableAdapter Query Configuration Wizard that you can use to add queries to a table adapter. The first step lets you specify whether you want to use a SQL statement, create a new stored procedure, or use an existing stored procedure. In this topic, you'll learn how to add a query that uses a SQL statement. You'll learn how to use stored procedures later in this chapter.

The second step of the wizard lets you specify the type of SQL statement you want to generate. Although most queries return rows, it's also common to create queries that return a single value. You'll see an example of this type of query in just a minute. You can also use this step to create a custom query that inserts, updates, or deletes a row. However, the standard Insert, Update, and Delete statements that are generated by default for a table adapter are adequate for most applications.

The wizard step for choosing a command type

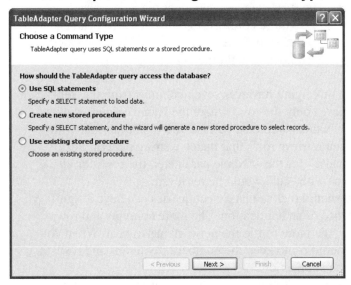

The wizard step for choosing a query type

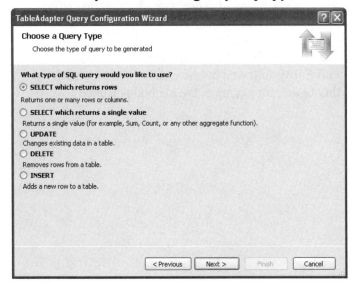

Description

- To add a query, you use the TableAdapter Query Configuration Wizard. The first step of this wizard lets you specify whether you want to use a SQL statement or a new or existing stored procedure for the query.

- If you choose to use an SQL statement, the second step of the wizard lets you choose what type of query you want to create. In most cases, you'll create a Select statement that retrieves one or more rows and columns from the database.

Figure 5-2   How to add a query that uses a SQL statement (part 1 of 2)

Part 2 of figure 5-2 shows the third and fourth steps of the TableAdapter Query Configuration Wizard. The third step lets you enter the Select statement you want to use to retrieve data. If you're comfortable with SQL, you can enter the Select statement directly into this step. Otherwise, you can click the Query Builder button to use the Query Builder to build the Select statement as described later in this chapter.

The Select statement in this figure retrieves seven columns from the Vendors table. However, it retrieves only the rows where the Name column is like the value specified by the @Name parameter. In case you're not familiar with the LIKE keyword, it lets you retrieve rows that match a string pattern. For example, if you specified "cal%" for the @Name parameter, the rows for all vendors with names that start with "cal" would be retrieved.

Before I continue, you should realize that Select queries can have a significant effect on the performance of an application. The more columns and rows that are returned by a query, the more traffic the network has to bear. When you design a query, then, you should try to keep the number of columns and rows to the minimum required by the application.

The fourth step of the wizard lets you select the types of methods that are generated for the table adapter. In this chapter, we'll only use Fill methods that fill a data table in a dataset. However, you can also generate methods that return DataTable objects that are independent of a dataset.

The fourth step also lets you enter a name for the method that's generated. When generating a parameterized query that fills a data table, it's a good practice to begin the name with FillBy followed by the name of the parameter that's used by the query. In this figure, for example, the method is named FillByName.

The wizard step for specifying a Select statement

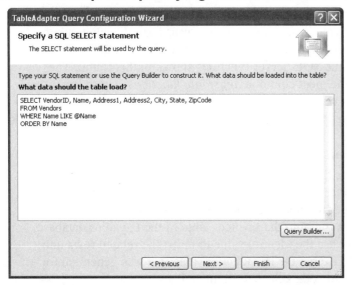

The wizard step for choosing and naming the methods

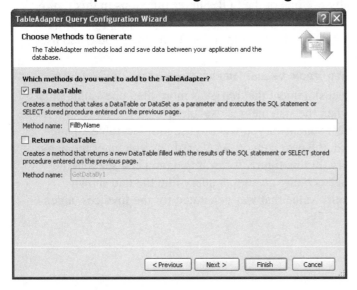

Description

- If you choose to create a Select statement that retrieves one or more rows, the third step of the wizard lets you specify the Select statement. You can either type the Select statement into the area provided, or you can click the Query Builder button to use the Query Builder as shown later in this chapter.

- The fourth step of the wizard lets you select and name the methods that will be added to the table adapter. In most cases, you can include just the method that fills the data table.

Figure 5-2   How to add a query that uses a SQL statement (part 2 of 2)

How to add a query that returns a single value

Figure 5-3 shows how you create a query that returns a single value rather than an entire result set. When you do that, you'll typically code a Select statement that uses one of the SQL Server functions shown in this figure. The first table shows some of the most common *aggregate functions*. These functions perform a calculation on the values in a set of selected rows. If you wanted to get a count of the invoices for a given vendor, for example, you could code a Select statement like this:

```
SELECT COUNT(*) FROM Invoices WHERE VendorID = @VendorID
```

The second table in this figure shows a SQL Server function you can use to get the last identity value that was generated for a table. You may need to do that if you need to use this value for another purpose, such as inserting rows into a related table. If you insert a row into the Invoices table of the Payables database, for example, you'll need to use the identity value to insert the related rows into the InvoiceLineItems table. To get the last identity value that was generated for the Invoices table, you would code a Select statement like this:

```
SELECT IDENT_CURRENT('Invoices') FROM Invoices
```

Although you'll typically use one of the SQL Server functions in this figure to return a single value, that's not always the case. For example, suppose you want to get the default terms ID for a selected vendor. To do that, you could use a Select statement like this:

```
SELECT DefaultTermsID FROM Vendor WHERE VendorID = @VendorID
```

Note that if you code a Select statement that retrieves more than one value, only the first value is returned when the statement is executed.

After you enter the Select statement you want to use into the TableAdapter Query Configuration Wizard, the next step of the wizard lets you enter the name you want to use for the query. In this figure, for example, you can see that the name "GetLastIdentityValue" is being given to a query like the one shown above that gets the last identity value that was generated for the Invoices table.

The wizard step for entering the name of the function

The SQL Server aggregate functions

Function syntax	Description
AVG([ALL|DISTINCT] expression)	The average of the non-null values in the expression.
SUM([ALL|DISTINCT] expression)	The total of the non-null values in the expression.
MIN([ALL|DISTINCT] expression)	The lowest non-null value in the expression.
MAX([ALL|DISTINCT] expression)	The highest non-null value in the expression.
COUNT([ALL|DISTINCT] expression)	The number of non-null values in the expression.
COUNT(*)	The number of rows selected by the query.

A SQL Server function that you can use to get an identity value

Function syntax	Description
IDENT_CURRENT('TableName')	Returns the last value generated for the identity column of the specified table.

Description

- If you choose to create a query that returns a single value from the second step of the wizard, the third step lets you enter the Select statement as shown in part 2 of figure 5-2. This Select statement can return the value of an *aggregate function*, any other SQL Server function that returns a single value, or any other single value.

- The fourth step lets you enter the name of the query, also called a *function* since it returns a single value.

Figure 5-3   How to add a query that returns a single value

How to add a query that uses an existing stored procedure

For illustrative purposes, all of the examples in this book use SQL statements rather than stored procedures. However, in a production environment, it's common to use stored procedures because they run more efficiently. In addition, stored procedures let you store the SQL statements that work with the database as part of the database. That way, other projects that use the same database can use the same SQL statements.

If a stored procedure already exists for the operation you want to perform, you can use the TableAdapter Query Configuration Wizard to identify that procedure. Figure 5-4 shows how to do that. To start, you select the stored procedure you want to use from the list of available procedures. Then, the parameters used by that procedure and any results returned by the procedure are displayed. In the first wizard step shown in this figure, for example, a stored procedure named spGetVendorAddress has been selected. As you can see, this procedure uses a parameter named @VendorID to identify the vendor to be retrieved, and it returns the seven columns shown here.

After you select the stored procedure you want to use, the next step of the wizard lets you choose the type of data that's returned by the procedure. For the procedure in this figure, the Tabular Data option is selected since the procedure returns one or more rows and columns. Then, when you click the Next button, the next step lets you select and name the methods you want to add to the TableAdapter just as it does if you had entered a Select statement that returns rows and columns.

If the stored procedure you select returns a single value, you can select the A Single Value option. Then, the wizard will display the step you saw in the last figure that lets you enter a name for the query.

Finally, if the query doesn't return any data, you can select the No Value option. This is the option you'll select if the stored procedure executes an Insert, Update, or Delete statement. Then, the next step lets you enter a name for the query just as it does for a stored procedure that returns a single value.

The wizard step for choosing an existing stored procedure

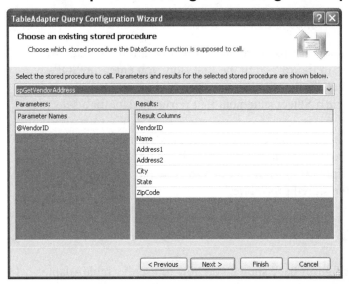

The wizard step for choosing the type of data that's returned

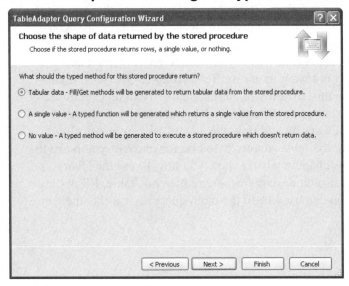

Description

- If you choose to use an existing stored procedure from the first step of the wizard, the second step lets you choose the stored procedure you want to use, and it displays the parameters and results for the selected procedure.
- The third step of the wizard lets you choose whether the stored procedure returns rows and columns, a single value, or no value. The step that's displayed next depends on the option you choose.

Figure 5-4   How to add a query that uses an existing stored procedure

How to add a query that creates a new stored procedure

If you want to create a new stored procedure for an operation, you can use the two wizard steps shown in figure 5-5. In the first step, you enter the SQL statement you want to include in the stored procedure. In this example, the stored procedure will contain a Select statement that retrieves data for a selected vendor.

After you enter the Select statement and click the Next button, the next step lets you name the stored procedure that the wizard will create. You can also click the Preview SQL Script button from this step to view the script that the wizard will use to create the stored procedure.

How to edit a query

Although the last four figures have shown you how to use the TableAdapter Query Configuration Wizard to add a new query, you can also use this wizard to edit an existing query. When you do that, however, the first two steps of the wizard shown in part 1 of figure 5-2 aren't displayed. That means that you can't change whether the query uses SQL statements or stored procedures, and you can't change the type of query that's generated.

Before I go on, you should realize that if you want to edit the main query for a table adapter, you may not want to use the TableAdapter Query Configuration Wizard. That's because this wizard will automatically try to regenerate the Insert, Update, and Delete statements from the Select statement you specify, which may not be what you want. In addition, the wizard will automatically update any other queries for the table adapter based on the changes you make to the main query. Later in this chapter, when I show you how to use the Query Builder to create queries that include data from more than one table, I'll describe another technique you can use to edit the main query so it works the way you want it to.

The wizard step for entering the Select statement

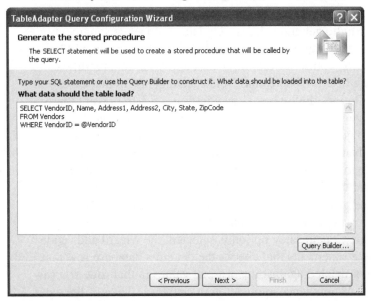

The wizard step for naming the stored procedure

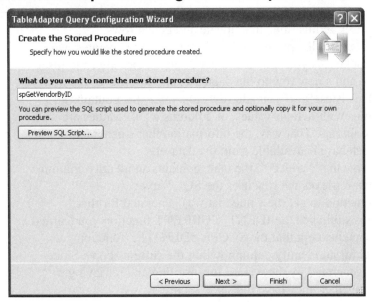

Description

- If you choose to create a stored procedure from the first step of the wizard, the second step lets you enter the Select statement that will be used to create the stored procedure.

- The third step of the wizard lets you enter the name for the stored procedure. You can also preview the SQL script that will be generated from this step.

Figure 5-5   How to add a query that creates a new stored procedure

How to set the advanced SQL generation options

By default, Visual Studio generates Insert, Update, and Delete statements from the main query for each TableAdapter object as described in chapter 3. However, if the application you're developing won't allow for data modification, you won't need the Insert, Update, and Delete statements. In that case, you can use the Advanced Options dialog box shown in figure 5-6 to prevent these statements from being generated. To do that, just deselect the first check box.

Even if you want to generate Insert, Update, and Delete statements, you may want to use the Advanced Options dialog box to control the statements that are generated. The second option, for example, determines whether optimistic concurrency is used, and the third option determines if the dataset will be refreshed after each insert or update operation. These options are selected by default, which is appropriate in most situations.

If the Use Optimistic Concurrency option is selected, the wizard adds code to the Update and Delete statements that checks the data in a database row that is going to be updated or deleted against the original values in that row. You saw this code for the Vendor Maintenance application in chapter 3. Then, if the data has changed, the update or delete is refused and a concurrency exception is thrown. That prevents one user from making changes to rows that have been changed by another user. For that reason, you almost always use optimistic concurrency for multi-user applications that update and delete rows.

If the Refresh the Data Table option is selected, the wizard generates two additional Select statements. As you saw in chapter 3, one comes after the Insert statement that's used to add a new row to the database, and it retrieves the new row into the dataset. This is useful if you add rows to a table that contains an identity column, columns with default values, or columns whose values are calculated from other columns. That way, the information that's generated for these columns by the database is available from the dataset.

By the way, if the row that's added to the table contains an identity column, the Select statement that retrieves the row uses the SQL Server SCOPE_IDENTITY function to get the value that was generated for that column. This function is similar to the IDENT_CURRENT function you learned about earlier in this chapter except that the SCOPE_IDENTITY function gets the last value generated for an identity column within the current scope. Since the statements that are generated by the wizard for inserting and retrieving a new row are executed together, they have the same scope.

The other Select statement that's generated by the wizard is added after the Update statement that's used to modify a row. This ensures that the dataset has current information following an update. Of course, if the values that are generated by the database aren't used by your application, it isn't necessary to refresh the dataset with this information. In fact, it would be inefficient to do that. In some cases, though, you need to refresh the dataset for your application if you want it to work properly.

The dialog boxes for setting advanced SQL generation options

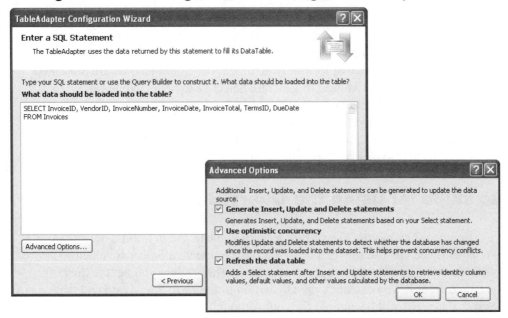

Description

- To display the Advanced Options dialog box, right-click on the main query for a table adapter in the Dataset Designer and select the Configure command to display the TableAdapter Configuration Wizard. Then, click the Advanced Options button.

- The Advanced Options dialog box lets you set the options related to the generation of the Insert, Update, and Delete statements that will be used to update the database.

- If your application doesn't need to add, change, or delete rows in the database table, you should remove the check mark from the Generate option. Then, the other options become unavailable.

- The Use Optimistic Concurrency option determines whether or not the application checks that the rows that are updated or deleted haven't been changed by another user since they were retrieved. If this option is selected, the wizard adds code to the Update and Delete statements to provide for this checking.

- If you remove the check mark from the Use Optimistic Concurrency option, rows are updated and deleted whether or not they've been changed by another user since they were retrieved.

- The Refresh the Data Table option determines whether or not the table in the dataset is refreshed after an insert or update operation. If this option is selected, a Select statement that retrieves the affected row is executed after each Insert and Update statement.

Figure 5-6   How to set the advanced SQL generation options

How to use the Query Builder

Instead of entering a SQL statement manually when you create a query, you can use the Query Builder to generate the statement for you. You'll learn how to do that in the two topics that follow. Note that in the examples that are presented here, the Query Builder is used to generate Select statements. However, you should know that you can also use it to generate Insert, Update, and Delete statements. Although the techniques for doing that are slightly different from the ones shown here, you shouldn't have any trouble figuring out how to generate these statements if you ever need to do that.

Basic skills for using the Query Builder

Figure 5-7 shows the Query Builder tool you can use to build a Select statement. You can use this graphical interface to create a Select statement without even knowing the proper syntax for it. Then, when you get the query the way you want it, you can click the OK button to return to the wizard and the Select statement will be entered for you. Although this is usually easier and more accurate than entering the code yourself, the statement that's generated often contains unnecessary parentheses and qualifiers that can make it more difficult to read. However, you can modify the statement any way you like once it's entered into the wizard.

When the Query Builder first opens, the current table is displayed in the *diagram pane*. In this figure, for example, the Vendors table is displayed in the diagram pane. If you need to add other tables to this pane, you can right-click on the pane and select the Add Table command. You'll learn more about creating queries with multiple tables in the next topic.

In the *grid pane*, you can see the columns that are going to be included in the query. To add columns to this pane, you just check the boxes before the column names listed in the diagram pane. Once the columns have been added to the grid pane, you can use the Sort Type column to identify any columns that should be used to sort the returned rows and the Sort Order column to give the order of precedence for the sort if more than one column is identified. Here, for example, the rows will be sorted in ascending sequence by the Name column.

Similarly, you can use the Filter column to establish the criteria to be used to select the rows that will be retrieved by the query. For example, to retrieve only the rows where the Name column matches a specified pattern, you can specify "LIKE @Name" in the Filter column for the Name column as shown here.

As you create the query, the *SQL pane* shows the resulting Select statement. You can also run this query at any time to display the selected rows in the *results pane*. That way, you can be sure that the query works the way you want it to. To run the query, click the Execute Query button. Then, you will be prompted to enter any parameters that are required by the query.

The Query Builder

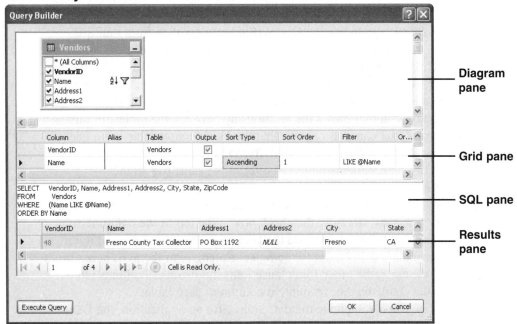

Diagram pane

Grid pane

SQL pane

Results pane

Description

- To display the Query Builder, click the Query Builder button from the wizard step that lets you enter a SQL statement. Or, in the Properties window, click on the ellipsis to the right of the CommandText property of a query.

- By default, the current table is displayed in the *diagram pane*.

- To include a column in a query, click on the box to its left. Then, that column is added to the *grid pane*. Or, select all the columns by checking the * (All Columns) item.

- To create a calculated column, enter an expression in the Column column and then enter the name you want to use for the column in the Alias column.

- To sort the returned rows by one or more columns, select the Ascending or Descending option from the Sort Type column for those columns in the sequence you want them sorted. You can also use the Sort Order column to set the sort sequence.

- To specify selection criteria (like a specific value that the column must contain to be selected), enter the criteria in the Filter column.

- To use a column for sorting or for specifying criteria without including it in the query results, remove the check mark from the Output column.

- As you select columns and specify sort and selection criteria, the Query Builder builds the SQL statement and displays it in the *SQL pane*.

- To display the results of a query, click the Execute Query button. Then, if necessary, enter any parameters required by the query. When you're done, the results are displayed in the *results pane*.

Figure 5-7   Basic skills for using the Query Builder

How to get data from multiple tables

Figure 5-8 shows how to use the Query Builder to get data from multiple tables. To start, you can add tables to the diagram pane by right-clicking in the pane and selecting the Add Table command. Then, you can use the Add Table dialog box that's displayed to select the tables you want to include in the query.

When you add related tables to the diagram pane, the Query Builder includes a connector icon that shows the relationship between the tables. In this figure, for example, the connector shows that the GLAccounts table has a one-to-many relationship with the InvoiceLineItems table. In other words, more than one row in the InvoiceLineItems table can refer to the same row in the GLAccounts table.

Once you've added a table to the diagram pane, you can add a column from that table to the query by selecting the check box to the left of the column's name. Then, the Query Builder will add the column to the grid pane, and it will add the necessary Inner Join clause to the Select statement in the SQL pane. In this figure, for example, the Inner Join clause joins the InvoiceLineItems table to the GLAccounts table on the AccountNo column in each table.

As you know, when you create the data source for an application, the Data Source Configuration Wizard creates a main query for each table you select that retrieves the data for that table. Most of the time, that's what you want. Occasionally, though, you'll want to include one or more columns from another table in the main query for a table. Later in this chapter, for example, you'll see a main query that uses the Select statement shown in this figure. Although you might think that you could create this query by modifying the main query using the TableAdapter Query Configuration Wizard, you don't usually want to do that because this wizard automatically attempts to generate Insert, Update, and Delete statements from the Select statement you specify. If the Select statement contains data from more than one table, however, it won't be able to do that. As a result, you won't be able to insert, update, or delete rows in the table.

To get around this problem, you can display the Query Builder for the main query from the Properties window. To do that, just select the query in the Dataset Designer and click on the ellipsis to the right of the CommandText property. When you finish editing the query and click the OK button, one or two dialog boxes will be displayed. The first dialog box will ask if you want to regenerate the updating commands based on the new command text. In other words, do you want to modify the Insert, Update, and Delete statements so that they match the Select statement. Since Visual Studio can't generate these statements from a Select statement that contains data from more than one table, you won't want to do that. Instead, you'll want the Insert, Update, and Delete statements to remain unchanged so they include only the columns from the main table. If additional queries are defined for the table adapter, the second dialog box will ask if you want to update the other queries based on the changes you made to the main query. In most cases, you won't want to do that.

A query that gets data from two tables

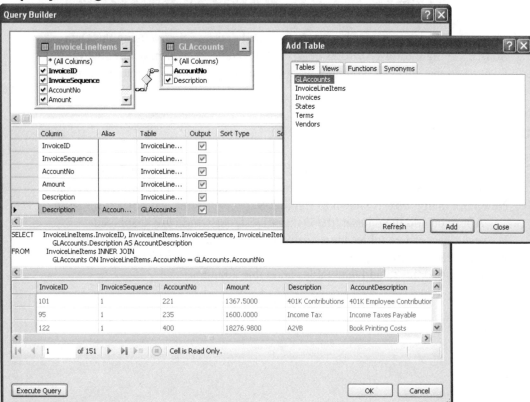

Description

- To add tables to the diagram pane, right-click in the diagram pane and select the Add Table command. Then, you can use the dialog box that's displayed to select the tables you want to include in the query.

- If the tables you add to a query are related, the Query Builder adds connector icons that show the relationships between the tables.

- To add a column from a table to the query, select the check box to the left of the column's name in the diagram pane. When you do, the Query Builder will add the column to the grid pane, and it will add the necessary Inner Join clause to the Select statement in the SQL pane.

- To edit the Select statement that's used by a main query so it includes data from more than one table, select the appropriate query in the Dataset Designer. Then, in the Properties window, click on the ellipsis to the right of the CommandText property, and use the Query Builder to edit the query. Finally, respond to the resulting dialog box to control whether the Insert, Update, and Delete statements for the query are updated.

- If you modify the main query for a table adapter that contains other queries, another dialog box will be displayed that asks if you want to update the other queries based on the changes made to the main query. In most cases, you'll respond No to this dialog box.

Figure 5-8   How to get data from multiple tables

How to create a new dataset schema

Although you can create a data source and dataset schema using the Data Source Configuration Wizard as described in chapter 3, you may not always want to do that. Instead, you may want to use the techniques that are presented in the topics that follow.

How to create a dataset

To create a dataset schema without using the Data Source Configuration Wizard, you start by adding a dataset to the project. To do that, you use the Add New Item dialog box as shown in figure 5-9.

After you add the dataset, the Dataset Designer window is displayed. However, because no tables have been added to the dataset at this point, the design surface is empty. Then, you can use one of the techniques presented in the next two topics to add data tables and table adapters.

The Dataset Designer window for a new dataset class

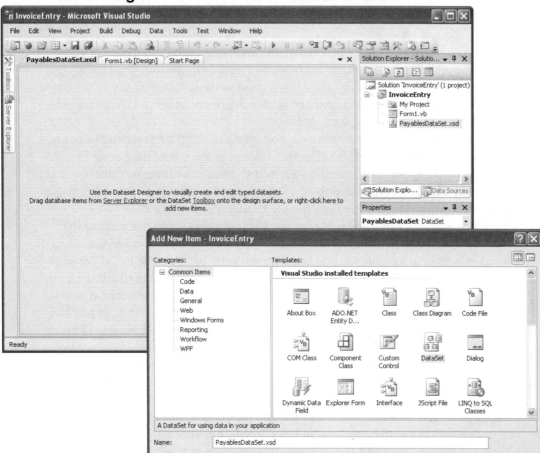

Description

- To display the Add New Item dialog box, right-click on the project in the Solution Explorer and select Add→New Item or select the Add New Item command from the Project menu.
- To create a dataset class, highlight the DataSet template, enter a name for the dataset, and click the Add button.
- To add items to the dataset, you can drag them from the Server Explorer as shown in figure 5-10. You can also drag components from the Toolbox or right-click on the design surface and use the shortcut menu that's displayed to add components as shown in figure 5-11.

Figure 5-9   How to use the Dataset Designer to create a dataset class

How to create a data table and table adapter using the Server Explorer

The easiest way to add a new data table and table adapter to a dataset is to drag it from the Server Explorer as shown in figure 5-10. Before you can do that, though, you must have established a connection to the database that you want to use. If you have established a connection, it will appear under the Data Connections node in the Server Explorer window.

If you haven't established a connection, you can use the Server Explorer to do that. Just click the Connect to Database button at the top of the Server Explorer window and then complete the Add Connection dialog box that's displayed. This is the same dialog box you saw in chapter 3 that lets you define a connection when you use the Data Source Configuration Wizard.

Once you've established a connection to the database, you can expand the database node and the Tables node. Then, if you want to include all of the columns in a table in the dataset, you can drag the node for the table to the designer window. Alternatively, if you want to include selected columns in the dataset, you can expand the node for the table, select the columns you want to include, and then drag those columns to the designer window. In this figure, for example, you can see that I created a data table that consists of the first seven columns in the Vendors table.

When you use this technique to create a dataset, Visual Studio creates a table adapter just as it does when you use the Data Source Configuration Wizard. This table adapter includes a Fill query that retrieves the selected columns from the database. It also includes Insert, Update, and Delete commands that can be used to update the data in the database. In other words, this technique creates a data table and table adapter just like the ones that are created when you use the wizard.

The Dataset Designer after columns are dragged from the Server Explorer

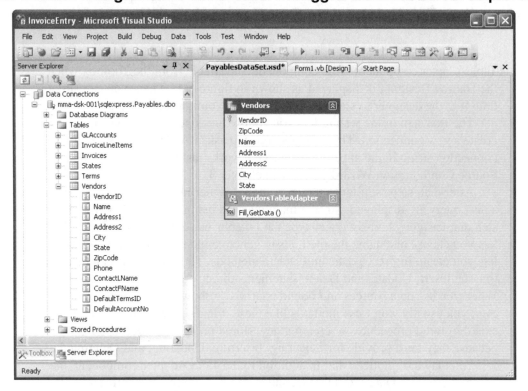

Description

- To display the Server Explorer, use the View→Server Explorer command.
- To use the Server Explorer to add a data table to a dataset, highlight the columns you want to include in the table and then drag them to the design surface. If you want to include all of the columns, you can drag the table rather than its columns.
- In addition to the data table, a table adapter is created with a Fill query that defines the Select statement that's used to retrieve data from the table. This query is also used to generate Insert, Update, and Delete statements for the table adapter.

Express Edition difference

- The Server Explorer is called the Database Explorer.

How to create a data table and table adapter using the TableAdapter Configuration Wizard

Another way to create a data table and table adapter is to use the TableAdapter component. This component is available from the Toolbox when the Dataset Designer is displayed as shown in figure 5-11. Then, you can simply drag it to the designer to start the TableAdapter Configuration Wizard.

The first step of the wizard lets you choose an existing data connection or create a new connection. Then, the second step asks if you want to save the connection string in the app.config file. This works just like it does for the Data Source Configuration Wizard you saw in chapter 3.

After that, steps similar to the ones shown earlier in this chapter for creating a new query are displayed. Since a main query is being created, however, the step that lets you choose a query type isn't displayed. In addition, the step that lets you choose and name the methods to generate includes a third option that lets you create Insert, Update, and Delete methods. These methods can be used to issue Insert, Update, and Delete statements directly against the database. When you use data sources and bound controls as shown in this chapter, however, you usually won't use methods like these. Finally, the steps for using existing stored procedures or creating new stored procedures are different because they must provide for Selecting, Inserting, Updating, and Deleting data.

You may have noticed that in addition to the TableAdapter component, the Toolbox provides Query, DataTable, and Relation components. You can use the Query component to add a query to a table adapter by dragging it from the Toolbox to the appropriate table. This works the same as using the Add Query command in the shortcut menu for a table adapter.

You can use the DataTable and Relation components to create a custom dataset schema. But if you use this technique to create a dataset, a table adapter isn't created. Because of that, you have to work with the dataset using a data adapter. Since you'll rarely need to create a custom dataset schema, I won't show you how to do that in this book.

At this point, you may be wondering when you would use the Data Source Configuration Wizard or the Server Explorer to create data tables and table adapters and when you would use the TableAdapter Configuration Wizard. In general, I think you should use the TableAdapter Configuration Wizard any time you want to generate Select, Insert, Update, and Delete statements other than the defaults. That's because when you use this wizard, you can make the necessary changes as you create the table adapter. If you don't want to refresh the data table after an insert or update operation, for example, you can set the appropriate option when you specify the Select statement. In contrast, if you use the Data Source Configuration Wizard or the Server Explorer to create the table adapter, you have to modify the main query as shown in figure 5-6 to change this option.

The Dataset Designer after a TableAdapter is dragged from the Toolbox

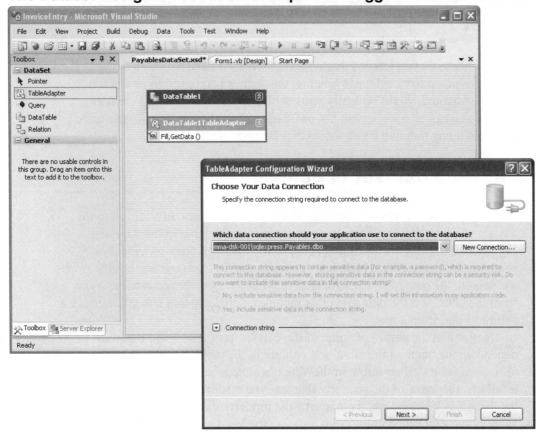

Description

- To start the TableAdapter Configuration Wizard, drag the TableAdapter component from the Toolbox or right-click in the Dataset Designer and select the Add→TableAdapter command.

- The first step of the TableAdapter Configuration Wizard lets you choose an existing data connection or create a new connection. Then, the second step asks you if you want to save the connection string in the application configuration file. The remaining steps are similar to the ones shown earlier in this chapter for adding and editing a query.

- The TableAdapter Configuration Wizard lets you specify the exact query you want to use to retrieve data, it lets you use an existing stored procedure for the main query, it lets you create and use a new stored procedure for the main query, and it lets you set the SQL generation options the way you want them. Because of that, you may want to use this wizard to create your data tables and table adapters instead of using the Data Source Configuration Wizard or the Server Explorer.

Figure 5-11   How to create a data table and table adapter using the
TableAdapter Configuration Wizard

How to use code to work with a typed dataset

In chapter 3, you learned that when you create a dataset from a dataset class that's generated from a dataset schema, the dataset is referred to as a typed dataset. Although you'll typically work with a typed dataset using a binding source, you can also work with a typed dataset directly. You'll learn the basic skills for doing that in the two topics that follow.

How a typed dataset is defined

A typed dataset includes definitions for several classes. In addition to the dataset class itself, two classes are generated for each table in the dataset. Figure 5-12 lists these classes and some of the members they provide. For example, the dataset class includes a property that lets you retrieve a table from the dataset, the data table class includes a property that lets you retrieve a row from the table, and the data row class includes a property that lets you retrieve a column value from a row.

Notice that the names of some of the classes, properties, and methods depend on the name of the table or a column in the table. For example, the name of the class that defines a row in the Vendors table is named VendorsRow. Similarly, the name of the property that lets you retrieve the Vendors table from the dataset is Vendors, and the name of the property that lets you retrieve the value of the ZipCode column from a row in the Vendors table is ZipCode.

Although it isn't necessary for you to understand the details of how a typed dataset is implemented, you do need to be aware of the properties and methods that are provided by a typed dataset so you can use them when necessary. In the next figure, for example, you'll see some typical code for working with typed datasets. This code should help you understand how to use these properties and methods.

Classes defined by a typed dataset

Class	Description	Example
Dataset	The dataset itself.	PayablesDataSet
Data table	A table in the dataset.	VendorsDataTable
Data row	A row in the data table.	VendorsRow

Property defined by a dataset class

Property	Description	Example
tablename	Gets a table.	Vendors

Members defined by a data table class

Property	Description	
Count	Gets the number of rows in the table.	
Item	Gets the row with the specified index.	

Method	Description	Example
New*tablename*Row	Creates a new row based on the table definition.	NewVendorsRow
Add*tablename*Row	Adds the specified data row to the table, or adds a row with the specified values to the table.	AddVendorsRow

Members defined by a data row class

Property	Description	Example
columnname	Gets or sets the value of a column.	ZipCode

Method	Description	
BeginEdit	Places the row in edit mode.	
EndEdit	Saves changes to the current row to the data table.	
CancelEdit	Cancels changes to the current row.	
Delete	Marks the row as deleted.	
Is*columnname*Null	Returns a Boolean value that indicates if the column contains a null value.	IsAddress2Null
Set*columnname*Null	Assigns a null value to the column.	SetAddress2Null

Description

- When you create a dataset schema, Visual Studio generates a typed dataset that includes definitions for the dataset class, the data table classes, and the data row classes.

- The Is…Null and Set…Null methods are generated only for data columns that allow null values. Then, if necessary, you can use these methods to determine what value is assigned to a control that displays the value of the column and what value is assigned to the column based on the value of the control.

Figure 5-12   How a typed dataset is defined

How to work with a typed dataset

Figure 5-13 shows how to work with the data in a typed dataset. To start, you declare a variable that will hold the row as illustrated by the first example in this figure. Here, a variable named vendorRow is declared with a type of PayablesDataSet.VendorsRow. That way, you can use the properties defined by the VendorsRow class to get and set the value of each column in a row as you'll see in a moment.

After you declare a variable to hold a row, you can retrieve a row and assign it to that variable. To retrieve a row, you can use the Item property of the table to refer to the row by its index as illustrated in the first example. Here, the row at index 0 is retrieved and assigned to the vendorRow variable. Notice that because Item is the default property of a table, it can be omitted as shown.

The rest of the code in this example retrieves values from individual columns of the row and assigns them to the appropriate properties of controls on a form. Here, you can see that the value of each column is retrieved using a property of the row. To retrieve the value of the Name column, for example, the Name property is used.

The second example illustrates how you modify the data in an existing row. This code starts by executing a BeginEdit method, which places the row in *edit mode*. Then, the statements that follow assign new values to the columns in the row. To do that, these statements use properties of the data row to refer to the columns just as in the first example. Once the new values have been assigned, the EndEdit method is executed to commit the changes.

The third example in this figure shows how you add new rows to a data table. To do that, you use the New…Row method of the table, and you assign the result to a data row variable. Then, you assign values to the columns in the row just as you do for an existing row. When you're done, you use the Add…Row method of the table to add the new row to the table.

The statement in the fourth example in this figure uses the Delete method to mark a row as deleted. However, this row isn't permanently deleted until you update the database. That makes sense because if the Delete method actually deleted the row, there would be no way of knowing it had been deleted and it wouldn't be deleted from the database.

The fifth example in this figure shows an UpdateAll method for the table adapter manager. As you've already learned, this method saves changes made to the dataset to the database.

If a table adapter manager isn't generated for a dataset, you can use the Update method of a table adapter to save the changes made to a single table to the database as shown in the sixth example. You'll see one situation where you'll want to use this method in the Invoice Entry application that's presented next.

By default, when you create a dataset object by dragging a data source to a form, the dataset object is given the same name as the dataset class it's created from. Because of that, it can be difficult to distinguish between the two when you refer to them in code. To make your code clear, then, you should always use the keyword Me to refer to a dataset object as shown in this figure.

Code that retrieves a row and assigns column values to form controls

```
Dim vendorRow As PayablesDataSet.VendorsRow
vendorRow = Me.PayablesDataSet.Vendors(0)
VendorIDTextBox.Text = vendorRow.VendorID.ToString
NameTextBox.Text = vendorRow.Name
...
ZipCodeTextBox.Text = vendorRow.ZipCode
```

Code that modifies the values in the data row

```
vendorRow.BeginEdit()
vendorRow.Name = NameTextBox.Text
...
vendorRow.ZipCode = ZipCodeTextBox.Text
vendorRow.EndEdit()
```

Code that adds a new row to a dataset

```
vendorRow = Me.PayablesDataSet.Vendors.NewVendorsRow
vendorRow.Name = NameTextBox.Text
...
vendorRow.ZipCode = ZipCodeTextBox.Text
Me.PayablesDataSet.Vendors.AddVendorsRow(vendorRow)
```

A statement that marks the row as deleted

```
vendorRow.Delete()
```

A statement that updates the database with the changes

```
TableAdapterManager.UpdateAll(Me.PayablesDataSet)
```

Another way to update the database

```
VendorsTableAdapter.Update(Me.PayablesDataSet.Vendors)
```

Description

- To declare a variable for a row in a data table, you use the class for the data row that's defined by the dataset.

- To retrieve a row from a data table, you can use the Item property of the table and the index of the row. Since Item is the default property, you can omit it as shown above.

- To get or set the values of the columns in a row, use the properties of the row that have the same names as the columns in the data table.

- After you assign new values to the columns in a row, you can use the EndEdit method to commit the changes. To cancel the changes, you can use the CancelEdit method.

- To create a new row based on the schema of a table, you use the New...Row method of the table and assign the result to a data row variable.

- After you assign values to the columns in the row, you use the Add...Row method of the table to add the row to the table.

- The Delete method of a row marks the row for deletion. The row isn't actually deleted until the UpdateAll method of the table adapter manager or the Update method of the table adapter is executed.

Figure 5-13   How to work with a typed dataset

The Invoice Entry application

Now that you've seen how to use the Dataset Designer to work with data tables and table adapters, you're ready to see an Invoice Entry application that uses a variety of custom queries. As you review this application, keep in mind that it isn't necessarily implemented using the most professional techniques. In fact, one of the main purposes for presenting this application is to illustrate how difficult it can be to implement an application using data sources and bound controls. That will help you better appreciate the skills you'll learn in the next section of this book.

The user interface

Figure 5-14 presents the two forms of the Invoice Entry application. When this application starts, it displays a blank Add Invoice form. Then, the user can use the toolbar to select a vendor by vendor ID or by name.

If the user enters all or part of a name and clicks the Find button next to the Name text box, the Select Vendor form is displayed. This form displays all the vendors with names that match the name pattern in a DataGridView control. The user can also click this Find button without entering a value in the Name text box, in which case all the vendors are listed in the DataGridView control. Then, the user can double-click on a row to select a vendor or click on the row and then click the OK button. In either case, control returns to the Add Invoice form and the information for the vendor is displayed.

Once a vendor is selected, the user can enter the data for an invoice into the remaining controls on the form. Specifically, the user must enter an invoice number and invoice date along with the line item information. In addition, the user can change the terms or leave them at the vendor's default. In either case, the due date for the invoice is calculated automatically based on the invoice date and the terms.

To enter a line item, the user selects an account from the Account combo box, enters a description and amount in the appropriate text boxes, and clicks the Add button. Then, a line item is added to the DataGridView control, and the invoice total is calculated and displayed. The user can also delete a line item from the grid by clicking the Delete button to the right of the line item. However, the user can't make any changes directly to the data in the grid.

When all the line items for the invoice have been added, the user can click the Accept Invoice button. Then, the new invoice and its line items are saved to the database and a blank Add Invoice form is displayed. The user can also click the Cancel Invoice button to clear the Add Invoice form without saving the invoice.

The Add Invoice form

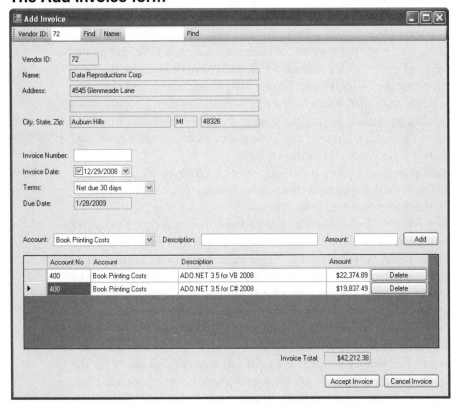

The Select Vendor form

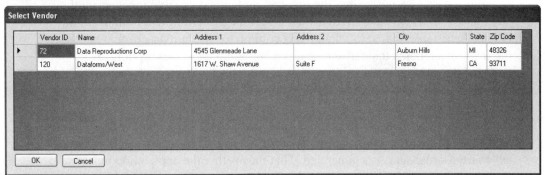

Description

- To add an invoice, the user must select a vendor, enter the invoice information, and enter one or more line items.
- To select a vendor, the user can enter a vendor ID in the toolbar and click the first Find button or enter all or part of the vendor name, click the second Find button, and then select the vendor from the Select Vendor form that's displayed.
- To enter a line item, the user selects an account, enters a description and amount, and clicks the Add button. The user can also delete a line item by clicking its Delete button.

Figure 5-14   The user interface for the Invoice Entry application

The dataset schema

Figure 5-15 shows the dataset schema for this application. The most important thing to notice here are the queries for each table adapter. First, notice that the Vendors table adapter doesn't contain a Fill query. That's because the table is loaded using either the FillByVendorID or FillByName query, and the table isn't updated. Because of that, when I created this table adapter, I modified the query that's created by default so that it retrieves the data for a vendor by vendor ID and so that Insert, Update, and Delete statements weren't generated. I named this query FillByVendorID as shown here.

The FillByVendorName query is similar except it retrieves all the vendors whose names start with the specified characters. This query is used to display the vendors on the Select Vendor form.

The last two queries for the Vendors table adapter return a single value. The first one returns the default account number for a vendor, and the second one returns the default terms ID for a vendor. These values are used to initialize the combo boxes on the Add Invoice form when the user selects a different vendor.

The GetDueDays query for the Terms table adapter also returns a single value. In this case, it returns the number of due days for the terms that are selected for the invoice. Then, this value can be used along with the invoice date to calculate the due date for the invoice.

The last query you should notice is the GetLastIdentityValue query for the Invoices table. This query is used to get the identity value that's generated for the InvoiceID column when a new invoice is added to the database. Then, this value can be used for the InvoiceID column of each line item for the invoice.

You should also notice that the InvoiceLineItems data table includes all the columns from the InvoiceLineItems table plus the Description column from the GLAccounts table. (I had to rename this column to AccountDescription because the InvoiceLineItems table also contains a column named Description.) I included the account description so that I could display it for each row in the line items data grid on the Add Invoice form. I'll explain how I created the query that's used to load this table in the next figure.

Although you can't see it in this figure, you should know that the Hierarchical Update property for this dataset has been set to False. Because of that, no table adapter manager was generated. That means that the application must use the table adapters that are generated for the Invoices and InvoiceLineItems tables to update the database.

The dataset schema

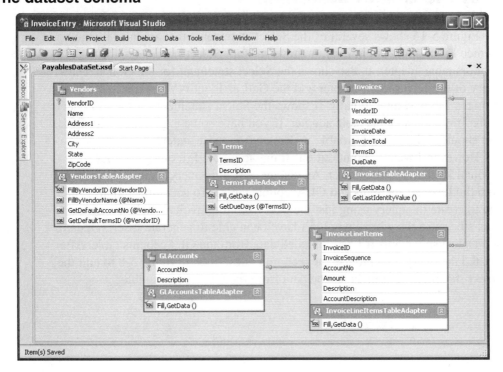

Description

- The FillByVendorID query for the Vendors table adapter is used to retrieve the vendor data that's displayed on the Add Invoice form. This query is based on the vendor ID entered by the user into the toolbar on the form.

- The FillByVendorName query for the Vendors table adapter is used to retrieve the vendors that are displayed in the Select Vendor form. This query is based on a name pattern entered by the user into the toolbar on the Add Invoice form.

- The GetDefaultAccountNo and GetDefaultTermsID queries for the Vendors table adapter are used to retrieve the default account number and terms ID for the selected vendor. These values are used to initialize the Account and Terms combo boxes. These queries are based on the vendor ID for the selected vendor.

- The GetDueDays query for the Terms table adapter is used to retrieve the due days for the selected terms. This value is used to calculate the due date for the invoice.

- The Fill queries for the Terms and GLAccounts table adapters are used to display the lists in the Terms and Account combo boxes on the Add Invoice form.

- The GetLastIdentityValue query for the Invoices table adapter is used to get the ID of the last invoice that was added to the database.

- The Fill query for the InvoiceLineItems table adapter has been modified so it includes the account description from the GLAccounts table. This description is included in the data grid on the Add Invoice form.

Figure 5-15   The dataset schema for the Invoice Entry application

Some of the Select statements

Figure 5-16 shows several of the Select statements that are used by the Invoice Entry application. First, it shows all four Select statements for the Vendors table adapter. It also shows the Select statement for the GetDueDays query of the Terms table adapter and the GetLastIdentityValue query for the Invoices Table adapter. Finally, it shows the Select statement for the Fill query of the InvoiceLineItems table adapter. If you have some experience with SQL, you shouldn't have much trouble understanding these statements.

However, I want to point out one thing about the Fill query for the InvoiceLineItems table adapter. As you can see, this query includes data from both the InvoiceLineItems and GLAccounts tables. To accomplish that, I first had to create the query using just the data from the InvoiceLineItems table. That's because the wizard wouldn't have been able to generate Insert, Update, and Delete statements if I had included data from the GLAccounts table. After I created the query, I had to use the technique described in figure 5-8 to edit the Select statement so it includes the data from the GLAccounts table.

The custom Select statements for the Vendors table adapter

FillByVendorID(@VendorID)

```
SELECT     VendorID, Name, Address1, Address2, City, State, ZipCode
FROM       Vendors
WHERE      VendorID = @VendorID
```

FillByName(@Name)

```
SELECT     VendorID, Name, Address1, Address2, City, State, ZipCode
FROM       Vendors
WHERE      Name LIKE @Name
ORDER BY   Name
```

GetDefaultAccountNo(@VendorID)

```
SELECT     DefaultAccountNo
FROM       Vendors
WHERE      VendorID = @VendorID
```

GetDefaultTermsID(@VendorID)

```
SELECT     DefaultTermsID
FROM       Vendors
WHERE      VendorID = @VendorID
```

The custom Select statement for the Terms table adapter

GetDueDays(@TermsID)

```
SELECT     DueDays
FROM       Terms
WHERE      TermsID = @TermsID
```

The custom Select statement for the Invoices table adapter

GetLastIdentityValue()

```
SELECT     IDENT_CURRENT('Invoices')
FROM       Invoices
```

The Select statement for the InvoiceLineItems table adapter

Fill()

```
SELECT     InvoiceLineItems.InvoiceID, InvoiceLineItems.InvoiceSequence,
           InvoiceLineItems.AccountNo, InvoiceLineItems.Amount,
           InvoiceLineItems.Description,
           GLAccounts.Description AS AccountDescription
FROM       InvoiceLineItems INNER JOIN GLAccounts
           ON InvoiceLineItems.AccountNo = GLAccounts.AccountNo
```

Notes

- The Fill queries for the Terms and GLAccounts table adapters have been configured so no Insert, Update, and Delete statements are generated.
- The Fill queries for the Invoices and InvoiceLineItems table adapters have been configured so the dataset isn't updated after an insert operation.

Figure 5-16   Some of the Select statements for the Invoice Entry application

The code for the Add Invoice form

Figure 5-17 shows the code for the Add Invoice form. To start, this class declares an Integer variable named invoiceSequence. This variable is used to keep track of the InvoiceSequence column that's added to the InvoiceLineItems table, with a value of 1 for the first line item for each invoice, 2 for the second line item, and so on. As a result, this variable is 0 when the application starts, increased by 1 as each line item is added, and reset to zero when an invoice is accepted or canceled.

At the start of the Load event handler for the form, you should notice that the wiring for the SelectedIndexChanged event of the Terms combo box is removed so the event handler for this event isn't executed when the combo box is loaded. Then, this wiring is added back at the end of the Load event handler. In practice, you often need to add this type of code to Load event handlers to prevent the unwanted execution of other event handlers.

The rest of the code in the Load event handler starts by loading the Terms and GLAccounts tables and then initializing the combo boxes that are bound to these tables so that no item is selected. In addition, the date that's displayed in the Invoice Date date time picker is set to the current date, and the checked property of this control is set to False. As you'll see, this property is checked later to determine if the user has selected an invoice date. This is necessary because the date that's initially displayed in this control isn't saved to the data table.

Finally, the Load event handler calls the DisableControls procedure. This procedure disables all of the controls on the form except for the toolbar. That way, the user must select a vendor before entering the data for an invoice.

To select a vendor, the user must enter a vendor ID or name pattern into the toolbar and then click the appropriate Find button. If the user enters a vendor ID and clicks the associated Find button, the Click event handler for this button uses the FillByVendorID method of the Vendors table adapter to fill this table with the appropriate row. Then, the Count property of the Vendors table is used to determine if a vendor with the ID the user entered was found. If not, an error message is displayed and the Vendor ID text box in the toolbar is cleared.

The code for the Add Invoice form   **Page 1**

```vb
Imports System.Data.SqlClient

Public Class frmAddInvoice

    Dim invoiceSequence As Integer

    Private Sub frmAddInvoice_Load(ByVal sender As System.Object, _
            ByVal e As System.EventArgs) Handles MyBase.Load

        RemoveHandler TermsIDComboBox.SelectedIndexChanged, _
            AddressOf TermsIDComboBox_SelectedIndexChanged

        ' Initialize the combo boxes and date time picker
        Me.TermsTableAdapter.Fill(Me.PayablesDataSet.Terms)
        TermsIDComboBox.SelectedIndex = -1

        Me.GLAccountsTableAdapter.Fill(Me.PayablesDataSet.GLAccounts)
        AccountNoComboBox.SelectedIndex = -1

        InvoiceDateDateTimePicker.Value = DateTime.Today
        InvoiceDateDateTimePicker.Checked = False

        ' Disable the controls on the form so the user can't enter
        ' any data until a vendor is selected
        Me.DisableControls()

        AddHandler TermsIDComboBox.SelectedIndexChanged, _
            AddressOf TermsIDComboBox_SelectedIndexChanged
    End Sub

    Private Sub DisableControls()
        InvoiceNumberTextBox.Enabled = False
        InvoiceDateDateTimePicker.Enabled = False
        TermsIDComboBox.Enabled = False
        AccountNoComboBox.Enabled = False
        DescriptionTextBox.Enabled = False
        AmountTextBox.Enabled = False
        btnAdd.Enabled = False
        btnAccept.Enabled = False
        btnCancel.Enabled = False
    End Sub

    Private Sub FillByVendorIDToolStripButton_Click( _
            ByVal sender As System.Object, ByVal e As System.EventArgs) _
            Handles FillByVendorIDToolStripButton.Click

        Try
            ' Load the Vendors table with the selected vendor
            Dim vendorID As Integer _
                = Convert.ToInt32(VendorIDToolStripTextBox.Text)
            Me.VendorsTableAdapter.FillByVendorID( _
                Me.PayablesDataSet.Vendors, vendorID)

            If Me.PayablesDataSet.Vendors.Rows.Count = 0 Then
                MessageBox.Show("No vendor found with ID " & vendorID & ".", _
                            "Vendor Not Found")
                VendorIDToolStripTextBox.Text = ""
```

Figure 5-17   The code for the Add Invoice form (part 1 of 7)

If the vendor is found, the event handler calls the EnableControls procedure to enable the form controls so the user can enter the invoice data. Then, it executes the CancelEdit method of the Invoices binding source to cancel any edit operation. This is necessary because a new invoice row is added later in this event handler. Then, if the user selects a different vendor without adding or canceling the invoice, this code must cancel the current edit before it adds another new row.

Similarly, the next statement removes any rows that may have been added to the line items data grid. To do that, it uses a For statement that loops through the rows in the grid. Notice that to get the number of rows in the grid, this statement uses the Count property of the Rows collection of the grid. Also notice that the loop moves from the last row in the data grid to the first. That's because if you removed the rows from first to last, the second row would become the first row when the first row was deleted and this loop wouldn't work correctly.

After the invoice is cancelled and the data grid is cleared, the Click event handler executes the AddNew method of the Invoices binding source to add a new invoice row. Then, it sets the value of the Vendor ID text box. This is necessary because this text box isn't bound to the VendorID column of the Vendors table. Instead, it's bound to the VendorID column of the Invoices table. That way, when an invoice is accepted, the value of the VendorID column can be taken from this control.

Next, this event handler sets the value of the Invoice Date date time picker to the current date and sets the Checked property to False. This is necessary because if the user has changed the date, the date won't be reset if a new vendor is selected.

The last group of statements in this event handler initializes the two combo boxes on the form. To do that, the GetDefaultTermsID and GetDefaultAccountNo queries are used to get the default terms ID and account number for the selected vendor. Then, these values are used to select the appropriate items in the combo boxes.

The code for the Add Invoice form   **Page 2**

```
            Else
                ' Enable the form controls so the user can enter the invoice
                Me.EnableControls()

                ' Remove the new invoice row that was added if a vendor
                ' was previously selected
                Me.InvoicesBindingSource.CancelEdit()

                ' Remove any line items that have been added
                For i As Integer _
                        = InvoiceLineItemsDataGridView.Rows.Count - 1 _
                        To 0 Step -1
                    InvoiceLineItemsDataGridView.Rows.RemoveAt(i)
                Next

                ' Add a new row to the Invoices table
                Me.InvoicesBindingSource.AddNew()

                VendorIDTextBox.Text = vendorID.ToString

                ' Initialize the invoice date to the current date
                InvoiceDateDateTimePicker.Value = DateTime.Today
                InvoiceDateDateTimePicker.Checked = False

                ' Get the vendor defaults and initialize the combo boxes
                Dim defaultTermsID As Integer _
                    = CInt(Me.VendorsTableAdapter.GetDefaultTermsID(vendorID))
                TermsIDComboBox.SelectedValue = defaultTermsID

                Dim defaultAccountNo As Integer = _
                    CInt(Me.VendorsTableAdapter.GetDefaultAccountNo(vendorID))
                AccountNoComboBox.SelectedValue = defaultAccountNo

                InvoiceNumberTextBox.Select()
            End If

        Catch ex As FormatException
            MessageBox.Show("Vendor ID must be an integer.", "Entry Error")
            VendorIDToolStripTextBox.Select()
        Catch ex As SqlException
            MessageBox.Show("Database error # " & ex.Number _
                & ": " & ex.Message, ex.GetType.ToString)
        End Try
    End Sub

    Private Sub EnableControls()
        InvoiceNumberTextBox.Enabled = True
        InvoiceDateDateTimePicker.Enabled = True
        TermsIDComboBox.Enabled = True
        AccountNoComboBox.Enabled = True
        DescriptionTextBox.Enabled = True
        AmountTextBox.Enabled = True
        btnAdd.Enabled = True
        btnAccept.Enabled = True
        btnCancel.Enabled = True
    End Sub
```

Figure 5-17   The code for the Add Invoice form (part 2 of 7)

When the item that's selected in the Terms combo box changes, the event handler for the SelectedIndexChanged event of this control is executed. This event handler calls the CalculateDueDate procedure, which uses the GetDueDays query of the Terms table adapter to get the due days for the selected terms. Then, it calculates the due date by adding the due days to the invoice date, and it displays the due date on the form.

If the user enters a name pattern in the toolbar and clicks the associated Find button, the Click event handler for this button displays the Select Vendor form as a dialog box so the user can select the vendor from those that match the pattern. This name pattern is passed to the Select Vendor form using its Tag property. Then, if the user selects a vendor, the vendor ID is retrieved from the Tag property. Finally, the Click event handler for the Find button associated with the Vendor ID text box is executed to get the selected vendor. Note that for this to work, the ID of the selected vendor must first be assigned to the Vendor ID text box. That's because the Click event handler uses the value in this text box in the methods it executes.

The next event handler is executed if the user changes the value of the invoice date. This event handler calls the CalculateDueDate procedure to recalculate the due date based on the new invoice date. Before it does that, though, it checks the Vendor ID text box to see if it contains a value. That's because the value of a date time picker control is set to the current date by default. And when that happens, the ValueChanged event is fired. But you don't want the code in the event handler for this event to be executed until after the user has selected a vendor.

The code for the Add Invoice form   **Page 3**

```vbnet
Private Sub TermsIDComboBox_SelectedIndexChanged( _
        ByVal sender As System.Object, ByVal e As System.EventArgs) _
        Handles TermsIDComboBox.SelectedIndexChanged
    Me.CalculateDueDate()
End Sub

Private Sub CalculateDueDate()
    Dim termsID As Integer = CInt(TermsIDComboBox.SelectedValue)
    Dim dueDays As Integer = CInt(Me.TermsTableAdapter.GetDueDays(termsID))
    Dim invoiceDate As Date = InvoiceDateDateTimePicker.Value
    Dim dueDate As Date = invoiceDate.AddDays(dueDays)
    DueDateTextBox.Text = dueDate.ToShortDateString
End Sub

Private Sub FillByNameToolStripButton_Click( _
        ByVal sender As System.Object, ByVal e As System.EventArgs) _
        Handles FillByNameToolStripButton.Click

    Try
        ' Create a search string for the name

        Dim name As String = NameToolStripTextBox.Text & "%"

        ' Display the Select Vendor form
        Dim selectVendorForm As New frmSelectVendor
        selectVendorForm.Tag = name
        Dim result As DialogResult = selectVendorForm.ShowDialog
        If result = DialogResult.OK Then

            ' Get the ID of the selected vendor
            Dim vendorID As Integer = CInt(selectVendorForm.Tag)

            If vendorID = -1 Then ' No rows matched the search string
                MessageBox.Show("No vendors were found with that name. " _
                    & "Please try again.", "No Vendors Found")
                NameToolStripTextBox.Select()
            Else
                ' Fill the dataset with the vendor row
                VendorIDToolStripTextBox.Text = vendorID.ToString
                FillByVendorIDToolStripButton.PerformClick()
                NameToolStripTextBox.Text = ""
            End If
        End If

    Catch ex As Exception
        MessageBox.Show(ex.Message, ex.GetType.ToString)
    End Try
End Sub

Private Sub InvoiceDateDateTimePicker_ValueChanged( _
        ByVal sender As System.Object, ByVal e As System.EventArgs) _
        Handles InvoiceDateDateTimePicker.ValueChanged
    If VendorIDTextBox.Text <> "" Then
        Me.CalculateDueDate()
    End If
End Sub
```

Figure 5-17   The code for the Add Invoice form (part 3 of 7)

When the user enters the data for a line item and clicks the Add button, the Click event handler for this button starts by calling the IsValidLineItem procedure. This procedure checks that the user has entered a description and an amount and that the amount is a decimal value. To do that, it uses the IsPresent and IsDecimal procedures on the next page.

If the data is valid, this event handler continues by executing the AddNew method of the InvoiceLineItems binding source to add a new row to the InvoiceLineItems table, which also adds a row to the data grid. Then, it gets the new row from the grid and sets the values of its cells. Notice that the value of the cell that contains the InvoiceID (cell 0, which isn't visible) is set to 1. That's because a value must be assigned to this cell before the row can be added to the table, but the actual value will be taken from the value that's generated by the database when the invoice is inserted. For now, then, a temporary value of 1 is assigned to this cell.

After the values of all the cells in the row are set, the EndEdit method of the binding source is executed to save the row to the dataset. Then, the GetInvoiceTotal procedure is called. This procedure loops through the rows in the data grid to accumulate the invoice total and then displays the total on the form. Finally, the Description and Amount text boxes are cleared and the focus is moved to the Description text box to prepare for the next entry.

The code for the Add Invoice form   **Page 4**

```vb
Private Sub btnAdd_Click(ByVal sender As System.Object, _
        ByVal e As System.EventArgs) Handles btnAdd.Click

    ' Check that the line item data is valid
    If IsValidLineItem() Then

        ' Add a new row to the InvoiceLineItems table
        InvoiceLineItemsBindingSource.AddNew()

        ' Set the values of the row in the data grid
        Dim rowIndex As Integer = InvoiceLineItemsDataGridView.Rows - 1
        Dim row As DataGridViewRow _
            = InvoiceLineItemsDataGridView.Rows(rowIndex)
        Dim cell As DataGridViewCell
        cell = row.Cells(0)
        cell.Value = 1
        invoiceSequence += 1
        cell = row.Cells(1)
        cell.Value = invoiceSequence
        cell = row.Cells(2)
        cell.Value = AccountNoComboBox.SelectedValue
        cell = row.Cells(3)
        cell.Value = AccountNoComboBox.Text
        cell = row.Cells(4)
        cell.Value = DescriptionTextBox.Text
        cell = row.Cells(5)
        cell.Value = AmountTextBox.Text

        ' Save the line item to the table
        InvoiceLineItemsBindingSource.EndEdit()

        ' Calculate the invoice total
        Me.GetInvoiceTotal()

        ' Prepare for the next entry
        DescriptionTextBox.Text = ""
        AmountTextBox.Text = ""
        DescriptionTextBox.Select()
    End If
End Sub

Private Function IsValidLineItem() As Boolean
    If IsPresent(DescriptionTextBox, "Description") AndAlso _
       IsPresent(AmountTextBox, "Amount") AndAlso _
       IsDecimal(AmountTextBox, "Amount") Then
        Return True
    Else
        Return False
    End If
End Function
```

Figure 5-17   The code for the Add Invoice form (part 4 of 7)

If the user clicks a cell in the data grid, the event handler for the CellContentClick event is executed. This event handler starts by checking if the column index of the column that was clicked is equal to 6, which means that the user clicked the Delete button. In that case, the event handler removes the row from the grid. In addition, it resets the sequence number for each line item so that the numbers are in sequence. For example, if the grid has two line items and the first line item is deleted, this code changes the sequence number for the second line item, which is now the first line item, to 1. Last, this event handler recalculates the invoice total and moves the focus to the Description text box.

If the user clicks the Accept Invoice button, the Click event handler for this button starts by calling the IsValidInvoice procedure to be sure that the user has entered an invoice number, selected an invoice date, and added at least one line item. If so, the event handler continues by executing the EndEdit method of the Invoices binding source to save the invoice to the dataset. Then, it adds the invoice to the database using the Update method of the Invoices table adapter.

Note that I couldn't use a table adapter manager to add both the invoice and line item rows at the same time. That's because before the line items can be added, the value of the InvoiceID column must be set. But this value isn't generated until the invoice is added to the database. So I had to add the invoice first and then get the generated invoice ID.

To get the value that was generated for the InvoiceID column, this event handler uses the GetLastIdentityValue query. Then, it assigns this value to the InvoiceID column of each line item, and it updates the InvoiceLineItems table using the Update method of the InvoiceLineItems table adapter.

The next three statements clear the Vendors, Invoices, and InvoiceLineItems tables. These tables must be cleared so that no data is displayed in the bound controls. Note that these operations are performed directly on the dataset. That's because, if you remove them using the binding source, they'll be marked as deleted in the dataset and not actually removed. Then, when the Update method is executed for the Invoices and InvoiceLineItems tables, it will try to delete the existing rows from the database and an error will occur.

The last three statements in this event handler prepare the form for the next entry. The first statement resets the value of the variable that holds the invoice sequence to zero. The second statement calls a procedure named ClearControls, which initializes some of the controls on the form. And the third statement calls the DisableControls procedure so the user must select another vendor before entering the next invoice.

The last event handler for this form is executed when the user clicks the Cancel Invoice button. This event handler starts by cancelling the edit operation on the Invoices table. Then, it clears the Vendors and InvoiceLineItems rows from the dataset. Finally, it prepares the form for another entry.

The code for the Add Invoice form   **Page 5**

```vb
Private Function IsPresent(ByVal textBox As TextBox, _
        ByVal name As String) As Boolean
    If textBox.Text = "" Then
        MessageBox.Show(name & " is a required field.", "Entry Error")
        textBox.Select()
        Return False
    Else
        Return True
    End If
End Function

Private Function IsDecimal(ByVal textbox As TextBox, _
        ByVal name As String) As Boolean
    Try
        Convert.ToDecimal(textbox.Text)
        Return True
    Catch ex As FormatException
        MessageBox.Show(name & " must be a decimal value.", "Entry Error")
        textbox.Select
        textbox.SelectAll()
        Return False
    End Try
End Function

Private Sub GetInvoiceTotal()
    Dim cell As DataGridViewCell
    Dim amount As Decimal
    Dim invoiceTotal As Decimal
    For Each row As DataGridViewRow In InvoiceLineItemsDataGridView.Rows
        cell = row.Cells(5)
        amount = CDec(cell.Value)
        invoiceTotal += amount
    Next
    InvoiceTotalTextBox.Text = FormatCurrency(invoiceTotal)
End Sub

Private Sub InvoiceLineItemsDataGridView_CellContentClick( _
        ByVal sender As System.Object, _
        ByVal e As System.Windows.Forms.DataGridViewCellEventArgs) _
        Handles InvoiceLineItemsDataGridView.CellContentClick

    If e.ColumnIndex = 6 Then

        ' Remove the line item when the user clicks the Delete button
        InvoiceLineItemsDataGridView.Rows.RemoveAt(e.RowIndex)

        ' Reset the invoice sequence for all line items
        Dim cell As DataGridViewCell
        Dim row As DataGridViewRow
        For i As Integer = 1 To InvoiceLineItemsDataGridView.Rows.Count
            row = InvoiceLineItemsDataGridView.Rows(i - 1)
            cell = row.Cells(1)
            invoiceSequence = i
            cell.Value = invoiceSequence
        Next
```

Figure 5-17   The code for the Add Invoice form (part 5 of 7)

The code for the Add Invoice form

```vb
            Me.GetInvoiceTotal()
            DescriptionTextBox.Select()
        End If
End Sub

Private Sub btnAccept_Click(ByVal sender As System.Object, _
        ByVal e As System.EventArgs) Handles btnAccept.Click

    If IsValidInvoice() Then
        Try

            ' Save the invoice to the Invoices data table
            InvoicesBindingSource.EndEdit()

            ' Update the Invoices table
            InvoicesTableAdapter.Update(Me.PayablesDataSet.Invoices)

            ' Get the generated invoice ID
            Dim invoiceID As Integer _
                = CInt(InvoicesTableAdapter.GetLastIdentityValue)

            ' Set the final invoice ID for all line items
            Dim cell As DataGridViewCell
            For Each row As DataGridViewRow _
                    In InvoiceLineItemsDataGridView.Rows
                cell = row.Cells(0)
                cell.Value = invoiceID
            Next

            ' Update the InvoiceLineItems table
            InvoiceLineItemsTableAdapter.Update( _
                Me.PayablesDataSet.InvoiceLineItems)

            ' Clear the data tables
            Me.PayablesDataSet.Vendors.Rows.Clear()
            Me.PayablesDataSet.Invoices.Rows.Clear()
            Me.PayablesDataSet.InvoiceLineItems.Rows.Clear()

            ' Prepare the form for another entry
            invoiceSequence = 0
            Me.ClearControls()
            Me.DisableControls()

        Catch ex As ConstraintException
            MessageBox.Show("A constraint violation has occurred. " _
                & "The row was not added.", "Constraint Error")
        Catch ex As DataException
            MessageBox.Show(ex.Message, ex.GetType.ToString)
        Catch ex As SqlException
            MessageBox.Show("Database error # " & ex.Number _
                & ": " & ex.Message, ex.GetType.ToString)
        End Try
    End If
End Sub
```

Figure 5-17   The code for the Add Invoice form (part 6 of 7)

The code for the Add Invoice form   **Page 7**

```
    Private Function IsValidInvoice() As Boolean
        If IsPresent(InvoiceNumberTextBox, "Invoice Number") Then
            If InvoiceDateDateTimePicker.Checked = True Then
                If InvoiceLineItemsDataGridView.Rows.Count > 0 Then
                    Return True
                Else
                    MessageBox.Show("You must enter at least one line item.", _
                        "Entry Error")
                    DescriptionTextBox.Select()
                    Return False
                End If
            Else
                MessageBox.Show("You must select an invoice date.", _
                    "Entry Error")
                InvoiceDateDateTimePicker.Select()
                Return False
            End If
        Else
            Return False
        End If
    End Function

    Private Sub ClearControls()
        VendorIDToolStripTextBox.Text = ""
        VendorIDTextBox.Text = ""
        InvoiceDateDateTimePicker.Value = DateTime.Today
        InvoiceDateDateTimePicker.Checked = False
        TermsIDComboBox.SelectedIndex = -1
        DueDateTextBox.Text = ""
        AccountNoComboBox.SelectedIndex = -1
    End Sub

    Private Sub btnCancel_Click(ByVal sender As System.Object, _
            ByVal e As System.EventArgs) Handles btnCancel.Click

        ' Cancel the current edit operation
        InvoicesBindingSource.CancelEdit()

        ' Clear the data tables
        Me.PayablesDataSet.Vendors.Rows.Clear()
        Me.PayablesDataSet.InvoiceLineItems.Rows.Clear()

        ' Prepare the form for another entry
        invoiceSequence = 0
        Me.ClearControls()
        Me.DisableControls()
    End Sub

End Class
```

Figure 5-17   The code for the Add Invoice form (part 7 of 7)

The code for the Select Vendor form

Figure 5-18 presents the code for the Select Vendor form. The Load event handler for this form starts by getting the name pattern that was assigned to the Tag property of the form. Then, it uses the FillByName method of the Vendors table adapter to retrieve all the vendors whose names match that pattern. If no names match the pattern, a value of -1 is assigned to the Tag property of the form and the DialogResult property of the form is set to DialogResult.OK, which closes the form.

If one or more vendor names match the pattern, the user can double-click in the DataGridView control to select a vendor. Then, the CellDoubleClick event handler gets the index of the selected row, and that index is passed to the GetVendorID function. This function gets the vendor ID from that row, which is then assigned to the Tag property of the form. Finally, the DialogResult property of the form is set to DialogResult.OK.

The GetVendorID function starts by using the index of the selected row to retrieve the row from the DataGridView control. Next, it gets the cell at index zero, which is the cell that contains the vendor ID. Then, it gets the value of this cell and returns this value.

If the user selects a row in the DataGridView control and clicks the OK button, the Click event handler uses the CurrentCell property of the grid and the RowIndex property of the cell to get the index of the selected row. Then, it calls the GetVendorID function to get the vendor ID from the row, it assigns that value to the Tag property of the form, and it sets the DialogResult property of the form to DialogResult.OK.

The code for the Select Vendor form

```
Public Class frmSelectVendor

    Private Sub frmSelectVendor_Load(ByVal sender As System.Object, _
            ByVal e As System.EventArgs) Handles MyBase.Load

        ' Get the vendor rows that match the search string
        Dim name As String = Me.Tag.ToString
        Me.VendorsTableAdapter.FillByName( _
            Me.PayablesDataSet.Vendors, name)

        If VendorsDataGridView.Rows.Count = 0 Then
            ' No rows matched the search string
            Me.Tag = -1
            Me.DialogResult = DialogResult.OK
        End If

    End Sub

    Private Sub VendorsDataGridView_CellDoubleClick( _
            ByVal sender As System.Object, _
            ByVal e As System.Windows.Forms.DataGridViewCellEventArgs) _
            Handles VendorsDataGridView.CellDoubleClick
        Dim rowIndex As Integer = e.RowIndex
        Me.Tag = Me.GetVendorID(rowIndex)
        Me.DialogResult = DialogResult.OK
    End Sub

    Private Function GetVendorID(ByVal rowindex As Integer) As Integer
        Dim row As DataGridViewRow = VendorsDataGridView.Rows(rowindex)
        Dim cell As DataGridViewCell = row.Cells(0)
        Dim vendorID As Integer = CInt(cell.Value)
        Return vendorID
    End Function

    Private Sub btnOK_Click(ByVal sender As System.Object, _
            ByVal e As System.EventArgs) Handles btnOK.Click
        Dim rowindex As Integer = VendorsDataGridView.CurrentCell.RowIndex
        Me.Tag = Me.GetVendorID(rowindex)
        Me.DialogResult = DialogResult.OK
    End Sub

End Class
```

Figure 5-18   The code for the Select Vendor form

Perspective

Now that you've completed this chapter, you should be able to use data sources, datasets, and bound controls to develop serious applications. And yet, you should also have a good feel for why you may not want to use this development technique as your applications get more complicated. In particular, you should realize that using bound controls limits the control you have over the operations that an application performs.

One alternative is to develop three-layer applications, and you'll learn how to do that in the five chapters of the next section. When you use that development technique, you have complete control over how your applications work. You can use the code in the database and business classes in more than one application. And your applications are often easier to debug and maintain.

In most companies, of course, there's a place for both development techniques. When you need to develop a "quick-and-dirty" application or prototype the user interface for a larger application, using data sources and datasets is often the best approach. But when you need to develop a sophisticated production application, using a three-layer approach usually makes sense. As a result, most developers need to learn both approaches to application development.

You also have some other alternatives to working with datasets and bound controls. First, you can use LINQ as described in section 4. Second, you can use the Entity Framework as described in section 5. As you'll see in those sections, each of these techniques has its own advantages and disadvantages.

Terms

aggregate function
diagram pane
grid pane
SQL pane
results pane
edit mode

Exercise 5-1   Build the Invoice Entry application

For this exercise, you'll build the application that's presented in figure 5-14 from scratch. That will give you a good feel for the strengths and limitations of using data sources and datasets. As you develop this application, you can of course refer to the documentation that's presented in figures 5-15 through 5-17. But even with that, it could take you two hours or more to build this application.

Before you start this application, you may want to run the book application that you've downloaded from our web site, which should be in your Book applications\Chapter 05 directory. That way, you'll have a better understanding of how this application works.

Development guidelines

- Use the Dataset Designer to create the dataset class for this application as shown in figure 5-9, and use the Server Explorer to add tables to the dataset as shown in figure 5-10.

- Like any form, you should build the Add Invoice form from the top down with the data for one table at a time: (1) the controls that present the vendor data; (2) the controls that get the data for a new invoice; (3) the controls that get the data for a line item; and (4) the DataGridView control that presents the line items that have been entered for the current invoice.

- For each portion of the form, you can: (1) use the Server Explorer to add the required data table to the dataset; (2) drag the table or columns from the Data Sources window onto the form; (3) use the Dataset Designer to add the required queries; (4) use the Form Designer to set the required properties and make the required adjustments to the form; and (5) add the event handlers and modify the generated code as needed.

- Since the Select Vendor form just provides another way to get the data for a specific vendor, you can build this form and write the related code any time after you get the FillByVendorID portion of the Add Invoice form working right.

- As you build the application, you don't need to set all the properties right or add all the code for error handling. You just need to set the properties and add the code that affect the way the application works. Once you get the application working right, you can add the finishing touches.

Development notes

- If you have any trouble figuring out how to do something, you can open the book application and see how it does it. In fact, you may want to open this application in a separate instance of Visual Studio. Then, you can switch back and forth between your application and the book application whenever you want to.

- If you make a mistake as you're building the application, you can often undo it by clicking the Undo button or pressing Ctrl+Z. That's often better than trying to fix your mistake.

- To display the check box in a DateTimePicker control like the Invoice Date control, set the ShowCheckBox property to True. This box is automatically checked when a user selects a date, so you can use the Checked property of the control to determine whether the user has selected a date.

- When you create the InvoiceLineItems data table, be sure to configure it so the table isn't refreshed after an insert operation. Then, you can use the technique described in figure 5-8 to edit the Select statement for the main query so it includes the Description column from the GLAccounts table. When you accept this query, be sure to click the No button in the dialog box that's displayed so that the Insert, Update, and Delete statements that are generated from the main query aren't modified based on the change you made.

Section 3

Three-layer Windows Forms applications

In section 2, you learned how to use data sources, datasets, and the Dataset Designer to build Windows Forms applications. Now, you'll learn a completely different way to develop Windows Forms applications.

In this section, you'll learn how to develop three-layer applications that consist of presentation, business, and database classes. When you use this approach to application development, you write Visual Basic code to do everything. As a result, you have complete control over the way your applications work, but you write a lot more code.

One of the benefits of this approach is that you are often able to use the code in your business and database classes for more than one application. Another benefit is that your applications are usually easier to test, debug, and maintain. For these reasons, this development approach is commonly used for serious production applications.

6

How to work with connections, commands, and data readers

In this chapter, you'll learn how to use connections, commands, and data readers for building three-layer applications. Then, you'll see these techniques used in a simple application. When you're done with this chapter, you'll be able to develop simple three-layer applications of your own.

How to create and work with connections and commands

Before you can execute a SQL statement, you must create the command object that will contain it. In addition, you must create the connection object that the command will use to connect to the database.

How to create and work with connections

Figure 6-1 shows how you create and work with a connection for a SQL Server database. As you can see from the syntax at the top of this figure, you can specify a connection string when you create the connection. If you do, this string is assigned to the ConnectionString property. Otherwise, you have to assign a value to this property after you create the connection object. This is illustrated by the first two examples in this figure.

The first example also shows how you can use the Open and Close methods to open and close a connection. Note, though, that instead of using the Close method to close a connection, you can use the Dispose method. This method closes the connection and releases all of the resources used by the connection, which means that you can no longer use the connection. Because of that, you'll want to use Dispose only when you no longer need to use a connection.

This figure also shows some of the common values that you specify in a connection string. For a SQL Server database, you typically specify the name of the server where the database resides, the name of the database, and the type of security to be used. You can also specify the additional values shown in this figure, as well as others. For more information on these values, see the Visual Studio documentation.

To create a connection for an OLE DB provider, you use code similar to that shown in this figure. The main difference is the information that you provide for the connection string. The connection string for a Jet (Access) OLE DB provider, for example, is shown in the last example in this figure. Because the requirements for each provider differ, you may need to consult the documentation for that provider to determine what values to specify.

Before I go on, you should realize that the connection strings for production applications are frequently stored in configuration files outside the application. That way, they can be accessed by any application that needs them, and they can be modified without having to modify each application that uses them. For example, you'll see an application that uses a connection string that's stored in an XML file in chapter 10.

Two constructors for the SqlConnection class

```
New SqlConnection()
New SqlConnection(connectionString)
```

Common properties and methods of the SqlConnection class

Property	Description
ConnectionString	Provides information for accessing a SQL Server database.

Method	Description
Open()	Opens the connection using the specified connection string.
Close()	Closes the connection.
Dispose()	Releases all resources used by the connection.

Common values used in the ConnectionString property

Name	Description
Data Source/Server	The name of the instance of SQL Server you want to connect to.
Initial Catalog/Database	The name of the database you want to access.
Integrated Security	Determines whether the connection is secure. Valid values are True, False, and SSPI. SSPI uses Windows integrated security and is equivalent to True.
User ID	The user ID that's used to log in to SQL Server.
Password/Pwd	The password that's used to log in to SQL Server.
Persist Security Info	A Boolean value that determines whether sensitive information, such as the password, is returned as part of the connection. The default is False.
Workstation ID	The name of the workstation that's connecting to SQL Server.

Code that creates, opens, and closes a SQL connection

```
Dim connectionString As String _
    = "Data Source=localhost\sqlexpress;Initial Catalog=Payables;" _
    & "Integrated Security=True"
Dim connection As New SqlConnection()
connection.ConnectionString = connectionString
connection.Open()
...
connection.Close()
```

Another way to create a SqlConnection object

```
Dim connection As New SqlConnection(connectionString)
```

A connection string for the Jet OLE DB provider

```
Provider=Microsoft.Jet.OLEDB.4.0;Data Source=C:\Databases\Payables.mdb
```

Description

- You can set the ConnectionString property after you create a connection or as you create it by passing the string to the constructor of the connection class.
- The values you specify for the ConnectionString property depend on the type of database you're connecting to.

Figure 6-1   How to create and work with connections

How to create a connection string using the SqlConnectionStringBuilder class

Figure 6-2 presents another technique you can use to create a connection string. This technique uses the SqlConnectionStringBuilder class. If you review the properties of this class in this figure, you'll see that, except for the ConnectionString property, they correspond with the values that you can include in a connection string.

The first example in this figure illustrates how you can use the SqlConnectionStringBuilder class to build the same connection string you saw in the last figure. The first statement in this example creates the connection string builder. Then, the next three statements set properties that identify the server, the database, and the security to be used to connect to the server.

The second example shows how you use a connection string builder with a connection. To do that, you use the ConnectionString property of the connection string builder to get the connection string it contains. Then, you use that value to assign a connection string to the connection.

Although this may seem like a roundabout way to create a connection string, it has some distinct advantages. First, you don't have to remember all the different values that you can code for a connection string. Instead, you can use IntelliSense to locate the properties you need. In addition, this technique makes it easy to construct connection strings at runtime. If you need to include a user ID and password that the user enters into a form, for example, you can do that easily by assigning the appropriate control properties to the UserID and Password properties of the connection string builder.

How to create a connection in a Using block

Figure 6-2 also shows how to use a Using block to create and dispose of a connection. As you can see, you create the connection as part of the Using statement, and you open the connection within the Using block. Then, when the Using block ends, the Dispose method of the connection is called automatically. This ensures that the resources for the connection are released as soon as it's no longer needed. This is particularly useful for connections that are only needed for a short period of time.

A constructor for the SqlConnectionStringBuilder class

```
New SqlConnectionStringBuilder()
```

Common properties for working with a SqlConnectionStringBuilder

Property	Description
ConnectionString	The connection string associated with the connection string builder.
DataSource	The name of the instance of SQL Server you want to connect to.
InitialCatalog	The name of the database you want to access.
IntegratedSecurity	A Boolean value that indicates if the connection is secure. False indicates that a user ID and password are included in the connection string, and True indicates that Windows integrated security is used.
UserID	The user ID that's used to log in to SQL Server.
Password	The password that's used to log in to SQL Server.
PersistSecurityInfo	A Boolean value that determines whether sensitive information, such as the password, is returned as part of the connection. The default is False.
WorkstationID	The name of the workstation that's connecting to SQL Server.

Code that creates a connection string using a connection string builder

```
Dim builder As New SqlConnectionStringBuilder
builder.DataSource = "localhost\sqlexpress"
builder.InitialCatalog = "Payables"
builder.IntegratedSecurity = True
```

Code that uses the connection string to create a connection

```
Dim connection As New SqlConnection(builder.ConnectionString)
```

Code that creates a connection in a Using block

```
Using connection As New SqlConnection(connectionString)
    connection.Open()
    ...
End Using
```

Description

- The SqlConnectionStringBuilder class provides an easy way to manage the information that's contained in a connection string. This class defines a collection of key/value pairs that correspond with the information that you can include in a connection string.

- You can access the connection values stored in a connection string builder by using its properties as shown above or by specifying the name of a key like this:

```
builder("Data Source") = "localhost\sqlexpress"
```

- After you define a connection string builder, you can use its ConnectionString property to access the connection string it defines.

- To be sure that the resources used by a connection are released when you're done using the connection, you can create the connection within a Using block. Then, the resources are released automatically when the Using block ends.

Figure 6-2   Two more techniques for working with connections

How to create and work with commands

After you define the connection to the database, you create the command objects that contain the SQL statements you want to execute against the database. Figure 6-3 shows three constructors for the SqlCommand class. The first one doesn't require arguments. When you use this constructor, you must set the Connection property to the connection to be used by the command, and you must set the CommandText property to the text of the SQL statement before you execute the command. This is illustrated by the first example in this figure.

The second constructor accepts the SQL command text as an argument. Then, you just have to set the Connection property before you execute the command. The third constructor accepts both the connection and the command text as arguments. The second code example in this figure uses this constructor.

Another property you may need to set is the CommandType property. This property determines how the value of the CommandText property is interpreted. The values you can specify for this property are members of the CommandType enumeration that's shown in this figure. The default value is Text, which causes the value of the CommandText property to be interpreted as a SQL statement. If the CommandText property contains the name of a stored procedure, however, you'll need to set this property to StoredProcedure. Finally, if the CommandText property contains the name of a table, you'll need to set this property to TableDirect. Then, all the rows and columns will be retrieved from the table. Note that this setting is available only for the OLE DB data provider.

The last property that's shown in this figure, Parameters, lets you work with the collection of parameters for a command. You'll see how to use this property in the next chapter.

To execute a query that a command contains, you use the Execute methods of the command shown in this figure. To execute a command that returns a result set, you use the ExecuteReader method of the command. In contrast, you use the ExecuteScalar method to execute a query that returns a single value, and you use the ExecuteNonQuery method to execute an action query. You'll learn how to use all three of these methods in the remaining topics of this chapter.

Three constructors for the SqlCommand class

```
New SqlCommand()
New SqlCommand(commandText)
New SqlCommand(commandText, connection)
```

Common properties and methods of the SqlCommand class

Property	Description
Connection	The connection used to connect to the database.
CommandText	A SQL statement or the name of a stored procedure.
CommandType	A member of the CommandType enumeration that determines how the value in the CommandText property is interpreted.
Parameters	The collection of parameters for the command (see chapter 7 for details).

Method	Description
ExecuteReader()	Executes the query identified by the CommandText property and returns the result as a SqlDataReader object.
ExecuteScalar()	Executes the query identified by the CommandText property and returns the first column of the first row of the result set.
ExecuteNonQuery()	Executes the query identified by the CommandText property and returns an integer that indicates the number of rows that were affected.

CommandType enumeration members

Member	Description
Text	The CommandText property contains a SQL statement. This is the default.
StoredProcedure	The CommandText property contains the name of a stored procedure.
TableDirect	The CommandText property contains the name of a table (OLE DB only).

Code that creates a SqlCommand object that executes a Select statement

```
Dim selectCommand As New SqlCommand()
selectCommand.Connection = connection
Dim selectStatement As String _
    = "SELECT VendorID, Name, Address1, Address2, City, State, ZipCode " _
    & "FROM Vendors ORDER BY Name"
selectCommand.CommandText = selectStatement
```

Another way to create a SqlCommand object

```
Dim selectCommand As New SqlCommand(selectStatement, connection)
```

Description

- The CommandText and Connection properties are set to the values you pass to the constructor of the command class. If you don't pass these values to the constructor, you must set the CommandText and Connection properties after you create the command object.

- If you set the CommandText property to the name of a stored procedure, you must set the CommandType property to StoredProcedure.

Figure 6-3   How to create and work with commands

How to work with queries that return a result set

When you execute a command object that contains a Select statement, the command object returns the result set in a data reader object. Then, to work with that result set, you use properties and methods of the data reader object. You'll learn how to do that in the topics that follow.

How to create and work with a data reader

Figure 6-4 presents the basic skills for creating and working with a data reader. To create a data reader, you use the ExecuteReader method of a command object that contains a Select statement. Notice that when you execute this method, you can specify a behavior. The behavior you specify must be a member of the CommandBehavior enumeration. Some of the most common members of this enumeration are listed in this figure. You can use these members to simplify your code or to improve the efficiency of your application.

After you create a data reader, you can use the properties and methods shown in this figure to work with it. To retrieve the next row of data in the result set, for example, you use the Read method. Note that you must execute the Read method to retrieve the first row of data. It's not retrieved automatically when the data reader is created.

To access a column in the most recently retrieved row, you use the Item property. Like many of the other objects you've seen previously, the Item property is the default property of a data reader. Because of that, you can omit it.

The code example in this figure illustrates how you use a data reader. First, the connection that's used by the SqlCommand object is opened. Although it's not shown here, this command contains a Select statement that retrieves columns from the States table. Then, the ExecuteReader method of the command is used to retrieve the data and create a data reader that can process the state rows. Because the CloseConnection behavior is included on this method, the connection will be closed automatically when the data reader is closed. The ExecuteReader method also opens the data reader and positions it before the first row in the result set.

Next, a List() object that can hold State objects is created and a Do While statement is used to loop through the rows in the result set. The condition on this statement executes the Read method of the data reader. This works because the Read method returns a Boolean value that indicates whether the result set contains additional rows. As long as this condition is true, the application processes the row that was retrieved. In this case, the application creates a State object for each row and adds it to the List() object. After all of the rows have been processed, the data reader is closed.

Two ways to create a SqlDataReader object

```
sqlCommand.ExecuteReader()
sqlCommand.ExecuteReader(behavior)
```

Common CommandBehavior enumeration members

Member	Description
CloseConnection	Closes the connection when the data reader is closed.
Default	Equivalent to specifying no command behavior.
SingleResult	Only a single result set is returned.
SingleRow	Only a single row is returned.

Common properties and methods of the SqlDataReader class

Property	Description
IsClosed	Gets a value that indicates if the data reader is closed.
Item(index)	Gets the value of the column with the specified name or position in the row.

Method	Description
Close()	Closes the data reader. If the command executes a stored procedure that includes output parameters or a return value, this method also sets these values.
NextResult()	Advances the data reader to the next result set and returns a Boolean value that indicates whether there are additional result sets.
Read()	Retrieves the next row and returns a Boolean value that indicates whether there are additional rows.

Code that uses a data reader to populate a list with State objects

```
connection.Open()
Dim reader As SqlDataReader _
    = selectCommand.ExecuteReader(CommandBehavior.CloseConnection)
Dim stateList As New List(Of State)
Do While reader.Read()
    Dim state As New State
    state.StateCode = reader("StateCode").ToString
    state.StateName = reader("StateName").ToString
    stateList.Add(state)
Loop
reader.Close()
```

Description

- You must open the connection that's used by the data reader before you execute the ExecuteReader method of the command object.

- The data reader is opened automatically when it's created. While it's open, no other data readers can be opened on the same connection. The exception is if you're using an Oracle data reader, in which case other Oracle data readers can be open at the same time.

- When you first create a data reader, it's positioned before the first row in the result set. To retrieve the first row, you have to execute the Read method.

- You can combine two or more command behavior members using the & operator.

Figure 6-4   How to create and work with a data reader

Although most commands execute a single Select statement and return a single result set, a command can also execute two or more Select statements and return two or more result sets. That way, only one trip is made to the server for all the statements. To combine two or more Select statements, you code a semicolon between them. For example, suppose you want to retrieve vendor, terms, and account information. To do that, you could code three Select statements in a single command like this:

```
SELECT * From Vendors;
SELECT TermsID, Description FROM Terms;
SELECT AccountNo, Description FROM GLAccounts
```

To process the three result sets returned by these statements, you would read the vendor rows in the first result set. Then, you would use the NextResult method to move to the result set that contains the terms, and you would read the rows in that result set. Finally, you would repeat this process for the rows in the third result set.

How to improve the efficiency of column lookups

When you retrieve a column from a data reader using the column name as shown in the previous figure, the data reader has to search for the appropriate column. To make the retrieval operation more efficient, you can specify the position of the column instead of its name. One way to do that is to use a literal value. For example, you can use a statement like this to retrieve the value of the first column in the States data reader:

```
state.StateCode = reader.Read(0).ToString
```

This technique is error prone, though, because you can easily specify the wrong position for a column. In addition, if the columns that are retrieved change, you may have to modify your code to accommodate the new column positions.

An alternative is to use the GetOrdinal method of the data reader to get the position, or *ordinal*, of a column with the specified name. Then, you can assign the result of that method to a variable and use the variable to refer to the column on the Read method. To understand how this works, take a look at the code example in figure 6-5. Here, the command contains a Select statement that will return a result set with three columns.

After the connection is opened and the ExecuteReader method is executed, the GetOrdinal method is used to get the position of each of the columns. Notice that this method must locate the column using its name just as the Read method in the previous figure did. In this case, though, the column is looked up by name only once. Then, within the Do While loop that processes the rows in the result set, the Read method uses the columns' ordinals.

When you refer to a column using its ordinal, you can also use the other methods listed in this figure. These methods let you specify the type of data that's retrieved. The three columns in the code in this figure, for example, are retrieved using the GetString, GetDateTime, and GetDecimal methods. This can improve the efficiency of the operation by eliminating unnecessary data conversion.

Common methods for improving the efficiency of column lookups

Method	Description
GetOrdinal(name)	Gets the position of the column with the specified name. The position is zero-based.
GetBoolean(position)	Gets the value of the column at the specified position as a Boolean.
GetDateTime(position)	Gets the value of the column at the specified position as a date and time.
GetDecimal(position)	Gets the value of the column at the specified position as a decimal.
GetInt16(position)	Gets the value of the column at the specified position as a 16-bit signed integer.
GetInt32(position)	Gets the value of the column at the specified position as a 32-bit signed integer.
GetInt64(position)	Gets the value of the column at the specified position as a 64-bit signed integer.
GetString(position)	Gets the value of the column at the specified position as a string.

Code that uses type-specific Get methods and ordinals

```
Dim selectStatement As String _
    = "SELECT InvoiceNumber, InvoiceDate, InvoiceTotal " _
    & "FROM Invoices " _
    & "WHERE InvoiceTotal - PaymentTotal - CreditTotal > 0"
Dim selectCommand As New SqlCommand(selectStatement, connection)
connection.Open()
Dim reader As SqlDataReader = selectCommand.ExecuteReader()
Dim invNoOrd As Integer = reader.GetOrdinal("InvoiceNumber")
Dim invDateOrd As Integer = reader.GetOrdinal("InvoiceDate")
Dim invTotalOrd As Integer = reader.GetOrdinal("InvoiceTotal")
Dim invoiceList As New List(Of Invoice)
Do While reader.Read
    Dim invoice As New Invoice
    invoice.InvoiceNumber = reader.GetString(invNoOrd)
    invoice.InvoiceDate = reader.GetDateTime(invDateOrd)
    invoice.InvoiceTotal = reader.GetDecimal(invTotalOrd)
    invoiceList.Add(invoice)
Loop
reader.Close()
connection.Close()
```

Description

- Instead of retrieving a column by name, you can retrieve it by its position, or *ordinal*, in the row. That improves the efficiency of the retrieval operation because the data reader can retrieve the column directly rather than looking for it by name.

- If you know that the position of a column won't change, you can specify the position as a literal value. Otherwise, you can use the GetOrdinal method to get its position.

- When you use the Item property to get the value of a column, the value is returned with the Object data type. To improve efficiency, you can use one of the type-specific Get methods to retrieve a column value with the appropriate type.

Figure 6-5   How to improve the efficiency of column lookups

An Invoices by Due Date application that uses a data reader

To illustrate how you can use a data reader to work with the data returned by a Select statement, I'll present an application that lists invoices by due date. Although this is a simple application, you'll see that it consists of three classes in addition to the form class. That will help you understand how you can separate the business and database processing from the processing for the user interface.

The user interface

Figure 6-6 presents the design of the Invoices by Due Date form. As you can see, this form includes information for each invoice with a balance due. This information is displayed in a ListView control, which can be used to display a collection of items in one of five different views. This control is a common control that's available from the Toolbox, not a data control.

To display the invoices, I set the View property of the ListView control to Details, which displays the data in a row and column format. In addition, I used the ColumnHeader Collection Editor for the control to specify the column headings and widths shown here. If you aren't familiar with the ListView control, you may want to consult the Visual Studio documentation on this control to learn more about how it works.

The class design

Figure 6-6 also summarizes the classes used by this application. Like all of the applications in this section of the book, this one has a three-layer architecture that consists of presentation, business, and database classes. To refresh your memory about how this works, please refer back to figure 2-11 in chapter 2.

For this application, the business and database classes are stored in a class library named PayablesData. That way, they can be used by other applications that require the data or operations they provide.

The Invoice class is a business class that represents a single invoice. It has six public properties that represent the data from the Invoices table that's used by this application and a method that calculates and returns the unpaid balance of an invoice.

The InvoiceDB and PayablesDB classes are database classes that contain one method each that works directly with the database. The GetInvoicesDue method in the InvoiceDB class returns a List() object that holds one Invoice object for each invoice in the Invoices table with a balance due. The GetConnection method in the PayablesDB class returns a connection to the Payables database.

The Invoices by Due Date form

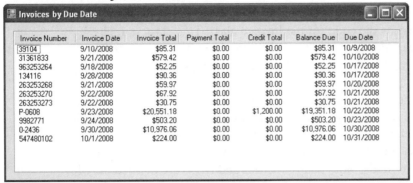

Properties and methods of the Invoice class

Property	Description
InvoiceNumber	The invoice number assigned by the vendor.
InvoiceDate	The date the invoice was issued.
InvoiceTotal	The total amount of the invoice.
PaymentTotal	The total payments that have been applied to the invoice.
CreditTotal	The total credits that have been applied to the invoice.
DueDate	The date the invoice is due.

Method	Description
BalanceDue()	The unpaid balance of the invoice.

Method of the InvoiceDB class

Method	Description
GetInvoicesDue()	Returns a List() object that contains all of the invoices in the Invoices table with unpaid balances.

Method of the PayablesDB class

Method	Description
GetConnection()	Returns a SqlConnection object for the Payables database.

Description

- The Invoices by Due Date form uses a ListView control to display a list of all the invoices with a balance due. A data reader is used to retrieve the rows that are displayed.

- To make this work, the View property of the ListView control is set to Details, which causes the data items to be displayed in columns. In addition, the column headers shown above were added using the ColumnHeader Collection Editor.

- The Invoice, InvoiceDB, and PayablesDB classes that are used by this application are stored in a class library named PayablesData.

Figure 6-6   An Invoices by Due Date application that uses a data reader

The code for the Invoice class

Figure 6-7 presents the code for the Invoice class. This class starts by defining the private fields for the class. When an object is created from this class, these fields can be used to store the values of the properties defined by the class.

This class also contains a single parameterless constructor. Because this constructor doesn't contain any statements, all of the fields defined by the class will be assigned default values when the class is instantiated.

Next, this class contains six properties that can be used to get or set the values of the private fields. Note that properties and fields are defined only for the data that's used by the Invoices by Due Date application. I did that just to keep this code as simple as possible. In a production application, however, this class would define properties for all of the columns in the Invoices table. That way, any application that accessed this table could use this class.

The Invoice class also contains one method. This method calculates the balance due for an invoice using the invoice total, payment total, and credit total fields and then returns the value to the calling procedure. If you look back at figure 6-6, you'll see that this is the value that's displayed in the next to last column of the ListView control.

The code for the Invoice class

```vbnet
Public Class Invoice
    Private m_InvoiceNumber As String
    Private m_InvoiceDate As Date
    Private m_InvoiceTotal As Decimal
    Private m_PaymentTotal As Decimal
    Private m_CreditTotal As Decimal
    Private m_DueDate As Date

    Public Sub New()

    End Sub

    Public Property InvoiceNumber() As String
        Get
            Return m_InvoiceNumber
        End Get
        Set(ByVal value As String)
            m_InvoiceNumber = value
        End Set
    End Property

    Public Property InvoiceDate() As Date
        Get
            Return m_InvoiceDate
        End Get
        Set(ByVal value As Date)
            m_InvoiceDate = value
        End Set
    End Property

    Public Property InvoiceTotal() As Decimal
        Get
            Return m_InvoiceTotal
        End Get
        Set(ByVal value As Decimal)
            m_InvoiceTotal = value
        End Set
    End Property
    .
    .
    Public Property DueDate() As Date
        Get
            Return m_DueDate
        End Get
        Set(ByVal value As Date)
            m_DueDate = value
        End Set
    End Property

    Public Function BalanceDue() As Decimal
        Return m_InvoiceTotal - m_PaymentTotal - m_CreditTotal
    End Function

End Class
```

Figure 6-7   The code for the Invoice class

The code for the InvoiceDB class

Figure 6-8 presents the code for the InvoiceDB class. This class consists of a single method named GetInvoicesDue that returns a list of Invoice objects. This method starts by creating a new List() object that can hold Invoice objects. Then, it creates a connection by calling the GetConnection method of the PayablesDB class. I'll describe the code for this class in just a minute.

Next, this method defines the Select statement that will be used to retrieve invoices from the Invoices table. Notice that this statement only retrieves invoices with a balance due (InvoiceTotal – PaymentTotal – CreditTotal > 0). In addition, it sorts the invoices by due date.

After it creates the connection and defines the Select statement, this method creates a command object that uses that Select statement and connection. Then, it opens the connection and uses the ExecuteReader method to execute the command. Next, it uses the data reader that's created by the ExecuteReader method to get each invoice that's returned by the Select statement. For each invoice, it creates a new Invoice object and adds it to the invoice list. Then, after all the invoices have been processed, it closes the data reader and the connection and then returns the list of Invoice objects to the calling procedure.

Notice that the statements that open the connection and data reader and process the rows in the data reader are coded within the Try block of a Try…Catch…Finally statement. Then, if a SqlException occurs, the Catch block throws the exception to the calling procedure. Because of that, the procedure that calls this method should catch this exception. Whether or not an exception occurs, the statement that closes the connection is coded within the Finally block. That way, if the statement that opens the connection is successful but the statement that executes the command isn't, the connection is still closed.

The code for the PayablesDB class

Figure 6-8 also presents the code for the PayablesDB class. This class contains a single method named GetConnection that returns a connection to the Payables database. As you've already seen, the InvoiceDB class calls this method to get the connection that's used by the command it executes. Note that the connection string is hard coded into this method. As I explained earlier, however, the connection string for a production application is typically stored in an external configuration file. Then, the GetConnection method would read the connection string from this file. That way, you could change the location of the database without recompiling the application.

At this point, you may be wondering why I coded the GetConnection method in a separate class rather than in the InvoiceDB class. The reason is that this method isn't specific to the Invoices table. Because of that, it can be used to get a connection for any method in any database class in the class library. Although this class library only contains one other database class, a complete class library would probably contain a database class for each table in the database.

The code for the InvoiceDB class

```vb
Imports System.Data.SqlClient

Public Class InvoiceDB

    Public Shared Function GetInvoicesDue() As List(Of Invoice)
        Dim invoiceList As New List(Of Invoice)
        Dim connection As SqlConnection = PayablesDB.GetConnection
        Dim selectStatement As String _
            = "SELECT InvoiceNumber, InvoiceDate, InvoiceTotal, " _
            & "PaymentTotal, CreditTotal, DueDate " _
            & "FROM Invoices " _
            & "WHERE InvoiceTotal - PaymentTotal - CreditTotal > 0 " _
            & "ORDER BY DueDate"
        Dim selectCommand As New SqlCommand(selectStatement, connection)
        Try
            connection.Open()
            Dim reader As SqlDataReader = selectCommand.ExecuteReader()
            Dim invoice As Invoice
            Do While reader.Read
                invoice = New Invoice
                invoice.InvoiceNumber = reader("InvoiceNumber").ToString
                invoice.InvoiceDate = CDate(reader("InvoiceDate"))
                invoice.InvoiceTotal = CDec(reader("InvoiceTotal"))
                invoice.PaymentTotal = CDec(reader("PaymentTotal"))
                invoice.CreditTotal = CDec(reader("CreditTotal"))
                invoice.DueDate = CDate(reader("DueDate"))
                invoiceList.Add(invoice)
            Loop
            reader.Close()
        Catch ex As SqlException
            Throw ex
        Finally
            connection.Close()
        End Try
        Return invoiceList
    End Function

End Class
```

The code for the PayablesDB class

```vb
Imports System.Data.SqlClient

Public Class PayablesDB

    Public Shared Function GetConnection() As SqlConnection
        Dim connectionString As String _
            = "Data Source=localhost\SqlExpress;Initial Catalog=Payables;" _
            & "Integrated Security=True"
        Return New SqlConnection(connectionString)
    End Function

End Class
```

Figure 6-8   The code for the InvoiceDB and PayablesDB classes

The code for the Invoices by Due Date form

Figure 6-9 presents the code for the Invoices by Due Date form. It is stored in a class named frmInvoicesDue, and this is the presentation class for this application.

To start, this form imports the PayablesData namespace, which is the namespace for the class library that contains the Invoice, InvoiceDB, and PayablesDB classes. For this to work, a reference to the class library must be added to the project that contains the Invoices by Due Date form. To do that, you can use the Project→Add Reference command.

The code within the form class provides for populating the ListView control when the form is loaded. To start, it declares a variable that will contain a list of Invoice objects and then assigns the list that's returned by the GetInvoicesDue method of the InvoiceDB class to that list. Because the GetInvoicesDue method can throw a SqlException, this method is coded within the Try block of a Try…Catch statement. Then, if an exception occurs, the Catch block displays an error message and closes the form.

After the invoices are loaded into the invoice list, this code checks to see if the list contains at least one item. If so, it loads the items into the ListView control. Otherwise, it displays a message indicating that all the invoices are paid in full and it closes the form.

To load the invoices into the ListView control, this code uses a For…Next statement that loops through the invoices in the invoice list. For each invoice, it adds the InvoiceNumber property to the list of items in the control. That causes the invoice number to be displayed in the first column of the control. Then, the other properties of each invoice are added as subitems. That causes these values to be displayed in columns following the invoice number.

If you aren't familiar with the ListView control, you may want to consult the Visual Studio documentation on this control to learn more about how it works. In general, though, when its View property is set to Details, it works like any collection of rows that contain columns.

The code for the Invoices by Due Date form

```
Imports PayablesData

Public Class frmInvoicesDue

    Private Sub frmInvoicesDue_Load(ByVal sender As System.Object, _
            ByVal e As System.EventArgs) Handles MyBase.Load
        Dim invoiceList As List(Of Invoice)
        Try
            invoiceList = InvoiceDB.GetInvoicesDue
            If invoiceList.Count > 0 Then
                Dim invoice As Invoice
                For i As Integer = 0 To invoiceList.Count - 1
                    invoice = invoiceList(i)
                    lvInvoices.Items.Add(invoice.InvoiceNumber)
                    lvInvoices.Items(i).SubItems.Add( _
                        CDate(invoice.InvoiceDate).ToShortDateString)
                    lvInvoices.Items(i).SubItems.Add( _
                        FormatCurrency(invoice.InvoiceTotal))
                    lvInvoices.Items(i).SubItems.Add( _
                        FormatCurrency(invoice.PaymentTotal))
                    lvInvoices.Items(i).SubItems.Add( _
                        FormatCurrency(invoice.CreditTotal))
                    lvInvoices.Items(i).SubItems.Add( _
                        FormatCurrency(invoice.BalanceDue))
                    lvInvoices.Items(i).SubItems.Add( _
                        CDate(invoice.DueDate).ToShortDateString)
                Next
            Else
                MessageBox.Show("All invoices are paid in full.", _
                    "No Balance Due")
                Me.Close()
            End If
        Catch ex As Exception
            MessageBox.Show(ex.Message, ex.GetType.ToString)
            Me.Close()
        End Try
    End Sub

End Class
```

Figure 6-9   The code for the Invoices by Due Date form

How to work with queries that don't return a result set

In addition to executing queries that return result sets, you can use a command to execute queries that return a single value or that perform an action against the database. You'll learn how to work with commands that execute these two types of queries in the last two topics of this chapter. And you'll get a chance to use queries that return scalar values if you do exercise 6-1.

How to execute a query that returns a scalar value

The first code example in figure 6-10 shows you how to execute a command that returns a single value, called a *scalar value*. To do that, you execute the ExecuteScalar method of the command. In this case, the command contains a Select statement that retrieves the total balance due for all the invoices in the Invoices table. This type of summary value is often called an *aggregate value*.

A scalar value can also be the value of a single column, a calculated value, or any other value that can be retrieved from the database. In the Vendor Maintenance application that's presented in the next chapter, for example, you'll see how the ExecuteScalar method is used to retrieve the value of an identity column that's generated for a row that's added to a database.

Since the ExecuteScalar method returns an Object type, you must cast that object to an appropriate data type to get its value. In this example, the object is cast to a Decimal value.

Before I go on, you should realize that you can use the ExecuteScalar method with a Select statement that retrieves more than one value. In that case, though, the ExecuteScalar method returns only the first value and the others are discarded.

How to execute an action query

As you know, you can use an Insert, Update, or Delete statement to perform actions against a database. For that reason, these statements are often referred to as *action queries*. To execute an action query, you use the ExecuteNonQuery method of a command as shown in the second code example in figure 6-10.

This example executes a command that contains a Delete statement that will delete all of the invoices in the Invoices table that have a balance due of zero. Notice that the ExecuteNonQuery method returns an integer that indicates the number of rows in the database that were affected by the operation. In this case, the value is used to display a message to the user. In other cases, you can use it to check if the operation was successful.

Code that creates and executes a command that returns an aggregate value

```
Dim selectCommand As New SqlCommand()
selectCommand.Connection = connection
selectCommand.CommandText _
    = "SELECT SUM(InvoiceTotal - PaymentTotal - CreditTotal) " _
    & "AS BalanceDue FROM Invoices"
connection.Open()
Dim balanceDue As Decimal = CDec(selectCommand.ExecuteScalar)
connection.Close()
```

Code that creates and executes a command that deletes rows

```
Dim deleteCommand As New SqlCommand()
deleteCommand.Connection = connection
deleteCommand.CommandText _
    = "DELETE FROM Invoices " _
    & "WHERE InvoiceTotal - PaymentTotal - CreditTotal = 0"
Try
    connection.Open()
    Dim rowCount As Integer = deleteCommand.ExecuteNonQuery()
    MessageBox.Show(rowCount & " rows deleted")
Catch ex As SqlException
    MessageBox.Show("SQL Server error # " & ex.Number _
        & ": " & ex.Message, ex.GetType.ToString)
Finally
    connection.Close()
End Try
```

How to execute queries that return a single value

- You use the ExecuteScalar method of a command object to retrieve a single value, called a *scalar value*.

- The value that's returned can be the value of a single column and row in the database, a calculated value, an *aggregate value* that summarizes data in the database, or any other value that can be retrieved from the database.

- If the Select statement returns more than one column or row, only the value in the first column and row is retrieved by the ExecuteScalar method.

How to execute action queries

- You use the ExecuteNonQuery method of a command object to execute an Insert, Update, or Delete statement, called an *action query*. This method returns an integer that indicates the number of rows that were affected by the query.

- You can also use the ExecuteNonQuery method to execute statements that affect the structure of a database object. For more information, see the documentation for your database management system.

Figure 6-10   How to execute queries that don't return a result set

Perspective

In this chapter, you learned the essential skills for working with commands and data readers in a three-layer application. When you work this way, your code has to do all of the functions that are done by the table adapter and table adapter manager when you use data sources and datasets. This means that you have to write more code, but it also means that you have complete control over how the data is processed.

Terms

ordinal
scalar value
aggregate value
action query

Exercise 6-1   Review the Invoices by Due Date application

In this exercise, you'll review the Invoices by Due Date application that's presented in this chapter. That will give you a better idea of how it works.

1. Open the DisplayInvoicesDue application that's in your Chapter 6 directory.

2. In the Solution Explorer, notice that this solution includes two projects: DisplayInvoicesDue and PayablesData. Then, expand the PayablesData project to see that it contains the business and database classes that are used by this application: Invoice, InvoiceDB, and PayablesDB.

3. Double-click on any one of the classes in the PayablesData project to review its code.

4. Display the code for the Invoices by Due Date form and note the Imports statement that it starts with. For this to work, the application must include a reference to the PayablesData project.

5. To see the required reference, expand the References folder for the project in the Solution Explorer. If you don't see this folder, select the project and then click the Show All Files button at the top of the Solution Explorer window.

6. Run the application to see how it works. Then, when you're done experimenting, close the application.

Exercise 6-2   Enhance the Invoices by Due Date application

In this exercise, you'll enhance the Invoices by Due Date application. This will give you a chance to work with commands that return scalar values. When you're done, the form for the application should look like this:

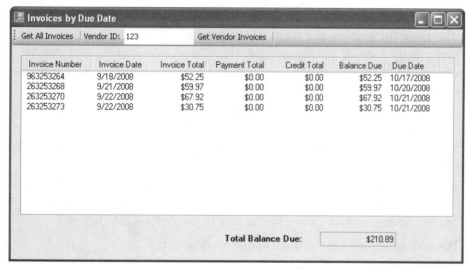

Enhance the interface

1. Open the DisplayInvoicesDue application in your Chapter 6 directory.

2. Add a ToolStrip control to the top of the Invoices by Date Due form and add the buttons, separators, label, and text box shown above to it. Then, set the properties for these controls.

3. Add a label and text box below the ListView control as shown above. Then, set the properties for these controls.

4. Modify the code for the form so it displays the unpaid invoices for all vendors when the user clicks on the Get All Invoices button in the toolbar instead of when the form is loaded. To do that, you just need to move the code from the Load event handler to the Click event handler for the Get All Invoices button. Or, if you prefer, you can copy the code from the Load event handler to the Click event handler and then comment out the code for the Load event handler.

5. Test this modification to see how it works.

Add the code for getting the invoices for a single vendor

6. Add a method named GetVendorInvoicesDue to the InvoiceDB class that gets the unpaid invoices for a single vendor. This method should have one parameter that accepts a vendor ID as an Integer, and it should return a list of Invoice objects that represent the unpaid invoices for that vendor ID. The easiest way to code this method is to copy and modify the code for the GetInvoicesDue method. For now, you can hardcode the parameter that contains the vender ID into the Select statement. Then, in the next chapter, you'll learn how to work with parameter objects.

7. Add an event handler to the code for the form that handles the Click event of the Get Vendor Invoices toolbar button. The easiest way to do that is to copy and modify the code for the Click event of the Get All Invoices button.

8. Test and debug this enhancement until it works right. Try vendor IDs 110 and 123, and make sure the ListView control is cleared before any invoices are added to it. To do that, you can use this command:

```
lvInvoices.Items.Clear()
```

Add the code for getting the total balances due

9. Add a method named GetTotalBalanceDue to the InvoiceDB class. It should use an aggregate query like the one in the first example in figure 6-10 to get the sum of all the unpaid invoices.

10. Add a method named GetVendorBalanceDue to the InvoiceDB class. It should have one parameter that receives a vendor ID, and it should get the sum of all of the unpaid invoices for that vendor. Again, you can hardcode the vendor ID parameter into the Select statement.

11. Add the code to the form class that uses the methods that you created in steps 9 and 10 to display the total balance due for all unpaid invoices or just one vendor's unpaid invoices when the buttons in the toolbars are clicked.

12. Test and debug this enhancement until it works right.

7

How to work with parameters and stored procedures

This chapter builds on the skills you learned in the last chapter by presenting some additional techniques for working with commands. Specifically, you'll learn how to work with commands that use parameters to retrieve, insert, update, and delete data. And you'll learn how to execute a stored procedure from a command. When you complete this chapter, you'll have all the skills you need for working with commands in the three-layer applications that you develop.

How to create and work with parameters

In chapter 4, you learned how to generate a parameterized query from a bound control that was created using a data source. In that case, the parameters were generated for you based on the Select statement you defined. When you work with commands directly, however, you have to create the parameters yourself. You'll learn how to do that in just a minute. But first, you need to know how to use parameters in the SQL statements you code.

How to use parameters in SQL statements

A *parameter* is a variable that's used in a SQL statement. Parameters let you create statements that retrieve or update database data based on variable information. For example, an application that maintains the Vendors table can use a parameter in the Where clause of a Select statement to retrieve a specific row from the Vendors table based on the value of the VendorID column. A Select statement that uses parameters in the Where clause is called a *parameterized query*. You can also use parameters in other types of SQL statements, including Insert, Update, and Delete statements.

To use parameters in a SQL statement, you use placeholders as shown in figure 7-1. These placeholders indicate where the parameters should be inserted when the statement is executed. Unfortunately, database management systems don't use a standard syntax for coding placeholders.

For example, the first Select statement in this figure is for SQL Server. As you can see, you use a *named variable* to identify a parameter. Note that the name of the variable must begin with an at sign (@) and is usually given the same name as the column it's associated with. Oracle also uses named variables, but the names must begin with a colon (:) as illustrated in the second Select statement. In contrast, the placeholder for an OLE DB or ODBC parameter is a question mark, as shown in the third Select statement.

The fourth example in this figure shows how you can use parameters in an Insert statement. Here, a row is being inserted into the Vendors table. To do that, a variable is included in the Values clause for each required column in the table.

All of the parameters in the first four examples are *input parameters* because they provide input to the database. In contrast, the last example uses *output parameters*, which receive values from the database. Here, the Select statement retrieves six columns from a single row of the Vendors table just as the Select statement in the first example does, but in this case the column values are stored in output parameters.

When you use output parameters, you don't have to use a data reader to get the values, which can improve the efficiency of an application. However, you'll probably want to use this technique only when you're retrieving a small number of values. Otherwise, the parameters can get unwieldy.

A SQL Server Select statement that uses a parameter

```
SELECT Name, Address1, Address2, City, State, ZipCode
FROM Vendors
WHERE VendorID = @VendorID
```

An Oracle Select statement that uses a parameter

```
SELECT Name, Address1, Address2, City, State, ZipCode
FROM Vendors
WHERE VendorID = :VendorID
```

An OLE DB or ODBC Select statement that uses a parameter

```
SELECT Name, Address1, Address2, City, State, ZipCode
FROM Vendors
WHERE VendorID = ?
```

A SQL Server Insert statement that uses parameters

```
INSERT Vendors (Name, Address1, Address2, City, State, ZipCode)
VALUES (@Name, @Address1, @Address2, @City, @State, @ZipCode)
```

A SQL Server Select statement that uses output parameters

```
SELECT @Name = Name, @Address1 = Address1, @Address2 = Address2,
    @City = City, @State = State, @ZipCode = ZipCode
FROM Vendors
WHERE VendorID = @VendorID
```

Description

- A *parameter* lets you place variable information into a SQL statement.

- When you use a parameter in the Where clause of a Select statement, the resulting query is often called a *parameterized query* because the results of the query depend on the value of the parameter.

- Parameters are often used in Insert or Update statements to provide the values for the database row or rows to be inserted or updated. Likewise, you can use parameters in a Delete statement to indicate which row or rows should be deleted.

- In most cases, you'll use *input parameters* to pass values to the database. However, you can also use *output parameters* in the Select clause of a Select statement to retrieve data from the database. This can be more efficient than using a data reader.

- To use parameters, you code a SQL statement with placeholders for the parameters. Then, you create a parameter object that defines each parameter, and you add it to the Parameters collection of the command object that contains the SQL statement.

- The placeholder for a parameter in a SQL Server command is a *named variable* whose name begins with an at sign (@). For Oracle, the variable name begins with a colon (:). In most cases, you'll give the variable the same name as the column it's associated with.

- If you're using the OLE DB or ODBC data provider, you code the placeholder for a parameter as a question mark. The question mark simply indicates the position of the parameter.

Figure 7-1   How to use parameters in SQL statements

How to create parameters

After you define a SQL statement that contains parameters, you create the parameter objects. Figure 7-2 shows you how to do that. Here, you can see four constructors for the SqlParameter class. Although there are others, these are the ones you're most likely to use. You can create a parameter for an OLE DB, ODBC, or Oracle command using similar techniques.

Before you can use a parameter, you must assign a name to it. In addition, if the parameter will be used for input, you must also assign a value to it. And if the parameter will be used for output and it will hold string data, you must assign a size to it. If you don't pass these values as arguments to the constructor when you create the parameter, you can do that using some of the properties shown in this figure.

Note here that you can specify the data type using either the DbType or SqlDbType property for a SQL Server parameter. Because the data type is inferred from the value of the parameter, you usually won't set the type for an input parameter. However, you may want to specify the type for an output parameter so you can specify the name when you create the parameter.

The first example in this figure shows how to create a parameter object using the first constructor for the SqlParameter class. This parameter is assigned to a variable named vendorIDParm. Then, this variable is used to set the parameter's properties.

The second example shows how to create a parameter using a single statement. This statement uses the second constructor for the SqlParameter class to create a parameter named @VendorID with the value specified by the vendorID variable.

In contrast to the first two examples, the third example creates an output parameter. To do that, it uses the fourth constructor to specify the name, type, and size for the parameter. Then, it sets the Direction property of the parameter to ParameterDirection.Output.

When you assign a name to a SQL Server or Oracle parameter, that name must be the same as the name that's specified in the SQL statement. That's because ADO.NET associates the parameters with the placeholders by name. As a result, if a statement uses two or more parameters, you can add them to the Parameters collection in any sequence. In contrast, OLE DB and ODBC parameters must be added to the collection in the same order that they appear in the SQL statement. In that case, ADO.NET associates the parameters with the placeholders by sequence since the placeholders aren't named.

Four constructors for the SqlParameter class

```
New SqlParameter()
New SqlParameter(name, value)
New SqlParameter(name, type)
New SqlParameter(name, type, size)
```

Common properties of the SqlParameter class

Property	Description
DbType	A member of the DbType enumeration that determines the type of data that the parameter can hold.
Direction	A member of the ParameterDirection enumeration that determines if the parameter will be used for input, output, both input or output, or to hold the return value from a stored procedure or function. The default is Input.
IsNullable	A Boolean value that indicates if the parameter accepts nulls. The default is False.
ParameterName	The name of the parameter.
Size	The maximum size of the value that the parameter can hold.
SqlDbType	A member of the SqlDbType enumeration that determines the type of data that the parameter can hold. This property is synchronized with the DbType property.
Value	The value of the parameter stored as an Object type.

Code that creates an input parameter

```
Dim vendorIDParm As New SqlParameter()
vendorIDParm.ParameterName = "@VendorID"
vendorIDParm.Value = vendorID
```

Another way to create an input parameter

```
Dim vendorIDParm As New SqlParameter("@VendorID", vendorID)
```

Code that creates an output parameter

```
Dim nameParm As New SqlParameter("@Name", SqlDbType.VarChar, 50)
nameParm.Direction = ParameterDirection.Output
```

Description

- When you create a parameter, you can specify the parameter name along with a value, a data type, or a data type and size. If you don't specify the appropriate values, you can set the values of the associated properties after you create the parameter.

- In addition to a name, you must set the value for an input parameter and a direction for an output parameter. You must also set the size for an output parameter if it will contain string data.

- When you create parameters for a SQL Server or Oracle command, you must give them the same names you used in the SQL statement. Then, you can add the parameters to the Parameters collection in any order you want since ADO.NET refers to them by name.

- Because the parameters for an OLE DB command aren't named in the SQL statement, the parameters can be given any name you want. However, they must be added to the Parameters collection in the same order that they appear in the statement.

Figure 7-2   How to create parameters

How to work with parameters

After you create a parameter, you must add it to the Parameters collection of the command that will use the parameter. This is illustrated in the first example in figure 7-3. Here, the Parameters property of the command is used to refer to the Parameters collection. Then, the Add method of that collection is used to add the vendorIDParm parameter that was created in the previous figure.

You can also use one of the overloaded Add methods to create a parameter and add it to the Parameters collection in a single statement. These methods let you specify a name and type or a name, type, and size, and they return the parameter that's created. That way, you can store the parameter in a variable so you can refer to it later if you need to.

Another way to create a parameter and add it to the Parameters collection is to use the AddWithValue method. This is illustrated in the second example in this figure, and this is the easiest way to create an imput parameter. Like the Add methods, the AddWithValue method returns the parameter that's created in case you want to refer to it later.

If you don't create a variable to hold a parameter, you can refer to it through the Parameters collection as illustrated in the third example. Here, the value of the @VendorID parameter is set to the value of a variable named vendorID.

The last example in this figure shows how to work with a command that uses output parameters. Although it's not shown here, this command contains the last Select statement shown in figure 7-1. The first thing you should notice is that the ExecuteNonQuery method is used to execute this command, even though it contains a Select statement. That's because you don't need a data reader to get the results of the query. Instead, the results will be stored in the output parameters.

After you execute a command that contains output parameters, you can refer to the parameters using the same techniques you use to refer to input parameters. In this example, parameter variables are used to display the parameter values in text boxes. Notice that the values of the parameters are converted to strings. That's necessary because the Value property is an Object type.

Common properties and methods of the Parameters collection

Property	Description
`Item(index)`	Gets the parameter with the specified name or position from the collection.

Method	Description
`Add(parameter)`	Adds the specified parameter to the collection.
`Add(name, type)`	Adds a parameter with the specified name and type to the collection.
`Add(name, type, size)`	Adds a parameter with the specified name, type, and size to the collection.
`AddWithValue(name, value)`	Adds a parameter with the specified name and value to the collection.

A statement that adds a parameter to the Parameters collection

```
selectCommand.Parameters.Add(vendorIDParm)
```

A statement that creates an input parameter and adds it to the Parameters collection

```
selectCommand.Parameters.AddWithValue("@VendorID", vendorID)
```

A statement that changes the value of an existing parameter

```
selectCommand.Parameters("@VendorID").Value = vendorID
```

Code that executes a command with a Select statement that uses output parameters

```
selectCommand.ExecuteNonQuery()
txtName.Text = nameParm.Value.ToString
txtAddress1.Text = address1Parm.Value.ToString
txtAddress2.Text = address2Parm.Value.ToString
txtCity.Text = cityParm.Value.ToString
txtState.Text = stateParm.Value.ToString
txtZipCode.Text = zipCodeParm.Value.ToString
```

Description

- To work with the parameters for a command, you use the Parameters property of the command. This property returns a SqlParameterCollection object that contains all the parameters for the command.

- To add an existing parameter to the Parameters collection, you use the Add method. You can also use the Add method to create a parameter with the specified name and type or name, type, and size, and add that parameter to the Parameters collection.

- You can use the AddWithValue method of the Parameters collection to create a parameter with the specified name and value and add that parameter to the collection.

- All the Add methods return the parameter that's created so you can assign it to a variable.

- To execute a command that contains a Select statement that uses output parameters, you use the ExecuteNonQuery method of the command. Then, when the method is executed, the returned values are stored in the output parameters.

Figure 7-3   How to work with parameters

A Vendor Maintenance application that uses parameters

To illustrate the use of parameters, the following topics present a Vendor Maintenance application. As you'll see, this application uses a parameter in the Select statement that retrieves a single vendor from the Vendors table. It uses parameters in the Insert statement to specify the column values for the new vendor. And it uses parameters in the Update statement to specify the new column values as well as parameters that provide the old column values that are used for concurrency checking. Although this presentation is lengthy, it's worth taking the time to go through it because it will give you a thorough understanding of how you build three-layer applications with commands.

The user interface

Figure 7-4 presents the user interface for the Vendor Maintenance application. As you can see, this application consists of two forms. The Vendor Maintenance form lets the user select an existing vendor and then displays the basic information for that vendor on the form. Then, the user can click the Modify button to modify the information for the vendor or the Add button to add a new vendor.

If the user clicks the Add or Modify button, the Add/Modify Vendor form is displayed. Note that the title of this form changes depending on whether a vendor is being added or modified. In this case, the user that was selected in the Vendor Maintenance form is being modified.

In addition to the name and address information that's displayed in the Vendor Maintenance form, the Add/Modify Vendor form lets the user enter contact information and select default terms and a default account. After entering the appropriate values, the user can click the Accept button or press the Enter key to accept the new or modified vendor. Alternatively, the user can click the Cancel button or press the Esc key to cancel the operation.

At this point, you may be wondering why I used two forms to implement the Vendor Maintenance application. The answer is that, in the real world, most maintenance applications aren't this simple. In many cases, in fact, the maintenance of a table will be combined with other functions. In chapter 10, for example, you'll see a Payable Entry application that lets you add and modify vendors at the same time that you enter new invoices. Even if the table maintenance is provided by a separate application, however, it can be easier to implement the application using two forms because it simplifies the program logic.

The Vendor Maintenance form

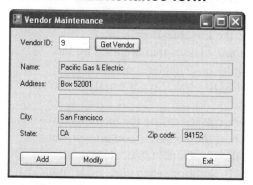

The Add/Modify Vendor form

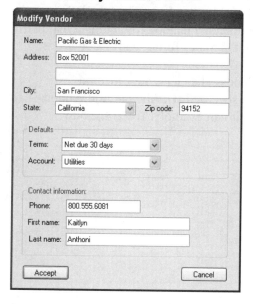

Description

- To add a new vendor, the user clicks the Add button on the Vendor Maintenance form to display a blank Add Vendor form. Then, the user enters the data for the new vendor and clicks the Accept button to return to the Vendor Maintenance form.

- To modify the data for an existing vendor, the user enters the vendor ID and clicks the Get Vendor button to display the basic information for that vendor. Then, the user clicks the Modify button to display the Modify Vendor form, makes the appropriate modifications, and clicks the Accept button to return to the Vendor Maintenance form.

Figure 7-4   The user interface for the Vendor Maintenance application

The class diagram for the PayablesData library

Figure 7-5 presents the class diagram for the PayablesData library. This diagram shows the business classes and database classes that are used by the Vendor Maintenance application. If you read the last chapter, you should already understand the purpose of the PayablesDB class. So I'll briefly describe the other classes here.

The Vendor, State, Terms, and GLAccount classes define the business objects that are used by this application. Each of these classes contains private fields that hold the values of the columns in the associated table, along with properties that provide access to these fields. In addition, each class is defined with a parameterless constructor.

The VendorDB, StateDB, TermsDB, and GLAccountDB classes provide methods for working with the tables in the Payables database. The StateDB, TermsDB, and GLAccountDB classes each contain a method for getting a list of objects. These lists are then used to populate the State, Terms, and Account combo boxes.

The VendorDB class contains three methods. The GetVendor method returns a Vendor object for the vendor with a specified ID. And the AddVendor and UpdateVendor methods do just what their names imply. You'll see how these methods work in the next figure.

The class diagram for the PayablesData library

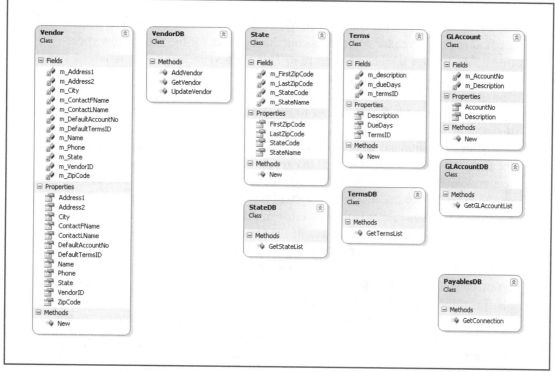

Description

- The PayablesData library contains the classes that define the business objects used by the Vendor Maintenance application and the database classes that are used to work with the Payables database.

- The business objects are defined by the Vendor, State, Terms, and GLAccount classes. These objects will hold data from the associated tables in the Payables database.

- The classes that end with DB, including VendorDB, StateDB, TermsDB, GLAccountDB, and PayablesDB, are the database classes. These classes provide shared members for working with the Payables database.

- The StateDB, TermsDB, and GLAccountDB classes provide public methods for getting lists of data from the States, Terms, and GLAccounts tables. The VendorDB class provides public methods for getting the data for a vendor, adding a vendor, and updating a vendor. And the PayablesDB class provides a public method for getting a connection to the Payables database.

Note

- To create a class diagram like this, right-click on a project or class in the Solution Explorer and select the View Class Diagram command.

Figure 7-5   The class diagram for the PayablesData library

The code for the VendorDB class

Figure 7-6 shows the code for the VendorDB class. To start, the GetVendor method returns a Vendor object that contains the data for the vendor row specified by the vendor ID that's passed to it. This method creates a SqlCommand object with a parameterized query that contains a placeholder for the vendor ID. Then, it creates the parameter, sets its value to the vendorID that was passed to the method, and adds the parameter to the Parameters collection of the command.

After the command and parameter are created, the connection is opened and the ExecuteReader method is used to execute the command and create a data reader object. Notice that the ExecuteReader method specifies the SingleRow command behavior because the query will return just one row. Then, the Read method of the data reader is used to retrieve that row, and the values of that row are assigned to a new Vendor object. If the reader doesn't contain a row, however, the Vendor object is set to Nothing to indicate that the vendor wasn't found. Then, the reader and connection are closed and the Vendor object is returned to the calling procedure.

Like the code you saw in the last chapter, these statements are coded within a Try...Catch...Finally statement. Then, if a SQL Server error occurs when any of these statements is executed, the exception is thrown to the calling procedure so it can handle the error. In addition, the statement that closes the connection is coded within the Finally block so the connection is closed whether or not an exception occurs.

The AddVendor method adds a new row to the Vendors table. This method receives a Vendor object that contains the data for the new row. Then, a command object that contains an Insert statement with a parameter for each column in the row is created.

The code for the VendorDB class

Page 1

```vbnet
Imports System.Data.SqlClient

Public Class VendorDB

    Public Shared Function GetVendor(ByVal vendorID As Integer) As Vendor
        Dim vendor As New Vendor
        Dim connection As SqlConnection = PayablesDB.GetConnection
        Dim selectStatement As String _
            = "SELECT VendorID, Name, Address1, Address2, City, State, " _
            & "ZipCode, Phone, ContactFName, ContactLName, " _
            & "DefaultAccountNo, DefaultTermsID " _
            & "FROM Vendors " _
            & "WHERE VendorID = @VendorID"
        Dim selectCommand As New SqlCommand(selectStatement, connection)
        selectCommand.Parameters.AddWithValue("@VendorID", vendorID)
        Try
            connection.Open()
            Dim reader As SqlDataReader _
                = selectCommand.ExecuteReader(CommandBehavior.SingleRow)
            If reader.Read Then
                vendor.VendorID = CInt(reader("VendorID"))
                vendor.Name = reader("Name").ToString
                vendor.Address1 = reader("Address1").ToString
                vendor.Address2 = reader("Address2").ToString
                vendor.City = reader("City").ToString
                vendor.State = reader("State").ToString
                vendor.ZipCode = reader("ZipCode").ToString
                vendor.Phone = reader("Phone").ToString
                vendor.ContactFName = reader("ContactFName").ToString
                vendor.ContactLName = reader("ContactLName").ToString
                vendor.DefaultAccountNo = CInt(reader("DefaultAccountNo"))
                vendor.DefaultTermsID = CInt(reader("DefaultTermsID"))
            Else
                vendor = Nothing
            End If
            reader.Close()
        Catch ex As SqlException
            Throw ex
        Finally
            connection.Close()
        End Try
        Return vendor
    End Function

    Public Shared Function AddVendor(ByVal vendor As Vendor) As Integer
        Dim connection As SqlConnection = PayablesDB.GetConnection
        Dim insertStatement As String _
            = "INSERT Vendors " _
            & "(Name, Address1, Address2, City, State, ZipCode, Phone, " _
            & "ContactFName, ContactLName, DefaultTermsID, DefaultAccountNo) " _
            & "VALUES (@Name, @Address1, @Address2, @City, @State, @ZipCode, " _
            & "@Phone, @ContactFName, @ContactLName, @DefaultTermsID, " _
            & "@DefaultAccountNo)"
        Dim insertCommand As New SqlCommand(insertStatement, connection)
```

Figure 7-6   The code for the VendorDB class (part 1 of 5)

After the command is created, the parameters for the command are created. If a column doesn't allow nulls, the appropriate property of the Vendor object is assigned to the parameter. But if a column allows nulls, the property is first checked to see if it contains an empty string. If so, the Value field of the DBNull class is used to assign a null value to the parameter. Otherwise, the value of the property is assigned to the parameter.

Next, the connection is opened and the ExecuteNonQuery method of the command object is executed within a Try…Catch…Finally statement that catches SQL Server exceptions. Then, if an exception occurs, this method throws the exception so it can be handled by the calling procedure. Otherwise, another command object that contains a Select statement that retrieves the ID of the vendor that was just added is created, and this command is executed using the ExecuteScalar method. The vendor ID that's returned by this statement is then returned to the calling procedure.

The code for the VendorDB class   Page 2

```vb
        insertCommand.Parameters.AddWithValue("@Name", vendor.Name)
        insertCommand.Parameters.AddWithValue("@Address1", vendor.Address1)
        If vendor.Address2 = "" Then
            insertCommand.Parameters.AddWithValue("@Address2", DBNull.Value)
        Else
            insertCommand.Parameters.AddWithValue("@Address2", _
                vendor.Address2)
        End If
        insertCommand.Parameters.AddWithValue("@City", vendor.City)
        insertCommand.Parameters.AddWithValue("@State", vendor.State)
        insertCommand.Parameters.AddWithValue("@ZipCode", vendor.ZipCode)
        If vendor.Phone = "" Then
            insertCommand.Parameters.AddWithValue("@Phone", DBNull.Value)
        Else
            insertCommand.Parameters.AddWithValue("@Phone", vendor.Phone)
        End If
        If vendor.ContactFName = "" Then
            insertCommand.Parameters.AddWithValue("@ContactFName", _
                DBNull.Value)
        Else
            insertCommand.Parameters.AddWithValue("@ContactFName", _
                vendor.ContactFName)
        End If
        If vendor.ContactLName = "" Then
            insertCommand.Parameters.AddWithValue("@ContactLName", _
                DBNull.Value)
        Else
            insertCommand.Parameters.AddWithValue("@ContactLName", _
                vendor.ContactLName)
        End If
        insertCommand.Parameters.AddWithValue("@DefaultTermsID", _
            vendor.DefaultTermsID)
        insertCommand.Parameters.AddWithValue("@DefaultAccountNo", _
            vendor.DefaultAccountNo)
        Try
            connection.Open()
            insertCommand.ExecuteNonQuery()
            Dim selectStatement As String _
                = "SELECT IDENT_CURRENT('Vendors') FROM Vendors"
            Dim selectCommand As New SqlCommand(selectStatement, connection)
            Dim vendorID As Integer = CInt(selectCommand.ExecuteScalar)
            Return vendorID
        Catch ex As SqlException
            Throw ex
        Finally
            connection.Close()
        End Try
    End Function
```

Figure 7-6   The code for the VendorDB class (part 2 of 5)

The UpdateVendor method receives two arguments: a Vendor object named oldVendor that contains the original data for the vendor row to be updated, and another Vendor object named newVendor that supplies the updated values for the vendor. The properties of these objects are used to set the values of the parameters defined by the Update statement associated with the command object. Notice that the properties of the oldVendor object are assigned to parameters in the Where clause of the Update statement. That way, the Update statement will update the row only if none of the vendor columns have been changed since the vendor was retrieved.

Also notice how the Update statement handles columns that can contain nulls. First, it checks if the value of the column in the database is equal to the value that was originally retrieved just as it does for the other columns. In addition, it checks if both the database value and the original value are equal to NULL. That's necessary because two nulls aren't considered equal.

After the parameter values are set, this method uses the ExecuteNonQuery method to execute the Update statement. If no error occurs, the value that's returned by the ExecuteNonQuery method is tested to determine whether the update was successful. If it wasn't, it probably means that the vendor has been modified or deleted by another user. In that case, this method returns False to the calling procedure. Otherwise, it returns True.

The code for the VendorDB class

```
Public Shared Function UpdateVendor(ByVal oldVendor As Vendor, _
        ByVal newVendor As Vendor) As Boolean
    Dim connection As SqlConnection = PayablesDB.GetConnection
    Dim updateStatement As String _
        = "UPDATE Vendors SET " _
        & "Name = @NewName, " _
        & "Address1 = @NewAddress1, " _
        & "Address2 = @NewAddress2, " _
        & "City = @NewCity, " _
        & "State = @NewState, " _
        & "ZipCode = @NewZipCode, " _
        & "Phone = @NewPhone, " _
        & "ContactFName = @NewContactFName, " _
        & "ContactLName = @NewContactLName, " _
        & "DefaultTermsID = @NewDefaultTermsID, " _
        & "DefaultAccountNo = @NewDefaultAccountNo " _
      & "WHERE VendorID = @OldVendorID " _
        & "AND Name = @OldName " _
        & "AND Address1 = @OldAddress1 " _
        & "AND (Address2 = @OldAddress2 " _
          & " OR Address2 IS NULL AND @OldAddress2 IS NULL) " _
        & "AND City = @OldCity " _
        & "AND State = @OldState " _
        & "AND ZipCode = @OldZipCode " _
        & "AND (Phone = @OldPhone " _
          & " OR Phone IS NULL AND @OldPhone IS NULL) " _
        & "AND (ContactFName = @OldContactFName " _
          & " OR ContactFName IS NULL AND @OldContactFName IS NULL) " _
        & "AND (ContactLName = @OldContactLName " _
          & " OR ContactLName IS NULL AND @OldContactLName IS NULL) " _
        & "AND DefaultTermsID = @OldDefaultTermsID " _
        & "AND DefaultAccountNo = @OldDefaultAccountNo"
    Dim updateCommand As New SqlCommand(updateStatement, connection)
    updateCommand.Parameters.AddWithValue("@NewName", _
        newVendor.Name)
    updateCommand.Parameters.AddWithValue("@NewAddress1", _
        newVendor.Address1)
    If newVendor.Address2 = "" Then
        updateCommand.Parameters.AddWithValue("@NewAddress2", _
            DBNull.Value)
    Else
        updateCommand.Parameters.AddWithValue("@NewAddress2", _
            newVendor.Address2)
    End If
    updateCommand.Parameters.AddWithValue("@NewCity", _
        newVendor.City)
    updateCommand.Parameters.AddWithValue("@NewState", _
        newVendor.State)
    updateCommand.Parameters.AddWithValue("@NewZipCode", _
        newVendor.ZipCode)
```

Figure 7-6   The code for the VendorDB class (part 3 of 5)

The code for the VendorDB class

```
If newVendor.Phone = "" Then
    updateCommand.Parameters.AddWithValue("@NewPhone", _
        DBNull.Value)
Else
    updateCommand.Parameters.AddWithValue("@NewPhone", _
        newVendor.Phone)
End If
If newVendor.ContactFName = "" Then
    updateCommand.Parameters.AddWithValue("@NewContactFName", _
        DBNull.Value)
Else
    updateCommand.Parameters.AddWithValue("@NewContactFName", _
        newVendor.ContactFName)
End If
If newVendor.ContactLName = "" Then
    updateCommand.Parameters.AddWithValue("@NewContactLName", _
        DBNull.Value)
Else
    updateCommand.Parameters.AddWithValue("@NewContactLName", _
        newVendor.ContactLName)
End If
updateCommand.Parameters.AddWithValue("@NewDefaultTermsID", _
    newVendor.DefaultTermsID)
updateCommand.Parameters.AddWithValue("@NewDefaultAccountNo", _
    newVendor.DefaultAccountNo)
updateCommand.Parameters.AddWithValue("@OldVendorID", _
    oldVendor.VendorID)
updateCommand.Parameters.AddWithValue("@OldName", _
    oldVendor.Name)
updateCommand.Parameters.AddWithValue("@OldAddress1", _
    oldVendor.Address1)
If oldVendor.Address2 = "" Then
    updateCommand.Parameters.AddWithValue("@OldAddress2", _
        DBNull.Value)
Else
    updateCommand.Parameters.AddWithValue("@OldAddress2", _
        oldVendor.Address2)
End If
updateCommand.Parameters.AddWithValue("@OldCity", _
    oldVendor.City)
updateCommand.Parameters.AddWithValue("@OldState", _
    oldVendor.State)
updateCommand.Parameters.AddWithValue("@OldZipCode", _
    oldVendor.ZipCode)
If oldVendor.Phone = "" Then
    updateCommand.Parameters.AddWithValue("@OldPhone", _
        DBNull.Value)
Else
    updateCommand.Parameters.AddWithValue("@OldPhone", _
        oldVendor.Phone)
End If
```

Figure 7-6   The code for the VendorDB class (part 4 of 5)

The code for the VendorDB class

```
        If oldVendor.ContactFName = "" Then
            updateCommand.Parameters.AddWithValue("@OldContactFName", _
                DBNull.Value)
        Else
            updateCommand.Parameters.AddWithValue("@OldContactFName", _
                oldVendor.ContactFName)
        End If
        If oldVendor.ContactLName = "" Then
            updateCommand.Parameters.AddWithValue("@OldContactLName", _
                DBNull.Value)
        Else
            updateCommand.Parameters.AddWithValue("@OldContactLName", _
                oldVendor.ContactLName)
        End If
        updateCommand.Parameters.AddWithValue("@OldDefaultTermsID", _
            oldVendor.DefaultTermsID)
        updateCommand.Parameters.AddWithValue("@OldDefaultAccountNo", _
            oldVendor.DefaultAccountNo)

        Try
            connection.Open()
            Dim count As Integer = updateCommand.ExecuteNonQuery
            If count > 0 Then
                Return True
            Else
                Return False
            End If
        Catch ex As SqlException
            Throw ex
        Finally
            connection.Close()
        End Try
    End Function

End Class
```

Figure 7-6   The code for the VendorDB class (part 5 of 5)

The code for the StateDB class

Figure 7-7 shows the code for the StateDB class. This class contains a single method named GetStateList that returns a generic List() object that contains one State object for each of the rows in the States table, sorted by state name.

To get this list, the GetStateList method creates a SqlCommand object with a Select statement that retrieves the appropriate data. Then, it calls the ExecuteReader method of this command to create a data reader that can be used to read each state. Once the data reader is created, this method uses this reader to read each row in the table, it creates a State object for each row, and it adds each State object to the List() object. Finally, it closes the data reader and returns the list of State objects.

Although they're not shown here, the TermsDB and GLAccountDB classes contain methods similar to the GetStateList method. Instead of creating a list of State objects, however, the GetTermsList method in the TermsDB class returns a list of Terms objects. And the GetGLAccountList method in the GLAccountDB class returns a list of GLAccount objects.

The code for the StateDB class

```vbnet
Imports System.Data.SqlClient

Public Class StateDB

    Public Shared Function GetStateList() As List(Of State)
        Dim stateList As New List(Of State)
        Dim connection As SqlConnection = PayablesDB.GetConnection
        Dim selectStatement As String _
            = "SELECT StateCode, StateName, FirstZipCode, LastZipCode " _
            & "FROM States " _
            & "ORDER BY StateName"
        Dim selectCommand As New SqlCommand(selectStatement, connection)
        Try
            connection.Open()
            Dim reader As SqlDataReader = selectCommand.ExecuteReader()
            Dim state As State
            Do While reader.Read
                state = New State
                state.StateCode = reader("StateCode").ToString
                state.StateName = reader("StateName").ToString
                state.FirstZipCode = CInt(reader("FirstZipCode"))
                state.LastZipCode = CInt(reader("LastZipCode"))
                stateList.Add(state)
            Loop
            reader.Close()
        Catch ex As SqlException
            Throw ex
        Finally
            connection.Close()
        End Try
        Return stateList
    End Function

End Class
```

Note

- The code for the TermsDB and GLAccountDB classes is similar to the code for the StateDB class. The GetTermsList method in the TermsDB class retrieves data from the Terms table and stores it in a list of Terms objects. The GetGLAccountList method in the GLAccountDB class retrieves data from the GLAccounts table and stores it in a list of GLAccount objects.

Figure 7-7   The code for the StateDB class

The code for the Vendor Maintenance form

Figure 7-8 shows the code for the Vendor Maintenance form. Because this form doesn't contain a Load event handler, no data is displayed when the form is first displayed. Then, the user must enter a vendor ID and click the Get Vendor button to retrieve the data for a vendor or click the Add button to add a new vendor.

The event handler for the Click event of the Get Vendor button starts by calling the IsPresent and IsInt32 methods in a class named Validator to check that the user entered a vendor ID and that the vendor ID is an integer. Although I won't show you the Validator class here, it contains shared methods that check for various data types and formats. These methods are similar to the procedures that were used in the Vendor Maintenance application in chapter 4 to validate the data for a vendor.

If the vendor ID is an integer, this value is passed to a procedure named GetVendor. This procedure starts by calling the GetVendor method of the VendorDB class to get the vendor with the specified ID, and the Vendor object that's returned by this method is stored in a variable named vendor. If the object contains a value of Nothing, a message is displayed indicating that the vendor wasn't found. Otherwise, a procedure named DisplayVendor is called to display the properties of the Vendor object in the text boxes on the form. This procedure also enables the Modify button so the user can modify the selected vendor. (This button is disabled when the form is first displayed.)

Notice that the statements of the GetVendor procedure are coded within a Try…Catch statement. That's because, if a SQL Server error occurs during the execution of the GetVendor method in the VendorDB class, the exception is thrown to the calling procedure. Because of that, this procedure must catch the exception. You'll see this same technique used for all the methods of the database classes that are called by this application.

If the user clicks the Add button, the Click event handler for this button displays the Add/Modify Vendor form as a dialog box. But first, it sets the public addVendor field of this form to True so the form will know that a new vendor is being added. If the vendor is added successfully, the new vendor is retrieved from the Add/Modify Vendor form. Then, the data for the new vendor is displayed on the form and the Modify button is enabled.

The code for the Vendor Maintenance form   **Page 1**

```
Imports PayablesData

Public Class frmVendorMaintenance

    Dim vendor As Vendor

    Private Sub btnGetVendor_Click(ByVal sender As System.Object, _
            ByVal e As System.EventArgs) Handles btnGetVendor.Click
        If Validator.IsPresent(txtVendorID) AndAlso _
           Validator.IsInt32(txtVendorID) Then
            Dim vendorID As Integer = CInt(txtVendorID.Text)
            Me.GetVendor(vendorID)
        End If
    End Sub

    Private Sub GetVendor(ByVal vendorID As Integer)
        Try
            vendor = VendorDB.GetVendor(vendorID)
            If vendor Is Nothing Then
                MessageBox.Show("No vendor found with this ID. " _
                    & "Please try again.", "Vendor Not Found")
            Else
                Me.DisplayVendor()
            End If
        Catch ex As Exception
            MessageBox.Show(ex.Message, ex.GetType.ToString)
        End Try
    End Sub

    Private Sub DisplayVendor()
        txtName.Text = vendor.Name
        txtAddress1.Text = vendor.Address1
        txtAddress2.Text = vendor.Address2
        txtCity.Text = vendor.City
        txtState.Text = vendor.State
        txtZipCode.Text = vendor.ZipCode
        btnModify.Enabled = True
    End Sub

    Private Sub btnAdd_Click(ByVal sender As System.Object, _
            ByVal e As System.EventArgs) Handles btnAdd.Click
        Dim addModifyVendorForm As New frmAddModifyVendor
        addModifyVendorForm.addVendor = True
        Dim result As DialogResult = addModifyVendorForm.ShowDialog
        If result = DialogResult.OK Then
            vendor = addModifyVendorForm.vendor
            txtVendorID.Text = vendor.VendorID.ToString
            Me.DisplayVendor()
        End If
    End Sub
```

Figure 7-8   The code for the Vendor Maintenance form (part 1 of 2)

The Click event handler for the Modify button is similar. However, it sets the addVendor field of the Add/Modify Vendor form to False to indicate that a vendor is being modified. In addition, it sets the public vendor field to the current Vendor object. That way, the form can display this data without having to retrieve it from the database again.

If the vendor is modified successfully, the updated vendor is retrieved from the Add/Modify Vendor form and the new data for the vendor is displayed on the form. If a concurrency error occurs, however, the result of the Add/Modify Vendor form is set to DialogResult.Retry. Then, a procedure named ClearControls is called. This procedure assigns empty strings to the text boxes on the form and disables the Modify button. Last, the GetVendor procedure is called to retrieve and display the current data for the vendor if that vendor still exists.

The code for the Vendor Maintenance form   **Page 2**

```vb
Private Sub btnModify_Click(ByVal sender As System.Object, _
        ByVal e As System.EventArgs) Handles btnModify.Click
    Dim addModifyVendorForm As New frmAddModifyVendor
    addModifyVendorForm.addVendor = False
    addModifyVendorForm.vendor = vendor
    Dim result As DialogResult = addModifyVendorForm.ShowDialog
    If result = DialogResult.OK Then
        vendor = addModifyVendorForm.vendor
        Me.DisplayVendor()
    ElseIf result = Windows.Forms.DialogResult.Retry Then
        Me.ClearControls()
        Me.GetVendor(vendor.VendorID)
    End If
End Sub

Private Sub ClearControls()
    txtName.Text = ""
    txtAddress1.Text = ""
    txtAddress2.Text = ""
    txtCity.Text = ""
    txtState.Text = ""
    txtZipCode.Text = ""
    btnModify.Enabled = False
End Sub

Private Sub btnExit_Click(ByVal sender As System.Object, _
        ByVal e As System.EventArgs) Handles btnExit.Click
    Me.Close()
End Sub

End Class
```

Figure 7-8   The code for the Vendor Maintenance form (part 2 of 2)

The code for the Add/Modify Vendor form

Figure 7-9 shows the code for the Add/Modify Vendor form. This form starts by declaring the two public fields that are also used by the Vendor Maintenance form.

When the form is first loaded, the Load event handler starts by calling the LoadComboBoxes procedure. This procedure uses the methods of the StateDB, TermsDB, and GLAccountDB classes to get generic lists that contain State, Terms, and GLAccount objects. Then, it binds the three combo boxes on the form to these lists. Note that the list that contains the State objects is declared at the module-level. That's because it's also used by the IsValidData function, which you can see on page 3 of this listing.

If a new vendor is being added, the Load event handler continues by setting the Text property of the form to "Add Vendor" and initializing the combo boxes so that no items are selected. Otherwise, it sets the Text property of the form to "Modify Vendor" and calls the DisplayVendorData procedure. This procedure displays the current data for the vendor on the form. Notice that if the Phone property of the Vendor object contains data, the phone number is formatted by calling the FormattedPhoneNumber function. After that, the user can enter the data for a new vendor or modify the data for an existing vendor.

If the user clicks the Accept button, the Click event handler for this button starts by calling the IsValidData function. This function calls the IsPresent, IsInt32, IsStateZipCode, and IsPhoneNumber methods of the Validator class to determine if the data is valid. Note that because a phone number isn't required, the IsPhoneNumber method is called only if a phone number has been entered.

If the data is valid, the event handler continues by checking whether a vendor is being added. If so, the vendor field is set to a new Vendor object and the PutVendorData procedure is called. This procedure sets the properties of the Vendor object to the values that the user entered on the form.

Next, the event handler executes the AddVendor method of the VendorDB class and assigns the new vendor ID that's returned by this method to the VendorID property of the Vendor object. Then, if no SQL Server error occurs, the DialogResult property of the form is set to DialogResult.OK, which causes the form to be closed and control to be returned to the Vendor Maintenance form. Otherwise, the exception is caught and an error message is displayed.

If a vendor is being modified, this procedure starts by creating a new Vendor object and storing it in the newVendor variable. Then, it sets the VendorID property of that object to the VendorID property of the current Vendor object since the vendor ID can't be changed, and it calls the PutVendorData procedure to set the rest of the properties. Next, it calls the UpdateVendor method of the VendorDB class and passes it both the old and new Vendor objects. If a concurrency error occurs, a value of False is returned. In that case, an error message is displayed and the DialogResult property of the form is set to DialogResult.Retry. Otherwise, the new Vendor object is assigned to the original Vendor object and the DialogResult property is set to DialogResult.OK. In either case, the form is closed.

The code for the Add/Modify Vendor form   **Page 1**

```
Imports PayablesData

Public Class frmAddModifyVendor
    Public addVendor As Boolean
    Public vendor As Vendor
    Private stateList As List(Of State)

    Private Sub frmAddModifyVendor_Load(ByVal sender As System.Object, _
            ByVal e As System.EventArgs) Handles MyBase.Load
        Me.LoadComboBoxes()
        If addVendor Then
            Me.Text = "Add Vendor"
            cboStates.SelectedIndex = -1
            cboTerms.SelectedIndex = -1
            cboAccounts.SelectedIndex = -1
        Else
            Me.Text = "Modify Vendor"
            Me.DisplayVendorData()
        End If
    End Sub

    Private Sub LoadComboBoxes()
        Try
            stateList = StateDB.GetStateList
            cboStates.DataSource = stateList
            cboStates.DisplayMember = "StateName"
            cboStates.ValueMember = "StateCode"

            Dim termsList As List(Of Terms)
            termsList = TermsDB.GetTermsList
            cboTerms.DataSource = termsList
            cboTerms.DisplayMember = "Description"
            cboTerms.ValueMember = "TermsID"

            Dim accountList As List(Of GLAccount)
            accountList = GLAccountDB.GetGLAccountList
            cboAccounts.DataSource = accountList
            cboAccounts.DisplayMember = "Description"
            cboAccounts.ValueMember = "AccountNo"
        Catch ex As Exception
            MessageBox.Show(ex.Message, ex.GetType.ToString)
        End Try
    End Sub

    Private Sub DisplayVendorData()
        txtName.Text = vendor.Name
        txtAddress1.Text = vendor.Address1
        txtAddress2.Text = vendor.Address2
        txtCity.Text = vendor.City
        cboStates.SelectedValue = vendor.State
        txtZipCode.Text = vendor.ZipCode
        cboTerms.SelectedValue = vendor.DefaultTermsID
        cboAccounts.SelectedValue = vendor.DefaultAccountNo
```

Figure 7-9   The code for the Add/Modify Vendor form (part 1 of 3)

The code for the Add/Modify Vendor form

```vb
        If vendor.Phone = "" Then
            txtPhone.Text = ""
        Else
            txtPhone.Text = FormattedPhoneNumber(vendor.Phone)
        End If
        txtFirstName.Text = vendor.ContactFName
        txtLastName.Text = vendor.ContactLName
    End Sub

    Private Function FormattedPhoneNumber(ByVal phone As String) As String
        Return phone.substring(0, 3) & "." _
            & phone.substring(3, 3) & "." _
            & phone.substring(6, 4)
    End Function

    Private Sub btnAccept_Click(ByVal sender As System.Object, _
            ByVal e As System.EventArgs) Handles btnAccept.Click
        If IsValidData() Then
            If addVendor Then
                vendor = New Vendor
                Me.PutVendorData(vendor)
                Try
                    vendor.VendorID = VendorDB.AddVendor(vendor)
                    Me.DialogResult = DialogResult.OK
                Catch ex As Exception
                    MessageBox.Show(ex.Message, ex.GetType.ToString)
                End Try
            Else
                Dim newVendor As New Vendor
                newVendor.VendorID = vendor.VendorID
                Me.PutVendorData(newVendor)
                Try
                    If Not VendorDB.UpdateVendor(vendor, newVendor) Then
                        MessageBox.Show("Another user has updated or " _
                            & "deleted that vendor.", "Database Error")
                        Me.DialogResult = DialogResult.Retry
                    Else
                        Vendor = newVendor
                        Me.DialogResult = DialogResult.OK
                    End If
                Catch ex As Exception
                    MessageBox.Show(ex.Message, ex.GetType.ToString)
                End Try
            End If
        End If
    End Sub
```

Figure 7-9   The code for the Add/Modify Vendor form (part 2 of 3)

The code for the Add/Modify Vendor form   **Page 3**

```
Private Function IsValidData() As Boolean
    If Validator.IsPresent(txtName) AndAlso _
            Validator.IsPresent(txtAddress1) AndAlso _
            Validator.IsPresent(txtCity) AndAlso _
            Validator.IsPresent(cboStates) AndAlso _
            Validator.IsPresent(txtZipCode) AndAlso _
            Validator.IsInt32(txtZipCode) AndAlso _
            Validator.IsPresent(cboTerms) AndAlso _
            Validator.IsPresent(cboAccounts) Then
        Dim firstZip As Integer _
            = statelist(cboStates.SelectedIndex).FirstZipCode
        Dim lastZip As Integer _
            = stateList(cboStates.SelectedIndex).LastZipCode
        If Validator.IsStateZipCode(txtZipCode, firstZip, lastZip) Then
            If txtPhone.Text <> "" Then
                If Validator.IsPhoneNumber(txtPhone) Then
                    Return True
                Else
                    Return False
                End If
            Else
                Return True
            End If
        Else
            Return False
        End If
    Else
        Return False
    End If
End Function

Private Sub PutVendorData(ByVal vendor As Vendor)
    vendor.Name = txtName.Text
    vendor.Address1 = txtAddress1.Text
    vendor.Address2 = txtAddress2.Text
    vendor.City = txtCity.Text
    vendor.State = cboStates.SelectedValue.ToString
    vendor.ZipCode = txtZipCode.Text
    vendor.DefaultTermsID = CInt(cboTerms.SelectedValue)
    vendor.DefaultAccountNo = CInt(cboAccounts.SelectedValue)
    vendor.Phone = txtPhone.Text.Replace(".", "")
    vendor.ContactFName = txtFirstName.Text
    vendor.ContactLName = txtLastName.Text
End Sub

End Class
```

Figure 7-9   The code for the Add/Modify Vendor form (part 3 of 3)

How to work with stored procedures

Instead of using Select, Insert, Update, and Delete statements that are coded in your application, you can use stored procedures that contain the statements you need. A *stored procedure* is a database object that contains one or more SQL statements.

In the topics that follow, you'll learn how to work with stored procedures. But keep in mind as you read these topics that they're not meant to teach you how to code stored procedures. They're just meant to give you an idea of how stored procedures work and how you can use them from Visual Basic applications. When you're ready to learn how to code your own stored procedures, please see our book, *Murach's SQL Server 2008 for Developers*.

An introduction to stored procedures

When you send a SQL statement to a database management system for processing, the DBMS must compile and optimize the query before it executes it. In contrast, because a stored procedure is stored with the database, it only has to be compiled and optimized the first time it's executed. Because of that, stored procedures can improve the efficiency of a database application.

Figure 7-10 illustrates how a stored procedure works. At the top of this figure, you can see a Create Procedure statement that creates a stored procedure named spGetVendorAddress. This stored procedure contains a Select statement that retrieves data for a vendor from the Vendors table based on the Vendor ID. Notice that this stored procedure requires a parameter, which is defined at the beginning of the procedure.

To execute a stored procedure, you use a command object as in this figure. Here, the CommandText property is set to the name of the stored procedure, and the CommandType property is set to CommandType.StoredProcedure. In addition, a parameter that will contain the value that's passed to the stored procedure is added to the Parameters collection of the command. Then, the connection is opened and the command is executed. Because the stored procedure in this example contains a Select statement, the ExecuteReader method is used to execute the command and store the result set in a data reader. But you can use the ExecuteNonQuery method to execute a stored procedure that contains an Insert, Update, or Delete statement, and you can use the ExecuteScalar method to execute a stored procedure that returns a single value.

When you use a stored procedure in a three-layer application, you execute it from a database class. In the Vendor Maintenance application, for example, the command in the GetVendor method in the VendorDB class in figure 7-6 (part 1) could be replaced with a command that uses a stored procedure. In other words, when you call a method in a database class, you can't tell whether it's going to use a stored procedure. And you can change a method in a database class so it uses a stored procedure without changing anything else in the application.

SQL code for creating a stored procedure that retrieves a row

```
CREATE PROCEDURE spGetVendorAddress (@VendorID int)
AS
SELECT VendorID, Name, Address1, Address2, City, State, ZipCode
FROM Vendors
WHERE (VendorID = @VendorID)
```

Visual Basic code that creates and executes a command that uses the stored procedure

```
Dim selectCommand As New SqlCommand()
selectCommand.Connection = connection
selectCommand.CommandText = "spGetVendorAddress"
selectCommand.CommandType = CommandType.StoredProcedure
selectCommand.Parameters.AddWithValue("@VendorID", vendorID)
connection.Open()
Dim reader As SqlDataReader = selectCommand.ExecuteReader()
    .
    .
```

Concepts

- A *stored procedure* consists of one or more SQL statements that have been compiled and stored with the database.

- Stored procedures can improve database performance because the SQL statements in each procedure are only compiled and optimized the first time they're executed. In contrast, SQL statements that are sent from a Visual Basic application have to be compiled and optimized every time they're executed.

- You can use parameters to pass values from an application to the stored procedure or from the stored procedure to the application. Stored procedures can also pass back a return value, which is typically used to indicate whether or not an error occurred.

How to use stored procedures from Visual Basic

- To use a stored procedure in a Visual Basic application, you set the CommandText property of a command to the name of the stored procedure, and you set the CommandType property to CommandType.StoredProcedure.

- If a stored procedure uses input parameters, you must add parameter objects to the Parameters collection just as you do when you use SQL statements directly. You must also add parameter objects for output parameters or a return value returned by the procedure. See figure 7-11 for details.

- To execute a stored procedure, you use the method of the command object that's appropriate for the processing that's done by the procedure. To execute a stored procedure that returns a result set, for example, you use the ExecuteReader method.

Figure 7-10   An introduction to stored procedures

How to work with output parameters and return values

The stored procedure you saw in the last figure used just an input parameter. But stored procedures can also use output parameters, and they can return a return value. Figure 7-11 illustrates how this works.

At the top of this figure, you can see a stored procedure that inserts a new row into the Vendors table. This procedure uses input parameters for each of the required columns in this table. In addition, it uses an output parameter that will return the identity value that's generated for the Vendor ID column. To assign a value to this parameter, the procedure uses a Set statement. As you can see, this statement assigns the value of the SCOPE_IDENTITY function to this parameter. SCOPE_IDENTITY is a SQL Server system function that returns the last value that was generated for an identity column within the current scope. In this case, the scope is the stored procedure.

This procedure also includes a Return statement that passes a return value back to the program. In this case, the procedure simply returns the value of the @@ERROR system function, which will contain the error number that was generated by the Insert statement. If no error was generated, this function will return a value of zero.

The Visual Basic code shown in this figure illustrates how you can use the output parameter and return value included in this stored procedure. To do that, you add parameter objects to the Parameters collection of the command that will execute the stored procedure. To indicate that a parameter will receive a return value or output from the stored procedure, you set its Direction property as shown here. Then, after the query is executed, you can get the values of the parameters through the Parameters collection. In this example, the @Error parameter is checked to see if it has a value of zero, which indicates that no error occurred. Then, the value of the @VendorID parameter is assigned to the VendorID property of a Vendor object. Otherwise, some other processing is performed.

If you understand how to use commands to execute queries, you shouldn't have any trouble using them with stored procedures. Before you use an existing stored procedure, though, you'll need to find out how it's defined, what parameters it uses, and whether it includes a Return statement. That way, you can define your command objects accordingly.

SQL code for creating a stored procedure that returns output parameters and a return value

```
CREATE PROCEDURE spInsertVendor
    ( @Name varchar(50), @Address1 varchar(50),
      @Address2 varchar(50), @City varchar(50),
      @State char(2), @ZipCode varchar(20),
      @VendorID int OUTPUT )
AS
INSERT INTO Vendors(Name, Address1, Address2, City, State, ZipCode)
VALUES (@Name, @Address1, @Address2, @City, @State, @ZipCode)
SET @VendorID = SCOPE_IDENTITY()
RETURN @@ERROR
```

Visual Basic code that executes the stored procedure

```
Dim insertCommand As New SqlCommand("spInsertVendor", connection)
insertCommand.CommandType = CommandType.StoredProcedure
insertCommand.Parameters.AddWithValue("@Name", vendor.Name)
insertCommand.Parameters.AddWithValue("@Address1", vendor.Address1)
insertCommand.Parameters.AddWithValue("@Address2", vendor.Address2)
insertCommand.Parameters.AddWithValue("@City", vendor.City)
insertCommand.Parameters.AddWithValue("@State", vendor.State)
insertCommand.Parameters.AddWithValue("@ZipCode", vendor.ZipCode)
insertCommand.Parameters.Add("@VendorID", SqlDbType.Int)
insertCommand.Parameters("@VendorID").Direction _
    = ParameterDirection.Output
insertCommand.Parameters.Add("@Error", SqlDbType.Int)
insertCommand.Parameters("@Error").Direction _
    = ParameterDirection.ReturnValue
 .
 .
connection.Open()
insertCommand.ExecuteNonQuery()
If CInt(insertCommand.Parameters("@Error").Value) = 0 Then
    vendor.VendorID = CInt(insertCommand.Parameters("@VendorID").Value)
Else
 .
 .
End If
connection.Close()
```

Description

- If a stored procedure includes output parameters or a Return statement, you must add parameters to the command that executes the stored procedure. These parameters will receive the values returned by the stored procedure.

- The Direction property of an output parameter must be set to ParameterDirection.Output. The Size property must also be set if the parameter is defined with a string data type.

- The Direction property of the parameter that receives the return value must be set to ParameterDirection.ReturnValue.

Figure 7-11   How to work with output parameters and return values

Perspective

In this chapter, you learned the skills for working with parameters and stored procedures. These are essential skills for working with commands as you develop database applications. In the next chapter, though, you'll learn an essential skill for working with a series of related commands.

Terms

parameter
parameterized query
input parameter
output parameter
stored procedure

Exercise 7-1   Enhance the Vendor Maintenance application

In this exercise, you'll enhance the Vendor Maintenance application that's presented in this chapter. That will give you a chance to work with parameters and stored procedures. It will also demonstrate that it's relatively easy to make changes to a three-layer application.

Review the application

1. Open the Vendor Maintenance application that's in your Chapter 7 directory. Then, use the Solution Explorer to review the files for this application.

2. In the PayablesData project, note that each business class is matched with a DB class. In the VendorMaintenace project, note that the Validator class provides the methods for validating data.

3. Test the application to see how it works. First, modify a row. Then, add a new row.

Add a delete function to the application

4. Add a Delete button to the Vendor Maintenance form to the right of the Modify button.

5. Add a DeleteVendor method to the VendorDB class that deletes the current vendor row. This method should have one parameter that accepts a Vendor object, and it should return a Boolean value of True if the deletion works and False if it doesn't. Like the UpdateVendor method in the VendorDB class, the deletion shouldn't be done if the vendor data has changed since it was retrieved from the database. Also, if a SQL exception occurs during the operation, the exception should be thrown to the calling class. The easiest way to code this method is to copy and modify the code for the UpdateVendor method.

6. Add a Click event handler for the Delete button. This event handler should start by using a message box to confirm that the user wants to delete the current vendor. If the user does, the event handler should execute the DeleteVendor method in the VendorDB class. Then, if the method returns True, the form controls should be cleared. If the method returns False, an error message should be displayed that indicates that another user updated or deleted the current vendor before the delete operation. And if the method throws a SQL exception, the exception message should be displayed.

7. Test and debug this enhancement until it works right.

Use a stored procedure for the GetVendor method in the VendorDB class

8. Use the View menu to display the Server Explorer. Then, expand the nodes for the Payables database until you reach Stored Procedures. There, you can see that the database includes a stored procedure named spGetVendor, and if you double-click on it you can see the stored procedure.

9. Modify the GetVendor method in the VendorDB class so it uses the spGetVendor stored procedure instead of the coded Select statement. To do that, comment out the statements that you won't need. Then, use figure 7-10 as a guide for writing the statements that you do need for using the stored procedure.

10. Test and debug this enhancement until it works right. And note that this enhancement doesn't require changes to any of the presentation or business classes.

8

How to work with transactions

In the last two chapters, you learned how to issue one database command at a time. Now, you'll learn how to work with groups of related commands so none of the commands in the group are applied to the database unless all of the commands are. This is an important skill for critical applications. And this is a feature that you can't implement when you use data sources and datasets.

How to use transactions

In chapter 5, you saw an Invoice Entry application that added one invoice row to the Invoices table and one or more line item rows to the InvoiceLineItems table for each invoice that the user entered. In a case like this, you want to be sure that all of the database commands for each invoice are executed successfully. For instance, you don't want the invoice row to get added to the database unless the line item rows are added too. To prevent that from happening, you can use transactions.

A *transaction* is a group of related database commands that you combine into a single logical unit. Then, you can make sure that all of the commands in the transaction are done successfully before you *commit* them. And if one or more of the commands aren't done successfully, you can *rollback* all of the commands.

How to start a transaction

Figure 8-1 presents the methods you use to create and work with transactions. To start a transaction, you use the BeginTransaction method of a connection object as shown in the first example in this figure. This creates a transaction object that you can use to work with the transaction.

Note that before you execute the BeginTransaction method, you must open the connection. Also note that the SqlTransaction class doesn't have a public constructor. As a result, the only way to create a SqlTransaction object is to use the BeginTransaction method of the connection object.

How to associate commands with a transaction

To use a transaction, you associate it with one or more commands. To do that, you assign the transaction object to the Transaction property of each command as shown in the second and third examples in figure 8-1. Note that each of the commands must be associated with the same connection object on which the transaction was started.

How to commit or rollback a transaction

After you associate a transaction with a command, any SQL statement you execute using that command becomes part of the transaction. Then, if all of the commands in the transaction execute without error, you can *commit* the transaction. That means that all of the changes that have been made to the database since the beginning of the transaction are made permanent. To commit a transaction, you use the Commit method of the transaction as shown in the fourth example in figure 8-1.

The syntax for creating a transaction object

```
sqlConnection.BeginTransaction()
```

Common methods of the SqlTransaction class

Method	Description
Commit()	Commits the changes to the database, making them permanent.
Rollback()	Reverses the changes made to the database to the beginning of the transaction.

Code that begins a transaction on a connection

```
Dim payableTransaction As SqlTransaction
connection.Open()
payableTransaction = connection.BeginTransaction
```

Code that associates the transaction with a command

```
Dim insertInvoiceCommand As New SqlCommand
insertInvoiceCommand.Connection = connection
insertInvoiceCommand.Transaction = payableTransaction
```

Code that associates the transaction with another command

```
Dim insertLineItemCommand As New SqlCommand
insertLineItemCommand.Connection = connection
insertLineItemCommand.Transaction = payableTransaction
```

Code that commits the transaction

```
payableTransaction.Commit()
```

Code that rolls back the transaction

```
payableTransaction.Rollback()
```

Description

- A *transaction* is a group of SQL statements that are combined into a logical unit. By default, each SQL statement is treated as a separate transaction.

- When you *commit* a transaction, the changes made to the database become permanent. Until it's committed, you can undo all of the changes since the beginning of the transaction by *rolling back* the transaction.

- The BeginTransaction method of a connection begins a transaction on an open connection and returns a transaction object. To associate a transaction with a command, you set the Transaction property of the command to the transaction object.

- If you close a connection while a transaction is pending, the changes are rolled back.

Figure 8-1   How to create and work with transactions

In contrast, if any of the commands cause an error, you can reverse, or *rollback*, all of the changes made to the database since the beginning of the transaction. To rollback a transaction, you use the Rollback method of the transaction as shown in the last example in figure 8-1.

How to work with save points

In most cases, if you need to rollback a transaction, you'll rollback the entire transaction. Occasionally, though, you may need to rollback just part of a transaction. To do that, you use *save points* as illustrated in figure 8-2.

To set a save point, you use the Save method of the transaction. On this method, you specify the name you want to use for the save point. Then, to roll a transaction back to a save point, you name the save point on the Rollback method. The example in this figure illustrates how this works.

The code in this example starts by creating a command that contains a Delete statement that deletes the vendor with a specified ID. This command is associated with a transaction named vendorTransaction. The next group of statements deletes the vendor with a vendor ID of 124 and then sets a save point named Vendor1. The next group of statements is similar except that it deletes the vendor with a vendor ID of 125 and then sets a save point named Vendor2. The two statements after that delete the vendor with a vendor ID of 126.

After that, the next statement rolls back the transaction to the Vendor2 save point. That means that any processing that was done after the Vendor2 save point is rolled back, which means that the third delete operation is rolled back. Then, the next statement rolls back the transaction to the Vendor1 save point, which rolls back the second delete operation. Finally, the transaction is committed. Since the only delete operation that hasn't already been rolled back is the one that deleted row 124, this row is deleted permanently.

Methods of the SqlTransaction class for working with save points

Method	Description
`Save(savePointName)`	Creates a save point with the specified name within the transaction.
`Rollback(savePointName)`	Reverses the changes made to the database to the specified save point.

Code that uses a transaction with two save points

```
Dim vendorTransaction As SqlTransaction
connection.Open()
vendorTransaction = connection.BeginTransaction

Dim deleteStatement As String _
    = "DELETE FROM Vendors WHERE VendorID = @VendorID"
Dim deleteCommand As New SqlCommand(deleteStatement, connection)
deleteCommand.Parameters.Add("@VendorID", SqlDbType.Int)
deleteCommand.Connection = connection
deleteCommand.Transaction = vendorTransaction

deleteCommand.Parameters("@VendorID").Value = 124
deleteCommand.ExecuteNonQuery()
vendorTransaction.Save("Vendor1")

deleteCommand.Parameters("@VendorID").Value = 125
deleteCommand.ExecuteNonQuery()
vendorTransaction.Save("Vendor2")

deleteCommand.Parameters("@VendorID").Value = 126
deleteCommand.ExecuteNonQuery()

vendorTransaction.Rollback("Vendor2")
vendorTransaction.Rollback("Vendor1")

vendorTransaction.Commit()
```

Description

- To partially rollback a transaction, you can use *save points*. To set a save point, you use the Save method of the transaction.
- To rollback a transaction to a save point, you code the save point name on the Rollback method. If you don't code a save point name on this method, the entire transaction is rolled back.
- After you rollback to a save point, you must still execute the Commit method if you want to commit the rest of the transaction.

Figure 8-2   How to work with save points

An introduction to concurrency and locking

When two or more users have access to the same database, it's possible for them to be working with the same data at the same time. As you learned in chapter 2, this is called *concurrency*. Concurrency isn't a problem when two users retrieve the same data at the same time. If they then try to update that data, however, that can be a problem. In the topics that follow, you'll learn how SQL Server uses locking to prevent concurrency problems. You'll also learn how you can control the types of problems that are allowed.

The four concurrency problems that locks can prevent

Figure 8-3 describes the four types of concurrency problems that locks can prevent. Depending on the nature of the data you're working with, these problems may not adversely affect a database. In fact, for many systems, these problems happen infrequently. Then, when they do occur, they can be corrected by simply resubmitting the query that caused the problem. On some database systems, however, these problems can affect data integrity in a serious way.

To help prevent concurrency problems, SQL Server uses *locking*. In most cases, the default locking behavior prevents serious data integrity problems from occurring. In some cases, though, you may want to change the default locking behavior. ADO.NET lets you do that by setting the transaction isolation level.

Four types of concurrency problems

Problem	Description
Lost updates	Occur when two transactions select the same row and then update the row based on the values originally selected. Since each transaction is unaware of the other, the later update overwrites the earlier update.
Dirty reads	Occur when a transaction selects data that isn't committed by another transaction. For example, transaction A changes a row. Transaction B then selects the changed row before transaction A commits the change. If transaction A then rolls back the change, transaction B has selected a row that doesn't exist in the database.
Nonrepeatable reads	Occur when two Select statements of the same data result in different values because another transaction has updated the data in the time between the two statements. For example, transaction A selects a row. Transaction B then updates the row. When transaction A selects the same row again, the data is different.
Phantom reads	Occur when you perform an update or delete on a set of rows when another transaction is performing an insert or delete that affects one or more rows in that same set of rows. For example, transaction A updates the payment total for each invoice that has a balance due. Transaction B inserts a new, unpaid, invoice while transaction A is still running. After transaction A finishes, there is still an invoice with a balance due.

Description

- SQL Server uses *locking* to help prevent concurrency problems. *Locks* delay the execution of a transaction if it conflicts with a transaction that's already running.

- In a large system with many users, you should expect for these kinds of problems to occur. In general, you don't need to take any action except to anticipate the problem. In many cases, if the query is resubmitted, the problem goes away.

- On some systems, if two transactions overwrite each other, the validity of the database is compromised and resubmitting one of the transactions won't eliminate the problem. If you're working on such a system, you must anticipate these concurrency problems and account for them in your code.

- You should consider concurrency problems as you write your code. If one of these problems would affect data integrity, you can change the default locking behavior by setting the transaction isolation level as shown in the next figure.

Note

- Although you can use locking to prevent lost updates, you can also prevent them by comparing the original values retrieved from the database with the current values in the database in the Where clause of the Update statement as you saw in the last chapter.

Figure 8-3   The four concurrency problems that locks can prevent

How to work with isolation levels

Figure 8-4 shows how you change the *transaction isolation level* for a transaction. To do that, you specify the isolation level on the BeginTransaction method using one of the members of the IsolationLevel enumeration. The table in this figure indicates which of the four concurrency problems each member will prevent or allow. For example, if you set the isolation level to Serializable as shown in the statement in this figure, all four concurrency problems will be prevented.

When you set the isolation level to Serializable, each transaction is completely isolated from every other transaction and concurrency is severely restricted. The server does this by locking each resource, preventing other transactions from accessing it. Since each transaction must wait for the previous transaction to commit, the transactions are executed serially, one after another.

Since the Serializable isolation level eliminates all possible concurrency problems, you may think that this is the best option. However, this option requires more server overhead to manage all of the locks. In addition, access time for each transaction is increased, since only one transaction can work with the data at a time. For most systems, this will actually eliminate few concurrency problems but will cause severe performance problems.

The lowest isolation level is ReadUncommitted, which allows all four of the concurrency problems to occur. It does this by performing Select queries without setting any locks and without honoring any existing locks. Since this means that your Select statements will always execute immediately, this setting provides the best performance. Since other transactions can retrieve and modify the same data, however, this setting can't prevent concurrency problems.

The default isolation level, ReadCommitted, is acceptable for most applications. However, the only concurrency problem it prevents is dirty reads. Although it can prevent some lost updates, it can't prevent them all.

The RepeatableRead level allows more concurrency than the Serializable level but less than the ReadCommitted level. As you might expect, then, it results in faster performance than Serializable and permits fewer concurrency problems than ReadCommitted.

The Snapshot level uses a SQL Server feature called *row versioning*. With row versioning, any data that's retrieved by a transaction that uses Snapshot isolation is consistent with the data that existed at the start of the transaction. To accomplish that, SQL Server maintains a snapshot of the original version of a row each time it's modified.

When you use row versioning, locks aren't required for read operations, which improves concurrency. However, the need to maintain row versions requires additional resources and can degrade performance. In most cases, then, you'll use row versioning only when data consistency is imperative.

The syntax for changing the isolation level for a transaction

```
connection.BeginTransaction(isolationLevel)
```

Members of the IsolationLevel enumeration

Member	Description
ReadUncommitted	Allows all concurrency problems.
ReadCommitted	Prevents dirty reads, but not lost updates, nonrepeatable reads, or phantom reads. This is the default isolation level for SQL Server.
RepeatableRead	Prevents dirty reads, lost updates, and nonrepeatable reads, but not phantom reads.
Snapshot	Prevents all concurrency problems by using row versioning instead of locking.
Serializable	Prevents all concurrency problems.

A statement that sets the isolation level for a transaction so that all concurrency problems are prevented

```
Connection.BeginTransaction(IsolationLevel.Serializable)
```

Description

- Since SQL Server manages locking automatically, you can't control every aspect of locking for your transactions. However, you can set the isolation level in your code.

- The *transaction isolation level* controls the degree to which transactions are isolated from one another. The server isolates transactions by using more restrictive locking behavior. If you isolate your transactions from other transactions, concurrency problems are reduced or eliminated.

- You specify the transaction isolation level by passing a member of the IsolationLevel enumeration to the BeginTransaction method. The default transaction isolation level is ReadCommitted. At this level, some lost updates, nonrepeatable reads, and phantom reads can occur, but this is acceptable for most transactions.

- The ReadUncommitted isolation level doesn't set any locks and ignores locks that are already held. This level results in the highest possible performance for your query, but at the risk of every kind of concurrency problem. For this reason, you should only use this level for data that is rarely updated.

- The RepeatableRead level places locks on all data that's used in a transaction, preventing other users from updating that data. However, this isolation level still allows inserts, so phantom reads can occur.

- The Snapshot level was introduced with SQL Server 2005. It uses *row versioning* rather than locks to provide read consistency. With row versioning, each time a transaction modifies a row, SQL Server stores an image of the row as it existed before the modification. That way, read operations that use row versioning retrieve the row as it existed at the start of the transaction.

- The Serializable level places a lock on all data that's used in a transaction. Since each transaction must wait for the previous transaction to commit, the transactions are handled in sequence. This is the most restrictive of the five isolation levels.

Figure 8-4   How to work with isolation levels

A Transfer Payment application that uses transactions

To illustrate the use of transactions, the rest of this chapter presents a simple application. It lets the user reverse an incorrect invoice payment and apply the payment to the correct invoice. For each transfer, a transaction is used to make sure that a payment isn't reversed unless it is also applied to the correct invoice.

The user interface

Figure 8-5 presents the user interface for this application. First, the user gets the invoice information for the invoice that the payment amount should be transferred from. Then, the user gets the invoice information for the invoice that the payment should be transferred to. At this point, if everything looks okay, the user can enter the transfer amount and click the Make Transfer button.

Of course, this application is unrealistically simple. For instance, you probably wouldn't get the invoice data without also getting some vendor data to make sure you've got the right invoice. So please keep in mind that the purpose of this application is to illustrate the use of transactions, not business practices.

Nevertheless, this application does represent a type of application that is relatively common. That is, an application that lets a user fix a clerical error. For no matter how well designed a user interface is, a careless user can make errors that need to be fixed with applications like this one.

The Transfer Payment form

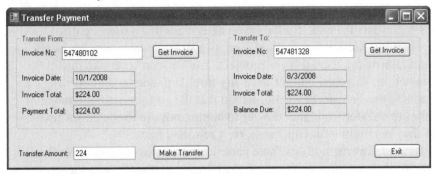

The dialog box that's displayed after the transfer is processed

Description

- Due to clerical errors, invoice payments are sometimes applied to the wrong invoices. In those cases, you need to reverse any payments that are applied to the wrong invoices and apply those amounts to the right invoices. That's what this application provides for.

- To transfer a payment from one invoice to another, the user enters the invoice number for the first invoice, clicks the first Get Invoice button, enters the invoice number for the second invoice, and clicks the second Get Invoice button. Then, if the data that's displayed is for the right invoices, the user enters the amount to be transferred and clicks the Make Transfer button.

- If the transfer is successful, the dialog box shown above is displayed. Otherwise, an error message is displayed. In either case, the form is cleared so the user can transfer another payment.

- This application requires the use of transactions because the transfer amount shouldn't be reversed from the first invoice without also applying it to the second invoice. If an error occurs during this process, the database operations should be rolled back.

Figure 8-5   The user interface for the Transfer Payment application

The code for the InvoiceDB class

Figure 8-6 presents the code for the InvoiceDB class that's used by this application. Here, the GetInvoice method accepts a string invoice number as a parameter and returns the related Invoice object. You've seen code like this several times before, so you shouldn't have any trouble understanding it.

It is of course the TransferPayment method that uses a transaction to make sure that both the transfer from and transfer to commands are executed successfully before they're committed. Otherwise, they're rolled back.

As you can see, this method has three parameters: an Invoice object for the transfer from invoice; an Invoice object for the transfer to invoice; and the payment amount as a Decimal type. To start, this method creates a connection object and a transaction object. These will be used later.

Next, this method creates the transfer from command object. In the Where clause of the Update statement for this command, you can see that parameters are used to make sure that the PaymentTotal column hasn't been changed since the row was retrieved. This prevents a concurrency problem. In the Set clause, you can see that the PaymentTotal column is reduced by the payment amount. This code is followed by code that sets the three parameters that are used by the Update statement.

The code for the InvoiceDB class

```vb
Imports System.Data.SqlClient

Public Class InvoiceDB

    Public Shared Function GetInvoice(ByVal invoiceNo As String) As Invoice
        Dim invoice As New Invoice
        Dim connection As SqlConnection = PayablesDB.GetConnection
        Dim selectStatement As String _
            = "SELECT InvoiceNumber, InvoiceDate, " _
            & "InvoiceTotal, PaymentTotal " _
            & "FROM Invoices " _
            & "WHERE InvoiceNumber = @InvoiceNumber"
        Dim selectCommand As New SqlCommand(selectStatement, connection)
        selectCommand.Parameters.AddWithValue("@InvoiceNumber", invoiceNo)
        Try
            connection.Open()
            Dim reader As SqlDataReader _
                = selectCommand.ExecuteReader(CommandBehavior.SingleRow)
            If reader.Read Then
                invoice.InvoiceNumber = reader("InvoiceNumber").ToString
                invoice.InvoiceDate = CDate(reader("InvoiceDate"))
                invoice.InvoiceTotal = CDec(reader("InvoiceTotal"))
                invoice.PaymentTotal = CDec(reader("PaymentTotal"))
            Else
                invoice = Nothing
            End If
            reader.Close()
        Catch ex As SqlException
            Throw ex
        Finally
            connection.Close()
        End Try
        Return invoice
    End Function

    Public Shared Function TransferPayment(ByVal fromInvoice As Invoice, _
            ByVal toInvoice As Invoice, ByVal payment As Decimal) As Boolean
        Dim connection As SqlConnection = PayablesDB.GetConnection
        Dim paymentTran As SqlTransaction = Nothing

        Dim fromCommand As New SqlCommand
        fromCommand.Connection = connection
        fromCommand.CommandText _
            = "UPDATE Invoices " _
            & "SET PaymentTotal = PaymentTotal - @Payment " _
            & "WHERE InvoiceNumber = @InvoiceNumber " _
            & "  AND PaymentTotal = @PaymentTotal"
        fromCommand.Parameters.AddWithValue("@Payment", payment)
        fromCommand.Parameters.AddWithValue("@InvoiceNumber", _
                fromInvoice.InvoiceNumber)
        fromCommand.Parameters.AddWithValue("@PaymentTotal", _
                fromInvoice.PaymentTotal)
```

Figure 8-6   The code for the InvoiceDB class (part 1 of 2)

The next set of statements creates the transfer to command object. This works like the statements for the transfer from command object, but the PaymentTotal column is increased by the payment amount.

The rest of the code in this method starts the transaction, associates the two commands with the transaction, and executes the commands. Then, if one of the commands doesn't return a value that's greater than zero, which indicates a concurrency problem, the transaction is rolled back and the method returns a value of False. Or, if a SQL exception is caught by the Catch block, the transaction is rolled back and the exception is thrown to the calling method. But if both commands are successful, the transaction is committed and the method returns a value of True.

The code for the InvoiceDB class

```vb
Dim toCommand As New SqlCommand
toCommand.Connection = connection
toCommand.CommandText _
    = "UPDATE Invoices " _
    & "SET PaymentTotal = PaymentTotal + @Payment " _
    & "WHERE InvoiceNumber = @InvoiceNumber " _
    & "   AND PaymentTotal = @PaymentTotal"
toCommand.Parameters.AddWithValue("@Payment", payment)
toCommand.Parameters.AddWithValue("@InvoiceNumber", _
        toInvoice.InvoiceNumber)
toCommand.Parameters.AddWithValue("@PaymentTotal", _
        toInvoice.PaymentTotal)

Try
    connection.Open()
    paymentTran = connection.BeginTransaction
    fromCommand.Transaction = paymentTran
    toCommand.Transaction = paymentTran

    Dim count As Integer = fromCommand.ExecuteNonQuery
    If count > 0 Then
        count = toCommand.ExecuteNonQuery
        If count > 0 Then
            paymentTran.Commit()
            Return True
        Else
            paymentTran.Rollback()
            Return False
        End If
    Else
        paymentTran.Rollback()
        Return False
    End If
Catch ex As SqlException
    If paymentTran IsNot Nothing Then
        paymentTran.Rollback()
    End If
    Throw ex
Finally
    connection.Close()
End Try
    End Function

End Class
```

Figure 8-6   The code for the InvoiceDB class (part 2 of 2)

The code for the Transfer Payment form

To show you how the TransferPayment method of the InvoiceDB database class is used by the Transfer Payment form, figure 8-7 presents the code for the Click event of its Make Transfer button. If you want to see the other event handlers for this form, you can of course open the application that you've downloaded from our web site. But you shouldn't have any trouble envisioning what the other event handlers do.

As you can see in this figure, the code for the Click event handler of the Make Transfer button consists of nested If statements that check the validity of all the data before executing the TransferPayment method of the InvoiceDB class. If anything is invalid, the related Else clause displays an appropriate error message. But if everything is valid, the TransferPayment method is executed.

When the TransferPayment method is executed, it returns True, returns False, or throws a SQL exception. As a result, the call for this method is coded as the condition for an If statement within the Try block of a Try...Catch statement. Then, if the method returns True, a message is displayed that documents the payment transfer. If the method returns False, a message is displayed that indicates that a concurrency error probably occurred. And if the method throws a SQL exception, the exception message is displayed.

The code for the Click event of the Make Transfer button

```
Private Sub btnTransfer_Click(ByVal sender As System.Object, _
        ByVal e As System.EventArgs) Handles btnTransfer.Click
    If Validator.IsPresent(txtTransferAmount) AndAlso _
        Validator.IsDecimal(txtTransferAmount) Then
        If fromInvoice IsNot Nothing AndAlso toInvoice IsNot Nothing Then
            Dim transferAmount As Decimal = CDec(txtTransferAmount.Text)
            If transferAmount <= fromInvoice.PaymentTotal Then
                If transferAmount <= toInvoice.BalanceDue Then
                    Try
                        If InvoiceDB.TransferPayment(fromInvoice, _
                                toInvoice, transferAmount) Then
                            Dim message As String _
                                = "A payment of " _
                                & FormatCurrency(transferAmount) _
                                & " has been transferred from " _
                                & "invoice number " _
                                & fromInvoice.InvoiceNumber _
                                & " to invoice number " _
                                & toInvoice.InvoiceNumber & "."
                            MessageBox.Show(message, "Transfer Complete")
                            Me.ClearControls()
                        Else
                            MessageBox.Show("The transfer was not " _
                                & "processed. Another user may have " _
                                & "posted a payment to one of the " _
                                & "invoices.", "Transfer Not Processed")
                            Me.ClearControls()
                        End If
                    Catch ex As Exception
                        MessageBox.Show(ex.Message, ex.GetType.ToString)
                    End Try
                Else
                    MessageBox.Show("Transfer amount cannot be more " _
                        & "than the balance due.", "Data Entry Error")
                End If
            Else
                MessageBox.Show("Transfer amount cannot be more " _
                    & "than the payment total.", "Data Entry Error")
            End If
        Else
            MessageBox.Show("You must select the From and To invoices " _
                & "before transferring a payment.", "Data Entry Error")
        End If
    End If
End Sub
```

Figure 8-7   The code for the Transfer Payment form

Perspective

In this chapter, you've learned how to use transactions, which is an important skill for critical database applications. Although the application in this chapter is simplistic, you'll see the use of transactions in a more realistic application in chapter 10. And the exercise for that chapter will give you a chance to work with the code for using transactions.

Now that you know how to use transactions, you have a complete set of skills for building three-layer database applications. When you use these skills, you have complete control over how your applications work. The code in your business and database classes can be used in more than one application. Your applications are relatively easy to test, debug, maintain, and enhance. And you can use transactions to make sure that all of the database commands in a group have been done successfully before you commit them.

In the next chapter, though, you'll learn how to use a feature of Visual Studio that lets you build three-layer applications and still get the benefits of using bound controls. This feature is called object data sources, and every professional should know how to use it.

Terms

transaction
commit
rollback
save point
locking
dirty read
nonrepeatable read
phantom read
transaction isolation level
row versioning
lost update

9

How to work with object data sources

In section 2 of this book, you learned how to use a database as a data source for your application. This lets you quickly create forms that use controls that are bound to the database. However, it doesn't give you as much control over how your applications work as you may like.

In the last three chapters, you learned how to use code to access a database. Although you can't build applications as quickly with this approach and you can't use data binding, you do have complete control over the way the data access code works.

In this chapter, you'll learn how you can get the best of both worlds by using object data sources, which are data sources that get their data from business objects. This lets you get the benefits of data binding and have complete control over how the data access code works.

An introduction to object data sources

The following topics introduce you to object data sources and the three-layer architecture that they let you implement.

How three-layer Windows applications work with object data sources

As you learned in chapter 2, most development experts recommend a *three-layer architecture* that separates the presentation, business, and data access components of the application. The *presentation layer* includes the forms that define the user interface. The *middle layer* includes classes that represent business entities. It may also include classes that implement business rules such as data validation requirements or discount policies. The *database layer* consists of the classes that manage the data access for the business objects and the database itself.

When you use *object data sources*, as figure 9-1 shows, you still use a three-layer architecture that includes business and database classes. Then, the object data source is stored in the presentation layer so it can be used for data binding. In this case, it's used to bind controls on a form to the data in a business object, which is created from a business class in the middle layer. This means that you can use data binding in the presentation layer and still use code to control the data access operations.

When you use an object data source, you create a database class to handle the data access for the business object. This class typically provides at least one method that retrieves data from the database and stores it in the business object. It can also provide methods to insert, update, and delete data.

The three-layer architecture in Visual Studio 2008

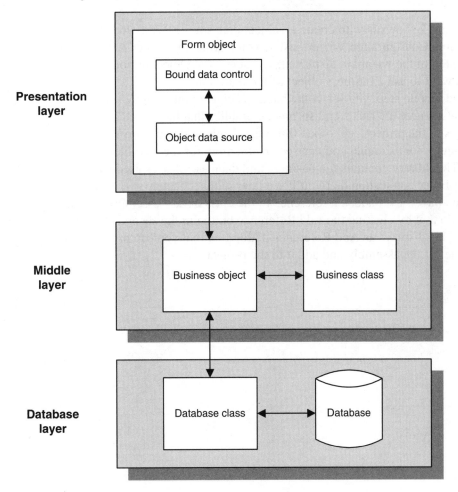

Description

- An *object data source* is a data source that gets its data from a business object rather than directly from a database. To work with the data in a business object, an application uses a database class.

- An application that uses object data sources has a *three-layer architecture* where the object data sources are part of the *presentation layer*, the business classes are part of the *middle layer*, and the database classes are part of the *database layer*.

- The business classes that define the business objects used by an application and the database classes that work with those objects are typically stored in a class library.

- Once you create an object data source, you can drag it to a form to create controls that are bound to the properties of the business object it's based on.

Figure 9-1   How three-layer Windows applications work with object data sources

How to create an object data source

Figure 9-2 shows how to create an object data source. First, you start the Data Source Configuration Wizard just as you learned in chapter 3. Then, when the first step of the wizard is displayed, you select the Object option to indicate that you want to use a business object as the data source.

In the second step, you select the business object you want to bind the object data source to. This step lists any assemblies that have been added as references to the project, other than those that begin with Microsoft or System. In this figure, for example, you can see an assembly for the PayablesData class library. This library contains the business and database classes used by the Payment Entry application that you'll see later in this chapter.

If you haven't yet added a reference to the class library assembly you need, you can do that by clicking the Add Reference button in the second step of the Wizard. This displays an Add Reference dialog box that you can use to locate the dll file for the assembly and add it to the project.

The first dialog box of the Data Source Configuration Wizard

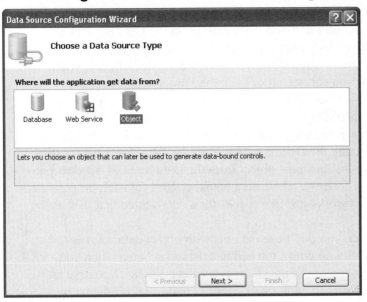

How to select the object for the data source

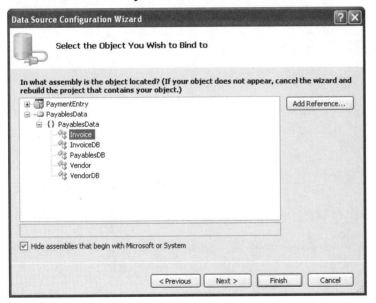

Description

- To create an object data source, select the Object option from the first step of the Data Source Configuration Wizard. Then, select the business object you want to use as the source of data from the list of objects in the second step.

Figure 9-2   How to create an object data source

How to use an object data source

After you create an object data source, it appears in the Data Sources window as shown in figure 9-3. Here, you can see the Invoice business object in the PayablesData class library that was selected in the previous figure. When you expand this object, you can see all of the public properties it defines.

To work with an object data source, you can drag a business object to a form. By default, a DataGridView control, binding source, and binding navigator are generated as shown here. You can also change the default control for a business object by selecting the Details option from the drop-down list for the table. Then, if you drag that business object from the Data Sources window onto a form, Visual Studio generates a label and a bound control for each property of the business object. This works just like it does for a data source that gets its data from a database.

As you might expect, you don't use datasets with object data sources. Because of that, Visual Studio doesn't generate a dataset schema when you create an object data source, and it doesn't create a dataset when you drag an object data source to a form. In addition, it doesn't create a table adapter or table adapter manager since they're used strictly with datasets.

A form after the Invoice data source has been dragged onto it

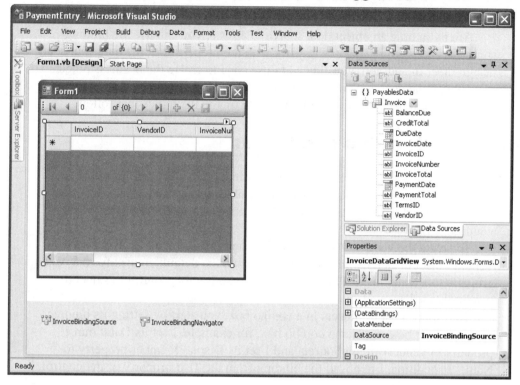

Description

- When you create an object data source, it appears in the Data Sources window. Then, you can drag the entire business object or individual properties of the business object to the form to create bound controls. This is identical to the way that you work with tables and columns in a data source that gets its data from a database.

- Unlike a data source that gets it data from a database, an object data source doesn't store its data in a dataset. Because of that, no dataset schema file is generated when the data source is created, and no dataset, table adapter, or table adapter manager are created when you drag the data source to a form.

- Although a binding navigator is added to the form when you drag an object data source onto it, you won't typically use this control.

- The binding source for an object data source provides for working with the properties of the data source at design time. At runtime, however, the application must create the object that contains the data that will be displayed in the controls and then bind the controls to the object. See figures 9-4 and 9-5 for details.

Figure 9-3   How to use an object data source

How to work with bound controls

After you drag an object data source to a form, you can use the binding source Visual Studio generates to work with the properties of the data source at design time. In addition, you'll need to use code to create the business objects that contain the data that you want to display and to bind the controls on the form to those objects. You'll learn how to do that in the topics that follow.

How to work with a combo box

Figure 9-4 shows a form that displays vendor data. This form uses an object data source that gets its data from a Vendor object. The Vendor class that this object is created from is defined with the properties listed in the Data Sources window.

To create the Vendor Display form, I changed the default control for the Vendor object to Details. In addition, I changed the default control for the Name property to a combo box. That way, the user can use this control to select the vendor that's displayed.

To display a list of objects in a combo box, you start by setting its binding properties. To bind the Name combo box, for example, I set its DataSource property to VendorBindingSource, and I set its DisplayMember property to Name. In addition, I removed the binding from the Text property of the control, which is set by default.

Note that I didn't set the ValueMember property of the combo box. That's because, when the user selects a vendor from the combo box, the selected vendor is retrieved from the list of vendors using the SelectedIndex property. Later in this chapter, when I present the Payment Entry application, I'll show you another way to retrieve a vendor by setting the ValueMember property.

Next, you use code like that shown in the first example in this figure to create the list of objects to be displayed and bind it to the combo box. The first statement in this example creates a variable that can store a list of Vendor objects. Then, the second statement uses the GetVendorList method of a class named VendorDB to get all the vendors from the database and store them in this list. Finally, the last statement sets the DataSource property of the combo box to this list.

Note that this last statement overrides the DataSource property that's set at design time. In contrast, you set this property to the binding source at design time so you can set the other binding properties of the control. That's necessary because the object you want to bind to isn't available at design time.

How to work with a text box

When you create a text box from an object data source, its Text property is automatically bound to the appropriate property of the binding source. Then, to display a value in the text box, you use code like that shown in the second example in figure 9-4.

A combo box and text boxes that are bound to an object data source

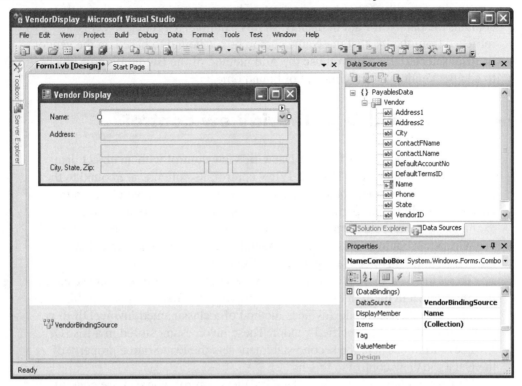

Code that creates a List() object and binds the combo box to it

```
Private vendorList As List(Of Vendor)
vendorList = VendorDB.GetVendorList
NameComboBox.DataSource = vendorList
```

Code that binds the text boxes to a Vendor object

```
VendorBindingSource.Clear()
Dim vendor As Vendor = vendorList(NameComboBox.SelectedIndex)
VendorBindingSource.Add(vendor)
```

Description

- If you generate a combo box from a property of an object data source, you'll need to set its binding properties as described in chapter 4.

- To bind a combo box to an object, you create the object from a class that implements the IList interface, such as the List() class. Then, you set the DataSource property of the combo box to that object.

- To bind text boxes to an object, you first clear the binding source to remove any existing object that the controls are bound to. Then, you create the object that contains the data you want to display and add it to the binding source.

Figure 9-4   How to use text boxes and combo boxes with an object data source

To start, you use the Clear method of the BindingSource object to remove any objects from the list of bound objects. Then, you create a new object that contains the data you want to display. In this example, a Vendor object is retrieved from the list that the Name combo box is bound to based on the vendor the user selected. Finally, you use the Add method of the BindingSource object to add the Vendor object to the list of bound objects.

How to work with a DataGridView control

Figure 9-5 shows how to use a DataGridView control with an object data source. When you create a DataGridView control, its columns are bound to the properties of the business object. Then, you can use the skills you learned in chapter 4 to edit the properties and columns of the control. In this figure, for example, you can see a form that displays the invoices for a selected vendor in a DataGridView control. This control is bound to an object data source that was created from the Invoice class you saw in figure 9-3.

To set the data source for a DataGridView control at runtime, you use code like that shown in the first example in this figure. The first statement in this example uses the GetVendorInvoices method of a class named InvoiceDB to get all the invoices for the specified vendor. These invoices are stored in a List(Of Invoice) variable. Then, the second statement sets the DataSource property of the DataGridView control to this list.

To work with the objects in a DataGridView control, you can use code like that shown in the second example. This code uses a For Each…Next loop to iterate through each row in the grid to calculate the total balance due for a vendor. Within this loop, it uses the DataBoundItem property of each row to get the business object that's stored in that row. Then, it casts the Object type that's returned by this property to the Invoice type so it can be stored in an Invoice variable. Finally, the BalanceDue property of the Invoice object is added to the balance due for the vendor.

When a DataGridView control is bound to an object data source, a CurrencyManager object is used to manage the list of business objects that's displayed by the control. If the list of objects changes, you can use the CurrencyManager object to synchronize the grid with the list. To do that, you use code like that shown in the third example in this figure.

The first statement in this example uses the BindingContext property of the DataGridView control to get the CurrencyManager object for this control. Notice that the object that's returned by this property must be cast to the CurrencyManager type. That's because the object type depends on the data source that's passed to the BindingContext property. Then, the second statement uses the Refresh method of the CurrencyManager object to display the current list of objects in the DataGridView control.

A form with a DataGridView control that's bound to an object data source

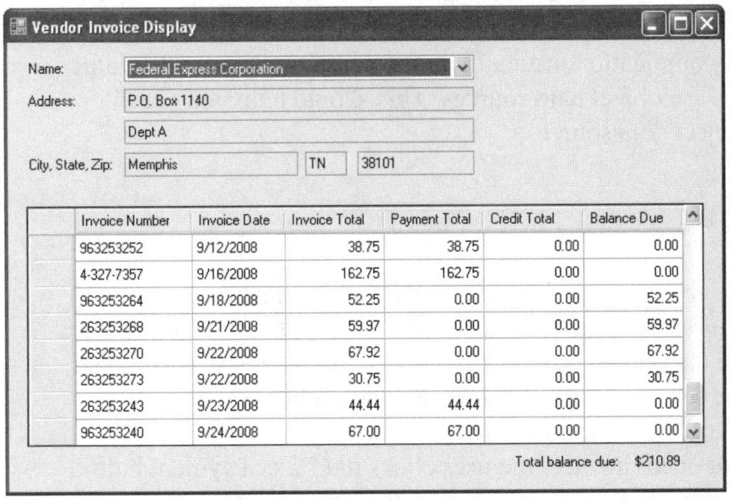

Code that creates a List() object and binds a DataGridView control to it

```
Dim invoiceList As List(Of Invoice) = InvoiceDB.GetVendorInvoices(vendorID)
InvoiceDataGridView.DataSource = invoiceList
```

Code that retrieves business objects from the DataGridView control

```
Dim balanceDue As Decimal = 0
For Each row As DataGridViewRow In InvoiceDataGridView.Rows
    Dim invoice As Invoice = CType(row.DataBoundItem, Invoice)
    balanceDue += invoice.BalanceDue
Next
```

Code that refreshes the data displayed in the DataGridView control

```
Dim cm As CurrencyManager = CType( _
    InvoiceDataGridView.BindingContext(invoiceList), CurrencyManager)
cm.Refresh()
```

Description

- When you generate a DataGridView control from an object data source, the columns in the control are bound to the properties of the business object. You can edit these columns as described in chapter 4.

- You can set the DataSource property of a DataGridView object to any class that implements a list. This includes the generic List() class and its subclasses as well as the older ArrayList class and the DataSet and DataTable classes.

- You can use the DataBoundItem property of a DataGridViewRow object to get the business object that's stored in that row.

- If an application lets you add, modify, or delete items in a DataGridView control, you can use the BindingContext property of the control to get the CurrencyManager object that manages the list of bound objects. Then, you can use the Refresh method of the CurrencyManager object to refresh the list so the current list is displayed.

Figure 9-5   How to use a DataGridView control with an object data source

A Payment Entry application

The Payment Entry application presented in the next few figures illustrates how an application can use object data sources. This should help you see the advantages of using object data sources.

The user interface

Figure 9-6 presents the two forms that make up the user interface for the Payment Entry application. To enter a payment, the user starts by selecting the vendor to be paid from the combo box. Then, the vendor's address is displayed in the text boxes on the form, and any invoices that have a balance due are displayed in the DataGridView control.

To make a payment on an invoice, the user clicks the Enter Payment button for that invoice. Then, the Payment Entry form is displayed. From this form, the user can enter the payment amount and then click the Accept button to post the payment and return to the Vendor Invoices form. Alternatively, the user can click the Cancel button to return to the Vendor Invoices form without posting a payment.

The Vendor Invoices form

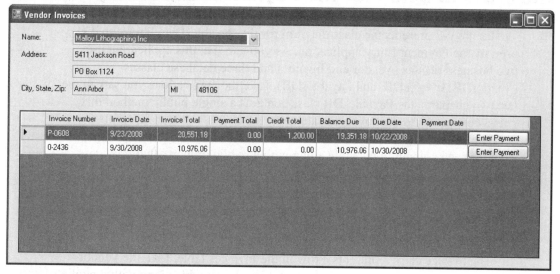

The Payment Entry form

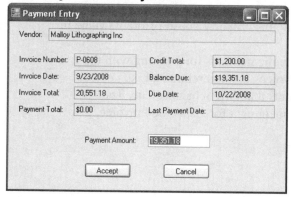

Description

- The Vendor Invoices form lets the user select a vendor from a combo box that lists all the vendors with unpaid invoices. Then, all the unpaid invoices are displayed in a DataGridView control.

- To enter a payment for an invoice, the user clicks the Enter Payment button for that invoice in the DataGridView control to display the Payment Entry form. Then, the user enters the payment amount and clicks the Accept button.

- The Name combo box is bound to a list of Vendor objects created from the Vendor class, the text boxes that display the vendor data are bound to a Vendor object that's created from the Vendor class, the DataGridView control is bound to a list of Invoice objects created from the Invoice class, and the text boxes that display the invoice data are bound to an Invoice object that's created from the Invoice class.

Figure 9-6   The user interface for the Payment Entry application

The class diagram for the PayablesData library

Figure 9-7 presents the class diagram for the PayablesData library that's used by the Payment Entry application. As you can see, this application uses two business classes (Vendor and Invoice) and three database classes (VendorDB, InvoiceDB, and PayablesDB). Like the applications you saw in the last two chapters, the PayablesDB class contains a single public method that gets a connection to the Payables database.

The Vendor class represents a row in the Vendors table. It contains a private field for each column in the table along with a public property that provides access to the field. The VendorDB class provides two public methods for working with the Vendors table. The GetVendorNameAndAddress method returns a single Vendor object with the specified Vendor ID. The GetVendorsWithBalanceDue method returns a List() object that contains a collection of Vendor objects with unpaid invoices.

The Invoice class represents a row in the Invoices table. Like the Vendor class, it contains a private field for each column in the table along with a public property that provides access to the field. In addition, it contains a property named BalanceDue that represents the unpaid amount of the invoice. When you see the code for this class, you'll see why this property doesn't store its value in a private field.

The InvoiceDB class provides two public methods for working with the Invoices table. The GetUnpaidVendorInvoices method returns a List() object that contains a collection of Invoice objects that have a balance due. The UpdatePayment method updates the payment data for a specified invoice.

The class diagram for the PayablesData library

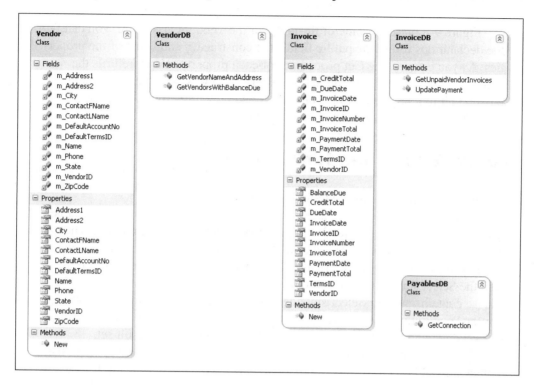

Description

- The PayablesData library contains the classes that define the business objects used by the Payment Entry application and the database classes that are used to work with the Payables database.

- The business objects are defined by the Vendor and Invoice classes. These objects will hold data from the Vendors and Invoices tables in the Payables database.

- The VendorDB, InvoiceDB, and PayablesDB classes are the database classes. These classes provide shared members for working with the Payables database.

- The VendorDB class provides public methods for getting a single vendor and a list of vendors that have unpaid invoices from the Vendors table. The InvoiceDB class provides public methods for getting the unpaid invoices for a vendor and for updating the payment data for an invoice. And the PayablesDB class provides a public method for getting a connection to the Payables database.

Figure 9-7   The class diagram for the PayablesData library

The code for the Vendor class

Figure 9-8 presents some of the code for the Vendor class. Here, you can see the declarations for all the public fields, the constructor, and some of the properties. As you can see, the Get procedure for each property simply returns the value of a private field, and the Set procedure simply assigns the value that's passed to it to a private field. If you understand how properties work, you shouldn't have any trouble understanding this code.

The code for the VendorDB class

Figure 9-9 presents the code for the VendorDB class. The GetVendorsWithBalanceDue method of this class starts by declaring a variable that will hold the List() of Vendor objects that's returned by the method. Then, it uses the GetConnection method of the PayablesDB class to get a connection to the Payables database, and it creates a command object using the connection and the Select statement that will retrieve the Vendors. In this case, the Where clause contains another Select statement that retrieves the sum of the invoices for the vendor and checks whether that sum is greater than zero. That way, only the vendors who have unpaid invoices will be included in the result set.

Once the command object is created, this method continues by opening the connection and executing the command to create a data reader. Then, for each vendor that's returned, it creates a Vendor object, sets the VendorID and Name properties of the object, and adds the object to the list of Vendor objects. Note that because this list will be used only to load the Name combo box on the Vendor Invoices form, it isn't necessary to set the other properties of the Vendor objects. Instead, the vendor ID of the selected vendor will be used to retrieve the vendor from the Vendors table. That makes the application more efficient because it retrieves only the data it needs. This method ends by closing the data reader and the connection and returning the list of vendors to the calling procedure.

The GetVendorNameAndAddress method is similar to the GetVendor method you saw in the Vendor Maintenance application in chapter 7. The only difference is that the GetVendor method retrieved all the columns from the Vendors table, because all the columns were used by the Vendor Maintenance application. In contrast, the Payment Entry application uses only the vendor ID and name and address columns. So that's all the GetVendorNameAndAddress method retrieves. That reduces network traffic and improves efficiency.

Also notice that if a row isn't returned—in other words, if a row isn't found with the specified vendor ID—the Vendor object is set to Nothing. Although this application doesn't check for this condition because a vendor wouldn't be deleted if it had unpaid invoices, this method could be used by other applications that retrieve a vendor by vendor ID.

The code for the Vendor class

```
Public Class Vendor
    Private m_VendorID As Integer
    Private m_Name As String
    Private m_Address1 As String
    Private m_Address2 As String
    Private m_City As String
    Private m_State As String
    Private m_ZipCode As String
    Private m_Phone As String
    Private m_ContactLName As String
    Private m_ContactFName As String
    Private m_DefaultTermsID As Integer
    Private m_DefaultAccountNo As Integer

    Public Sub New()

    End Sub

    Public Property VendorID() As Integer
        Get
            Return m_VendorID
        End Get
        Set(ByVal value As Integer)
            m_VendorID = value
        End Set
    End Property

    Public Property Name() As String
        Get
            Return m_Name
        End Get
        Set(ByVal value As String)
            m_Name = value
        End Set
    End Property

    Public Property Address1() As String
        Get
            Return m_Address1
        End Get
        Set(ByVal value As String)
            m_Address1 = value
        End Set
    End Property
    .
    .
    .
    Public Property DefaultAccountNo() As Integer
        Get
            Return m_DefaultAccountNo
        End Get
        Set(ByVal value As Integer)
            m_DefaultAccountNo = value
        End Set
    End Property

End Class
```

Figure 9-8   The code for the Vendor class

The code for the VendorDB class

```vb
Imports System.Data.SqlClient

Public Class VendorDB

    Public Shared Function GetVendorsWithBalanceDue() As List(Of Vendor)
        Dim vendorList As New List(Of Vendor)

        Dim connection As SqlConnection = PayablesDB.GetConnection
        Dim selectStatement As String _
            = "SELECT VendorID, Name " _
            & "FROM Vendors " _
            & "WHERE (SELECT SUM(InvoiceTotal - PaymentTotal " _
            & "             - CreditTotal) " _
            & "        FROM Invoices " _
            & "        WHERE Invoices.VendorID = Vendors.VendorID) " _
            & "      > 0 " _
            & "ORDER BY Name"
        Dim selectCommand As New SqlCommand(selectStatement, connection)

        Try
            connection.Open()
            Dim reader As SqlDataReader = selectCommand.ExecuteReader()
            Dim vendor As Vendor
            Do While reader.Read
                vendor = New Vendor
                vendor.VendorID = CInt(reader("VendorID"))
                vendor.Name = reader("Name").ToString
                vendorList.Add(vendor)
            Loop
            reader.Close()
        Catch ex As SqlException
            Throw ex
        Finally
            connection.Close()
        End Try

        Return vendorList
    End Function
```

Figure 9-9   The code for the Vendor class (part 1 of 2)

The code for the VendorDB class   **Page 2**

```
Public Shared Function GetVendorNameAndAddress(ByVal vendorID As Integer) _
        As Vendor
    Dim vendor As New Vendor

    Dim connection As SqlConnection = PayablesDB.GetConnection
    Dim selectStatement As String _
        = "SELECT VendorID, Name, Address1, Address2, " _
        & "City, State, ZipCode " -_
        & "FROM Vendors " _
        & "WHERE VendorID = @VendorID"
    Dim selectCommand As New SqlCommand(selectStatement, connection)
    selectCommand.Parameters.AddWithValue("@VendorID", vendorID)

    Try
        connection.Open()
        Dim reader As SqlDataReader _
            = selectCommand.ExecuteReader(CommandBehavior.SingleRow)
        If reader.Read Then
            vendor.VendorID = CInt(reader("VendorID"))
            vendor.Name = reader("Name").ToString
            vendor.Address1 = reader("Address1").ToString
            vendor.Address2 = reader("Address2").ToString
            vendor.City = reader("City").ToString
            vendor.State = reader("State").ToString
            vendor.ZipCode = reader("ZipCode").ToString
        Else
            vendor = Nothing
        End If
        reader.close
    Catch ex As SqlException
        Throw ex
    Finally
        connection.Close()
    End Try

    Return vendor
End Function

End Class
```

Figure 9-9   The code for the VendorDB class (part 2 of 2)

The code for the Invoice class

Like the Vendor class, the Invoice class shown in figure 9-10 contains private fields, a constructor, and public properties that provide access to the private fields. I want to point out two things about this class, though. First, in addition to the properties that provide access to the private fields, this class contains a property named BalanceDue that returns the balance due for an invoice. To do that, it returns the result of subtracting the payment total and the credit total from the invoice total. Because the value of this property can't be set directly, it's defined as a read-only property.

Second, the m_PaymentDate field and the PaymentDate property are declared as nullable types. That's necessary because the PaymentDate column in the Invoices table can contain a null. If you didn't define this field and property as nullable and the column contained a null value, the field would be set to the default date of 01/01/01. Then, this value would be returned by the property and displayed in the DataGridView control, which isn't what you want.

For the PaymentDate property to work correctly, the Get procedure uses the HasValue property of the field to determine if it stores a value or contains a null. Then, if it stores a value, the procedure returns the date. Otherwise, it returns Nothing.

The code for the InvoiceDB class

Figure 9-11 presents the code for the InvoiceDB class. The GetUnpaidVendorInvoices method of this class receives a vendor ID and returns a List() that contains a collection of Invoice objects for the vendor that have a balance due. Because you've seen code like this before, you shouldn't have any trouble understanding it. However, I do want to point out that to determine if the payment date is null, this method uses the IsDBNull function. Then, if it is null, the PaymentDate property is set to Nothing. Otherwise, it's set to the payment date.

The UpdatePayment method of this class receives two Invoice objects named oldInvoice and newInvoice. The oldInvoice object contains the original data for the invoice and is used to check that another user hasn't modified or deleted the invoice since it was retrieved. The newInvoice object is used to assign new values to the PaymentTotal and PaymentDate columns.

After the connection and command are created, this method creates the necessary parameters and adds them to the Parameters collection. Then, it opens the connection and executes the command. If the command is successful, True is returned to the calling procedure. If the command in unsuccessful, however, it most likely means that a concurrency error occurred. In that case, False is returned to the calling procedure. In either case, the connection is closed.

The code for the Invoice class

```
Public Class Invoice
    Private m_InvoiceID As Integer
    Private m_VendorID As Integer
    Private m_InvoiceNumber As String
    Private m_InvoiceDate As Date
    Private m_InvoiceTotal As Decimal
    Private m_PaymentTotal As Decimal
    Private m_CreditTotal As Decimal
    Private m_TermsID As Integer
    Private m_DueDate As Date
    Private m_PaymentDate As Nullable(Of Date)

    Public Sub New()

    End Sub

    Public Property InvoiceID() As Integer
        Get
            Return m_InvoiceID
        End Get
        Set(ByVal value As Integer)
            m_InvoiceID = value
        End Set
    End Property

    Public Property VendorID() As Integer
        Get
            Return m_VendorID
        End Get
        Set(ByVal value As Integer)
            m_VendorID = value
        End Set
    End Property
    .
    .
    .
    Public Property PaymentDate() As Nullable(Of Date)
        Get
            If m_PaymentDate.HasValue Then
                Return CDate(m_PaymentDate)
            Else
                Return Nothing
            End If
        End Get
        Set(ByVal value As Nullable(Of Date))
            m_PaymentDate = value
        End Set
    End Property

    Public ReadOnly Property BalanceDue() As Decimal
        Get
            Return m_InvoiceTotal - m_PaymentTotal - m_CreditTotal
        End Get
    End Property

End Class
```

Figure 9-10   The code for the Invoice class

The code for the InvoiceDB class

```vbnet
Imports System.Data.SqlClient

Public Class InvoiceDB

    Public Shared Function GetUnpaidVendorInvoices(ByVal vendorID As Integer) _
            As List(Of Invoice)
        Dim invoiceList As New List(Of Invoice)

        Dim connection As SqlConnection = PayablesDB.GetConnection
        Dim selectStatement As String _
            = "SELECT InvoiceID, VendorID, InvoiceNumber, InvoiceDate, " _
            & "InvoiceTotal, PaymentTotal, CreditTotal, " _
            & "TermsID, DueDate, PaymentDate " _
            & "FROM Invoices " _
            & "WHERE VendorID = @VendorID " _
            & "  AND InvoiceTotal - PaymentTotal - CreditTotal > 0 " _
            & "ORDER BY InvoiceDate"
        Dim selectCommand As New SqlCommand(selectStatement, connection)
        selectCommand.Parameters.AddWithValue("@VendorID", vendorID)

        Try
            connection.Open()
            Dim reader As SqlDataReader = selectCommand.ExecuteReader()
            Dim invoice As Invoice
            Do While reader.Read
                invoice = New Invoice
                invoice.InvoiceID = CInt(reader("InvoiceID"))
                invoice.VendorID = CInt(reader("VendorID"))
                invoice.InvoiceNumber = reader("InvoiceNumber").ToString
                invoice.InvoiceDate = CDate(reader("InvoiceDate"))
                invoice.InvoiceTotal = CDec(reader("InvoiceTotal"))
                invoice.PaymentTotal = CDec(reader("PaymentTotal"))
                invoice.CreditTotal = CDec(reader("CreditTotal"))
                invoice.TermsID = CInt(reader("TermsID"))
                invoice.DueDate = CDate(reader("DueDate"))
                If IsDBNull(reader("PaymentDate")) Then
                    invoice.PaymentDate = Nothing
                Else
                    invoice.PaymentDate = CDate(reader("PaymentDate"))
                End If
                invoiceList.Add(invoice)
            Loop
            reader.Close()
        Catch ex As SqlException
            Throw ex
        Finally
            connection.Close()
        End Try

        Return invoiceList
    End Function
```

Figure 9-11   The code for the InvoiceDB class (part 1 of 2)

The code for the InvoiceDB class

```
Public Shared Function UpdatePayment(ByVal oldInvoice As Invoice, _
        ByVal newInvoice As Invoice) As Boolean
    Dim connection As SqlConnection = PayablesDB.GetConnection
    Dim updateStatement As String _
        = "UPDATE Invoices " _
        & "SET PaymentTotal = @NewPaymentTotal, " _
        & "PaymentDate = @NewPaymentDate " _
        & "WHERE InvoiceID = @OldInvoiceID " _
        & "   AND VendorID = @OldVendorID " _
        & "   AND InvoiceNumber = @OldInvoiceNumber " _
        & "   AND InvoiceDate = @OldInvoiceDate " _
        & "   AND InvoiceTotal = @OldInvoiceTotal " _
        & "   AND PaymentTotal = @OldPaymentTotal " _
        & "   AND CreditTotal = @OldCreditTotal " _
        & "   AND TermsID = @OldTermsID " _
        & "   AND DueDate = @OldDueDate " _
        & "   AND (PaymentDate = @OldPaymentDate " _
        & "    OR PaymentDate IS NULL AND @OldPaymentDate IS NULL)"
    Dim updateCommand As New SqlCommand(updateStatement, connection)
    updateCommand.Parameters.AddWithValue("@NewPaymentTotal", _
        newInvoice.PaymentTotal)
    updateCommand.Parameters.AddWithValue("@NewPaymentDate", _
        newInvoice.PaymentDate)
    updateCommand.Parameters.AddWithValue("@OldInvoiceID", _
        oldInvoice.InvoiceID)
    updateCommand.Parameters.AddWithValue("@OldVendorID", _
        oldInvoice.VendorID)
    .
    .
    updateCommand.Parameters.AddWithValue("@OldDueDate", oldInvoice.DueDate)
    If Not oldInvoice.PaymentDate.HasValue Then
        updateCommand.Parameters.AddWithValue("@OldPaymentDate", _
            DBNull.Value)
    Else
        updateCommand.Parameters.AddWithValue("@OldPaymentDate", _
            oldInvoice.PaymentDate)
    End If

    Try
        connection.Open()
        Dim count As Integer = updateCommand.ExecuteNonQuery
        If count > 0 Then
            Return True
        Else
            Return False
        End If
    Catch ex As SqlException
        Throw ex
    Finally
        connection.Close()
    End Try
End Function

End Class
```

Figure 9-11   The code for the InvoiceDB class (part 2 of 2)

The code for the Vendor Invoices form

Figure 9-12 presents the code for the Vendor Invoices form. This form starts by declaring three variables. The first variable, named vendor, will store a Vendor object that the text boxes on the form are bound to. The second variable, named vendorList, will store the list of Vendor objects that the Name combo box will be bound to. The third variable, named invoiceList, will store the list of Invoice objects that the DataGridView control will be bound to.

The event handler for the Load event of the form populates these three variables. To do that, it calls two procedures named GetVendorList and GetVendorData. The GetVendorList procedure uses the GetVendorsWithBalanceDue method of the VendorDB class to populate the vendorList variable with all the vendors that have unpaid invoices. Then, it sets the DataSource property of the Name combo box to this list so that the combo box displays a list of vendor names. This works because the DisplayMember property of the combo box was set to the Name property of the Vendor object at design time using the BindingSource object.

The GetVendorData procedure displays the data for the currently selected vendor, which is the first vendor when this application starts. This procedure starts by getting the vendor ID from the Name combo box. This works because the ValueMember property of the combo box was set to the VendorID property of the Vendor object at design time. Then, it calls the GetVendorNameAndAddress method of the VendorDB class to get the data for the selected vendor, and it stores the Vendor object that's returned in the vendor variable. Next, it clears the vendor binding source and adds the Vendor object to that binding source. This binds the text boxes on the form to the Vendor object so they display the vendor data.

The next statement in the GetVendorData procedure calls the GetUnpaidVendorInvoices method of the InvoiceDB class to populate the invoiceList variable with all the unpaid invoices for the vendor. Then, it sets the DataSource property of the DataGridView control to this list, which causes the invoices to be displayed in this control.

If the user selects a different vendor from the combo box, the event handler for the SelectedIndexChanged event is executed. This event handler calls the GetVendorData procedure to retrieve the data for the selected vendor along with a list of the vendor's unpaid invoices.

The code for the Vendor Invoices form   Page 1

```
Imports PayablesData

Public Class frmVendorInvoices

    Private vendor As Vendor
    Private vendorList As List(Of Vendor)
    Private invoiceList As List(Of Invoice)

    Private Sub frmVendorInvoices_Load(ByVal sender As System.Object, _
            ByVal e As System.EventArgs) Handles MyBase.Load

        Me.GetVendorList()
        Me.GetVendorData()

    End Sub

    Private Sub GetVendorList()
        Try
            ' Get the list of Vendor objects
            ' and bind the combo box to the list
            vendorList = VendorDB.GetVendorsWithBalanceDue
            NameComboBox.DataSource = vendorList
        Catch ex As Exception
            MessageBox.Show(ex.Message, ex.GetType.ToString)
        End Try
    End Sub

    Private Sub GetVendorData()
        Dim vendorID As Integer = CInt(NameComboBox.SelectedValue)
        Try
            ' Get a Vendor object for the selected vendor
            ' and bind the text boxes to the object
            vendor = VendorDB.GetVendorNameAndAddress(vendorID)
            VendorBindingSource.Clear()
            VendorBindingSource.Add(vendor)

            ' Get the list of Invoice objects
            ' and bind the DataGridView control to the list
            invoiceList = InvoiceDB.GetUnpaidVendorInvoices(vendorID)
            InvoiceDataGridView.DataSource = invoiceList
        Catch ex As Exception
            MessageBox.Show(ex.Message, ex.GetType.ToString)
        End Try
    End Sub

    Private Sub NameComboBox_SelectedIndexChanged( _
            ByVal sender As System.Object, _
            ByVal e As System.EventArgs) _
            Handles NameComboBox.SelectedIndexChanged

        Me.GetVendorData()

    End Sub
```

Figure 9-12   The code for the Vendor Invoices form (part 1 of 2)

If the user clicks an Enter Payment button in the DataGridView control, the event handler for the CellContentClick event is executed. This event handler starts by checking that the user clicked in the column with this button and not another column in the grid. If the button column was clicked, it gets the index for the row that was clicked and retrieves the row. Then, it uses the DataBoundItem property of the row to get the Invoice object that's stored in the row.

After that, this event handler creates a new instance of the Payment Entry form. Then, it sets the public vendorName field of this form to the name of the selected vendor, it sets the public invoice field to the selected invoice, and it displays the form as a dialog box.

If the payment is posted successfully, the BindingContext property of the DataGridView control is used to get the CurrencyManager object for this control. Then, if the invoice was paid in full, the invoice is removed from the list of invoices. If additional invoices remain in the list, the currency manager is then refreshed so the invoice that was removed is no longer displayed in the data grid. If no more invoices remain in the list, however, the GetVendorList and GetVendorData procedures are called to refresh the list of names in the combo box and display the data for the first vendor. If the invoice is not paid in full, the invoice in the invoice list is replaced with the new invoice, and the currency manager is refreshed so it displays the updated data for the invoice.

If a concurrency error occurs during the update of the invoice, the DialogResult property of the Payment Entry form is set to DialogResult.Retry. Then, the GetUnpaidVendorInvoices method is called to get an updated list of invoices. If there is still at least one unpaid invoice, the DataSource property of the DataGridView control is set to this list. Otherwise, the GetVendorList and GetVendorData procedures are called to refresh the vendor list and display the data for the first vendor.

The code for the Vendor Invoices form   **Page 2**

```
Private Sub InvoiceDataGridView_CellContentClick( _
        ByVal sender As System.Object, _
        ByVal e As System.Windows.Forms.DataGridViewCellEventArgs) _
        Handles InvoiceDataGridView.CellContentClick

    If e.ColumnIndex = 11 Then ' The Enter Payment button was clicked

            ' Get the invoice from the row
            Dim i As Integer = e.RowIndex
            Dim row As DataGridViewRow = InvoiceDataGridView.Rows(i)
            Dim invoice As Invoice = CType(row.DataBoundItem, Invoice)

            ' Display the Payment Entry form to accept the payment
            Dim paymentEntryForm As New frmPaymentEntry
            paymentEntryForm.vendorName = NameComboBox.Text
            paymentEntryForm.invoice = invoice
            Dim result As DialogResult = paymentEntryForm.ShowDialog

        If result = DialogResult.OK Then
            Dim cm As CurrencyManager = CType( _
                InvoiceDataGridView.BindingContext(invoiceList), _
                CurrencyManager)
            If paymentEntryForm.invoice.BalanceDue = 0 Then
                ' Remove the invoice from the list
                invoiceList.RemoveAt(i)
                If invoiceList.Count > 0 Then
                    ' Refresh the data grid
                    cm.Refresh()
                Else
                    ' Get a current vendor list and refresh the display
                    Me.GetVendorList()
                    Me.GetVendorData()
                End If
            Else
                ' Replace the invoice and refresh the data grid
                invoiceList(i) = paymentEntryForm.invoice
                cm.Refresh()
            End If
        ElseIf result = DialogResult.Retry Then
            ' A concurrency exception occurred
            invoiceList = InvoiceDB.GetUnpaidVendorInvoices(vendor.VendorID)
            If invoiceList.Count > 0 Then
                InvoiceDataGridView.DataSource = invoiceList
            Else
                Me.GetVendorList()
                Me.GetVendorData()
            End If
        End If

    End If

    End Sub

End Class
```

Figure 9-12   The code for the Vendor Invoices form (part 2 of 2)

The code for the Payment Entry form

Figure 9-13 presents the code for the Payment Entry form. This form starts by declaring the two public fields whose values are set by the Vendor Invoices form: vendorName and invoice. Then, the event handler for the Load event of the form assigns the vendor name to the appropriate text box on the form, and it adds the Invoice object in the invoice variable to the invoice binding source so that the invoice data is displayed on the form. Finally, it displays the balance due for the invoice in the Payment text box. That way, the user can just press the Enter key to pay the invoice in full.

When the user presses the Enter key or clicks the Accept button, the event handler for the Click event of this button starts by checking that the payment amount the user entered is valid. To do that, it uses three methods of the Validator class. First, it calls the IsPresent method to check that the user entered a value. Second, it calls the IsDecimal method to check that the user entered a decimal value. Third, it calls the IsWithinRange method to check that the user entered a value between 1 and the balance due.

If the payment amount is valid, this event handler continues by creating a new Invoice object. Then, it calls the PutNewInvoice procedure to assign values to the properties of that object. Notice that because only the payment total and payment date values will be updated, most of the values for the new invoice are taken from the original invoice. Also notice that the payment date is set to the current date.

After the appropriate values are assigned to the new invoice, the UpdatePayment method of the InvoiceDB class is called to update the payment information for the invoice. If the update is unsuccessful, a message is displayed indicating that another user updated or deleted the invoice, and the DialogResult property of the form is set to DialogResult.Retry. If the update is successful, however, the new Invoice object is assigned to the original Invoice object and the DialogResult property of the form is set to DialogResult.OK.

The code for the Payment Entry form

```
Imports PayablesData

Public Class frmPaymentEntry

    Public vendorName As String
    Public invoice As Invoice

    Private Sub frmPaymentEntry_Load(ByVal sender As System.Object, _
            ByVal e As System.EventArgs) Handles MyBase.Load
        txtVendor.Text = vendorName
        InvoiceBindingSource.Add(invoice)
        txtPayment.Text = FormatNumber(invoice.BalanceDue)
    End Sub

    Private Sub btnAccept_Click(ByVal sender As System.Object, _
            ByVal e As System.EventArgs) Handles btnAccept.Click
        If Validator.IsPresent(txtPayment) AndAlso _
            Validator.IsDecimal(txtPayment) AndAlso _
            Validator.IsWithinRange(txtPayment, 1, _
                CDec(FormatNumber(invoice.BalanceDue))) Then
            Dim newInvoice As New Invoice
            Me.PutNewInvoice(newInvoice)
            Try
                If Not InvoiceDB.UpdatePayment(invoice, newInvoice) Then
                    MessageBox.Show("Another user has updated or deleted " _
                        & "that invoice.", "Database Error")
                    Me.DialogResult = DialogResult.Retry
                Else
                    invoice = newInvoice
                    Me.DialogResult = DialogResult.OK
                End If
            Catch ex As Exception
                MessageBox.Show(ex.Message, ex.GetType.ToString)
            End Try
        End If
    End Sub

    Private Sub PutNewInvoice(ByVal newInvoice As Invoice)
        newInvoice.InvoiceID = invoice.InvoiceID
        newInvoice.VendorID = invoice.VendorID
        newInvoice.InvoiceNumber = invoice.InvoiceNumber
        newInvoice.InvoiceDate = invoice.InvoiceDate
        newInvoice.InvoiceTotal = invoice.InvoiceTotal
        Dim payment As Decimal = CDec(txtPayment.Text)
        newInvoice.PaymentTotal = invoice.PaymentTotal + payment
        newInvoice.CreditTotal = invoice.CreditTotal
        newInvoice.TermsID = invoice.TermsID
        newInvoice.DueDate = invoice.DueDate
        newInvoice.PaymentDate = DateTime.Today
    End Sub

End Class
```

Figure 9-13   The code for the Payment Entry form

Perspective

As you've seen in this chapter, object data sources provide a powerful way to develop database applications. Like standard data sources, they let you develop forms that use bound controls. Unlike standard data sources, however, they let you write your own data access code, which gives you complete control over how the data is processed.

Terms

three-layer architecture
presentation layer
middle layer
database layer
object data source

Exercise 9-1   Build the Payment Entry application

In this exercise, you'll start to build the application that's presented in this chapter, but you'll use the existing PayablesData library. As a result, you won't have to code the business or database classes. This exercise will demonstrate how the use of object data sources can make it easier for you to build three-layer applications.

Start the application and set up the PayablesData library

1. Start a new project named PaymentEntry in your chapter 9 directory.

2. Add a new class library project to the solution named PayablesData. To do that, you can right-click on the solution in the Solution Explorer, select Add→New Project, click on the Class Library template, and proceed from there.

3. Add the five classes in the PayablesData library that's in the PaymentEntry application in the Book applications\Chapter 09 directory to the new PayablesData project. To do that, you can right-click on the PayablesData project in the Solution Explorer, select Add→Existing Item, and proceed from there.

4. Use the Build→Build PayablesData command to build the PayablesData project and create the DLL file for the class library.

Build the Vendor Invoices form

5. Use the procedure in figure 9-2 to create an object data source for the Vendor class in the PayablesData library. In the step for selecting the object, click on the Add Reference button and add a reference to the PayablesData library. Then, create another object data source for the Invoice class.

6. Use the procedure in figure 9-3 to drag the properties for the Vendor class onto the form so they look like the ones in figure 9-6. Then, drag the Invoice class onto the form so it creates a DataGridView control like the one in this figure.

7. Set the properties for the Name combo box using the procedure shown in figure 4-3 of chapter 4. In this case, you set DataSource to VendorBindingSource, DisplayMember to Name, and ValueMember to VendorID. Also, set the DropDownStyle property to DropDownList, and *be sure to change the (DataBindings) – Text property to none to remove the binding from the text box portion of the combo box.*

8. Test the application to see how it works. At this time, no data is displayed because the business objects that are bound to the controls haven't been populated with data.

9. Add the code for the Load event handler that's shown in figure 9-12 (part 1), and add the code for the two procedures that it calls. That will populate the business objects. Then, add the event handler for the SelectedIndexChanged event for the Name combo box.

10. Test the application to see that the form shows the data for any vendor that you select from the combo box. This should give you some idea of how the use of object data sources can help you build three-layer applications more quickly.

Build the Payment Entry form and complete the application

11. If you think you can learn more by building the rest of this application, you should be able to do so without much trouble. And if you have problems, you can refer to the complete application in the Book applications\Chapter 09 directory.

10

A complete Payable Entry application

In the last four chapters, you've seen examples of applications that use business and database classes. However, the examples in those chapters have been relatively simple so you could focus on the database programming skills that they require.

Now that you've learned those skills, you're ready to see how they all fit together in a comprehensive, real-world application. To help you do that, this chapter presents a Payable Entry application that's significantly more complicated than any of the examples you've seen so far. This application uses object data sources and transactions, and it should give you many programming ideas that you can apply to your own applications.

The user interface and class diagram

The Payable Entry application lets the user enter a new invoice (or payable) for a selected vendor, and each invoice consists of invoice data and line item data. This application lets the user add or modify vendors. And it lets the user display the line items for an existing invoice.

For each new invoice, one row is added to the Invoices table in the database, and for each line item for that invoice, one row is added to the InvoiceLineItems table. To make sure that all of the rows for a related invoice are added successfully, this application uses transactions.

This is a three-layer application that uses object data sources, because I think that's the best way to develop applications like this. As you will see, using object data sources reduces the amount of code that you have to write, but still retains the benefits that you get from developing three-layer applications.

The user interface

Figure 10-1 presents four of the forms that make up the user interface for the Payable Entry application. When this application starts, the Vendor Invoices form is displayed. From this form, the user can enter a vendor ID and click the Get Vendor button to retrieve the vendor and invoice information for that vendor and display it on the form.

Instead of entering a vendor ID, the user can search for a vendor by clicking the Find Vendor button. This displays the Find Vendor form, which lets the user enter a name and state for the search criteria. In this figure, for example, all of the vendors whose names start with the letter "w" are displayed. Then, the user can select a vendor from this list.

The user can also add or modify a vendor by clicking the Add Vendor or Modify Vendor button on the Vendor Invoices form. This displays the Add/ Modify Vendor form you saw in chapter 7. Because this form works just like the form presented in that chapter, it's not repeated here.

If the selected vendor has any existing invoices, the user can click the View Line Items button for that invoice on the Vendor Invoices form. Then, a Line Items form like the one shown in the second part of this figure is displayed.

The Vendor Invoices form

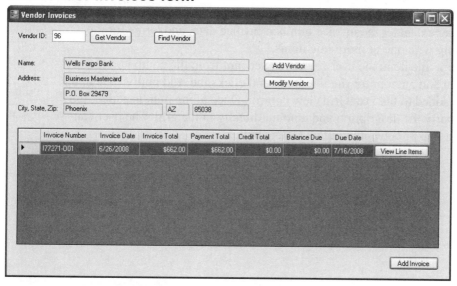

The Find Vendor form

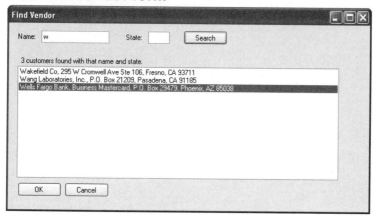

Description

- To select a vendor, the user can enter the vendor ID and click the Get Vendor button or click the Find Vendor button to display the Find Vendor form.

- From the Find Vendor form, the user can enter all or part of a name and a state code and then click the Search button to list all the vendors that match the criteria. Then, the user can highlight a vendor and click the OK button or double-click a vendor to select that vendor.

- After a vendor is selected, the name and address information for that vendor is displayed on the Vendor Invoices form, along with any existing invoices for that vendor.

- The user can also add or modify a vendor by clicking the Add Vendor or Modify Vendor button on the Vendor Invoices form. This displays a form like the one used by the Vendor Maintenance application in chapter 7.

Figure 10-1   The user interface for the Payable Entry application (part 1 of 2)

To add an invoice for a selected vendor, the user clicks the Add Invoice button on the Vendor Invoices form to display the Add Invoice form. From this form, the user can enter the invoice number, invoice date, and terms for the invoice, along with one or more line items.

To enter a line item, the user selects an account from the combo box, enters a description and amount for the line item, and clicks the Add button. Then, the line item is added to the DataGridView control. Once a line item is added, the user can modify the description and amount directly in the grid. The user can also delete a line item by clicking its Delete button.

The Line Items form

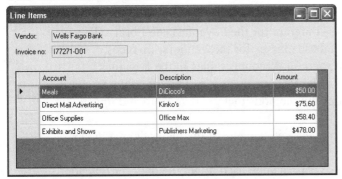

The Add Invoice form

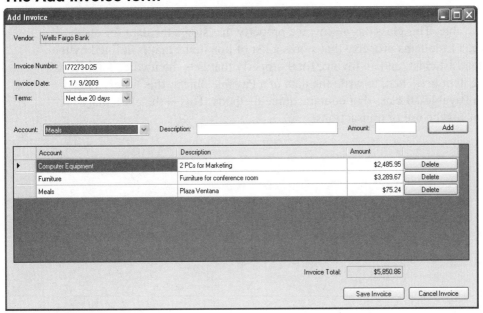

Description

- To display the line items for an invoice, the user clicks the View Line Items button for the invoice on the Vendor Invoices form.

- To enter a new invoice for a vendor, the user clicks the Add Invoice button on the Vendor Invoices form to display the Add Invoice form. Then, the user enters the invoice information and clicks the Save Invoice button.

- To enter a line item, the user selects an account, enters a description and amount, and clicks the Add button. The user can also modify the description and amount for a line item directly in the DataGridView control or delete a line item by clicking its Delete button.

- After an invoice is processed, the Add Invoice form is closed and the Vendor Invoices form is redisplayed with the new invoice. To return to the Vendor Invoices form without processing the invoice, the user can click the Cancel Invoice button.

Figure 10-1   The user interface for the Payable Entry application (part 2 of 2)

The class diagram for the PayablesData library

Figure 10-2 presents the class diagram for the PayablesData library. This library includes business and database classes for the Vendors, Invoices, InvoiceLineItems, States, Terms, and GLAccounts tables in the Payables database. For each business class like Vendor, there is a corresponding database class like VendorDB that provides the methods that get data from and update the data in the related table.

When you use object data sources, you use one of the methods in a database class to get the data for the related business object. For instance, the GetVendor method in the VendorDB database class can be used to get the data for a Vendor business object. Then, the business object is the data source for the controls that are bound to it.

The PayablesData library also contains a Payable class that defines the data for a payable. This class has an Invoice property that stores the data for one invoice, a LineItems property that stores a list of line items that is defined by the LineItemList class, and an InvoiceTotal property that gets the invoice total from the line item list. Then, to write the data in a Payable object, this library provides a PayableDB class that contains three methods. This is the class that implements the use of transactions.

The class diagram for the PayablesData library

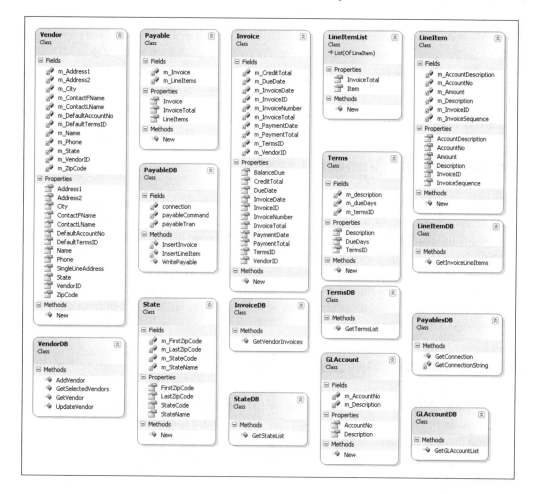

Description

- The Payable Entry application uses a business class named Payable to create a business object that holds the invoice and line item data for a payable. Then, it uses the public, shared WritePayable method of the PayableDB class to add the payable to the Invoice and InvoiceLineItems tables of the Payables database.

- The line items that are stored in a Payable object are defined by the LineItemList class. This class inherits the List() class, overloads the Item property of that class, and adds a custom InvoiceTotal property.

- Each line item is defined by the LineItem class. This class contains a property for each column in the InvoiceLineItems table, plus a property for the Description column of the GLAccounts table.

Figure 10-2   The class diagram for the PayablesData library

The code for the business classes

Most of the business classes for the Payable Entry application are like those that you've seen in the last four chapters. As a result, the topics that follow present just the code for the most important business classes used by the Payable Entry application. If you want to review the code for any of the classes that aren't presented in this chapter, though, you can review the complete application that you've downloaded from our web site.

The code for the Vendor class

The Vendor class is identical to the Vendor class used by the Payment Entry application in chapter 9 with one difference. It includes an additional property named SingleLineAddress that formats a vendor's name and address into a single line. This property is presented in figure 10-3.

The list control on the Find Vendor form is bound to this property. In contrast, the text boxes that display the vendor name and address on the Vendor Invoices form are bound to other properties of this class, as are the controls on the Add/Modify Vendor form.

The code for the Payable class

Figure 10-3 also presents the code for the Payable class. This class declares two private fields that can store an Invoice object and a LineItemList object. Notice that the constructor for this class initializes these fields to instances of the appropriate class. Then, you can use the Invoice and LineItems properties to retrieve these objects, and you can use the properties of these objects to work with the values they contain.

The last property of the Payable class, InvoiceTotal, gets the total of the line items. To do that, it uses the InvoiceTotal property of the LineItemList object. You'll see the code for this property in just a minute.

The code for the SingleLineAddress property in the Vendor class

```
Public Class Vendor

    .
    .
    .

    Public ReadOnly Property SingleLineAddress() As String
        Get
            Dim s As String
            s = Name & ", " & Address1 & ", "
            If Address2 <> "" Then
                s &= Address2 & ", "
            End If
            s &= City & ", " & State & " " & ZipCode
            Return s
        End Get
    End Property
End Class
```

The code for the Payable class

```
Public Class Payable
    Private m_Invoice As Invoice
    Private m_LineItems As LineItemList

    Public Sub New()
        m_Invoice = New Invoice
        m_LineItems = New LineItemList
    End Sub

    Public ReadOnly Property Invoice() As Invoice
        Get
            Return m_Invoice
        End Get
    End Property

    Public ReadOnly Property LineItems() As LineItemList
        Get
            Return m_LineItems
        End Get
    End Property

    Public ReadOnly Property InvoiceTotal() As Decimal
        Get
            Return m_LineItems.InvoiceTotal
        End Get
    End Property
End Class
```

Figure 10-3   The code for the Vendor and Payable classes

The code for the LineItem class

Figure 10-4 presents the code for the LineItem class. This class declares one private field and one public property for each column in the InvoiceLineItems table. In addition, it declares a private field and a public property for the Description column in the GLAccounts table. That way, this column can be displayed in the DataGridView control on the Add Invoice form, which is bound to the LineItem class.

The code for the LineItemList class

Figure 10-4 also presents the code for the LineItemList class. This class inherits the List() class and defines a list of LineItem objects. It consists of a constructor that calls the default constructor of the base class and two properties.

The Item property overloads the Item property defined by the List() class. It returns a line item from the list based on the index that's passed to it. Notice that if the index value doesn't fall within the range of indexes for the list, a value of Nothing is returned.

The InvoiceTotal property returns the total of all the line items in the list. To do that, it uses a For...Next statement to loop through the line items and accumulate a total of the Amount property.

The code for the State class

Figure 10-5 presents the code for the State class. It declares a private field and a public property for each column in the States table. The State combo box on the Add/Modify Vendor form displays the values of the StateName property and stores the values of the StateCode property of this class. The code in this class is typical of the code in the Terms and GLAccount classes.

The code for the LineItem class   **Page 1**

```
Public Class LineItem

    Private m_InvoiceID As Integer
    Private m_InvoiceSequence As Integer
    Private m_AccountNo As Integer
    Private m_AccountDescription As String
    Private m_Amount As Decimal
    Private m_Description As String

    Public Sub New()

    End Sub

    Public Property InvoiceID() As Integer
        Get
            Return m_InvoiceID
        End Get
        Set(ByVal value As Integer)
            m_InvoiceID = value
        End Set
    End Property

    Public Property InvoiceSequence() As Integer
        Get
            Return m_InvoiceSequence
        End Get
        Set(ByVal value As Integer)
            m_InvoiceSequence = value
        End Set
    End Property

    Public Property AccountNo() As Integer
        Get
            Return m_AccountNo
        End Get
        Set(ByVal value As Integer)
            m_AccountNo = value
        End Set
    End Property

    Public Property AccountDescription() As String
        Get
            Return m_AccountDescription
        End Get
        Set(ByVal value As String)
            m_AccountDescription = value
        End Set
    End Property
```

Figure 10-4   The code for the LineItem and LineItemList classes (part 1 of 2)

The code for the LineItem class

```
Public Property Amount() As Decimal
    Get
        Return m_Amount
    End Get
    Set(ByVal value As Decimal)
        m_Amount = value
    End Set
End Property

Public Property Description() As String
    Get
        Return m_Description
    End Get
    Set(ByVal value As String)
        m_Description = value
    End Set
End Property

End Class
```

The code for the LineItemList class

```
Public Class LineItemList
    Inherits List(Of LineItem)

    Public Sub New()
        MyBase.New()
    End Sub

    Default Public Overloads ReadOnly Property Item(ByVal i As Integer) _
            As LineItem
        Get
            If i < 0 OrElse i > MyBase.Count - 1 Then
                Return Nothing
            Else
                Return MyBase.Item(i)
            End If
        End Get
    End Property

    Public ReadOnly Property InvoiceTotal() As Decimal
        Get
            Dim total As Decimal
            Dim lineItem As LineItem
            For i As Integer = 0 To MyBase.Count - 1
                lineItem = MyBase.Item(i)
                total += lineItem.Amount
            Next
            Return total
        End Get
    End Property

End Class
```

Figure 10-4 The code for the LineItem and LineItemList classes (part 2 of 2)

The code for the State class

```
Public Class State
    Private m_StateCode As String
    Private m_StateName As String
    Private m_FirstZipCode As Integer
    Private m_LastZipCode As Integer

    Public Sub New()

    End Sub

    Public Property StateCode() As String
        Get
            Return m_StateCode
        End Get
        Set(ByVal value As String)
            m_StateCode = value
        End Set
    End Property

    Public Property StateName() As String
        Get
            Return m_StateName
        End Get
        Set(ByVal value As String)
            m_StateName = value
        End Set
    End Property

    Public Property FirstZipCode() As Integer
        Get
            Return m_FirstZipCode
        End Get
        Set(ByVal value As Integer)
            m_FirstZipCode = value
        End Set
    End Property

    Public Property LastZipCode() As Integer
        Get
            Return m_LastZipCode
        End Get
        Set(ByVal value As Integer)
            m_LastZipCode = value
        End Set
    End Property

End Class
```

Figure 10-5   The code for the State class

The code for the database classes

Most of the database classes for the Payable Entry application use methods like the ones that you've been studying in the last four chapters. As a result, the topics that follow present just the code for the most important database classes and methods. If you want to review the code for any of the classes that aren't presented in this chapter, though, you can review the complete application that you've downloaded from our web site.

The code for the VendorDB class

Figure 10-6 presents the code for just the GetSelectedVendors method in the VendorDB class. The other methods in this class are like the ones that you've seen in the last four chapters.

The GetSelectedVendors method is used by the Find Vendor form to retrieve the vendors that meet the name and state criteria the user enters. Notice how the Where clause of the Select statement for this method is coded. It uses the Like operator to retrieve vendors with a name and state *like* the name and state the user enters. Then, a percent sign (%) is added at the end of the values for the @Name and @State parameters. This indicates that any characters can follow the characters the user enters.

If, for example, the user enters "comp" for the name and doesn't enter anything for the state, this statement retrieves all the vendors that have a name that begins with "comp", such as Compuserve and Computerworld. However, if the user also enters "ca" for the state, the search will be further refined so it only retrieves vendors that have a name that begins with "comp" in a state that begins with "ca".

For each vendor that's retrieved, a Vendor object is created and added to a list of Vendor objects. Then, when all the vendors have been retrieved, the vendor list is returned to the calling procedure.

The code for the GetSelectedVendors method

```
Imports System.Data.SqlClient

Public Class VendorDB

    Public Shared Function GetSelectedVendors(ByVal name As String, _
            ByVal state As String) As List(Of Vendor)
        Dim vendorList As List(Of Vendor) = New List(Of Vendor)
        Dim connection As SqlConnection = PayablesDB.GetConnection
        Dim selectStatement As String _
            = "SELECT VendorID, Name, Address1, Address2, City, State, " _
            & "ZipCode, Phone, ContactFName, ContactLName, " _
            & "DefaultAccountNo, DefaultTermsID " _
            & "FROM Vendors " _
            & "WHERE (Name LIKE @Name) AND (State LIKE @State) " _
            & "ORDER BY Name"
        Dim selectCommand As SqlCommand _
            = New SqlCommand(selectStatement, connection)
        selectCommand.Parameters.AddWithValue("@Name", name & "%")
        selectCommand.Parameters.AddWithValue("@State", state & "%")
        Try
            connection.Open()
            Dim reader As SqlDataReader = selectCommand.ExecuteReader()
            Dim vendor As Vendor
            Do While reader.Read
                vendor = New Vendor
                vendor.VendorID = CInt(reader("VendorID"))
                vendor.Name = reader("Name").ToString.Trim
                vendor.Address1 = reader("Address1").ToString
                vendor.Address2 = reader("Address2").ToString
                vendor.City = reader("City").ToString.Trim
                vendor.State = reader("State").ToString.Trim
                vendor.ZipCode = reader("ZipCode").ToString.Trim
                vendor.Phone = reader("Phone").ToString
                vendor.ContactFName = reader("ContactFName").ToString
                vendor.ContactLName = reader("ContactLName").ToString
                vendor.DefaultAccountNo = CInt(reader("DefaultAccountNo"))
                vendor.DefaultTermsID = CInt(reader("DefaultTermsID"))
                vendorList.Add(vendor)
            Loop
            reader.Close()
        Catch ex As SqlException
            Throw ex
        Finally
            connection.Close()
        End Try
        Return vendorList
    End Function

    .
    .
    .


End Class
```

Figure 10-6   The code for the VendorDB class

The code for the PayableDB class

Figure 10-7 presents the code for the PayableDB class. Since this class uses transactions and performs the main function of the Payable Entry application, I'll describe it in detail. To start, this class declares three private fields that will hold the connection, command, and transaction objects.

The WritePayable method gets a Payable object as a parameter and returns an integer value that represents an invoice ID. It starts by calling the GetConnection method of the PayablesDB class to get a connection to the Payables database. Next, it opens the connection, starts a transaction on the connection, creates a command object, and sets its Connection and Transaction properties.

At this point, a SQL statement has not been assigned to the command object. That's because the same command object will be used to insert rows into the Invoices and InvoiceLineItems tables. That way, you only have to associate the transaction with a single command object. Another way to do this, however, would be to use two command objects: one for inserting a row into the Invoices table and one for inserting a row into the InvoiceLineItems table. Then, you would have to associate the transaction with both command objects if you wanted them to be executed as part of the same transaction.

After the connection and command objects are established, the WritePayable method writes the payable data to the database. To do that, it starts by calling the InsertInvoice procedure to insert the invoice into the Invoices table. Because this procedure uses properties of the Payable object, that object is passed to it. Then, the invoice ID for the new invoice that's returned by this procedure is saved in a local variable named invoiceID.

If the InsertInvoice procedure is successful, the WritePayable method continues by calling the InsertLineItem procedure for each line item in the Payable object's LineItems collection. Before it does that, though, it sets the Invoice ID property of each line item to the value that was returned by the InsertInvoice procedure, and it sets the InvoiceSequence property to the appropriate value.

If the invoice and all of the line items are written successfully, the WritePayable method commits the transaction and returns the generated invoice ID to the calling procedure. However, if an error occurs while inserting a row into the Invoices or InvoiceLineItems table, the code in the Catch block rolls back the transaction and throws the exception to the calling procedure.

The InsertInvoice procedure starts by setting the CommandText property of the command object to the Insert statement that will be used to insert the invoice. As you can see, this statement will use parameters to specify the values that are assigned to the columns in the invoice row. Then, the next statement clears the Parameters collection of the command object. That's necessary because this command is used to insert rows into both the Invoices and InvoiceLineItems tables. So different parameters will need to be created for each Insert statement. The next group of statements creates the parameters used by the statement that inserts an invoice.

The code for the PayableDB class

```
Imports System.Data.SqlClient

Public Class PayableDB
    Private Shared connection As SqlConnection
    Private Shared payableCommand As SqlCommand
    Private Shared payableTran As SqlTransaction

    Public Shared Function WritePayable(ByVal payable As Payable) As Integer

        Try
            connection = PayablesDB.GetConnection
            connection.Open()
            payableTran = connection.BeginTransaction

            payableCommand = New SqlCommand
            payableCommand.Connection = connection
            payableCommand.Transaction = payableTran

            Dim invoiceID As Integer = InsertInvoice(payable)
            Dim invoiceSequence As Integer = 0
            For Each li As LineItem In payable.LineItems
                li.InvoiceID = invoiceID
                invoiceSequence += 1
                li.InvoiceSequence = invoiceSequence
                InsertLineItem(li)
            Next
            payableTran.Commit()
            Return invoiceID
        Catch ex As SqlException
            payableTran.Rollback()
            Throw ex
        Finally
            connection.Close()
        End Try

    End Function

    Private Shared Function InsertInvoice(ByVal payable As Payable) As Integer
        payableCommand.CommandText _
            = "INSERT INTO Invoices " _
            & "(VendorID, InvoiceNumber, InvoiceDate, InvoiceTotal, " _
            & "TermsID, DueDate) " _
            & "VALUES (@VendorID, @InvoiceNumber, @InvoiceDate, " _
            & "@InvoiceTotal, @TermsID, @DueDate)"
        payableCommand.Parameters.Clear()

        payableCommand.Parameters.AddWithValue("@VendorID", _
            payable.Invoice.VendorID)
        payableCommand.Parameters.AddWithValue("@InvoiceNumber", _
            payable.Invoice.InvoiceNumber)
        payableCommand.Parameters.AddWithValue("@InvoiceDate", _
            payable.Invoice.InvoiceDate)
        payableCommand.Parameters.AddWithValue("@InvoiceTotal", _
            payable.Invoice.InvoiceTotal)
```

Figure 10-7   The code for the PayableDB class (part 1 of 2)

After the parameters have been created, the InsertInvoice procedure calls the command's ExecuteNonQuery method to execute the Insert statement. Then, it changes the command's CommandText property to "SELECT IDENT_CURRENT('Invoices') FROM Invoices" and executes this statement using the ExecuteScalar method. This SQL statement returns the identity value that was generated for the invoice. This value is then returned to the WritePayable method.

The InsertLineItem procedure works similarly. It sets the CommandText property of the command object to an Insert statement that can be used to insert a line item. Then, it clears the Parameters collection of the command and creates the required parameters. Finally, it calls the ExecuteNonQuery method to insert the row.

Notice that neither the InsertInvoice nor the InsertLineItem procedure uses a Try...Catch statement to catch SQL Server exceptions. That's because each of these procedures is called within the scope of the Try...Catch statement in the WritePayable method. As a result, if a SQL Server exception occurs within either of these procedures, the Catch block in the WritePayable method will be executed.

The code for the PayableDB class   **Page 2**

```vb
        payableCommand.Parameters.AddWithValue("@TermsID", _
            payable.Invoice.TermsID)
        payableCommand.Parameters.AddWithValue("@DueDate", _
            payable.Invoice.DueDate)

        payableCommand.ExecuteNonQuery()

        payableCommand.CommandText _
            = "SELECT IDENT_CURRENT('Invoices') FROM Invoices"
        Dim invoiceID As Integer = CInt(payableCommand.ExecuteScalar)
        Return invoiceID

    End Function

    Private Shared Sub InsertLineItem(ByVal li As LineItem)
        payableCommand.CommandText _
            = "INSERT INTO InvoiceLineItems " _
            & "(InvoiceID, InvoiceSequence, AccountNo, Description, Amount) " _
            & "VALUES (@InvoiceID, @InvoiceSequence, @AccountNo, " _
            & "@Description, @Amount)"
        payableCommand.Parameters.Clear()

        payableCommand.Parameters.AddWithValue("@InvoiceID", li.InvoiceID)
        payableCommand.Parameters.AddWithValue("@InvoiceSequence", _
            li.InvoiceSequence)
        payableCommand.Parameters.AddWithValue("@AccountNo", li.AccountNo)
        payableCommand.Parameters.AddWithValue("@Description", li.Description)
        payableCommand.Parameters.AddWithValue("@Amount", li.Amount)

        payableCommand.ExecuteNonQuery()

    End Sub

End Class
```

Figure 10-7   The code for the PayableDB class (part 2 of 2)

The code for the PayablesDB class

Figure 10-8 presents the code for the PayablesDB class. Unlike the PayablesDB class used by the applications in the last four chapters, the GetConnection method in this class gets the connection string from an XML file. This file is stored in the bin\Debug directory for the application, but it would normally be stored in a central location. That way, the connection string could be used by other applications.

The code for the StateDB class

Figure 10-8 also presents the code for the StateDB class. This class contains a method named GetStateList that returns a list of all the states in the States table. This method is used to get the list of states that's displayed in the State combo box on the Add/Modify Vendor form. This code is typical of the code in the TermsDB and GLAccountDB classes.

The code for the PayablesDB class

```
Imports System.Data.SqlClient
Imports System.Xml

Public Class PayablesDB

    Public Shared Function GetConnection() As SqlConnection
        Return New SqlConnection(GetConnectionString)
    End Function

    Private Shared Function GetConnectionString() As String
        Dim xmlReader As New XmlTextReader("csPayables.xml")
        Return xmlReader.ReadElementString("Connection")
    End Function

End Class
```

The code for the StateDB class

```
Imports System.Data.SqlClient

Public Class StateDB

    Public Shared Function GetStateList() As List(Of State)
        Dim stateList As New List(Of State)
        Dim connection As SqlConnection = PayablesDB.GetConnection
        Dim selectStatement As String _
            = "SELECT StateCode, StateName, FirstZipCode, LastZipCode " _
            & "FROM States " _
            & "ORDER BY StateName"
        Dim selectCommand As New SqlCommand(selectStatement, connection)
        Try
            connection.Open()
            Dim reader As SqlDataReader = selectCommand.ExecuteReader()
            Dim state As State
            Do While reader.Read
                state = New State
                state.StateCode = reader("StateCode").ToString
                state.StateName = reader("StateName").ToString
                state.FirstZipCode = CInt(reader("FirstZipCode"))
                state.LastZipCode = CInt(reader("LastZipCode"))
                stateList.Add(state)
            Loop
            reader.Close()
        Catch ex As SqlException
            Throw ex
        Finally
            connection.Close()
        End Try
        Return stateList
    End Function

End Class
```

Figure 10-8   The code for the PayablesDB and StateDB classes

The code for the forms

The code for the forms used by the Payable Entry application follows.

The code for the Vendor Invoices form

Figure 10-9 presents the code for the Vendor Invoices form. This form starts by declaring a public variable named vendor that will store the Vendor object for the currently selected vendor. This variable is declared as public so it can be used by other forms of this application.

If the user enters a vendor ID and clicks the Get Vendor button, the Click event handler for that button calls the GetVendor procedure. This procedure calls the GetVendor method of the VendorDB class. If the vendor is found, the Vendor binding source is cleared, the new vendor is added to the binding source so its data is displayed on the form, and the Modify Vendor button is enabled. (This button is disabled when the form is first displayed.) If the vendor isn't found, an error message is displayed, the Vendor binding source is cleared so no data is displayed on the form, and the Modify Vendor button is disabled.

If the vendor is found, the Click event handler for the Get Vendor button continues by calling the GetVendorInvoices procedure. This procedure calls the GetVendorInvoices method of the InvoiceDB class to get a list of the invoices for the selected vendor. Then, the DataSource property of the DataGridView control is set to this list, the CurrencyManager object for this control is retrieved, and the currency manager is refreshed so the invoices are displayed.

If the vendor isn't found, the event handler checks if the invoice list is not equal to nothing. In other words, it checks if the GetVendorInvoices method has been called previously so the invoice list has been initialized. If it has, the invoice list is cleared and the currency manager for the DataGridView control is refreshed so no invoices are displayed.

If the user clicks the Find Vendor button, the Click event handler for that button creates an instance of the Find Vendor form and displays it as a dialog box. Then, if the user selects a vendor, that vendor is added to the Vendor binding source and the vendor's invoices are retrieved.

The event handlers for the Add Vendor and Modify Vendor buttons are similar to those event handlers in the Vendor Maintenance application you saw in chapter 7. The main difference is that, in this application, the data for a vendor is displayed by adding the Vendor object to the Vendor binding source.

If the user clicks the View Line Items button for an invoice, the CellContentClick event handler for the data grid starts by retrieving the invoice from the selected row. Then, it creates an instance of the Line Items form, sets the public invoiceID and invoiceNumber variables of that form, and displays the form.

Finally, the Click event handler for the Add Invoice button first checks that a vendor has been selected. If not, an error message is displayed. Otherwise, an instance of the Add Invoice form is created and displayed as a dialog box. Then, if an invoice is added successfully, it's added to the invoice list and the currency manager for the DataGridView control is refreshed so the invoice is displayed.

The code for the Vendor Invoices form   **Page 1**

```vb
Imports PayablesData

Public Class frmVendorInvoices
    Public vendor As Vendor
    Private invoiceList As List(Of Invoice)
    Private cm As CurrencyManager

    Private Sub btnGetVendor_Click(ByVal sender As System.Object, _
            ByVal e As System.EventArgs) Handles btnGetVendor.Click
        If Validator.IsPresent(txtVendorID) AndAlso _
           Validator.IsInt32(txtVendorID) Then
            Dim vendorID As Integer = CInt(txtVendorID.Text)
            Me.GetVendor(vendorID)
            If vendor IsNot Nothing Then
                Me.GetVendorInvoices(vendorID)
            Else
                If invoiceList IsNot Nothing Then
                    invoiceList.Clear()
                    cm.Refresh()
                End If
            End If
        End If
    End Sub

    Private Sub GetVendor(ByVal vendorID As Integer)
        Try
            vendor = VendorDB.GetVendor(vendorID)
            If vendor IsNot Nothing Then
                VendorBindingSource.Clear()
                VendorBindingSource.Add(vendor)
                btnModifyVendor.Enabled = True
            Else
                MessageBox.Show("No vendor found with this ID. " _
                    & "Please try again.", "Vendor Not Found")
                VendorBindingSource.Clear()
                btnModifyVendor.Enabled = False
            End If
        Catch ex As Exception
            MessageBox.Show(ex.Message, ex.GetType.ToString)
        End Try
    End Sub

    Private Sub GetVendorInvoices(ByVal vendorID As Integer)
        Try
            invoiceList = InvoiceDB.GetVendorInvoices(vendorID)
            InvoiceDataGridView.DataSource = invoiceList
            cm = CType(InvoiceDataGridView.BindingContext(invoiceList), _
                CurrencyManager)
            cm.Refresh()
        Catch ex As Exception
            MessageBox.Show(ex.Message, ex.GetType.ToString)
        End Try
    End Sub
```

Figure 10-9   The code for the Vendor Invoices form (part 1 of 3)

The code for the Vendor Invoices form   **Page 2**

```
Private Sub btnFindVendor_Click(ByVal sender As System.Object, _
        ByVal e As System.EventArgs) Handles btnFindVendor.Click
    Dim findVendorForm As New frmFindVendor
    Dim result As DialogResult = findVendorForm.ShowDialog()
    If result = DialogResult.OK Then
        txtVendorID.Text = vendor.VendorID.ToString
        VendorBindingSource.Clear()
        VendorBindingSource.Add(vendor)
        Me.GetVendorInvoices(vendor.VendorID)
        btnModifyVendor.Enabled = True
    End If
End Sub

Private Sub btnAddVendor_Click(ByVal sender As System.Object, _
        ByVal e As System.EventArgs) Handles btnAddVendor.Click
    Dim addModifyVendorForm As New frmAddModifyVendor
    addModifyVendorForm.addVendor = True
    Dim result As DialogResult = addModifyVendorForm.ShowDialog
    If result = DialogResult.OK Then
        txtVendorID.Text = vendor.VendorID.ToString
        VendorBindingSource.Clear()
        VendorBindingSource.Add(vendor)
        btnModifyVendor.Enabled = True
    End If
End Sub

Private Sub btnModifyVendor_Click(ByVal sender As System.Object, _
        ByVal e As System.EventArgs) Handles btnModifyVendor.Click
    Dim addModifyVendorForm As New frmAddModifyVendor
    addModifyVendorForm.addVendor = False
    Dim result As DialogResult = addModifyVendorForm.ShowDialog
    If result = DialogResult.OK Then
        VendorBindingSource.Clear()
        VendorBindingSource.Add(vendor)
    ElseIf result = DialogResult.Retry Then
        Me.GetVendor(vendor.VendorID)
        Me.GetVendorInvoices(vendor.VendorID)
    End If
End Sub
```

Figure 10-9   The code for the Vendor Invoices form (part 2 of 3)

The code for the Vendor Invoices form   **Page 3**

```
Private Sub InvoiceDataGridView_CellContentClick( _
        ByVal sender As System.Object, _
        ByVal e As System.Windows.Forms.DataGridViewCellEventArgs) _
        Handles InvoiceDataGridView.CellContentClick
    If e.ColumnIndex = 9 Then
        Dim i As Integer = e.RowIndex
        Dim row As DataGridViewRow = InvoiceDataGridView.Rows(i)
        Dim invoice As Invoice = CType(row.DataBoundItem, Invoice)

        Dim lineItemsForm As New frmLineItems
        lineItemsForm.invoiceID = invoice.InvoiceID
        lineItemsForm.invoiceNumber = invoice.InvoiceNumber
        lineItemsForm.ShowDialog()
    End If
End Sub

Private Sub btnAddInvoice_Click(ByVal sender As System.Object, _
        ByVal e As System.EventArgs) Handles btnAddInvoice.Click
    If txtVendorID.Text = "" Then
        MessageBox.Show("You must select a vendor.", "Entry Error")
    Else
        Dim AddInvoiceForm As New frmAddInvoice
        Dim result As DialogResult = frmAddInvoice.ShowDialog
        If result = DialogResult.OK Then
            invoiceList.Add(frmAddInvoice.payable.Invoice)
            cm.Refresh()
        End If
    End If
End Sub

End Class
```

Figure 10-9   The code for the Vendor Invoices form (part 3 of 3)

The code for the Find Vendor form

Figure 10-10 presents the code for the Find Vendor form. The first event handler for this form is executed when the user enters the name and state criteria for the vendors to be displayed and clicks the Search button. This event handler starts by calling the GetSelectedVendors method of the VendorDB class to get a list of Vendor objects.

As you saw earlier in this chapter, the GetSelectedVendors method uses the values the user entered into the Name and State text boxes to determine which Vendor objects to return. Then, this list of Vendor objects is stored in the vendorList variable that's declared at the module level, and the DataSource property of the list box is set to this list. Because the DisplayMember property of the list box was set to the SingleLineAddress property of the Vendor class at design time, the information for each vendor will be displayed as shown in figure 10-1.

After it sets the DataSource property of the list box, this event handler uses a Select Case statement to display a message in the label above the list box. This message indicates whether any vendors were found with the specified name and state and, if so, how many were found.

Once a list of vendors is displayed, the user can highlight a vendor and click the OK button. Then, the event handler for the Click event of this button sets the vendor variable that's declared in the Vendor Invoices form to the selected Vendor object and sets the DialogResult property of the form to DialogResult.OK. The same processing is performed if the user double-clicks on a vendor. If the user clicks the Cancel button, however, the DialogResult property of the form is automatically set to DialogResult.Cancel since the CancelButton property of the form is set to this button.

The code for the Find Vendor form

```
Imports PayablesData

Public Class frmFindVendor

    Private vendorList As List(Of Vendor)

    Private Sub btnSearch_Click(ByVal sender As System.Object, _
            ByVal e As System.EventArgs) Handles btnSearch.Click

        vendorList = VendorDB.GetSelectedVendors(txtLastName.Text, txtState.Text)
        SingleLineAddressListBox.DataSource = vendorList

        Select Case vendorList.Count
            Case 0
                lblMessage.Text = "No vendors found with that name and state."
            Case 1
                lblMessage.Text = "One vendor found with that name and state."
            Case Else
                lblMessage.Text = SingleLineAddressListBox.Items.Count _
                    & " vendors found with that name and state."
        End Select

        SingleLineAddressListBox.SelectedIndex = -1
        btnOK.Enabled = False

    End Sub

    Private Sub SingleLineAddressListBox_SelectedIndexChanged( _
            ByVal sender As System.Object, ByVal e As System.EventArgs) _
            Handles SingleLineAddressListBox.SelectedIndexChanged
        btnOK.Enabled = True
    End Sub

    Private Sub btnOK_Click(ByVal sender As System.Object, _
            ByVal e As System.EventArgs) Handles btnOK.Click
        frmVendorInvoices.vendor _
            = vendorList(SingleLineAddressListBox.SelectedIndex)
        Me.DialogResult = DialogResult.OK
    End Sub

    Private Sub SingleLineAddressListBox_DoubleClick( _
            ByVal sender As System.Object, ByVal e As System.EventArgs) _
            Handles SingleLineAddressListBox.DoubleClick
        frmVendorInvoices.vendor _
            = vendorList(SingleLineAddressListBox.SelectedIndex)
        Me.DialogResult = DialogResult.OK
    End Sub

End Class
```

Figure 10-10   The code for the Find Vendor form

The code for the Add Invoice form

Figure 10-11 presents the code for the Add Invoice form. This form starts by declaring a public variable named payable that will hold a Payable object. It's declared as public so that after a payable is added, the Vendor Invoices form can retrieve the Invoice object from the Payable object and add it to the list of invoices that are displayed on the form.

When this form is displayed, the Load event handler starts by displaying the vendor name in the Vendor text box, initializing the Text property of the Invoice Number text box to an empty string, and initializing the Value property of the Invoice Date date time picker to the current date. This is necessary because these controls are unbound. Then, it calls the GetTermsList method of the TermsDB class to get a list of terms, and it assigns this list to the DataSource property of the Terms combo box. It also sets the SelectedValue property of the combo box to the DefaultTermsID property of the Vendor object so the default terms are selected by default. Similar processing is performed for the Account combo box. Finally, a new Payable object is created and assigned to the payable variable; the LineItems property of this object, which contains a collection of LineItem objects, is assigned to the DataSource property of the DataGridView control; and the CurrencyManager object is retrieved from this control.

If the user clicks the Add button to add a line item, the Click event handler for that button starts by checking that the description and amount are valid. If so, a new LineItem object is created, its properties are set, and it's added to the LineItems collection of the Payable object. Then, the CurrencyManager object for the DataGridView control is refreshed so the new line item is displayed. Finally, the invoice total is retrieved from the Payable object and displayed on the form, the Description and Amount text boxes are cleared, and the focus is moved to the Account combo box so another line item can be entered.

If the user clicks the Delete button for a line item, the event handler for the CellContentClick event of the DataGridView control removes the line item from the LineItems collection of the Payable object. Then, it refreshes the CurrencyManager object so the line item is no longer displayed, it displays the new invoice total, and it moves the focus to the Account combo box.

The code for the Add Invoice form   **Page 1**

```
Imports PayablesData
Public Class frmAddInvoice
    Public payable As Payable
    Private cm As CurrencyManager
    Private termsList As List(Of Terms)

    Private Sub frmAddInvoice_Load(ByVal sender As System.Object, _
            ByVal e As System.EventArgs) Handles MyBase.Load
        txtVendor.Text = frmVendorInvoices.vendor.Name
        txtInvoiceNo.Text = ""
        dtpInvoiceDate.Value = DateTime.Today

        termsList = TermsDB.GetTermsList
        cboTerms.DataSource = termsList
        cboTerms.SelectedValue = frmVendorInvoices.vendor.DefaultTermsID

        Dim accountList As List(Of GLAccount) = GLAccountDB.GetGLAccountList
        AccountNoComboBox.DataSource = accountList
        cboAccountNo.SelectedValue = frmVendorInvoices.vendor.DefaultAccountNo

        payable = New Payable

        LineItemDataGridView.DataSource = payable.LineItems
        cm = CType(LineItemDataGridView.BindingContext(payable.LineItems), _
            CurrencyManager)

        txtInvoiceNo.Select()
    End Sub

    Private Sub btnAdd_Click(ByVal sender As System.Object, _
            ByVal e As System.EventArgs) Handles btnAdd.Click
        If IsValidData() Then
            Dim lineItem As New LineItem
            lineItem.AccountNo = CInt(AccountNoComboBox.SelectedValue)
            lineItem.AccountDescription = AccountNoComboBox.Text
            lineItem.Description = txtDescription.Text
            lineItem.Amount = CDec(txtAmount.Text)
            payable.LineItems.Add(lineItem)
            cm.Refresh()
            txtInvoiceTotal.Text = FormatCurrency(payable.InvoiceTotal)
            txtDescription.Text = ""
            txtAmount.Text = ""
            AccountNoComboBox.Select()
        End If
    End Sub

    Private Sub LineItemDataGridView_CellContentClick( _
            ByVal sender As System.Object, _
            ByVal e As System.Windows.Forms.DataGridViewCellEventArgs) _
            Handles LineItemDataGridView.CellContentClick
        If e.ColumnIndex = 6 Then
            payable.LineItems.RemoveAt(e.RowIndex)
            cm.Refresh()
            txtInvoiceTotal.Text = FormatCurrency(payable.InvoiceTotal)
            AccountNoComboBox.Select()
        End If
    End Sub
```

Figure 10-11   The code for the Add Invoice and Line Items forms (part 1 of 2)

The last event handler is executed when the user clicks the Save Invoice button. This event handler starts by making sure that at least one line item has been entered. If so, it sets the properties of the Invoice object that's stored in the Payable object. Then, it calls the WritePayable method of the PayableDB class to add the invoice and line items to the Payables database. If the invoice ID that's returned by this method is equal to zero, it indicates that the invoice wasn't added. In that case, an error message is displayed and the DialogResult property of the form is set to DialogResult.Cancel. Otherwise, the invoiceID property of the Invoice object is set to the new invoice ID and the DialogResult property of the form is set to DialogResult.OK.

The code for the Line Items form

Figure 10-11 also presents the code for the Line Items form. This form declares two public variables: invoiceID and invoiceNumber. The values of these variables are set by the Vendor Invoices form before this form is displayed.

The Load event for this form starts by calling the GetInvoiceLineItems method of the LineItemDB class to get the line items for the selected invoice and store them in a list. Then, the DataSource property of the DataGridView control is set to this list so it displays the line items. Finally, the vendor name and invoice number are displayed in the text boxes on the form.

The code for the Add Invoice form   **Page 2**

```vb
    Private Sub btnSave_Click(ByVal sender As System.Object, _
            ByVal e As System.EventArgs) Handles btnSave.Click
        If payable.LineItems.Count = 0 Then
            MessageBox.Show("You must add at least one line item.", _
                "Entry Error")
            AccountNoComboBox.Select()
        Else
            payable.Invoice.VendorID = frmVendorInvoices.vendor.VendorID
            payable.Invoice.InvoiceNumber = InvoiceNumberTextBox.Text
            payable.Invoice.InvoiceDate = InvoiceDateDateTimePicker.Value
            payable.Invoice.InvoiceTotal = payable.LineItems.InvoiceTotal
            payable.Invoice.TermsID = CInt(TermsIDComboBox.SelectedValue)
            Dim dueDays As Integer _
                = termsList(TermsIDComboBox.SelectedIndex).DueDays
            payable.Invoice.DueDate _
                = payable.Invoice.InvoiceDate.AddDays(dueDays)
            Try
                Dim invoiceID As Integer = PayableDB.WritePayable(payable)
                If invoiceID = 0 Then
                    MessageBox.Show("A database error occurred. " _
                        & "The invoice was not posted.", "Database Error")
                    Me.DialogResult = DialogResult.Cancel
                Else
                    payable.Invoice.InvoiceID = invoiceID
                    Me.DialogResult = DialogResult.OK
                End If
            Catch ex As Exception
                MessageBox.Show(ex.Message, ex.GetType.ToString)
            End Try
        End If
    End Sub

    Private Function IsValidData() As Boolean
        Return Validator.IsPresent(txtDescription) AndAlso _
               Validator.IsPresent(txtAmount) AndAlso _
               Validator.IsDecimal(txtAmount)
    End Function

End Class
```

The code for the Line Items form

```vb
Imports PayablesData
Public Class frmLineItems
    Public invoiceID As Integer
    Public invoiceNumber As String

    Private Sub frmLineItems_Load(ByVal sender As System.Object, _
            ByVal e As System.EventArgs) Handles MyBase.Load
        Dim lineItemList As List(Of LineItem) _
            = LineItemDB.GetInvoiceLineItems(invoiceID)
        LineItemDataGridView.DataSource = lineItemList
        txtVendor.Text = frmVendorInvoices.vendor.Name
        txtInvoiceNo.Text = invoiceNumber
    End Sub
End Class
```

Figure 10-11   The code for the Add Invoice and Line Items forms (part 2 of 2)

The code for the Add/Modify Vendor form

Figure 10-12 presents the code for the Add/Modify Vendor form. Although this form works like the Add/Modify Vendor form in chapter 7, its code is somewhat different since it uses object data sources. As a result, you may want to compare the code in this chapter to the code in chapter 7.

This form starts by declaring a public variable named addVendor that indicates whether a vendor is being added or modified. This variable is set by the Vendor Invoices form before the form is displayed. In addition, three private variables are declared: newVendor will store a Vendor object that contains any changes the user makes; oldVendor will store a Vendor object that contains the original data for the vendor, and phoneBinding will store the Binding object for the Phone text box.

The Load event handler for the form starts by calling the LoadComboBoxes procedure, which gets the list of objects to be displayed in each box and sets its DataSource property to the list. Here, the DisplayMember and ValueMember properties of the boxes don't have to be set because they're set at design time.

Next, if a vendor is being added, an instance of the Vendor object is created and stored in the newVendor variable. But if a vendor is being modified, the Vendor object for the current vendor is stored in the oldVendor variable. In addition, a new Vendor object is created and stored in the newVendor variable, and the PutNewVendor procedure is called to assign the properties of the oldVendor object to the newVendor object. At this point, the oldVendor and newVendor objects have identical data.

The next set of statements retrieve the Binding object for the Phone text box and wire its Format and Parse events to event handlers. The Format event handler formats the phone number when it's displayed in the text box. In contrast, the Parse event handler removes the formatting when the value in the control changes so it won't be stored in the database. Finally, the Load event handler adds the newVendor object to the Vendor binding source. This causes the current data for the vendor to be displayed on the form.

If the user clicks the Accept button, the Click event handler for this button starts by checking if the data is valid. If it is and a vendor is being added, the AddVendor method of the VendorDB class is called to add the vendor to the database, and the vendorID that's returned by this method is stored in the VendorID property of the newVendor object. Then, this object is assigned to the Vendor object declared by the Vendor Invoices form, and the DialogResult property of the form is set to DialogResult.OK.

If a vendor is being modified, this event handler calls the UpdateVendor method of the VendorDB class, and both the oldVendor and newVendor objects are passed to this method. That way, the oldVendor object can be used to perform concurrency checking. If the update is successful, the Vendor object declared by the Vendor Invoices form is set to the newVendor object, and the DialogResult property of the form is set to DialogResult.OK. Otherwise, an error message is displayed indicating that the vendor row has been updated or deleted, and the DialogResult property is set to DialogResult.Retry.

The code for the Add/Modify Vendor form

```
Imports PayablesData

Public Class frmAddModifyVendor

    Public addVendor As Boolean
    Private oldVendor As Vendor
    Private newVendor As Vendor
    Private phoneBinding As Binding

    Private Sub frmAddModifyVendor_Load(ByVal sender As System.Object, _
            ByVal e As System.EventArgs) Handles MyBase.Load

        Me.LoadComboBoxes()

        If addVendor Then
            Me.Text = "Add Vendor"
            newVendor = New Vendor
        Else
            Me.Text = "Modify Vendor"
            oldVendor = frmVendorInvoices.vendor
            newVendor = New Vendor
            Me.PutNewVendor()
        End If

        phoneBinding = PhoneTextBox.DataBindings("Text")
        AddHandler phoneBinding.Format, AddressOf FormatPhoneNumber
        AddHandler phoneBinding.Parse, AddressOf UnformatPhoneNumber

        VendorBindingSource.Add(newVendor)

    End Sub

    Private Sub LoadComboBoxes()
        Try
            Dim stateList As List(Of State)
            stateList = StateDB.GetStateList
            StateComboBox.DataSource = stateList

            Dim termsList As List(Of Terms)
            termsList = TermsDB.GetTermsList
            cboTerms.DataSource = termsList

            Dim accountList As List(Of GLAccount)
            accountList = GLAccountDB.GetGLAccountList
            cboAccounts.DataSource = accountList
        Catch ex As Exception
            MessageBox.Show(ex.Message, ex.GetType.ToString)
        End Try
    End Sub
```

Figure 10-12   The code for the Add/Modify Vendor form (part 1 of 3)

The code for the Add/Modify Vendor form

```
Private Sub FormatPhoneNumber(ByVal sender As Object, _
        ByVal e As ConvertEventArgs)
    If e.Value IsNot Nothing Then
        If e.Value.GetType.ToString = "System.String" Then
            Dim s As String = e.Value.ToString
            If IsNumeric(s) Then
                If s.Length = 10 Then
                    e.Value = s.Substring(0, 3) & "." _
                            & s.Substring(3, 3) & "." _
                            & s.Substring(6, 4)
                End If
            End If
        End If
    End If
End Sub

Private Sub UnformatPhoneNumber(ByVal sender As Object, _
        ByVal e As ConvertEventArgs)
    Dim s As String = e.Value.ToString
    e.Value = s.Substring(0, 3) _
            & s.Substring(4, 3) _
            & s.Substring(8, 4)
End Sub

Private Sub PutNewVendor()
    newVendor.VendorID = oldVendor.VendorID
    newVendor.Name = oldVendor.Name
    newVendor.Address1 = oldVendor.Address1
    newVendor.Address2 = oldVendor.Address2
    newVendor.City = oldVendor.City
    newVendor.State = oldVendor.State
    newVendor.ZipCode = oldVendor.ZipCode
    newVendor.DefaultTermsID = oldVendor.DefaultTermsID
    newVendor.DefaultAccountNo = oldVendor.DefaultAccountNo
    newVendor.Phone = oldVendor.Phone
    newVendor.ContactFName = oldVendor.ContactFName
    newVendor.ContactLName = oldVendor.ContactLName
End Sub
```

Figure 10-12   The code for the Add/Modify Vendor form (part 2 of 3)

The code for the Add/Modify Vendor form   **Page 3**

```
Private Sub btnAccept_Click(ByVal sender As System.Object, _
        ByVal e As System.EventArgs) Handles btnAccept.Click
    If IsValidData() Then
        If addVendor Then
            Try
                newVendor.VendorID = VendorDB.AddVendor(newVendor)
                frmVendorInvoices.vendor = newVendor
                Me.DialogResult = DialogResult.OK
            Catch ex As Exception
                MessageBox.Show(ex.Message, ex.GetType.ToString)
            End Try
        Else
            Try
                If VendorDB.UpdateVendor(oldVendor, newVendor) Then
                    frmVendorInvoices.vendor = newVendor
                    Me.DialogResult = DialogResult.OK
                Else
                    MessageBox.Show("Another user has updated or deleted " _
                        & "that vendor.", "Database Error")
                    Me.DialogResult = DialogResult.Retry
                End If
            Catch ex As Exception
                MessageBox.Show(ex.Message, ex.GetType.ToString)
            End Try
        End If
    End If
End Sub

Private Function IsValidData() As Boolean
    If Validator.IsPresent(NameTextBox) AndAlso _
            Validator.IsPresent(Address1TextBox) AndAlso _
            Validator.IsPresent(CityTextBox) AndAlso _
            Validator.IsPresent(StateComboBox) AndAlso _
            Validator.IsPresent(ZipCodeTextBox) AndAlso _
            Validator.IsPresent(cboTerms) AndAlso _
            Validator.IsPresent(cboAccounts) Then
        If PhoneTextBox.Text <> "" Then
            If Validator.IsPhoneNumber(PhoneTextBox) Then
                Return True
            Else
                Return False
            End If
        Else
            Return True
        End If
    Else
        Return False
    End If

End Function
```

Figure 10-12   The code for the Add/Modify Vendor form (part 3 of 3)

Perspective

Now that you've seen the code for the Payable Entry application, you should have a better feel for how you can use object data sources. As you've seen, they're particularly useful for working with controls like the DataGridView control that's designed for working with bound data. But they also make it easier to work with the data in standard controls like text boxes and combo boxes.

You should also have a better idea of when and how transactions should be used. In particular, you've seen how you can use special database classes to implement the use of transactions.

At this point, you may also be thinking that developing all of the code that's required for a three-layer application is a lot of hard work. Although that's true, you should keep in mind that all of the code for the business and database classes can be reused by other applications. So you only have to write this code once.

In fact, if you work in a shop with other programmers, some of this code may already be written for you. In that case, you may need to add new properties and methods to these classes to provide additional functionality, but that should be easy to do once you develop some basic properties and methods like the ones shown in this chapter.

Exercise 10-1   Revise the code for using transactions in the Payable Entry application

In this exercise, you'll modify the way transactions are used by the Payable Entry application that has been presented in this chapter. That will give you some practice working with transactions.

1. Open the Payable Entry application in your chapter 10 directory.

2. Review the code in the PayableDB class that implements the use of transactions. Note that it uses just one command object for three different types of SQL statements, so the properties of the command have to be changed each time a new type of SQL statement is executed.

3. Modify the code in the PayableDB class so it uses a separate command object for each type of SQL statement that is executed, but still implements the use of transactions.

4. Test your modifications.

Section 4

How to use LINQ

In the last three sections of this book, you learned the basic techniques for using ADO.NET in your Windows applications. With that as background, the chapters in this section will show you how you to use a new feature of Visual Basic 2008 called LINQ. As you'll see, you can use LINQ to query a data source using constructs that are built into the Visual Basic language.

In chapter 11, you'll learn how LINQ works and how to code basic LINQ queries to retrieve data from generic lists. Then, in chapter 12, you'll learn how to use LINQ to query a dataset. In chapters 13 and 14, you'll learn how to use LINQ to query and update a SQL Server database. In chapter 15, you'll learn how to use the LINQ data source control to work with a SQL Server database from a web application. And in chapter 16, you'll learn how to use LINQ to query and work with XML. When you're done with this section, you'll have the skills you need to use LINQ in your own business applications.

11

An introduction to LINQ

In this chapter, you'll learn the basic concepts and skills for using a new feature of Visual Basic 2008 called LINQ. To illustrate these concepts and skills, I'll use an implementation of LINQ called LINQ to Objects. You use LINQ to Objects to work with in-memory data structures such as generic lists and arrays.

In section 3 of this book, for example, you saw that you frequently return the data from a database in a generic list. When you do that, you can use LINQ to Objects to query the data in that list. Although this implementation of LINQ isn't technically part of ADO.NET, it will help you understand the basic skills for using LINQ. And that will prepare you for learning how to use LINQ with datasets, relational databases, and XML.

Basic concepts for working with LINQ

As its name implies, *LINQ*, or *Language-Integrated Query*, lets you query a data source using the Visual Basic language. Before you learn how to code LINQ queries, you need to learn some concepts related to LINQ, such as how LINQ is implemented and what the three stages of a query operation are. You'll also want to know about the new features of Visual Basic 2008 that support LINQ and the LINQ providers that are included with Visual Basic 2008. And you'll want to know about the advantages you'll get from using LINQ so you can decide for yourself if it's a feature you want to use.

How LINQ is implemented

LINQ is implemented as a set of methods that are defined by the Enumerable and Queryable classes. Because these methods can only be used in a query operation, they're referred to as *query operators*. Although you can call the query operators directly by coding a *method-based query*, you're more likely to use the clauses Visual Basic provides that give you access to the operators. When you use Visual Basic clauses to code a LINQ query, the result is called a *query expression*.

Figure 11-1 presents the Visual Basic clauses you're most likely to use in a query expression. If you've ever coded a query using SQL, you shouldn't have any trouble understanding what most of these clauses do. For example, you use the From clause to identify the data source for the query. You use the Where clause to filter the data that's returned by the query. And you use the Select clause to identify the fields you want to be returned by the query. You'll learn how to code queries that use all of these clauses later in this chapter.

Advantages of using LINQ

Figure 11-1 also lists several advantages of LINQ. Probably the biggest advantage is that it lets you query different types of data sources using the same language. In this chapter, for example, you'll see how to use LINQ to query a generic list of objects. Then, in the chapters that follow, you'll see how to use LINQ to query datasets, SQL Server databases, and XML.

The key to making this work is that the query language is integrated into Visual Basic. Because of that, you don't have to learn a different query language for each type of data source you want to query. In addition, as you enter your queries, you can take advantage of the IntelliSense features that are provided for the Visual Basic language. The compiler can catch errors in the query, such as a field that doesn't exist in the data source, so that you don't get errors at runtime. And when a runtime error does occur, you can use the Visual Studio debugging features to determine its cause.

Some of the Visual Basic clauses for working with LINQ

Clause	Description
From	Identifies the source of data for the query.
Where	Provides a condition that specifies which elements are retrieved from the data source.
Order By	Indicates how the elements that are returned by the query are sorted.
Select	Specifies the content of the returned elements.
Let	Performs a calculation and assigns an alias to the result that can then be used within the query.
Join	Combines data from two data sources.
Aggregate	Lets you include aggregate functions, such as Sum, Average, and Count, in a query.
Group By	Groups the returned elements and, optionally, applies aggregate functions to each group.

Advantages of using LINQ

- Makes it easier for you to query a data source by integrating the query language with Visual Basic.

- Makes it easier to develop applications that query a data source by providing IntelliSense, compile-time syntax checking, and debugging support.

- Makes it easier for you to query different types of data sources because you use the same basic syntax for each type.

- Makes it easier for you to use objects to work with relational data sources by providing designer tools that create *object-relational mappings*.

Description

- *Language-Integrated Query* (*LINQ*) provides a set of *query operators* that are implemented using *extension methods*. These methods are static members of the Enumerable and Queryable classes.

- You can work with LINQ by calling the extension methods directly or by using Visual Basic clauses that are converted to calls to the methods at compile time.

- A query that calls LINQ methods directly is called a *method-based query*. A query that uses Visual Basic clauses is called a *query expression*. You use a method-based query or query expression to identify the data you want to retrieve from a data source.

- To use LINQ with a data source, the data source must implement the IEnumerable(Of T) interface or another interface that implements IEnumerable(Of T) such as IQueryable(Of T). A data source that implements one of these interfaces is called an *enumerable type*.

Figure 11-1   An introduction to LINQ

Finally, if you're working with a relational data source such as a SQL Server database, you can use designer tools provided by Visual Studio to develop an *object-relational mapping*. Then, you can use LINQ to query the objects defined by this mapping, and the query will be converted to the form required by the data source. This can make it significantly easier to work with relational data sources.

Visual Basic 2008 features that support LINQ

Visual Basic 2008 introduced a variety of new features to support LINQ. These features are listed in the first table in figure 11-2. Most of these features can be used outside of LINQ. For the most part, though, you'll use these features when you code LINQ queries. You'll learn more about these features later in this chapter.

LINQ providers included with Visual Basic 2008

Figure 11-2 also presents the LINQ providers that are included with Visual Basic 2008. As I've already mentioned, you'll learn how to use the *LINQ to Objects* provider in this chapter to query generic lists. Then, in chapter 12, you'll learn how to use the *LINQ to DataSet* provider to query the data in a dataset. In chapter 13, you'll learn how to use the Object Relational Designer to create an object model for use with the *LINQ to SQL* provider, and you'll learn how to use that model to query a SQL Server database. Then, in chapter 14, you'll learn how to update the data in a SQL Server database using LINQ to SQL with an object model. In chapter 16, you'll learn how to use the *LINQ to XML* provider to load XML from a file, query and modify the XML in your application, and save the updated XML to a file. You'll also learn how to create XML documents and elements from scratch or from other documents and elements.

Another provider you can use with Visual Basic is *LINQ to Entities*. This provider works with an Entity Data Model that maps the data in a relational database to the objects used by your application. In chapter 17, you'll learn how to use the Entity Data Model Designer to create an Entity Data Model. Then, in chapter 18, you'll learn how to use LINQ to Entities to work with this model.

Visual Basic 2008 features that support LINQ

Feature	Description
Query expressions	Expressions with a syntax similar to SQL that can be used to retrieve and update data. Converted into method calls at compile time.
Implicitly typed variables	Variables whose types are inferred from the data that's assigned to them. Used frequently in query expressions and with query variables.
Anonymous types	An unnamed type that's created temporarily when a query returns selected fields from the data source.
Object initializers	Used with query expressions that return anonymous types to assign values to the properties of the anonymous type.
Extension methods	Provide for adding methods to a data type from outside the definition of the data type.

LINQ providers included with Visual Basic 2008

Provider	Description
LINQ to Objects	Lets you query in-memory data structures such as generic lists and arrays.
LINQ to DataSet	Lets you query the data in a typed or untyped dataset. See chapter 12 for more information.
LINQ to SQL	Lets you query and update the data in a SQL Server database. See chapters 13 and 14 for more information.
LINQ to XML	Lets you query and modify in-memory XML or the XML stored in a file. See chapter 16 for more information.
LINQ to Entities	Lets you query and update the data in any relational database. See chapter 18 for more information.

Description

- Visual Basic 2008 provides several new features that are used to implement and work with LINQ. Most of these features can also be used outside of LINQ.

- The LINQ providers perform three main functions: 1) They translate your queries into commands that the data source can execute; 2) They convert the data that's returned from the data source to the objects defined by the query; and 3) They convert objects to data when you update a data source.

- *LINQ to DataSet*, *LINQ to SQL*, and *LINQ to Entities* are collectively known as *LINQ to ADO.NET* because they work with ADO.NET objects.

- You can use the Object Relational Designer provided by Visual Studio to generate an object model for use with LINQ to SQL. See chapter 13 for information on how to use this designer.

- You can use the Entity Data Model Designer provided by Visual Studio to generate an Entity Data Model for use with LINQ to Entities. See chapter 17 for information on how to use this designer.

Figure 11-2   Visual Basic features and providers that support LINQ

The three stages of a query operation

Figure 11-3 presents the three stages of a query operation and illustrates these stages using a generic list. The first stage is to get the data source. How you do that depends on the type of data source you're working with. For the generic list shown here, getting the data source means declaring a variable to hold the list and then calling a method that returns a List(Of Invoice) objects.

The second stage is to define the *query expression*. This expression identifies the data source and the data to be retrieved from that data source. The query expression in this figure, for example, retrieves all the invoices with an invoice total greater than 20,000. It also sorts those invoices by invoice total in descending sequence. (Don't worry if you don't understand the syntax of this query expression. You'll learn how to code query expressions in the topics that follow.)

Notice here that the query expression is stored in a *query variable*. That's necessary because this query isn't executed when it's defined. Also notice that the query variable isn't declared with a type. Instead, it's given a type implicitly based on the type of elements returned by the query. As you learned in the previous figure, this is one of the new features of Visual Basic. In this case, because the query returns Invoice objects, the query variable is given the type IEnumerable(Of Invoice).

For this to work, the data source must be an *enumerable type*, which means that it implements the IEnumerable(Of T) interface. The data source can also implement the IQueryable(Of T) interface since this interface implements IEnumerable(Of T). In case you're not familiar with interfaces, they consist of a set of declarations for one or more properties, methods, and events, but they don't provide implementation for those properties, methods, and events. For the example in this figure, however, all you need to know is that the List() class implements the IEnumerable(Of T) interface.

The third stage of a query operation is to execute the query. To do that, you typically use a For Each statement like the one shown in this figure. Here, each element that's returned by the query expression is added to a string variable. Then, after all the elements have been processed, the string is displayed in a message box. As you can see, this message box lists the invoice numbers and invoice totals for all invoices with totals greater than 20,000.

When a query is defined and executed separately as shown here, the process is referred to as *deferred execution*. In contrast, queries that are executed when they're defined use *immediate execution*. Immediate execution typically occurs when a method that requires access to the individual elements returned by the query is executed on the query expression. For example, to get a count of the number of elements returned by a query, you can execute the Count method on the query expression. Then, the query will be executed immediately so the count can be calculated. You'll learn about some of the methods for returning these types of values later in this chapter.

The three stages of a query operation

1. Get the data source. If the data source is a generic list, for example, you must declare and populate the list object.

2. Define the query expression.

3. Execute the query to return the results.

A LINQ query that retrieves data from a generic list of invoices

A statement that declares and populates the list

```
Dim invoiceList As List(Of Invoice) = InvoiceDB.GetInvoices
```

A statement that defines the query expression

```
Dim invoices = From invoice In invoiceList _
               Where invoice.InvoiceTotal > 20000 _
               Order By invoice.InvoiceTotal Descending _
               Select invoice
```

Code that executes the query

```
Dim invoiceDisplay As String = "Invoice No." & vbTab _
                             & "Invoice Total" & vbCrLf
For Each invoice In invoices
    invoiceDisplay &= invoice.InvoiceNumber & vbTab & vbTab _
                    & FormatCurrency(invoice.InvoiceTotal) & vbCrLf
Next
MessageBox.Show(invoiceDisplay, "Invoices Over $20,000")
```

The resulting dialog box

Description

- The process described above is called *deferred execution* because the query isn't executed when it's defined. Instead, it's executed when the application tries to access the individual elements returned by the query, such as when the query is used in a For Each statement.

- If a query isn't executed when it's defined, it's stored in a *query variable*. In that case, the query variable is implicitly typed as IEnumerable(Of T) where T is the type of each element. In the example above, the invoices variable is assigned the type IEnumerable(Of Invoice) since the invoice list contains Invoice objects.

- If a query requires access to the individual elements identified by the query expression, such as when an aggregate value is requested, *immediate execution* occurs. In that case, the query expression isn't saved in a query variable.

Figure 11-3   The three stages of a query operation

How to code query expressions

Now that you have a basic understanding of what a LINQ query is, you need to learn the syntax for coding query expressions. That's what you'll learn in the topics that follow.

How to identify the data source for a query

To identify the source of data for a query, you use the From clause shown in figure 11-4. As you can see, this clause declares a *range variable* that will be used to represent each element of the data source, and it names the data source, which must be an enumerable type. Note that because the result of a query is an enumerable type, the data source can be a previously declared query variable. The From clause can also declare a type for the range variable, although the type is usually omitted. If it is omitted, it's determined by the type of elements in the data source.

The example in this figure shows how to use the From clause with a generic list of invoices. The first statement in this example creates a list that's based on the Invoice class and loads invoices into it using the GetInvoices method of the InvoiceDB class. Note that the Invoice class used in this example and other examples in this chapter is identical to the class presented in figure 6-7 of chapter 6, except that it doesn't include a BalanceDue method. Also note that it's not important for you to know how the GetInvoices method of the InvoiceDB class works. All you need to know is that this method returns a List(Of Invoice) object. This object is then assigned to a variable named invoiceList.

The second statement defines the query expression, which consists of just the From clause. This clause uses the name invoice for the range variable, and it identifies invoiceList as the data source. This expression is then stored in a query variable named invoices. Finally, the code that follows uses a For Each statement to loop through the invoices and calculate a sum of the InvoiceTotal field for each invoice.

At this point, you may be wondering why you would use a query expression like this. The answer is, you wouldn't. That's because you could just as easily use the For Each statement on the generic list itself. Because of that, you won't typically code the From clause by itself. It's shown by itself here to illustrate that it's the only required clause. (One exception is if you code the Aggregate clause, in which case you can omit the From clause.)

If you include other clauses in a query expression, the From clause must always be coded first. That way, Visual Basic knows what the source of data for the query is, and it can help you construct the rest of the query based on that data source. You can also code more than one From clause in a query expression to join data from two or more data sources.

The syntax of the From clause

```
From elementName1 [As type1] In collectionName1
    [, elementName2 [As type2] In collectionName2]...
```

A LINQ query that includes just a From clause

A statement that declares and populates a generic list of invoices

```
Dim invoiceList As List(Of Invoice) = InvoiceDB.GetInvoices
```

A statement that defines the query expression

```
Dim invoices = From invoice In invoiceList
```

Code that executes the query

```
Dim sum As Decimal = 0
For Each invoice In invoices
    sum += invoice.InvoiceTotal
Next
MessageBox.Show(FormatCurrency(sum), "Sum of Invoices")
```

The resulting dialog box

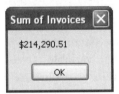

Description

- The From clause identifies the source of data for a query and declares a *range variable* that's used to iterate through the elements of the data source.

- If the range variable you use in a query expression and the range variable you use in the For Each statement that executes the query refer to the same type of elements, you should give them the same name for clarity. Otherwise, you should give them different names to indicate the type of elements they refer to.

- The From clause can identify two or more data sources, each with its own range variable. In that case, data from the two sources is joined based on the condition you specify in the Where clause. See figure 11-9 for more information on joining data.

- The From clause is required in a query expression unless the Aggregate clause is coded (see figure 11-10). If the From clause is coded with other clauses, it must be the first clause in the expression.

Figure 11-4   How to identify the data source for a query

You may have noticed in this example that the variable that's used in the query expression and the variable that's used in the For Each loop have the same name. That makes sense because they both refer to an element in the data source. However, you should know that you don't have to use the same names for these variables. In fact, when you code more sophisticated query expressions, you'll want to use different variable names to indicate the differences between the elements they refer to. That'll make more sense when you see the Group By clause later in this chapter.

How to filter the results of a query

To filter the results of a query, you use the Where clause shown in figure 11-5. On this clause, you specify a condition that an element must meet to be returned by the query. The condition is coded as a Boolean expression. The example in this figure illustrates how this works.

The Where clause in this example specifies that for an element to be returned from the generic list of invoices, the invoice's balance due, which is calculated by subtracting its PaymentTotal and CreditTotal columns from its InvoiceTotal column, must be greater than zero. In addition, the due date must be less than 15 days from the current date. Notice here that the range variable that's declared by the From clause is used in the Where clause to refer to each Invoice object. Then, the For Each statement that executes the query refers to the VendorID, InvoiceNumber, InvoiceTotal, PaymentTotal, and CreditTotal properties of each Invoice object that's returned by the query to create a string that's displayed in a message box.

The syntax of the Where clause

```
Where condition
```

A LINQ query that filters the generic list of invoices

A query expression that returns invoices with a balance due within the next 15 days

```
Dim invoices = From invoice In invoiceList _
               Where invoice.InvoiceTotal _
                   - invoice.PaymentTotal _
                   - invoice.CreditTotal > 0 _
               And invoice.DueDate < DateTime.Today.AddDays(15)
```

Code that executes the query

```
Dim invoiceDisplay As String _
    = "Vendor ID" & vbTab & "Invoice No." & vbTab & "Balance Due" & vbCrLf
For Each invoice In invoices
    invoiceDisplay &= invoice.VendorID & vbTab & vbTab _
                  & invoice.InvoiceNumber & vbTab _
                  & IIf(invoice.InvoiceNumber.Length < 8, _
                        vbTab, "").ToString _
                  & FormatCurrency(invoice.InvoiceTotal _
                  - invoice.PaymentTotal - invoice.CreditTotal) & vbCrLf
Next
MessageBox.Show(invoiceDisplay, "Vendor Invoices Due")
```

The resulting dialog box

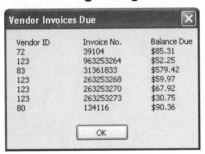

Description

- The Where clause lets you filter the data in a data source by specifying a condition that the elements of the data source must meet to be returned by the query.

- The condition is coded as a Boolean expression that can contain one or more relational and logical operators.

Figure 11-5   How to filter the results of a query

How to sort the results of a query

If you want the results of a query to be returned in a particular sequence, you can include the Order By clause in the query expression. The syntax of this clause is shown at the top of figure 11-6. This syntax indicates that you can sort by one or more expressions in either ascending or descending sequence.

To understand how this works, the example in this figure shows how you might sort the Invoice objects retrieved from a generic list of invoices. Here, the query expression includes an Order By clause that sorts the invoices by vendor ID in ascending sequence (the default), followed by balance due in descending sequence. To do that, it uses the range variable that's declared by the From clause to refer to each Invoice object just like the Where clause does. If you compare the results of this query with the results shown in the previous figure, you'll see how the sequence has changed.

To start, the vendor IDs are listed from smallest to largest. Then, within each vendor ID, the invoices are listed from those with the largest balances due to those with the smallest balances due. For example, the first invoice for vendor ID 123 has a balance due of $67.92, and the second invoice for that vendor ID has a balance due of $59.97.

The syntax of the Order By clause

```
Order By expression1 [Ascending|Descending]
        [, expression2 [Ascending|Descending]]...
```

A LINQ query that sorts the generic list of invoices

A query expression that sorts the invoices by vendor ID, due date, and balance due

```
Dim invoices = From invoice In invoiceList _
               Where invoice.InvoiceTotal _
                   - invoice.PaymentTotal _
                   - invoice.CreditTotal > 0 _
                 And invoice.DueDate < DateTime.Today.AddDays(15) _
               Order By invoice.VendorID, _
                        invoice.InvoiceTotal _
                      - invoice.PaymentTotal _
                      - invoice.CreditTotal Descending
```

Code that executes the query

```
Dim invoiceDisplay As String _
    = "Vendor ID" & vbTab & "Invoice No." & vbTab & "Balance Due" & vbCrLf
For Each invoice In invoices
    invoiceDisplay &= invoice.VendorID & vbTab & vbTab _
                    & invoice.InvoiceNumber & vbTab _
                    & IIf(invoice.InvoiceNumber.Length < 8, _
                          vbTab, "").ToString _
                    & FormatCurrency(invoice.InvoiceTotal _
                    - invoice.PaymentTotal - invoice.CreditTotal) & vbCrLf
Next
MessageBox.Show(invoiceDisplay, "Sorted Vendor Invoices Due")
```

The resulting dialog box

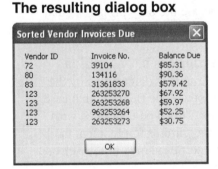

Description

- The Order By clause lets you specify how the results of the query are sorted. You can specify one or more expressions on this clause, and each expression can be sorted in ascending or descending sequence.

Figure 11-6   How to sort the results of a query

How to select fields from a query

By default, a query returns entire elements from the data source. In the examples you saw in the last three figures, the queries returned Invoice objects because the data source consisted of a generic list of Invoice objects. But you can also return selected fields of the elements. To do that, you use the Select clause shown in figure 11-7. This clause lets you identify one or more fields to be included in the query results. A query that returns something other than entire source elements is called a *projection*.

Before I show you how to return selected fields, you should know that you can include the Select clause even if you want to return entire elements. For example, assuming that the data source is a generic list of invoices and that the range variable in the From clause is named invoice, you could use the first Select clause in this figure to return Invoice objects. That means that the results of the queries in the last three figures would be the same regardless of whether this Select clause was included. Although the Select clause isn't required when you want to return entire elements from the data source, it's often included for completeness.

The second Select clause in this figure returns a single field of each element. In this case, it returns the InvoiceTotal property of an Invoice object. Note that because the InvoiceTotal property is defined as a Decimal type, the query variable is declared implicitly as an IEnumerable(Of Decimal) type.

The third example shows a query expression that returns selected properties from the Invoice objects. Specifically, it returns the VendorID, InvoiceNumber, InvoiceTotal, PaymentTotal, and CreditTotal properties. If you look back at the example in the previous figure, you'll see that these are the only properties that are used when the query is executed. Because of that, these are the only properties that need to be retrieved.

As I mentioned when I described the second example in this figure, if a query returns a single field, the type of the query variable is determined by the type of the field. But what if the query returns more than one field? In that case, the query variable is declared as an *anonymous type*. This type is defined with properties that are based on the selected fields. In the third example, then, the anonymous type would be defined with the five properties named in the Select clause. Note that an anonymous type doesn't have a usable name, so you can't refer to it from your code.

The last example in this figure shows how you can assign an *alias* to a column in the query results. Here, the alias Number is assigned to the InvoiceNumber column, and the alias BalanceDue is assigned to the expression that calculates the balance due. These aliases are then used as the names of the properties in the anonymous type that's created, and you can refer to them when you execute the query. In this case, the result is the same as in figure 11-6.

The syntax of the Select clause

```
Select [alias1 =] columnExpression1
    [, [alias2 =] columnExpression2]...
```

A Select clause that returns Invoice objects

```
Select invoice
```

A Select clause that returns a single field

```
Select invoice.InvoiceTotal
```

A Select clause that creates an anonymous type

```
Select invoice.VendorID, invoice.InvoiceNumber, invoice.InvoiceTotal, _
    invoice.PaymentTotal, invoice.CreditTotal
```

A LINQ query that uses aliases in the Select clause

A query expression that assigns aliases to a column and a calculated value

```
Dim invoices = From invoice In invoiceList _
               Where invoice.InvoiceTotal - invoice.PaymentTotal _
                   - invoice.CreditTotal > 0 _
                 And invoice.DueDate < DateTime.Today.AddDays(15) _
               Order By invoice.VendorID, _
                   invoice.InvoiceTotal _
                   - invoice.PaymentTotal _
                   - invoice.CreditTotal Descending _
               Select invoice.VendorID, Number = invoice.InvoiceNumber, _
                   BalanceDue = invoice.InvoiceTotal _
                       - invoice.PaymentTotal _
                       - invoice.CreditTotal
```

Code that executes the query

```
Dim invoiceDisplay As String _
    = "Vendor ID" & vbTab & "Invoice No." & vbTab & "Balance Due" & vbCrLf
For Each invoice In invoices
    invoiceDisplay &= invoice.VendorID & vbTab & vbTab _
                  & invoice.Number & vbTab _
                  & IIf(invoice.Number.Length < 8, vbTab, "").ToString _
                  & FormatCurrency(invoice.BalanceDue) & vbCrLf
Next
MessageBox.Show(invoiceDisplay, "Sorted Vendor Invoices Due")
```

Description

- The Select clause indicates the data you want to return from each element of the query results.

- A query that returns anything other than entire source elements is called a *projection*. The second, third, and fourth examples above illustrate projections.

- If a projection returns two or more fields, an *anonymous type* that contains those fields as its properties is created. This is illustrated by the third and fourth examples above.

- You can assign an *alias* to a field by coding the alias name, followed by an equals sign, followed by a column expression. You can assign an alias to an existing column in the data source or to a calculated column as shown in the fourth example above.

Figure 11-7   How to select fields from a query

How to assign an alias to the result of a calculation

In the last figure, you saw one way to assign an alias to the result of a calculation. If you look back at the example in that figure, however, you'll see that the same calculation is performed in the Where, Order By, and Select clauses. To avoid that, you can use the Let clause shown in figure 11-8.

As you can see, you can use the Let clause to assign aliases to one or more expressions. In the query expression in this figure, the Let clause calculates the balance due for each invoice and assigns the alias BalanceDue to the result of that calculation. Then, the Where, Order By, and Select clauses that follow all refer to this alias.

If you look at the code that executes this query, you'll see that it's identical to the code in figure 11-7. That's possible because both queries return an anonymous type with VendorID, Number, and BalanceDue properties. However, the query expression in this figure is much simpler because the balance due is calculated only once.

The syntax of the Let clause

```
Let alias1 = expression1 [, alias2 = expression2]...
```

A LINQ query that assigns the result of a calculation to a variable

A query expression that calculates the balance due

```
Dim invoices = From invoice In invoiceList _
               Let BalanceDue = invoice.InvoiceTotal _
                   - invoice.PaymentTotal _
                   - invoice.CreditTotal _
               Where BalanceDue > 0 _
                 And invoice.DueDate < DateTime.Today.AddDays(15) _
               Order By invoice.VendorID, _
                     BalanceDue Descending_
               Select invoice.VendorID, Number = invoice.InvoiceNumber, _
                     BalanceDue
```

Code that executes the query

```
Dim invoiceDisplay As String _
    = "Vendor ID" & vbTab & "Invoice No." & vbTab & "Balance Due" & vbCrLf
For Each invoice In invoices
    invoiceDisplay &= invoice.VendorID & vbTab & vbTab _
                   & invoice.Number & vbTab _
                   & IIf(invoice.Number.Length < 8, vbTab, "").ToString _
                   & FormatCurrency(invoice.BalanceDue) & vbCrLf
Next
MessageBox.Show(invoiceDisplay, "Sorted Vendor Invoices Due")
```

The resulting dialog box

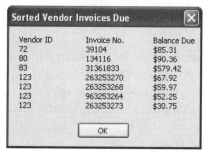

Description

- The Let clause lets you assign an alias to a calculation that you perform within a query. Then, you can use that alias in other clauses of the query that follow the Let clause.

- The Let clause can simplify a query expression because it eliminates the need to include a calculation two or more times in the same query.

Figure 11-8   How to assign an alias to the result of a calculation

How to join data from two or more data sources

Figure 11-9 shows how you can include data from two or more data sources in a query. To do that, you typically use the Join clause shown at the top of this figure. To start, this clause declares a range variable and names a data source just like the From clause does. Then, it indicates how the two data sources are related.

To illustrate, the first example in this figure joins data from the list of Invoice objects you've seen in the previous figures with a list of Vendor objects. To do that, it names the invoice list on the From clause, and it names the vendor list on the Join clause. Then, the On condition indicates that only vendors in the vendor list with vendor IDs that match vendor IDs in the invoice list should be included in the results.

Because both the invoice and vendor lists are included as data sources in this query expression, the rest of the query can refer to properties of both Invoice and Vendor objects. For example, the Order By clause in this query expression sorts the results by the BalanceDue property of the Invoice objects within the Name property of the Vendor objects. Similarly, the Select clause selects the Name property from the Vendor objects and the InvoiceNumber property from the Invoice objects. (Both clauses also include the balance due, which is defined by a Let clause.)

The remaining code in this example executes the query and displays a list that includes the vendor names, invoice numbers, and balances due. This is similar to the lists you saw in figures 11-6 and 11-8. Because the list in this figure includes the vendor names instead of the vendor IDs, however, it provides more useful information.

You can also join data without using the Join clause. To do that, you list the data sources in the From clause, as shown in the second example in this figure. Then, you code the condition that indicates how the two data sources are related on the Where clause. For instance, the query expression in this example names both the invoice and vendor lists on the From clause, and it indicates that the VendorID fields in the two lists must be equal on the Where clause.

Although this figure only shows how to join data from two data sources, you can extend this syntax to join data from additional data sources. For example, suppose you have three data sources named vendorList, invoiceList, and lineItemList. Then, you could join the data in these lists using code like this:

```
From vendor In vendorList _
Join invoice In invoiceList _
  On vendor.vendorID Equals invoice.vendorID _
Join lineItem In lineItemList _
  On invoice.invoiceID Equals lineItem.invoiceID...
```

You could also perform this join by naming all three lists in the From clause and then coding both join conditions in the Where clause. In either case, you could then refer to properties from any of the three lists in the query expression.

The basic syntax of the Join clause

```
Join elementName In collectionName On keyName1 Equals keyName2
```

A LINQ query that joins data from two data sources

A query expression that joins data from generic lists of invoices and vendors

```
Dim invoices = From invoice In invoiceList _
               Join vendor In vendorList _
               On invoice.VendorID Equals vendor.VendorID _
               Let BalanceDue = invoice.InvoiceTotal _
                              - invoice.PaymentTotal _
                              - invoice.CreditTotal _
               Where BalanceDue > 0 _
                 And invoice.DueDate < DateTime.Today.AddDays(15) _
               Order By vendor.Name, BalanceDue Descending _
               Select vendor.Name, Number = invoice.InvoiceNumber, _
                      BalanceDue
```

Code that executes the query

```
Dim invoiceDisplay As String _
    = "Vendor Name" & vbTab & vbTab & vbTab & "Invoice No." & vbTab _
    & "Balance Due" & vbCrLf
For Each invoice In invoices
    invoiceDisplay &= invoice.Name & vbTab & vbTab _
                    & IIf(invoice.Name.Length < 10, vbTab, "").ToString _
                    & IIf(invoice.Name.Length < 20, vbTab, "").ToString _
                    & invoice.Number & vbTab _
                    & IIf(invoice.Number.Length < 8, vbTab, "").ToString _
                    & FormatCurrency(invoice.BalanceDue) & vbCrLf
Next
MessageBox.Show(invoiceDisplay, "Joined Vendor and Invoice Data")
```

The resulting dialog box

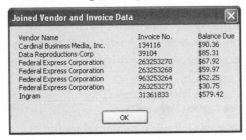

Another way to join the data in the two data sources

```
Dim invoices = From invoice In invoiceList, vendor In vendorList _
               Where invoice.VendorID = vendor.VendorID...
```

Description

- The Join clause lets you combine data from two or more data sources based on matching key values. The query results will include only those elements that meet the condition specified by the Equals operator.

- You can also join data without using the Join clause by coding the join condition as illustrated by the second example above.

Figure 11-9   How to join data from two or more data sources

How to use aggregate functions

If you want to summarize the data returned by a query, you can use the Aggregate clause shown in figure 11-10. On this clause, you name a range variable and a collection just as you do on a From clause. In fact, you'll frequently code the Aggregate clause in place of a From clause.

To identify the summary calculations you want to perform, you code the Into keyword followed by one or more expressions. Each expression must use one of the *aggregate functions* listed in this figure. These functions perform an operation on a set of selected elements. If you review the descriptions of these functions, you shouldn't have any trouble understanding how they work.

The query expression in this figure includes an Aggregate clause that uses two aggregate functions. The Average function calculates an average of the invoice totals in a list of generic invoices, and the Sum function calculates the total of all the invoices. The result is a single instance of an anonymous type that includes properties named Average and Sum. You can see how these properties are used in the code that displays the results of the query. If you want to use different names for these properties, you can assign aliases to the aggregate functions.

Note that the Into clause doesn't have to be coded immediately after the Aggregate clause. In this query expression, for example, a Where clause is coded between the Aggregate and Into clauses. Also note that a query expression that includes the Aggregate clause is executed immediately. That's because the aggregate functions require access to the individual elements of the query result.

Although you'll typically code the Aggregate clause in place of the From clause, you can also code it in addition to the From clause. For example, suppose that the Vendor class is defined with a property named Invoices that provides access to all a vendor's invoices. Then, if you wanted to calculate the total of all the invoices, you could code a query expression like this:

```
Dim invoiceTotal = From vendor In vendorList _
                   Aggregate invoice In vendor.Invoices _
                   Into Sum(invoice.InvoiceTotal)
```

If you can access the invoices directly, of course, you wouldn't want to access them through the vendors instead. As you'll see in later chapters, however, this technique becomes more useful when you're using LINQ to SQL or LINQ to Entities.

The syntax of the Aggregate clause

```
Aggregate elementName1 [As type1] In collectionName1
    [, elementName2 [As type2] In collectionName2]...
    [queryClause]...
  Into [alias1 = ] aggregateFunction1
    [, [alias2 = ] aggregateFunction2]...
```

Aggregate functions

Function	Description
All	Returns a Boolean value that specifies if all the elements of a collection satisfy a condition.
Any	Returns a Boolean value that specifies if any of the elements of a collection satisfy a condition.
Average	Calculates the average of a given field or expression.
Count	Counts the number of elements in a collection or the number of elements that satisfy a condition.
LongCount	Same as Count, but returns the count as a Long type.
Max	Calculates the maximum value of a given field or expression.
Min	Calculates the minimum value of a given field or expression.
Sum	Calculates the sum of a given field or expression.

A LINQ query that includes aggregates

A query expression that calculates the average and sum of invoice totals

```
Dim invoiceSummary = Aggregate invoice In invoiceList _
                     Where invoice.InvoiceDate > #1/1/2008# _
                     Into Average(invoice.InvoiceTotal), _
                          Sum(invoice.InvoiceTotal)
```

Code that displays the query results

```
Dim summaryDisplay As String = ""
summaryDisplay &= "Average invoice total:" & vbTab _
        & FormatCurrency(invoiceSummary.Average) & vbCrLf _
        & "Total invoices:" & vbTab & vbTab _
        & FormatCurrency(invoiceSummary.Sum)
MessageBox.Show(summaryDisplay, "Invoice Total Summary")
```

The resulting dialog box

Description

- The Aggregate clause lets you include *aggregate functions* in a query. It can be used in place of the From clause or as an additional clause in a query.

- The use of the Aggregate clause causes the query to be executed immediately.

Figure 11-10   How to use aggregate functions

How to group query results

If you want to group the elements returned by a query, you can use the Group By clause presented in figure 11-11. To start, you can list the fields or elements you want to use in the group following the Group keyword. In the query expression in this figure, I named the range variable for the query, invoice, which represents an Invoice object. That way, I can use any of the properties of the Invoice object in the Group By clause. Since this is the default, however, I could have omitted this variable.

Next, you code the By keyword followed by one or more expressions that identify the fields you want to use to group the elements. In this example, the invoices will be grouped by vendor ID. You can also assign an alias to an expression. In most cases, you'll only do that if the expression is a calculated value.

Finally, you code the Into keyword followed by one or more aggregate expressions. Each aggregate expression can use one of the aggregate functions you learned about in the previous figure. For example, the first aggregate expression shown here uses the Count() function, which returns a count of the items returned by the query.

By default, an aggregate expression is given the same name as the aggregate function it uses. If that's not what you want, you can assign an alias to the expression. In this example, I assigned the alias InvoiceCount to the Count function.

Instead of an aggregate function, one of the aggregate expressions in a Group By clause can use the Group keyword. This keyword refers to the elements that are being grouped. In this case, the Group keyword refers to Invoice objects. Because of that, I assigned an alias of Invoices to the group. Notice that I also included the Invoices alias in the Select clause. That way, the query results are defined as an anonymous type that includes the Invoice objects as well as the vendor ID and count.

You can see how this works in the code that executes this query. This code uses nested For Each statements to retrieve the query results. The outer statement uses a variable named vendor to refer to each vendor so the vendor ID and count of invoices can be retrieved for that vendor. Then, the inner statement uses the Invoices property, which refers to the invoice objects for the current vendor. This property is used to get the invoice total for each invoice. As you can see in the dialog box that's displayed, the output includes the vendor ID for each vendor, followed by a count of invoices for that vendor and a list of the invoice totals.

The syntax of the Group By clause

```
Group [listField1 [, listField2]...]
   By [alias1 = ] keyExpression1
   [, [alias2 = ] keyExpression2]...
 Into [alias3 = ] {Group|aggregateExpression1}
   [, [alias4 = ] aggregateExpression2]...
```

A LINQ query that groups data by vendor

A query expression that calculates the balance due for each vendor

```
Dim vendorsDue = From invoice In invoiceList _
               Where invoice.InvoiceTotal > 20000 _
               Group invoice By invoice.VendorID _
                Into InvoiceCount = Count(), Invoices = Group _
               Order By VendorID _
               Select VendorID, InvoiceCount, Invoices
```

Code that executes the query

```
Dim vendorDisplay As String = "Vendor ID (Invoices)" & vbTab _
                            & "Invoice Total" & vbCrLf
For Each vendor In vendorsDue
    vendorDisplay &= vendor.VendorID & " (" _
                  & vendor.InvoiceCount & ")" & vbCrLf
    For Each invoice In vendor.Invoices
        vendorDisplay &= vbTab & vbTab & vbTab _
                      & FormatCurrency(invoice.InvoiceTotal) & vbCrLf
    Next
Next
MessageBox.Show(vendorDisplay, "Invoices Due By Vendor")
```

The resulting dialog box

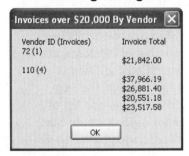

Description

- The Group By clause lets you group the elements returned by a query. It's typically used to calculate aggregate values for the grouped elements. For a list of the aggregate functions you can use, see figure 11-10.

- You can use the Group keyword in the Into clause to refer to the element that's being grouped. Then, when you execute the query, you can use the Group keyword or the alias that's assigned to it to refer to individual elements within the group.

Figure 11-11   How to group query results

How to use additional Visual Basic clauses in query expressions

In addition to the Visual Basic clauses you've already learned about, LINQ provides some additional clauses you can use in your query expressions. These clauses are summarized in figure 11-12. Although you may not use them often, you should at least know they're available in case you ever need them.

The first clause is Distinct. You can use this clause to eliminate duplicate elements from the results of a query. The first query expression in this figure illustrates how this works. This expression retrieves all the cities from the generic list of vendors. If you coded this query without the Distinct clause, the results would include the city for each vendor whether or not the vendor was in the same city as another vendor. To include each city just once, you can use the Distinct clause.

The second clause, Group Join, is a combination of the Join and Group By clauses. Like the Join clause, it lets you combine elements from two data sources. Like the Group By clause, it lets you group the elements retrieved by the query. The second query expression in this figure illustrates how this works. This expression groups invoices by vendor and returns the vendor name and the total of the invoices for each vendor.

Note that when you use the Group Join clause, all of the elements in the data source that's named on the From clause are included in the result whether or not the data source named on the Group Join clause has any matching elements. This is different from the way the Join clause works. Also note that you can include the Group keyword on the Into clause to refer to the elements that are being grouped just like you can on the Group By clause.

The next two clauses, Skip and Skip While, let you skip over elements in the data source. The Skip clause skips over a specified number of elements, and the Skip While clause skips over elements as long as a specified condition is true. The third query expression in this figure illustrates how to code the Skip While clause. This expression retrieves Vendor objects from the generic list of vendors. Here, the Skip While clause skips over any Vendor objects whose State property isn't equal to "FL". Because the Vendor objects are sorted by the State property in ascending sequence, that means that vendors with states that come before Florida, such as Arizona (AZ) and California (CA), will be skipped over.

The last two clauses, Take and Take While, let you retrieve selected elements from the beginning of the data source. The Take clause lets you retrieve a specified number of elements, and the Take While clause lets you retrieve elements as long as a condition is true. The last query expression in this figure illustrates how you might use the Take clause. Here, Invoice objects are grouped by vendor, the invoice total for each vendor is calculated, and the invoice totals for all the vendors are sorted in descending sequence. Then, the Take clause returns the first ten vendors, which are the vendors with the highest invoice totals.

Additional Visual Basic clauses for coding query expressions

Clause	Description
Distinct	Eliminates duplicate elements from the query results.
Group Join	Combines the elements from the data source named on the From clause with the elements from the data source named on the Group Join clause based on matching key values. All the elements in the From data source are included in the results, and the results are grouped by these elements.
Skip	Skips a specified number of elements from the beginning of a data source and then returns the remaining elements.
Skip While	Skips elements from the beginning of a data source as long as a specified condition is true and then returns the remaining elements.
Take	Returns a specified number of elements from the beginning of a data source.
Take While	Returns elements from the beginning of a data source as long as a specified condition is true and then skips the remaining elements.

A query that uses the Distinct clause to eliminate duplicate vendor cities

```
Dim vendorCities = From vendor In vendorList _
                   Order By vendor.City _
                   Select vendor.City _
                   Distinct
```

A query that uses the Group Join clause to get the invoice total for every vendor

```
Dim vendorTotals = From vendor In vendorList _
                   Group Join invoice In invoiceList _
                       On vendor.VendorID Equals invoice.VendorID _
                   Into InvoiceTotal = Sum(invoice.InvoiceTotal) _
                   Order By InvoiceTotal Descending _
                   Select vendor.Name, InvoiceTotal
```

A query that uses the Skip While clause to only retrieve vendors in states from Florida on

```
Dim vendors = From vendor In vendorList _
              Order By vendor.State _
              Skip While vendor.State <> "FL"
```

A query that uses the Take clause to get the 10 vendors with the largest invoice totals

```
Dim top10Vendors = From invoice In invoiceList _
                   Group invoice By invoice.VendorID _
                    Into InvoiceTotal = Sum(invoice.InvoiceTotal) _
                   Order By invoiceTotal Descending _
                   Take 10
```

Description

- Although you may not use the clauses shown here often, you should understand how they work in case you ever need to use them.

Figure 11-12   How to use additional Visual Basic clauses in query expressions

How to use extension methods and lambda expressions

Earlier in this chapter, I mentioned that the query operators provided by LINQ are implemented as methods and that you can call these methods directly rather than use the Visual Basic clauses for LINQ. In the topics that follow, you'll learn how these methods work and how you use them to implement LINQ functionality.

How extension methods work

Most of the methods that provide for LINQ functionality are implemented as *extension methods*. An extension method is similar to a regular method except that it's defined outside the data type that it's used with. The example in figure 11-13 shows how this works. Here, a function named FormattedPhoneNumber is implemented as an extension method of the String class.

You should notice several things about the code that implements this method. First, it's stored in a module, which is a requirement for extension methods. Second, the method starts with the <Extension> attribute, which identifies it as an extension method. You can also code this attribute at the start of the module to indicate that the module contains extension methods, but that's not required. Note that to use this attribute, you must import the System.Runtime.CompilerServices namespace.

The most important thing to notice here is the data type of the first parameter of the method. It identifies the .NET class or structure that the method extends. In this case, the parameter is a string, so the method extends the String class.

Once you've defined an extension method, you can use it as shown in this figure. To start, you declare a variable with the same type as the first parameter of the method. In this case, a String variable is declared and assigned the digits of a phone number. Then, the extension method is executed as a method of that string. Notice that you don't pass a value to the first parameter of the method. Instead, the value of the object on which the method is executed is assigned to this parameter. If any additional parameters are defined by the method, though, their values are passed to the method as shown here.

Extension methods used to implement LINQ functionality

Now that you have an idea of how extension methods work, you may want to know what methods are used to implement some of the common Visual Basic clauses for LINQ. These methods are listed in the table in figure 11-13. In the next figure, you'll see how you can use some of these methods in a query. Please note that there are other extension methods that aren't associated with Visual Basic clauses. You'll learn about some of these methods later in this book.

Extension methods used to implement common Visual Basic clauses for LINQ

Clause	Method
Where	Where
Order By	OrderBy, OrderByDescending, ThenBy, ThenByDescending
Select	Select
Join	Join
Group By	GroupBy
Aggregate	All, Any, Average, Count, LongCount, Max, Min, Sum

An extension method that extends the String data type

A module with an extension method that formats a phone number

```
Imports System.Runtime.CompilerServices
Module StringExtensions

    <Extension()> _
    Public Function FormattedPhoneNumber(ByVal phone As String, _
            ByVal separator As String) As String
        Return phone.Substring(0, 3) & separator _
            & phone.Substring(3, 3) & separator _
            & phone.Substring(6, 4)
    End Function

End Module
```

Code that uses the extension method

```
Dim phoneNumber As String = "5595551212"
Dim formattedPhoneNumber = phoneNumber.FormattedPhoneNumber(".")
MessageBox.Show(formattedPhoneNumber, "Extension Method")
```

The resulting dialog box

Description

- Visual Basic uses *extension methods* to implement the standard query operators provided by LINQ. These methods are defined for the Enumerable and Queryable classes.

- Extension methods provide for adding Sub or Function procedures to a data type from outside the definition of that data type. Extension methods must be coded within a module, and each extension method must be marked with the Extension attribute, which is a member of the System.Runtime.CompilerServices namespace.

- The first parameter of an extension method identifies the data type it extends. You don't pass a value to this parameter when you call the method. Instead, you call the method on an instance of the data type identified by the first parameter.

Figure 11-13   How to use extension methods

How lambda expressions work

When you code a query using extension methods, you need to know how to code lambda expressions. In short, a *lambda expression* is a function without a name that evaluates an expression and returns its value. Figure 11-14 presents the syntax of a lambda expression, which consists of the Function keyword, followed by a parameter list enclosed in parentheses and an expression.

The first example in this figure illustrates how lambda expressions work. Here, the lambda expression is a function that accepts a decimal value and then checks to see if that value is greater than 20,000. If so, it returns a True value. Otherwise, it returns a False value. Note that the lambda expression doesn't explicitly specify its return type like a standard function does. Instead, the type is inferred from the value that results when the expression is evaluated.

In this example, the lambda expression is assigned to a variable. Then, in the code that executes the lambda expression, that variable is used to refer to the lambda expression and pass in the decimal value. However, you can also code the lambda expression in-line. You'll see how that works next.

How to use lambda expressions with extension methods

Several of the extension methods that are used to implement LINQ define one or more parameters that accept lambda expressions. These parameters represent *delegates* that specify the signature of a method. For example, the second parameter of the Where method is defined as a delegate that accepts a function with two parameters. The first parameter is the source element, and the second parameter is a Boolean expression.

The second example in this figure should help you understand how this works. Here, the query uses extension methods and lambda expressions instead of Visual Basic clauses. As you review this query, remember that when you use an extension method, you execute it on an instance of the data type it extends. In this case, the extension methods are executed on the invoiceList object, which is an Enumerable type.

The query shown here uses three extension methods, and each method accepts a lambda expression that identifies two parameters. In each case, the first parameter is the source element, which is an invoice in this example. Then, the second parameter of the lambda expression for the Where method is a Boolean expression, the second parameter for the OrderBy method is an expression that specifies the key that's used for sorting, and the second parameter for the Select method is an object that identifies the values to be returned by the query. This object is an anonymous type that's declared using an *object initializer*. In this case, the object initializer includes the New and With keywords, followed by the names of the properties to be included in the type enclosed in braces.

The last example is a query that performs the same function as the previous query but uses Visual Basic clauses instead of extension methods. If you compare these two queries, I think you'll agree that the one that uses Visual Basic clauses is much simpler. Because of that, we recommend you use this technique whenever possible.

The syntax of a lambda expression

```
Function(parameterList) expression
```

A lambda expression that tests a condition

A statement that defines the lambda expression

```
Dim invoiceOver20000 = Function(total As Decimal) total > 20000
```

Code that executes the lambda expression

```
Dim invoiceTotal As Decimal = 22438.19
Dim invoiceMessage As String = ""
invoiceMessage &= "Invoice Total: " _
            & FormatCurrency(invoiceTotal) & vbCrLf _
            & "Invoice over $20,000: " _
            & invoiceOver20000(invoiceTotal)
MessageBox.Show(invoiceMessage, "Invoice Test")
```

The resulting dialog box

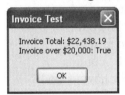

A query that uses extension methods and lambda expressions

```
Dim invoices = invoiceList _
            .Where(Function(invoice) invoice.InvoiceTotal > 20000) _
            .OrderBy(Function(invoice) invoice.VendorID) _
            .Select(Function(invoice) New With {invoice.VendorID, _
                                        invoice.InvoiceTotal})
```

The same query using Visual Basic clauses

```
Dim invoices = From invoice In invoiceList _
            Where invoice.InvoiceTotal > 20000 _
            Order By invoice.VendorID _
            Select invoice.VendorID, invoice.InvoiceTotal
```

Description

- When a LINQ query is compiled, it's translated into a method-based query. You can also code method-based queries explicitly.

- To code a method-based query, you use lambda expressions. A *lambda expression* consists of an unnamed function that evaluates a single expression and returns its value.

- Lambda expressions are typically passed as arguments to methods that accept a *delegate*, which specifies the signature of a method. Many of the LINQ methods, including the Where, OrderBy, and Select methods shown above, accept delegates as parameters.

- Because method-based queries and lambda expressions are more difficult to work with than queries that use Visual Basic clauses, we don't include the details for using them in this book. For more information, see the Visual Studio documentation for the individual query methods.

Figure 11-14   How to use lambda expressions

A Vendor Balances application that uses LINQ

The next three topics of this chapter present a simple application that uses a LINQ query to display vendor and invoice information on a form. This will help you see how you can use a query from within a Visual Basic application.

The user interface for the application

Figure 11-15 shows the user interface for the Vendor Balances application. As you can see, this interface consists of a single form that lists the balance due for each vendor that has a balance due. This list is sorted by balance due in descending sequence.

The list in this form is displayed in a ListView control. If you aren't familiar with this control, you may want to refer to Visual Studio help to find out how it works. For the purposes of this application, though, you just need to set the View property of this control to Details, and you need to define the column headings as described in this figure. In addition, you need to know how to load data into the control as shown in the next figure.

The classes used by the application

Figure 11-15 also summarizes the classes used by this application. As you can see, the Invoice class represents a single invoice in the Invoices table, and the Vendor class represents a single vendor in the Vendors table. Then, the InvoiceDB class contains a single method named GetInvoices that retrieves all the invoices from the Invoices table and returns them as a List(Of Invoice) object. Similarly, the VendorDB class contains a single method named GetVendors that retrieves all the vendors from the Vendors table and returns them as a List(Of Vendor) object. Finally, the PayablesDB class contains a method named GetConnection that returns a connection to the Payables database.

All of these classes are stored in a class library named PayablesData. Because you saw classes like these in the previous section of this book, I won't show you the code for these classes here. Instead, I'll just present the code for the form so you can see the query that's used by this application.

The Vendor Balances form

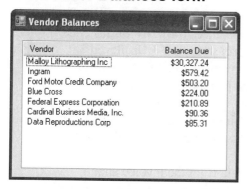

Classes used by the application

Class	Description
Invoice	Defines one property for each column in the Invoices table.
Vendor	Defines one property for each column in the Vendors table.
InvoiceDB	Defines a single method named GetInvoices that retrieves all the columns and rows from the Invoices table and stores them in a List(Of Invoice) object.
VendorDB	Defines a single method named GetVendors that retrieves all the columns and rows from the Vendors table and stores them in a List(Of Vendor) object.
PayablesDB	Defines a single method named GetConnection that's used by the GetInvoices and GetVendors methods to get a connection to the Payables database.

Description

- The Vendor Balances form uses a ListView control to display a list of the balance due for each vendor with unpaid invoices. The list is sorted by balance due in descending sequence.

- To make this work, the View property of the ListView control is set to Details, which causes the data items to be displayed in columns. In addition, the column headers for the control were added using the ColumnHeader Collection Editor. To display this editor, you can select Edit Columns from the smart tag menu for the control. Then, you can set the Text, TextAlign, and Width properties for each column as necessary.

- The Vendor Balances application uses a class library named PayablesData that contains the classes listed above.

Figure 11-15   A Vendor Balances application that uses LINQ

The code for the form

Figure 11-16 shows the code for the Vendor Balances form. All of this code is placed within the Load event handler for the form so the list is displayed when the form is loaded. To start, this code declares the variables that will store the lists of vendors and invoices. Then, it uses the methods of the InvoiceDB and VendorDB classes to load data into these lists. The next statement defines the query expression. Because this expression is similar to others you've seen in this chapter, you shouldn't have any trouble understanding how it works. So I'll just summarize it for you.

First, notice that the query expression joins data from the invoice and vendor lists. That's necessary because the vendor name will be displayed on the form along with the balance due. Second, notice that the invoices are grouped by vendor using the Name property of each vendor. Then, the balance due is calculated for each vendor using the Sum function. The result of this function is given the alias BalanceDue. This alias is used in the Where clause to restrict the elements that are returned to vendors who have a balance, and it's used in the Order By clause to sort the list by the balance due so that the largest balances are displayed first. Finally, only the vendor name and balance due are returned by the query since these are the only two values that are displayed on the form.

To load data into the ListView control, this code uses a For Each statement that loops through the query results. But first, this code checks that at least one element was returned by the query. If not, it displays a message indicating that all invoices are paid in full. Otherwise, it declares a variable named i that will be used as an index for the items that are added to the ListView control.

For each element in the query results, the For Each loop starts by adding the Name property to the Items collection of the ListView control. That causes the name to be displayed in the first column of the control. Then, the next statement adds the BalanceDue property as a subitem of the item that was just added. That causes this value to be displayed in the column following the vendor name column. Notice that this statement refers to the item by its index. Then, the last statement in the loop increments the index variable.

The code for the Vendor Balances form

```
Imports PayablesData

Public Class Form1

    Private Sub Form1_Load(ByVal sender As System.Object, _
            ByVal e As System.EventArgs) Handles MyBase.Load
        Dim invoiceList As List(Of Invoice)
        Dim vendorList As List(Of Vendor)
        Try
            invoiceList = InvoiceDB.GetInvoices
            vendorList = VendorDB.GetVendors
            Dim vendorsDue = _
                From invoice In invoiceList Join vendor In vendorList _
                  On invoice.VendorID Equals vendor.VendorID _
                Group invoice By vendor.Name _
                 Into BalanceDue = Sum(invoice.InvoiceTotal _
                                     - invoice.PaymentTotal _
                                     - invoice.CreditTotal) _
                Where BalanceDue > 0 _
                Order By BalanceDue Descending _
                Select Name, BalanceDue
            If vendorsDue.Count > 0 Then
                Dim i As Integer = 0
                For Each vendor In vendorsDue
                    lvVendorsDue.Items.Add(vendor.Name)
                    lvVendorsDue.Items(i).SubItems.Add( _
                        FormatCurrency(vendor.BalanceDue))
                    i += 1
                Next
            Else
                MessageBox.Show("All invoices are paid in full.", _
                    "No Balances Due")
                Me.Close()
            End If
        Catch ex As Exception
            MessageBox.Show(ex.Message, ex.GetType.ToString)
            Me.Close()
        End Try
    End Sub
End Class
```

Description

- The LINQ query used by this application joins data from the Vendors and Invoices tables, groups the data by vendor, and calculates the balance due for each vendor. Only vendors with a balance due greater than zero are included in the query results.

Figure 11-16   The code for the Vendor Balances form

Perspective

In this chapter, you learned the basic skills for coding and executing LINQ queries that work with generic lists. With these skills, you should be able to create queries that perform a variety of functions. However, there's a lot more to learn about LINQ than what's presented here. In particular, you'll want to learn about the three implementations of LINQ for ADO.NET. You'll learn about two of these implementations, LINQ to DataSet and LINQ to SQL, in the next three chapters. Then, in chapter 18, you'll learn how to use LINQ to Entities, which uses the new Entity Framework.

Terms

Language-Integrated Query (LINQ)	LINQ to XML
object-relational mapping	deferred execution
query operator	query variable
extension method	immediate execution
method-based query	range variable
query expression	projection
enumerable type	anonymous type
LINQ to Objects	alias
LINQ to DataSet	aggregate function
LINQ to SQL	lambda expression
LINQ to Entities	delegate
LINQ to ADO.NET	object initializer

Exercise 11-1   Create the Vendor Balances application

In this exercise, you'll develop and test the Vendor Balances application that was presented in this chapter.

Design the form

1. Open the project that's in the C:\ADO.NET 3.5 VB\Chapter 11\DisplayVendorsDue directory. In addition to the default form, this project contains the business and database classes needed by the application.

2. Add a ListView control to the form, and set the View property of this control to Details.

3. Use the smart tag menu for the ListView control to display the ColumnHeader Collection Editor. Then, define the column headings for this control so they look like the ones shown in figure 11-15.

Add code to display the invoice data

4. Open the Invoice, InvoiceDB, and PayablesDB classes and review the code that they contain. In particular, notice that the GetInvoices method in the InvoiceDB class returns the invoices in a List(Of Invoice) object.

5. Add an event handler for the Load event of the form. Then, use the GetInvoices method to get the list of invoices, and store this list in a variable.

6. Define a query expression that returns all the invoices in the invoice list that have a balance due greater than zero. Sort the invoices by balance due in descending sequence within vendor ID.

7. Use a For Each statement to execute the query and load the results into the ListView control.

8. Run the application to see how it works. At this point, the list should include one item for each invoice with a balance due. Make any necessary corrections, and then end the application.

Enhance the application to display the vendor names

9. Open the Vendor and VendorDB classes and review the code they contain. In particular, notice that the GetVendors method in the VendorDB class returns the vendors in a List(Of Vendor) object.

10. Add code at the beginning of the Load event handler that uses the GetVendors method to get the list of vendors, and store this list in a variable.

11. Modify the query expression so it joins the data in the vendor list with the data in the invoice list, so it sorts the results by balance due in descending sequence within vendor name, and so only the fields that are needed by the form are returned by the query.

12. Modify the For Each statement so it adds the vendor name instead of the vendor ID to the ListView control.

13. Run the application to make sure it works correctly. Although the list will still include one item for each invoice with a balance due, the items will be listed by vendor name instead of vendor ID.

Enhance the application to group the invoices by vendor

14. Modify the query expression so it groups the invoices by vendor name and calculates the balance due for each group. In addition, modify the sort sequence so it doesn't include the vendor name.

15. Run the application to make sure it works correctly. If it does, the form should look like the one shown in figure 11-15. When you're done, close the solution.

12

How to use LINQ to DataSet

In the last chapter, you learned the basic skills for creating and using LINQ queries. These are the skills you'll need regardless of the implementation of LINQ you're using. Now, in this chapter, you'll learn the skills that are specific to using LINQ with datasets. As you'll see, using LINQ to DataSet makes querying datasets quick and easy.

Although you learned some of the skills for working with typed datasets in section 2 of this book, you'll need to learn some additional skills before you can use LINQ with typed datasets. Specifically, you'll need to know how to work with typed datasets and table adapters in code. So I'll present those skills in this chapter. I'll also present the basic skills for working with untyped datasets so I can show you how to use LINQ to work with untyped datasets as well as typed datasets.

An introduction to LINQ to DataSet

Before I show you how to use LINQ to query a dataset, you should have a
general idea of how LINQ to DataSet works. In addition, you'll want to know
how the features that are specific to LINQ to DataSet are implemented.

How LINQ to DataSet works

LINQ to DataSet is built on the existing ADO.NET architecture. That means
that when you use LINQ to DataSet, you still use ADO.NET to work with the
database. This is illustrated in figure 12-1.

Here, you can see that when a query is performed on a dataset, it's processed by the LINQ to DataSet provider. This provider retrieves the requested
data from the dataset and returns the query results. Then, you can work with the
query results from your application.

Note that the dataset is still loaded using the objects provided by one of the
.NET data providers. In other words, LINQ to DataSet affects only how you
retrieve data from the dataset, not how you retrieve data from the database. In
fact, before you query a dataset, you have to load data into the dataset.

Extension methods for working with datasets

The two tables in figure 12-1 present the extension methods for using LINQ
with datasets. The three methods in the first table extend the DataTable class,
and the two methods in the second table extend the DataRow class. You'll learn
how to use all these methods except for SetField later in this chapter. Because
you won't use SetField often, it's not presented here. For more information on
this method, please see the Visual Studio documentation.

How LINQ to DataSet works with ADO.NET

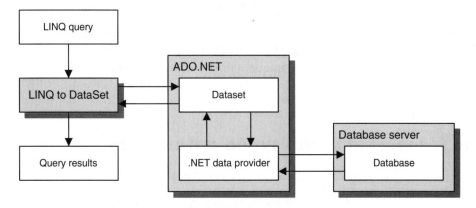

Extension methods of the DataTableExtensions class

Method	Description
AsDataView	Creates a data view from the results of a LINQ query. See figure 12-5 for details.
AsEnumerable	Returns an IEnumerable(Of DataRow) object for a table in an untyped dataset. See figure 12-11 for details.
CopyToDataTable	Creates a data table from the results of a LINQ query. See figure 12-6 for details.

Extension methods of the DataRowExtensions class

Method	Description
Field	Provides access to a column of a data row in an untyped dataset. See figure 12-11 for details.
SetField	Assigns a new value to a column of a data row in an untyped dataset.

Description

- LINQ to DataSet makes it easy to query the data in a dataset. It builds on ADO.NET and uses the existing ADO.NET architecture.

- The functionality that's provided specifically for LINQ to DataSet is made available primarily through the extension methods of the DataTableExtensions and DataRowExtensions classes shown above.

- LINQ to DataSet also provides a DataRowComparer class that lets you compare rows by their values. For more information, see the Visual Studio documentation.

- When you use LINQ to DataSet, you are querying an enumeration of DataRow objects. Because of that, you can use members of the DataRow class in your queries.

Figure 12-1   An introduction to LINQ to DataSet

How to use LINQ with typed datasets

To use LINQ with typed datasets, you need to know some basic skills for working with typed datasets and table adapters in code. Once you have these skills, you can query the dataset using techniques similar to those you use to query a generic list. In addition, you can create data views and data tables from the results of your LINQ queries.

Basic skills for working with typed datasets in code

Figure 12-2 presents some basic skills for working with typed datasets in code. Before you can use the skills shown here, you need to create a typed dataset class. To do that, you can use the Data Source Configuration Wizard or the Dataset Designer.

In chapter 5, you learned about some of the classes, properties, and methods that are defined within a typed dataset. This figure repeats some of the most important of these classes and members and illustrates how you work with them in code. To create an instance of a typed dataset, for example, you declare a variable with the dataset class as its type as shown in the first example in this figure.

The second example shows how you can work with the rows and columns in a data table. To start, you declare a variable that will hold the row. Here, a variable named vendorRow is declared with a type of PayablesDataSet.VendorsRow, which defines a row in the Vendors table. Then, a variable named rowIndex that will hold the index of the row to be retrieved is declared. After some additional processing, the row with the specified index is retrieved and assigned to the vendorRow variable. To do that, the Vendors property of the payablesDataSet object is used to get the Vendors table, and the Item property, which is the default property, is used to get the row.

After the row is retrieved, the next two statements get the values of two of the columns in the row and assign them to the Text property of two text boxes. To get the values of the columns, these statements use the properties of the vendorRow object that have the same names as the columns. In this case, the Name and Address1 properties are used.

Classes defined by a typed dataset

Class	Description	Example
Dataset	The dataset itself.	PayablesDataSet
Data table	A table in the dataset.	VendorsDataTable
Data row	A row in the data table.	VendorsRow

Property defined by the dataset class

Property	Description	Example
tablename	Gets a table.	Vendors

Property defined by the data table class

Property	Description
Item	Gets the row with the specified index.

Property and method defined by the data row class

Property	Description	Example
columnname	Gets or sets the value of a column.	VendorName
Method	**Description**	**Example**
Is*columnname*Null	Determines whether a column contains a null.	IsAddress2Null

A statement that creates a typed dataset

```
Dim payablesDataSet As New PayablesDataSet
```

Code that retrieves a row and assigns column values to form controls

```
Dim vendorRow As PayablesDataSet.VendorsRow
Dim rowIndex As Integer
...
vendorRow = payablesDataSet.Vendors(rowIndex)
txtName.Text = vendorRow.Name
txtAddress1.Text = vendorRow.Address1
...
```

Description

- You can create a typed dataset class using the Data Source Configuration Wizard as shown in chapter 3 or the Dataset Designer as shown in chapter 5.

- After you create a typed dataset class, you can create an instance of that class and refer to the tables it contains using properties with the same names as the tables.

- To declare a variable for a row in a data table, you use the class for the data row that's defined by the dataset. Then, you can retrieve a row from the table using the Item property of the table and the index of the row.

- To get the values of the columns in a row, you use the properties of the row that have the same names as the columns in the data table.

Figure 12-2   Basic skills for working with typed datasets in code

Basic skills for working with table adapters in code

When you use the Data Source Configuration Wizard or the Dataset Designer to create a typed dataset, Visual Studio generates a table adapter class for each table in the dataset. The code for this class is stored in a separate namespace within the file that defines the typed dataset. The name that's assigned to this namespace is the name of the dataset class, followed by "TableAdapters". For example, the table adapters for the PayablesDataSet class are defined in a namespace named PayablesDataSetTableAdapters as shown in the first example in figure 12-3.

Within the table adapters namespace, one class is defined for each table adapter. As you saw in section 2, a table adapter is given the name of the table followed by "TableAdapter". For example, the table adapter for the Vendors table is named VendorsTableAdapter as shown in the second example in this figure.

When you work with table adapters in code, you'll typically want to include an Imports statement for the namespace that contains them as shown in the third example in this figure. That way, you won't have to include the name of the namespace every time you refer to a table adapter. And that can simplify your code.

The fourth example in this figure shows how to create an instance of a table adapter in code and use it to load the associated data table. Here, the first statement creates an instance of the Vendors table adapter. Then, the second statement uses the Fill method to load data into the Vendors table. You saw examples of this method in the chapters in section 2. The only difference here is that the table adapter is created in code.

Common property and method of a table adapter

Property	Description
Connection	The connection object associated with the table adapter.
Method	**Description**
Fill(dataset.DataTable)	Retrieves rows from the database using the Select statement associated with the main query for the table adapter and stores them in a data table.

The Namespace statement for the table adapters in a typed dataset named PayablesDataSet

```
Namespace PayablesDataSetTableAdapters
```

The Class statement for a table adapter class

```
Partial Public Class VendorsTableAdapter
```

An Imports statement for a table adapter namespace

```
Imports VendorDisplay.PayablesDataSetTableAdapters
```

Code that creates a table adapter and then loads the data table

```
Dim vendorsTableAdapter As New VendorsTableAdapter
vendorsTableAdapter.Fill(payablesDataSet.Vendors)
```

Description

- You can create a table adapter class using the Data Source Configuration Wizard as shown in chapter 3 or the Dataset Designer as shown in chapter 5. Each table adapter is defined by a class that's declared within a namespace in the file that defines the typed dataset class.

- A table adapter class is given a name that consists of the table it's associated with, followed by "TableAdapter". The namespace that contains the table adapter classes is given a name that consists of the name of the dataset class, followed by "TableAdapters".

- To avoid having to include the name of the namespace on each statement that refers to a table adapter class in the namespace, you can code an Imports statement for the namespace. To do that, you refer to it through the name of the project that contains it.

- After you create a table adapter class, you can create an instance of it as shown above. Then, you can use it to retrieve data from the database by executing its Fill method.

Figure 12-3   Basic skills for working with table adapters in code

How to retrieve data from a typed dataset

Figure 12-4 shows how to use LINQ to DataSet to retrieve data from a typed dataset. To start, you have to load data into the dataset. Then, you can code a query expression like the one in this figure.

This query expression queries a dataset named payablesDataSet that contains tables named Vendors and Invoices and returns the name and balance due for each vendor. If you compare this query expression with the query expression you saw in the Vendors Due application at the end of the last chapter, you'll see that they're almost identical. The only difference is that the source of data for this query is the two tables in the dataset rather than two generic lists.

To understand how you can use LINQ with typed datasets, you need to realize that each DataTable class in a typed dataset class is derived from the TypedTableBase(Of T) class where T is a DataRow object. The TypedTableBase(Of T) class, in turn, implements the IEnumerable(Of T) interface. That means that each data table in a typed dataset is an enumerable type that can be used in a LINQ query.

A LINQ query that retrieves data from a typed dataset

Code that creates and loads the dataset

```
Dim payablesDataSet As New PayablesDataSet
Dim vendorsTableAdapter As New VendorsTableAdapter
Dim invoicesTableAdapter As New InvoicesTableAdapter
...
vendorsTableAdapter.Fill(payablesDataSet.Vendors)
invoicesTableAdapter.Fill(payablesDataSet.Invoices)
```

A query expression that gets the balance due for each vendor

```
Dim vendorsDue = _
    From invoice In payablesDataSet.Invoices _
    Join vendor In payablesDataSet.Vendors _
      On invoice.VendorID Equals vendor.VendorID _
    Group invoice By vendor.Name _
     Into BalanceDue = Sum(invoice.InvoiceTotal _
                        - invoice.PaymentTotal _
                        - invoice.CreditTotal) _
    Where BalanceDue > 0 _
    Order By BalanceDue Descending _
    Select Name, BalanceDue
```

Code that executes the query

```
Dim vendorDisplay As String = "Name" & vbTab & vbTab & vbTab & vbTab _
                            & "Balance Due" & vbCrLf
For Each vendor In vendorsDue
    vendorDisplay &= vendor.Name & vbTab & vbTab _
                & IIf(vendor.Name.Length < 10, vbTab, "").ToString _
                & IIf(vendor.Name.Length < 20, vbTab, "").ToString _
                & FormatCurrency(vendor.BalanceDue) & vbCrLf
Next
MessageBox.Show(vendorDisplay, "Vendor Balances")
```

The resulting dialog box

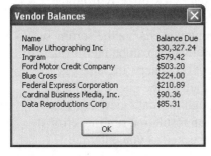

Description

- When Visual Studio generates a typed dataset class, the DataTable classes are derived from the TypedTableBase(Of T) class where T is a DataRow object. Because the TypedTableBase(Of T) class implements the IEnumerable(Of T) interface, you can use LINQ to query a data table directly.

- Before you can execute a query that retrieves data from a typed dataset, you must load data into the dataset.

Figure 12-4   How to retrieve data from a typed dataset

How to create a data view from the results of a LINQ query

In ADO.NET, a *data view* is an object that provides for filtering and sorting the data in a data table. One way to create a data view is to create an instance of the DataView class, assign the name of the table it's associated with to the Table property of the data view, and set the Sort and RowFilter properties to the appropriate expressions. Another way to create a data view is to execute the AsDataView method of the DataTableExtensions class on the results of a query. Figure 12-5 illustrates how this works.

The form at the top of this figure includes a combo box that lists all the vendors in the Vendors table. When the user selects a vendor from the combo box, the invoices in the Invoices table are filtered so that only the invoices for the selected vendor that have a balance due greater than zero are displayed in the DataGridView control. In addition, the invoices are sorted by invoice date.

The code in this figure shows how the filtering and sorting for this form is implemented. It starts by defining a query expression with the appropriate Where and Order By clauses. Then, the next statement calls the AsDataView method on the query variable, which causes the query to be executed and the data view to be created. This data view inherits the sorting and filtering that's specified by the query expression. Then, the result is stored in a variable that's declared with the DataView type.

Finally, the data view is assigned to the DataSource property of the Invoices binding source. Although it's not shown here, the DataSource property of the DataGridView control is set to this binding source. Because of that, the invoice data is displayed in the DataGridView control.

At this point, you may be wondering why you would use a query expression like the one shown here rather than just creating a data view directly from the Invoice table. One reason is that when you create a data view from a data table, an index is built over the entire table. Then, each time you change the sorting or filtering for the data view, the index has to be rebuilt, which can be inefficient. In contrast, if you create a data view from the results of a query, the index is built only once using the filtering and sorting specified by the query. Another reason is that the sort and filter expressions you assign to a data view can't be checked when the application is compiled, which can result in a runtime error. In contrast, the sorting and filtering for a query is checked as you enter the query expression.

Because a data view represents a view of a data table, you can create a data view only from a query that returns complete data rows. In other words, the query can't return a projection. In addition, other than specifying the source table, the query can only specify filter and sort information. That makes sense because this is the only information that applies to a data view.

A form with a DataGridView control that's bound to a data view created from the results of a query

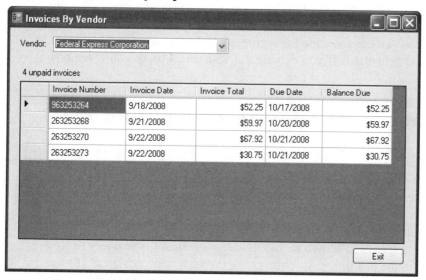

Code that creates the data view and binds it to the DataGridView control

```
Dim vendorInvoices _
    = From invoice In PayablesDataSet.Invoices _
      Where invoice.VendorID = CInt(cboVendor.SelectedValue) _
          And invoice.BalanceDue > 0 _
      Order By invoice.InvoiceDate _
      Select invoice

Dim invoiceView As DataView = vendorInvoices.AsDataView
InvoicesBindingSource.DataSource = invoiceView
```

Description

- A *data view* provides a customized view of the data in a data table. Data views can be used to sort or filter the rows in a data table.

- To create a data view from the results of a LINQ query, you use the AsDataView method of the DataTableExtensions class. This method creates an instance of the LinqDataView class, which inherits the DataView class.

- When you create a data view from the results of a query, the LinqDataView object inherits the sorting and filtering specified by the query. If you change the properties of the data view that specify how the data view is sorted (Sort) and filtered (RowFilter), the sorting or filtering specified by the query is overridden.

- To create a data view from the results of a query, the query can include only the From, Where, Order By, and Select clauses, and the Select clause can only select entire rows.

- Data views are typically used in situations where you need to bind a control to the results of a query.

Figure 12-5   How to create a data view from the results of a LINQ query

When you create a data view from the results of a query, you should realize that the data view is stored in a LinqDataView object. This works because the LinqDataView class inherits the DataView class. However, the RowFilter and Sort properties of the LinqDataView object aren't set based on the query. Because of that, you can override the sorting and filtering specified by the query by setting these properties. If you experiment with this, I think you'll see how it works.

How to create a data table from the results of a LINQ query

Instead of creating a data view from the results of a query, you can create a data table. Then, you can bind a control to the new data table. To create a data table from the results of a query, you use the CopyToDataTable method of the DataTableExtensions class as shown in figure 12-6.

The query expression shown in this figure is identical to the query expression you saw in the last figure. It retrieves the invoices with a balance due for the selected vendor and sorts the invoices by due date. Then, a new data table that will hold the results of the query is declared.

Next, the Count property of the query variable is called to determine whether one or more rows are returned by the query. This is necessary because an InvalidOperationException will occur if you execute the CopyToDataTable method on a query that doesn't return any rows. If the query returns one or more rows, the CopyToDataTable method is called to create a data table from the results of the query. Finally, the data table is assigned to the DataSource property of the Invoices binding source.

Just as when you create a data view from the results of a query, you can create a data table from the results of a query only if the query returns entire data rows. The query can also specify sorting and filtering just like it can for a query that's used to create a data view. In addition, a query that's used to create a data table can include a Let clause that assigns an alias to the result of a calculation.

In most cases, you probably won't create a data table from the results of a query like the one shown here. Instead, you'll create a data view as shown in the previous figure that works with the original table. If you ever need to create a separate table that contains selected rows from another table, however, you can use the technique shown here.

A form with a DataGridView control that's bound to a data table created from the results of a query

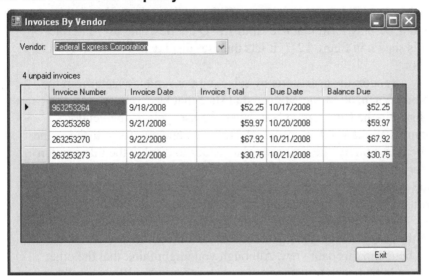

Code that creates the data table and binds it to the DataGridView control

```
Dim vendorInvoices _
    = From invoice In PayablesDataSet.Invoices _
      Where invoice.VendorID = CInt(cboVendor.SelectedValue) _
        And invoice.BalanceDue > 0 _
      Order By invoice.DueDate _
      Select invoice

Dim vendorInvoicesTable As New DataTable
If vendorInvoices.Count > 0 Then
    vendorInvoicesTable = vendorInvoices.CopyToDataTable
End If
InvoicesBindingSource.DataSource = vendorInvoicesTable
```

Description

- To create a data table from the results of a LINQ query, you use the CopyToDataTable method of the DataTableExtensions class. You'll typically do this if you need to bind a control to the results of the query.

- To create a data table from the results of a query, the query can include only the From, Where, Order By, Let, and Select clauses, and the Select clause can only select entire rows.

- You can't use the CopyToDataTable method with a LINQ query that doesn't return any rows. Because of that, you should check that the query results contain at least one row before you create a data table from the query.

Figure 12-6   How to create a data table from the results of a LINQ query

The user interface for the Vendor Display form

To give you a better idea of how to use LINQ with a typed dataset, I'll present a Vendor Display form that uses four LINQ queries. The user interface for this form is shown in figure 12-7. It lets the user display information for a selected vendor.

To display a vendor, the user starts by selecting the vendor's state from the State combo box. Then, all of the cities in that state that have one or more vendors are listed in the City combo box. Next, the user selects the vendor's city, which causes all the vendors in the selected state and city to be listed in the Vendor combo box. Finally, the user selects a vendor to display the information for that vendor on the form.

To get the data for each combo box, this form uses a LINQ query. A LINQ query is also used to get the information for the selected vendor. You'll see the code for these queries in the next figure. This form also creates a data view from the results of the query that gets the data for the Vendor combo box. Then, the combo box is bound to this data view. Although you might think that the other combo boxes could be bound to data views too, they can't. You'll see why that is in just a minute.

The Vendor Display form

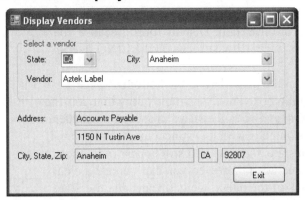

Description

- The Vendor Display form lets the user display vendor information based on the selections made from the three combo boxes at the top of the form.

- When the form is first loaded, each state with at least one vendor is included in the State combo box, each city in the first state with at least one vendor is included in the City combo box, each vendor in the selected state and city is included in the Vendor combo box, and the information for the first vendor is displayed on the form.

- When the user selects a different state, the City combo box is updated to include the cities in that state, the Vendor combo box is updated to include the vendors in the first city in that state, and the information for the first vendor in the state and city is displayed.

- When the user selects a different city, the Vendor combo box is updated to include the vendors in the selected state and city, and the information for the first vendor in that state and city is displayed.

- When the user selects a different vendor, the information for that vendor is displayed.

- A LINQ query is used to get the data for each combo box and to get the data for the currently selected vendor.

- A data view is created from the results of the LINQ query that gets the data for the Vendor combo box, and the combo box is bound to this data view.

Figure 12-7   The user interface for the Vendor Display form

The code for the Vendor Display form

Figure 12-8 presents the code for the Vendor Display form. Because you should be familiar with most of this code, I'll just focus on the LINQ queries here.

The first LINQ query appears in the procedure at the bottom of page 1 of this listing that loads the State combo box. This is a simple query that gets the State column from the Vendors table and sorts the states in ascending sequence. Notice here that the query expression ends with a Distinct clause. That way, if there is more than one vendor in a state, the state will still appear only once in the results. Because this clause is included, however, you can't create a data view or a data table from the results of the query, which means that the State combo box can't be bound. Instead, a For Each loop is used to load the states into the combo box.

The second LINQ query appears in the first procedure on page 2 that loads the City combo box. This query is similar to the query that's used to get the states for the State combo box. It gets the City column for each city in the selected state and sorts the results by city. It also includes a Distinct clause, which means that a data view or data table can't be created from the query results. Because of that, the cities are loaded into the combo box using a For Each loop.

The second procedure on page 2 loads the Vendor combo box. It uses a query that retrieves all the vendors in the selected state and city and sorts them by vendor name. This time, a data view can be created from the results of the query. Then, the DataSource property of the combo box is set to this data view, the DisplayMember property is set to the Name column, and the ValueMember property is set to the VendorID column.

The last LINQ query is used in the procedure at the top of page 3 that displays the information for the selected vendor. This query specifies that only vendors with a vendor ID that's equal to the vendor ID of the vendor selected from the Vendor combo box should be retrieved. Because only one vendor will be retrieved by this query, the Single method is called on the query results. That causes the query to be executed immediately, and the vendor row that's returned is assigned to the selectedVendor variable. If I hadn't called the Single method, this query would have returned a collection of data rows containing a single row. Then, I would have had to retrieve the first and only row of that collection to work with that row. So using the Single method simplifies this process.

After the row for the selected vendor is retrieved, the rest of the code in this procedure assigns the data in that row to the text boxes on the form. Notice that this code uses the IsAddress2Null property of the Vendor object to determine whether the Address2 column contains a null. If so, an empty string is displayed in the associated text box. Otherwise, the column value is displayed.

The code for the Vendor Display form

```vb
Imports System.Data.SqlClient
Imports VendorDisplay.PayablesDataSetTableAdapters

Public Class Form1

    Dim payablesDataSet As New PayablesDataSet
    Dim vendorsTableAdapter As New VendorsTableAdapter

    Private Sub Form1_Load(ByVal sender As System.Object, _
            ByVal e As System.EventArgs) Handles MyBase.Load
        Me.FillVendorsTable()
        Me.LoadStatesComboBox()
        Me.LoadCitiesComboBox()
        Me.LoadVendorsComboBox()
        Me.DisplayVendor()
    End Sub

    Private Sub FillVendorsTable()
        Try
            vendorsTableAdapter.Fill(payablesDataSet.Vendors)
        Catch ex As SqlException
            MessageBox.Show("Database error # " & ex.Number _
                & "; " & ex.Message, ex.GetType.ToString)
        End Try
    End Sub

    Private Sub LoadStatesComboBox()
        RemoveHandler cboState.SelectedIndexChanged, _
            AddressOf cboState_SelectedIndexChanged

        Dim selectedStates = From vendor In payablesDataSet.Vendors _
                             Order By vendor.State _
                             Select vendor.State _
                             Distinct

        cboState.Items.Clear()
        For Each state In selectedStates
            cboState.Items.Add(state)
        Next
        cboState.SelectedIndex = 0

        AddHandler cboState.SelectedIndexChanged, _
            AddressOf cboState_SelectedIndexChanged
    End Sub
```

Figure 12-8   The code for a Vendor Display form that uses a typed dataset (part 1 of 3)

The code for the Vendor Display form

```vb
Private Sub LoadCitiesComboBox()
    RemoveHandler cboCity.SelectedIndexChanged, _
        AddressOf cboCity_SelectedIndexChanged

    Dim vendorCities _
        = From vendor In payablesDataSet.Vendors _
          Where vendor.State = cboState.SelectedItem.ToString _
          Order By vendor.City _
          Select vendor.City _
          Distinct

    cboCity.Items.Clear()
    For Each city In vendorCities
        cboCity.Items.Add(city)
    Next
    cboCity.SelectedIndex = 0

    AddHandler cboCity.SelectedIndexChanged, _
        AddressOf cboCity_SelectedIndexChanged
End Sub

Private Sub LoadVendorsComboBox()
    RemoveHandler cboVendor.SelectedIndexChanged, _
        AddressOf cboVendor_SelectedIndexChanged

    Dim selectedVendors _
        = From vendor In payablesDataSet.Vendors _
          Where vendor.State = cboState.SelectedItem.ToString _
            And vendor.City = cboCity.SelectedItem.ToString _
          Order By vendor.Name

    Dim vendorsView As DataView = selectedVendors.AsDataView
    cboVendor.DataSource = vendorsView
    cboVendor.DisplayMember = "Name"
    cboVendor.ValueMember = "VendorID"

    AddHandler cboVendor.SelectedIndexChanged, _
        AddressOf cboVendor_SelectedIndexChanged
End Sub
```

Figure 12-8   The code for a Vendor Display form that uses a typed dataset (part 2 of 3)

The code for the Vendor Display form   **Page 3**

```vb
    Private Sub DisplayVendor()
        Dim selectedVendor _
            = (From vendor In payablesDataSet.Vendors _
               Where vendor.VendorID = CInt(cboVendor.SelectedValue)).Single

        txtAddress1.Text = selectedVendor.Address1
        If selectedVendor.IsAddress2Null Then
            txtAddress2.Text = ""
        Else
            txtAddress2.Text = selectedVendor.Address2
        End If
        txtCity.Text = selectedVendor.City
        txtState.Text = selectedVendor.State
        txtZipCode.Text = selectedVendor.ZipCode

    End Sub

    Private Sub cboState_SelectedIndexChanged(ByVal sender As System.Object, _
            ByVal e As System.EventArgs) Handles cboState.SelectedIndexChanged
        Me.LoadCitiesComboBox()
        Me.LoadVendorsComboBox()
        Me.DisplayVendor()
    End Sub

    Private Sub cboCity_SelectedIndexChanged(ByVal sender As System.Object, _
            ByVal e As System.EventArgs) Handles cboCity.SelectedIndexChanged
        Me.LoadVendorsComboBox()
        Me.DisplayVendor()
    End Sub

    Private Sub cboVendor_SelectedIndexChanged( _
            ByVal sender As System.Object, ByVal e As System.EventArgs) _
            Handles cboVendor.SelectedIndexChanged
        Me.DisplayVendor()
    End Sub

    Private Sub btnExit_Click(ByVal sender As System.Object, _
            ByVal e As System.EventArgs) Handles btnExit.Click
        Me.Close()
    End Sub

End Class
```

Figure 12-8   The code for a Vendor Display form that uses a typed dataset (part 3 of 3)

How to use LINQ with untyped datasets

An *untyped dataset* is one that isn't based on a dataset schema and a custom dataset class. Instead, it's based on the generic DataSet class. In the topics that follow, you'll learn the basic skills for creating and working with untyped datasets and for retrieving data from an untyped dataset with LINQ. Then, you'll see the code for a Vendor Display form that uses LINQ with an untyped dataset to see how it differs from the code you saw in the last topic.

Basic skills for working with untyped datasets

Figure 12-9 presents the basic skills for working with an untyped dataset. To create an untyped dataset, you create an instance of the DataSet class. The first statement in this figure, for example, creates an untyped dataset and assigns it to a variable named payablesDataSet.

To access the collections of objects contained within a dataset, you use the properties listed in this figure. To access the collection of tables in a dataset, for example, you use the Tables property of the dataset. This is illustrated in the second example in this figure. Here, the Tables property of the dataset in the payablesDataSet variable is used to access a table named Vendors. This table is then assigned to a variable that's declared using the generic DataTable type. That's necessary because a custom data table class isn't available for an untyped dataset like it is for a typed dataset.

The third example in this figure shows how to work with the rows and columns in a table. The first statement in this example declares a variable that will hold a data row. Like the variable for the data table in the second example, the variable in this example is declared using a generic data type, in this case, DataRow. That's because a custom data row class isn't available for an untyped dataset. That also means that you can't use properties of the data row to refer to its columns, as you'll see in a moment.

After you declare a variable to hold a row, you can retrieve the row using its index. In this example, the Tables property of the dataset is used to get the table that contains the row, and the Rows property of the table is used to get the row with the specified index.

The rest of the code in this example retrieves values from individual columns of the row and assigns them to the appropriate properties of controls on a form. To do that, it uses the Item property of the data row and specifies the name of the column as an argument. Note that because the Item property is the default property of a row, it can be omitted as shown here. Also note that the ToString method is used to convert the value of each column to a string. That's necessary only if the Option Strict setting is on, which is what we recommend. In that case, the Object type that's returned when you refer to a column can't be converted implicitly to a string. The ToString method is also useful if a column can contain a null value. Then, this method converts the null to an empty string.

A constructor for the DataSet class

```
New DataSet()
```

Common properties used to access collections in an untyped dataset

Object	Property	Description
Dataset	Tables	A collection of the tables in the dataset.
Data table	Rows	A collection of the rows in a data table.
	Columns	A collection of the columns in a data table.

A statement that creates an untyped dataset

```
Dim payablesDataSet As New DataSet
```

A statement that refers to a table in the dataset by name

```
Dim vendorsTable As DataTable = payablesDataSet.Tables("Vendors")
```

Code that retrieves a row and assigns column values to form controls

```
Dim vendorRow As DataRow
Dim rowIndex As Integer
  .
  .
vendorRow = payablesDataSet.Tables("Vendors").Rows(rowIndex)
txtName.Text = vendorRow("Name").ToString
txtAddress1.Text = vendorRow("Address1").ToString
txtAddress2.Text = vendorRow("Address2").ToString
  .
  .
```

Description

- An *untyped dataset* is one that's created from the generic ADO.NET DataSet class. You use the properties and methods of this class to work with an untyped dataset and the objects it contains.

- The information within a dataset is stored in collections. To refer to a collection, you can use a property of the parent object.

- To refer to a table in a dataset, you use the Tables property of the dataset and specify the table's name or its index value as the argument. Then, you can assign that table to a variable that's declared with the DataTable type.

- To retrieve a row from a data table, you use the Rows property of the table and specify the row's index as the argument. Then, you can assign that row to a variable that's declared with the DataRow type.

- To get the value of a column in a row, you can use the Item property of the row and specify the name of the column as the argument. Since Item is the default property of a data row, you can omit it as shown above.

Figure 12-9   Basic skills for working with untyped datasets

Basic skills for working with data adapters

As you learned in chapter 2, a data adapter manages the flow between a database and a dataset. Before you can work with an untyped dataset, then, you must create a data adapter and use it to load data into a data table. Figure 12-10 presents the basic skills for doing that.

You can use two techniques to create SqlDataAdapter objects, as illustrated by the syntax diagrams at the top of this figure. If you use the first technique, you don't pass an argument to the constructor. Then, you have to set the value of the SelectCommand property after you create the object. This property identifies the command object that will be used to retrieve data. If you use the second technique, you pass the value of the SelectCommand property to the constructor.

This figure also presents the Fill method that you use to load a data table with data from a database. Notice here that a second argument is included on the Fill method that names the data table where the data that's retrieved is stored. By default, if you don't include a table name on the Fill method, the data is placed in a table named "Table", which usually isn't what you want.

The code example in this figure illustrates how this works. This code starts by creating a connection to the Payables database. Then, it creates a command object that will be used to retrieve data from that database. Next, it creates an untyped dataset that will hold the data that's retrieved from the database. Finally, it creates a data adapter, assigns the command to the SelectCommand property of the data adapter, and then executes the Fill method of the data adapter to retrieve the data and store it in a table named Vendors in the dataset.

Two constructors for the SqlDataAdapter class

```
New SqlDataAdapter()
New SqlDataAdapter(selectCommand)
```

Common property and method of the SqlDataAdapter class

Property	Description
SelectCommand	The command object used to retrieve data from the database.

Method	Description
Fill(dataset, "TableName")	Retrieves rows from the database using the command specified by the SelectCommand property and stores them in a data table.

Code that creates a SqlDataAdapter object and then loads the dataset

```
Dim connectionString As String _
    = "Data Source=localhost\SqlExpress;Initial Catalog=Payables;" _
    & "Integrated Security=True"
Dim payablesConnection As New SqlConnection(connectionString)

Dim vendorsCommand As New SqlCommand
vendorsCommand.Connection = payablesConnection
Dim vendorSelect As String _
    = "SELECT VendorID, Name, Address1, Address2, City, State, ZipCode " _
    & "FROM Vendors"
vendorsCommand.CommandText = vendorSelect

Dim payablesDataSet As New DataSet

Dim vendorsDataAdapter As New SqlDataAdapter
vendorsDataAdapter.SelectCommand = vendorsCommand
vendorsDataAdapter.Fill(payablesDataSet, "Vendors")
```

Description

- When you create a data adapter, the SelectCommand property is set to the command object you pass to the constructor. If you don't pass a command object to the constructor, you must set this property after you create the data adapter.

- Before you can set the SelectCommand property, you must create the command object that contains the Select statement you want to associate with the data adapter.

- You can use the Fill method of a data adapter to retrieve data from the database. By default, this method maps the data in the source table to a data table named "Table". Since that's not usually what you want, you should include the name of the data table as the second argument of the Fill method.

Figure 12-10   Basic skills for working with data adapters

How to retrieve data from an untyped dataset

Figure 12-11 presents a query expression that returns the same results as the query expression in figure 12-4 that uses a typed dataset. If you compare these two query expressions, you'll notice three differences. First, the tables in the dataset are referred to through the Tables collection. For example, the From clause uses this code to refer to the Invoices table:

```
payablesDataSet.Tables("Invoices")
```

Second, the AsEnumerable method is called on both the Invoices and Vendors tables. This method converts a DataTable object, which doesn't implement the IEnumerable(Of T) interface, to an IEnumerable(Of DataRow) object that can be used in a query. Note that if you don't call this method explicitly, the Visual Basic compiler will call it for you. Even so, we recommend that you code it for clarity.

Third, to get the value of a column in a data row, you use the Field method. On this method, you specify the type of data that the column contains. If you don't do that, the column is returned as an Object type, which isn't usually what you want.

Although you could cast the object that's returned for a column to the appropriate type instead of using the Field method, using this method has another advantage. That is, this method handles null values. That means that if a column contains the value DBNull.Value, the Field method returns a null value that you can use in your application code.

A LINQ query that retrieves data from an untyped dataset

Code that creates and loads the dataset

```
Dim payablesDataSet As New DataSet
Dim vendorsDataAdapter As New SqlDataAdapter
Dim invoicesDataAdapter As New SqlDataAdapter
...
vendorsDataAdapter.Fill(payablesDataSet, "Vendors")
invoicesDataAdapter.Fill(payablesDataSet, "Invoices")
```

A query expression that gets the balance due for each vendor

```
Dim vendorsDue = _
    From invoice In payablesDataSet.Tables("Invoices").AsEnumerable _
    Join vendor In payablesDataSet.Tables("Vendors").AsEnumerable _
      On invoice.Field(Of Integer)("VendorID") _
          Equals vendor.Field(Of Integer)("VendorID")
    Group invoice By Name = vendor.Field(Of String)("Name") _
      Into BalanceDue = Sum(invoice.Field(Of Decimal)("InvoiceTotal") _
                      - invoice.Field(Of Decimal)("PaymentTotal") _
                      - invoice.Field(Of Decimal)("CreditTotal")) _
    Where BalanceDue > 0 _
    Order By BalanceDue Descending _
    Select Name, BalanceDue
```

Code that executes the query

```
Dim vendorDisplay As String = "Name" & vbTab & vbTab & vbTab & vbTab _
                                & "Balance Due" & vbCrLf
For Each vendor In vendorsDue
    vendorDisplay &= vendor.Name & vbTab & vbTab _
                & IIf(vendor.Name.Length < 10, vbTab, "").ToString _
                & IIf(vendor.Name.Length < 20, vbTab, "").ToString _
                & FormatCurrency(vendor.BalanceDue) & vbCrLf
Next
MessageBox.Show(vendorDisplay, "Vendor Balances")
```

The resulting dialog box

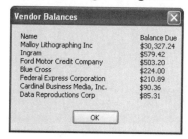

Description

- When you use a data table as the data source in a LINQ query, the compiler automatically calls the AsEnumerable method to convert it to an IEnumerable(Of DataRow) object. You can also call this method explicitly as shown above.

- To get a column value from a row in an untyped dataset, you use the Field method of the DataRowExtensions class. On this method, you specify the type of the field being retrieved. If the column value can't be cast to this type, an InvalidCastException occurs.

- If a column contains the value DBNull.Value, the Field method returns a null value.

Figure 12-11   How to retrieve data from an untyped dataset

The code for the Vendor Display form

Figure 12-12 presents the code for a Vendor Display form that uses an untyped dataset. This code works just like the code you saw in figure 12-8. It uses three queries to get the data for the three combo boxes and a fourth query to get the row for the selected vendor. If you review these four queries, you'll see that they use the AsEnumerable and Field methods as described in the last topic.

You'll also notice that each of these queries uses a variable named vendorsTable to refer to the table of vendors. This variable is defined at the class level so it can be used by any procedure of the form. Then, after the Load event handler for the form fills the Vendors table, that table is assigned to the vendorsTable variable. That makes it easier to use this table in the LINQ queries.

The code for the Vendor Display form

```
Imports System.Data.SqlClient

Public Class Form1

    Dim payablesDataSet As New DataSet
    Dim vendorsDataAdapter As New SqlDataAdapter
    Dim vendorsTable As DataTable

    Private Sub Form1_Load(ByVal sender As System.Object, _
            ByVal e As System.EventArgs) Handles MyBase.Load
        Me.CreateDataProviderObjects()
        Me.FillVendorsTable()
        vendorsTable = payablesDataSet.Tables("Vendors")
        Me.LoadStatesComboBox()
        Me.LoadCitiesComboBox()
        Me.LoadVendorsComboBox()
        Me.DisplayVendor()
    End Sub

    Private Sub CreateDataProviderObjects()
        Dim connectionString As String _
            = "Data Source=localhost\SqlExpress;Initial Catalog=Payables;" _
            & "Integrated Security=True"
        Dim payablesConnection As New SqlConnection(connectionString)

        Dim vendorsCommand As New SqlCommand
        vendorsCommand.Connection = payablesConnection
        Dim vendorSelect As String _
            = "SELECT VendorID, Name, Address1, Address2, " _
            & "City, State, ZipCode " _
            & "FROM Vendors"
        vendorsCommand.CommandText = vendorSelect
        vendorsDataAdapter.SelectCommand = vendorsCommand
    End Sub

    Private Sub FillVendorsTable()
        Try
            vendorsDataAdapter.Fill(payablesDataSet, "Vendors")
        Catch ex As SqlException
            MessageBox.Show("Database error # " & ex.Number _
                & ": " & ex.Message, ex.GetType.ToString)
        End Try
    End Sub

    Private Sub LoadStatesComboBox()
        RemoveHandler cboState.SelectedIndexChanged, _
            AddressOf cboState_SelectedIndexChanged

        Dim selectedStates = From vendor In vendorsTable.AsEnumerable _
                             Order By vendor.Field(Of String)("State") _
                             Select vendor.Field(Of String)("State") _
                             Distinct
```

Figure 12-12   The code for a Vendor Display form that uses an untyped dataset (part 1 of 3)

The code for the Vendor Display form

```vb
        cboState.Items.Clear()
        For Each state In selectedStates
            cboState.Items.Add(state)
        Next
        cboState.SelectedIndex = 0

        AddHandler cboState.SelectedIndexChanged, _
            AddressOf cboState_SelectedIndexChanged
    End Sub

    Private Sub LoadCitiesComboBox()
        RemoveHandler cboCity.SelectedIndexChanged, _
            AddressOf cboCity_SelectedIndexChanged

        Dim vendorCities = From vendor In vendorsTable.AsEnumerable _
                           Where vendor.Field(Of String)("State") _
                               = cboState.SelectedItem.ToString _
                           Order By vendor.Field(Of String)("City") _
                           Select vendor.Field(Of String)("City") _
                           Distinct

        cboCity.Items.Clear()
        For Each city In vendorCities
            cboCity.Items.Add(city)
        Next
        cboCity.SelectedIndex = 0

        AddHandler cboCity.SelectedIndexChanged, _
            AddressOf cboCity_SelectedIndexChanged
    End Sub

    Private Sub LoadVendorsComboBox()
        RemoveHandler cboVendor.SelectedIndexChanged, _
            AddressOf cboVendor_SelectedIndexChanged

        Dim selectedVendors = From vendor In vendorsTable.AsEnumerable _
                              Where vendor.Field(Of String)("State") _
                                  = cboState.SelectedItem.ToString _
                              And vendor.Field(Of String)("City") _
                                  = cboCity.SelectedItem.ToString _
                              Order By vendor.Field(Of String)("Name")

        Dim vendorsView As DataView = selectedVendors.AsDataView
        cboVendor.DataSource = vendorsView
        cboVendor.DisplayMember = "Name"
        cboVendor.ValueMember = "VendorID"

        AddHandler cboVendor.SelectedIndexChanged, _
            AddressOf cboVendor_SelectedIndexChanged
    End Sub
```

Figure 12-12   The code for a Vendor Display form that uses an untyped dataset (part 2 of 3)

The code for the Vendor Display form   **Page 3**

```
    Private Sub DisplayVendor()
        Dim selectedVendor _
            = (From vendor In vendorsTable.AsEnumerable _
                Where vendor.Field(Of Integer)("VendorID") _
                    = CInt(cboVendor.SelectedValue)).Single

        txtAddress1.Text = selectedVendor("Address1").ToString
        txtAddress2.Text = selectedVendor("Address2").ToString
        txtCity.Text = selectedVendor("City").ToString
        txtState.Text = selectedVendor("State").ToString
        txtZipCode.Text = selectedVendor("ZipCode").ToString

    End Sub

    Private Sub cboState_SelectedIndexChanged(ByVal sender As System.Object, _
            ByVal e As System.EventArgs) Handles cboState.SelectedIndexChanged
        Me.LoadCitiesComboBox()
        Me.LoadVendorsComboBox()
        Me.DisplayVendor()
    End Sub

    Private Sub cboCity_SelectedIndexChanged(ByVal sender As System.Object, _
            ByVal e As System.EventArgs) Handles cboCity.SelectedIndexChanged
        Me.LoadVendorsComboBox()
        Me.DisplayVendor()
    End Sub

    Private Sub cboVendor_SelectedIndexChanged( _
            ByVal sender As System.Object, ByVal e As System.EventArgs) _
            Handles cboVendor.SelectedIndexChanged
        Me.DisplayVendor()
    End Sub

    Private Sub btnExit_Click(ByVal sender As System.Object, _
            ByVal e As System.EventArgs) Handles btnExit.Click
        Me.Close()
    End Sub

End Class
```

Figure 12-12   The code for a Vendor Display form that uses an untyped dataset (part 3 of 3)

Perspective

As you've seen in this chapter, the skills you need to use LINQ to query a dataset are relatively simple. If you're going to query a typed dataset, however, you also need to have some basic skills for working with typed datasets and tables adapters in code. And if you're going to query an untyped dataset, you need to have some basic skills for working with untyped datasets and data adapters. That's why I presented these skills in this chapter. With these skills and the skills you learned in the last chapter, you shouldn't have any trouble using LINQ to DataSet.

Terms

data view
untyped dataset

Exercise 12-1   Implement the LINQ queries for the Vendor Display form that uses a typed dataset

In this exercise, you'll write the code that implements the LINQ queries and displays the results on the Vendor Display form that uses a typed dataset.

Run the application and review the form

1. Open the project that's in the C\:ADO.NET 3.5 VB\Chapter 12\VendorDisplay (Typed) directory. This project contains the data source used by the project, the design for the Vendor Display form, and the starting code for all the procedures used by the form.

2. Review the starting code and then run the application. Drop down the three combo boxes to see that they don't contain any data. Then, exit from the form.

Add a query to load the State combo box

3. Add a query expression to the LoadStatesComboBox procedure that retrieves all the states from the Vendors table and sorts them alphabetically. Be sure that each state is included in the results only once.

4. Clear any items that are currently in the State combo box. Then, code a For Each statement that executes the query and adds the state in each row that's returned to the State combo box. Set the SelectedIndex property of the combo box to 0 so that the first state is displayed.

5. Run the application and check that the State combo box is loaded correctly and that the first state is displayed.

Add a query to load the City combo box

6. Add a query expression to the LoadCitiesComboBox procedure that retrieves all the cities from the Vendors table for the state selected from the State combo box and sorts the cities alphabetically. Be sure that each city is included in the results only once.

7. Clear the City combo box, and then code a For Each statement that adds the city in each row that's returned by the query to the combo box. Set the SelectedIndex property of the combo box so that the first state is displayed.

8. Run the application again and check that the City combo box was loaded correctly. Then, select CA from the State combo box and check that the City combo box is updated correctly.

Add a query to load the Vendor combo box

9. Add a query expression to the LoadVendorsComboBox procedure that retrieves all the vendors from the Vendors table for the state and city selected from the State and City combo boxes. Sort the results by vendor name.

10. Create a data view from the query results. Then, bind the Vendor combo box to the data view so that the name for each vendor is displayed in the list and the ID for each vendor is stored in the list.

11. Run the application again and check that the Vendor combo box is loaded correctly. Select CA from the State combo box and check the Vendor combo to be sure it was updated correctly. Finally, select Fresno from the City combo box and check the Vendor combo box again.

Add a query to get the data for a vendor

12. Add a query expression to the DisplayVendor procedure that gets the vendor row for the vendor that's selected from the Vendor combo box. (Remember that the Vendor combo box is a bound control, so you can get the vendor ID for the selected vendor using the SelectedValue property of the control.) To get a single row, you'll need to use the Single method.

13. Assign the column values of the row that's returned to the text boxes on the form, making sure to account for null values in the Address2 column.

14. Run the application one more time. If you coded it correctly, the information for the selected vendor should be displayed on the form. Select a different vendor from the combo box to be sure that the information for that vendor is displayed.

15. Continue experimenting until you're sure that the application works correctly. Then, end the application and close the solution.

Exercise 12-2   Modify the queries for the Vendor Display form to use an untyped dataset

In this exercise, you'll modify the LINQ queries you coded in the last exercise so they work with an untyped dataset.

Review the application

1. Open the project that's in the C\:ADO.NET 3.5 VB\Chapter 12\VendorDisplay (Untyped) directory. This project contains the design for the Vendor Display form and the starting code for all the procedures used by the form, including the code that creates and loads the untyped dataset.

2. Review the code for the LoadStatesComboBox, LoadCitiesComboBox, LoadVendorsComboBox, and DisplayVendor procedures. Notice that the LINQ queries in these procedures are written to work with a typed dataset. Because of that, the code contains numerous errors.

Modify the query expressions to use an untyped dataset

3. Declare a class variable that you can use to store the Vendors table. Then, add a statement after the call to the FillVendorsTable procedure in the Load event handler that assigns the Vendors table to this variable.

4. Modify the query expression in the LoadStatesComboBox procedure so it gets data from the vendors table. Use the AsEnumerable method to convert the data table to an IEnumerable(Of DataRow) object.

5. After you correct the data source, a new error will be displayed indicating that the State column referred to in the Order By clause isn't a member of System.Data.DataRow. To fix this error, you can use the Field method to get the value of the field as the correct type. Make these same changes to the code that accesses the State column in the Select clause.

6. Make the necessary changes to the query expressions in the LoadCitiesComboBox, LoadVendorsComboBox, and DisplayVendor procedures, including using the AsEnumerable and Field methods.

Test the application

7. Run the application to make sure it works correctly. Then, end the application and close the solution.

13

How to use LINQ to SQL (part 1)

In section 3 of this book, you learned how to develop three-layer applications that store data in business objects. When you use this technique, you must code the business classes that define these objects as well as the database classes that provide for working with the data in the database. With LINQ to SQL, you can perform many of the same functions without having to write the code for the business and database classes.

In this chapter, you'll learn how to create the object model that LINQ to SQL uses to work with the data for an application. In addition, you'll learn how to retrieve data from a SQL Server database by executing queries against this object model. Then, in the next chapter, you'll learn how to modify the data that you retrieve.

An introduction to LINQ to SQL

Before I show you how to use LINQ to SQL, you should have a general idea of how it works. You should also understand the basic components of the object model that is at the core of LINQ to SQL.

How LINQ to SQL works

The illustration in figure 13-1 provides an overview of LINQ to SQL. As you can see, LINQ to SQL consists of two main components: an *object model* and the *LINQ to SQL runtime*. I'll have more to say about the object model in just a minute. For now, you can think of it as a set of business classes that define business objects that are directly related to tables or views in a database.

To retrieve data from a database, you code a query expression similar to the ones you've seen in the previous chapters. The main difference is that instead of querying against a collection or a dataset, you query against objects created from the classes defined by the object model. When you execute the query, the LINQ to SQL runtime translates it into a SQL Select statement and then sends it to ADO.NET, which sends it on to SQL Server for processing. Then, when the requested data is returned, the LINQ to SQL runtime translates it back to the objects used by the application. Note that currently, LINQ to SQL can only be used with SQL Server databases.

You can also change the data in a database using LINQ to SQL. To do that, you first change the related objects defined by the object model. Then, when you submit the changes, the LINQ to SQL runtime generates the required Insert, Update, and Delete statements and passes them on for processing. LINQ to SQL also detects concurrency errors so you can handle them in your applications.

The basic components of an object model

Before you can use LINQ to SQL, you have to create an object model. The table in figure 13-1 describes the basic components of an object model.

To start, an object model contains a *data context* that defines the connection to the database. The data context also provides for retrieving data from the database. If the application changes that data, the data context tracks those changes and submits them to the database when requested.

An object model also contains *entity classes* that have a one-to-one mapping with tables or views in the database. Each entity class has one or more members that map to columns in the table or view. If two tables in a database are related by a foreign key, an *association* defines the relationship in the object model.

In addition to entity classes, an object model can include *data context methods*. These methods are mapped to stored procedures or functions in the database. You can use stored procedures and functions to retrieve data from the database. You can also use stored procedures to update the data in a database.

How LINQ to SQL works

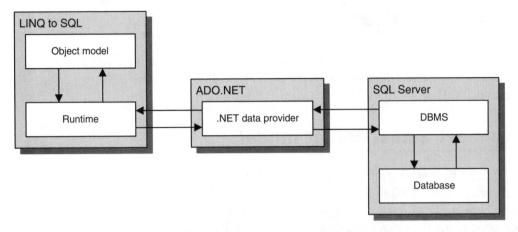

Basic components of an object model

Component	Description
Data context	Defines the connection to the database and provides for retrieving data from the database, tracking changes made to the data, and submitting the changes to the database.
Entity class	Maps to a table or view in the database.
Class member	Maps to a column in a table or view.
Association	Defines a relationship between two tables in the object model.
Method	Maps to a stored procedure or function in the database.

Description

- To use LINQ to SQL, you create an *object model* that represents the objects used by your applications and maps them to objects in a database. An object model can be defined in either Visual Basic or C#.

- When you execute a query against an object model, the *LINQ to SQL runtime* translates the query into a SQL Select statement and sends it to the .NET data provider for execution. The .NET data provider sends the statement on to the DBMS for processing. When the results are returned from the DBMS through the .NET data provider, the LINQ to SQL runtime translates them back to the objects defined by the object model.

- When you submit changes to the database based on changes made to the objects defined by the object model, the LINQ to SQL runtime generates the required Insert, Update, and Delete statements and passes them to ADO.NET for processing.

- An object model consists of a *data context class* that manages the flow of data to and from the database and *entity classes* that map to tables and views in the database.

- Each entity class can define one or more class members that represent columns in the table or view.

- If two tables in a database are related by a foreign key, an *association* is created between the two tables in the object model.

Figure 13-1   An introduction to LINQ to SQL

How to create an object model using the O/R Designer

The easiest way to create an object model is to use the Object Relational Designer. You'll learn the basic skills for working with this designer in the topics that follow.

How to start a new object model

Figure 13-2 presents the basic skills for creating an object model. To do that, you use the LINQ to SQL Classes template in the Add New Item dialog box. Then, a file with the name you specify and the extension *dbml* is added to the project, and the *Object Relational Designer*, or just *O/R Designer*, is displayed as shown here.

As you can see, the O/R Designer consists of two panes: the entities pane on the left side of the designer and the methods pane on the right. As their names imply, the *entities pane* displays the entity classes of the model, and the *methods pane* displays the data context methods. You'll learn how to create entity classes and data context methods in the figures that follow.

If an object model won't include any data context methods or you aren't currently working with these methods, you can close the methods pane as described in this figure. You can't close the entities pane, however. If you need to, though, you can change its size by dragging the border between the two panes.

Note that when the O/R Designer is displayed, the Toolbox contains components that you can use to work with an object model. As you'll see in the next figure, however, you won't typically use these tools.

The Object Relational Designer for a new object model

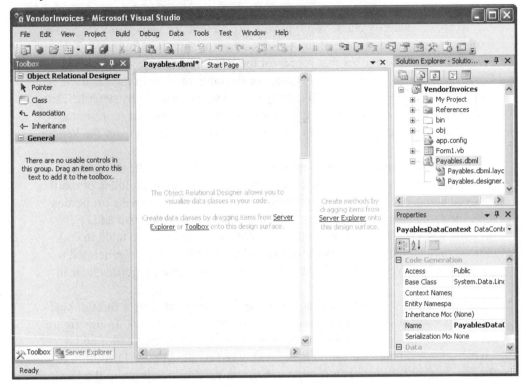

Description

- To create an object model, display the Add New Item dialog box, select the LINQ to SQL Classes template, and enter a name for the *dbml* file that will define the object model.

- After you create an object model, the *Object Relational Designer* (*O/R Designer*) is displayed. You can use this designer to create entity classes or to create data context methods that map to stored procedures or functions.

- The O/R Designer consists of two panes. The *entities pane* on the left is where the entity classes you create are displayed, and the *methods pane* on the right is where the data context methods you create are displayed.

- If you close the O/R Designer, you can open it again by double-clicking on the dbml file in the Solution Explorer.

- If you won't be creating data context methods, you can hide the methods pane by right-clicking anywhere in the designer and choosing the Hide Methods Pane command. To redisplay this pane, right-click and choose the Show Methods Pane command.

- You can use the tools in the Toolbox to create entity classes manually, to add relationships (associations), and to use inheritance. For more information, see the Visual Studio documentation.

Figure 13-2   How to start a new object model

How to create entity classes

To create an entity class, you typically drag a table or view from the Server Explorer to the entities pane of the O/R Designer as shown in figure 13-3. Here, I created two entity classes that represent the Vendors and Invoices tables in the Payables database. Note that if the name of the table or view in the database is plural, the O/R Designer gives the entity class a singular name by default. That makes sense because the class will be used to create objects that represent a single item in the table or view. For example, an object created from the Vendor class represents a single vendor.

When you create an entity class using the O/R Designer, the designer generates Visual Basic code that defines the class. That code includes properties that you can use to refer to each column in the table or view. These properties have the same names as the columns by default. The designer also adds a property to the data context class that you can use to refer to the table in code. When I created the Vendor class, for example, the O/R Designer generated a property named Vendors. You'll see how to use all of these properties later in this chapter.

If you create entity classes for two tables that are related by a foreign key, the O/R Designer creates an *association* between the two classes. In this figure, for example, the arrow represents the association between the Vendor and Invoice classes. This association is defined based on the VendorID column in the Invoices table, which is a foreign key to the VendorID column in the Vendors table. Because the association between the Vendor and Invoice classes represents a one-to-many relationship, the Invoice class will include a property named Vendor that you can use in a query to refer to columns in the Vendors table. Similarly, the Vendor class will include a property named Invoices that you can use to refer to the collection of invoices for a vendor.

If all this sounds a little confusing, it may help to take a look at the code that's generated for an object model. I'll show you some of this code a little later. But first, I want to show you how to create data context methods that retrieve data.

The O/R Designer for an object model that contains two entity classes

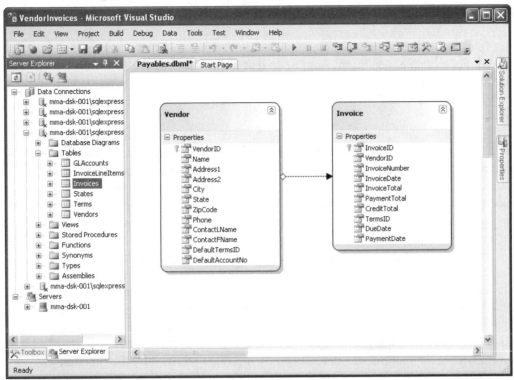

Description

- To create an entity class, display the Server Explorer and then drag a table or view or selected columns of a table or view from the Server Explorer to the O/R Designer. The first time you do that, the connection for the data context is set to the database that contains the table or view.

- Each time you add an entity class, a property is added to the data context that you can use to refer to the table that the class is mapped to. In addition, a property is added to the entity class for each column in the table or view the class is created from that you can use to refer to the class member.

- If two tables that you add to an object model are related by a foreign key, the O/R Designer defines an association between the entity classes based on that relationship. An association is defined by properties in the entity classes, and you can use these properties to refer to one class from the other class.

- By default, if the name of a table or view in the database is plural, the O/R Designer creates a class with a singular name. If that's not what you want, display the Options dialog box (Tools→Options), expand the Database Tools node, select O/R Designer, and select False from the Enabled drop-down list in the Pluralization of Names group.

- You can display the properties of a member in an entity class by clicking on the member in the O/R Designer. However, you won't usually change these properties since they're based on the definition of the column in the database.

Figure 13-3   How to create entity classes

How to create data context methods that retrieve data

In addition to entity classes, you can add data context methods to an object model. For example, you might want to do that if the database you're working with already contains stored procedures or functions that get the data needed by an application. In many shops, this technique is used to restrict access to the database.

Figure 13-4 shows you how to create a data context method that retrieves data from a database. To do that, you simply drag a stored procedure or function that returns data from the Server Explorer to the O/R Designer. Note that if the stored procedure or function returns data that maps to a class in the object model, you should drop the stored procedure or function on that class in the entities pane. That way, the return type of the data context method will be set to the type of that class.

For example, the stored procedure named spGetVendor returns the data for the vendor with the ID that's passed to the procedure. When I created a data context method from this stored procedure, then, I dropped the stored procedure onto the Vendor class so it was given a return type of Vendor. In contrast, when I created a method from the fnVendorBalance function, I dropped the function on an empty area of the designer because it returns a single value. In that case, the return type of the method was determined by the value returned by the function, which in this case is a decimal value. Note that if you need to, you can change the return type of a data context method by changing the Return Type property of the method as described in this figure.

By the way, you can also create data context methods that insert, update, and delete data. You'll learn how to do that in the next chapter.

An object model with two data context methods that retrieve data

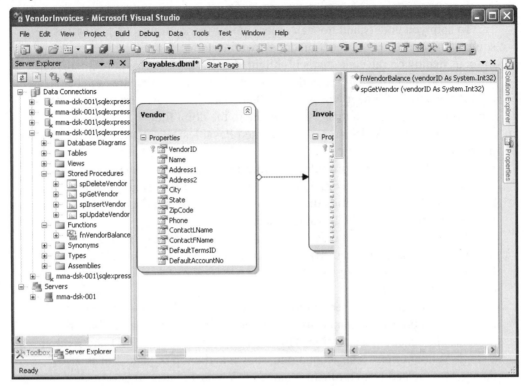

Description

- To create a data context method that retrieves data, locate the stored procedure or function that returns the data in the Server Explorer and drag it to either pane of the O/R Designer. The data context method appears in the methods pane.

- The return type of a data context method is determined by where you drop the stored procedure or function on the design surface. If you drop it on an entity class, the method has the return type of that class. If you drop it on an empty area of the design surface, the return type is determined by the type specified in the stored procedure or function.

- If you need to change the return type of a data context method after it's created, you can do that by selecting the method in the methods pane and then changing the Return Type property in the Properties window. For a method that has a return type of an entity class, you can select any class in the object model as the return type. For any other method, you can select from a variety of system data types.

- When you create a data context method that retrieves data, it's defined by a Function procedure within the data context class. Then, you can use that procedure to call the stored procedure or function.

Figure 13-4   How to create a data context method that retrieves data

The code that's generated for an object model

To help you understand how an object model works, figure 13-5 presents some of the code for the object model shown in figure 13-4. For now, I'm going to focus mainly on the code that's highlighted in this figure. If you're interested, though, you can look at all the code for an object model you create to get a complete picture of how it works. To do that, just double-click on the file with the designer.vb extension that's subordinate to the dbml file.

To start, this code declares a class named PayablesDataContext that defines the data context for the object model. Notice that this class inherits the DataContext class, which provides for working with the entity classes and data context methods of the object model. Also notice that the attribute that precedes the class declaration identifies the name of the database that the object model is mapped to, in this case, the Payables database.

Within the data context class, you can see the code for two properties named Vendors and Invoices. These properties return a collection of Vendor and Invoice objects respectively. You'll see the code for the classes that define these objects in just a moment.

Next, you can see the declaration for two methods. The first one was created from a stored procedure named spGetVendor as indicated by the attribute that precedes the function declaration. This method accepts a vendor ID and returns a single Vendor object. The second one, shown at the top of page 2 of this listing, was created from a function named fnVendorBalance. It accepts a vendor ID and returns a decimal value.

After the data context class, a class named Vendor that's mapped to the Vendors table is declared. This class contains a private field for each column of the table as well as a property that provides access to that field. Notice that the Column attribute for each column declaration provides information about the column. For example, the information for the VendorID column indicates that it's the primary key and an identity column that's generated by the database. It also indicates that on an insert operation, the generated ID will be sent back to the application so it remains synchronized with the database.

In addition to the fields and properties for the columns of the Vendors table, the Vendor class includes a field and a property that define the relationship (association) between the Vendors and Invoices tables. In this case, the Invoices property provides access to the invoices for a vendor. Similarly, the Invoice class that's defined following the Vendor class includes a property named Vendor that provides access to the vendor for an invoice. You'll see how you use these properties as well as the properties for the tables and columns in just a minute.

But first, you should realize that you can modify the generated code to enhance the object model. Keep in mind, though, that if you use the O/R Designer to modify the object model after making changes directly to this code, the changes will be lost. In most cases, then, you won't modify the generated code directly. However, you might want to enhance this code with code that's stored in separate classes. This is possible because the classes within an object model are partial classes that can be extended by other partial classes.

Some of the generated code for the object model in figure 13-4   Page 1

```vb
Option Strict On
Option Explicit On

Imports System
Imports System.Collections.Generic
Imports System.ComponentModel
Imports System.Data
Imports System.Data.Linq
Imports System.Data.Linq.Mapping
Imports System.Linq
Imports System.Linq.Expressions
Imports System.Reflection


<System.Data.Linq.Mapping.DatabaseAttribute(Name:="Payables")> _
Partial Public Class PayablesDataContext _
    Inherits System.Data.Linq.DataContext

    Private Shared mappingSource As System.Data.Linq.Mapping.MappingSource _
        = New AttributeMappingSource

    Public Sub New()
        MyBase.New(Global.VendorMaintenance.My.MySettings.Default. _
                   PayablesConnectionString, mappingSource)
        OnCreated
    End Sub
    .
    .
    Public Sub New(ByVal connection As System.Data.IDbConnection, _
            ByVal mappingSource As System.Data.Linq.Mapping.MappingSource)
        MyBase.New(connection, mappingSource)
        OnCreated
    End Sub

    Public ReadOnly Property Vendors() As System.Data.Linq.Table(Of Vendor)
        Get
            Return Me.GetTable(Of Vendor)
        End Get
    End Property

    Public ReadOnly Property Invoices() As System.Data.Linq.Table(Of Invoice)
        Get
            Return Me.GetTable(Of Invoice)
        End Get
    End Property
    .
    .
    <FunctionAttribute(Name:="dbo.spGetVendor")> _
    Public Function spGetVendor(<Parameter(Name:="VendorID", DbType:="Int")> _
    ByVal vendorID As System.Nullable(Of Integer)) As ISingleResult(Of Vendor)
        Dim result As IExecuteResult = Me.ExecuteMethodCall(Me, _
            CType(MethodInfo.GetCurrentMethod,MethodInfo), vendorID)
        Return CType(result.ReturnValue,ISingleResult(Of Vendor))
    End Function
```

Figure 13-5   The code that's generated for an object model (part 1 of 3)

Some of the generated code for the object model in figure 13-4   Page 2

```vb
<FunctionAttribute(Name:="dbo.fnVendorBalance", IsComposable:=true)> _
Public Function fnVendorBalance(<Parameter(Name:="VendorID", DbType:="Int")> _
ByVal vendorID As System.Nullable(Of Integer)) As System.Nullable(Of Decimal)
    Return CType(Me.ExecuteMethodCall(Me, _
        CType(MethodInfo.GetCurrentMethod,MethodInfo), _
        vendorID).ReturnValue,System.Nullable(Of Decimal))
End Function
    .
    .
    .
End Class

<Table(Name:="dbo.Vendors")> _
Partial Public Class Vendor
    Implements System.ComponentModel.INotifyPropertyChanging, _
    System.ComponentModel.INotifyPropertyChanged
    .
    .
    Private _VendorID As Integer
    Private _Name As String
    .
    .
    Private _DefaultAccountNo As Integer

    Private _Invoices As EntitySet(Of Invoice)

    Public Sub New()
        MyBase.New
        Me._Invoices = New EntitySet(Of Invoice) _
            (AddressOf Me.attach_Invoices, AddressOf Me.detach_Invoices)
        OnCreated
    End Sub

    <Column(Storage:="_VendorID", AutoSync:=AutoSync.OnInsert, _
        DbType:="Int NOT NULL IDENTITY", IsPrimaryKey:=true, _
        IsDbGenerated:=true)> _
    Public Property VendorID() As Integer
        Get
            Return Me._VendorID
        End Get
        Set(ByVal value As Integer)
            ...
        End Set
    End Property

    <Column(Storage:="_Name", DbType:="VarChar(50) NOT NULL", _
        CanBeNull:=false)> _
    Public Property Name() As String
        Get
            Return Me._Name
        End Get
        Set
            ...
        End Set
    End Property
    .
    .
```

Figure 13-5   The code that's generated for an object model (part 2 of 3)

Some of the generated code for the object model in figure 13-4   Page 3

```vb
<Column(Storage:="_DefaultAccountNo", DbType:="Int NOT NULL")> _
Public Property DefaultAccountNo() As Integer
    Get
        Return Me._DefaultAccountNo
    End Get
    Set
        ...
    End Set
End Property

<Association(Name:="Vendor_Invoice", Storage:="_Invoices", _
            ThisKey:="VendorID", OtherKey:="VendorID")> _
Public Property Invoices() As EntitySet(Of Invoice)
    Get
        Return Me._Invoices
    End Get
    Set
        Me._Invoices.Assign(value)
    End Set
End Property
    .
    .
End Class

<Table(Name:="dbo.Invoices")> _
Partial Public Class Invoice
    Implements System.ComponentModel.INotifyPropertyChanging, _
    System.ComponentModel.INotifyPropertyChanged
        .
        .
    Private _Vendor As EntityRef(Of Vendor)
        .
        .
    <Association(Name:="Vendor_Invoice", Storage:="_Vendor", _
                ThisKey:="VendorID", OtherKey:="VendorID", _
                IsForeignKey:=true)> _
    Public Property Vendor() As Vendor
        Get
            Return Me._Vendor.Entity
        End Get
        Set
            ...
        End Set
    End Property
    .
    .
End Class
```

Description

- To see the Visual Basic code that defines an object model, click the plus sign to the left of the dbml file and then double-click the designer.vb file.

Figure 13-5   The code that's generated for an object model (part 3 of 3)

How to retrieve data from a database

To retrieve data from a database using LINQ to SQL, you use techniques similar to the techniques you use to retrieve data using LINQ to Objects and LINQ to DataSet. When you use LINQ to SQL, however, you work with the classes, properties, and methods defined by the object model. You'll see how to do that in the topics that follow.

How to retrieve data from a single table

Figure 13-6 shows how to retrieve data from a single table. To start, you create an instance of the data context class as shown in the first statement in this figure. This statement creates an instance of the PayablesDataContext class and assigns it to a variable named payables. Then, you can use the properties of the data context object to refer to the tables in the database that the data context is mapped to. This is illustrated in the query expression shown here.

This query expression is similar to query expressions you've seen in the last two chapters. It retrieves the vendor ID, invoice number, and balance due for each invoice in the Invoices table with a balance due greater than zero that's due within the next 15 days. The results are sorted by balance due in descending sequence within vendor ID. The only difference here is that the data source for the query is the Invoices table in the Payables database. To refer to this table, the query expression uses the Invoices property of the payables variable that contains a reference to the data context object.

Notice that this query expression also uses several of the properties defined by the Invoice class within the object model. For example, the Let clause refers to the InvoiceTotal, PaymentTotal, and CreditTotal properties. This works because the range variable in this query represents a single Invoice object.

A LINQ query that retrieves data from the Invoices table

A statement that creates an instance of the data context

```
Dim payables As New PayablesDataContext
```

A query expression that gets invoice balances due

```
Dim invoicesDue = _
    From invoice In payables.Invoices _
    Let BalanceDue = invoice.InvoiceTotal - invoice.PaymentTotal _
                   - invoice.CreditTotal _
    Where BalanceDue > 0 _
      And invoice.DueDate < DateTime.Today.AddDays(15) _
    Order By invoice.VendorID, BalanceDue Descending _
    Select invoice.VendorID, Number = invoice.InvoiceNumber, BalanceDue
```

Code that executes the query

```
Dim invoiceDisplay As String _
    = "Vendor ID" & vbTab & "Invoice No." & vbTab & "Balance Due" & vbCrLf
For Each invoice In invoicesDue
    invoiceDisplay &= invoice.VendorID & vbTab & vbTab _
                    & invoice.Number & vbTab _
                    & IIf(invoice.Number.Length < 8, vbTab, "").ToString _
                    & FormatCurrency(invoice.BalanceDue) & vbCrLf
Next
MessageBox.Show(invoiceDisplay, "Sorted Vendor Invoices Due")
```

The resulting dialog box

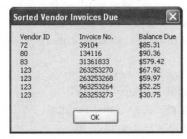

Description

- Before you can work with the entity classes in an object model, you have to create an instance of the data context for the model.

- To refer to a database table in a query expression, you use the property of the data context class that returns data from the table as a collection of entity objects.

- To refer to a member of an entity object, you use the property that defines the member. In a LINQ query, you refer to that member through the range variable.

- By default, an object model tracks changes to the objects it defines. If an application won't change the data it retrieves, you can improve the performance of a query by setting the ObjectTrackingEnabled property of the data context to False.

- Unlike LINQ to Objects and LINQ to DataSet queries, LINQ to SQL queries return an IQueryable(Of T) object.

Figure 13-6   How to retrieve data from a single table

How to query across relationships

As you saw when I showed you some of the code for an object model, the entity classes of the object model contain properties that provide access to the relationships between the classes. You can use these properties to query across relationships as shown in figure 13-7. The examples in this figure use the one-to-many relationship between the Vendor and Invoice classes.

The first query expression in this figure gets information for a vendor through the Invoice objects. To do that, it uses the Vendor property of the Invoice class. In this case, the Vendor property is used to get the Name property of the Vendor object. This property is included in the query results, and it's used to sort those results.

The second query expression in this figure gets invoice information through the Vendor objects. To do that, it uses the Invoices property of the Vendor class. Note that this query expression includes the relationship in the From clause. That works because the Invoices property returns a queryable type. Then, the properties of the related class can be accessed through the range variable for that relationship. This is similar to the way you use joins with LINQ to Objects and LINQ to DataSet. In fact, you can use standard join syntax with LINQ to SQL as well. However, it's more common to use the relationships that are defined by the object model as shown here.

You can also use a technique called *deferred loading* when you work with relationships. In some cases, deferred loading can make your applications more efficient because related data isn't loaded into memory until it's needed. This is illustrated in the third example in this figure.

The query expression in this example is similar to the query expression in the first example except that it doesn't refer to the Vendor property of the Invoice objects. Because of that, this query doesn't retrieve the related vendor data. Instead, the vendor data isn't retrieved until the query is executed as illustrated by the code that follows the query expression in this example.

Note that when you use this technique, the query expression must not return a projection. The query expression shown here, for example, returns entire invoice rows, which are stored in Invoice objects. That's necessary because the Vendor property is available only from an Invoice object. It's not available from anonymous types like the ones returned by the first two query expressions.

A query expression that gets vendor data through the Invoice objects

```
Dim invoicesDue = From invoice In payables.Invoices _
                  Let BalanceDue = invoice.InvoiceTotal _
                              - invoice.PaymentTotal _
                              - invoice.CreditTotal _
                  Where BalanceDue > 0 _
                    And invoice.DueDate < DateTime.Today.AddDays(15) _
                  Order By invoice.Vendor.Name, BalanceDue Descending _
                  Select invoice.Vendor.Name, _
                         Number = invoice.InvoiceNumber, BalanceDue
```

A query expression that gets invoice data through the Vendor objects

```
Dim invoicesDue = From vendor In payables.Vendors, _
                       invoice In vendor.Invoices _
                  Let BalanceDue = invoice.InvoiceTotal _
                              - invoice.PaymentTotal _
                              - invoice.CreditTotal _
                  Where BalanceDue > 0 _
                    And invoice.DueDate < DateTime.Today.AddDays(15) _
                  Order By vendor.Name, BalanceDue Descending _
                  Select vendor.Name, Number = invoice.InvoiceNumber, _
                         BalanceDue
```

Code that defers the loading of vendor data

```
Dim invoicesDue = From invoice In payables.Invoices _
                  Let BalanceDue = invoice.InvoiceTotal _
                              - invoice.PaymentTotal _
                              - invoice.CreditTotal _
                  Where BalanceDue > 0 _
                    And invoice.DueDate < DateTime.Today.AddDays(15) _
                  Order By BalanceDue Descending _
                  Select invoice
        .
        .
        .
For Each invoice In invoicesDue
    Dim vendor As Vendor = invoice.Vendor
        .
        .
        .
Next
```

Description

- Instead of using joins in LINQ to SQL queries, you typically use the associations defined by the object model that identify the relationships between the classes. To refer to an association, you use the property of an entity class that defines the association.

- You can simplify the reference to objects on the many side of a relationship by including the association in the From clause as shown in the second example above.

- You can defer the loading of related objects by omitting references to those objects from the query expression. Then, the objects aren't loaded until you refer to them from the query results. For this to work, the query must not return a projection.

Figure 13-7   How to query across relationships

How to load related objects

In the last figure, you saw how you can use the properties that define the relationships between objects to get data from related objects, and you saw how you can defer the loading of related objects until they're needed. But you can also load the child objects related to parent objects when a query that retrieves the parent objects is executed. Figure 13-8 illustrates how this works.

To load related objects, you must set the load options for the data context object as shown in the first example in this figure. The first statement in this example creates a new DataLoadOptions object. Then, the second statement uses the LoadWith(Of T) method of this object to specify the objects to be loaded. Here, T represents the parent object, in this case, a Vendor object. The argument for this method is a lambda expression that identifies the related objects that will be loaded when a Vendor object is loaded. In this case, the Invoice objects for the vendor will be loaded. The last statement in this example sets the LoadOptions property of the data context object to the DataLoadOptions object.

The second example in this figure shows a query expression that retrieves the vendors in a specified state. Then, the third example executes this query. To do that, it uses nested For Each statements. The outer statement loops through the Vendor objects in the query results, and the inner statement loops through the invoices for each vendor. Although you can't tell from these statements, the invoices for the vendors in the query results are loaded when the outer For Each statement is executed. In contrast, if I hadn't set the load options as shown in the first example, the invoices for each vendor would have been loaded when the inner For Each statement was executed. Since that requires more round trips to the server, it's less efficient than the technique shown here.

Code that sets the load options for the data context object

```
Dim loadOptions As New DataLoadOptions
loadOptions.LoadWith(Of Vendor)(Function(v) v.Invoices)
payables.LoadOptions = loadOptions
```

A query expression that gets Vendor objects

```
Dim vendors = From vendor In payables.Vendors _
              Where vendor.State = CInt(cboStates.SelectedValue) _
              Select vendor
```

Code that executes the query

```
Dim vendorBalanceDisplay As String _
    = "Invoice No." & vbTab & "Invoice Date" & vbTab _
    & "Invoice Total" & vbCrLf
For Each vendor In vendors
    For Each invoice In vendor.Invoices
        vendorBalanceDisplay _
            &= invoice.InvoiceNumber & vbTab _
            & IIf(invoice.InvoiceNumber.Length < 8, vbTab, "").ToString _
            & invoice.InvoiceDate & vbTab _
            & IIf(invoice.InvoiceDate.ToShortDateString.Length < 9, _
                vbTab, "").ToString _
            & FormatCurrency(invoice.InvoiceTotal) & vbCrLf
    Next
    MessageBox.Show(vendorBalanceDisplay, vendor.Name)
Next
```

A resulting dialog box

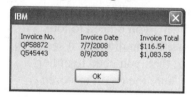

Description

- By default, only the entity objects that are specifically requested in a query are loaded into the data context object. Related objects aren't automatically loaded.

- To load related objects, you can use the LoadWith(Of T) method of a DataLoadOptions object where T is the parent object. On this method, you specify a lambda expression that uses the association property of the parent object to identify the related child objects to be loaded. Then, you set the LoadOptions property of the data context object to the DataLoadOptions object.

- When you execute a query that retrieves parent objects, the related child objects are also loaded. For this to work, the query must not return a projection.

- The DataLoadOptions class is a member of the System.Data.Linq namespace.

Figure 13-8   How to load related objects

How to retrieve data using data context methods

When you create a data context method that retrieves data, it's defined by a Function procedure within the data context class as you saw in figure 13-5. Then, you can execute the stored procedure or function associated with the data context method by calling the Function procedure. How you do that depends on the type of data the procedure returns.

The first example in figure 13-9 shows how you can execute a data context method named fnVendorBalance that returns a single value. As you can see, this method is created from a function that returns the balance due for a vendor. Then, the query expression that follows executes the method for each vendor in the Vendors table. To do that, it refers to the method through the data context, and it assigns an alias to the result in the Select clause of the query.

You should notice two things about this query expression. First, because the data context method expects a vendor ID, that ID is passed to the method as an argument. Second, Where and Order By clauses are coded after the Select clause. That way, the result of the method can be used within these clauses. When you include clauses after the Select clause in a query expression, you should realize that they can refer only to the fields that are named on the Select clause. That's because any other fields that may have been available before the Select clause are no longer in scope after the Select clause.

You can also execute a data context method that returns a single value directly. To do that, you use a statement like the one shown in this figure. Here, the value that's returned by the fnVendorBalance method is assigned to a variable with the Decimal type. Notice in this example that the result of the method is converted to a decimal value. To understand why, you'd need to look at the return type of this method in the data context class. If you did, you'd see that the return type is Nullable(Of Decimal). Because of that, you need to either convert the result to a Decimal or declare the variable where the result is stored as a nullable type.

The second example in this figure shows how to execute a data context method named spVendorInvoices that returns a queryable object. In this case, the method is created from a stored procedure that retrieves all the invoices for a vendor. Then, the query expression uses this method as a data source.

Once again, you can look at the return type for the data context method to see how this works. If you do, you'll see that the return type is ISingleResult(Of spVendorInvoices). Since the ISingleResult(Of T) interface implements the IEnumerable(Of T) interface, it can be used as a data source in a query.

A data context method that gets the balance due for a vendor

Code that creates the function that gets the balance due

```
CREATE FUNCTION dbo.fnVendorBalance
    (@VendorID int)
RETURNS decimal
BEGIN
    RETURN (SELECT SUM(InvoiceTotal - PaymentTotal - CreditTotal)
            FROM Invoices
            WHERE VendorID = @VendorID)
END
```

A query that uses the method generated from the function

```
Dim vendorBalances _
    = From vendor In payables.Vendors _
      Select vendor.Name, _
             BalanceDue = payables.fnVendorBalance(vendor.VendorID) _
      Where BalanceDue > 0 _
      Order By BalanceDue Descending
```

A statement that calls the method directly

```
Dim vendorBalance As Decimal _
    = CDec(payables.fnVendorBalance(CInt(txtVendorID.Text)))
```

A data context method that gets the invoices for a vendor

Code that creates the stored procedure that gets the invoices

```
CREATE PROCEDURE dbo.spVendorInvoices
    (@VendorID int)
AS
    SELECT * FROM Invoices WHERE VendorID = @VendorID
```

A query that uses the method generated from the stored procedure

```
Dim vendorInvoices = _
    From invoice In payables.spVendorInvoices(CInt(txtVendorID.Text)) _
    Let BalanceDue = invoice.InvoiceTotal _
                   - invoice.PaymentTotal _
                   - invoice.CreditTotal _
    Where BalanceDue > 0 _
    Order By BalanceDue Descending _
    Select invoice.VendorID, Number = invoice.InvoiceNumber, _
           BalanceDue
```

Description

- When you create a data context method, it's defined by a procedure within the data context class. Then, you can call that procedure from an instance of the class.

- If the stored procedure or function that's called by a data context method requires arguments, you pass those arguments to the data context method just as you would if you were calling a method of any class.

- Any value types that are returned by a data context method are returned as nullable types. Because of that, you have to either store the value in a nullable type or convert the value to the appropriate type.

Figure 13-9   How to retrieve data using data context methods

How to get information about the SQL command for a query

When you execute a query against an object model, LINQ to SQL translates the query to a SQL statement and then passes it on to ADO.NET for processing. If the data that's returned by a query isn't what you expect, you may be able to determine the problem by reviewing the information in the generated command object. Figure 13-10 shows how to do that.

To get the command object for a query, you use the GetCommand method of the DataContext class. For example, the first statement in the example in this figure gets the command object that's generated for the query expression you saw in figure 13-6. Notice that the result of this command is assigned to a variable that's declared with the DbCommand type. This is the type that's returned by the GetCommand method, and it's the base class for all the provider-specific command classes.

Once you've retrieved the command object for a query, you can get information about the command using the properties of the DbCommand class. The three properties you're most likely to use are shown in this figure. In particular, you'll want to use the CommandText property to display the SQL statement for the command.

The code in this figure uses all three of these properties to display information about the command in a dialog box. Notice that after it uses the Connection property to get the connection object, it uses the Connection string property of that object to get the connection string. Also notice that the CommandType property is converted to a string. That way, the command type is displayed as a string rather than an integer that represents the command type.

If you review the information that's displayed by this code, you'll see how this works. Here, after the connection string and command type are displayed, the Select statement that's stored in the CommandText property is displayed. As you can see, this statement is relatively complicated. In particular, the From clause uses a subquery to get the data used by the query from the Invoices table. (In case you're not familiar with subqueries, they're just Select statements that are coded within other clauses of a SQL statement.)

At this point, you should realize that the Select statement shown here is more complicated than one you would write yourself to retrieve the same data. For example, the Select statement shown here could be written like this:

```
SELECT VendorID, InvoiceNumber, InvoiceTotal - PaymentTotal
       - CreditTotal AS BalanceDue
FROM Invoices
WHERE InvoiceTotal - PaymentTotal - CreditTotal > 0
  AND DueDate < @DueDate
ORDER BY VendorID, BalanceDue DESC
```

That illustrates that although using LINQ to SQL makes it easy to query a SQL Server database, the SQL statements it generates are often more complicated, which makes them less efficient. In most cases, though, the ease of use outweighs the slight inefficiency.

Method of the DataContext class for getting a SQL command

Method	Description
GetCommand(query)	Returns a DbCommand object that provides information about the SQL command that's generated by LINQ to SQL for a query.

Properties of the DbCommand class that provide information about a command

Property	Description
CommandText	The text of the SQL statement that's generated.
CommandType	A member of the CommandType enumeration that indicates if the CommandText property contains a SQL statement or a stored procedure.
Connection	The connection used to connect to the database.

Code that displays information about the SQL command that's generated for the query expression in figure 13-6

```
Dim selectCommand As DbCommand = payables.GetCommand(invoicesDue)
Dim commandDisplay As String _
    = "Connection string: " _
    & selectCommand.Connection.ConnectionString & vbCrLf & vbCrLf _
    & "Command type: " _
    & selectCommand.CommandType.ToString & vbCrLf & vbCrLf _
    & "Command text:" & vbCrLf _
    & selectCommand.CommandText
MessageBox.Show(commandDisplay, "Generated SQL Command")
```

The resulting dialog box

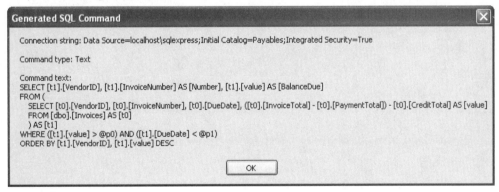

```
Generated SQL Command                                          [X]

Connection string: Data Source=localhost\sqlexpress;Initial Catalog=Payables;Integrated Security=True

Command type: Text

Command text:
SELECT [t1].[VendorID], [t1].[InvoiceNumber] AS [Number], [t1].[value] AS [BalanceDue]
FROM (
    SELECT [t0].[VendorID], [t0].[InvoiceNumber], [t0].[DueDate], ([t0].[InvoiceTotal] - [t0].[PaymentTotal]) - [t0].[CreditTotal] AS [value]
    FROM [dbo].[Invoices] AS [t0]
    ) AS [t1]
WHERE ([t1].[value] > @p0) AND ([t1].[DueDate] < @p1)
ORDER BY [t1].[VendorID], [t1].[value] DESC

                        [  OK  ]
```

Description

- If you want to review the SQL command that's generated for a query, you can use the GetCommand method of the DataContext class to get that command. Then, you can use properties of the DbCommand class to get information about the command.

- The DbCommand class is the base class for provider-specific command classes such as the SqlCommand class. It can be found in the System.Data.Common namespace.

Figure 13-10   How to get information about the SQL command for a query

How to work with bound controls

When you use LINQ to SQL, you can bind controls to an entity collection, to the results of a query, and to an object data source that's created from an entity class. You'll learn about these binding techniques in the next two topics.

How to create an object data source from an entity class

In chapter 9, you learned how to create an object data source from a business class that you develop. You can also create an object data source from an entity class in an object model. Figure 13-11 shows you how to do that.

As you can see, you use the Data Source Configuration Wizard just as you do for any other data source. From the first step of this wizard, you select the Object option. Then, from the second step, you select the entity type you want to use as the source of data. In this figure, for example, I selected the Vendor entity. When I clicked the Finish button, the Vendor data source appeared in the Data Sources window.

After you create an object data source, you can use it to create bound controls as described in chapter 9. Then, you can work with the bound controls using techniques that are similar to the techniques presented in that chapter. Instead of using database classes to access the data in a database, however, you can use LINQ to SQL as shown in the next figure.

The first step of the Data Source Configuration Wizard

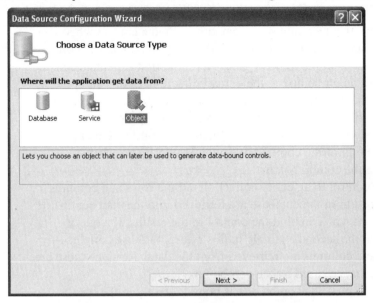

The second step of the Data Source Configuration Wizard

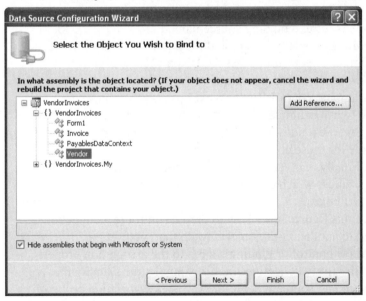

Description

- To create an object data source from an entity class, select the Object option from the first step of the Data Source Configuration Wizard. Then, select the entity type you want to use from the list that's displayed in the second step.

Figure 13-11   How to create an object data source from an entity class

How to bind controls

Figure 13-12 shows five techniques you can use to bind a control when you use LINQ to SQL. To start, you can complex-bind a control to an entity collection as shown in the first example in this figure. Here, the first statement sets the DataSource property of a combo box to the entity collection, in this case, the Vendors collection in the payables data context. Then, the second statement sets the DisplayMember property of the combo box so the Name property of the entity will be displayed in the combo box list. Finally, the third statement sets the ValueMember property of the combo box so the VendorID property of the entity will be stored in the combo box list.

When you bind a control to an entity collection, all the rows and columns that the entity is mapped to in the database are retrieved into the data context. If that's not what you want, you can bind the control to the results of a query instead as illustrated in the second example in this figure. In this example, only the VendorID and Name columns are retrieved from the database since these are the only two columns that are used by the combo box.

In the first two examples, the combo box is bound directly to the data source through its DataSource property. If a control is created from an object data source, however, you can also bind it to the data source by setting the DataSource property of the binding source for the control. If the DataSource property of a combo box is set to a binding source named VendorBindingSource, for example, you can bind the control as shown in the third example in this figure. This assumes that the DisplayMember and ValueMember properties were set at design time.

If you want to simple-bind controls such as text boxes, you can use the technique shown in the fourth example. The code in this example starts by getting a Vendor object whose values will be displayed in the bound controls. Then, the binding source for those controls is cleared so that no data is displayed in the controls. Finally, the Vendor object is added to the list of bound objects for the binding source, which causes the properties of the Vendor object to be displayed in the text boxes.

The last example in this figure shows how to bind a control to a collection of entity objects related to another entity object. To do that, you set the DataSource property of the control or binding source to the association property that provides access to the entity collection. In this example, the DataSource property of an Invoice binding source is set to the Invoices association property for a vendor. Note that when this statement is executed, the invoices for the vendor are loaded automatically if necessary.

Code that binds a combo box to an entity collection

```
cboVendors.DataSource = payables.Vendors
cboVendors.DisplayMember = "Name"
cboVendors.ValueMember = "VendorID"
```

Code that binds a combo box to the results of a query

```
Dim vendors = From vendor In payables.Vendors _
              Order By vendor.Name _
              Select vendor.VendorID, vendor.Name

cboVendors.DataSource = vendors
cboVendors.DisplayMember = "Name"
cboVendors.ValueMember = "VendorID"
```

A statement that binds a combo box using its binding source

```
VendorBindingSource.DataSource = vendors
```

Code that binds text boxes to an entity object

```
Dim vendorID As Integer = CInt(NameComboBox.SelectedValue)
Dim selectedVendor = (From vendor In payables.Vendors _
                      Where vendor.VendorID = vendorID).Single

VendorBindingSource.Clear()
VendorBindingSource.Add(selectedVendor)
```

A statement that binds a DataGridView control to related objects

```
InvoiceBindingSource.DataSource = selectedVendor.Invoices
```

Description

- You can complex-bind a control such as a combo box or a DataGridView control to an entity collection or to the results of a query by setting the DataSource property of the control or the binding source associated with the control to the collection or results.

- You can simple-bind controls such as text boxes that are created from an object data source to the properties of an entity object by clearing the binding source for the controls and then adding the object to the list of bound objects for the binding source.

- If an object has a one-to-many relationship with other objects, you can complex-bind a control to the objects on the many side by setting the DataSource property of the control or the binding source associated with the control to the association property of the object on the one side. If the objects on the many side haven't already been loaded, they're loaded automatically.

- You can use bound controls to display, add, modify, and delete data.

Figure 13-12   How to bind controls

A Vendor Invoices application

Now that you've seen how to retrieve data and bind controls using LINQ to SQL, you're ready to see how to use LINQ to SQL in an application. In the topics that follow, then, I'll present an application that displays vendor and invoice data.

The user interface

Figure 13-13 presents the user interface for the Vendor Invoices application. As you can see, the Vendor Invoices form includes a combo box that lets the user select a vendor. Then, the address information for that vendor is displayed in the text boxes on the form, and the invoices for that vendor are displayed in the DataGridView control.

The object model

Figure 13-13 also presents the object model for this application. It includes just Vendor and Invoice entity classes. Note that I included only the columns needed by the application in these two classes.

Although you can't tell from the user interface and object model, this application uses two object data sources for the Vendor and Invoice objects. I used the Vendor object to generate the combo box and text boxes along with a Vendor binding source, and I used the Invoice object to generate the DataGridView control along with an Invoice binding source. That way, I was able to set the DisplayMember and ValueMember properties of the combo box at design time, and I was able to format the DataGridView control so it looked the way I wanted it to. (Remember from chapter 4 that if you bind a combo box this way, you need to remove the binding from the Text property of the combo box. Otherwise, the combo box won't work correctly.)

The Vendor Invoices form

The object model

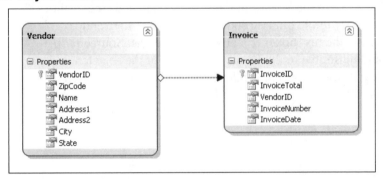

Description

- When the user selects a vendor from the combo box, the vendor address is displayed in the text boxes and the invoices for the vendor are displayed in the DataGridView control.

- The object model for this application consists of just the Vendor and Invoice classes. These classes have a one-to-one correspondence with the Vendors and Invoices tables in the Payables database. Only the columns that are used by this application are included in the object model, however.

- A one-to-many association is defined between the Vendor and Invoice classes based on the foreign key defined between the Vendors and Invoices tables in the database.

- This application uses two object data sources that were created from the Vendor and Invoice classes. The Vendor object is used to generate the combo box and text boxes on the form, and the Invoice object is used to generate the DataGridView control.

Figure 13-13   The user interface and object model for the Vendor Invoices application

The code for the Vendor Invoices form

Figure 13-14 presents the code for the Vendor Invoices form. This code starts by creating an instance of the PayablesDataContext class. The application can then use this data context in any of the three procedures it contains.

When the form is first loaded, a query that retrieves the vendor ID and names for all the vendors is bound to the combo box. Note that this binding is accomplished by setting the DataSource property of the combo box to the results of the query rather than by setting the DataSource property of the Vendor binding source to the results of the query. That's because the text boxes use the Vendor binding source to display the data for the selected vendor, so you don't want to use this binding source for the combo box.

After binding the combo box, the Load event handler calls the GetVendorInvoices procedure to display the address and invoices for the vendor that's selected in the combo box. This procedure is also called whenever the user selects a different vendor. It starts by declaring a query expression that retrieves the vendor with the vendor ID that's selected in the combo box. Notice that the Single method is executed on this query expression so that only one Vendor object is returned.

Next, this procedure clears the Vendor binding source and adds the vendor that's retrieved by the query to the binding source. That causes the vendor address to be displayed in the text boxes. Finally, it sets the DataSource property of the Invoice binding source to the Invoices property of the selected vendor. That causes the invoices for that vendor to be loaded and displayed in the DataGridView control.

The code for the Vendor Invoices form

```
Public Class Form1

    Dim payables As New PayablesDataContext

    Private Sub Form1_Load(ByVal sender As System.Object, _
            ByVal e As System.EventArgs) Handles MyBase.Load
        RemoveHandler NameComboBox.SelectedIndexChanged, _
            AddressOf NameComboBox_SelectedIndexChanged

        Dim vendors = From vendor In payables.Vendors _
                      Order By vendor.Name _
                      Select vendor.VendorID, vendor.Name
        NameComboBox.DataSource = vendors

        Me.GetVendorInvoices()

        AddHandler NameComboBox.SelectedIndexChanged, _
            AddressOf NameComboBox_SelectedIndexChanged
    End Sub

    Private Sub NameComboBox_SelectedIndexChanged( _
            ByVal sender As System.Object, ByVal e As System.EventArgs) _
            Handles NameComboBox.SelectedIndexChanged
        Me.GetVendorInvoices()
    End Sub

    Private Sub GetVendorInvoices()
        Dim selectedVendor = _
            (From vendor In payables.Vendors _
            Where vendor.VendorID = CInt(NameComboBox.SelectedValue) _
            Select vendor).Single

        VendorBindingSource.Clear()
        VendorBindingSource.Add(selectedVendor)

        InvoiceBindingSource.DataSource = selectedVendor.Invoices
    End Sub

End Class
```

Notes

- The DisplayMember and ValueMember properties of the combo box are set at design time.
- This application uses deferred loading to load the invoices for a selected vendor.

Figure 13-14   The code for the Vendor Invoices form

Perspective

As you've seen in this chapter, LINQ to SQL makes it quick and easy to develop database applications that work with SQL Server data. That's because you don't have to code the business classes or write the data access code when you use LINQ to SQL. Instead, the business classes are generated for you when you use the O/R Designer. And the data access code is generated for you when you execute a query.

Keep in mind if you use LINQ to SQL that the classes in the object models you create have a direct relationship with the tables and views in a database. In other words, LINQ to SQL does nothing to address the mismatch between a relational database and the objects used in an application. Because of that, you may want to use LINQ to SQL only for Rapid Application Development. Then, if you want to address the mismatch between a relational database and the objects in an application, you can use the Entity Framework as described in section 5 of this book.

Terms

object model	O/R (Object Relational) Designer
LINQ to SQL runtime	data context method
data context class	entities pane
entity class	methods pane
association	deferred loading

Exercise 13-1   Develop the Vendor Invoices application

In this exercise, you'll develop the Vendor Invoices application presented in this chapter. That will show you how to build a simple application that uses LINQ to SQL.

Create the object model for the application

1. Start a new application named VendorInvoices in your chapter 13 directory.

2. Start a new object model as described in figure 13-2. Then, close the methods pane so you have more room to work in the entities pane.

3. Use the Server Explorer to create entity classes from the Vendors and Invoices tables in the Payables database as described in figure 13-3. Include just the columns needed by the application. When you're done, the object model should look like the one shown in figure 13-13.

Create and use the object data sources for the application

4. Use the Data Source Configuration Wizard as shown in figure 13-11 to create object data sources for the Vendor and Invoice entities in the object model you just created.

5. In the Data Sources window, change the default control for the Vendor object to Detail, and change the default control for the Name property to a combo box. Then, drag the vendor object to the form and delete the navigation toolbar that's generated.

6. Set the binding properties for the combo box so the value of the Name property is displayed in the control and the value of the ID property is stored in the control. In addition, set the DropDownStyle property of the control to DropDownList, and remove the binding from the Text property of the control.

7. Drag the Invoice object from the Data Sources window to the form to generate a DataGridView control.

8. Make the necessary adjustments to the form and its controls so the form looks like the one shown in figure 13-13.

Code and test the application

9. Start an event handler for the Load event of the form. Then, create an instance of the Payables data context and store it in a variable that's declared at the class level.

10. Code a query expression in the Load event handler that will retrieve the VendorID and Name columns from the Vendors table and sort the results by the Name column. Assign the results to the DataSource property of the combo box.

11. Run the application. At this point, the combo box list should include all the vendor names. However, the address and invoices for the selected vendor won't be displayed.

12. Add a procedure that uses a query to get the vendor that's selected in the combo box. This procedure should also include code that binds the selected vendor to the text boxes on the form and binds the invoices for the vendor to the DataGridView. Call this procedure from the Load event handler and from the event handler for the SelectedIndexChanged event of the combo box.

13. Add a RemoveHandler statement at the beginning of the Load event handler that prevents the SelectedIndexChanged event of the combo box from firing as the combo box is loaded. Then, add an AddHandler statement to rewire this event at the end of the Load event handler.

14. Run the application again. This time, the address information should be displayed for the first vendor. In addition, if the vendor has any invoices, those invoices should be displayed in the DataGridView control.

15. Select a different vendor such as IBM to be sure that the correct invoices are displayed. When you're sure this is working correctly, end the application.

Display the command text for the vendors query

16. Add an Imports statement for the System.Data.Common namespace. Then, add code to the Load event handler to get the command object for the vendors query before the combo box is bound to the query results.

17. Display a dialog box with the Select statement for the command like this:

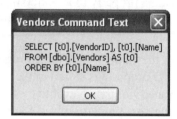

When you click the OK button in this dialog box, the vendor and invoice information should be displayed as before. When you have this working correctly, close the solution.

14

How to use LINQ to SQL (part 2)

In the last chapter, you learned how to create an object model for use with LINQ to SQL, and you learned how to use LINQ to SQL to retrieve data from a database. But you can also use LINQ to SQL to insert, update, and delete data in a database and to provide for concurrency during update and delete operations. These are the skills you'll learn in this chapter.

How to insert, update, and delete data in a database

When you execute a query against an object model, the LINQ to SQL runtime translates the query into a Select statement that can be executed by the database. Then, if you make changes to the query results, you can use LINQ to SQL to submit those changes back to the database. That includes modifying and deleting existing rows as well as adding new rows. You'll learn how to perform these operations in the topics that follow.

How to modify an existing row

Before you can modify a row, you must retrieve the row from the database. To do that, you can use a query like the one shown at the top of figure 14-1. This query retrieves the vendor with the specified ID.

After you retrieve a vendor, you can modify the data in the Vendor object as shown in the second example in this figure. This code simply assigns values from controls on a form to the appropriate properties of the Vendor object. Finally, you can submit the changes to the database by executing the SubmitChanges method of the data context object as shown in the third example.

If you need to change the parent object of a child object, you can do that using one of the techniques shown in the fourth and fifth examples. In the fourth example, an invoice is retrieved and then the Vendor property of that invoice is set to the new Vendor object. An invoice is also retrieved in the fifth example. Instead of changing the Vendor property, though, this code gets the current vendor for the invoice using the Vendor property. Then, it removes the invoice from the collection of invoices for the vendor using the Invoices property of the Vendor object. Finally, the invoice is added to the Invoices collection of another vendor.

Code that retrieves a vendor row from the Payables database

```
Dim selectedVendor = (From vendor In payables.Vendors _
                      Where vendor.VendorID = CInt(txtVendorID.Text) _
                      Select vendor).Single
```

Code that modifies the data in the Vendor object

```
selectedVendor.Name = txtName.Text
selectedVendor.Address1 = txtAddress1.Text
selectedVendor.Address2 = txtAddress2.Text
selectedVendor.City = txtCity.Text
selectedVendor.State = cboStates.SelectedValue.ToString
selectedVendor.ZipCode = txtZipCode.Text
selectedVendor.DefaultTermsID = CInt(cboTerms.SelectedValue)
selectedVendor.DefaultAccountNo = CInt(cboAccounts.SelectedValue)
selectedVendor.Phone = txtPhone.Text.Replace(".", "")
selectedVendor.ContactFName = txtFirstName.Text
selectedVendor.ContactLName = txtLastName.Text
```

A statement that saves the changes to the database

```
payables.SubmitChanges()
```

Code that assigns an invoice to a different vendor

```
Dim selectedInvoice _
    = (From invoice In payables.Invoices _
       Where invoice.InvoiceID = CInt(cboInvoices.SelectedValue)).Single

selectedInvoice.Vendor = selectedVendor
```

Another way to assign an invoice to a different vendor

```
Dim selectedInvoice _
    = (From invoice In payables.Invoices _
       Where invoice.InvoiceID = CInt(cboInvoices.SelectedValue)).Single

Dim oldVendor As Vendor = selectedInvoice.Vendor
oldVendor.Invoices.Remove(selectedInvoice)
selectedVendor.Invoices.Add(selectedInvoice)
```

Description

- To modify a row in the database, you retrieve the row and store it in an object created from a class in the object model. Then, you assign new values to the properties of the object. Finally, you execute the SubmitChanges method of the data context object.

- When you execute the SubmitChanges method, LINQ to SQL generates a SQL Update statement for each object that was modified and then passes those statements to the DBMS for processing.

- If you need to change the parent object that a child object is associated with, you can do that by updating the child object's reference to the parent object or by updating the collection of child objects for the old and new parent objects.

Figure 14-1   How to modify an existing row

How to delete an existing row

Figure 14-2 shows how to delete an existing row from the database. Just as when you modify a row, you start by retrieving the row you want to delete. To do that, you use a query expression like the one in the first example. This query expression retrieves an invoice based on its ID.

Next, you execute the DeleteOnSubmit method of the object collection that contains the object you want to delete as illustrated in the second example. On this method, you specify the object you want to delete. Then, that object is marked for deletion. In this case, the object is the invoice that was retrieved by the query expression. When the SubmitChanges method is executed, the invoice is deleted from the database table and marked as permanently deleted in the object collection.

If you want to delete a row from a table in a database that has a one-to-many relationship with another table in the database, you should realize that LINQ to SQL doesn't support cascading deletes. Unless the database handles cascading deletes, then, you'll need to retrieve all the child objects associated with the parent object and then mark them for deletion. This figure shows two ways to do that for the line items for an invoice.

First, you can use a For Each statement to loop through the line items and mark each one as deleted. Second, you can use the DeleteAllOnSubmit method to mark all the line items for the invoice at once. Note that regardless of which technique you use, the line items aren't retrieved until you refer to them on the DeleteOnSubmit or DeleteAllOnSubmit method. This is another example of deferred loading that you learned about in the last chapter.

Code that retrieves an invoice row from the Payables database

```
Dim selectedInvoice _
    = (From invoice In payables.Invoices _
        Where invoice.InvoiceID = CInt(cboInvoices.SelectedValue)).Single
```

A statement that marks the Invoice object for deletion

```
payables.Invoices.DeleteOnSubmit(selectedInvoice)
```

A statement that deletes the invoice from the database

```
payables.SubmitChanges()
```

Code that marks associated InvoiceLineItem objects for deletion

```
For Each lineItem In selectedInvoice.InvoiceLineItems
    payables.InvoiceLineItems.DeleteOnSubmit(lineItem)
Next
```

Another way to mark associated InvoiceLineItem objects for deletion

```
payables.InvoiceLineItems.DeleteAllOnSubmit( _
    selectedInvoice.InvoiceLineItems)
```

Description

- To delete a row from a database, you retrieve the row and store it in an object created from a class in the object model. Then, you execute the DeleteOnSubmit method of the object collection to mark the object for deletion. Finally, you execute the SubmitChanges method of the data context object.

- LINQ to SQL doesn't support cascading for delete operations. Because of that, you must either implement the operation in the database or mark the child objects for deletion along with the parent object.

- To mark child objects for deletion, you can either iterate through the collection of child objects for the parent object and execute the DeleteOnSubmit method for each one, or you can use the DeleteAllOnSubmit method to mark all the child objects associated with a parent object at once.

- When you execute the SubmitChanges method, LINQ to SQL generates a SQL Delete statement for each object that was marked for deletion and then passes those statements to the DBMS for processing

Figure 14-2   How to delete an existing row

How to add a new row

Figure 14-3 shows how to add a new row to a table in the database. To do that, you start by creating a new object from the class in the object model that's mapped to the table. Then, you set the properties of that object. For example, the code at the top of this figure creates a new Invoice object and sets its property values using an object initializer. Then, the next statement uses the InsertOnSubmit method to add the invoice to the collection of invoices in a pending state. Finally, when the SubmitChanges method is executed, the invoice is added to the Invoices table in the database.

In some cases, you'll need to add rows to a table that has a one-to-many relationship with the rows in another table. When you add an invoice to the Invoices table, for example, you'll want to add one or more line items to the InvoiceLineItems table. To do that, you can use code like that shown in the third example in this figure.

In this example, the line item data is stored in a DataGridView control. Then, a For statement is used to get each row in the grid, and an InvoiceLineItem object is created from the data in that row. Notice that the last property for each line item is the Invoice property, which is the property that associates the line item with an invoice. This property is set to the Invoice object that was created in the first example. That way, when the SubmitChanges method is executed, the invoice and all the line items associated with it will be added to the database.

You can also accomplish this without setting the Invoice property of each line item. Instead, you can add each line item to the collection of line items for the invoice as shown in the fourth example in this figure. Then, each line item in the collection will be added to the database after the invoice is added.

Note that LINQ to SQL determines the order in which the rows are added. If new, modified, and deleted rows are submitted at the same time, it also determines the order in which the operations are processed. This is done to maintain the integrity of the data in the database.

Code that creates a new Invoice object

```
Dim invoice As New Invoice With _
    {.VendorID = CInt(cboVendors.SelectedValue), _
     .InvoiceNumber = txtInvoiceNumber.Text, _
     .InvoiceDate = CDate(txtInvoiceDate.Text), _
     .InvoiceTotal = invoiceTotal, _
     .DueDate = CDate(txtDueDate.Text), _
     .TermsID = CInt(cboTerms.SelectedValue)}
```

A statement that adds the object to the Invoices collection

```
payables.Invoices.InsertOnSubmit(invoice)
```

Code that creates InvoiceLineItem objects and adds them to the InvoiceLineItems collection

```
Dim row As DataGridViewRow
For i As Integer = 1 To dgvLineItems.Rows.Count
    row = dgvLineItems.Rows(i - 1)
    Dim lineItem As New InvoiceLineItem With _
        {.InvoiceSequence = CShort(i), _
         .AccountNo = CInt(row.Cells(0).Value), _
         .Description = row.Cells(1).Value.ToString, _
         .Amount = CDec(row.Cells(2).Value), _
         .Invoice = invoice}
Next
```

Another way to add each line item to the InvoiceLineItems collection

```
invoice.InvoiceLineItems.Add(lineItem)
```

A statement that adds the invoice and line items to the database

```
payables.SubmitChanges()
```

Description

- To add a row to the database, you create an object from a class in the object model and assign values to its properties. Then, you execute the InsertOnSubmit method of the object collection to add the new object to the collection. Finally, you execute the SubmitChanges method of the data context object.

- If you need to insert child objects that are related to a parent object, you can do that by setting the association property of the child object to the parent object or by using the association property of the parent object to add the child object to the collection of child objects for the parent object.

- When you execute the SubmitChanges method, LINQ to SQL generates a SQL Insert statement for each object that was added to an object collection and then passes those statements to the DBMS for processing.

- If you set the property of the parent object that represents the primary key and the property of the child objects that represent the foreign key, you can use the InsertAllOnSubmit method to insert the child objects.

Figure 14-3   How to add a new row

How to provide for concurrency

When you use LINQ to SQL, optimistic concurrency is provided automatically. To accomplish that, the data context object maintains the original and current values of each object that's retrieved. Then, when changes are submitted to the database, LINQ to SQL can check the original values against the current values in the database. If the values in a row have changed or a row has been deleted, LINQ to SQL throws a ChangeConflictException. Then, you can handle this exception in your application. You'll see how to do that in the topics that follow.

How to detect concurrency conflicts

To detect a concurrency conflict, you code the SubmitChanges method within the Try block of a Try...Catch statement as shown in the example at the top of figure 14-4. Then, you include a Catch block for the ChangeConflictException. Within this block, you include the code you want to execute when a concurrency conflict occurs. You'll see some code like this in the next two topics.

If an application provides for updating or deleting more than one row in a database at a time, you may want to change when a ChangeConflictException is thrown. By default, this exception is thrown the first time an exception occurs, which means that the remaining rows aren't updated. If that's not what you want, you can specify ContinueOnConflict for the conflict mode on the SubmitChanges method as shown in the second example in this figure. Then, LINQ to SQL will attempt to process each change even if a concurrency conflict occurs. If a concurrency conflict does occur, a ChangeConflictException will be thrown after all changes have been attempted.

By default, LINQ to SQL checks each column in a table to be sure it hasn't changed since the data was retrieved. If you want to change how this works, you can change the UpdateCheck property of individual columns using the O/R Designer. If you set this property to Never, the value of the column will never be checked for changes. If you set it to When Changed, it will be checked only if the value of the column is changed by the application.

A Try...Catch statement that catches concurrency exceptions

```
Try
    payables.SubmitChanges()
Catch ex As ChangeConflictException
    .
    .
    .
End Try
```

Members of the ConflictMode enumeration

Member	Description
FailOnFirstConflict	A ConcurrencyConflictException is thrown and database processing is stopped when the first concurrency conflict occurs. This is the default.
ContinueOnConflict	A ConcurrencyConflictException isn't thrown until all updates have been attempted.

A statement that causes all updates to be attempted

```
payables.SubmitChanges(ConflictMode.ContinueOnConflict)
```

Description

- To implement optimistic currency, the data context object maintains the original and current values of each object property. That way, the original values can be checked against the current database values to determine if the row has been changed or deleted.

- If an update or delete operation isn't performed because of a concurrency conflict, a ChangeConflictException is thrown.

- To detect concurrency conflicts, you code the SubmitChanges method within the Try block of a Try...Catch statement, and you include a Catch block that catches the ChangeConflictException.

- By default, each column in a table is checked for concurrency when that table is updated. If that's not what you want, you can use the O/R Designer to change the UpdateCheck property of individual columns. The available options are Always, Never, and When Changed.

- If you submit more than one change to the database at the same time, you can specify a member of the ConflictMode enumeration on the SubmitChanges method to indicate when concurrency exceptions should be thrown.

- The classes and enumerations you use to work with concurrency conflicts are in the System.Data.Linq namespace. Because of that, you should include an Imports statement for this namespace in any class that performs concurrency checking.

Figure 14-4   How to detect concurrency conflicts

How to get conflict information

When a concurrency conflict occurs, LINQ to SQL provides information about this conflict. You might want to use this information to display a message to the user or to add an entry to an error log. Figure 14-5 shows how to access this information.

To get a collection of the objects that caused concurrency conflicts, you use the ChangeConflicts property of the data context object. Each item in this collection is an ObjectChangeConflict object. Because of that, you can use the properties of the ObjectChangeConflict class shown in this figure to work with an object conflict. To start, you can use the Object property to get the object that caused the conflict. In this example, the object is a vendor.

Next, you can use the MemberConflicts property to get a collection of the object members that caused the concurrency conflict. Notice that the code in this figure starts by checking whether there are any items in this collection. If there aren't, it means that the concurrency conflict was caused by the row being deleted from the database. In that case, no member conflicts occurred because the original values that were retrieved from the database couldn't be compared against the current values in the database.

If the MemberConflicts collection contains one or more items, you can use the MemberChangeConflict class to work with them. The Member property of this class gets information about the member, such as the member's name. This information is stored in a MemberInfo object, which is available from the System.Reflection namespace. The remaining three properties of the MemberChangeConflict class shown here provide the current value, database value, and original value of the member. You can see how all of these properties are used in the code in this figure.

Code that displays object and member conflict information

```
Public Sub DisplayConcurrencyConflicts()
    Dim conflictDisplay As String = ""
    For Each objConflict As ObjectChangeConflict In payables.ChangeConflicts
        Dim vendor As Vendor = CType(objConflict.Object, Vendor)
        If objConflict.MemberConflicts.Count = 0 Then
            conflictDisplay = "Vendor " & vendor.Name & " has been deleted."
        Else
            conflictDisplay &= "Columns changed for vendor " _
                            & vendor.Name & vbCrLf & vbCrLf
            For Each memberConflict As MemberChangeConflict _
                    In objConflict.MemberConflicts
                Dim memberInfo As MemberInfo = memberConflict.Member
                conflictDisplay &= "Member: " & memberInfo.Name & vbCrLf _
                    & "Original value: " _
                    & memberConflict.OriginalValue.ToString & vbCrLf _
                    & "Current value: " _
                    & memberConflict.CurrentValue.ToString & vbCrLf _
                    & "Database value: " _
                    & memberConflict.DatabaseValue.ToString & vbCrLf _
                    & vbCrLf
            Next
        End If
    Next
    MessageBox.Show(conflictDisplay, "Concurrency Conflicts")
End Sub
```

Common properties of the ObjectChangeConflict class

Property	Description
Object	Gets the object that caused the conflict.
MemberConflicts	Gets a collection of MemberChangeConflict objects that contain information about each conflict.

Common properties of the MemberChangeConflict class

Property	Description
Member	Gets a MemberInfo object that contains information about the member that caused the conflict.
CurrentValue	Gets the current value of the member that caused the conflict.
DatabaseValue	Gets the database value of the member that caused the conflict.
OriginalValue	Gets the original value of the member that caused the conflict.

Description

- To get the object conflicts for an object model, you use the ChangeConflicts property of the data context object. This property returns a collection of ObjectChangeConflict objects.

- You can use the properties of the ObjectChangeConflict and MemberChangeConflict classes to get information about the objects and members that caused a conflict.

- To use the MemberInfo class, you must import the System.Reflection namespace.

Figure 14-5   How to get conflict information

How to resolve concurrency conflicts

When a concurrency conflict occurs, you need to decide how you want to resolve the conflict. LINQ to SQL provides three options. These options, which are members of the RefreshMode enumeration, are summarized in the table at the top of figure 14-6.

To help you understand how these three options work, the second table in this figure shows you what the current values of three members of an object would be when you use each option. The first row in this table shows the original values of these members in the database. In other words, these are the values that were originally retrieved from the database and stored in the object. The second row of the table shows the current values in the database. As you can see, the last name and phone have been changed. The third row of the table shows the current values of the objects. Here, the first name and phone have been changed, but the last name has not.

The next three rows in this table show what the object values will be using each of the three RefreshMode options. If you use OverwriteCurrentValues, the current values of the object are replaced with the current values in the database. In contrast, if you use KeepCurrentValues, all of the current object values are retained. KeepChanges is similar except that only the object values that have changed are retained. That means that if a value has changed in the database but not in the object, the value in the object is replaced with the value in the database. In this example, that applies to the last name column.

The examples in this figure show two ways you can use the RefreshMode options. First, you can use them as the argument on the Resolve method of an ObjectChangeConflict object. In this example, the values in the object will be replaced by the values in the database. Second, you can use them on the Refresh method of the data context object. In addition to the RefreshMode option, you specify the object or object collection you want to refresh on this method. In this example, a Vendor object is refreshed so that if any values in the database have changed and those values haven't changed in the object, the object values are updated with the database values.

Members of the RefreshMode enumeration

Member	Description
OverwriteCurrentValues	The current values in the object model are overwritten by the current values in the database.
KeepCurrentValues	The current values in the object model are maintained regardless of whether the values have changed in the database. This is the default.
KeepChanges	The current values in the object model that haven't changed are overwritten by the current values in the database. The current values in the object model that have changed are maintained.

How the refresh modes affect the current values of an object

	FirstName	LastName	Phone
Original database values	Angela	Williams	559-555-1974
Current database values	Angela	**Neil**	**559-555-9328**
Current object values	**Angie**	Williams	**559-555-9382**
Object values after OverwriteCurrentValues	Angela	Neil	559-555-9328
Object values after KeepCurrentValues	Angie	Williams	559-555-9382
Object values after KeepChanges	Angie	Neil	559-555-9382

Code that uses the Resolve method to retain all database values

```
For Each objConflict As ObjectChangeConflict In payables.ChangeConflicts
    objConflict.Resolve(RefreshMode.OverwriteCurrentValues)
Next
```

Code that uses the Refresh method to retain changed object values

```
payables.Refresh(RefreshMode.KeepChanges, vendor)
```

Description

- You can use the Resolve method of an ObjectChangeConflict object to determine how concurrency conflicts are resolved. On this method, you specify one of the members of the RefreshMode enumeration.

- Regardless of which member you specify on the Resolve method, the original values in the object model are updated to the values in the database. That way, the same concurrency conflict won't occur again.

- You can also resolve a concurrency conflict by using the Refresh method of the data context object. This method accepts a member of the RefreshMode enumeration along with an entity object or a collection of entity objects.

Figure 14-6   How to resolve concurrency conflicts

How to use stored procedures to insert, update, and delete data

As you know, LINQ to SQL automatically generates SQL Insert, Update, and Delete statements when you submit changes to the database. If that's not what you want, you can use stored procedures to perform these operations instead. To do that, you add data context methods to the object model that are based on the stored procedures you want to use.

How to create and use data context methods that insert, update, and delete data

To create a data context method for a stored procedure that inserts, updates, or deletes data, you drag the stored procedure to an empty area of the O/R Designer. After you do that, you need to configure the entity so it uses the data context method. Figure 14-7 shows you how to do that.

To start, you display the Configure Behavior dialog box. Then, you select the Customize option and the method you want to use to perform the selected operation. When you do, the properties of the entity class are mapped to the arguments of the method that have the same name. Because the argument names are the same as the names you use for the parameters in the stored procedure, you should give the parameters the same names as the class properties. If you don't, you'll have to map the class properties to the method arguments manually using the combo box that's available for each property.

If you customize an update or delete operation by using a stored procedure, you'll notice that both current and original values are available for the class properties as shown here. By default, the method arguments with the same names as the class properties are mapped to the current version of the properties. Then, if the stored procedure uses optimistic concurrency, you can map the arguments that provide the original values to the original class properties. Note that if a stored procedure uses optimistic concurrency, you must provide for throwing a ChangeConflictException in your code. You'll see how to do that in a few minutes.

In addition to parameters that provide input to a stored procedure, some stored procedures use output parameters. For example, if you insert a row into a table that has an identity column, you'll want to return the value of that column so it can be used by the application. If you include output parameters in a stored procedure, those parameters will be included as arguments in the data context method along with the arguments for the input parameters. Then, you can map those arguments to the appropriate class properties.

Once you're sure that the mapping is correct, you can click the OK or Apply button to accept the settings. If you click Apply, the Configure Behavior dialog box remains open and you can select another behavior to customize from the Behavior combo box. Otherwise, the dialog box is closed.

The dialog box for customizing insert, update, and delete operations

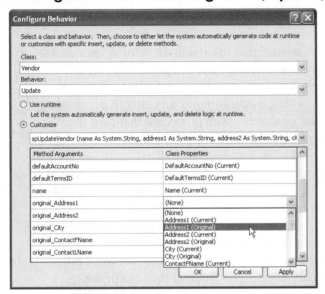

How to create a data context method that inserts, updates, or deletes data

1. Drag the appropriate stored procedure from the Server Explorer to the O/R Designer.

2. Select the entity class you want to use the method with in the O/R Designer, select the Insert, Update, or Delete property from the Properties window, and click the ellipsis button to display the Configure Behavior dialog box.

3. Select the Customize option, and then select the method you want to use from the combo box that becomes available. When you do, the arguments required by that method and the properties of the entity class that are mapped to those arguments are displayed.

4. Review the list of arguments to be sure they're mapped properly. To change or specify mappings, select a property and then use the combo box that's displayed to select a value.

5. Click OK or Apply to accept the changes.

Description

- You can override the default behavior for inserting, updating, and deleting data by using stored procedures that perform these operations. To do that, you create data context methods from the stored procedures and then configure the entity they work with.

- LINQ to SQL automatically maps method arguments to the current values of class properties that have the same name. If a stored procedure includes arguments for concurrency checking, you can map those arguments to the original values of the class properties.

- If a table contains values that are generated by the database, you can return those values as output parameters and then assign them to class properties.

Figure 14-7   How to create data context methods that insert, update, and delete data

The code that's generated for a data context method

When you add a data context method that inserts, updates, or deletes data to an object model, the O/R Designer generates a Function procedure just like it does when you add a data context method that retrieves data. In addition, when you customize an insert, update, or delete operation for an entity to use the data context method, the O/R Designer generates a Sub procedure that calls the Function procedure. It's this Sub procedure that's called when the SubmitChanges method is executed.

To help you understand how this code works, figure 14-8 presents some of the code that was generated for the data context method I created in figure 14-7 that updates a vendor. Here, you can see that the Function procedure receives each of the parameters that were mapped in figure 14-7. Note that these parameters include the current values of the class properties for the Vendor object as well as the original values of these properties. That's because the stored procedure implements optimistic concurrency, as you'll see in the next figure.

The code within the Function procedure executes the stored procedure, passing the required parameters. Then, it returns the value that's returned by the stored procedure to the calling procedure. In this case, the calling procedure is the Sub procedure that's generated by the O/R Designer.

Because the stored procedure that's used to update a vendor uses optimistic concurrency, the Sub procedure starts by getting the original Vendor object. Then, it calls the Function procedure and passes the properties of both the current Vendor object and the original Vendor object. Of course, if the stored procedure didn't use optimistic concurrency, the Sub procedure wouldn't include the code that works with the original Vendor object. Similarly, the Function procedure wouldn't include parameters for the original values.

The code for the spUpdateVendor function

```
<FunctionAttribute(Name:="dbo.spUpdateVendor")> _
Public Function spUpdateVendor( _
    <Parameter(Name:="Name", DbType:="VarChar(50)")> _
        ByVal name As String, _
    <Parameter(Name:="Address1", DbType:="VarChar(50)")> _
        ByVal address1 As String, _
        .
        .
        .
    <Parameter(Name:="DefaultAccountNo", DbType:="Int")> _
        ByVal defaultAccountNo As System.Nullable(Of Integer), _
    <Parameter(DbType:="Int")> ByVal original_VendorID _
        As System.Nullable(Of Integer), _
    <Parameter(DbType:="VarChar(50)")> ByVal original_Name As String, _
    <Parameter(DbType:="VarChar(50)")> ByVal original_Address1 As String, _
        .
        .
        .
    <Parameter(DbType:="Int")> ByVal original_DefaultAccountNo _
        As System.Nullable(Of Integer)) As Integer
    Dim result As IExecuteResult = Me.ExecuteMethodCall(Me, _
        CType(MethodInfo.GetCurrentMethod,MethodInfo), name, address1, ...
        original_VendorID, original_Name, original_Address1, ...,
        original_DefaultAccountNo)
    Return CType(result.ReturnValue,Integer)
End Function
```

The code for the UpdateVendor procedure

```
Private Sub UpdateVendor(ByVal obj As Vendor)
    Dim original As Vendor _
        = CType(Vendors.GetOriginalEntityState(obj),Vendor)
    Me.spUpdateVendor( _
        obj.Name, obj.Address1, ...,
        CType(obj.DefaultAccountNo,System.Nullable(Of Integer)),
        CType(original.VendorID,System.Nullable(Of Integer)),
        original.Name, original.Address1, ...,
        CType(original.DefaultAccountNo,System.Nullable(Of Integer)))
End Sub
```

Description

- When you add a data context method, a Function procedure that calls the stored procedure is added to the data context class. This function accepts the parameters required by the stored procedure and then executes the stored procedure and passes the parameters. If the stored procedure returns a value, it returns that value to the calling procedure.

- When you customize an insert, update, or delete operation to use a data context method, a Sub procedure that calls the Function procedure is added to the data context class. This procedure passes the parameter values required by the stored procedure to the Function procedure.

- If the stored procedure provides for concurrency, the Sub procedure also gets the original object and passes its values to the Function procedure.

Figure 14-8   The code that's generated for a data context method that inserts, updates, or deletes data

How to handle concurrency conflicts

Although the O/R Designer generates the code for executing a stored procedure that uses optimistic concurrency, it doesn't provide for detecting concurrency conflicts. Instead, you have to provide this code yourself. The easiest way to do that is to modify the Sub procedure that's called when the SubmitChanges method is executed.

Figure 14-9 illustrates how this works. To start, this figure shows some of the code for a stored procedure that updates a vendor row. As you can see, this procedure accepts parameters for both the current and original values for a vendor. Then, it uses the original values in the Where clause of the Update statement to provide for optimistic concurrency. When it's done, it returns the value of the @@ROWCOUNT system function, which gets the number of rows that were affected by the Update statement. If an optimistic concurrency conflict occurs, this value will be 0. Otherwise, it will be 1.

To check for concurrency conflicts in the Sub procedure that updates the vendor, you must first get the value that's returned by the stored procedure. As I mentioned in the previous topic, the Function procedure that calls the stored procedure returns this value to the Sub procedure. However, the Sub procedure discards this value by default. So you must modify the procedure so it stores this value in a variable as shown in the second example in this figure. Then, you can check this value to see if it's zero. If it is, you should throw a ChangeConflictException that can be caught by your application code.

Note that because you're modifying code that's generated by the O/R Designer, you should place this code in a partial class for the data context. The easiest way to do that is to create the partial class, cut the generated Sub procedure, and then paste it into the partial class. Then, you can modify the generated code and it won't be overwritten if you change the object model. However, a Sub procedure with the same name as your customized Sub procedure will still be generated, and you'll need to delete this procedure so you don't have two procedures with the same name.

The code for a stored procedure that updates a vendor row

```
CREATE PROCEDURE dbo.spUpdateVendor
    (@Name varchar(50),
     @Address1 varchar(50),
        .
        .
     @DefaultAccountNo int,
     @original_VendorID int,
     @original_Name varchar(50),
     @original_Address1 varchar(50),
        .
        .
     @original_DefaultAccountNo int)
AS
    UPDATE Vendors
      SET Name = @Name,
          Address1 = @Address1,
             .
             .
          DefaultAccountNo = @DefaultAccountNo,
        WHERE VendorID = @original_VendorID
          AND Name = @original_Name
          AND Address1 = @original_Address1,
             .
             .
          AND DefaultAccountNo = @original_DefaultAccountNo

RETURN @@ROWCOUNT
```

The procedure that executes the data context method for the stored procedure

```
Private Sub UpdateVendor(ByVal obj As Vendor)
    Dim original As Vendor _
        = CType(Vendors.GetOriginalEntityState(obj),Vendor)
    Dim count As Integer = Me.spUpdateVendor( _
        obj.Name, obj.Address1, ...,
        CType(obj.DefaultAccountNo,System.Nullable(Of Integer)),
        CType(original.VendorID,System.Nullable(Of Integer)),
        original.Name, original.Address1, ...,
        CType(original.DefaultAccountNo,System.Nullable(Of Integer)))
    If count = 0 Then
        Throw New ChangeConflictException
End Sub
```

Description

- A stored procedure that provides for concurrency typically returns a value that indicates the number of rows that were affected by the operation. Then, you can include code in the Sub procedure that calls the data context method that checks this value and throws a ChangeConflictException if it's 0.

- When you use this technique, you should move the Sub procedure that calls the data context method to a partial class so it's not overwritten if the object model is regenerated.

Figure 14-9   How to handle concurrency conflicts with stored procedures

A Vendor Maintenance application

To illustrate how you can use many of the skills you've learned in this chapter, the topics that follow present a Vendor Maintenance application. As you'll see, this application is similar to the Vendor Maintenance application you saw in chapter 7. When you use LINQ to SQL, though, you don't have to define your own business objects or write your own data access code. And that can save you a lot of time.

The user interface

Figure 14-10 presents the user interface for the Vendor Maintenance application. As you can see, it consists of two forms. The Vendor Maintenance form lets you retrieve an existing vendor and then modify or delete that vendor. If you click the Modify button, the Modify Vendor form is displayed. Then, you can use this form to make changes to any of the vendor information. When you click the Accept button, the changes are saved to the database.

In contrast, if you click the Delete button, a dialog box is displayed to confirm the operation. If the operation is confirmed, the row is deleted from the database.

The Vendor Maintenance form also lets you add a new vendor. To do that, you click the Add button to display the Add Vendor form. This form is identical to the Modify Vendor form shown here except that no data is displayed initially. Then, you can enter the data for the new vendor and click the Accept button to add it to the database.

The Vendor Maintenance form

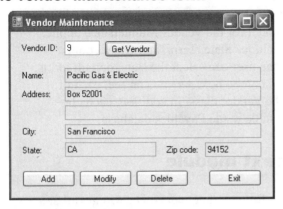

The Add/Modify Vendor form

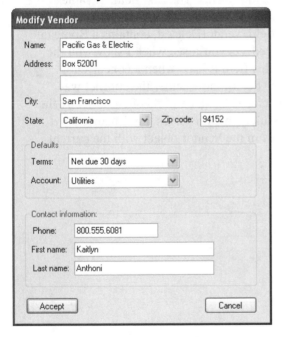

Description

- To add a new vendor, the user clicks the Add button on the Vendor Maintenance form to display a blank Add Vendor form. Then, the user enters the data for the new vendor and clicks the Accept button to return to the Vendor Maintenance form.

- To modify the data for an existing vendor, the user enters the vendor ID and clicks the Get Vendor button to display the basic information for that vendor. Then, the user clicks the Modify button to display the Modify Vendor form, makes the appropriate modifications, and clicks the Accept button to return to the Vendor Maintenance form.

- To delete an existing vendor, the user enters the vendor ID, clicks the Get Vendor button, and then clicks the Delete button.

Figure 14-10   The user interface for the Vendor Maintenance application

The object model

Figure 14-11 presents the object model for the Vendor Maintenance application. In addition to a Vendor class, it includes State, Term, and GLAccount classes. These classes are included so the user can select the state, default terms, and default account for a vendor from a combo box. As you can see, each of these classes has an association with the Vendor class. In addition, each class corresponds directly with the data in a table in the Payables database.

The code for the DataContext module

Figure 14-11 also presents the code for a module named DataContext that's used by this application. This module contains code that's used by both the Vendor Maintenance and Add/Modify Vendor forms. The first field, payables, contains a reference to a data context object that's created from the data context class for the object model. The second field, vendorDeleted, contains a Boolean value that indicates if a vendor was deleted. As you'll see when I show you the code for the Add/Modify Vendor form, this field is used when a concurrency conflict occurs on an update operation to determine whether the conflict was caused by the row being modified or deleted. The value of this field is set by the GetCurrentValues procedure in this module, which resolves the concurrency conflict by overwriting the current values in the Vendor object with the current values in the database.

The object model for the Vendor Maintenance application

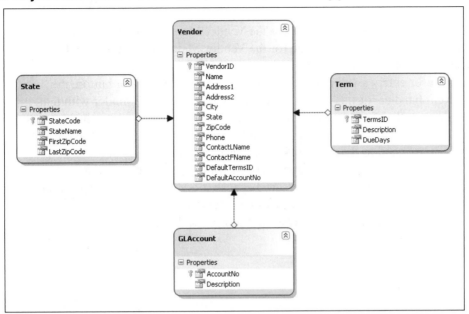

The code for the DataContext module

```
Imports System.Data.Linq

Module DataContext

    Public payables As New PayablesDataContext
    Public vendorDeleted As Boolean

    Public Sub GetCurrentValues()
        For Each objConflict As ObjectChangeConflict _
                In payables.ChangeConflicts
            If objConflict.MemberConflicts.Count = 0 Then
                vendorDeleted = True
            Else
                objConflict.Resolve(RefreshMode.OverwriteCurrentValues)
                vendorDeleted = False
            End If
        Next
    End Sub

End Module
```

Description

- The object model contains the classes that define the business objects used by the Vendor Maintenance application. These classes have a one-to-one correspondence with tables in the Payables database.
- Associations are defined between the Vendor class and the State, GLAccount, and Term classes based on the foreign keys defined between the associated tables in the database.

Figure 14-11   The object model and the code for the DataContext module

The code for the Vendor Maintenance form

Figure 14-12 presents the code for the Vendor Maintenance form. As you'll see, this code is similar to the code for the Vendor Maintenance form of chapter 7. Because of that, I'll just point out the main differences here.

If the user enters a valid vendor ID and clicks the Get Vendor button, the Click event handler for this button uses a query to retrieve the vendor with that ID. To do that, the Single method is called on the query expression, which causes the query to be executed immediately. Then, the Vendor object that's returned is assigned to the selectedVendor class variable.

Notice that the query expression is coded within the Try block of a Try...Catch statement. That's necessary because if a vendor with the specified ID isn't found, the Single method causes an InvalidOperationException to occur. So the first Catch block catches and processes this error.

The code for the Vendor Maintenance form   **Page 1**

```
Imports System.Data.Linq

Public Class frmVendorMaintenance

    Dim selectedVendor As Vendor

    Private Sub btnGetVendor_Click(ByVal sender As System.Object, _
            ByVal e As System.EventArgs) Handles btnGetVendor.Click
        If Validator.IsPresent(txtVendorID) AndAlso _
            Validator.IsInt32(txtVendorID) Then
            Try
                selectedVendor _
                    = (From vendor In payables.Vendors _
                        Where vendor.VendorID = CInt(txtVendorID.Text) _
                        Select vendor).Single
                Me.DisplayVendor()
            Catch ex As InvalidOperationException
                MessageBox.Show("No vendor found with this ID. " _
                    & "Please try again.", "Vendor Not Found")
                Me.ClearControls()
                txtVendorID.Select()
            Catch ex As Exception
                MessageBox.Show(ex.Message, ex.GetType.ToString)
            End Try
        End If
    End Sub

    Private Sub DisplayVendor()
        txtName.Text = selectedVendor.Name
        txtAddress1.Text = selectedVendor.Address1
        txtAddress2.Text = selectedVendor.Address2
        txtCity.Text = selectedVendor.City
        txtState.Text = selectedVendor.State
        txtZipCode.Text = selectedVendor.ZipCode
        btnModify.Enabled = True
        btnDelete.Enabled = True
    End Sub

    Private Sub ClearControls()
        txtName.Text = ""
        txtAddress1.Text = ""
        txtAddress2.Text = ""
        txtCity.Text = ""
        txtState.Text = ""
        txtZipCode.Text = ""
        btnModify.Enabled = False
        btnDelete.Enabled = False
    End Sub
```

Figure 14-12   The code for the Vendor Maintenance form (part 1 of 2)

If the user clicks the Add button, the Click event handler for this button is executed. Like the Vendor Maintenance application in chapter 7, this event handler displays the Add/Modify Vendor form and then processes the result depending on whether the add operation was successful.

The Click event handler for the Modify button is similar. However, you should notice that it checks for three possible results from the Add/Modify Vendor form. If the result is OK, it indicates that the update operation was successful. If it's Retry, it indicates that a concurrency conflict occurred because the data for the vendor changed. As you'll see in a minute, this conflict is resolved by the Add/Modify Vendor form. In either case, the updated Vendor object is retrieved from the Add/Modify Vendor form and displayed on the Vendor Maintenance form.

If the result is Abort, it indicates that a concurrency conflict occurred because the vendor was deleted. In that case, the Vendor Maintenance form simply clears all the controls on the form.

If the user clicks the Delete button and confirms the operation, the Click event handler for this button executes the DeleteOnSubmit method to mark the vendor for deletion. Then, it executes the SubmitChanges method to delete the vendor from the database. If the deletion is successful, the controls on the form are cleared.

If a concurrency conflict occurs when SubmitChanges is executed, a ChangeConflictException is thrown. Because of that, this method is coded within the Try block of a Try...Catch statement. Then, if a concurrency conflict occurs, the GetCurrentValues procedure in the DataContext module is called to resolve the conflict, an error message is displayed, and the data for the vendor is redisplayed on the form.

Notice that when a concurrency conflict occurs, this code doesn't check whether it was caused by the row being modified or deleted. That's because if the user is attempting to delete a row that has already been deleted, a ChangeConflictException isn't thrown. Because of that, the code that clears the form controls following the SubmitChanges method is executed so the application appears to have deleted the vendor.

The code for the Vendor Maintenance form   **Page 2**

```vb
Private Sub btnAdd_Click(ByVal sender As System.Object, _
        ByVal e As System.EventArgs) Handles btnAdd.Click
    Dim addModifyVendorForm As New frmAddModifyVendor
    addModifyVendorForm.addVendor = True
    Dim result As DialogResult = addModifyVendorForm.ShowDialog
    If result = DialogResult.OK Then
        selectedVendor = addModifyVendorForm.vendor
        txtVendorID.Text = selectedVendor.VendorID.ToString
        Me.DisplayVendor()
    End If
End Sub

Private Sub btnModify_Click(ByVal sender As System.Object, _
        ByVal e As System.EventArgs) Handles btnModify.Click
    Dim addModifyVendorForm As New frmAddModifyVendor
    addModifyVendorForm.addVendor = False
    addModifyVendorForm.vendor = selectedVendor
    Dim result As DialogResult = addModifyVendorForm.ShowDialog
    If result = DialogResult.OK OrElse _
        result = DialogResult.Retry Then
        selectedVendor = addModifyVendorForm.vendor
        Me.DisplayVendor()
    ElseIf result = DialogResult.Abort Then
        txtVendorID.Text = ""
        Me.ClearControls()
    End If
End Sub

Private Sub btnDelete_Click(ByVal sender As System.Object, _
        ByVal e As System.EventArgs) Handles btnDelete.Click
    Dim result As DialogResult _
        = MessageBox.Show("Delete " & selectedVendor.Name & "?", _
            "Confirm Delete", MessageBoxButtons.YesNo, _
            MessageBoxIcon.Question)
    If result = DialogResult.Yes Then
        Try
            payables.Vendors.DeleteOnSubmit(selectedVendor)
            payables.SubmitChanges()
            txtVendorID.Text = ""
            Me.ClearControls()
        Catch ex As ChangeConflictException
            GetCurrentValues()
            MessageBox.Show("Another user has updated that vendor.", _
                            "Database Error")
            Me.DisplayVendor()
        Catch ex As Exception
            MessageBox.Show(ex.Message, ex.GetType.ToString)
        End Try
    End If
End Sub

Private Sub btnExit_Click(ByVal sender As System.Object, _
        ByVal e As System.EventArgs) Handles btnExit.Click
    Me.Close()
End Sub
End Class
```

Figure 14-12   The code for the Vendor Maintenance form (part 2 of 2)

The code for the Add/Modify Vendor form

Figure 14-13 presents the code for the Add/Modify Vendor form. Like the code for the Vendor Maintenance form, the code for this form is similar to the code for the Add/Modify Vendor form you saw in chapter 7. Because of that, I'll just focus on the differences here.

First, you should notice how the LoadComboBoxes procedure uses query expressions to get the data for the State, Terms, and Account combo boxes. These queries retrieve and sort the required data from the States, Terms, and GLAccounts tables. Then, the combo boxes are bound to the query results. Note that if I hadn't needed to sort the rows, I wouldn't have had to use the queries. Instead, I could have just set the DataSource properties of the combo boxes to the tables in the data context object. For example, I could have set the DataSource property of the Terms combo box to payables.Terms. If I had done that, however, all the columns would have been retrieved from each table. Since these tables are relatively small, that's probably okay. For larger tables, though, you'll want to select just the columns you need as shown here.

On page 2 of this listing, you can see the code that's executed if the user clicks the Accept button. This code starts by calling the IsValidData procedure to determine if the data on the form is valid. If you look at this procedure on page 3, you'll see that it includes a query expression. This expression gets the FirstZipCode and LastZipCode columns from the States table for the state that's selected in the State combo box. Then, these values are used to validate the zip code.

If the data is valid and a vendor is being added, a new Vendor object is created, the PutVendorData procedure is called to set its property values, and the InsertOnSubmit method is executed to insert the vendor into the collection of Vendor objects in a pending state. Finally, the SubmitChanges method is executed to add the vendor to the database, and the DialogResult property of the form is set to DialogResult.OK.

If the vendor is being modified, the PutVendorData procedure is called to update the properties of the Vendor object. Notice here that it's not necessary to create a new Vendor object to hold the updated values like the application in chapter 7 did. That's because the original values of this object are maintained by the data context object, and modifying the object properties doesn't affect these values.

After the Vendor object is updated, the SubmitChanges method is executed to update the database. If this method is successful, the DialogResult property of the form is set to DialogResult.OK. If a concurrency conflict occurs, however, the GetCurrentValues procedure is called to handle the conflict. Then, the vendorDeleted variable is checked to determine if the conflict occurred because the vendor row was deleted or because it was modified. If the vendor row was deleted, an appropriate error message is displayed and the DialogResult property of the form is set to DialogResult.Abort. Otherwise, this property is set to DialogResult.Retry so the user can reenter the changes based on the current data in the database.

The code for the Add/Modify Vendor form   **Page 1**

```
Imports System.Data.Linq

Public Class frmAddModifyVendor
    Public addVendor As Boolean
    Public vendor As Vendor

    Private Sub frmAddModifyVendor_Load(ByVal sender As System.Object, _
            ByVal e As System.EventArgs) Handles MyBase.Load
        Me.LoadComboBoxes()
        If addVendor Then
            Me.Text = "Add Vendor"
            cboStates.SelectedIndex = -1
            cboTerms.SelectedIndex = -1
            cboAccounts.SelectedIndex = -1
        Else
            Me.Text = "Modify Vendor"
            Me.DisplayVendorData()
        End If
    End Sub

    Private Sub LoadComboBoxes()
        Try
            Dim states = From state In payables.States _
                         Order By state.StateName _
                         Select state.StateCode, state.StateName
            cboStates.DataSource = states
            cboStates.DisplayMember = "StateName"
            cboStates.ValueMember = "StateCode"

            Dim terms = From term In payables.Terms _
                        Order By term.Description _
                        Select term.TermsID, term.Description
            cboTerms.DataSource = terms
            cboTerms.DisplayMember = "Description"
            cboTerms.ValueMember = "TermsID"

            Dim accounts = From account In payables.GLAccounts _
                           Order By account.Description
            cboAccounts.DataSource = accounts
            cboAccounts.DisplayMember = "Description"
            cboAccounts.ValueMember = "AccountNo"
        Catch ex As Exception
            MessageBox.Show(ex.Message, ex.GetType.ToString)
        End Try
    End Sub

    Private Sub DisplayVendorData()
        txtName.Text = vendor.Name
        txtAddress1.Text = vendor.Address1
        txtAddress2.Text = vendor.Address2
        txtCity.Text = vendor.City
        cboStates.SelectedValue = vendor.State
        txtZipCode.Text = vendor.ZipCode
        cboTerms.SelectedValue = vendor.DefaultTermsID
        cboAccounts.SelectedValue = vendor.DefaultAccountNo
```

Figure 14-13   The code for the Add/Modify Vendor form (part 1 of 3)

```vb
        If vendor.Phone = "" Then
            txtPhone.Text = ""
        Else
            txtPhone.Text = FormattedPhoneNumber(vendor.Phone)
        End If
        txtFirstName.Text = vendor.ContactFName
        txtLastName.Text = vendor.ContactLName
    End Sub

    Private Function FormattedPhoneNumber(ByVal phone As String) As String
        Return phone.Substring(0, 3) & "." _
            & phone.Substring(3, 3) & "." _
            & phone.Substring(6, 4)
    End Function

    Private Sub btnAccept_Click(ByVal sender As System.Object, _
            ByVal e As System.EventArgs) Handles btnAccept.Click
        If IsValidData() Then
            If addVendor Then
                vendor = New Vendor
                Me.PutVendorData(vendor)
                payables.Vendors.InsertOnSubmit(vendor)
                Try
                    payables.SubmitChanges()
                    Me.DialogResult = DialogResult.OK
                Catch ex As Exception
                    MessageBox.Show(ex.Message, ex.GetType.ToString)
                End Try
            Else
                Me.PutVendorData(vendor)
                Try
                    payables.SubmitChanges()
                    Me.DialogResult = DialogResult.OK
                Catch ex As ChangeConflictException
                    GetCurrentValues()
                    If vendorDeleted Then
                        MessageBox.Show("Another user has deleted " _
                            & "that vendor.", "Database Error")
                        Me.DialogResult = DialogResult.Abort
                    Else
                        MessageBox.Show("Another user has updated " _
                            & "that vendor.", "Database Error")
                        Me.DialogResult = DialogResult.Retry
                    End If
                Catch ex As Exception
                    MessageBox.Show(ex.Message, ex.GetType.ToString)
                End Try
            End If
        End If
    End Sub
```

Figure 14-13   The code for the Add/Modify Vendor form (part 2 of 3)

The code for the Add/Modify Vendor form   **Page 3**

```vb
    Private Function IsValidData() As Boolean
        If Validator.IsPresent(txtName) AndAlso _
                Validator.IsPresent(txtAddress1) AndAlso _
                Validator.IsPresent(txtCity) AndAlso _
                Validator.IsPresent(cboStates) AndAlso _
                Validator.IsPresent(txtZipCode) AndAlso _
                Validator.IsInt32(txtZipCode) AndAlso _
                Validator.IsPresent(cboTerms) AndAlso _
                Validator.IsPresent(cboAccounts) Then
            Dim state = cboStates.SelectedValue.ToString
            Dim zipRange = (From s In payables.States _
                        Where s.StateCode = state _
                        Select s.FirstZipCode, s.LastZipCode).Single
            If Validator.IsStateZipCode(txtZipCode, zipRange.FirstZipCode, _
                    zipRange.LastZipCode) Then
                If txtPhone.Text <> "" Then
                    If Validator.IsPhoneNumber(txtPhone) Then
                        Return True
                    Else
                        Return False
                    End If
                Else
                    Return True
                End If
            Else
                Return False
            End If
        Else
            Return False
        End If

    End Function

    Private Sub PutVendorData(ByVal vendor As Vendor)
        vendor.Name = txtName.Text
        vendor.Address1 = txtAddress1.Text
        vendor.Address2 = txtAddress2.Text
        vendor.City = txtCity.Text
        vendor.State = cboStates.SelectedValue.ToString
        vendor.ZipCode = txtZipCode.Text
        vendor.DefaultTermsID = CInt(cboTerms.SelectedValue)
        vendor.DefaultAccountNo = CInt(cboAccounts.SelectedValue)
        vendor.Phone = txtPhone.Text.Replace(".", "")
        vendor.ContactFName = txtFirstName.Text
        vendor.ContactLName = txtLastName.Text
    End Sub

End Class
```

Figure 14-13   The code for the Add/Modify Vendor form (part 3 of 3)

Perspective

In this chapter, you've seen how to use LINQ to SQL to maintain the data in a SQL Server database. With these skills and the skills you learned in the last chapter, you should be able to develop a complete maintenance application of your own. To make sure you can do that, the exercise that follows has you develop the Vendor Maintenance application you saw in this chapter.

Exercise 14-1   Develop the Vendor Maintenance application

In this exercise, you'll create the object model for the Vendor Maintenance application and then write code that uses that model to retrieve, insert, update and delete data from the Vendors table.

Run the application and review the form

1. Open the project that's in the C\:ADO.NET 3.5 VB\Chapter 14\VendorMaintenance directory. This project contains the forms and starting code for the Vendor Maintenance application.

2. Review the code for the forms and note the errors in the Error List window that indicate that the Vendor type isn't defined. These errors occur because an object model isn't defined for the application.

Define the object model and create an instance of the data context class

3. Use the LINQ to SQL Classes template to add an object model named Payables to the project. When the O/R Designer is displayed, close the methods pane.

4. Drag the Vendors table from the Server Explorer to the O/R Designer. Do the same for the States, GLAccounts, and Terms tables. When you're done, the object model should look like the one shown in figure 14-11.

5. Close the O/R Designer and save the changes. When you do, the syntax errors should be removed from the Error List window because the project now contains a class named Vendor.

6. Add a module named DataContext to the project. Declare a public variable named payables within this class and assign an instance of the data context class to it.

7. Close the module and save the changes.

Add code to retrieve a vendor

8. Display the code for the Vendor Maintenance form.

9. Add a query to the event handler for the Click event of the Get Vendor button that retrieves the data for the vendor with the ID that's entered in the Vendor ID text box, and assign the result to the selectedVendor class variable.

10. Run the application, enter 9 for the vendor ID, and click the Get Vendor button. If you coded the query correctly, the information for the vendor will be displayed on the form as shown in figure 14-10.

11. Enter a vendor ID such as 999 that doesn't exist in the Vendors table. When you click the Get Vendor button, an InvalidOperationException should occur. Respond to the dialog box that's displayed and then end the application.

12. Add code to catch an InvalidOperationException. When this exception occurs, the application should display a message indicating that a vendor with the specified ID wasn't found. Then, it should call the ClearControls procedure and move the focus to the Vendor ID text box.

Add code to load the combo boxes on the Add/Modify Vendor form

13. Display the code for the Add/Modify Vendor form.

14. Add a query to the LoadComboBoxes procedure that retrieves the required data from the States table and sorts the results by state name. Then, bind the State combo box to the results of the query.

15. Add a query to the LoadComboBoxes procedure that retrieves the required data from the Terms table and sorts the results by description. Then, bind the Terms combo box to the results of the query.

16. Add a query to the LoadComboBoxes procedure that retrieves the required data from the GLAccounts table and sorts the results by description. Then, bind the Account combo box to the results of the query.

17. Run the application, retrieve the data for vendor ID 9, and then click the Modify button to display the Modify Vendor form. Then, drop down the three combo box lists to be sure they were loaded correctly.

Add code to add a new vendor

18. Add code to the event handler for the Click event of the Accept button that adds a new vendor to the Vendors collection of the data context object and then updates the database.

19. Run the application and click the Add button on the Vendor Maintenance form to display the Add Vendor form.

20. Enter the data for a new vendor and then click the Accept button to return to the Vendor Maintenance form. Notice that the vendor ID for the vendor, which was generated by the database, is displayed. Make a note of this ID, and then end the application.

Add code to modify a vendor

21. Add a statement to the event handler for the Click event of the Accept button that updates the database when changes are made to a vendor.

22. Run the application, enter the ID for the vendor you added in step 21, and click the Get Vendor button.

23. Click the Modify button to display the Modify Vendor form. Make one or more changes to the vendor's address, accept the changes, and make sure the changes are reflected on the Vendor Maintenance form.

Add code to delete a vendor

24. Return to the code for the Vendor Maintenance form. Then, add code to the event handler for the Click event of the Delete button to mark the selected vendor for deletion and to delete the vendor from the database.

25. Run the application, enter the ID for the vendor you added in step 21 and modified in step 24, and click the Get Vendor button.

26. Click the Delete button and then click Yes when you're asked to confirm the operation. The data for the vendor should be cleared from the form.

27. Enter the same vendor ID and click the Get Vendor button to confirm that the vendor has been deleted.

Add the remaining code

28. At this point, the application can perform the basic retrieval, insert, update and delete operations. Now, you just need to add code to validate the zip code and provide for concurrency conflicts. Add this code if you want to and then test the application. When you're done, close the solution.

15

How to use LINQ data source controls with web applications

In the last three chapters, you learned how to use LINQ from a Windows application. Although you can use some of those same techniques in a web application, ASP.NET 3.5 also provides a LINQ data source control that you can use to work with SQL Server databases. You'll learn the basic skills for using LINQ data source controls in this chapter.

Note that this chapter assumes that you already know how to develop web applications with Visual Studio and ASP.NET. It also assumes that you know how to work with data source controls such as the SQL Server data source control. If you don't have these skills, you can get them by reading our book, *Murach's ASP.NET 3.5 Web Programming with VB 2008*.

An introduction to the LINQ data source control

When you use the LINQ data source control, it uses LINQ to SQL to work with a SQL Server database. Before you create a LINQ data source control, then, you need to define the object model you want to work with as shown in chapter 13. Then, you can create a LINQ data source control that works with that object model.

How the LINQ data source control works

When you use a LINQ data source control, you don't code query expressions. Instead, you assign values to the attributes of the control that identify the data you want to retrieve. This is illustrated in the example at the top of figure 15-1. Here, a LINQ data source control provides the data for a drop-down list.

The ContextTypeName attribute names the DataContext class in the object model you want to use. For this LINQ data source control, the DataContext class is named PayablesDataContext, which is mapped to the Payables database. Then, the TableName attribute names the property in the DataContext class that maps to the database table you want to access. In this case, the LINQ data source control will access the Vendors table. This is equivalent to coding a table name on the From clause of a query expression.

The Select and OrderBy attributes are equivalent to the Select and Order By clauses of a query expression. The Select attribute identifies the columns that will be included in the query results, and the OrderBy attribute indicates how the results are sorted. In this case, the VendorID and Name columns from the Vendors table will be included in the results, and the results will be sorted by the Name column.

Notice that just as when you use query expressions, a LINQ data source control can return an anonymous type. Here, the anonymous type will consist of just VendorID and Name properties. Although the syntax that's used for an anonymous type in the Select attribute of a LINQ data source control is different from the syntax that's used in a query expression, it should be clear how this works.

In addition to these attributes, you can use the Where attribute to filter the rows that are retrieved, you can use the GroupBy and OrderGroupsBy attributes to group the rows that are retrieved, and you can use the EnableInsert, EnableUpdate, and EnableDelete attributes to provide for inserting, updating, and deleting rows using the data source control. You'll learn how to use these attributes later in this chapter.

A drop-down list that's bound to a LINQ data source control

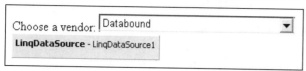

The code for the drop-down list and the LINQ data source control

```
<asp:DropDownList ID="DropDownList1" runat="server"
    DataSourceID="LinqDataSource1" DataTextField="Name"
    DataValueField="VendorID" Width="250px" AutoPostBack="True">
</asp:DropDownList>
<asp:LinqDataSource ID="LinqDataSource1" runat="server"
    ContextTypeName="PayablesDataContext"
    Select="new (VendorID, Name)"
    OrderBy="Name"
    TableName="Vendors">
</asp:LinqDataSource>
```

Basic attributes of the LINQ data source control

Attribute	Description
ID	The ID of the control.
Runat	Must specify "server."
ContextTypeName	The name of the DataContext class that represents the data in the database.
TableName	The property in the DataContext class that represents the table whose data you want to work with.
Select	Identifies the columns to be included in the query results. If this attribute is omitted, all the columns are retrieved from the table.
Where	Specifies the conditions that must be met for a row to be retrieved from the table. If this attribute is omitted, all the rows are retrieved from the table.
OrderBy	Names the columns that are used to sort the data that's retrieved and whether each column is sorted in ascending or descending sequence.
GroupBy	Names the columns that are used to group the data that's retrieved.
OrderGroupsBy	Names the columns that are used to sort the groups of data specified by the GroupBy attribute.
EnableInsert	Indicates if the control provides for inserting rows into the table.
EnableUpdate	Indicates if the control provides for updating rows in the table.
EnableDelete	Indicates if the control provides for deleting rows from the table.

Description

- The LINQ data source control uses LINQ to SQL to work with the data in a SQL Server database. Before you create a LINQ data source control, then, you must create an object model.

- The LINQ data source control names the DataContext class and table you want to work with, identifies the data to be retrieved, specifies how the data is sorted and grouped, and indicates whether the control will provide for insert, update, and delete operations.

Figure 15-1   How the LINQ data source control works

How to configure a LINQ data source control

Figure 15-2 shows you the two steps of the Data Source Configuration Wizard for configuring a LINQ data source control. The first step is displayed when you drag a LinqDataSource control from the Toolbox to a form and then select Configure Data Source from its smart tag menu. This step lets you choose the DataContext class you want to use with the control.

The second step of the wizard lets you select the table you want to retrieve data from and the columns whose data you want to retrieve. When this step is first displayed, the check box in the Select list that has an asterisk next to it is selected. This indicates that all the columns will be retrieved. If that's not what you want, you can select individual columns.

In this example, I selected the InvoiceNumber, InvoiceDate, and InvoiceTotal columns from the Invoices table. In addition, I selected the column named Vendor, which provides access to the vendor for a given Invoice. This is possible because I included both the Vendors and Invoices tables in the object model, so an association is defined between these tables.

The second step of the wizard also lets you specify a condition that determines what rows are returned as well as a sort sequence for the rows that are returned. To do that, you use the Where and OrderBy buttons. The dialog boxes that are displayed when you click these buttons work just like the ones that are displayed for other data source controls. So if you know how to use other data source controls, you shouldn't have any trouble using these dialog boxes.

The Advanced button displays a dialog box that lets you specify whether the data source provides for insert, update, and delete operations. You'll learn how this works later in this chapter.

Finally, the GroupBy drop-down list lets you select a column that the returned rows are grouped by. You'll learn how this works later in this chapter too.

By the way, you can also start the Data Source Configuration Wizard using the Choose Data Source command in the smart tag menu of a bindable control. Then, when the Choose a Data Source Type dialog box is displayed, you can select the LINQ icon and click the OK button to display the first dialog box shown here.

The Data Source Configuration Wizard

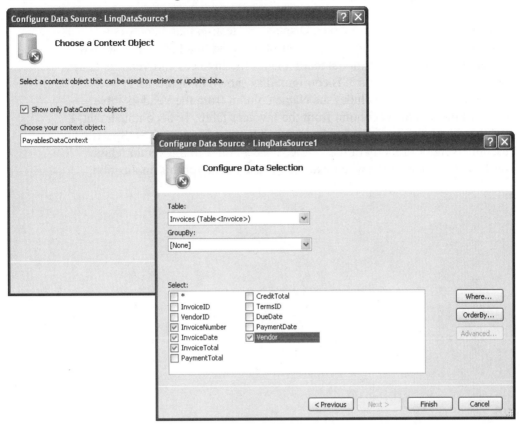

Description

- You can use the Data Source Configuration Wizard to configure a LINQ data source control by choosing Configure Data Source from its smart tag menu.

- The Choose a Context Object step of the wizard lets you select the DataContext class you want to use.

- The Configure Data Selection step of the wizard lets you select the table and columns you want to retrieve. By default, the first check box (*) is selected, which means that all the columns will be retrieved.

- The Select list includes the properties that are defined by the entity class for the table you select. If that table is related to another table in the data context, the property that provides access to the other table is also included in the Select list.

- To specify selection criteria, click the Where button. To specify the sort order, click the OrderBy button. To insert, update, or delete rows, click the Advanced button. See figures 15-5, 15-6, and 15-7 for more information on inserting, updating, and deleting rows.

- To group the rows that are retrieved, select a column from the GroupBy drop-down list. See figure 15-11 for more information.

Figure 15-2   How to configure a LINQ data source control

An Invoice Display application

Figure 15-3 presents an Invoice Display application that displays the list of invoices in a GridView control. This control is bound to a LINQ data source control that uses an object model that includes the Invoices and Vendors tables. The LINQ data source control is configured as shown in figure 15-2.

Notice that this list includes the Name column from the Vendors table instead of the VendorID column from the Invoices table. To accomplish that, I used the association between the Invoice and Vendor entity classes. Specifically, I used the Vendor property of the Invoice class to refer to the Vendor class. You'll see how that works when you see the aspx code for this application.

The Invoice Display application

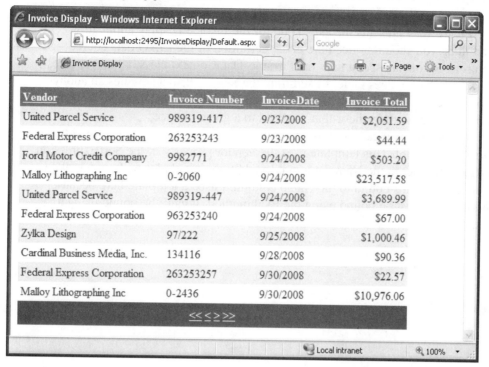

Description

- The Invoice Display application uses a GridView control that's bound to a LINQ data source control. The LINQ data source control retrieves selected columns from all the invoices in the Invoices table.

- The LINQ data source control uses an object model that includes two entity classes named Vendor and Invoice. The Vendor class is mapped to the Vendors table of the Payables database, and the Invoice class is mapped to the Invoices table.

- The Vendor class is included so that the Name column in the Vendors table can be displayed for each invoice instead of the VendorID column in the Invoices table. This is possible because of the foreign key relationship between the two tables in the database and the association that defines this relationship in the object model.

Figure 15-3   An Invoice Display application

The aspx file for the Invoice Display application

Figure 15-4 presents the aspx code for the Invoice Display application. The first thing you should notice here is the definition of the LINQ data source control. As you can see, it uses the PayablesDataContext class, and it retrieves data from the Invoices table. In addition, the Select attribute creates an anonymous type that includes four properties of the Invoice class. The last property, Vendor, refers to the vendor that's related to a given invoice.

To see how you can use this property, take a look at the template field in the GridView control. This template uses the Vendor property in the SortExpression attribute to refer to the Name column. In addition, it includes an Item template with a label that's bound to the Name column. I used a template here because this column must be bound using the Eval method. It can't be bound using a bound field.

The body of the Default.aspx file

```
<body>
    <form id="form1" runat="server">
    <div>
        <asp:GridView ID="GridView1" runat="server" AllowPaging="True"
            AllowSorting="True" AutoGenerateColumns="False" CellPadding="4"
            DataSourceID="LinqDataSource1" ForeColor="#333333"
            GridLines="None">
            <Columns>
                <asp:TemplateField HeaderText="Vendor"
                    SortExpression="Vendor.Name, InvoiceDate">
                    <ItemTemplate>
                        <asp:Label ID="Label1" runat="server"
                            Text='<%# Eval("Vendor.Name") %>'></asp:Label>
                    </ItemTemplate>
                    <HeaderStyle HorizontalAlign="Left" Width="200px" />
                </asp:TemplateField>
                <asp:BoundField DataField="InvoiceNumber"
                    HeaderText="Invoice Number" ReadOnly="True"
                    SortExpression="InvoiceNumber" >
                    <HeaderStyle HorizontalAlign="Left" Width="125px" />
                </asp:BoundField>
                <asp:BoundField DataField="InvoiceDate"
                    HeaderText="InvoiceDate" SortExpression="InvoiceDate"
                    DataFormatString="{0:d}" >
                    <HeaderStyle HorizontalAlign="Left" Width="90px" />
                </asp:BoundField>
                <asp:BoundField DataField="InvoiceTotal"
                    HeaderText="Invoice Total" SortExpression="InvoiceTotal"
                    DataFormatString="{0:c}" >
                    <HeaderStyle HorizontalAlign="Right" Width="110px" />
                    <ItemStyle HorizontalAlign="Right" />
                </asp:BoundField>
            </Columns>
            <HeaderStyle BackColor="#507CD1" Font-Bold="True"
                ForeColor="White" />
            <RowStyle BackColor="#EFF3FB" />
            <AlternatingRowStyle BackColor="White" />
            <PagerStyle BackColor="#2461BF" ForeColor="White"
                HorizontalAlign="Center" />
        </asp:GridView>
        <asp:LinqDataSource ID="LinqDataSource1" runat="server"
            ContextTypeName="PayablesDataContext"
            OrderBy="InvoiceDate"
            Select="new (InvoiceNumber, InvoiceDate, InvoiceTotal, Vendor)"
            TableName="Invoices">
        </asp:LinqDataSource>
    </div>
    </form>
</body>
```

Figure 15-4   The aspx file for the Invoice Display application

How to update data

If you want to use a LINQ data source control to update data, you need to set the appropriate attributes for enabling insert, update, and delete operations. In addition, you need to know how to provide for optimistic concurrency. And, if the bound control doesn't provide for inserting rows into the data source, you need to know how to insert rows using the LINQ data source control. That's what you'll learn in the topics that follow.

How to configure a LINQ data source control for updates

To configure a LINQ data source control so it provides for insert, update, and delete operations, you can use the Advanced Options dialog box shown in figure 15-5. As you can see, this dialog box simply lets you select the operations you want to perform. Then, the EnableDelete, EnableInsert, and EnableUpdate attributes of the LINQ data source control are set depending on which options you choose.

The control shown here illustrates how this works. This control can be used to insert, update, and delete rows from the Terms table. Notice that this control doesn't include a Select attribute. This is a requirement for controls that update data because the control must return an object that contains all the properties defined by the entity class.

Once you enable updating for the data source control, you can use it with any bound control that provides for updating. Then, when the data source control receives a request to perform an insert, update, or delete operation, it automatically creates the command needed to perform that operation. Because of that, you don't need to provide any additional aspx or Visual Basic code.

However, you may want to respond to events of the control that's bound to the LINQ data source control to perform processing before or after an insert, update, or delete operation. For example, you may want to use the before-action events to provide data validation. And you may want to use the after-action events to check that the operation completed successfully.

The Advanced Options dialog box

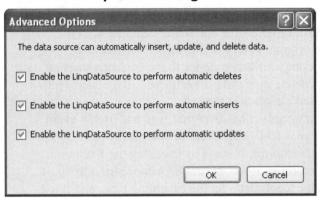

The aspx code for a LINQ data source control that performs insert, update, and delete operations

```
<asp:LinqDataSource ID="LinqDataSource1" runat="server"
    ContextTypeName="PayablesDataContext"
    EnableDelete="True" EnableInsert="True" EnableUpdate="True"
    OrderBy="Description" TableName="Terms">
</asp:LinqDataSource>
```

How to configure a LINQ data source for updates

- Display the Advanced Options dialog box and then select the appropriate options. Or, select the Enable Delete, Enable Insert, and Enable Update options from the LINQ data source control's smart tag menu.

- To display the Advanced Options dialog box, click the Advanced button in the Configure Data Selection step of the Data Source Configuration Wizard. This button is available only if you select the first check box (*) to select all the columns in the table.

- When you enable inserting, updating, or deleting for a LINQ data source control, the control automatically generates the commands needed to perform these operations.

- You can use the events of a control that's bound to a LINQ data source to perform processing before or after an insert, update, or delete operation.

Figure 15-5   How to configure a LINQ data source control for updates

How to provide for optimistic concurrency

The LINQ data source control provides for optimistic concurrency by default. To do that, it stores the original values of any columns that can be changed in view state. Then, it compares those values to the current values in the database when an update or delete operation is performed. If a concurrency conflict occurs, a ChangeConflictException is thrown.

To determine if a concurrency conflict has occurred, you can use an event handler like the one shown in figure 15-6. This event handler is for the RowUpdated event of a GridView control. It starts by checking the Exception property of the e argument to determine if any exception has occurred. If so, it uses the GetType method of that exception to get the exception type, and it uses the ToString method of the type to get the type name. Then, it compares this name to a string literal that contains the name of a ChangeConflictException. If the names are the same, an error message that indicates that the row has been updated or deleted is displayed. Otherwise, the Message property of the exception is displayed and the KeepInEditMode property of the e argument is set to True to keep the GridView control in edit mode. In either case, the ExceptionHandled property of the e argument is set to True to indicate that the exception has been handled.

An event handler for the RowUpdated event of a GridView control

```
Protected Sub grdTerms_RowUpdated(ByVal sender As Object, _
        ByVal e As System.Web.UI.WebControls.GridViewUpdatedEventArgs) _
        Handles grdTerms.RowUpdated
    If e.Exception IsNot Nothing Then
        If e.Exception.GetType.ToString _
                = "System.Data.Linq.ChangeConflictException" Then
            lblError.Text = "Another user has updated or deleted " _
                & "those terms. Please try again."
        Else
            lblError.Text = "A database error has occurred. " _
                & e.Exception.Message
            e.KeepInEditMode = True
        End If
        e.ExceptionHandled = True
    End If
End Sub
```

Description

- By default, the LINQ data source control provides for optimistic concurrency by storing the original values of the data on a page in view state. Then, when an update or delete operation is performed, the original values are compared to the values in the database. If the values have changed, a ChangeConflictException occurs.

- You can handle a ChangeConflictException in the event handlers for the control that the LINQ data source control is bound to. For a GridView control, you use the RowUpdated and RowDeleted events. For a DetailsView, FormView, or ListView control, you use the ItemUpdated and ItemDeleted events.

- To determine the type of exception that was thrown from the event handler for a bound control, use the Exception property of the e argument to get the exception. Then, use the GetType method of the exception to get its type, and use the ToString property of the type to get the type name. To determine if the exception is for a concurrency conflict, check this name to see if it's System.Data.Linq.ChangeConflictException.

- If you handle a ChangeConflictException in the event handler for a bound control, you should set the ExceptionHandled property of the e argument to True to suppress the exception.

- If a ChangeConflictException occurs, you shouldn't set the KeepInEditMode property of the e argument to True. That's because the new values for the row aren't displayed until the row leaves edit mode.

- You can determine which column values are checked when an update or delete operation is performed by changing the UpdateCheck property of the columns. For more information, see figure 14-4 in the last chapter.

- If you don't need to store the original values of the data in an object model in view state, you can set the StoreOriginalValuesInViewState property of the LINQ data source control to False.

Figure 15-6   How to provide for optimistic concurrency

How to insert a row using a LINQ data source control

As you may know, the DetailsView, FormView, and ListView controls provide for inserting rows as well as for modifying and deleting rows. Because of that, these controls are used most often for maintenance applications. Then, you can bind the control to a LINQ data source control, and the data source control will generate the commands for performing the insert, update, and delete operations.

In contrast, the GridView control doesn't provide for insert operations. If you want to use a GridView control to maintain the data in a table, then, you need to work directly with the LINQ data source control to insert a row. Figure 15-7 explains how to do that.

To start, you create a set of input controls such as text boxes in which the user can enter the data for the row to be inserted. Next, you provide a button that the user can click to start the insertion. Then, in the event handler for the Click event of this button, you can create a list with elements that contain the name and value for each column to be inserted. Finally, you can call the Insert method of the LINQ data source control to add the new row based on the values in the list.

This is illustrated by the event handler in this figure. This event handler starts by creating a variable named columnValues from the ListDictionary class. Then, it uses the Add method of that class to add two elements to the list. The first element contains the name and value for the Description column of the Terms table, and the second element contains the name and value for the DueDays column. Notice that an element isn't included for the TermsID column. That's because the value of this column is generated by the database.

Before I go on, you should realize that you can store the column names and values in any object that implements the IDictionary interface. In this case, I used the ListDictionary class because it's a simple class that's efficient for working with lists that have ten or fewer elements. For lists with more elements, you'll want to use the Hashtable class instead.

After the elements are added to the list, the Insert method of the LINQ data source control is executed. As you can see, the name of the list is specified as an argument on this method. Then, if the insert operation is successful, the DataBind method of the GridView control is executed so the new row is displayed.

Code that uses the LINQ data source control to insert a row

```
Protected Sub btnAdd_Click(ByVal sender As Object, _
        ByVal e As System.EventArgs) Handles btnAdd.Click
    Dim columnValues As New ListDictionary
    columnValues.Add("Description", txtDescription.Text)
    columnValues.Add("DueDays", txtDueDays.Text)
    Try
        LinqDataSource1.Insert(columnValues)
        grdTerms.DataBind()
        txtDescription.Text = ""
        txtDueDays.Text = ""
    Catch ex As Exception
        lblError.Text = "An error has occurred. " & ex.Message
    End Try
End Sub
```

Description

- If a control that's bound to a LINQ data source control doesn't support insert operations, you can use the data source control to insert rows into the database.

- To provide for inserts, the page should include controls such as text boxes for the user to enter data and a button that the user can click to insert the data.

- To use a LINQ data source control to insert a database row, first create a list with elements that contain the name and value for each column. Then, call the Insert method of the LINQ data source control and pass this list as an argument.

- After you insert a row using a LINQ data source control, you should call the DataBind method of the control that the LINQ data source control is bound to so the new row is displayed in that control.

- You can use any list that implements the IDictionary interface to store the column names and values. A simple class that implements this interface is the ListDictionary class. You can use the Add method of the ListDictionary class to add items to a ListDictionary object.

- The ListDictionary class is typically used only if the list will contain ten or fewer elements. For a list with more elements, use the Hashtable class.

- The ListDictionary and Hashtable classes are members of the System.Collections.Specialized namespace.

Figure 15-7   How to insert a row using a LINQ data source control

A Terms Maintenance application

To give you a better idea of how you can use a LINQ data source control to update, delete, and insert data, figure 15-8 presents a Terms Maintenance application that maintains the Terms table in the Payables database. This application uses an object model that consists of just one entity class that is mapped to the Terms table. Then, a GridView control is used to display the rows in the Terms table along with Edit and Delete buttons. In this figure, the user has clicked the Edit button for the last row, placing that row in edit mode.

Beneath the GridView control, two text boxes let the user enter data for a new terms row. Then, if the user clicks the Add New Terms button, the data entered in these text boxes is used to add the row to the database. Although it isn't apparent from this figure, a required field validator is used for the Description text box, and required field and compare validators are used for the Due Days text box. (For simplicity, I didn't use validation controls for the Description and Due Days columns in the GridView control.) Also, there's a label control beneath the GridView control that's used to display error messages when an update, delete, or insert operation fails.

The aspx file for the Terms Maintenance application

Figure 15-9 shows the aspx code for this application. The only thing of interest here is the code for the LINQ data source control that the GridView control is bound to. This data source control works with the table named Terms defined by the data context class named PayablesDataContext. Because this data source control doesn't include Where or Select attributes, all the rows and columns will be retrieved from the Terms table. In addition, the rows will be sorted by the TermsID column. Finally, the EnableDelete, EnableInsert, and EnableUpdate attributes indicate that this control will provide for insert, update, and delete operations.

The Terms Maintenance application

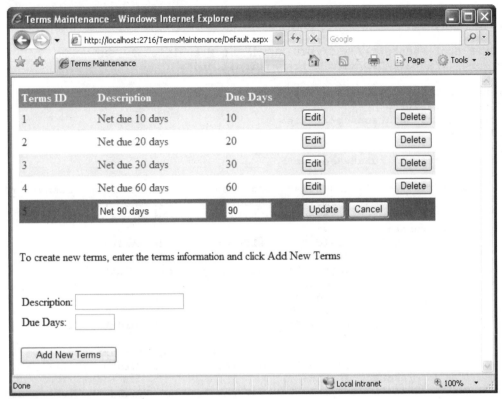

Description

- The Terms Maintenance application uses a LINQ data source control to work with the Terms table in the Payables database. This control provides for retrieving, inserting, updating, and deleting the terms data.

- The GridView control is bound to the LINQ data source control and provides for updating and deleting rows from the Terms table.

- To edit terms, the user clicks the Edit button. This places the GridView control into edit mode. The user can then change the Description and Due Days and click Update. Or, the user can click Cancel to leave edit mode.

- To delete terms, the user clicks the Delete button.

- Because the GridView control doesn't provide for inserting rows, the user must enter the description and due days for a new row into the text boxes on the form and then click the Add New Terms button to insert a row.

- If an insert, update, or delete operation is unsuccessful, an error message is displayed.

Figure 15-8   A Terms Maintenance application

The default.aspx file

```
<%@ Page Language="VB" AutoEventWireup="false" CodeFile="Default.aspx.vb"
Inherits="_Default" %>

<!DOCTYPE html PUBLIC "-//W3C//DTD XHTML 1.0 Transitional//EN" "http://
www.w3.org/TR/xhtml1/DTD/xhtml1-transitional.dtd">

<html xmlns="http://www.w3.org/1999/xhtml">
<head runat="server">
    <title>Terms Maintenance</title>
</head>
<body>
    <form id="form1" runat="server">
    <div>
        <asp:GridView ID="grdTerms" runat="server" AutoGenerateColumns="False"
            DataKeyNames="TermsID" DataSourceID="LinqDataSource1"
            CellPadding="4" ForeColor="#333333" GridLines="None">
            <Columns>
                <asp:BoundField DataField="TermsID" HeaderText="Terms ID"
                    InsertVisible="False" ReadOnly="True">
                    <HeaderStyle HorizontalAlign="Left" Width="100px" />
                </asp:BoundField>
                <asp:BoundField DataField="Description"
                    HeaderText="Description">
                    <HeaderStyle HorizontalAlign="Left" Width="175px" />
                </asp:BoundField>
                <asp:BoundField DataField="DueDays" HeaderText="Due Days">
                    <HeaderStyle HorizontalAlign="Left" Width="100px" />
                </asp:BoundField>
                <asp:CommandField ButtonType="Button" ShowEditButton="True" />
                <asp:CommandField ButtonType="Button" CausesValidation="False"
                    ShowDeleteButton="True" />
            </Columns>
            <HeaderStyle BackColor="#507CD1" Font-Bold="True"
             ForeColor="White" />
            <RowStyle BackColor="#EFF3FB" />
            <AlternatingRowStyle BackColor="White" />
            <EditRowStyle BackColor="#2461BF" />
        </asp:GridView>
        <asp:LinqDataSource ID="LinqDataSource1" runat="server"
            ContextTypeName="PayablesDataContext"
            EnableDelete="True"
            EnableInsert="True"
            EnableUpdate="True"
            OrderBy="TermsID"
            TableName="Terms">
        </asp:LinqDataSource>
        <br /><br />
```

Figure 15-9   The aspx file for the Terms Maintenance application (part 1 of 2)

The default.aspx file   **Page 2**

```
        To create new terms, enter the terms information
        and click Add New Terms<br />
        <asp:Label ID="lblError" runat="server" EnableViewState="False"
            ForeColor="Red">
        </asp:Label>
        <br /><br />
        <table>
            <tr>
                <td>
                    Description:</td>
                <td>
                    <asp:TextBox ID="txtDescription" runat="server">
                    </asp:TextBox>
                </td>
                <td>
                    <asp:RequiredFieldValidator ID="RequiredFieldValidator1"
                        runat="server" Display="Dynamic"
                        ControlToValidate="txtDescription"
                        ErrorMessage="Description is a required field."
                        ValidationGroup="Add">
                    </asp:RequiredFieldValidator>
                </td>
            </tr>
            <tr>
                <td>
                    Due Days:</td>
                <td>
                    <asp:TextBox ID="txtDueDays" runat="server" Width="50px">
                    </asp:TextBox>
                </td>
                <td>
                    <asp:RequiredFieldValidator ID="RequiredFieldValidator2"
                        runat="server" Display="Dynamic"
                        ControlToValidate="txtDueDays"
                        ErrorMessage="Due days is a required field."
                        ValidationGroup="Add">
                    </asp:RequiredFieldValidator>
                    <asp:CompareValidator ID="CompareValidator1"
                        runat="server" Display="Dynamic"
                        ControlToValidate="txtDueDays"
                        ErrorMessage="Due days must be an integer
                        greater than zero." Operator="GreaterThan"
                        Type="Integer" ValueToCompare="0"
                        ValidationGroup="Add">
                    </asp:CompareValidator>
                </td>
            </tr>
        </table>
        <br />
        <asp:Button ID="btnAdd" runat="server" Text="Add New Terms"
            ValidationGroup="Add" />
    </div>
    </form>
</body>
</html>
```

Figure 15-9   The aspx file for the Terms Maintenance application (part 2 of 2)

The Visual Basic code for the Terms Maintenance application

Figure 15-10 presents the Visual Basic code for the Terms Maintenance application. Since you've already seen most of this code, I'll just summarize it here.

First, you should notice the Imports statement at the beginning of this file. The namespace that's imported, System.Collections.Specialized, contains the ListDictionary class that's used by the Click event handler for the Add button. When this event handler is executed, a ListDictionary object is used to store the column values that were entered by the user into the text boxes on the form. Then, this list is passed to the Insert method of the data source control so that a row with those values is inserted into the database. If the insert operation is successful, the DataBind method of the GridView control is executed so the new row is displayed, and the two text boxes are cleared. Otherwise, an appropriate error message is displayed.

The second event handler is called after each update operation. It starts by checking if an exception has occurred. If so, it checks whether a ChangeConflictException or some other exception occurred. In either case, an appropriate error message is displayed and the ExceptionHandled property of the e argument is set to True. In addition, if an error other than a ChangeConflictException occurred, the KeepInEditMode property of the e argument is set to True so the control remains in edit mode.

The third event handler is called after each delete operation. Like the event handler that's called after an update operation, this event handler checks if an exception occurred and, if so, if it was a ChangeConflictException. Notice that this event handler doesn't set the KeepInEditMode property, though, since the control isn't in edit mode when the Delete button is clicked. Also notice that the error message that's displayed when a ChangeConflictException occurs indicates only that another user has updated the row, not that the row may have been deleted. That's because an exception doesn't occur if the user tries to delete a rows that's already been deleted.

The default.aspx.vb file

```vb
Imports System.Collections.Specialized

Partial Class _Default
    Inherits System.Web.UI.Page

    Protected Sub btnAdd_Click(ByVal sender As Object, _
            ByVal e As System.EventArgs) Handles btnAdd.Click
        Dim columnValues As New ListDictionary
        columnValues.Add("Description", txtDescription.Text)
        columnValues.Add("DueDays", txtDueDays.Text)
        Try
            LinqDataSource1.Insert(columnValues)
            grdTerms.DataBind()
            txtDescription.Text = ""
            txtDueDays.Text = ""
        Catch ex As Exception
            lblError.Text = "An error has occurred. " & ex.Message
        End Try
    End Sub

    Protected Sub grdTerms_RowUpdated(ByVal sender As Object, _
            ByVal e As System.Web.UI.WebControls.GridViewUpdatedEventArgs) _
            Handles grdTerms.RowUpdated
        If e.Exception IsNot Nothing Then
            If e.Exception.GetType.ToString _
                = "System.Data.Linq.ChangeConflictException" Then
                lblError.Text = "Another user has updated or deleted " _
                    & "those terms. Please try again."
            Else
                lblError.Text = "A database error has occurred. " _
                    & e.Exception.Message
                e.KeepInEditMode = True
            End If
            e.ExceptionHandled = True
        End If
    End Sub

    Protected Sub grdTerms_RowDeleted(ByVal sender As Object, _
            ByVal e As System.Web.UI.WebControls.GridViewDeletedEventArgs) _
            Handles grdTerms.RowDeleted
        If e.Exception IsNot Nothing Then
            If e.Exception.GetType.ToString _
                = "System.Data.Linq.ChangeConflictException" Then
                lblError.Text = "Another user has updated those terms. " _
                    & "Please try again."
            Else
                lblError.Text = "A database error has occurred. " _
                    & e.Exception.Message
            End If
            e.ExceptionHandled = True
        End If
    End Sub

End Class
```

Figure 15-10   The Visual Basic code for the Terms Maintenance application

How to group data

When you retrieve data from a table, you can group the results based on one of the columns in the table. Then, you can summarize the results for each group. You'll learn how to accomplish that in the topic that follows. Then, you'll see an application that uses groups to summarize the data in a table of invoices.

How to configure groups

If you select a column from the GroupBy drop-down list in the Configure Data Selection step of the Data Source Configuration Wizard, the dialog box changes to look like the one shown in figure 15-11. You can use this dialog box to identify the columns you want to include in the query results and to specify a sort order for the groups. You can sort the groups by the column that's used to group the results in ascending or descending sequence or not sort at all.

When this dialog box is first displayed, two columns are included in the Select list. The first one is for the column that's used for grouping, and it's represented by the *key* keyword. Since an *alias* is specified for this column, however, you'll refer to it in your application using this alias. By default, the alias is the name of the column, but you can change it to anything you want.

When you group data, you'll sometimes want to access the individual rows in the groups. To do that, you use the second column that's automatically included in the Select list. This column is represented by the *it* keyword, and its default alias is the name of the table.

In addition to the key and it columns, you can include one or more *aggregate columns*. An aggregate column is a column that summarizes the data in one of the columns of the table or provides a count of the number of rows returned by the query. To create an aggregate column that summarizes data, you simply select the column you want to summarize from the Column drop-down list, select the type of summary you want to perform from the Function drop-down list, and then enter an alias for the column. To create an aggregate column that provides a count of rows, you select (Count) from the Column drop-down list and then enter an alias.

The LINQ data source control in this figure illustrates how this works. Here, the rows in the Invoices table of the Payables database are grouped by the InvoiceDate column, and the groups are sorted by that column in ascending sequence. In addition to this column and the column that represents the individual invoices, the query includes aggregate columns named Count and Sum_InvoiceTotal. The first column will contain a count of the number of invoices in each group, and the second column will contain the sum of the InvoiceTotal column for the invoices in each group. You'll see how this LINQ data source control is used in the application that follows.

The dialog box for configuring a LINQ data source control that uses groups

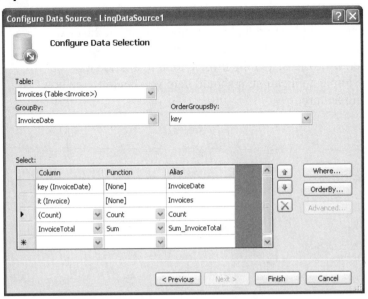

The aspx code for the data source control

```
<asp:LinqDataSource ID="LinqDataSource1" runat="server"
    ContextTypeName="PayablesDataContext" GroupBy="InvoiceDate"
    OrderGroupsBy="key" Select="new (key as InvoiceDate, it as Invoices,
    Count() as Count, Sum(InvoiceTotal) as Sum_InvoiceTotal)"
    TableName="Invoices">
</asp:LinqDataSource>
```

Description

- To group the rows that are returned by a LINQ data source control, select a column from the GroupBy drop-down list in the Configure Data Selection step of the Data Source Configuration Wizard. Then, this step changes to the one shown above.

- The LINQ data source control uses the *key* keyword to refer to the column that's used for grouping, and it uses the *it* keyword to refer to the individual rows in a group. Both of these columns are automatically included in the selected columns. The key column is given an *alias* that is the same as the name of the column that's used for grouping, and the it column is given an alias that is the same as the name of the table.

- A LINQ data source control that groups data typically includes one or more *aggregate columns* that summarize the data in the groups. An aggregate column can return the sum of the values in the column, the average of the values, the largest value, or the smallest value. It can also return a count of the number of rows returned in each group.

- To create an aggregate column that summarizes a value, select the column you want to summarize and the summary function you want to perform from the drop-down lists in a row of the Select grid, and enter an alias for the column. To create an aggregate column that returns a count, select (Count) for the column and then enter an alias.

Figure 15-11   How to configure groups

An Invoice Totals By Date application that uses groups

Figure 15-12 presents an application that groups the data in the Invoices table of the Payables database by invoice date. For each group, it displays the invoice date, the number of invoices, and the invoice total in a GridView control. Although this is a simple application, it should help you begin to see how you can use the grouping feature.

The Invoice Totals By Date application

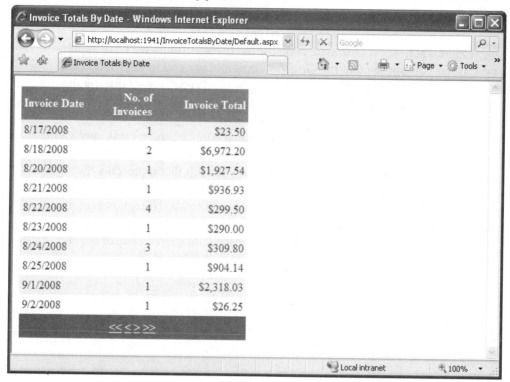

Description

- The Invoice Totals By Date application uses an object model that includes just the Invoices table from the Payables database.

- This application groups the data in the Invoices table by the invoice date. Then, it displays the invoice date, number of invoices, and invoice total for each group in a GridView control.

Figure 15-12   An Invoice Totals By Date application that uses groups

The aspx file for the Invoice Totals By Date application

Figure 15-13 shows the aspx code for the Invoice Totals By Date application. Here, you can see that the GridView control is bound to the LINQ data source control. Then, the three columns of the GridView control display the InvoiceDate, Count, and Sum_InvoiceTotal fields that are returned by the LINQ data source control.

If you compare the code for the data source control used by this application with the code shown in figure 15-11, you'll notice just one difference. That is, the field that the data source control returns by default that represents the individual invoices has been omitted. That's because this application doesn't display the invoices for each group, only the group totals. Note, however, that you can't omit this column using the Data Source Configuration Wizard. Instead, you have to omit it after the code for the data source control is generated.

The body of the Default.aspx file

```
<body>
    <form id="form1" runat="server">
    <div>
        <asp:GridView ID="GridView1" runat="server" AllowPaging="True"
            AutoGenerateColumns="False" DataSourceID="LinqDataSource1"
            CellPadding="4" ForeColor="#333333" GridLines="None">
            <PagerSettings Mode="NextPreviousFirstLast" />
            <RowStyle BackColor="#EFF3FB" />
            <Columns>
                <asp:BoundField DataField="InvoiceDate"
                    DataFormatString="{0:d}" HeaderText="Invoice Date">
                    <HeaderStyle HorizontalAlign="Left" Width="100px" />
                </asp:BoundField>
                <asp:BoundField DataField="Count" HeaderText="No. of Invoices">
                    <HeaderStyle HorizontalAlign="Right" Width="75px" />
                    <ItemStyle HorizontalAlign="Right" />
                </asp:BoundField>
                <asp:BoundField DataField="Sum_InvoiceTotal"
                    DataFormatString="{0:c}" HeaderText="Invoice Total">
                    <HeaderStyle HorizontalAlign="Right" Width="125px" />
                    <ItemStyle HorizontalAlign="Right" />
                </asp:BoundField>
            </Columns>
            <FooterStyle BackColor="#507CD1" Font-Bold="True"
             ForeColor="White" />
            <PagerStyle BackColor="#2461BF" ForeColor="White"
             HorizontalAlign="Center" />
            <SelectedRowStyle BackColor="#D1DDF1" Font-Bold="True"
             ForeColor="#333333" />
            <HeaderStyle BackColor="#507CD1" Font-Bold="True"
             ForeColor="White" />
            <EditRowStyle BackColor="#2461BF" />
            <AlternatingRowStyle BackColor="White" />
        </asp:GridView>
        <asp:LinqDataSource ID="LinqDataSource1" runat="server"
            ContextTypeName="PayablesDataContext"
            GroupBy="InvoiceDate" OrderGroupsBy="key"
            Select="new (key as InvoiceDate, Count() as Count,
                         Sum(InvoiceTotal) as Sum_InvoiceTotal)"
            TableName="Invoices">
        </asp:LinqDataSource>
    </div>
    </form>
</body>
```

Figure 15-13   The aspx file for the Invoice Totals By Date application

Perspective

The purpose of this chapter has been to present the basic skills for using the LINQ data source control to work with the data in a SQL Server database. As you've seen, this control is easy to configure, particularly if you use the Data Source Configuration Wizard as shown in this chapter. It's also easy to use, whether you're displaying individual rows, displaying groups, or maintaining data. Because of that, it's the preferred technique for using LINQ in a web application.

In some cases, though, you may find that the LINQ data source control won't provide the flexibility you need. In those cases, you should consider using code to work with LINQ to SQL instead as shown in the last two chapters. Although this technique requires more work, it still allows you to use an object model that provides the code for working with the database.

Terms

alias
aggregate column

16

How to use LINQ to XML

In addition to using LINQ to work with datasets and SQL Server databases, you can use it to work with XML. As you'll see in this chapter, LINQ to XML provides a complete application programming interface for working with XML. That means that you can use LINQ to XML to load XML from a file, query and modify the XML that's retrieved, and save the XML back to a file. You can also use LINQ to XML to create XML documents and elements. In most cases, LINQ to XML provides a simpler approach to working with XML than traditional methods.

An introduction to LINQ to XML

Before you use LINQ to XML, you need to be familiar with the basic structure of an XML document and the object model that LINQ to XML is based on. I'll present that information in the two topics that follow. Then, I'll present some basic techniques you can use with LINQ to XML. When you're done with these topics, you'll be ready to learn about the specific features of LINQ to XML.

The basic structure of an XML document

XML, the *Extensible Markup Language*, provides a standardized way of structuring text information by using *tags* that identify each data element. For example, figure 16-1 shows a simple *XML document* that contains information about two vendors. Each vendor has ID, name, address, city, state, and zip code data.

As you can see, each XML tag begins with the character < and ends with the character >, so the first line in the XML document in this figure contains a complete XML tag. Similarly, the next two lines contain complete tags. In contrast, the fourth line contains two tags, <Name> and </Name>, with a text value in between. You'll see how this works in a moment.

The first tag in any XML document is an *XML declaration*. This declaration identifies the document as an XML document. It typically indicates which XML version the document conforms to (1.0 in this example) and identifies the character set (encoding) that's being used for the document (utf-8).

Elements are the building blocks of XML. Each element in an XML document represents a single data item and is identified by two tags: a *start tag* and an *end tag*. The start tag marks the beginning of the element and provides the element's name. The end tag marks the end of the element and repeats the name, prefixed by a slash. For example, <Name> is the start tag for an element named Name, and </Name> is the corresponding end tag.

A complete element consists of the element's start tag, its end tag, and the *content* between the tags. For example, <City>Madison</City> indicates that the content of the City element is *Madison*. And <Address1>Attn: Supt. Window Services</Address1> indicates that the content of the Address1 element is *Attn: Supt. Window Services*.

Besides content, elements can contain other elements, known as *child elements*. This lets you add structure to a *parent element*. For example, a parent Vendor element can have child elements that provide details about each vendor, such as the vendor's name and address. In this figure, for example, you can see that the start tags, end tags, and values for the Name, Address1, Address2, City, State, and ZipCode elements are contained between the start and end tags for the Vendor element. As a result, these elements are children of the Vendor element, and the Vendor element is the parent of each of these elements.

An XML document that contains vendor data

```xml
<?xml version="1.0" encoding="utf-8"?>
<Vendors>
  <Vendor ID="1">
    <Name>U.S. Postal Service</Name>
    <Address1>Attn: Supt. Window Services</Address1>
    <Address2>PO Box 7005</Address2>
    <City>Madison</City>
    <State>WI</State>
    <ZipCode>53707</ZipCode>
  </Vendor>
  <Vendor ID="9">
    <Name>Pacific Gas and Electric</Name>
    <Address1>Box 52001</Address1>
    <City>San Francisco</City>
    <State>CA</State>
    <ZipCode>94152</ZipCode>
  </Vendor>
</Vendors>
```

Vendor element

ID attribute

City element

Description

- *XML*, the *Extensible Markup Language*, provides a method of structuring information using special *tags*. A file that contains XML is known as an *XML document*.

- An XML document consists of tags that begin with < and end with >.

- The first line in an XML document is an *XML declaration* that indicates which version of the XML standard is being used. This declaration can also identify the character set that's being used, and it can indicate whether all entity declarations are included.

- An *element* is a unit of XML data that begins with a *start tag* and ends with an *end tag*. The start tag provides the name of the element and contains any attributes assigned to the element. The end tag repeats the name, prefixed with a slash (/).

- An *attribute* consists of an attribute name, an equal sign, and a literal value that is coded within the start tag of an element. If an element has more than one attribute, the attributes must be separated by one or more spaces.

- The *content* for an element is coded between the element's start and end tags.

- Elements can contain other elements. An element that's contained within another element is a *child element*. An element that contains other child elements is a *parent element*.

- The highest-level parent element in an XML document is known as the *root element*. An XML document can have only one root element.

- XML was designed as a way to represent information so it can be exchanged between dissimilar systems or applications. The .NET Framework uses XML internally for many different purposes. In particular, ADO.NET relies extensively on XML.

Figure 16-1   The basic structure of an XML document

The highest-level parent element in an XML document is known as the *root element*, and an XML document can have only one root element. In the example in figure 16-1, the root element is Vendors. For XML documents that contain repeating information, it's common to use a plural name for the root element to indicate that it contains multiple child elements.

Attributes are a concise way to provide data for XML elements. In the Vendors XML document, for example, each Vendor element has an ID attribute that provides an identifying number for the vendor. Thus, <Vendor ID="1"> contains an attribute named ID whose value is 1.

It's important to realize that XML doesn't provide a predefined set of element and attribute names. Instead, the element names are created so they describe the contents of each element. Similarly, the attribute names are created so they describe the value of each attribute.

The LINQ to XML object model

If you've used the *Document Object Model* (*DOM*) to work with XML, you know that it isn't easy to work with and it frequently requires a lot of cumbersome code to accomplish a simple task. That's because it's designed to work with the text strings within an XML document. In addition, it's based on the XML document as the central object. Because of that, you can't create an XML element separate from an XML document using DOM.

The LINQ to XML object model changes how this works. As figure 16-2 illustrates, this object model consists of classes that are defined in the System.Xml.Linq namespace. You use these classes to work with XML data using an object-oriented approach rather than a text-based approach. When you see the examples that are presented throughout this chapter, you'll see how this simplifies the code for working with XML.

Notice that the XDocument and XElement classes, which are used to create documents and elements, are defined at the same level in the namespace hierarchy. That makes it possible to create XML elements as standalone objects. In other words, you can create an XML element without first creating an XML document. And that can simplify the coding requirements for an application.

Some of the objects in the LINQ to XML object model

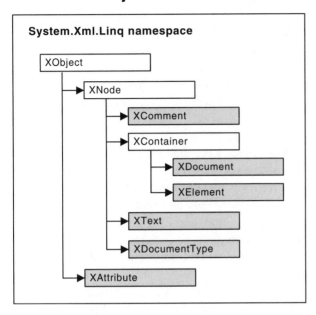

Description

- The LINQ to XML object model provides classes you can use to work with XML data using an object-oriented approach.

- Most of the objects in the object model inherit the abstract XNode class, which represents a *node* of an XML tree. See figure 16-9 for more information on XML trees.

- The objects you'll work with most often are XDocument, which represents an XML document; XElement, which represents an XML element; XText, which represents the content of an element; and XAttribute, which represents an attribute of an XML element.

- The XDocument and XElement classes inherit the abstract XContainer class, which represents a node that can contain other nodes.

- Unlike when you work with the *Document Object Model* (*DOM*), XML elements can exist separately from XML documents in the LINQ to XML object model.

Figure 16-2   The LINQ to XML object model

An introduction to programming with LINQ to XML

To give you an idea of how you can use LINQ to XML, figure 16-3 starts by presenting code that creates an XElement object. To do that, it simply assigns an XML literal to a variable named vendors that's declared with the XElement type. This literal includes a root element named Vendors and two Vendor elements. Within each Vendor element are elements that specify the name and address of the vendor.

The second example shows how you can create an XElement object that contains just some of the data in the vendors object. Like the first example, the code in this example assigns an XML literal to an XElement object. Embedded within this literal, however, is a query that retrieves just the vendors from California. In addition, the Select clause of this query indicates that the new Vendor elements should contain only Name, City, State, and ZipCode elements. The Address1 and Address2 elements have been omitted. To indicate that the values of these elements and the ID attribute should come from the original Vendor elements, embedded expressions are used.

The third example shows the contents of the new object. As you can see, it includes the root element named Vendors that was included in the XML literal in the second example. Then, within this element is a Vendor element that contains the data for the vendor in California. Note that the Address1 element that was included in the original Vendor element isn't included in the new Vendor element.

Before I go on, you should realize that XML literals are a new feature of Visual Basic 2008. They make it easy to create XElement and XDocument objects without using the constructors of those objects. You'll learn more about XML literals later in this chapter. You'll also learn more about coding embedded expressions and embedded queries. So don't worry if you don't fully understand the code in this figure.

The examples in this figure illustrate just some of the features that are provided by LINQ to XML. Because LINQ to XML is a complete application programming interface, you can use it to perform functions such as loading XML from a file, modifying the XML, and saving the modified XML to a file. Of course, you can also use it to query XML documents and elements. You'll learn how to perform all of these functions later in this chapter.

Code that creates an XElement object

```
Dim vendors As XElement = _
    <Vendors>
        <Vendor ID="1">
            <Name>U.S. Postal Service</Name>
            <Address1>Attn: Supt. Window Services</Address1>
            <Address2>PO Box 7005</Address2>
            <City>Madison</City>
            <State>WI</State>
            <ZipCode>53707</ZipCode>
        </Vendor>
        <Vendor ID="9">
            <Name>Pacific Gas and Electric</Name>
            <Address1>Box 52001</Address1>
            <City>San Francisco</City>
            <State>CA</State>
            <ZipCode>94152</ZipCode>
        </Vendor>
    </Vendors>
```

Code that queries the XElement object to create a new XElement object

```
Dim caVendors As XElement = _
    <Vendors>
        <%= From vendor In vendors.<Vendor> _
        Where vendor.<State>.Value = "CA" _
        Select _
        <Vendor ID=<%= vendor.@ID %>>
            <Name><%= vendor.<Name>.Value %></Name>
            <City><%= vendor.<City>.Value %></City>
            <State><%= vendor.<State>.Value %></State>
            <ZipCode><%= vendor.<ZipCode>.Value %></ZipCode>
        </Vendor> %>
    </Vendors>
```

The contents of the new XElement object

```
<Vendors>
    <Vendor ID="9">
        <Name>Pacific Gas and Electric</Name>
        <City>San Francisco</City>
        <State>CA</State>
        <ZipCode>94152</ZipCode>
    </Vendor>
</Vendors>
```

Description

- LINQ to XML provides a complete API that you can use to create, modify, and query XML documents and elements. You can also load an XML document or element from a file, and you can save the changes you make to the document or element to a file.

- You can use LINQ to retrieve XML elements or the values of XML elements or attributes from an XML document or element. You can also embed expressions and queries in XML literals to include content in a document or element you create.

Figure 16-3   An introduction to programming with LINQ to XML

How to work with existing XML data

In the topics that follow, you'll learn some basic skills for working with XML data. That includes loading XML data from a file and accessing and querying XML after it's been loaded.

How to load XML data from a file

To load data from an XML file, you use the Load method shown in figure 16-4. As you can see, this method is a member of both the XDocument and XElement classes. Because of that, you can use it to load an XML file into either an XDocument or an XElement object.

The first code example in this figure presents part of an XML document that stores invoice data. As you can see, the root element of this document, named Invoices, contains a number of child elements named Invoice. The opening tag for each Invoice element includes an attribute named ID that specifies the invoice ID value. In addition, each Invoice element contains several child elements that provide additional information about the invoice.

The next two examples load data into XDocument and XElement objects respectively. Note that the results of these two statements are identical. If you displayed the invoices object that's created by each statement, for example, you'd see that the XML looks just like the XML document shown in this figure except that the XML declaration isn't included. The way you refer to elements in XDocument and XElement objects is slightly different, however. You'll see an example of that later in this chapter.

At this point, you might want to know how you can display the data in an XDocument or XElement object to be sure it contains the data you want. To do that, you can use a statement like the last one shown in this figure. Notice here that the ToString method is used to convert the object to its string representation.

The syntax for loading XML data from a file

```
{XDocument|XElement}.Load(filename)
```

An XML document that stores invoice data

```xml
<?xml version="1.0" encoding="utf-8"?>
<Invoices>
  <Invoice ID="1">
    <VendorID>122</VendorID>
    <InvoiceNumber>989319-457</InvoiceNumber>
    <InvoiceDate>2008-06-08</InvoiceDate>
    <InvoiceTotal>3813.33</InvoiceTotal>
    <PaymentTotal>3813.33</PaymentTotal>
    <CreditTotal>0.00</CreditTotal>
    <DueDate>2008-07-08</DueDate>
  </Invoice>
    .
    .
    .
  <Invoice ID="114">
    <VendorID>123</VendorID>
    <InvoiceNumber>963253249</InvoiceNumber>
    <InvoiceDate>2008-10-02</InvoiceDate>
    <InvoiceTotal>127.75</InvoiceTotal>
    <PaymentTotal>127.75</PaymentTotal>
    <CreditTotal>0.00</CreditTotal>
    <DueDate>2008-11-01</DueDate>
  </Invoice>
</Invoices>
```

A statement that loads a file that contains the XML into an XDocument object

```
Dim invoices As XDocument = XDocument.Load("Invoices.xml")
```

A statement that loads a file that contains the XML into an XElement object

```
Dim invoices As XElement = XElement.Load("Invoices.xml")
```

A statement that displays the invoices

```
MessageBox.Show(invoices.ToString, "Invoices")
```

Description

- You can use the Load method of the XDocument or XElement class to load XML data from a file. On this method, you specify the file name for the file along with the path if necessary.

- In most cases, you'll want to load XML data into an XElement object because it can simplify the way you refer to elements within the XML.

- You can also use an XmlReader or TextReader object with the Load method, and you can specify load options. For more information, see the Visual Studio documentation.

Figure 16-4   How to load XML data from a file

How to use axis properties to work with XML

The XML *axis properties* provide an easy way for you to work with the XML in an XDocument or XElement object. Figure 16-5 presents these properties and shows you how to use them.

The first axis property lets you access the value of an attribute. The second axis property lets you access child elements. The third axis property lets you access *descendants*, which are child elements that are indirectly subordinate to an object. The fourth axis property lets you access an element by its index. And the fifth axis property gets the content of the first element in a collection of objects.

The examples in this figure show how to use some of these properties. The first example calculates the sum of the invoice totals of the invoices in the Invoices.xml file. To do that, this example starts by loading the invoices into an XDocument object. Then, it declares a variable named invoiceTotal that will hold the invoice total.

Next, a For Each statement is used to loop through the collection of Invoice elements in that document. To refer to this collection, the For Each statement uses two child axis properties. The first one refers to the Invoices element of the invoices document, and the second one refers to the Invoice element of the Invoices element.

Within the For Each loop, a child axis property is used to get the InvoiceTotal element for each invoice. Then, the value axis property is used to get the value of that element. Because this value is returned as a string, the CDec function is used to convert it to a decimal value so it can be added to the invoiceTotal variable. You can see the result of this code in the dialog box shown in this figure.

The statement in the second example in this figure shows how you can refer to the value of an attribute. This statement gets the value of the ID attribute for the first Invoice element. If you wanted to get the value of the ID attribute for another Invoice element, you could include an indexer property. For example, this statement would return the ID attribute for the second invoice:

```
Dim invoiceID As Integer =
    CInt(invoices.<Invoices>.<Invoice>(1).@ID)
```

Of course, you could also use a query to return data based on the condition you specify. You'll learn how to do that in a few minutes.

The last example in this figure shows another way you can get the value of the ID attribute for the first invoice. Here, the child axis property that was used to access the Invoices element in the second example has been replaced by a descendant axis property. This works because the Invoice element is a descendant of the invoices document.

XML axis properties

Property	Syntax	Description
Attribute	`object.@attributename`	Gets the value of the specified attribute from an XElement object or from the first element in a collection of XElement objects and returns it as a string. If the name of an attribute isn't a valid name for a Visual Basic identifier, you must enclose the attribute name in angle brackets(<>).
Child	`object.<childname>`	Gets the specified children of an XDocument object, an XElement object, or a collection of XDocument or XElement objects and returns them as a collection of XElement objects.
Descendant	`object...<descendantname>`	Gets the specified descendants of an XDocument object, an XElement object, or a collection of XDocument or XElement objects and returns them as a collection of XElement objects.
Indexer	`object(index)`	Gets the element at the specified index from a collection of XDocument or XElement objects.
Value	`object.Value`	Gets the content of the first element in a collection of XElement objects and returns it as a string.

Code that gets and displays the total of the invoices in the Invoices.xml file

```
Dim invoices As XDocument = XDocument.Load("Invoices.xml")
Dim invoiceTotal As Decimal = 0
For Each invoice As XElement In invoices.<Invoices>.<Invoice>
    invoiceTotal += CDec(invoice.<InvoiceTotal>.Value)
Next
MessageBox.Show(FormatCurrency(invoiceTotal), "Invoice Total")
```

The resulting dialog box

A statement that gets the value of the ID attribute for the first invoice

```
Dim invoiceID As Integer = CInt(invoices.<Invoices>.<Invoice>.@ID)
```

Another way to get the value of the ID attribute

```
Dim invoiceID As Integer = CInt(invoices...<Invoice>.@ID)
```

Description

- You can use the XML *axis properties* to access XML in your code. You can use these properties within LINQ to XML queries as shown in figure 16-7 or outside of a query as shown above.

Figure 16-5   How to use axis properties to work with XML

How to use axis methods to work with XML

In addition to using axis properties to work with XML, you can use *axis methods*. Axis methods are methods of the XContainer, XDocument, and XElement classes that provide access to the elements and attributes of a document or element. Figure 16-6 presents the axis methods you're most likely to use.

The first table in this figure presents methods you can use with both an XDocument and an XElement object. As their names imply, the Descendants method lets you get the descendants of a document or element, and the Elements method lets you get the child elements of a document or element. Notice that these methods each have two formats. The first one returns all of the descendants or elements, and the second one returns the descendants or elements with the specified name. You can also use the Element method of these classes to get the first child element with the specified name.

The first example in this figure shows how you can use the Element and Elements methods. The code in this example calculates the total of the invoices just like the first example in figure 16-5 did. If you compare these two examples, you'll see that the code that uses the axis properties is somewhat simpler. Because of that, I prefer to use the axis properties whenever possible.

The second table in this figure presents two additional methods of the XElement class. You can use these methods to get an attribute of an element with the specified name or to get all the attributes of an element. The second and third examples illustrate how you can use the Attribute method.

The second example gets the value of the attribute named ID from the first Invoice element. To get the first Invoice element, the first statement uses the Element method. Then, the second statement uses the Attribute method to get the ID attribute of that invoice, and it uses the value axis property to get the value of that attribute. Again, you may want to compare this example to the second example in figure 16-5 to see how much easier it is to use axis properties.

The third example is similar to the second one, except that it gets the ID attribute, not its value. Note that you can't get an attribute using axis properties. That's because the attribute axis property automatically returns the value of the attribute, not the attribute itself.

Common methods of the XDocument and XElement classes for getting elements

Method	Description
Descendants()	Returns a collection of the descendant elements in a document or element.
Descendants(name)	Returns a collection of the descendant elements with the specified name in a document or element.
Element(name)	Returns the first child element of a document or element with the specified name.
Elements()	Returns a collection of the child elements in a document or element.
Elements(name)	Returns a collection of the child elements with the specified name in a document or element.

Additional methods of the XElement class for getting attributes

Method	Description
Attribute(name)	Returns the attribute of an element with the specified name.
Attributes()	Returns a collection of the attributes of an element.

Code that gets the total of the invoices in the Invoices.xml file

```
Dim invoices As XDocument = XDocument.Load("Invoices.xml")
Dim invoiceTotal As Decimal = 0
For Each Invoice As XElement _
        In invoices.Element("Invoices").Elements("Invoice")
    invoiceTotal += CDec(Invoice.Element("InvoiceTotal").Value)
Next
```

Code that gets the value of the ID attribute for the first invoice

```
Dim invoice As XElement = invoices.Element("Invoices").Element("Invoice")
Dim invoiceID As Integer = CInt(invoice.Attribute("ID").Value)
```

Code that gets and displays the ID attribute for the first invoice

```
Dim IDAttribute As XAttribute = _
    invoices.Element("Invoices").Element("Invoice").Attribute("ID")
MessageBox.Show(IDAttribute.ToString, "ID Attribute")
```

The resulting dialog box

Description

- The XDocument and XElement classes provide a variety of methods for accessing XML elements and attributes. These methods are called *axis methods*, and you can use many of these methods in place of axis properties.

Figure 16-6   How to axis methods to work with XML

How to query a single XML collection

Now that you understand how to use axis properties and methods, you shouldn't have any trouble learning how to code query expressions that retrieve XML from an XDocument or XElement object. Figure 16-7 presents the basic techniques for doing that.

The first example in this figure shows how to retrieve data from an XElement object. The query expression in this example is similar to ones you've seen in previous chapters. It retrieves the values of the VendorID and InvoiceNumber elements, along with a calculated value that's given the alias BalanceDue, from each Invoice element that has a balance due that's greater than zero and that's due in less than 15 days. It sorts the results by balance due in descending sequence within vendor ID.

You should notice a couple of things about this query expression. To start, the Invoices element is omitted from the data source that's identified in the From clause. That's because it's not necessary to include the root element when you query an XElement object. In contrast, when you query an XDocument object, you must include the root element. For example, if I had stored the XML used by this example in an XDocument object instead of an XElement object, I would have had to code the From clause like the second one shown in this figure.

Like any query expression, the source of data for a query expression that works with XML must be an enumerable type. If you look back to figure 16-5, you'll see that both the child and descendant axis properties return a collection of XElement objects. And if you look back at figure 16-6, you'll see that the Descendants, Elements, and Attributes methods all return collections. Since a collection is an enumerable type, you can use any of these properties or methods as the source of data for a query. In this case, the data source is the collection of Invoice elements.

Because attribute and element values are always returned as strings, this query expression uses Visual Basic conversion functions to convert some of the values to the appropriate type. It uses the CDec function to convert the values of the InvoiceTotal, PaymentTotal, and CreditTotal elements to decimals so the balance due can be calculated. It uses the CDate function to convert the value of the DueDate element to a date so it can be compared to another date. And it uses the CInt function to convert the value of the VendorID element to an integer so the IDs will be sorted numerically rather than alphabetically.

The results of this query expression are also shown in this figure. As you can see, they look just like the query results you've seen in previous chapters.

A LINQ query that retrieves data from an XElement object

Code that loads the XElement object from an XML file

```
Dim invoices As XElement = XElement.Load("Invoices.xml")
```

A query expression that gets invoice balances by vendor

```
Dim invoicesDue = From invoice In invoices.<Invoice> _
                Let BalanceDue = CDec(invoice.<InvoiceTotal>.Value) _
                                - CDec(invoice.<PaymentTotal>.Value) _
                                - CDec(invoice.<CreditTotal>.Value) _
                Where BalanceDue > 0 _
                  And CDate(invoice.<DueDate>.Value) _
                    < DateTime.Today.AddDays(15) _
                Order By CInt(invoice.<VendorID>.Value), _
                        BalanceDue Descending _
                Select invoice.<VendorID>.Value, _
                        Number = invoice.<InvoiceNumber>.Value, BalanceDue
```

Code that executes the query

```
Dim invoiceDisplay As String _
    = "Vendor ID" & vbTab & "Invoice No." & vbTab & "Balance Due" & vbCrLf
For Each invoice In invoicesDue
    invoiceDisplay &= invoice.VendorID & vbTab & vbTab _
                    & invoice.Number & vbTab _
                    & IIf(invoice.Number.Length < 8, vbTab, "").ToString _
                    & FormatCurrency(invoice.BalanceDue) & vbCrLf
Next
MessageBox.Show(invoiceDisplay, "Vendor Invoices Due")
```

The resulting dialog box

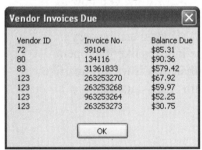

The From clause for a query that retrieves data from an XDocument object

```
From invoice In invoices.<Invoices>.<Invoice>
```

Description

- To code a LINQ to XML query, you use the Visual Basic keywords just as you do for any other type of query.
- Because the child and descendant properties return an enumerable collection of XElement objects, you can use them in the From clause of a query.
- Because the attribute and value axis properties return a string, you must convert the string to the appropriate type before you perform a non-string operation on it.

Figure 16-7   How to query a single XML collection

How to join data from two or more XML collections

In the last figure, you saw a query that retrieved data from the collection of Invoice elements in an XElement object. But you can also join data from two or more XML collections. This is illustrated in figure 16-8.

The first example in this figure shows part of the XML file that's used by the query in this figure. As you can see, this file contains both vendor and invoice data. That way, when the file is loaded into an XElement object, that object contains both the Vendor and Invoice elements. That's a requirement for coding a query that joins these elements.

The query expression in this figure is similar to the one in the previous figure. The main difference is that it joins the Vendor and Invoice elements based on the values of the ID attribute of the Vendor elements and the values of the VendorID elements of the Invoice elements. In addition, it sorts the results by the value of the Name elements of the Vendor elements, and it includes the value of the Name elements in the results.

Before I go on, you should realize that the Vendor and Invoice elements used by this example don't have to be in the same XML file as shown here. They just have to be included in the same XDocument or XElement object in your application. If the collections of elements you're joining are in separate files, you can load them into separate XDocument or XElement objects and then create another XDocument or XElement object that contains both collections. You'll learn one way to do that later in this chapter when I show you how to transform an XML tree.

You should also realize that join operations on XML data can be very inefficient. That's because these operations don't use indexes like join operations on other types of data sources do. Because of that, you'll want to restrict your use of join operations when you're working with XML data.

An XML file that contains vendor and invoice data

```xml
<?xml version="1.0" encoding="utf-8"?>
<VendorInvoices>
  <Vendor VendorID="1">
    <Name>US Postal Service</Name>
    <Address1>Attn:  Supt. Window Services</Address1>
    <Address2>PO Box 7005</Address2>
    <City>Madison</City>
    <State>WI</State>
    <ZipCode>53707</ZipCode>
  </Vendor>
  .
  .
  .
  <Invoice ID="1">
    <VendorID>122</VendorID>
    <InvoiceNumber>989319-457</InvoiceNumber>
    <InvoiceDate>2008-06-08</InvoiceDate>
    <InvoiceTotal>3813.33</InvoiceTotal>
    <PaymentTotal>3813.33</PaymentTotal>
    <CreditTotal>0.00</CreditTotal>
    <DueDate>2008-07-08</DueDate>
  </Invoice>
  .
  .
  .
</VendorInvoices>
```

A LINQ query that retrieves data from the file

Code that loads the file into an XElement object

```vb
Dim vendorInvoices As XElement = XElement.Load("VendorInvoices.xml")
```

A query expression that joins data from the Vendor and Invoice elements

```vb
Dim invoicesDue = From vendor In vendorInvoices.<Vendor> _
                  Join invoice In vendorInvoices.<Invoice> _
                    On vendor.@ID Equals invoice.<VendorID>.Value _
                  Let BalanceDue = CDec(invoice.<InvoiceTotal>.Value) _
                                 - CDec(invoice.<PaymentTotal>.Value) _
                                 - CDec(invoice.<CreditTotal>.Value) _
                  Where BalanceDue > 0 _
                    And CDate(invoice.<DueDate>.Value) _
                      < DateTime.Today.AddDays(15) _
                  Order By vendor.<Name>.Value, BalanceDue Descending _
                  Select vendor.<Name>.Value, _
                         Number = invoice.<InvoiceNumber>.Value, BalanceDue
```

Description

- To join two or more XML collections, the collections must be defined within the same XElement or XDocument object. If the collections are defined within the same file, you can just load the file as shown above. Otherwise, you can create an XDocument or XElement object that contains the collections that you've loaded from separate files using the technique presented in figure 16-14.

- Because join operations between XML collections don't use indexes, they can be very slow. So you should only use them when you have no other way to get the data you need.

Figure 16-8   How to query two or more XML collections

How to create and work with XML trees

When you load a file into an XDocument or XElement object, Visual Studio creates an in-memory representation of the file called an *XML tree*. You can also create an XML tree using Visual Basic code. Then, you can add, modify, and delete elements and attributes in the tree, you can transform the tree into a tree with a different structure, and you can save the tree to an XML file. That's what you'll learn in the topics that follow.

How to create an XML tree

One way to create an XML tree is to use the constructors of the classes in the LINQ to XML object model. This technique is illustrated in the first example in figure 16-9. The statement in this example creates a tree that contains invoice data. If you review this statement, you'll see that it uses the constructors of the XElement and XAttribute classes. Here, the first argument of each XElement constructor is the name of the element, and the second argument is the content of the element. Similarly, the first argument of each XAttribute constructor is the name of the attribute, and the second argument is the value of the attribute.

Notice in this example that, except for the first XElement constructor, the constructors are nested within the constructor for the element that contains them. For example, the two constructors that create the Invoice elements are nested within the constructor that creates the Invoices element. Similarly, the constructors that create the attribute and elements for each Invoice element are nested within the Invoice element. That makes it possible to create the XML tree using a single statement.

The second example in this figure shows you how to create an XML tree using *XML literals*. As you can see, XML literals let you include XML directly in your code. When you use XML literals, it's easy to see the exact structure of the XML tree. Because of that, I recommend you use XML literals to create your XML trees whenever possible.

A statement that uses constructors to create an XML tree

```
Dim invoices As XElement = _
    New XElement("Invoices", _
        New XElement("Invoice", _
            New XAttribute("ID", "1"), _
            New XElement("VendorID", "122"), _
            New XElement("InvoiceNumber", "989319-457"), _
            New XElement("InvoiceDate", "2008-06-08"), _
            New XElement("InvoiceTotal", "3813.33"), _
            New XElement("PaymentTotal", "3813.33"), _
            New XElement("CreditTotal", "0.00"), _
            New XElement("DueDate", "2008-07-08")), _
        New XElement("Invoice", _
            New XAttribute("ID", "2"), _
            New XElement("VendorID", "123"), _
            New XElement("InvoiceNumber", "263253241"), _
            New XElement("InvoiceDate", "2008-06-10"), _
            New XElement("InvoiceTotal", "40.20"), _
            New XElement("PaymentTotal", "40.20"), _
            New XElement("CreditTotal", "0.00"), _
            New XElement("DueDate", "2008-07-10")))
```

A statement that uses XML literals to create the same tree

```
Dim invoices As XElement = _
    <Invoices>
        <Invoice ID="1">
            <VendorID>122</VendorID>
            <InvoiceNumber>989319-457</InvoiceNumber>
            <InvoiceDate>2008-06-08</InvoiceDate>
            <InvoiceTotal>3813.33</InvoiceTotal>
            <PaymentTotal>3813.33</PaymentTotal>
            <CreditTotal>0.00</CreditTotal>
            <DueDate>2008-07-08</DueDate>
        </Invoice>
        <Invoice ID="2">
            <VendorID>123</VendorID>
            <InvoiceNumber>263253241</InvoiceNumber>
            <InvoiceDate>2008-06-10</InvoiceDate>
            <InvoiceTotal>40.20</InvoiceTotal>
            <PaymentTotal>40.20</PaymentTotal>
            <CreditTotal>0.00</CreditTotal>
            <DueDate>2008-07-10</DueDate>
        </Invoice>
    </Invoices>
```

Description

- An *XML tree* is an in-memory representation of an XML document or element. You can create an XML tree by using the constructors of the classes in the LINQ to XML object model or by using XML literals.

- *XML literals* let you include XML directly in your Visual Basic code. That makes it easy to see the structure of the resulting XML tree.

Figure 16-9   How to create an XML tree

How to embed expressions in XML literals

When you use XML literals to create an XML tree, you can include variable information by using *embedded expressions*. To code an embedded expression, you enter the characters "<%=". Then, Visual Studio enters the closing characters "%>" for you, and you can enter an expression between these characters. Figure 16-10 shows a variety of ways that you can use embedded expressions.

In the first example, embedded expressions are used to specify the value of the ID attribute for an Invoice element and to specify the values of the child elements for that element. Here, each expression except for the last one is simply the property of an object named invoice that contains the values for the Invoice element. The last expression is a calculation that's based on the values of three of the properties of the invoice object.

The second example shows how to use an expression to specify the name of an attribute for an element. Here, the name has been stored in a variable. Then, the embedded expression is coded before the equal sign and the attribute value. The third example is similar, but it uses an expression to embed the name of an element.

Notice that the two elements in these examples don't have an end tag. Instead, the start tag ends with the characters "/>". This type of tag is called a *self-closing tag*, and I've used it here for simplicity. Note that when you use a self-closing tag, the element can't contain any content.

The fourth example shows how to embed an entire attribute in an element. To do that, you start by creating an XAttribute object. Then, you name that object in the embedded expression.

You use a similar technique to embed an element within another element as illustrated by the fifth example. Here, the first statement creates an XElement object that contains a single Invoice element. Then, the second statement embeds that object in an XML literal for an XElement object named Invoices.

The last example shows how you can use an expression to embed a root element in an XDocument object. To do that, you start by creating the XElement object that contains the root element. Then, you create the XDocument object and name the XElement object in the embedded expression. Note that for this to work, you must include an XML declaration at the beginning of the document.

Code that uses expressions to embed attribute and element values

```
Dim invoice As New Invoice With {...}
Dim invoiceXML As XElement = _
    <Invoice ID=<%= invoice.InvoiceID %>>
        <VendorID><%= invoice.VendorID %></VendorID>
        <InvoiceNumber><%= invoice.InvoiceNumber %></InvoiceNumber>
        <InvoiceDate><%= invoice.InvoiceDate %></InvoiceDate>
        <InvoiceTotal><%= invoice.InvoiceTotal %></InvoiceTotal>
        <PaymentTotal><%= invoice.PaymentTotal %></PaymentTotal>
        <CreditTotal><%= invoice.CreditTotal %></CreditTotal>
        <DueDate><%= invoice.DueDate %></DueDate>
        <BalanceDue><%= invoice.InvoiceTotal - invoice.PaymentTotal _
                    - invoice.CreditTotal %></BalanceDue>
    </Invoice>
```

Code that uses an expression to embed an attribute name

```
Dim invoiceIDName As String = "ID"
Dim invoice As XElement = <Invoice <%= invoiceIDName %>="1"/>
```

Code that uses an expression to embed an element name

```
Dim invoiceElementName As String = "Invoice"
Dim invoice As XElement = <<%= invoiceElementName %> ID="1"/>
```

Code that uses an expression to embed an attribute in an element

```
Dim invoiceIDAttribute As New XAttribute("ID", "1")
Dim invoice As XElement = <Invoice <%= invoiceIDAttribute %>/>
```

Code that uses an expression to embed an element in another element

```
Dim invoice As XElement = _
    <Invoice ID="1">
        <VendorID>122</VendorID>
        .
        .
        <DueDate>2008-07-08</DueDate>
    </Invoice>
Dim invoices As XElement = <Invoices><%= invoice %></Invoices>
```

Code that uses an expression to embed a root element in a document

```
Dim invoices As XElement = <Invoices></Invoices>
Dim invoiceDocument As XDocument = _
    <?xml version="1.0" encoding="utf-8"?>
    <%= invoices %>
```

Description

- You can use *embedded expressions* in XML literals to insert element and attribute names, element content, and attribute values into an element. You can also use embedded expressions to insert an element into another element or a root element into a document.

- An embedded expression starts with the characters "<%=" and ends with the characters "%>". Between these characters, you code the expression you want to insert.

- In addition to standard Visual Basic expressions like the ones shown above, you can embed query expressions in XML literals. See figure 16-14 for more information.

Figure 16-10   How to embed expressions in XML literals

How to add elements and attributes to an XML tree

After you create an XML tree, you can add elements and attributes to it using the methods of the XElement and XDocument classes shown in figure 16-11. The first example in this figure shows two ways you can add elements. Here, the first statement creates an XElement object with an Invoices element that contains a single Invoice child element. Note that the value of the ID attribute of this Invoice element is 1.

The next two statements create an Invoice element with an ID attribute value of 3 and add it to the Invoices element. Because the Add method is used here, the new Invoice element is added after the existing Invoice element. At this point, the XML looks like this:

```
<Invoices>
    <Invoice ID="1"></Invoice>
    <Invoice ID="3"></Invoice>
</Invoices>
```

The last two statements add another Invoice element between the two existing Invoice elements. To do that, the first statement uses a query to retrieve the Invoice element whose ID attribute value is equal to 1. Then, the second statement uses the AddAfterSelf method of this element to add another Invoice element after this element. The resulting XML is shown in this figure.

Notice here that because the query returns a collection of XElement objects, I had to use an index to refer to the first item in this collection. Another way to do this would be to execute the First method on the query results. Then, the first and only Invoice element with an ID value of 1 would be returned, and the index wouldn't be required.

The second example in this figure shows one way to add an attribute to an element. To do that, you start by creating the XAttribute object. Then, you use the Add method of the element you want to add the attribute to.

You can also add an attribute to an element without using the Add method. To do that, you simply assign a value to an attribute axis property as shown in the last example in this figure. Then, if the attribute doesn't already exist, it's created. Otherwise, the specified value is assigned to the existing attribute.

Common methods of the XElement and XDocument classes for adding elements and attributes

Method	Description
`Add(content)`	Adds the specified object to the end of the child content of an element or document. If the object is an attribute, adds the attribute to the element.
`AddFirst(content)`	Adds the specified object to the beginning of the child content of an element or document.
`AddAfterSelf(content)`	Adds the specified object after a child node of an element or document.
`AddBeforeSelf(content)`	Adds the specified object before a child node of an element or document.

Code that adds two child elements to a parent element

```
Dim invoices As XElement = _
    <Invoices>
        <Invoice ID="1"></Invoice>
    </Invoices>

Dim invoice3 As XElement = <Invoice ID="3"></Invoice>
invoices.Add(invoice3)

Dim currentInvoice = From invoice In invoices.<Invoice> _
                     Where invoice.@ID = "1"
currentInvoice(0).AddAfterSelf(<Invoice ID="2"></Invoice>)
```

The resulting XML

```
<Invoices>
    <Invoice ID="1"></Invoice>
    <Invoice ID="2"></Invoice>
    <Invoice ID="3"></Invoice>
</Invoices>
```

Code that adds an attribute to an element

```
Dim invoice As XElement = <Invoice ID="1"/>
Dim vendorID As New XAttribute("VendorID", "122")
invoice.Add(vendorID)
```

Another way to add an attribute to an element

```
Dim invoice As XElement = <Invoice ID="1"/>
invoice.@VendorID = "122"
```

Description

- The Add methods let you add content before or after the current content of an element or document or before or after a specific child node of an element or document. You can also use the Add method to add an attribute to an element.

- Instead of using the Add method to add an attribute to an element, you can assign a value to an attribute axis property. If the attribute doesn't already exist, it's created.

Figure 16-11   How to add elements and attributes to an XML tree

How to modify documents, elements, and attributes in an XML tree

LINQ to XML provides a variety of properties and methods for modifying a document, element, or attribute in an XML tree. Figure 16-12 summarizes many of these properties and methods. In most cases, you shouldn't have any trouble understanding how these properties and methods work. So I'll just present a couple of examples here. For additional information and examples, please see the Visual Studio documentation for each property and method.

The first example in this figure shows how you can use the ReplaceAll method of the XElement class to replace the contents of an element. The first statement in this example retrieves the first (and only) DueDate element from the first Invoice element in the invoices element you saw back in figure 16-9. If you look back at this figure, you'll see that this DueDate element contains the value "2008-07-08". Then, the second statement uses the ReplaceAll method of the DueDate element to change the value to "2008-07-15".

The second example in this figure shows how you can replace an entire element instead of just changing its value. Here, the first statement retrieves the first DueDate element of the first Invoice element just as the first statement in the first example does. Then, the second statement uses the ReplaceWith method of the DueDate element to replace this element with an element named DueDays.

Methods of the XDocument class for modifying documents

Method	Description
`ReplaceWith`(content)	Replaces the document with the specified content.
`ReplaceNodes`(content)	Replaces the child nodes of the document with the specified content.

Properties and methods of the XElement class for modifying elements

Property	Description
`Value`(value)	Sets the value of an element to the specified string.

Method	Description
`ReplaceAll`(content)	Replaces the nodes and attributes of the element with the specified content.
`ReplaceAttributes`(content)	Replaces the attributes of the element with the specified content.
`ReplaceWith`(content)	Replaces the element with the specified content.
`ReplaceNodes`(content)	Replaces the child nodes of the element with the specified content.
`SetAttributeValue`(name, value)	Sets the value of an existing attribute, removes the attribute if the value is null, or adds the attribute if it doesn't exist.
`SetElementValue`(name, value)	Sets the value of a child element, removes the child element if the value is null, or adds the child element if it doesn't exist.
`SetValue`(value)	Sets the value of an element to the specified object.

Property and method of the XAttribute class for modifying attributes

Property	Description
`Value`(value)	Sets the value of the attribute to the specified string.

Method	Description
`SetValue`(value)	Sets the value of the attribute to the specified object.

Code that replaces the content of the DueDate element for the first invoice

```
Dim dueDate As XElement = invoices.<Invoice>(0).<DueDate>(0)
dueDate.ReplaceAll("2008-07-15")
```

The resulting element

```
<DueDate>2008-07-15</DueDate>
```

Code that replaces the entire DueDate element for the first invoice

```
Dim dueDate As XElement = invoices.<Invoice>(0).<DueDate>(0)
dueDate.ReplaceWith(<DueDays>30</DueDays>)
```

The resulting element

```
<DueDays>30</DueDays>
```

Description

- You can use the properties and methods of the XDocument, XElement, and XAttribute classes to modify an XML tree.

Figure 16-12   How to modify documents, elements, and attributes in an XML tree

How to remove elements and attributes from an XML tree

Figure 16-13 summarizes the methods you can use to remove elements and attributes from an XML tree. The examples in this figure work with the XML tree you saw back in figure 16-9.

To remove a single node from its parent or a single attribute from the element that contains it, you can use the Remove method of an XDocument, XElement, XText, or XAttribute object. The first example in this figure illustrates how this method works. Here, the first statement gets the first Invoice element in the XML tree. Then, the second statement uses the SetAttributeValue method you learned about in the last figure to add a new attribute named VendorID to the invoice. The value of this attribute is the value of the VendorID element. Then, the Remove method is used to remove the VendorID element. The result is that VendorID is now an attribute rather than an element.

To remove all the child nodes from a document or element, you can use the RemoveNodes method of an XDocument or XElement object. This is illustrated in the second example in this figure. The statement in this example removes all the nodes from the Invoices element, which leaves just the Invoices node.

To remove all the nodes and attributes from an element, you can use the RemoveAll method of the element. And to remove just the attributes from an element, you can use the RemoveAttributes method. Although these methods aren't illustrated here, you shouldn't have any trouble using them if you need to.

If you need to remove a collection of nodes from a parent node, you can use the Remove method of the Extensions class. This class contains the LINQ to XML extension methods. The third example in this figure illustrates how to use this method. Here, the first statement uses a query that gets a collection of the Invoice elements that are paid in full. Then, the second statement uses the Remove method of this collection to remove the Invoice elements. Notice that the result of this code is the same as the result of the statement in the second example. That's because the XML tree that's used by this example only contains two invoices and both are paid in full. If you executed this code on the entire Invoices.xml file, however, you'd see that the invoices that have a balance due wouldn't be deleted.

At this point, you might be thinking that you could use a For Each statement to loop through the Invoice elements and remove them one at a time. If you try that, however, you'll see that it won't work. That's because when you remove the first element, the pointers that are used to enumerate through the collection are corrupted. And that means that the remaining elements can't be removed.

Methods for removing nodes, elements, and attributes

Class	Method	Description
XDocument, XElement, XText, XAttribute	`Remove()`	Removes a node from its parent or an attribute from the element that contains it.
XDocument, XElement	`RemoveNodes()`	Removes the child nodes from a document or element.
XElement	`RemoveAll`	Removes all nodes and attributes from the element.
	`RemoveAttributes`	Removes all attributes from the element.
Extensions	`Remove`	Removes the nodes in a collection of nodes from the parent node.

Code that removes the VendorID element for the first invoice after adding a VendorID attribute

```
Dim invoice As XElement = invoices.<Invoice>(0)
invoice.SetAttributeValue("VendorID", invoice.<VendorID>.Value)
invoice.<VendorID>.Remove()
```

The resulting element

```
<Invoice ID="1" VendorID = "122">
    <InvoiceNumber>989319-457</InvoiceNumber>
    ...
</Invoice>
```

A statement that removes all the nodes from the Invoices element

```
invoices.RemoveNodes()
```

The resulting XML

```
<Invoices />
```

Code that removes paid invoices

```
Dim paidInvoices = From invoice In invoices.<Invoice> _
                Where CDec(invoice.<InvoiceTotal>.Value) _
                    - CDec(invoice.<PaymentTotal>.Value) _
                    - CDec(invoice.<CreditTotal>.Value) = 0
paidInvoices.Remove()
```

The resulting XML

```
<Invoices />
```

Description

- You can use the Remove methods of the XDocument, XElement, XText, and XAttribute classes to remove nodes and attributes from an XML tree. You can also use the Remove method of the Extensions class, which defines the extension methods for LINQ to XML, to remove a collection of nodes from the parent node.

- You can also remove an attribute or element using the SetAttributeValue or SetElementValue method and specifying Nothing for the value.

Figure 16-13   How to remove elements and attributes from an XML tree

How to transform an XML tree

When you use the techniques you learned in the last three topics, the XML tree is modified in-place. In some cases, though, it's easier to *transform* an XML tree. That just means that you create a new tree from the existing tree. To create the new tree, you use a process called *functional construction*. Figure 16-14 illustrates how this works.

The first example in this figure shows a transformation of the XML tree you saw in figure 16-9. The first thing you should notice about the statement in this example is that it uses XML literals and embedded expressions. In this case, the embedded expressions refer to the original XML tree. For example, the embedded expression that's used to specify the value of the ID attribute for an Invoice element refers to the ID attribute of the original tree. And the embedded expression that's used to specify the value of the InvoiceNumber element refers to the InvoiceNumber element of the original tree.

Within the Invoices element of the tree, an *embedded query* is used to determine which of the Invoice elements in the original tree are included in the transformed tree. In this case, the query retrieves all the Invoice elements from the original tree for invoices that have been paid in full.

On the Select clause of the query, you specify the structure you want to use for the Invoice elements. In this case, each Invoice element will include an ID attribute like the Invoice elements in the original tree. In addition, each Invoice element will include a VendorID attribute whose value is taken from the VendorID child element in the original tree. Each Invoice element will also contain the InvoiceNumber, InvoiceDate, and InvoiceTotal child elements from the original tree.

Notice that when you transform an XML tree, you define its new structure and content. In contrast, when you modify an XML tree in-place, you indicate what changes you want to make to it. For instance, the second example in this figure shows code you could use to modify the original XML tree so it contains the same XML as the transformed tree. Here, the first two statements remove all the unpaid invoices from the tree. Then, the For Each statement loops through the Invoice elements, adding a VendorID attribute to each element and removing the VendorID, PaymentTotal, CreditTotal, and DueDate elements.

By the way, when you transform an XML tree, you can also change the names of the elements and attributes that were used in the original tree. I used the same names here just to make it easy to see the relationships between the original tree and the transformed tree.

Code that transforms the XML tree of invoices

```
Dim paidInvoices As XElement = _
    <Invoices>
        <%= From invoice In invoices.<Invoice> _
            Where CDec(invoice.<InvoiceTotal>.Value) _
                - CDec(invoice.<PaymentTotal>.Value) _
                - CDec(invoice.<CreditTotal>.Value) = 0 _
            Select _
            <Invoice ID=<%= invoice.@ID %>
                VendorID=<%= invoice.<VendorID>.Value %>>
                <InvoiceNumber><%= invoice.<InvoiceNumber>.Value %>
                </InvoiceNumber>
                <InvoiceDate><%= invoice.<InvoiceDate>.Value %>
                </InvoiceDate>
                <InvoiceTotal><%= invoice.<InvoiceTotal>.Value %>
                </InvoiceTotal>
            </Invoice> %>
    </Invoices>
```

Code that modifies the XML tree in-place

```
Dim unpaidInvoices = From invoice In invoices.<Invoice> _
                     Where CDec(invoice.<InvoiceTotal>.Value) _
                         - CDec(invoice.<PaymentTotal>.Value) _
                         - CDec(invoice.<CreditTotal>.Value) > 0
unpaidInvoices.Remove()

For Each invoice In invoices.<Invoice>
    invoice.SetAttributeValue("VendorID", invoice.<VendorID>.Value)
    invoice.<VendorID>.Remove()
    invoice.<PaymentTotal>.Remove()
    invoice.<CreditTotal>.Remove()
    invoice.<DueDate>.Remove()
Next
```

The resulting XML

```
<Invoices>
  <Invoice ID="1" VendorID="122">
    <InvoiceNumber>989319-457</InvoiceNumber>
    <InvoiceDate>2008-06-08</InvoiceDate>
    <InvoiceTotal>3813.33</InvoiceTotal>
  </Invoice>
  <Invoice ID="2" VendorID="123">
    <InvoiceNumber>263253241</InvoiceNumber>
    <InvoiceDate>2008-06-10</InvoiceDate>
    <InvoiceTotal>40.20</InvoiceTotal>
  </Invoice>
</Invoices>
```

Description

- Instead of modifying an XML tree, you can *transform* it using code that creates a new tree. To do that, you use a feature called *functional construction*.

- To use functional construction, you code XML literals that indicate the format of the transformed tree, and you embed queries in the literals that select the data you want to include in the new XML tree.

Figure 16-14   How to transform an XML tree

How to save XML data to a file

After you modify an XML tree or create a new XML tree, you may want to save it to a file. To do that, you can use the Save method shown in figure 16-15. As you can see, you can use this method with either an XDocument or XElement object.

The example in this figure illustrates how this works. Here, an XElement object that contains an Invoices element with two Invoice elements is created. Then, the Save method is used to save this element to a file named NewInvoices.xml. The contents of this file are shown in this figure. Notice that an XML declaration is automatically added to the beginning of the file. That's true whether you save an XDocument or an XElement object.

The syntax for saving data to an XML file

```
{xDocument|xElement}.Save(filename)
```

Code that creates an XML element and saves it to an XML file

```vb
Dim invoices As XElement = _
    <Invoices>
        <Invoice ID="113">
            <VendorID>37</VendorID>
            <InvoiceNumber>547480102</InvoiceNumber>
            <InvoiceDate>2008-10-01</InvoiceDate>
            <InvoiceTotal>224.00</InvoiceTotal>
            <PaymentTotal>0.00</PaymentTotal>
            <CreditTotal>0.00</CreditTotal>
            <DueDate>2008-10-31</DueDate>
        </Invoice>
        <Invoice ID="114">
            <VendorID>123</VendorID>
            <InvoiceNumber>963253249</InvoiceNumber>
            <InvoiceDate>2008-10-02</InvoiceDate>
            <InvoiceTotal>127.75</InvoiceTotal>
            <PaymentTotal>127.75</PaymentTotal>
            <CreditTotal>0.00</CreditTotal>
            <DueDate>2008-11-01</DueDate>
        </Invoice>
    </Invoices>
invoices.Save("NewInvoices.xml")
```

The resulting XML file

```xml
<?xml version="1.0" encoding="utf-8"?>
<Invoices>
  <Invoice ID="113">
    <VendorID>37</VendorID>
    <InvoiceNumber>547480102</InvoiceNumber>
    <InvoiceDate>2008-10-01</InvoiceDate>
    <InvoiceTotal>224.00</InvoiceTotal>
    <PaymentTotal>0.00</PaymentTotal>
    <CreditTotal>0.00</CreditTotal>
    <DueDate>2008-10-31</DueDate>
  </Invoice>
  <Invoice ID="114">
    <VendorID>123</VendorID>
    <InvoiceNumber>963253249</InvoiceNumber>
    <InvoiceDate>2008-10-02</InvoiceDate>
    <InvoiceTotal>127.75</InvoiceTotal>
    <PaymentTotal>127.75</PaymentTotal>
    <CreditTotal>0.00</CreditTotal>
    <DueDate>2008-11-01</DueDate>
  </Invoice>
</Invoices>
```

Description

- You can use the Save method of an XDocument or XElement object to save XML data to a file. On this method, you specify the name for the file along with the path if necessary.
- You can also use an XmlWriter or TextWriter object with the Save method, and you can specify save options. For more information, see the Visual Studio documentation.

Figure 16-15   How to save XML data to a file

Visual Studio features for working with XML

When you create an XML tree, Visual Studio assists you by entering the end tag for an element after you enter the start tag and by entering the ending characters for an embedded expression after you enter the starting characters. In addition, Visual Studio uses different colors to identify the different parts of an XML tree that you create using XML literals. To make it easier to work with the XML in a tree, however, you'll need to add an *XML schema* to the project that defines the structure of the XML tree. Then, Visual Studio provides XML IntelliSense for working with the tree.

How to generate an XML schema

Figure 16-16 shows two ways you can generate an XML schema. First, if you're loading XML from an existing file, you can generate the schema from that file. The schema shown in this figure, for example, was generated from the Invoices.xml file. Once you create this schema, you can save it to a file and then add that file to your project.

Second, you can generate the schema from an XML literal in your application. To do that, you use the XML to Schema Wizard. The main dialog box for this wizard is shown in this figure. To use this dialog box with an XML literal, you copy the literal to the clipboard before you start the wizard. Then, you click the Type or Paste XML button and paste the literal into the dialog box that's displayed. When you click the OK button, you'll see the XML literal as shown here. When you click OK from this dialog box, the schema is generated and added to the project.

If you review the schema shown here, you should get a general idea of how it works. As you'll see in a minute, though, you don't need to understand the schema to take advantage of it in your applications.

An XML schema for the Invoices document

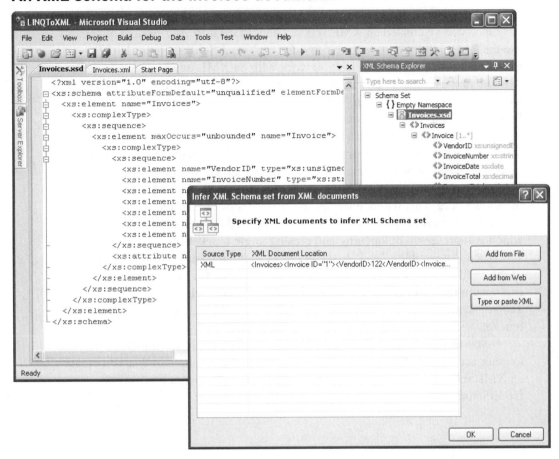

How to generate an XML schema from an XML file

- Use the File→Open File command to open the XML file in the XML Editor.
- Use the XML→Create Schema command to generate the schema and display it in the XML Editor.
- Save the schema to a file using the File→Save *filename* command, and add it to your project using the Project→Add Existing Item command.

How to generate an XML schema from an XML literal

- Copy the XML literal to the clipboard.
- Display the Add New Item dialog box, select the XML to Schema template, enter a name for the schema, and click the Add button.
- Click the Type or Paste XML button in the Infer XML Schema set from XML documents dialog box that's displayed to display the Add XML dialog box.
- Paste the XML into the dialog box, click the OK button, and click the OK button in the Infer XML Schema set dialog box to generate the schema file and add it to the project.

Figure 16-16   How to generate an XML schema

How to use XML IntelliSense

Once you've created an XML schema and added it to your project, you can use the XML IntelliSense feature provided by Visual Studio. Figure 16-17 illustrates how this feature helps you work with an XML tree.

The first example in this figure shows the completion list that's displayed when you enter a period in an XML reference. In this case, the invoices in the Invoices.xml file have been loaded into an XElement object named invoices. Then, a query expression that will get the unpaid invoices is being entered. Here, you can see that the From clause uses a variable named invoice to iterate over the collection of Invoice elements. When I entered the invoice variable in the Where clause followed by a period, Visual Studio displayed the completion list shown here. This list includes all the members of the XElement class, including the axis properties. In this case, I selected the child axis property, which is represented by opening and closing angle brackets.

When I pressed the Tab key, the opening angle bracket was entered and all of the child elements of the Invoice element were listed as shown in the second example in this figure. Then, I selected the InvoiceTotal element and pressed the Tab key again. When I did that, the element was entered along with its closing bracket.

If you use the XML IntelliSense feature, you'll quickly see how it helps you to enter accurate XML references. Because of that, I recommend that you create an XML schema anytime you work with XML in code so you can use the IntelliSense feature.

The list that's displayed when you enter a period in an XML reference

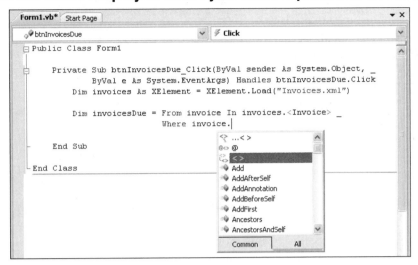

The list that's displayed when you enter an opening bracket in an XML reference

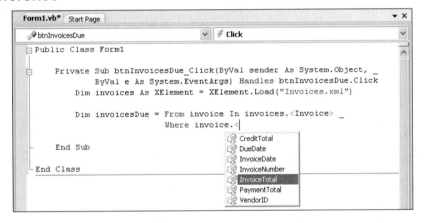

Description

- The XML IntelliSense feature can help you enter XML references correctly. To use this feature, you must include the XML schema for the XML data in the project.

- When you enter a period following the name of a collection or element, Visual Studio displays a list that includes the members of the collection or class as well as items you can use to identify a descendant, an attribute, or a child element.

- If you select the item for entering a descendant, attribute, or child element, Visual Studio enters the starting characters and then displays a list of the available descendants, attributes, and child elements. If you select a descendant or child element, Visual Studio adds the item along with the closing bracket.

Figure 16-17   How to use XML IntelliSense

Perspective

In this chapter, you learned about many of the features of LINQ to XML. As you've seen, LINQ to XML provides much more than a way to query XML data. It provides a complete object model that lets you load XML data from a file, work with that data in an XML tree, and save the data back to a file. If you've used DOM to work with XML in the past, you'll realize that LINQ to XML is a vast improvement over DOM.

Terms

XML (Extensible Markup Language)	DOM (Document Object Model)
	node
tag	axis property
XML document	descendant
XML declaration	axis method
element	XML tree
start tag	XML literal
end tag	embedded expression
attribute	self-closing tag
content	transform an XML tree
child element	functional construction
parent element	embedded query
root element	XML schema

Exercise 16-1   Query an XML file

In this exercise, you'll build an application that executes a query against an XML file that contains vendor data. This application will retrieve the names of all the vendors in the state you enter. When you're done, the form for the application should look like this:

Start the application, get the XML file, and create the XML schema

1.   Start a new application named VendorsByState in your chapter 16 directory.

2. Use Windows Explorer to copy the Vendors.xml file in your C:\ADO.NET 3.5 VB\Files directory to the bin\Debug directory of the application. When you return to Visual Studio, click the Show All Files button at the top of the Solution Explorer, and expand the bin\Debug directory. Click the Refresh button to see the Vendors.xml file you just added.

3. Double-click on the Vendors.xml file to open it in the XML Editor. Then, generate an XML schema from the file as described in figure 16-16, save the file, and add it to your project.

Design and code the form

4. Add controls to the default form so it looks like the form shown above. To allow users to enter lowercase letters for the state, set the CharacterCasing property of the text box to Upper so that lowercase letters are converted to uppercase as they're entered.

5. Start a Load event handler for the form. Define a module-level variable that will store the data in the Vendors.xml file as an XDocument object. Then, load the file into this object in the Load event handler. Note that because the Vendors.xml file has been copied to the bin\Debug directory, you don't have to specify a path for the file.

6. Start an event handler for the Click event of the button. Add a query expression to this event handler that retrieves the vendor names from the XElement object for all the vendors in the state the user enters into the text box. (Don't worry about validating the user entry.) Sort the results by the vendor name. Notice as you enter the query how XML IntelliSense helps you enter the XML references accurately.

7. Add code to the Click event handler that clears the list box and then adds each name in the query results to the list. Note that because the query retrieves only the vendor names, the result is an IEnumerable(Of String) object.

8. Test the application by entering "CA" for the state code. If this works, try other state codes. Otherwise, make the changes necessary to get it to work.

Change the code to use an XElement object

9. Change the code in the Load event handler so the Vendors.xml file is loaded into an XElement object instead of an XDocument object. Then, make the necessary changes to the query expression so it works with an XElement object.

10. Test the application again to be sure it still works. When you have it working correctly, end the application. If you're not going to continue with the next exercise, close the project.

Exercise 16-2   Transform an XML tree

In this exercise, you'll modify the application you developed in exercise 16-1 so it transforms the XML tree that contains the data from the Vendors.xml file and then saves the transformed tree to a new file.

Add and test the code to transform the XML tree

1. If it isn't already open, open the project you created in exercise 16-1.

2. Add a button below the list box that will transform the Vendors.xml file when it's clicked. This button should be disabled when the application starts, and it should be enabled and disabled depending on whether the list box contains any vendors.

3. Start an event handler for the Click event of the Transform button. Add code to this event handler that transforms the XML tree so it contains only the vendors in the state the user enters and so the state is included as an attribute rather than an element.

4. Add a statement that displays a dialog box with the transformed tree. To do that, use the ToString method of the tree to convert it to a string.

5. Run the application and display the vendors in New York (NY). Then, click the Transform XML button and review the XML in the dialog box that's displayed. If the XML is structured correctly and contains the correct vendors, end the application and continue with the next step. Otherwise, correct the application until the XML is transformed correctly.

Add and test the code to save the transformed tree

6. Comment out the statement that displays the dialog box. Then, add a statement that saves the transformed tree to a file that has the name "Vendors" appended with the two-letter state code. For example, the name of the file that contains the vendors in New York should be "VendorsNY". Don't specify a path for the file so it'll be saved in the bin\Debug directory for the application.

7. Add a statement that displays a dialog box when the transformation is complete. The message in this dialog box should include the name of the file that was created.

8. Run the application again, display the vendors for New York, and then click the Transform button. When the dialog box is displayed, close it and then end the application.

9. Click the Refresh button at the top of the Solution Explorer. Then, Locate the VendorsNY.xml file in the bin\Debug directory and double-click on it to display the file in the XML Editor. Review the file to be sure it's formatted properly. When you're sure it is, close the project.

Section 5

How to use the Entity Framework

The Entity Framework is a component of ADO.NET that became available with .NET Framework 3.5 Service Pack 1. It provides new techniques for developing applications that work with the data in a database.

The Entity Framework is Microsoft's first attempt to address the mismatch that often exists between the structure of a database and the objects used in an application. This is often referred to as the "impedance mismatch." To resolve this mismatch, the Framework uses an Entity Data Model that maps the conceptual model used by the application to the storage model for the database.

In chapter 17, you'll learn how to create an Entity Data Model. After you create this model, you can use several techniques to work with it. First, you can use LINQ to Entities as described in chapter 18. Second, you can use Entity SQL as described in chapter 19. Third, if you're developing an ASP.NET application, you can use an Entity data source control as described in chapter 20.

17

How to create an Entity Data Model

To use the Entity Framework, you start by creating an Entity Data Model. That's what you'll learn to do in this chapter. Then, in the chapters that follow, you'll learn how to use an Entity Data Model to work with the data in a database.

An introduction to the Entity Framework

The *Entity Framework* provides a new way to use ADO.NET to work with the data in a database. In the topic that follows, I'll present an overview of how the Entity Framework works. Then, I'll describe three ways you can implement queries when you use the Entity Framework.

How the Entity Framework works

Figure 17-1 presents the basic components that are used to implement database access with the Entity Framework. As you can see, the two basic components of the Entity Framework are *Object Services* and the EntityClient data provider. These two components work together to manage the transfer of data to and from the ADO.NET data provider, which provides direct access to the database.

As you'll see in the chapters that follow, you use queries to retrieve data from a database when you use the Entity Framework. These queries are executed against a conceptual model that is part of an *Entity Data Model*. The *conceptual model* defines the objects, or *entities*, used by the application and the relationships between those entities. The Entity Data Model also includes a *storage model* that defines the structure of the objects in the database. Finally, the Entity Data Model defines the *mappings* between the conceptual model and the storage model.

The Entity Framework uses the Entity Data Model to determine how to translate a query into a form that the DBMS understands. It also uses the Entity Data Model to translate the data that's returned by the query into the objects that are used by the application. Then, it tracks any changes made to those objects and provides for submitting those changes to the database.

Three techniques for performing query operations

Figure 17-1 also list three ways you can query a conceptual model. First, you can use LINQ to Entities, which is very similar to using LINQ to SQL. You'll learn how to use LINQ to Entities in chapter 18.

Second, you can use Entity SQL to query a conceptual model. Entity SQL works by using a dialect of SQL that's not specific to the database. You'll learn how to use Entity SQL in chapter 19.

Third, you can use query builder methods. These queries are like the method-based queries you use with LINQ, but they use Entity SQL. You'll learn how to code these types of queries in chapter 19 too.

How the Entity Framework works

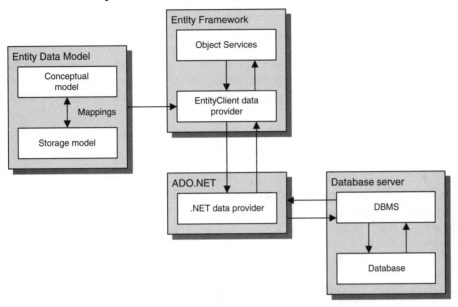

Three techniques for performing query operations

Technique	Description
LINQ to Entities	Uses LINQ to query entities in the conceptual model.
Entity SQL	Uses a dialect of SQL that's independent of the database and that can be used to work directly with the entities in the conceptual model.
Query builder methods	Entity SQL queries that use LINQ-style query methods.

Description

- The *Entity Framework* provides a layer of abstraction between the database used by an application and the objects used by an application. To do that, it uses an *Entity Data Model* that defines a conceptual model, a storage model, and mappings between the two.

- The *conceptual model* defines the entities and relationships used by the application. The *storage model* defines the structure of the database that's used by the application. And the *mappings* define how the conceptual and storage model are related.

- When you execute a query against a conceptual model, *Object Services* works in conjunction with the EntityClient data provider and the Entity Data Model to translate the query into a query that can be executed by the database. When the results are returned from the database, Object Services translates them back to objects defined by the conceptual model.

- You can use any of the three techniques listed above to query a conceptual model. See chapters 18 and 19 for details.

- The Entity Framework also provides for tracking changes to objects created from the conceptual model and for submitting those changes to the database.

Figure 17-1   An introduction to the Entity Framework

How to use the Entity Data Model Wizard

The easiest way to create an Entity Data Model from Visual Studio is to use the Entity Data Model Wizard. You'll learn how to use this wizard in the topics that follow. Then, you'll see the Entity Data Model and code that are generated.

How to start the wizard

To start the Entity Data Model Wizard, you can use any of the standard techniques to display the Add New Item dialog box. From this dialog box, you select the ADO.NET Entity Data Model template and then enter the name you want to use for the model. When you click the Add button, the first step of the wizard is displayed.

How to choose the model contents

The first step of the Entity Data Model Wizard, shown at the top of figure 17-2, lets you choose whether you want to create the model from a database or create an empty data model. In most cases, we recommend that you create the model from a database. If you create an empty model instead, you'll have to manually select the data source, database, and database objects.

How to choose a data connection

The second step of the Entity Data Model Wizard, also shown in figure 17-2, lets you specify the database connection you want to use. If the connection already exists, you can select it from the drop-down list. In this figure, for example, I selected the connection to the Payables database that I used in section 2 of this book.

Notice the connection string that was generated when I selected the Payables database. This string includes the names of the conceptual model, the storage model, and the mappings as well information about the provider and the database to be accessed. You'll see some of the code for the conceptual model, storage model, and mappings that this string refers to later in this chapter.

If the connection doesn't already exist, you can click the New Connection button and then use the Connection Properties dialog box that's displayed to create a connection. This dialog box is identical to the dialog box that's displayed when you create a new connection from the Data Source Configuration Wizard, so you shouldn't have any trouble using it.

The first two steps of the Entity Data Model Wizard

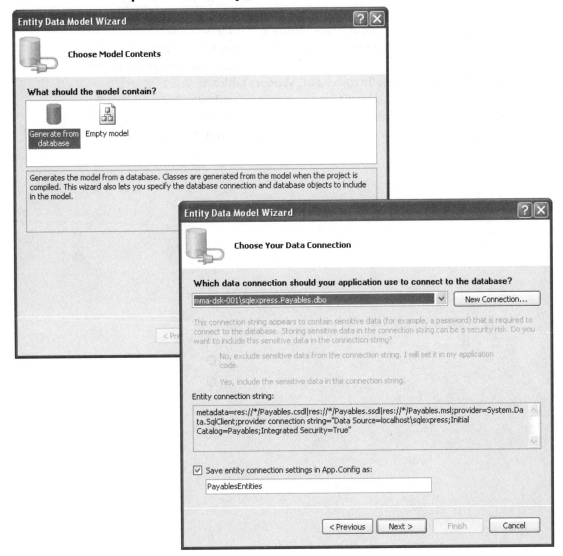

Description

- To start the Entity Data Model Wizard, display the Add New Item dialog box, select the ADO.NET Entity Data Model template, and enter a name for the model.

- The Choose Model Contents step of the wizard lets you choose whether you want to create the model from scratch or from an existing database.

- The Choose Your Data Connection step of the wizard lets you choose the database connection you want to use or create a new connection. It also lets you select whether the connection settings are saved in the App.Config file, and it lets you enter the name that's used for the connection string. The default is the name of the database appended with "Entities".

Figure 17-2   How to choose the contents and data connection for an object model

How to choose the database objects

The third step of the Entity Data Model Wizard lets you select the database objects you want to include in the model. As you can see in figure 17-3, you can select any of the tables, views, and stored procedures in the database. In this example, I've selected the Invoices and Vendors tables.

Note that the wizard doesn't let you select individual columns from tables and views. Instead, the entire table or view is included in the model. If that's not what you want, you can edit the model after it's generated as shown later in this chapter.

The third step of the Entity Data Model Wizard

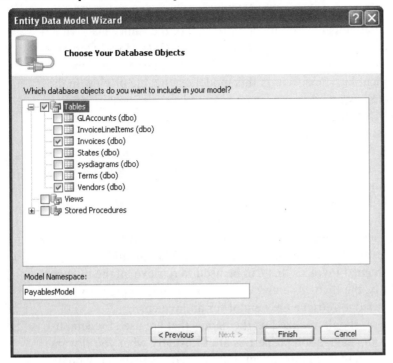

Description

- The Choose Your Database Objects step of the wizard lets you choose the tables, views, and stored procedures you want to include in the Entity Data Model.

- To include an object, expand the node that contains that object and then click in its check box.

- You can also enter the name you want to use for the model's namespace from this step of the wizard. By default, this is the name of the database appended with "Model".

- When you click the Finish button, the Entity Data Model Designer is displayed. You can use this designer to work with the object model.

Figure 17-3   How to choose the database objects for an object model

The Entity Data Model

When you click the Finish button in the third step of the Entity Data Model Wizard, the Entity Data Model is displayed in the *Entity Data Model Designer*, or just *Entity Designer*, as shown in figure 17-4. This designer presents the model using a graphical interface. Within this model, each table or view in the database is represented by an entity, and each foreign key relationship is represented by an *association*. In this figure, for example, you can see the Vendors and Invoices entities and the association between the two. Here, the 1 at the left side of the connector that represents the association indicates that there is a single vendor for each invoice, and the asterisk at the right side of the connector indicates that there can be many invoices for a single vendor.

Each entity in an Entity Data Model contains one or more *scalar properties* that represent the columns in the associated table or view. In addition, if two entities are related, they contain *navigation properties* that provide access to the related objects. For example, the Vendors entity in this figure includes a navigation property named Invoices that can be used to retrieve all the invoices for a vendor. Similarly, the Invoices entity contains a navigation property named Vendors that can be used to retrieve the Vendor for an invoice.

Before I go on, you should realize that the names that are used by default for entities and for some navigation properties aren't usually what you'll want. For example, since the entities in this model will be used to create individual vendor and invoice objects, you'll probably want to give them singular names. And since each invoice is related to only one vendor, you'll probably want to change the navigation property for the invoice entity to Vendor. You'll learn how to make changes like this later in this chapter.

The definition of an Entity Data Model, which includes the conceptual model, the storage model, and the mappings between the two, is stored in a file with the *.edmx* extension. You can see this file in the Solution Explorer in this figure. It's the graphical view of this file that's displayed in the Entity Designer.

Subordinate to the edmx file is a file with the Designer.vb extension. This file contains Visual Basic code that's generated from the conceptual model in the edmx file. It contains the classes that you'll use to work with the Entity Data Model from within your application.

The Entity Data Model displayed in the Entity Data Model Designer

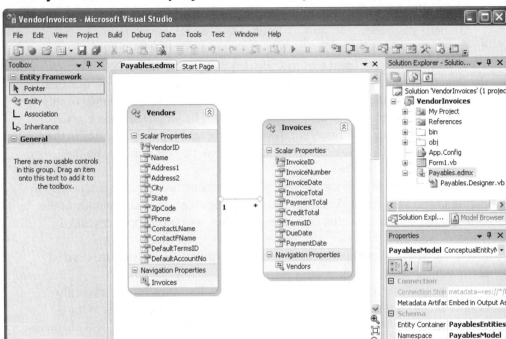

Description

- When you use the Entity Data Model Wizard to create an Entity Data Model, Visual Studio generates a file with the extension *edmx* that defines the model. This file encapsulates the storage model, the conceptual model, and the mappings between the two.

- Visual Studio also generates Visual Basic code that defines the classes that you use in your application to work with the model. This code is stored in the file with the Designer.vb extension that's subordinate to the edmx file.

- Each table or view you add to an Entity Data Model is defined by an *entity class*. Each entity class contains *scalar properties* that map to the columns in the table or view.

- If two tables you add to an Entity Data Model are related by a foreign key, Visual Studio defines an *association* between the entity classes based on that relationship. An association is represented in the model by a line between the two tables with a diamond at each end and an indication of the type of relationship.

- An association is defined by *navigation properties* in the entity classes. These properties let you refer to one class from the other class.

Figure 17-4   The Entity Data Model

The generated code

To help you understand how an Entity Data Model works, figure 17-5 presents some of the Visual Basic code that's generated for the model in figure 17-4. The first class defined by this code is the class named PayablesEntities that represents the container for the Vendors and Invoices entities. Notice that this class inherits the ObjectContext class. Because of that, an instance of this class is typically referred to as an *object context*. The ObjectContext class provides the facilities for querying the objects created from the entities in the conceptual model, tracking changes made to those objects, and saving the changes to the database.

Within the PayablesEntities class, you'll find one property for each entity in the conceptual model. By default, these properties have the same names as the tables in the database. In this case, the properties are named Invoices and Vendors, and they return a collection of Invoices and Vendors objects respectively. These collections are stored in the private fields that are defined after the properties.

On page 2 of this listing, you can see that the PayablesEntities class also defines methods that you can use to add invoice and vendor objects to the collection of objects. You'll learn how to use these methods in the next chapter.

In addition to the PayablesEntities class, the code for the Entity Data Model includes one class for each entity in the conceptual model. You can see the beginning of the Invoices entity starting near the middle of page 2. This class inherits the EntityObject class, which provides the basic functionality that's required by Object Services.

The Invoices class contains a method named CreateInvoices that you can use to create a new invoice object. In addition, it contains one property for each column in the associated database table, along with a private variable to store the value of that property. These are the scalar properties you saw in the last figure, and you can see the definitions for three of these properties on page 3 of this listing.

After the definitions for the scalar properties and fields is the definition for the navigation property. You can see this property, named Vendors, on page 4 of this listing. You can use this property to get the vendor object for an invoice.

In addition to the navigation property, the Invoices class includes a property named VendorsReference that represents the association that the class has with the Vendors class. You'll see one way to use this property in the next chapter.

The contents of the Vendors class are similar to the contents of the Invoices class. The main difference is that the navigation property, shown on page 5, returns a collection of invoice objects. That makes sense because a vendor can have more than one invoice.

Some of the generated code for the model in figure 17-4   Page 1

```vb
Option Strict Off
Option Explicit On

<Assembly: Global.System.Data.Objects.DataClasses.EdmSchemaAttribute( _
"a5b69783-8e2d-4145-9aee-f3773989b39c"), _
 Assembly: Global.System.Data.Objects.DataClasses.EdmRelationshipAttribute( _
"PayablesModel", "FK_Invoices_Vendors", "Vendors", _
Global.System.Data.Metadata.Edm.RelationshipMultiplicity.One, _
GetType(Vendors), "Invoices", _
Global.System.Data.Metadata.Edm.RelationshipMultiplicity.Many, _
GetType(Invoices))>


'Original file name:
'Generation date: 11/6/2008 1:32:39 PM
'''<summary>
'''There are no comments for PayablesEntities in the schema.
'''</summary>
Partial Public Class PayablesEntities
    Inherits Global.System.Data.Objects.ObjectContext
    '''<summary>
    '''Initializes a new PayablesEntities object using the connection string
    '''found in the 'PayablesEntities' section of the application
    '''configuration file.
    '''</summary>
    Public Sub New()
        MyBase.New("name=PayablesEntities", "PayablesEntities")
        Me.OnContextCreated
    End Sub
    .

    .
    '''<summary>
    '''There are no comments for Invoices in the schema.
    '''</summary>
    Public ReadOnly Property Invoices() _
    As Global.System.Data.Objects.ObjectQuery(Of Invoices)
        Get
            If (Me._Invoices Is Nothing) Then
                Me._Invoices = MyBase.CreateQuery(Of Invoices)("[Invoices]")
            End If
            Return Me._Invoices
        End Get
    End Property
    Private _Invoices As Global.System.Data.Objects.ObjectQuery(Of Invoices)
    '''<summary>
    '''There are no comments for Vendors in the schema.
    '''</summary>
    Public ReadOnly Property Vendors() _
    As Global.System.Data.Objects.ObjectQuery(Of Vendors)
        Get
            If (Me._Vendors Is Nothing) Then
                Me._Vendors = MyBase.CreateQuery(Of Vendors)("[Vendors]")
            End If
            Return Me._Vendors
        End Get
    End Property
    Private _Vendors As Global.System.Data.Objects.ObjectQuery(Of Vendors)
```

Figure 17-5   The code that's generated for the Entity Data Model (part 1 of 5)

Some of the generated code for the model in figure 17-4   **Page 2**

```vb
'''<summary>
'''There are no comments for Invoices in the schema.
'''</summary>
Public Sub AddToInvoices(ByVal invoices As Invoices)
    MyBase.AddObject("Invoices", invoices)
End Sub
'''<summary>
'''There are no comments for Vendors in the schema.
'''</summary>
Public Sub AddToVendors(ByVal vendors As Vendors)
    MyBase.AddObject("Vendors", vendors)
End Sub
End Class

'''<summary>
'''There are no comments for PayablesModel.Invoices in the schema.
'''</summary>
'''<KeyProperties>
'''InvoiceID
'''</KeyProperties>
<Global.System.Data.Objects.DataClasses.EdmEntityTypeAttribute( _
 NamespaceName:="PayablesModel", Name:="Invoices"), _
 Global.System.Runtime.Serialization.DataContractAttribute(IsReference:=true), _
 Global.System.Serializable()> _
Partial Public Class Invoices
    Inherits Global.System.Data.Objects.DataClasses.EntityObject
    '''<summary>
    '''Create a new Invoices object.
    '''</summary>
    '''<param name="invoiceID">Initial value of InvoiceID.</param>
    '''<param name="invoiceNumber">Initial value of InvoiceNumber.</param>
    '''<param name="invoiceDate">Initial value of InvoiceDate.</param>
    '''<param name="invoiceTotal">Initial value of InvoiceTotal.</param>
    '''<param name="paymentTotal">Initial value of PaymentTotal.</param>
    '''<param name="creditTotal">Initial value of CreditTotal.</param>
    '''<param name="termsID">Initial value of TermsID.</param>
    '''<param name="dueDate">Initial value of DueDate.</param>
    Public Shared Function CreateInvoices(ByVal invoiceID As Integer, _
    ByVal invoiceNumber As String, ByVal invoiceDate As Date, _
    ByVal invoiceTotal As Decimal, ByVal paymentTotal As Decimal, _
    ByVal creditTotal As Decimal, ByVal termsID As Integer, _
    ByVal dueDate As Date) As Invoices
        Dim invoices As Invoices = New Invoices
        invoices.InvoiceID = invoiceID
        invoices.InvoiceNumber = invoiceNumber
        invoices.InvoiceDate = invoiceDate
        invoices.InvoiceTotal = invoiceTotal
        invoices.PaymentTotal = paymentTotal
        invoices.CreditTotal = creditTotal
        invoices.TermsID = termsID
        invoices.DueDate = dueDate
        Return invoices
    End Function
```

Figure 17-5   The code that's generated for the Entity Data Model (part 2 of 5)

Some of the generated code for the model in figure 17-4   **Page 3**

```
'''<summary>
'''There are no comments for Property InvoiceID in the schema.
'''</summary>
<Global.System.Data.Objects.DataClasses.EdmScalarPropertyAttribute( _
 EntityKeyProperty:=true, IsNullable:=false), _
 Global.System.Runtime.Serialization.DataMemberAttribute()> _
Public Property InvoiceID() As Integer
    Get
        Return Me._InvoiceID
    End Get
    Set
        ...
    End Set
End Property
Private _InvoiceID As Integer
Partial Private Sub OnInvoiceIDChanging(ByVal value As Integer)
    End Sub
Partial Private Sub OnInvoiceIDChanged()
    End Sub
'''<summary>
'''There are no comments for Property InvoiceNumber in the schema.
'''</summary>
<Global.System.Data.Objects.DataClasses.EdmScalarPropertyAttribute( _
 IsNullable:=false), _
 Global.System.Runtime.Serialization.DataMemberAttribute()> _
Public Property InvoiceNumber() As String
    Get
        Return Me._InvoiceNumber
    End Get
    Set
        ...
    End Set
End Property
Private _InvoiceNumber As String
Partial Private Sub OnInvoiceNumberChanging(ByVal value As String)
    End Sub
Partial Private Sub OnInvoiceNumberChanged()
    End Sub
.
.
.
'''<summary>
'''There are no comments for Property PaymentDate in the schema.
'''</summary>
<Global.System.Data.Objects.DataClasses.EdmScalarPropertyAttribute(), _
 Global.System.Runtime.Serialization.DataMemberAttribute()> _
Public Property PaymentDate() As Global.System.Nullable(Of Date)
    Get
        Return Me._PaymentDate
    End Get
    Set
        ...
    End Set
End Property
Private _PaymentDate As Global.System.Nullable(Of Date)
Partial Private Sub OnPaymentDateChanging( _
        ByVal value As Global.System.Nullable(Of Date))
    End Sub
Partial Private Sub OnPaymentDateChanged()
    End Sub
```

Figure 17-5   The code that's generated for the Entity Data Model (part 3 of 5)

Some of the generated code for the model in figure 17-4   Page 4

```
'''<summary>
'''There are no comments for Vendors in the schema.
'''</summary>
<Global.System.Data.Objects.DataClasses.EdmRelationshipNavigationPropertyAttribute( _
"PayablesModel", "FK_Invoices_Vendors", "Vendors"), _
    Global.System.Xml.Serialization.XmlIgnoreAttribute(), _
    Global.System.Xml.Serialization.SoapIgnoreAttribute(), _
    Global.System.Runtime.Serialization.DataMemberAttribute()> _
Public Property Vendors() As Vendors
    Get
        ...
    End Get
    Set
        ...
    End Set
End Property
'''<summary>
'''There are no comments for Vendors in the schema.
'''</summary>
<Global.System.ComponentModel.BrowsableAttribute(false), _
  Global.System.Runtime.Serialization.DataMemberAttribute()> _
Public Property VendorsReference() _
As Global.System.Data.Objects.DataClasses.EntityReference(Of Vendors)
    Get
        ...
    End Get
    Set
        ...
    End Set
End Property
End Class

'''<summary>
'''There are no comments for PayablesModel.Vendors in the schema.
'''</summary>
'''<KeyProperties>
'''VendorID
'''</KeyProperties>
<Global.System.Data.Objects.DataClasses.EdmEntityTypeAttribute( _
  NamespaceName:="PayablesModel", Name:="Vendors"), _
  Global.System.Runtime.Serialization.DataContractAttribute(IsReference:=true), _
  Global.System.Serializable()> _
Partial Public Class Vendors
    Inherits Global.System.Data.Objects.DataClasses.EntityObject
    .
    .
    Public Shared Function CreateVendors(ByVal vendorID As Integer, _
    ByVal name As String, ByVal address1 As String, ByVal city As String, _
    ByVal state As String, ByVal zipCode As String, _
    ByVal defaultTermsID As Integer, ByVal defaultAccountNo As Integer) _
    As Vendors
        Dim vendors As Vendors = New Vendors
        vendors.VendorID = vendorID
        vendors.Name = name
        ...
        vendors.DefaultAccountNo = defaultAccountNo
        Return vendors
    End Function
```

Figure 17-5   The code that's generated for the Entity Data Model (part 4 of 5)

Some of the generated code for the model in figure 17-4   **Page 5**

```vb
    '''<summary>
    '''There are no comments for Property VendorID in the schema.
    '''</summary>
    <Global.System.Data.Objects.DataClasses.EdmScalarPropertyAttribute( _
     EntityKeyProperty:=true, IsNullable:=false), _
     Global.System.Runtime.Serialization.DataMemberAttribute()> _
    Public Property VendorID() As Integer
        Get
            Return Me._VendorID
        End Get
        Set
            ...
        End Set
    End Property
    Private _VendorID As Integer
    Partial Private Sub OnVendorIDChanging(ByVal value As Integer)
        End Sub
    Partial Private Sub OnVendorIDChanged()
        End Sub
    .
    .
    .
    '''<summary>
    '''There are no comments for Invoices in the schema.
    '''</summary>
    <Global.System.Data.Objects.DataClasses.EdmRelationshipNavigationPropertyAttribute( _
    "PayablesModel", "FK_Invoices_Vendors", "Invoices"), _
     Global.System.Xml.Serialization.XmlIgnoreAttribute(), _
     Global.System.Xml.Serialization.SoapIgnoreAttribute(), _
     Global.System.Runtime.Serialization.DataMemberAttribute()> _
    Public Property Invoices() _
    As Global.System.Data.Objects.DataClasses.EntityCollection(Of Invoices)
        Get
            ...
        End Get
        Set
            ...
        End Set
    End Property
    '''<summary>
    '''There are no comments for Invoices in the schema.
    '''</summary>
    <Global.System.ComponentModel.BrowsableAttribute(false), _
     Global.System.Runtime.Serialization.DataMemberAttribute()> _
    Public Property InvoicesReference() _
    As Global.System.Data.Objects.DataClasses.EntityReference(Of Invoices)
        Get
            ...
        End Get
        Set
            ...
        End Set
    End Property
End Class
```

Description

- To display the Visual Basic code for an Entity Data Model, click the plus sign to the left of the edmx file in the Solution Explorer and then double-click the Designer.vb file.

Figure 17-5   The code that's generated for the Entity Data Model (part 5 of 5)

How to use the Entity Data Model Designer

Once you create an Entity Data Model, you can use the Entity Data Model Designer to work with it. The topics that follow show you how.

Basic skills for using the designer

Figure 17-6 presents some basic skills for using the Entity Data Model Designer. When you first display this designer, the Model Browser window is displayed in the tabbed window with the Solution Explorer, and the Mapping Details window is displayed below the main design window. You'll learn how to use the Model Browser and Mapping Windows in the next two figures.

The Entity Framework Toolbox is also displayed in this figure. You can use the components in this Toolbox to create new entities and associations and to implement inheritance. Although I won't show you how to use these components in this chapter, you shouldn't have any trouble using them if you ever need to do that.

In general, the skills for using the designer are straightforward. So I just want to point out one thing here. That is, if you change the Name property of an entity, Visual Studio automatically changes the Entity Set Name property so it's the same as the Name property appended with "Set". When I changed the Name property of the Vendors entity to Vendor, for example, the Entity Set Name property was changed to VendorSet. Because the value of this property is used for the name of the property in the PayablesEntities class that accesses the vendor objects, this wasn't what I wanted. So I changed the Entity Set Name property to Vendors, which was its original value.

In addition to changing the names of the entities in this model, I also changed the name of the navigation property that's defined for the Invoice entity so it's singular rather than plural. That makes sense because this property returns a single vendor object.

The Entity Data Model Designer

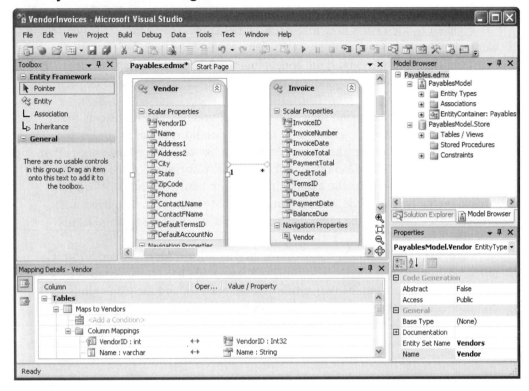

Description

- To display the *Entity Data Model Designer* for an Entity Data Model, double-click the edmx file in the Solution Explorer.

- To change the properties for an entity or for a scalar or navigation property, click the entity or property to display its settings in the Properties window. The only property you'll typically change is the Name property for an entity or a navigation property on the many side of a relationship to make them singular.

- To delete an entity, property, or association, click on it and then press the Delete key.

- To add an entity, right-click on the design surface, select Add→Entity, and then complete the Add Entity dialog box that's displayed.

- To add a scalar property to an entity, right-click on the entity and select Add→Scalar Property. Then, enter the name for the property and use the Properties window to set its properties.

- You can use the controls in the lower right corner of the designer window to change the zoom level for the model.

- To view and work with the conceptual and storage models using a tree view, use the Model Browser window. See figure 17-7 for details.

- To work with the mappings for an Entity Data Model, use the Mapping Details window. See figure 17-8 for details.

Figure 17-6   Basic skills for using the Entity Data Model Designer

How to use the Model Browser window

Figure 17-7 describes how to use the Model Browser window. This window can make it easy to work with an Entity Data Model, particularly if it contains many entities. It displays both the conceptual model and the storage model in a tree view. Then, you can expand and collapse the nodes of the tree to display just the items you want.

In this figure, I expanded the PayablesModel node, which represents the conceptual model, and the Entity Types and Associations nodes subordinate to that node. As you can see, the Entity Types node has two subordinate nodes that represent the Invoice and Vendor entities, and the Associations node contains a single item that represents the association between the two entities. When I clicked on the Invoice node, the properties for that entity were displayed in the Properties window, and the mappings were displayed in the Mapping Details window.

I also expanded some of the nodes in the PayablesModel.Store node, which represents the storage model. The Tables / Views node has two subordinate nodes for the tables that the two entities are mapped to, and the Constraints node contains the foreign key that the association is mapped to. If you experiment with the items and nodes in the Model Browser window, you should quickly see how this window works.

The Model Browser window with some of its nodes expanded

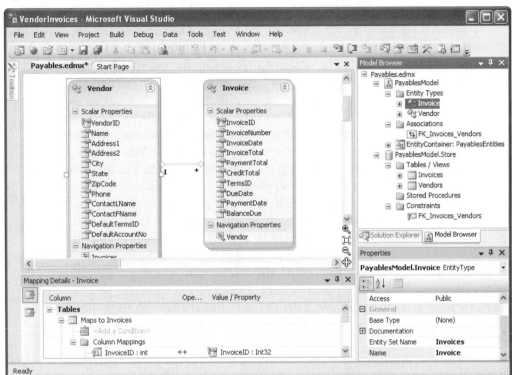

Description

- The *Model Browser window* displays the Entity Data Model in a tree view. The tree is divided into two nodes that represent the conceptual model and the storage model.

- You can expand the child nodes for the conceptual model to display the entity types and associations in the model. You can expand the child nodes for the storage model to display the tables, views, stored procedures, and constraints the conceptual model is mapped to.

- If you click an entity type, a property for an entity type, or an association in the Model Browser, the properties for that object are displayed in the Properties window so you can view or modify them.

- If you click an entity type or a property for an entity type in the Model Browser, the mappings for that entity are displayed in the Mapping Details window. If you click an association, the mappings for that association are displayed in the Mapping Details window. Then, you can use that window to work with the mappings.

- To locate an entity on the design surface, right-click the entity name in the Model Browser and select Show in Designer.

- You can also use the Model Browser to import a stored procedure (see figure 17-9) and update the Entity Data Model based on changes made to the underlying database (see figure 17-11).

Figure 17-7   How to use the Model Browser window

How to use the Mapping Details window

Figure 17-8 shows two ways to use the Mapping Details window. First, you can use it to work with the mappings between the columns in a table or view in the storage model and the properties of an entity in the conceptual model. Second, you can use it to work with the associations between the entities in the conceptual model.

In most cases, the columns and properties are mapped the way you want them by default. If you need to change the mapping for a column, however, you can do that by selecting a property from the drop-down list. You can also select <Delete> from this list to remove the mapping for a column. You might want to do that if a column isn't used by an application. Then, you can remove the corresponding property from the entity.

If you remove a property and its column mapping, you should realize that the column must allow nulls or it must be defined with a default value. If it's not, you'll get a syntax error when you build the project indicating that the column must be mapped. You should also realize that the column definitions in the conceptual model don't include default values by default. But you can add them if you need to by including the DefaultValue attribute on the column definition in the storage model. You'll learn more about how to do that later in this chapter.

Notice in this figure that the VendorID column in the Invoices table isn't mapped to a property in the Invoice entity. That's because the Invoice entity doesn't include a VendorID property. Instead, it contains a navigation property that provides access to the vendor for an invoice.

One useful feature of the Mapping Details windows is that it lets you map an entity to selected rows in a table or view. To do that, you specify one or more conditions for the rows you want to include. For example, suppose the Vendors table could contain both U.S. and foreign vendors. In addition, suppose it contained a Boolean column that indicated whether a vendor was foreign. Then, if you wanted to work with just foreign vendors, you could specify a condition as described in this figure so that only the rows for foreign vendors were retrieved.

Note that if you include a condition in the mappings for a table, you must delete the entity property that corresponds with the column that's used in the mapping. If you don't, you'll get an error when you build the project.

Another useful feature of the Mapping Details window is that it lets you map a single entity to two or more tables. For example, suppose the Vendors table has a one-to-one relationship with a table named VendorsSummary that contains summary information for each vendor. Then, you could create an Entity Data Model with a single entity that maps to both of these tables. You'll get a chance to see how this works when you do exercise 17-2 at the end of this chapter. This is just one way that you can provide a layer of abstraction between the conceptual model used by an application and the storage model used by a database.

A Mapping Details window that displays the mappings for the Invoice entity

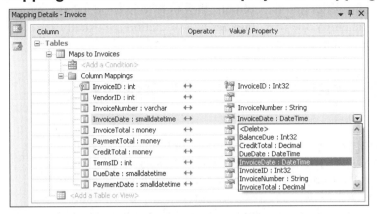

A Mappings Details window that displays the mappings for the association between the Vendor and Invoice entities

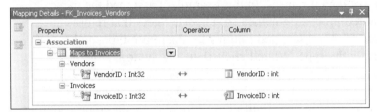

Description

- To display the mappings for an entity or association, click on it in the Model Browser window or on the design surface to display the mappings in the *Mapping Details window*.

- The mappings for an entity show the columns in the underlying table or view and the properties in the entity that they map to. If a column isn't mapped to a property, it typically means that the column is a foreign key.

- To change the mapping for a column, use the drop-down list for the property. To delete a mapping, select <Delete> from the drop-down list.

- You can map an entity to selected rows in a table or view by entering one or more conditions. To do that, select <Add a Condition>, select the column you want the condition based on, select an operator (= or Is), and enter or select a value. You must also delete the entity property that the condition is based on.

- To delete a condition, select <Delete> from the drop-down list for the column.

- If you want to map an entity to more than one table or view, you can do that by clicking <Add a Table or View> and then selecting a table or view from the drop-down list that's displayed.

- The mappings for an association show the table in the underlying database that the association is mapped to, the tables at both ends of the association, and the key properties for each table and the columns in the tables that they map to.

- Although you can change the table and column mappings for an association, you usually won't need to do that.

Figure 17-8   How to use the Mapping Details window

The mappings for an association show the properties that define the relationship between the entities and the columns they map to in the database. Like the mappings for an entity, the mappings for an association are usually set the way you want them by default.

How to add a stored procedure that retrieves data

If you want to use stored procedures with the Entity Framework, you can select those procedures when you use the Entity Data Model Wizard. When Visual Studio generates the Entity Data Model, it includes the stored procedures in the storage model but not in the conceptual model. If a stored procedure retrieves data, you can add it to the conceptual model as shown in figure 17-9.

To add a stored procedure to the conceptual model, you create a *function import*. To do that, you enter the name you want to use for the function import, and you select the type of data it returns. In this example, I assigned the name VendorInvoices to a stored procedure named spVendorInvoices that returns all the invoices for a vendor. Then, I selected Entities for the return type, and I selected Invoice for the entity type. When I clicked the OK button, a method named VendorInvoices was added to the PayablesEntities class of the Entity Data Model. I was then able to use this method to call the stored procedure.

Although a method is added to the Entity Data Model for a stored procedure that returns an entity type, a method isn't added for a stored procedure that returns a scalar value or no value. Because of that, you have to add a method yourself if you want to use the import function. You'll see how to do that later in this chapter.

The dialog box for adding a function import

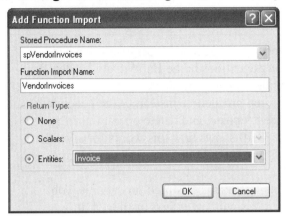

Description

- If you select stored procedures when you use the Entity Data Model Wizard to create an Entity Data Model, you must import those stored procedures before you can use them in your application.

- A stored procedure that's imported into an Entity Data Model is called a *function import*. To create a function import, you use the Add Function Import dialog box.

- To display the Add Function Import dialog box, right-click on the stored procedure in the storage model node of the Model Browser and select Create Function Import.

- By default, the function import name is the same as the name of the stored procedure. You can change this name if you want to.

- If the stored procedure returns a scalar value, select the Scalars option and then select a data type from the drop-down list. If the stored procedure returns an entity type, select the Entities option and then select the entity from the drop-down list.

- When you create a function import that returns an entity type, it's defined by a Function procedure within the Entity Data Model. Then, you can use that procedure to call the stored procedure.

- Visual Basic code isn't generated automatically for a function import that returns a scalar value or no value. Because of that, you have to write your own code if you want to use this type of function import.

Figure 17-9   How to add a stored procedure that retrieves data

How to add stored procedures that insert, update, and delete data

When you use the Entity Framework, it can generate SQL Insert, Update, and Delete statements for you based on the entities in the Entity Data Model. If the database you're working with provides stored procedures for these functions, though, you can use these stored procedures instead of the generated statements. To do that, you map the insert, update, and delete operations of an entity to the stored procedures. Figure 17-10 shows how this works for a Vendor Maintenance application that uses an Entity Data Model that includes Vendor, State, and GLAccount entities.

To map the insert, update and delete operations to stored procedures, you use the Mapping Details window. When this window is first displayed, it includes an item for each of these operations. At the bottom of the window shown here, for example, you can see that the item for the delete operation has been selected. Then, you can select the stored procedure you want to use from the drop-down list. When you do, the parameters of the stored procedure are automatically mapped to properties of the entity that have the same name. If any parameters don't have properties with matching names, you can click in the Property column for each parameter and then select the property you want to map it to.

If a stored procedure that performs an update or delete operation provides parameters for optimistic concurrency, you'll need to map them to the appropriate properties as well. You can see how this works for the update operation shown in this figure. Here, the parameters that are used for optimistic concurrency have names that are the same as the properties in the entity, preceded by "original_". Then, these parameters are mapped to the appropriate properties, and the Use Original Value option for each of these parameters is checked. That way, when this operation is performed, the current values of the properties will be assigned to the parameters with the same names as the properties, and the original values of the properties will be assigned to the parameters whose names start with "original_".

You should also notice here how the State, DefaultAccountNo, original_State, and original_DefaultAccountNo are mapped. Because the Entity Data Model includes State and GLAccount entities as well as a Vendor entity, the State and DefaultAccountNo columns that are included in the Vendors table aren't included in the Vendor entity. So the parameters that refer to these columns must be mapped to properties of the State and GLAccount entities, which are accessed through navigation properties of the Vendor entity.

You can also provide for stored procedures that return values generated by the database. For example, the stored procedure that inserts a vendor returns the value of the VendorID column for the new row. To update the vendor object with this value, you can create a column binding as described in this figure.

The Mapping Details window for mapping stored procedures

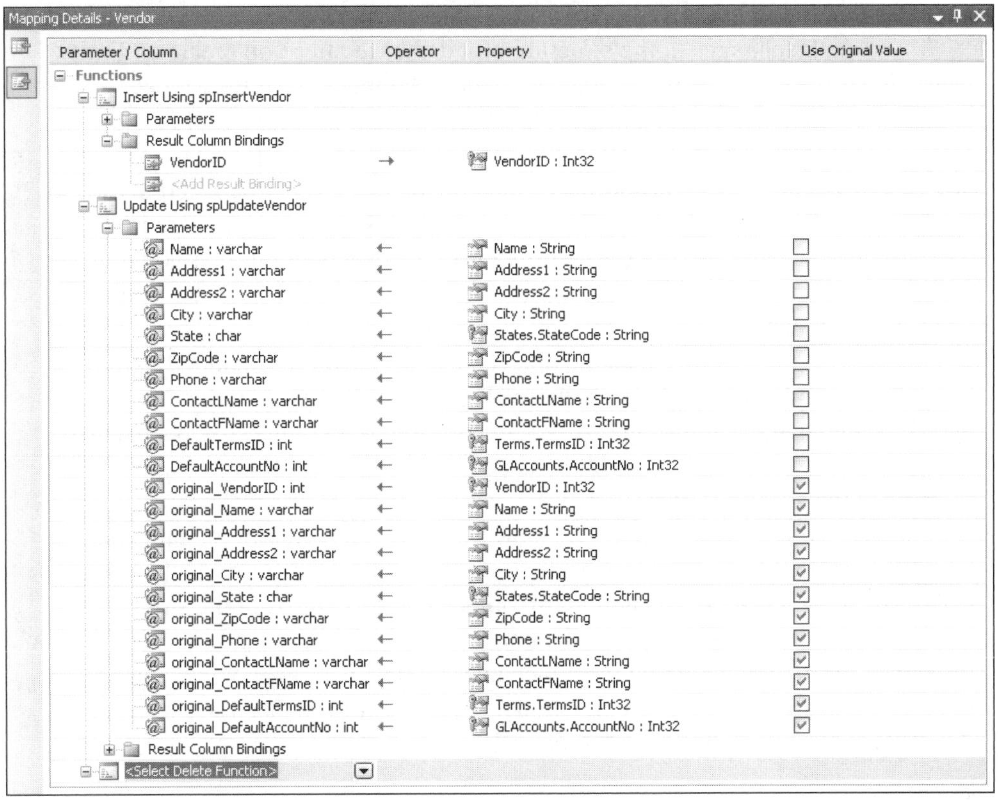

How to map an insert, update, or delete operation to a stored procedure

1. Right-click the entity and select Stored Procedure Mappings to display the Map to Entity Functions pane of the Mapping Details window.

2. Click <Select Insert Function>, <Select Update Function>, or <Select Delete Function>, and select the stored procedure you want to use from the drop-down list that's displayed. When you do, the parameters required by the stored procedure are mapped to entity properties with the same name.

3. Review the mappings and make any necessary changes or additions. If a stored procedure uses parameters for optimistic concurrency, select the Use Original Value check box.

4. If a stored procedure returns a value such as an identity value for an insert operation, click <Add Result Binding>. Then, enter the name of the column in the result set and map it to an entity property.

Description

- By default, the Entity Framework generates SQL statements for insert, update, and delete operations. If you need to, you can override this behavior with stored procedures that you include in the Entity Data Model.

- If you use stored procedures, you must use them for all three operations (insert, update, and delete).

Figure 17-10   How to add stored procedures that insert, update, and delete data

How to update an Entity Data Model

If you make changes to the structure of a database after you create an Entity Data Model from that database, you can update the model to reflect those changes. To do that, you use the Update Wizard shown in figure 17-11.

As you can see, the Update Wizard consists of three tabs. If you've added any tables, views, or stored procedures to the database, they'll be listed in the Add tab. In addition, any tables, views, and stored procedures that were in the database when you originally created the Entity Data Model but that you didn't include in the model are listed in this tab. Then, you can select the items you want to add to the model.

The Refresh tab simply lists the objects that are currently included in the Entity Data Model. Then, if any of these objects have changed in the database, they'll be updated in the storage model. In addition, if a column has been added to a table or view, that column will be added to the conceptual model and mapped to the storage model.

Finally, the Delete table lists any tables, views, and stored procedures that have been deleted from the database that are included in the Entity Data Model. Then, when the model is updated, these objects are deleted from the storage model along with the mappings to the conceptual model. Note, however, that the objects aren't deleted from the conceptual model. That way, you can map them to other objects in the storage model if you want to. Otherwise, you can delete them from the object model manually.

The Add tab of the Update Wizard dialog box

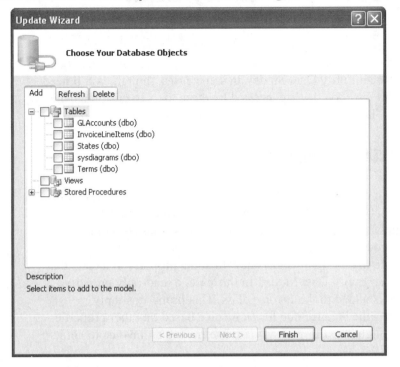

Description

- The Update Wizard lets you update an Entity Data Model based on changes made to the database. To display this wizard, right-click the edmx file in the Model Browser window and select Update Model from Database.

- The Add tab of the Update Wizard dialog box lets you select the tables, views, and stored procedures you want to add to the Entity Data Model. That can include tables, views, and stored procedures that have been added to the database or tables, views, and stored procedures that weren't originally included in the Entity Data Model.

- The Refresh tab lists the tables, views, and stored procedures from the database that are currently included in the Entity Data Model. If any changes have been made to these objects in the database, those changes will be reflected in the storage model. The conceptual model and mappings are affected only if a column is added to a table or view.

- The Delete tab lists the tables, views, and stored procedures that are currently included in the Entity Data Model and that have been deleted from the database. These objects will be deleted from the storage model along with any mappings to the conceptual model. These objects will not be deleted from the conceptual model, however.

Figure 17-11   How to update an Entity Data Model

How to customize an Entity Data Model

So far in this chapter, you've seen how to use the designer and wizards to create and work with an Entity Data Model. In some cases, though, you'll need to work directly with the code that's generated by these tools to customize the Entity Data Model. The topics that follow show you two ways you can do that.

How to use partial classes

One way to customize an Entity Data Model is to add your own Visual Basic code. To do that, you create partial classes as shown in figure 17-12. Then, when the application is compiled, the code in these classes will be combined with the code that's generated by Visual Studio.

The first example in this figure shows how to add a property to a class that defines an entity in an Entity Data Model. In this case, a read-only property named BalanceDue is added to the Invoice class. This property simply calculates and returns the balance due for an invoice based on other properties of the invoice. You might use this property after retrieving an invoice to get its balance.

The second example in this figure shows how to add a procedure to the container class for the Entity Data Model. This code executes a function import named VendorBalance that returns the balance due for the vendor with the specified ID. Because the stored procedure that's associated with this function import returns a scalar value, no Visual Basic code is generated for it.

If you review the code for this procedure, you'll see that it's similar to the code you saw in chapters 6 and 7. You should notice four differences, however. First, this code uses the CreateCommand method of the connection that's defined by the Entity Data Model to create the command object. This method returns a generic DbCommand object that can be used with any database. You could also convert the object to an EntityCommand object to make it clear that it's being used with an Entity Data Model, but that's not necessary.

Second, the CommandText property of the command includes the name of the class that defines the Entity Data model, in this case, PayablesEntities, and the name of the function import, in this case, VendorBalance. Third, the parameter that will hold the value of the vendor ID is created from the EntityParameter class. That's necessary because the DbParameter class is declared as MustInherit, which means it can't be used directly. Since the EntityParameter class inherits the DbParameter class, the EntityParameter class can be used to define a parameter for a DbCommand object. And Fourth, before opening the connection, the state of the connection is checked to be sure it isn't already open.

Code that adds a property to the Invoice class

```
Partial Public Class Invoice

    Public ReadOnly Property BalanceDue() As Decimal
        Get
            Return Me.InvoiceTotal - Me.PaymentTotal - Me.CreditTotal
        End Get
    End Property

End Class
```

Code that provides for calling a function import that returns a scalar value

```
Imports System.Data.Common
Imports System.Data.EntityClient

Partial Public Class PayablesEntities

    Public Function VendorBalance(ByVal vendorID As Integer) As Decimal
        Dim command As DbCommand = Me.Connection.CreateCommand
        command.CommandType = CommandType.StoredProcedure
        command.CommandText = "PayablesEntities.VendorBalance"
        Dim vendorIDParm As New EntityParameter
        vendorIDParm.ParameterName = "VendorID"
        vendorIDParm.Value = vendorID
        command.Parameters.Add(vendorIDParm)

        If command.Connection.State = ConnectionState.Closed Then
            command.Connection.Open()
        End If
        Dim balanceDue = CDec(command.ExecuteScalar)
        command.Connection.Close()

        Return balanceDue
    End Function

End Class
```

Description

- The classes that are generated for an Entity Data Model are implemented as partial classes. Because of that, you can extend these classes by adding custom properties and methods in separate files. That way, these custom members aren't overwritten if the Entity Data Model is regenerated.

- If you add a partial class for an entity, you can add properties and methods that perform calculations. You can also extend the On*Property*Changing and On*Property*Changed partial methods that are defined for each property in an entity class. For more information, see the Visual Studio documentation.

- If you include a function import that returns a scalar value or no value in an Entity Data Model, Visual Studio doesn't generate code to execute that function. Because of that, you have to add this code in a partial class for the object context.

Figure 17-12   How to use partial classes

How to modify the XML

When you create an Entity Data Model using the wizard and the Entity Designer, Visual Studio generates a file that contains the XML that defines the model. Then, if necessary, you can modify the XML for the model.

To modify the XML, you can display the XML in the *XML Editor* as shown in figure 17-13. If you do, you'll see that the code is divided into three main sections: the *SSDL* code that defines the storage model, the *CSDL* code that defines the conceptual model, and the *MSL* code that defines the mappings.

In this figure, you can see some of the SSDL code for the Entity Data Model that was presented back in figure 17-6. In particular, at the bottom of this figure, you can see the definitions for some of the columns in the Invoices table. As I mentioned earlier in this chapter, it's here that you could specify a default value for a column if necessary.

Before you modify any of this code, of course, you should have a thorough understanding of what it does. You can get much of the knowledge you need by reading the Visual Studio documentation. You should also realize that if you make modifications that aren't supported by the designer, the designer will no longer be able to display the Entity Data Model. In that case, you'll be able to work with the model only by changing the XML directly.

Some of the XML for an Entity Data Model

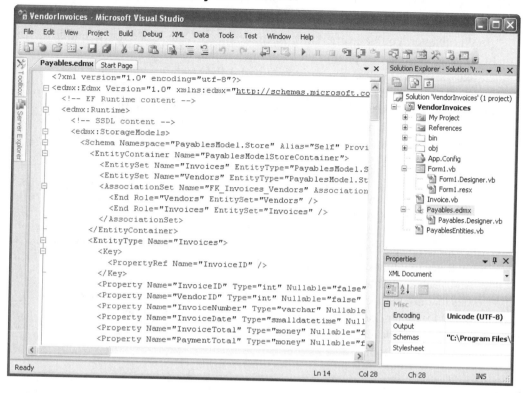

Description

- When you create an Entity Data Model using the wizard and the Entity Designer, Visual Studio generates a file that contains the XML that defines the model.

- To display the XML for an Entity Data Model, right-click on the edmx file in the Solution Explorer, select Open With, and select XML Editor from the dialog box that's displayed.

- The edmx file contains the XML that defines the storage model, which is written in the *Storage Schema Definition language* (*SSDL*); the conceptual model, which is written in the *Conceptual Schema Definition Language* (*CSDL*); and the mapping between the two, which is written in the *Mapping Specification Language* (*MSL*).

- If you need to make a change to an Entity Data Model that isn't supported by the Entity Designer, you can make changes directly to the edmx file. After you do that, the Entity Designer may no longer be able to display the Entity Data Model.

Figure 17-13   How to modify the XML for an Entity Data Model

Perspective

In this chapter, you've learned how to create Entity Data Models with entities that have a one-to-one mapping to the tables in a database. These models work much like the object models you can create with LINQ to SQL, and they have many of the same benefits. In particular, when you create an Entity Data Model, it includes all the properties and methods you need for working with the entities it defines. In addition, when you use the Entity Framework to work with an Entity Data Model as shown in the next three chapters, the Entity Framework generates all the required code. That means that you have to write a minimum of code, which makes applications that use the Entity Framework quick and easy to develop.

The real power of the Entity Framework, though, is its flexibility. For example, you learned in this chapter that you can map a single entity to two or more tables in a database that have a one-to-one relationship. You can also map a single entity to two or more tables that have the same structure. You can use inheritance to map all of the types in a hierarchy to a single table or to map each type to a different table. And you can define an entity with a complex type that contains scalar properties that are mapped to columns in the database. Unfortunately, the Entity Data Model Designer doesn't currently support all of these features. Because of that, you have to work directly with the XML for an Entity Data Model to implement some of them.

Terms

Entity Framework
Entity Data Model
conceptual model
storage model
entity
mappings
Object Services
entity class
Entity Data Model Designer
Entity Designer
scalar property
association

navigation property
object context
Model Browser window
Mapping Details window
function import
XML Editor
Storage Schema Definition Language
(SSDL)
Conceptual Schema Definition Language
(CSDL)
Mapping Specification Language (MSL)

Exercise 17-1   Create an Entity Data Model

In this exercise, you'll create an Entity Data Model that consists of four entities. Then, you'll experiment with this model to see what you can do.

Create the Entity Data Model

1. Start a new project named InvoiceLineItems in your chapter 17 directory.

2. Use the Entity Data Model Wizard as described in figures 17-2 and 17-3 to create an Entity Data Model that includes the Invoices, InvoiceLineItems, GLAccounts, and Terms tables from the Payables database.

3. Review the entities in the Entity Data Model Designer. In particular, notice the navigation properties that are defined for each table and the associations between the tables.

4. Select the Invoices entity and then use the Properties window to change its Name property to Invoice and its Entity Set Name property to Invoices. Make similar changes to the InvoiceLineItems and GLAccounts entities, but don't change the name of the Terms entity.

5. Change the names of the GLAccounts and Invoices navigation properties of the InvoiceLineItem entity so they're singular since they define many-to-one relationships.

Use the Mapping Details window

6. Display the Mapping Details window. Then, select the Invoice entity in the Entity Data Model, and review its mappings. Notice that the TermsID column isn't mapped to a property because the Invoice entity doesn't include a TermsID property.

7. Click on <Add a Condition> and then on the drop-down arrow that's displayed. Select the PaymentDate column, select Is for the operator, and select Null for the condition to restrict the invoices that are retrieved to only those for which payments haven't been received.

8. Build the project and notice the error that's displayed. Then, delete the PaymentDate column from the Invoice entity and build the project again to see that the error is no longer displayed.

9. Click on the Terms navigation property and review its mappings.

Use the Model Browser window

10. Display the Model Browser window by clicking on its tab. Expand the Entity Types folder in the node for the conceptual model. Then, click on any entity to see that its mappings are displayed in the Mapping Details window.

11. Expand the Associations folder and click on any association to see that its mappings are displayed in the Mapping Details window.

12. Use the Update Wizard as described in figure 17-11 to add the spGetInvoicesDue stored procedure to the Entity Data Model.

13. Expand the Stored Procedures folder in the node for the storage model so you can see the stored procedure you just added. Then, create a function import for the stored procedure as described in figure 17-9. Set the return type of the function import to the Invoice entity.

14. Open the EntityContainer node and then the Function Import folder in the node for the conceptual model to see that the stored procedure is now included in this model.

15. Close the Entity Data Model Designer and save the changes.

Review the XML for the Entity Data Model

16. Display the XML for the Entity Data Model as described in figure 17-13.

17. Review this code to see that it contains definitions for the storage model, the conceptual model, and the mappings between the two. When you're done, close the file and then close the solution.

Exercise 17-2   Create an entity that maps to two tables

In this exercise, you'll create an Entity Data Model with a single entity that maps to two tables in the database.

1. Start a new project named VendorsSummary in your chapter 17 directory.

2. Create an Entity Data Model that includes the Vendors and VendorsSummary tables from the Payables database.

3. Change the name of the Vendors entity to Vendor and the name of its entity set to Vendors.

4. Add a scalar property to the Vendor entity for each of the scalar properties in the VendorsSummary entity except for VendorID. Use the Properties window to define each property so it's identical to the property in the VendorsSummary entity.

5. Use the MappingDetails window to add the VendorsSummary table to the mappings for the Vendor entity. If you added the scalar properties to the Vendor entity correctly, they should be mapped to the corresponding columns in the VendorsSummary table.

6. Delete the VendorsSummary entity. Then, build the solution to be sure that no errors are displayed.

7. At this point, you have created an entity that maps to both the Vendors and the VendorsSummary tables. If this works correctly, close the solution.

18

How to use LINQ to Entities

Now that you know how to create an Entity Data Model, you're ready to learn how to use it to work with the data in a database. In this chapter, you'll learn how to use LINQ to Entities to retrieve data using an Entity Data Model. In addition, you'll learn how to insert, update, and delete data, and you'll learn how to work with bound controls.

How to retrieve data

LINQ to Entities lets you retrieve data using a syntax that's similar to the other implementations of LINQ that you learned about in section 4 of this book. When you use LINQ to Entities, however, you work with the classes, properties, and methods defined by the Entity Data Model. You'll see how to do that in the topics that follow.

How to retrieve data from a single table

To help you understand the basics of using LINQ to Entities, figure 18-1 shows you how to use it to retrieve data from a single table. To start, you create an instance of the object context for the Entity Data Model as shown in the first statement in this figure. This statement creates an instance of the PayablesEntities context and stores it in a variable named payables. Then, you can use the properties of this object to refer to the entity collections in the Entity Data Model that are mapped to tables in the database. The query expression in this figure illustrates how this works.

The first thing you should notice here is that the From clause specifies the Invoices property of the object context as the data source for the query. This property returns a collection of Invoice objects in an ObjectQuery(Of Invoice) object. You'll learn more about how the ObjectQuery(Of T) class works in the next chapter. For now, you just need to realize that since the Invoice entity in the Entity Data Model is mapped to the Invoices table in the Payables database, the query expression in this figure retrieves data from that table.

Once you specify the source of data for a query on the From clause, you can refer to the properties of the entities in the data source on the other clauses. To do that, you use the range variable that's specified on the From clause. In this query expression, for example, the Let clause refers to the InvoiceTotal, PaymentTotal, and CreditTotal properties, the Where clause refers to the DueDate property, and the Select clause refers to the InvoiceNumber and DueDate properties.

You should also notice that the date that's compared to the due date on the second condition in the Where clause is coded as a variable rather than as a Visual Basic expression that adds 15 days to the current date. As you can see, this variable is set to the appropriate date in the statement that precedes the query expression. This is necessary because Object Services doesn't recognize the Visual Basic expression.

A LINQ query that retrieves data from the Invoices table

A statement that creates an instance of the object context

```
Dim payables As New PayablesEntities
```

A query expression that gets invoice balances due

```
Dim payDate As DateTime = DateTime.Today.AddDays(15)

Dim invoicesDue = _
    From invoice In payables.Invoices _
    Let BalanceDue = invoice.InvoiceTotal - invoice.PaymentTotal _
                   - invoice.CreditTotal _
    Where BalanceDue > 0 _
      And invoice.DueDate < payDate _
    Order By invoice.DueDate, BalanceDue Descending _
    Select Number = invoice.InvoiceNumber, invoice.DueDate, BalanceDue
```

Code that executes the query

```
Dim invoiceDisplay As String = "Invoice No." & vbTab & "Due Date" & vbTab _
                               & vbTab & "Balance Due" & vbCrLf
For Each invoice In invoicesDue
    invoiceDisplay &= invoice.Number & vbTab _
                   & IIf(invoice.Number.Length < 8, vbTab, "").ToString _
                   & invoice.dueDate & vbTab _
                   & FormatCurrency(invoice.BalanceDue) & vbCrLf
Next
MessageBox.Show(invoiceDisplay, "Sorted Invoices Due")
```

The resulting dialog box

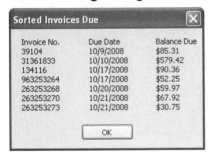

Description

- Before you can work with the entities in an Entity Data Model, you have to create an instance of the object context for the model.

- The data source for a LINQ to Entities query that retrieves data from a single table is a collection of entity objects. To refer to a collection, you use a property of the object context that represents an entity set. This property returns an ObjectQuery(Of T) object.

- To refer to a member of an entity object, you use the property that defines the member. In a LINQ to Entities query, you refer to that property through the range variable.

- A LINQ to Entities query always returns an ObjectQuery(Of T) object, where T can be a primitive type, an entity type, or an anonymous type. The ObjectQuery(Of T) class implements both the IEnumerable(Of T) and IQueryable(Of T) interfaces.

Figure 18-1   How to retrieve data from a single table

How to query across relationships

As you saw in the last chapter, if an entity is related to another entity in the Entity Data Model, it contains a navigation property that provides access to the related entity objects. You can use these properties to query across relationships as shown in figure 18-2.

The first query expression in this figure shows how to get data from an object on the one side of a relationship from an object on the many side of the relationship. In this example, a Vendor object is accessed through the Vendor property of an Invoice object. Then, the Name property of the Vendor object is used in the Order By and Select clauses.

The second query expression produces the same results, but it gets data from Invoice objects through the navigation property in the Vendor object. To do that, it includes the navigation property as a data source on the From clause. Then, it refers to properties of the Invoice objects in the Let, Where, Order By, and Select clauses.

Note that you don't have to include the navigation property on the From clause as shown in this example. If you don't, however, you'll have to include the navigation property on each reference to an invoice property. For example, the Let clause in this query expression would look like this:

```
Let BalanceDue = vendor.Invoices.InvoiceTotal _
              - vendor.Invoices.PaymentTotal _
              - vendor.Invoices.CreditTotal
```

Since including the navigation property on the From clause simplifies the query expression, we recommend you do that whenever it makes sense.

A query expression that gets vendor data through the Invoice objects

```
Dim invoicesDue = _
    From invoice In payables.Invoices _
    Let BalanceDue = invoice.InvoiceTotal - invoice.PaymentTotal _
                   - invoice.CreditTotal _
    Where BalanceDue > 0 _
      And invoice.DueDate < payDate _
    Order By invoice.Vendor.Name, BalanceDue Descending _
    Select invoice.Vendor.Name, _
           Number = invoice.InvoiceNumber, BalanceDue
```

A query expression that gets invoice data through the Vendor objects

```
Dim invoicesDue = _
    From vendor In payables.Vendors, _
        invoice In vendor.Invoices _
    Let BalanceDue = invoice.InvoiceTotal - invoice.PaymentTotal _
                   - invoice.CreditTotal _
    Where BalanceDue > 0 _
      And invoice.DueDate < payDate _
    Order By invoice.Vendor.Name, BalanceDue Descending _
    Select vendor.Name, Number = invoice.InvoiceNumber, BalanceDue
```

Code that executes the queries

```
Dim invoiceDisplay As String = "Vendor Name" & vbTab & vbTab & vbTab _
    & "Invoice No." & vbTab & "Balance Due" & vbCrLf
For Each invoice In invoicesDue
    invoiceDisplay &= invoice.Name & vbTab & vbTab _
                    & IIf(invoice.Name.Length < 10, vbTab, "").ToString _
                    & IIf(invoice.Name.Length < 20, vbTab, "").ToString _
                    & invoice.Number & vbTab _
                    & IIf(invoice.Number.Length < 8, vbTab, "").ToString _
                    & FormatCurrency(invoice.BalanceDue) & vbCrLf
Next
MessageBox.Show(invoiceDisplay, "Vendor Invoice Relationship")
```

The resulting dialog box

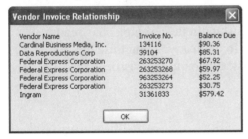

Description

- Instead of using joins in LINQ to Entities queries, you typically use the navigation properties defined by the Entity Data Model that identify the relationships between the entities.

- You can simplify the reference to objects on the many side of a relationship by including the navigation property in the From clause as shown in the second example above.

Figure 18-2   How to query across relationships

How to load related objects

In addition to using relationships to refer to properties of a related object, you can use them to load related objects. For example, suppose an application lets the user retrieve the data for a selected vendor and then displays the vendor data along with the invoices for that vendor. To do that, the application must load the invoice data as well as the vendor data. Figure 18-3 shows three ways you can do that.

The first example in this figure includes the invoices for a vendor in the query results. To do that, it includes the Invoices navigation property on the Select clause. Notice here that the First method is used to execute the query. That makes sense because the query returns the data for a single vendor, and the Single method isn't supported by LINQ to Entities.

The second example shows how to use the Include method to load related objects. As you can see, you code this method on the data source for the query, and you code a *query path* as an argument. In most cases, the query path is the name of the navigation property that identifies the related objects to be loaded. Note that when you use this technique, the related objects aren't included in the query results. Instead, they're simply loaded into the object context so you can access them later.

You can also load related objects explicitly using the Load method. The technique you use to do that depends on whether you want to load the objects on the one side of a relationship or the many side of a relationship. The third example in this figure shows how to load the objects on the many side of a relationship. Here, after the query that retrieves the Vendor object is executed, the IsLoaded property of the Invoices navigation property for that object checks that the invoices for that vendor aren't already loaded. That ensures that any existing data isn't overwritten, and it improves the efficiency of the application. If the invoices haven't been loaded, the Load method of the Invoices navigation property is used to load them.

The fourth example in this figure shows how to use the Load method to load the related object on the one side of a relationship. In this example, the Vendor object for an Invoice object is being loaded. To do that, you don't use the navigation property of the Invoice object. Instead, you use the association property, in this case, VendorReference.

A query expression that uses a navigation property to load related objects

```
Dim vendorInvoices = (From vendor In payables.Vendors _
                      Where vendor.VendorID = CInt(txtVendorID.Text) _
                      Select vendor.Name, vendor.Invoices).First
```

A query expression that uses the Include method to load related objects

```
Dim selectedVendor = (From vendor In payables.Vendors.Include("Invoices") _
                      Where vendor.VendorID = CInt(txtVendorID.Text) _
                      Select vendor).First
```

Code that explicitly loads the objects on the many side of a relationship

```
Dim selectedVendor = (From vendor In payables.Vendors _
                      Where vendor.VendorID = CInt(txtVendorID.Text) _
                      Select vendor).First

If Not selectedVendor.Invoices.IsLoaded Then
    selectedVendor.Invoices.Load()
End If
```

Code that explicitly loads the object on the one side of a relationship

```
Dim invoiceID As Integer = CInt(cboInvoices.SelectedValue)
Dim selectedInvoice _
    = (From invoice In payables.Invoices _
       Where invoice.InvoiceID = invoiceID _
       Select invoice).First

If Not selectedInvoice.VendorReference.IsLoaded Then
    selectedInvoice.VendorReference.Load()
End If
```

Description

- By default, only the entity objects that are specifically requested in a query are loaded into the object context. Related entity objects aren't automatically loaded.
- To load related objects, you can include the navigation property for the relationship in the query results, you can use the Include method with a *query path* that specifies the related objects to include in the query results, or you can use the Load method to load the related objects explicitly.
- To load the related objects on the many side of a relationship using the Load method, you use the navigation property for the object on the one side of the relationship. To load the related object on the one side of a relationship, you use the association property for the object on the many side of the relationship.
- Before you load related objects explicitly, you should use the IsLoaded property to check that the objects aren't already loaded. Otherwise, the current data will be overwritten, which may not be what you want.
- To use the Include or Load method, the query must return an entity type.

Figure 18-3   How to load related objects

How to use a stored procedure

When you import a stored procedure that returns an entity type into an Entity Data Model, it's defined by a method within the object context class as you saw in the last chapter. When you import a stored procedure that returns a scalar type or no type, you have to code the method yourself. You saw how to do that in the last chapter too. Now, figure 18-4 shows how to execute stored procedures using these methods.

The first example in this figure uses a stored procedure that returns a scalar value. Specifically, it returns the balance due for a vendor. The statement that executes the stored procedure does that by calling the method named VendorBalance that I added to the class that defines the object context. You can see the code for this method in figure 17-12 of the last chapter. Because this method and the stored procedure it calls accept a vendor ID, that vendor ID is passed as an argument to the method.

Before I go on, you should realize that you can't use a method that returns a scalar value within a query expression. For example, LINQ to Entities doesn't support a query like this that gets the balance due for all vendors:

```
Dim vendorBalances = _
    From vendor In payables.Vendors _
    Select vendor.Name, _
        BalanceDue = _
            payables.VendorBalance(vendor.VendorID)
```

So you can only call a method that returns a scalar value from outside a query expression.

The second example shows how to use a stored procedure that returns an entity type. In this case, the stored procedure returns the invoices for a vendor. Then, the query retrieves selected rows and columns from those invoices. To do that, it uses the method named VendorInvoices that was generated for the stored procedure when it was imported as the data source for the query. Like the method in the first example, this method accepts a vendor ID that's passed on to the stored procedure.

A stored procedure that gets the balance due for a vendor

Code that creates the stored procedure

```
CREATE PROCEDURE dbo.spVendorBalance
    (@VendorID int)
AS
    SELECT SUM(InvoiceTotal - PaymentTotal - CreditTotal)
    FROM Invoices
    WHERE VendorID = @VendorID
```

A statement that calls the method that executes the stored procedure

```
Dim balanceDue As Decimal = payables.VendorBalance(CInt(txtVendorID.Text))
```

A stored procedure that gets the invoices for a vendor

Code that creates the stored procedure

```
CREATE PROCEDURE dbo.spVendorInvoices
    (@VendorID int)
AS
    SELECT * FROM Invoices WHERE VendorID = @VendorID
```

A query that uses the method generated from the stored procedure

```
Dim vendorInvoices = _
    From invoice In payables.VendorInvoices(CInt(txtVendorID.Text)) _
    Let BalanceDue = invoice.InvoiceTotal _
                   - invoice.PaymentTotal _
                   - invoice.CreditTotal _
    Where BalanceDue > 0 _
    Order By invoice.DueDate, BalanceDue Descending _
    Select Number = invoice.InvoiceNumber, invoice.DueDate, BalanceDue
```

Description

- To execute a stored procedure that returns an entity type, you call the method that's generated when you import the stored procedure. Because this method is added to the class that defines the object context, you can call it from an instance of this class.

- Before you can execute a stored procedure that returns a scalar value, you must add your own method to the object context class as shown in figure 17-12 of the last chapter. Then, you can call the method to execute the stored procedure.

- A stored procedure that returns an entity type is typically used within a query. A stored procedure that returns a scalar type can't be used within a query because LINQ to Entities doesn't recognize it.

- If a stored procedure requires arguments, you pass those arguments to the method just as you would if you were calling any procedure.

Figure 18-4   How to use a stored procedure

How to insert, update, and delete data

In addition to retrieving data using the Entity Framework, you can use it to insert, update, and delete data. You'll learn how to do that in the topics that follow. As you read these topics, keep in mind that you can use these techniques regardless of how you retrieve the data. Since this chapter is about LINQ to Entities, the examples you'll see here will use LINQ to Entities to retrieve data. But you can also use these techniques when you retrieve data using Entity SQL as shown in the next chapter.

How to modify an existing row

To modify the data in an existing row of a database, you use the techniques shown in figure 18-5. To start, you must retrieve the row you want to modify. For example, the query at the top of this figure retrieves the vendor with the specified ID.

After you retrieve the row, you can modify the data in the entity object as shown in the second code example in this figure. This code simply assigns values from controls on a form to the appropriate properties of the Vendor object. Then, the statement that follows saves the changes to the database by calling the SaveChanges method of the object context.

If you need to, you can also change the parent object of a child object. To do that, you can use one of the techniques in the last two examples in this figure. In the next to last example, an invoice is retrieved and then the Vendor property of that invoice is set to the new Vendor object.

An invoice is also retrieved in the last example. Instead of changing the Vendor property, though, this code gets the current vendor for the invoice using the Vendor property. Then, it removes the invoice from the collection of invoices for the vendor using the Invoices property of the Vendor object. Finally, the invoice is added to the Invoices collection of another vendor.

Code that retrieves a vendor row from the Payables database

```
Dim selectedVendor = (From vendor In payables.Vendors _
                      Where vendor.VendorID = CInt(txtVendorID.Text) _
                      Select vendor).First
```

Code that modifies the data in the Vendor object

```
vendor.Name = txtName.Text
vendor.Address1 = txtAddress1.Text
vendor.Address2 = txtAddress2.Text
vendor.City = txtCity.Text
vendor.State = cboStates.SelectedValue.ToString
vendor.ZipCode = txtZipCode.Text
vendor.DefaultTermsID = CInt(cboTerms.SelectedValue)
vendor.DefaultAccountNo = CInt(cboAccounts.SelectedValue)
vendor.Phone = txtPhone.Text.Replace(".", "")
vendor.ContactFName = txtFirstName.Text
vendor.ContactLName = txtLastName.Text
```

A statement that saves the changes to the database

```
payables.SaveChanges()
```

Code that assigns an invoice to a different vendor

```
Dim invoiceID As Integer = CInt(cboInvoices.SelectedValue)
Dim selectedInvoice _
    = (From invoice In payables.Invoices _
       Where invoice.InvoiceID = invoiceID).First
selectedInvoice.Vendor = selectedVendor
```

Another way to assign an invoice to a different vendor

```
Dim selectedInvoice _
    = (From invoice In payables.Invoices _
       Where invoice.InvoiceID = invoiceID).First

If Not selectedInvoice.VendorReference.IsLoaded Then
    selectedInvoice.VendorReference.Load()
End If

Dim oldVendor As Vendor = selectedInvoice.Vendor
oldVendor.Invoices.Remove(selectedInvoice)
selectedVendor.Invoices.Add(selectedInvoice)
```

Description

- To modify a row in the database, you retrieve the row and store it in an object created from a class in the Entity Data Model. Then, you assign new values to the properties of the object. Finally, you execute the SaveChanges method of the object context.

- When you execute the SaveChanges method, the Entity Framework generates a SQL Update statement for each object that was modified and then passes those statements to the DBMS for processing.

- If you need to change the parent object that a child object is associated with, you can do that by using the child object's navigation property to change its parent object or by updating the collection of child objects for the old and new parent objects.

Figure 18-5   How to modify an existing row

How to delete an existing row

Figure 18-6 shows how to delete an existing row from a database. To start, you retrieve the row you want to delete just as you do when you modify a row. In this figure, the invoice with the specified ID is retrieved. In addition, the Load method is used to load the line items for the invoice. You'll learn why that's done in a minute.

After you retrieve the object you want to delete, you call the DeleteObject method of the object context and pass that object as an argument. In this figure, for example, the Invoice object that's retrieved by the query in the first example is deleted. Finally, you call the SaveChanges method of the object context.

In most cases, when you delete a row that has a one-to-many relationship with other rows in the database, you'll want to delete the related rows as well. One way to do that is to define the foreign key relationship between the two tables in the database so that it provides for cascading deletes. Then, the related rows will be deleted automatically, and you don't have to load them into the object context.

Even if the database doesn't provide for cascading deletes, you can still delete the related rows. To do that, you must load the related objects as shown in this figure. Then, when you call the SaveChanges method, these objects are deleted along with the parent object.

Code that retrieves an invoice row and its related line item rows from the Payables database

```
Dim invoiceID As Integer = CInt(cboInvoices.SelectedValue)
Dim selectedInvoice _
    = (From invoice In payables.Invoices _
        Where invoice.InvoiceID = invoiceID).First

selectedInvoice.InvoiceLineItems.Load()
```

A statement that marks the Invoice object for deletion

```
payables.DeleteObject(selectedInvoice)
```

A statement that deletes the invoice and line items from the database

```
payables.SaveChanges()
```

Description

- To delete a row from a database, you retrieve the row and store it in an object created from a class in the Entity Data Model. Then, you execute the DeleteObject method of the object context to mark the object for deletion. Finally, you execute the SaveChanges method of the object context.

- If you want to delete the child objects along with its parent object, you can do that by loading the child objects. Then, when the SaveChanges method is executed, the objects and the related rows in the database are deleted. This works even if the foreign key constraint in the database doesn't provide for cascading deletes.

- If a foreign key relationship in a database provides for cascading deletes, you don't need to load the child objects to delete the related rows in the database.

- When you execute the SubmitChanges method, the Entity Framework generates a SQL Delete statement for each object that was marked for deletion and then passes those statements to the DBMS for processing.

Figure 18-6   How to delete an existing row

How to add a new row

When you create an Entity Data Model, the code that's generated includes methods for each entity that let you create a new entity object and add an entity object to the collection of objects for that entity. Figure 18-7 shows how to use these methods. Note that you can also create an entity object from an entity class using standard techniques. You'll see an example of that in the Vendor Maintenance application that's presented later in this chapter.

To create a new instance of an entity class and assign values to its properties, you can use the Create*ObjectName* method of the entity class. The first example in this figure shows how to use the CreateInvoice method to create an Invoice object. On this method, you specify a value for each non-nullable column in the database. In this case, the PaymentDate column is nullable, so it's omitted from the list of arguments. If you want to set its value, you can do that after you create the invoice.

One drawback of using the Create*ObjectName* method is that you must specify a value for a column even if the value is generated by the database. For an invoice, that applies to the InvoiceID column, which is an identity column. You can specify any value you want for this column, as long as an invoice with that value doesn't already exist in the object context. You also have to specify a value for a column that has a default value, such as the PaymentTotal and CreditTotal columns. In this example, I specified 0 for both of these columns.

If an entity has a many-to-one relationship with other entities in the Entity Data Model, you also need to set the navigation properties of the new object that provide access to the related objects. For example, the two statements that follow the CreateInvoice method set the Vendor and Terms navigation properties of the Invoice object. That way, when the invoice is added to the database, the VendorID and TermsID columns for the invoice will be set to the VendorID and TermsID properties of the associated Vendor and Terms objects. Note that this code assumes that the Vendor and Terms objects have already been retrieved and stored in selectedVendor and selectedTerms variables.

After you create a new object, you need to add it to the collection of objects in the object context. To do that, you use the AddTo*EntitySetName* method of the object context as shown in the second example. On this method, you name the object you want to add. Here, the AddToInvoices method is used to add the Invoice object created in the first example to the Invoices collection.

The third example in this figure shows how to add objects on the many side of a one-to-many relationship. Here, line items are added for the invoice that was created in the first example and added to the collection of invoices in the second example. In this case, the line item data is stored in a DataGridView control. Then, a For statement is used to get each row in the grid, and the CreateInvoiceLineItem method is used to create an InvoiceLineItem object from the data in that row. Next, a query is used to get the GLAccount object for the line item, and the GLAccount navigation property of the InvoiceLineItem object is set to the GLAccount object. Finally, the Add method of the InvoiceLineItems

Code that creates a new Invoice object

```
Dim invoice As Invoice = Invoice.CreateInvoice( _
    1, txtInvoiceNumber.Text, CDate(txtInvoiceDate.Text), _
    invoiceTotal, 0, 0, CInt(cboTerms.SelectedValue), _
    CDate(txtDueDate.Text))
invoice.Vendor = selectedVendor
invoice.Terms = selectedTerms
```

A statement that adds the object to the Invoices collection

```
payables.AddToInvoices(invoice)
```

Code that creates InvoiceLineItem objects and adds them to the InvoiceLineItems collection

```
Dim row As DataGridViewRow
For i As Integer = 1 To dgvLineItems.Rows.Count
    row = dgvLineItems.Rows(i - 1)
    Dim lineItem As InvoiceLineItem _
        = InvoiceLineItem.CreateInvoiceLineItem( _
        1, CShort(i), CInt(row.Cells(0).Value), _
        CDec(row.Cells(2).Value), row.Cells(1).Value.ToString)
    Dim accountNo As Integer = CInt(row.Cells(0).Value)
    Dim selectedAccount _
        = (From account In payables.GLAccounts _
            Where account.AccountNo = accountNo).First
    lineItem.GLAccount = selectedAccount
    invoice.InvoiceLineItems.Add(lineItem)
Next
```

A statement that adds the invoice and line items to the database

```
payables.SaveChanges()
```

Description

- To add a row to the database, you can use the Create*ObjectName* method of an entity class to create a new instance of that class and assign values to its properties. Then, you can use the AddTo*EntitySetName* method to add the object to the collection of objects in the object context. Finally, you execute the SaveChanges method of the object context.

- If the value of a column is generated by the database, you can specify any value for that column on the Create*ObjectName* method as long as it's unique.

- The Create*ObjectName* methods only provide for setting properties that can't be null. You can set the values of nullable properties after you create the object.

- You can also create a new entity object by creating an instance of the entity class and then setting the values of its properties.

- To insert child objects that are related to a parent object, set the navigation property of the child object to the parent object, or use the navigation property of the parent object to add the child object to the collection of child objects for the parent object.

- When you execute the SaveChanges method, the Entity Framework generates a SQL Insert statement for each object that was added to an object collection and then passes those statements to the DBMS for processing.

Figure 18-7   How to add a new row

collection of the Invoice object is used to add the line item to the collection of line items in the object context. Then, when the SaveChanges method is called, the invoice and all of its related line items are added to the database.

How to provide for concurrency

By default, optimistic concurrency isn't used when you modify or delete a row from a database when you use the Entity Framework. However, Objects Services maintains the original values in the rows you retrieve from the database so you can use optimistic concurrency if you need to. Figure 18-8 shows you how to provide for concurrency.

To start, you need to identify the columns that you want to check for concurrency. To do that, you can use the Entity Designer to change the Concurrency Mode property for those columns from None to Fixed. Then, you code the SaveChanges method within the Try block of a Try...Catch statement, and you use the OptimisticConcurrencyException class to catch any concurrency exceptions that occur. Finally, you use the Refresh method of the object context to refresh the data if a concurrency exception occurs. On this method, you specify a refresh mode and the name of the object or object collection you want to refresh. The refresh mode indicates whether or not changes that have been made to the object or object collection are replaced with the current values in the database.

In some cases, you'll need to know whether a concurrency exception occurred due to the row being deleted or updated. To do that, you can check the EntityState property of the object after it's refreshed. If the row was deleted, the value of this property will be EntityState.Detached. This state indicates that the object has been removed from the object context. You'll see how the EntityState property is used in the Vendor Maintenance application that's presented later in this chapter.

If you use stored procedures to perform insert, update, and delete operations, you should realize that you don't have to set the Concurrency Mode property for the columns whose values you want to check. Instead, the stored procedures should include code that checks the column values. In addition, the stored procedures must return a value that indicates the number of rows that were affected by the operation. Then, if this value is zero, it indicates that a concurrency exception has occurred.

A Try...Catch statement that catches concurrency exceptions

```
Try
    payables.SaveChanges()
Catch ex As OptimisticConcurrencyException
    payables.Refresh(RefreshMode.StoreWins, selectedVendor)
        .
        .
End Try
```

Code that checks if a currency exception occurred due to the row being deleted

```
If selectedVendor.EntityState = EntityState.Detached Then ...
```

Members of the RefreshMode enumeration

Member	Description
ClientWins	Changes made to the objects in the object context are not replaced by the current values in the database.
StoreWins	Changes made to the objects in the object context are replaced by the current values in the database.

Description

- By default, Object Services saves changes made to objects in the object context to the database without checking for concurrency.

- If you want to check columns for concurrency, you can use the Entity Data Model Designer to set the Concurrency Mode property for those columns to Fixed. Then, the original values of the columns will be checked against the current database values to determine if the row has been changed or deleted.

- If you use stored procedures for insert, update, and delete operations, you don't have to set the Concurrency Mode property. Instead, you include parameters in the update and delete stored procedures that check the original values against the current values in the database. In addition, the stored procedures must return a count of the rows that were affected by the operation.

- If an update or delete operation isn't performed because of a concurrency conflict, an OptimisticConcurrencyException is thrown. To handle this exception, you code the SaveChanges method within the Try block of a Try...Catch statement, and you include a Catch block that catches the OptimisticConcurrencyException.

- If a concurrency exception occurs, you can use the Refresh method of the object context to refresh the object or collection of objects that were being updated. On this method, you specify a member of the RefreshMode enumeration.

- To check whether a concurrency exception occurred due to the row being updated or the row being deleted, you can check the EntityState property of the object after it's refreshed. If the row was deleted, the value of this property will be Detached.

- The Refresh method and the RefreshMode enumeration are members of the System.Data.Objects namespace.

Figure 18-8   How to provide for concurrency

How to work with bound controls

When you use the Entity Framework, you can bind controls to an entity collection, to the results of a query, and to an object data source that's created from an entity class. You'll learn about these binding techniques in the next two topics.

How to create an object data source

In chapter 9, you learned how to create an object data source from a business class that you develop. You can also create an object data source from an entity class in an Entity Data Model. Figure 18-9 shows you how to do that.

As you can see, you use the Data Source Configuration Wizard just as you do for any other data source. From the first step of this wizard, you select the Object option. Then, from the second step, you select the entity type you want to use as the source of data. In this figure, for example, I selected the Vendor entity. When I clicked the Finish button, the Vendor data source appeared in the Data Sources window.

After you create an object data source, you can use it to create bound controls as described in chapter 9. Then, you can work with the bound controls using techniques that are similar to the techniques presented in that chapter. Instead of using database classes to access the data in a database, however, you can use LINQ to Entities as shown in the next figure.

The first step of the Data Source Configuration Wizard

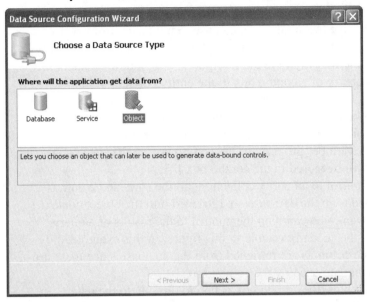

The second step of the Data Source Configuration Wizard

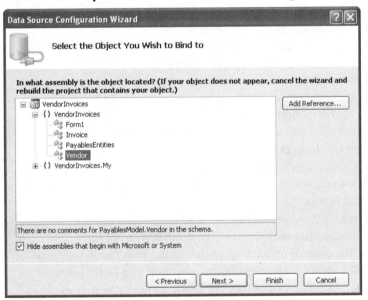

Description

- To create an object data source from an Entity Data Model, select the Object option from the first step of the Data Source Configuration Wizard. Then, select the entity type you want to use from the list that's displayed in the second step.

Figure 18-9   How to create an object data source

How to bind controls

Figure 18-10 shows five techniques you can use to bind a control when you use the Entity Framework. To start, you can complex-bind a control to an entity collection as shown in the first example in this figure. Here, the first statement sets the DataSource property of a combo box to the entity collection, in this case, the Vendors collection in the payables object context. Then, the second statement sets the DisplayMember property of the combo box so the Name property of the entity will be displayed in the combo box list. Finally, the third statement sets the ValueMember property of the combo box so the VendorID property of the entity will be stored in the combo box list.

When you bind a control to an entity collection, all the rows and columns that the entity is mapped to in the database are retrieved into the object context. If that's not what you want, you can bind the control to the results of a query instead as illustrated in the second example in this figure. In this example, only the VendorID and Name columns are retrieved from the database since these are the only two columns that are used by the combo box.

In the first two examples, the combo box is bound directly to the data source through its DataSource property. If a control is created from an object data source, however, you can also bind it to the data source by setting the DataSource property of the binding source for the control. If the DataSource property of a combo box is set to a binding source named VendorBindingSource, for example, you can bind the control as shown in the third example in this figure. This assumes that the DisplayMember and ValueMember properties were set at design time.

If you want to simple-bind controls such as text boxes, you can use the technique shown in the fourth example. The code in this example starts by getting a Vendor object whose values will be displayed in the bound controls. Then, the binding source for those controls is cleared so that no data is displayed in the controls. Finally, the Vendor object is added to the list of bound objects for the binding source, which causes the properties of the Vendor object to be displayed in the text boxes.

The last example in this figure shows how to bind a control to a collection of entity objects related to another entity object. To do that, you set the DataSource property of the control or binding source to the navigation property that provides access to the entity collection. In this example, the DataSource property of an Invoice binding source is set to the Invoices navigation property for a vendor. Note that before this property is set, the invoices for the vendor are loaded if necessary.

Code that binds a combo box to an entity collection

```
cboVendors.DataSource = payables.Vendors
cboVendors.DisplayMember = "Name"
cboVendors.ValueMember = "VendorID"
```

Code that binds the combo box to the results of a query

```
Dim vendors = From vendor In payables.Vendors _
              Order By vendor.Name _
              Select vendor.VendorID, vendor.Name

cboVendors.DataSource = vendors
cboVendors.DisplayMember = "Name"
cboVendors.ValueMember = "VendorID"
```

A statement that binds a combo box using its binding source

```
VendorBindingSource.DataSource = vendors
```

Code that binds text boxes to an entity object

```
Dim vendorID As Integer = CInt(NameComboBox.SelectedValue)
Dim selectedVendor = (From vendor In payables.Vendors _
                      Where vendor.VendorID = vendorID).First

VendorBindingSource.Clear()
VendorBindingSource.Add(selectedVendor)
```

Code that binds a DataGridView control to related objects

```
If Not selectedVendor.Invoices.IsLoaded Then
    selectedVendor.Invoices.Load()
End If

InvoiceBindingSource.DataSource = selectedVendor.Invoices
```

Description

- You can complex-bind a control such as a combo box or a DataGridView control to an entity collection or to the results of a query by setting the DataSource property of the control or the binding source associated with the control to the collection or results.

- You can simple-bind controls such as text boxes that are created from an object data source to the properties of an entity object by clearing the binding source for the controls and then adding the object to the list of bound objects for the binding source.

- If an object has a one-to-many relationship with another object, you can complex-bind a control to the objects on the many side by setting the DataSource property of the control or the binding source associated with the control to the navigation property of the object on the one side. Before you do that, you must load the related objects.

- You can use bound controls to display, add, modify, and delete data. Then, you can use the SaveChanges method of the object context to save the changes to the database.

Figure 18-10   How to bind controls

A Vendor Maintenance application

Now that you've seen how to use LINQ to Entities to retrieve data from a database and how to use the Entity Framework to insert, update, and delete data, you're ready to see a Vendor Maintenance application that uses these skills. As you'll see, this application works just like the Vendor Maintenance application you saw in chapter 14 that uses LINQ to SQL. And, like that application, it requires much less code than an application that uses standard Windows techniques like the ones you saw in section 3 of this book.

The user interface

Figure 18-11 presents the user interface for the Vendor Maintenance application, which consists of two forms. The Vendor Maintenance form lets you retrieve an existing vendor by vendor ID. Then, you can modify the data for that vendor by clicking the Modify button to display the Modify Vendor form. You can also delete an existing vendor by clicking the Delete button on the Vendor Maintenance form. And you can add a new vendor by clicking the Add button to display the Add Vendor form.

You should notice one difference between the Vendor Maintenance form shown here and the Vendor Maintenance forms you saw in chapters 7 and 14. That is, the form shown here displays the state name rather than the state code. That's possible because of the relationship that's defined between the Vendor and State entities in the Entity Data Model. You'll see this model in the next figure, and you'll see how the relationship between the Vendor and State entities is used in the code for the Vendor Maintenance form.

The Vendor Maintenance form

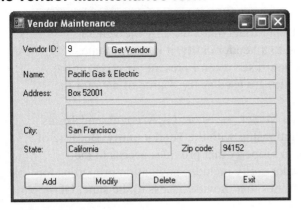

The Add/Modify Vendor form

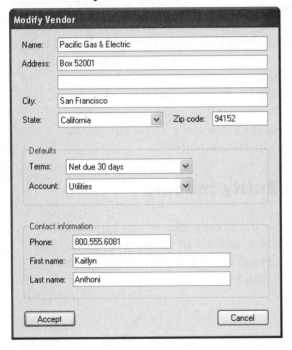

Description

- To add a new vendor, the user clicks the Add button on the Vendor Maintenance form to display a blank Add Vendor form. Then, the user enters the data for the new vendor and clicks the Accept button to return to the Vendor Maintenance form.

- To modify the data for an existing vendor, the user enters the vendor ID and clicks the Get Vendor button to display the basic information for that vendor. Then, the user clicks the Modify button to display the Modify Vendor form, makes the appropriate modifications, and clicks the Accept button to return to the Vendor Maintenance form.

- To delete an existing vendor, the user enters the vendor ID, clicks the Get Vendor button, and then clicks the Delete button.

Figure 18-11   The user interface for the Vendor Maintenance application

The Entity Data Model

Figure 18-12 shows the Entity Data Model that's used by the Vendor Maintenance application. In addition to a Vendor entity, it includes State, GLAccount, and Terms entities. As you'll see when I present the code for the Add/Modify Vendor form, these entities are used as the source of data for the three combo boxes on the form.

As you can see in the Entity Data Model, the State, GLAccount, and Terms entities each have a one-to-many relationship with the Vendor entity. Because of that, each entity includes a navigation property that provides access to the related vendors. In addition, the Vendor entity includes navigation properties for the State, GLAccount, and Terms entities that provide access to the state, GL account, and terms for the vendor.

Note that after the Entity Data Model was generated, I changed the names of all the entities except for Terms from plural to singular. (I didn't change the name of the Terms entity because the word "terms" is often used to refer to a single item.) That caused the entity set names for these entities to be changed to values like VendorSet and StateSet. So I changed these names back to values like Vendors and States. Finally, I changed the names of the States and GLAccounts navigation properties for the Vendor entity to State and GLAccount since they provide access to a single state and G/L account. Like the Terms entity, though, I didn't change the name of the Terms navigation property even though it provides access to a single object.

The code for the PayablesEntity module

Figure 18-12 also shows the code for the module used by this application. It consists of a single statement that creates an instance of the object context. This statement is coded in a module so the object context can be accessed by both the Vendor Maintenance and Add/Modify Vendor forms.

The Entity Data Model for the Vendor Maintenance application

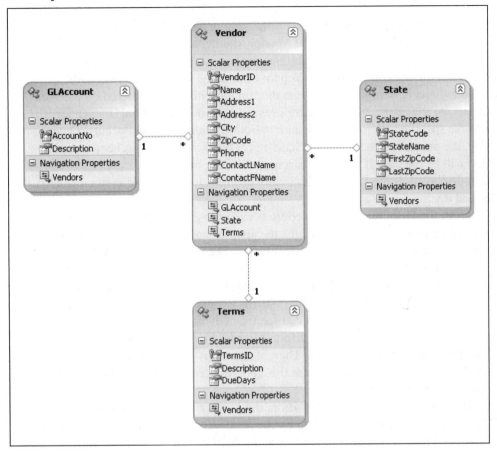

The code for the PayablesEntity module

```
Module PayablesEntity
    Public payables As New PayablesEntities
End Module
```

Description

- The Entity Data Model contains the entity classes that define the entities used by the Vendor Maintenance application. These classes correspond with tables in the Payables database.

- Associations are defined between the Vendor class and the State, GLAccount, and Terms classes based on the foreign keys defined between the related tables in the database.

- The entity and navigation property names have been modified as shown above. In addition, the entity set names for the Vendor, State, and GLAccount classes have been changed back to their original values of Vendors, States, and GLAccounts.

- The object context that's used by this application is created in the PayablesEntity module so it's available to both the Vendor Maintenance and the Add/Modify Vendor forms.

Figure 18-12   The Entity Data Model and the code for the PayablesEntity module

The code for the Vendor Maintenance form

Figure 18-13 presents the code for the Vendor Maintenance form. It works much like the code you saw for the Vendor Maintenance forms in chapters 7 and 14. So I'll just point out some highlights here.

When the user clicks the Get Vendor button, the GetVendor procedure executes a query expression that gets the vendor with the ID entered by the user. To execute the query, this procedure uses the First method. Then, if a vendor with the specified ID isn't found, an InvalidOperationException occurs. Otherwise, the procedure checks if the State object for that vendor has been loaded. That will be the case if the data for another vendor in the same state has already been displayed. If the state hasn't already been loaded, the Load method is used to load it.

Next, the DisplayVendor procedure is called to display the data for the selected vendor. To do that, it assigns the appropriate properties of the Vendor object to the Text properties of the text boxes. The exception is the value that's assigned to the State text box. In that case, the value is retrieved from the related State object. That's why the State object for the vendor had to be loaded. Then, the StateName property of the State object is assigned to the State text box.

On page 2 of this listing, you can see the code that's executed if the user clicks the Add button. This code displays the Add Vendor form so the user can enter the data for the new vendor. Then, if the insert operation is successful, the new Vendor object is retrieved from the Add Vendor form and displayed on the Vendor Maintenance form.

If the user clicks the Modify button, the Modify Vendor form is displayed. Then, the processing is determined by the result of that form. If the result is OK, it indicates that the update operation was successful. If it's Retry, it indicates that a concurrency error occurred because the data for the vendor changed. As you'll see in a minute, the Vendor object is refreshed when a concurrency error occurs. Then, the updated or refreshed Vendor object is retrieved from the Modify Vendor form and displayed on the Vendor Maintenance form.

If the result of the Modify Vendor form is Abort, it indicates that a concurrency error occurred because the vendor was deleted. In that case, all the controls on the Vendor Maintenance form are cleared.

On page 3, you can see the code that's executed if the user clicks the Delete button. This code starts by confirming the operation. If it's confirmed, the DeleteObject method of the object context is executed to mark the selected vendor for deletion. Then, the SaveChanges method is executed to delete the vendor from the database, and the controls on the form are cleared.

If a concurrency error occurs, the Vendor object is refreshed with the data in the database. Then, the state of the object is checked to determine if the vendor was updated or deleted. If it was deleted, the state of the object is Detached. In that case, a message is displayed and the controls on the form are cleared. If the object was updated, a message is displayed and the current values are displayed on the form.

The code for the Vendor Maintenance form

```vb
Imports System.Data.Objects

Class frmVendorMaintenance

    Private selectedVendor As Vendor

    Private Sub btnGetVendor_Click(ByVal sender As System.Object, _
            ByVal e As System.EventArgs) Handles btnGetVendor.Click
        If Validator.IsPresent(txtVendorID) AndAlso _
            Validator.IsInt32(txtVendorID) Then
            Dim vendorID As Integer = CInt(txtVendorID.Text)
            Me.GetVendor(vendorID)
        End If
    End Sub

    Private Sub GetVendor(ByVal vendorID As Integer)
        Try
            selectedVendor = (From vendor In payables.Vendors _
                              Where vendor.VendorID = vendorID _
                              Select vendor).First
            If Not selectedVendor.StateReference.IsLoaded Then
                selectedVendor.StateReference.Load()
            End If
            Me.DisplayVendor()
        Catch ex As InvalidOperationException
            MessageBox.Show("No vendor found with this ID. " _
                & "Please try again.", "Vendor Not Found")
            Me.ClearControls()
            txtVendorID.Select()
        Catch ex As Exception
            MessageBox.Show(ex.Message, ex.GetType.ToString)
        End Try
    End Sub

    Private Sub DisplayVendor()
        txtName.Text = selectedVendor.Name
        txtAddress1.Text = selectedVendor.Address1
        txtAddress2.Text = selectedVendor.Address2
        txtCity.Text = selectedVendor.City
        txtState.Text = selectedVendor.State.StateName
        txtZipCode.Text = selectedVendor.ZipCode
        btnModify.Enabled = True
        btnDelete.Enabled = True
    End Sub
```

Figure 18-13   The code for the Vendor Maintenance form (part 1 of 3)

The code for the Vendor Maintenance form

```vb
Private Sub ClearControls()
    txtName.Text = ""
    txtAddress1.Text = ""
    txtAddress2.Text = ""
    txtCity.Text = ""
    txtState.Text = ""
    txtZipCode.Text = ""
    btnModify.Enabled = False
    btnDelete.Enabled = False
End Sub

Private Sub btnAdd_Click(ByVal sender As System.Object, _
        ByVal e As System.EventArgs) Handles btnAdd.Click
    Dim addModifyVendorForm As New frmAddModifyVendor
    addModifyVendorForm.addVendor = True
    Dim result As DialogResult = addModifyVendorForm.ShowDialog()
    If result = DialogResult.OK Then
        selectedVendor = addModifyVendorForm.vendor
        txtVendorID.Text = selectedVendor.VendorID.ToString
        Me.DisplayVendor()
    End If
End Sub

Private Sub btnModify_Click(ByVal sender As System.Object, _
        ByVal e As System.EventArgs) Handles btnModify.Click
    Dim addModifyVendorForm As New frmAddModifyVendor
    addModifyVendorForm.addVendor = False
    addModifyVendorForm.vendor = selectedVendor
    Dim result As DialogResult = addModifyVendorForm.ShowDialog()
    If result = DialogResult.OK OrElse _
       result = DialogResult.Retry Then
        selectedVendor = addModifyVendorForm.vendor
        Me.DisplayVendor()
    ElseIf result = DialogResult.Abort Then
        txtVendorID.Text = ""
        Me.ClearControls()
    End If
End Sub
```

Figure 18-13   The code for the Vendor Maintenance form (part 2 of 3)

The code for the Vendor Maintenance form   Page 3

```
Private Sub btnDelete_Click(ByVal sender As System.Object, _
        ByVal e As System.EventArgs) Handles btnDelete.Click
    Dim result As DialogResult _
        = MessageBox.Show("Delete " & selectedVendor.Name & "?", _
          "Confirm Delete", MessageBoxButtons.YesNo, _
          MessageBoxIcon.Question)
    If result = DialogResult.Yes Then
        Try
            payables.DeleteObject(selectedVendor)
            payables.SaveChanges()
            txtVendorID.Text = ""
            Me.ClearControls()
        Catch ex As OptimisticConcurrencyException
            payables.Refresh(RefreshMode.StoreWins, selectedVendor)
            If selectedVendor.EntityState = EntityState.Detached Then
                MessageBox.Show("Another user has deleted that vendor.", _
                                "Concurrency Error")
                txtVendorID.Text = ""
                Me.ClearControls()
            Else
                MessageBox.Show("Another user has updated that vendor.", _
                                "Concurrency Error")
                Me.DisplayVendor()
            End If
        Catch ex As Exception
            MessageBox.Show(ex.Message, ex.GetType.ToString)
        End Try
    End If
End Sub

Private Sub btnExit_Click(ByVal sender As System.Object, _
        ByVal e As System.EventArgs) Handles btnExit.Click
    Me.Close()
End Sub

End Class
```

Figure 18-13   The code for the Vendor Maintenance form (part 3 of 3)

The code for the Add/Modify Vendor form

Figure 18-14 presents the code for the Add/Modify Vendor form. When this form is first loaded, the LoadComboBoxes procedure is called to get the data for the State, Terms, and Account combo boxes. To do that, this procedure uses query expressions that retrieve and sort the required data. Then, the combo boxes are bound to the query results.

If a vendor is being modified, the DisplayVendorData procedure is called to display the data for that vendor. This procedure is similar to the DisplayVendor procedure of the Vendor Maintenance form. It assigns properties of the Vendor object to the Text property of the text boxes on the form. It also assigns properties of the State, Terms, and GLAccount objects that are accessed through navigation properties of the Vendor object to the SelectedValue property of the combo boxes on the form.

On page 2 of this listing, you can see the code that's executed if the user clicks the Accept button. This code starts by calling the IsValidData procedure to determine if the data on the form is valid. If the data is valid and a vendor is being added, a new Vendor object is created, the PutVendorData procedure is called to set its property values, and the AddToVendors method of the object context is called to add the Vendor object to the Vendors collection. Finally, the SaveChanges method is executed to add the vendor to the database, and the DialogResult property of the form is set to DialogResult.OK.

If the vendor is being modified, the PutVendorData procedure is called to update the properties of the Vendor object. Then, the SaveChanges method is executed to update the database. If this method is successful, the DialogResult property of the form is set to DialogResult.OK. If a concurrency error occurs, however, the Vendor object is refreshed with the data in the database. Then, the state of the object is checked to determine if the vendor was updated or deleted, an appropriate message is displayed, and the DialogResult property of the form is set accordingly.

On page 3 of this listing, you can see the IsValidData procedure. Here, you should notice the statement that follows the last call to the IsPresent method. This statement retrieves the State object for the vendor from the State combo box using its SelectedItem property. Then, it uses the FirstZipCode and LastZipCode properties of that object to check that the zip code the user entered is valid for the state.

The PutVendorData procedure also uses this technique to get the State, Terms, and GLAccount objects for the vendor. Then, it sets the State, Terms, and GLAccount navigation properties of the Vendor object to these objects. That way, the appropriate values will be saved in the State, DefaultTermsID, and DefaultAccountNo columns of the row in the Vendors table.

The code for the Add/Modify Vendor form   **Page 1**

```vb
Imports System.Data.Objects

Public Class frmAddModifyVendor

    Public addVendor As Boolean
    Public vendor As Vendor

    Private Sub frmAddModifyVendor_Load(ByVal sender As System.Object, _
            ByVal e As System.EventArgs) Handles MyBase.Load

        Me.LoadComboBoxes()

        If addVendor Then
            Me.Text = "Add Vendor"
            cboStates.SelectedIndex = -1
            cboTerms.SelectedIndex = -1
            cboAccounts.SelectedIndex = -1
        Else
            Me.Text = "Modify Vendor"
            Me.DisplayVendorData()
        End If
    End Sub

    Private Sub LoadComboBoxes()
        Try
            Dim states = From state In payables.States _
                        Order By state.StateName
            cboStates.DataSource = states
            cboStates.DisplayMember = "StateName"
            cboStates.ValueMember = "StateCode"

            Dim terms = From term In payables.Terms _
                        Order By term.Description
            cboTerms.DataSource = terms
            cboTerms.DisplayMember = "Description"
            cboTerms.ValueMember = "TermsID"

            Dim accounts = From account In payables.GLAccounts _
                        Order By account.Description
            cboAccounts.DataSource = accounts
            cboAccounts.DisplayMember = "Description"
            cboAccounts.ValueMember = "AccountNo"
        Catch ex As Exception
            MessageBox.Show(ex.Message, ex.GetType.ToString)
        End Try
    End Sub

    Private Sub DisplayVendorData()
        txtName.Text = vendor.Name
        txtAddress1.Text = vendor.Address1
        txtAddress2.Text = vendor.Address2
        txtCity.Text = vendor.City
        cboStates.SelectedValue = vendor.State.StateCode
        txtZipCode.Text = vendor.ZipCode
```

Figure 18-14   The code for the Add/Modify Vendor form (part 1 of 3)

The code for the Add/Modify Vendor form

```vb
        cboTerms.SelectedValue = vendor.Terms.TermsID
        cboAccounts.SelectedValue = vendor.GLAccount.AccountNo
        If vendor.Phone = "" Then
            txtPhone.Text = ""
        Else
            txtPhone.Text = FormattedPhoneNumber(vendor.Phone)
        End If
        txtFirstName.Text = vendor.ContactFName
        txtLastName.Text = vendor.ContactLName
    End Sub

    Private Function FormattedPhoneNumber(ByVal phone As String) As String
        Return phone.Substring(0, 3) & "." _
            & phone.Substring(3, 3) & "." _
            & phone.Substring(6, 4)
    End Function

    Private Sub btnAccept_Click(ByVal sender As System.Object, _
            ByVal e As System.EventArgs) Handles btnAccept.Click
        If IsValidData() Then
            If addVendor Then
                vendor = New Vendor
                Me.PutVendorData(vendor)
                payables.AddToVendors(vendor)
                Try
                    payables.SaveChanges()
                    Me.DialogResult = DialogResult.OK
                Catch ex As Exception
                    MessageBox.Show(ex.Message, ex.GetType.ToString)
                End Try
            Else
                Me.PutVendorData(vendor)
                Try
                    payables.SaveChanges()
                    Me.DialogResult = DialogResult.OK
                Catch ex As OptimisticConcurrencyException
                    payables.Refresh(RefreshMode.StoreWins, vendor)
                    If vendor.EntityState = EntityState.Detached Then
                        MessageBox.Show("Another user has deleted " _
                            & "that vendor.", "Concurrency Error")
                        Me.DialogResult = DialogResult.Abort
                    Else
                        MessageBox.Show("Another user has updated " _
                            & "that vendor.", "Concurrency Error")
                        Me.DialogResult = DialogResult.Retry
                    End If
                Catch ex As Exception
                    MessageBox.Show(ex.Message, ex.GetType.ToString)
                End Try
            End If
        End If
    End Sub
```

Figure 18-14   The code for the Add/Modify Vendor form (part 2 of 3)

The code for the Add/Modify Vendor form   **Page 3**

```vb
    Private Function IsValidData() As Boolean
        If Validator.IsPresent(txtName) AndAlso _
            Validator.IsPresent(txtAddress1) AndAlso _
            Validator.IsPresent(txtCity) AndAlso _
            Validator.IsPresent(cboStates) AndAlso _
            Validator.IsPresent(txtZipCode) AndAlso _
            Validator.IsInt32(txtZipCode) AndAlso _
            Validator.IsPresent(cboTerms) AndAlso _
            Validator.IsPresent(cboAccounts) Then
            Dim state As State = CType(cboStates.SelectedItem, State)
            If Validator.IsStateZipCode(txtZipCode, state.FirstZipCode, _
                    state.LastZipCode) Then
                If txtPhone.Text <> "" Then
                    If Validator.IsPhoneNumber(txtPhone) Then
                        Return True
                    Else
                        Return False
                    End If
                Else
                    Return True
                End If
            Else
                Return False
            End If
        Else
            Return False
        End If
    End Function

    Private Sub PutVendorData(ByVal vendor As Vendor)
        vendor.Name = txtName.Text
        vendor.Address1 = txtAddress1.Text
        vendor.Address2 = txtAddress2.Text
        vendor.City = txtCity.Text
        Dim state As State = CType(cboStates.SelectedItem, State)
        vendor.State = state
        vendor.ZipCode = txtZipCode.Text
        Dim terms As Terms = CType(cboTerms.SelectedItem, Terms)
        vendor.Terms = terms
        Dim account As GLAccount = CType(cboAccounts.SelectedItem, GLAccount)
        vendor.GLAccount = account
        vendor.Phone = txtPhone.Text.Replace(".", "")
        vendor.ContactFName = txtFirstName.Text
        vendor.ContactLName = txtLastName.Text
    End Sub

End Class
```

Figure 18-14   The code for the Add/Modify Vendor form (part 3 of 3)

Perspective

Now that you've read this chapter, you should be able to use LINQ to Entities to retrieve the data you need for your applications. In addition, you should be able to use the features provided by the Entity Framework to insert, update, and delete data. You should be able to use stored procedures. And you should be able to use object data sources and bound controls.

Although using LINQ to Entities is the easiest way to retrieve data from a database using an Entity Data Model, it's not the only way. In the next chapter, then, you'll learn how to use Entity SQL to retrieve data using an Entity Data Model. Then, in chapter 20, you'll learn how to use Entity data source controls to work with an Entity Data Model from a web application.

Term

query path

Exercise 18-1   Implement the Vendors Summary application

In this exercise, you'll use the Entity Data Model you created in exercise 17-2 to retrieve data from the Vendors and VendorsSummary tables and display it in a DataGridView control like this:

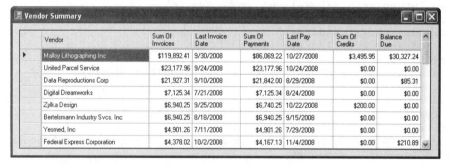

1. Copy the VendorsSummary directory from your chapter 17 directory to your chapter 18 directory, and then open the VendorsSummary project in the chapter 18 directory.

2. Create an object data source from the vendor entity as described in figure 18-9, and then drag this data source to the form to generate a DataGridView control, a navigation toolbar, and a binding source.

3. Delete the navigation toolbar and then format the DataGridView control and the form so they appear as shown above.

4. Start an event handler for the Load event of the form, and create an instance of the object context.

5. Code a query that retrieves just the vendors with invoices (sum of invoices greater than zero) and just the columns required by the application. Sort the results by the SumOfInvoices column in descending sequence.

6. Execute the query by binding its results to the DataSource property of the binding source.

7. Run the application to see how it works, make any necessary adjustments, and then close the solution. You've now developed an application that uses a single entity to get data from two separate tables.

Exercise 18-2   Develop the Vendor Maintenance application

In this exercise, you'll write code that uses the Entity Data Model for the Vendor Maintenance application to retrieve, insert, update and delete data from the Vendors table.

Review the application and add a module

1. Open the project that's in the C\:ADO.NET 3.5 VB\Chapter 18\VendorMaintenance directory. This project contains the Entity Data Model, forms, and starting code for the Vendor Maintenance application.

2. Review the Entity Data Model and notice the names it uses for the entities and navigation properties.

3. Add a module named PayablesEntity to the project. Declare a public variable named payables within this class and assign an instance of the object context class to it.

4. Close the module and save the changes.

Add code to retrieve a vendor

5. Display the code for the Vendor Maintenance form.

6. Add a query to the event handler for the Click event of the Get Vendor button that retrieves the data for the vendor with the ID that's entered in the Vendor ID text box, and assign the result to the selectedVendor class variable.

7. Add code to the Click event handler that checks if the State object has been loaded and that loads it if it hasn't.

8. Run the application, enter 9 for the vendor ID, and click the Get Vendor button. If you coded the query correctly, the information for the vendor will be displayed on the form as shown in figure 18-11.

Add code to load the combo boxes on the Add/Modify Vendor form

9. Display the code for the Add/Modify Vendor form.

10. Add a query to the LoadComboBoxes procedure that retrieves the required data from the States table and sorts the results by state name. Do the same for the Terms and GLAccounts tables, but sort the results by description. Then, bind the three combo boxes on the form to the results of the appropriate query.

11. Run the application, retrieve the data for vendor ID 9, and then click the Modify button to display the Modify Vendor form. Then, drop-down the three combo box lists to be sure they were loaded correctly.

Add code to add a new vendor

12. Add code to the event handler for the Click event of the Accept button that adds a new vendor to the Vendors collection of the object context and then updates the database.

13. Run the application and click the Add button on the Vendor Maintenance form to display the Add Vendor form.

14. Enter the data for a new vendor and then click the Accept button to return to the Vendor Maintenance form. Make a note of the ID for the new vendor and then end the application.

Add code to modify a vendor

15. Add a statement to the event handler for the Click event of the Accept button that updates the database when changes are made to a vendor.

16. Run the application, enter the ID for the vendor you added in step 14, and click the Get Vendor button.

17. Click the Modify button to display the Modify Vendor form. Make one or more changes to the vendor's address, accept the changes, and make sure the changes are reflected on the Vendor Maintenance form.

Add code to delete a vendor

18. Return to the code for the Vendor Maintenance form. Then, add code to the event handler for the Click event of the Delete button to mark the selected vendor for deletion and to delete the vendor from the database.

19. Run the application, enter the ID for the vendor you added in step 14 and modified in step 17, and click the Get Vendor button.

20. Click the Delete button and then click Yes when you're asked to confirm the operation. The data for the vendor should be cleared from the form.

21. Enter the same vendor ID and click the Get Vendor button to confirm that the vendor has been deleted.

Add the remaining code

22. At this point, the application can perform the basic retrieval, insert, update and delete operations. Now, you just need to add code to validate the zip code and provide for concurrency conflicts. Add this code if you want to and then test the application. When you're done, close the solution.

19

How to use Entity SQL

In the last chapter, you saw that LINQ to Entities provides an easy way to retrieve data using an Entity Data Model. In some cases, though, you'll need to code queries that are more complex than what you can code with LINQ to Entities. In that case, you can use Entity SQL instead. In this chapter, you'll learn the basic techniques for using Entity SQL.

An introduction to Entity SQL

To use Entity SQL, you start by coding a Select statement that specifies the data you want to retrieve. Then, you execute that statement using an object query. You'll see how to do that in the topics that follow.

How to code a Select statement

Figure 19-1 presents the basic syntax of the Select statement. If you're familiar with *Transact-SQL*, which is the dialect of SQL that's used by SQL Server, you'll see that this statement is quite similar. The main difference is that the Select statement for Entity SQL works with query expressions and entity collections rather than column expressions and tables. That's because this statement is executed against an Entity Data Model rather than a database.

Another difference between the Select statement for Entity SQL and the Select statement for Transact-SQL is the Value keyword that you can code on the Select clause. You use this keyword if the statement retrieves an entity type or a primitive type. For example, the Select statement in this figure retrieves Invoice entities. Because of that, the Value keyword must be included. In contrast, it must be omitted if the statement retrieves an anonymous type. You'll learn more about retrieving all three of these types later in this chapter.

The From clause on an Entity SQL statement names a property that's defined by the object context that returns an entity collection. In this example, that property is named Invoices. This works just like it does in LINQ to Entities. Note, however, that you don't specify the object context that defines the property when you use Entity SQL. Instead, you specify the object context when you create the object query as you'll see in the next figure.

Before I go on, you should realize that the entity collection that's returned by the property named on the From clause is stored in an ObjectQuery(Of T) object. For example, the From clause in the statement in this figure returns an ObjectQuery(Of Invoice) object. If you're interested, you can refer to the code that's generated for an object context to see how this works.

Just like you can with LINQ to Entities, you can refer to any property of an entity in the entity collection that's named on the From clause in the other clauses of the Select statement. For example, both the Where and Order By clauses shown in this figure refer to the InvoiceTotal property of the Invoice entity. Notice that these properties are referred to through the alias that's assigned to the entity collection on the From clause. If you don't assign an alias, you refer to the properties through the name of the entity collection instead.

The basic syntax of the Select statement

```
SELECT [VALUE] query-expression-1 [AS alias-1]
          [, query-expression-2 [AS alias-2]] ...
FROM entity-collection [AS alias-3]
WHERE selection-criteria
ORDER BY sort-expression-1 [ASC|DESC]
        [, sort-expression-2 [ASC|DESC]] ...
```

The four clauses of the Select statement

Clause	Description
SELECT	Specifies the content of the returned elements.
FROM	Identifies the source of data for the query.
WHERE	Provides a condition that specifies which elements are retrieved from the data source.
ORDER BY	Indicates how the elements that are returned by the query are sorted.

A Select statement that retrieves data from the Invoices table

```
SELECT VALUE Invoice
FROM Invoices AS Invoice
WHERE Invoice.InvoiceTotal > 5000
ORDER BY Invoice.InvoiceTotal DESC
```

Description

- Entity SQL provides a Select statement that you can use to retrieve data using the Entity Data Model. This statement is based on the Select statement that's included in the SQL Server dialect of SQL, called *Transact-SQL*.

- The Select statement lets you retrieve entity types, primitive types, and anonymous types. To retrieve an entity or primitive type, you must include the Value keyword on the Select clause.

- The From clause names an entity collection that's defined by an ObjectQuery(Of T) class in the object context. You refer to this collection using a property of the object context.

- You can refer to properties of the entities in the entity collection named on the From clause in the other clauses of a Select statement. You refer to these properties through the alias specified on the From clause. If an alias isn't specified, a name is generated based on the name of the entity collection.

- The Select statement includes clauses in addition to those shown above. For more information, see the Visual Studio documentation.

Note

- Currently, Entity SQL provides only for retrieving data. To insert, update, and delete data, you have to use the techniques presented in chapter 18.

Figure 19-1   How to code a Select statement

How to execute a Select statement using an object query

To execute an Entity SQL statement, you create an object query for the statement and then execute the object query. Figure 19-2 shows how this works.

The first code example in this figure starts by creating an instance of the object context. Then, it declares a string that contains the Select statement to be executed. Finally, it creates an *object query* using a constructor of the ObjectQuery class.

At the least, this constructor must identify the Select statement and the object context. In addition, it can specify one of the merge options listed in the table in this figure. This option indicates how the data that's retrieved is merged with the data in the object context if the object context already contains data. If an application doesn't provide for changing the data that's retrieved, you can specify the NoTracking option as shown in this example so that changes aren't tracked. This can increase the efficiency of the application.

The second code example in this figure shows one way to execute an object query. To do that, it uses a For Each statement like the others you've seen in this book. You can also execute an object query by executing a method of the ObjectQuery class that causes immediate execution. For example, you could use the First method to return the first entity in a collection. Finally, you can use the Execute method of the ObjectQuery class. You'll typically use this method when you want to bind a control to the results of a query. You'll see how to do that later in this chapter.

Two constructors for the ObjectQuery class

```
New ObjectQuery(Of T)(selectStatement, objectContext)
New ObjectQuery(Of T)(selectStatement, objectContext, MergeOption)
```

MergeOption enumeration members

Member	Description
AppendOnly	Only objects that don't already exist in the object context are loaded from the database. This is the default.
OverwriteChanges	All objects are loaded from the database, overwriting changes made to objects in the object context.
PreserveChanges	All objects are loaded from the database, but changes made to objects in the object context are preserved.
NoTracking	Changes to objects in the object context aren't tracked.

Code that creates an object query

```
Dim payables As New PayablesEntities

Dim selectStatement As String _
    = "SELECT VALUE Invoice FROM Invoices AS Invoice " _
    & "WHERE Invoice.InvoiceTotal > 5000 " _
    & "ORDER BY Invoice.InvoiceTotal DESC"

Dim invoiceTotals As New ObjectQuery(Of Invoice) _
    (selectStatement, payables, MergeOption.NoTracking)
```

Code that executes the object query

```
Dim invoiceDisplay As String _
    = "Invoice No." & vbTab & "Invoice Total" & vbCrLf
For Each invoice In invoiceTotals
    invoiceDisplay &= invoice.InvoiceNumber & vbTab _
                   & IIf(invoice.InvoiceNumber.Length <= 8, _
                         vbTab, "").ToString _
                   & FormatCurrency(invoice.InvoiceTotal) & vbCrLf
Next
MessageBox.Show(invoiceDisplay, "Invoice totals over $5000")
```

Description

- To execute a Select statement that's written using Entity SQL, you can create an *object query* and then execute it using a For Each statement, the Execute method of the object query, or another method of the object query that causes it to be executed immediately.

- To create an object query, you use a constructor of the ObjectQuery(Of T) class where T represents the type of data that's returned by the query.

- The ObjectQuery(Of T) constructor specifies the statement to be executed and the object context it should be executed against. It can also specify a merge option that indicates how the data that's retrieved is merged with the data currently in the object context.

- The ObjectQuery class is a member of the System.Data.Objects namespace.

Figure 19-2   How to execute a Select statement using an object query

How to retrieve data using Entity SQL

The code you use to define an Entity SQL Select statement and to create an object query depend on whether the query returns an entity type, a primitive type, or an anonymous type. You'll learn how to retrieve all three of these types in the topics that follow. Then, you'll learn some additional skills for retrieving data.

How to retrieve an entity type

Figure 19-3 shows how to create and execute a query that retrieves an entity type. To start, the Select clause must include the Value keyword. When you use this keyword, you specify a single expression on the Select clause. For a statement that returns an entity type, the expression is the name of the entity class. In the Select statement in this figure, for example, you can see that the Invoice class is named on the Select clause.

When a Select statement retrieves an entity type, you must create an object query that declares entities of that type. You can see how this works in the second example in this figure. Here, the object query is declared as an ObjectQuery(Of Invoice) object.

The third code example executes the query and then displays the results. If you review this code and the resulting dialog box, you'll see that it works just like other examples you've seen in this book.

A Select statement that retrieves an entity type

```
Dim selectStatement As String _
    = "SELECT VALUE Invoice " _
    & "FROM Invoices AS Invoice " _
    & "WHERE Invoice.InvoiceTotal - Invoice.PaymentTotal " _
    & "    - Invoice.CreditTotal > 0 " _
    & "ORDER BY Invoice.DueDate, " _
    & "           Invoice.InvoiceTotal - Invoice.PaymentTotal " _
    & "           - Invoice.CreditTotal DESC"
```

An object query that uses the Select the statement

```
Dim unpaidInvoices As New ObjectQuery(Of Invoice)(selectStatement, payables)
```

Code that executes the query

```
Dim invoiceDisplay As String _
    = "Invoice No." & vbTab & "Due Date" & vbTab & vbTab _
    & "Balance Due" & vbCrLf
For Each invoice In unpaidInvoices
    invoiceDisplay &= invoice.InvoiceNumber & vbTab _
                & IIf(invoice.InvoiceNumber.Length < 8, _
                    vbTab, "").ToString _
                & invoice.DueDate & vbTab _
                & FormatCurrency(invoice.InvoiceTotal _
                - invoice.PaymentTotal - invoice.CreditTotal) & vbCrLf
Next
MessageBox.Show(invoiceDisplay, "Sorted Invoices Due")
```

The resulting dialog box

Description

- If an object query retrieves an entity type, the Select clause must include the Value keyword, and you must name the entity type on the ObjectQuery(Of T) constructor.

Note

- Entity SQL doesn't support the use of * in the Select clause to retrieve all the columns from a data source. Instead, you must select an entity type that's mapped to a table in the database.

Figure 19-3   How to retrieve an entity type

How to retrieve a primitive type

Figure 19-4 shows how to create and execute an object query that retrieves a primitive type. Like a query that retrieves an entity type, the Select clause for a query that retrieves a primitive type must include the Value keyword and it must specify a single expression. In this example, the expression is a calculation that uses three properties of the entity named on the From clause to return the balance due for the selected invoices.

When a Select statement retrieves a primitive type, the object query must be declared as an object of that type. Because the calculation in the Select clause in this figure will return a decimal value, for example, the object query is declared so that it can store decimal values. Then, the code that executes the query simply iterates through the decimal values.

A Select statement that retrieves a primitive type

```
Dim selectStatement As String _
    = "SELECT VALUE Invoice.InvoiceTotal - Invoice.PaymentTotal " _
    & "            - Invoice.CreditTotal " _
    & "FROM Invoices AS Invoice " _
    & "WHERE Invoice.InvoiceTotal - Invoice.PaymentTotal " _
    & "    - Invoice.CreditTotal > 0 " _
    & "ORDER BY Invoice.InvoiceTotal - Invoice.PaymentTotal " _
    & "           - Invoice.CreditTotal DESC"
```

An object query that uses the Select statement

```
Dim invoiceBalances As New ObjectQuery(Of Decimal) _
    (selectStatement, payables, MergeOption.NoTracking)
```

Code that executes the query

```
Dim balanceDisplay As String = "Balance Due" & vbCrLf
For Each balance In invoiceBalances
    balanceDisplay &= FormatCurrency(balance) & vbCrLf
Next
MessageBox.Show(balanceDisplay, "Sorted Invoice Balances")
```

The resulting dialog box

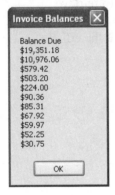

Description

- If an object query retrieves a primitive type, the Select clause must include the Value keyword, and you must name the primitive type on the ObjectQuery(Of T) constructor.

Figure 19-4   How to retrieve a primitive type

How to retrieve an anonymous type

The technique you use to retrieve an anonymous type using Entity SQL is somewhat more complicated. This technique is illustrated in figure 19-5. To start, you can include one or more expressions on the Select clause, and you must omit the Value keyword. The Select clause in this figure, for example, includes three expressions. The first two are properties of the entity that's named on the From clause, and the third is a calculation that uses three additional properties of that entity.

Next, because anonymous types are stored in DbDataRecord objects, you must create an object query that can store this type of object. When you execute the query, each column in the DbDataRecord object contains a value that's returned by the query. Then, you can retrieve those values by using the column names, which are the same as the names specified on the Select clause, or the position of the column in the record. In this example, I used the column names to make it clear which columns are being accessed.

Although it's not shown here, you can also use Get methods to retrieve the values in a DbDataRecord object. For example, you can use the GetOrdinal method to get the position of a column with the specified name. Then, if the column contains a string value, you can use the GetString method to retrieve that value based on its position. This works just like it does for retrieving the values of columns from a SqlDataReader object, and it can improve the efficiency of retrieval operations.

A Select statement that retrieves an anonymous type

```
Dim selectStatement As String _
    = "SELECT Invoice.InvoiceNumber, Invoice.DueDate, " _
    & "        Invoice.InvoiceTotal - Invoice.PaymentTotal " _
    & "      - Invoice.CreditTotal AS BalanceDue " _
    & "FROM Invoices AS Invoice " _
    & "WHERE Invoice.InvoiceTotal - Invoice.PaymentTotal " _
    & "      - Invoice.CreditTotal > 0 " _
    & "ORDER BY Invoice.DueDate, " _
    & "        Invoice.InvoiceTotal - Invoice.PaymentTotal " _
    & "      - Invoice.CreditTotal DESC"
```

An object query that uses the Select statement

```
Dim unpaidInvoices As New ObjectQuery(Of DbDataRecord) _
    (selectStatement, payables, MergeOption.NoTracking)
```

Code that executes the query

```
Dim invoiceDisplay As String _
    = "Invoice No." & vbTab & "Due Date" & vbTab & vbTab _
    & "Balance Due" & vbCrLf
For Each invoice In unpaidInvoices
    invoiceDisplay &= invoice("InvoiceNumber").ToString & vbTab _
                    & IIf(invoice("InvoiceNumber").ToString.Length < 8, _
                        vbTab, "").ToString _
                    & CDate(invoice("DueDate")).ToShortDateString & vbTab _
                    & FormatCurrency(CDec(invoice("BalanceDue"))) & vbCrLf
Next
MessageBox.Show(invoiceDisplay, "Unpaid Invoices")
```

The resulting dialog box

Description

- If an object query retrieves an anonymous type, the data is returned as DbDataRecord objects, so you must name this type on the ObjectQuery(Of T) constructor. DbDataRecord is a member of the System.Data.Common namespace.

- To retrieve a column value from a DbDataRecord object, you can specify the name or index of the column on the Item property (the default).

Figure 19-5   How to retrieve an anonymous type

How to use query parameters

In the last chapter, you saw that you can include variables in a LINQ to Entities query to specify the condition that must be met for a row to be retrieved from the database. When you use Entity SQL, however, you use parameters instead of variables. Figure 19-6 shows how this works.

The Select statement at the top of this figure uses a parameter named PayDate that's compared with the due date of each invoice. The parameter in this statement is identified by a placeholder whose name starts with an at sign (@). This is identical to the way you identify a parameter in a SQL Select statement.

The second example in this figure shows how you set the value of the parameter. To start, you create the object query that that will store the results of the Select statement. Then, you create a new ObjectParameter object and specify the parameter's name and value. Note that the parameter name is the same as the placeholder name without the at sign.

After you create the parameter, you add it to the collection of parameters for the object query. To do that, you use the Parameters property of the query to get the collection and then use the Add method of the collection to add the parameter.

In this example, the parameter is created when it's added to the Parameters collection. You can also create the parameter using a separate statement like this:

```
Dim payDateParm As New ObjectParameter("PayDate", payDate)
```

Then, you can add it to the collection using a statement like this:

```
invoicesDue.Parameters.Add(payDateParm)
```

You might want to do that if you need to change the value of the parameter as the application executes. To change the value of a parameter, you simply assign the value to the parameter's Value property.

A Select statement that includes a parameter

```
Dim selectStatement As String _
    = "SELECT VALUE Invoice FROM Invoices AS Invoice " _
    & "WHERE Invoice.InvoiceTotal - Invoice.PaymentTotal " _
    & "    - Invoice.CreditTotal > 0 " _
    & "  AND Invoice.DueDate < @PayDate " _
    & "ORDER BY Invoice.DueDate, " _
    & "          Invoice.InvoiceTotal - Invoice.PaymentTotal " _
    & "          - Invoice.CreditTotal DESC"
```

Code that creates an object query from the statement and adds the parameter

```
Dim invoicesDue As New ObjectQuery(Of Invoice)(selectStatement, payables)
invoicesDue.Parameters.Add(New ObjectParameter("PayDate", payDate))
```

Code that executes the query

```
Dim invoiceDisplay As String _
    = "Invoice No." & vbTab & "Due Date" & vbTab & vbTab _
    & "Balance Due" & vbCrLf
For Each invoice In invoicesDue
    invoiceDisplay &= invoice.InvoiceNumber & vbTab _
                    & IIf(invoice.InvoiceNumber.Length < 8, _
                        vbTab, "").ToString _
                    & invoice.DueDate & vbTab _
                    & FormatCurrency(invoice.InvoiceTotal _
                    - invoice.PaymentTotal - invoice.CreditTotal) & vbCrLf
Next
MessageBox.Show(invoiceDisplay, "Invoices Due")
```

The resulting dialog box

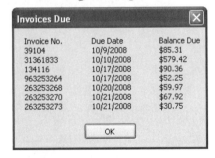

Description

- To include parameters in an Entity SQL statement, you code placeholders for the parameters. Each placeholder is a named variable whose name begins with an at sign (@).

- To create a parameter object, you use the constructor for the ObjectParameter class. On this constructor, you can specify the name and value of the parameter.

- To add a parameter to the collection of parameters for an object query, you use the Parameters property of the object query to get the collection and then use the Add method of the collection to add the parameter.

Figure 19-6   How to use query parameters

How to query across relationships

When you use Entity SQL, you can query across relationships using techniques similar to the techniques you use with LINQ to Entities. This is illustrated in figure 19-7. Here, the first Select statement retrieves the Name property of a Vendor object through the Invoice object. To do that, it uses the Vendor navigation property of the Invoice object. The same expression is used in the Order By clause to sort the rows by vendor name.

The second Select statement returns the same results, but it retrieves invoice data through the Vendor object. To do that, it names two entity collections on the From clause. The first one is the collection of Vendor entities, and the second one is the collection of Invoice entities for the vendor. This collection is referred to using the Invoices navigation property of the Vendor object. Then, the other clauses in the statement can refer to either of these collections.

A Select statement that gets vendor data through the Invoice objects

```
Dim selectStatement As String _
    = "SELECT Invoice.Vendor.Name, Invoice.InvoiceNumber, " _
    & "        Invoice.InvoiceTotal - Invoice.PaymentTotal " _
    & "        - Invoice.CreditTotal AS BalanceDue " _
    & "FROM Invoices AS Invoice " _
    & "WHERE Invoice.InvoiceTotal - Invoice.PaymentTotal " _
    & "        - Invoice.CreditTotal > 0 " _
    & "   AND Invoice.DueDate < @PayDate " _
    & "ORDER BY Invoice.Vendor.Name, " _
    & "            Invoice.InvoiceTotal - Invoice.PaymentTotal " _
    & "        - Invoice.CreditTotal DESC"
```

A Select statement that gets invoice data through the Vendor objects

```
Dim selectStatement As String _
    = "SELECT Vendor.Name, Invoice.InvoiceNumber, " _
    & "        Invoice.InvoiceTotal - Invoice.PaymentTotal " _
    & "        - Invoice.CreditTotal AS BalanceDue " _
    & "FROM Vendors AS Vendor, Vendor.Invoices AS Invoice " _
    & "WHERE Invoice.InvoiceTotal - Invoice.PaymentTotal " _
    & "        - Invoice.CreditTotal > 0 " _
    & "   AND Invoice.DueDate < @PayDate " _
    & "ORDER BY Vendor.Name, " _
    & "            Invoice.InvoiceTotal - Invoice.PaymentTotal " _
    & "        - Invoice.CreditTotal DESC"
```

Code that creates and executes the Select statements

```
Dim invoicesDue As New ObjectQuery(Of DbDataRecord) _
    (selectStatement, payables, MergeOption.NoTracking)
invoicesDue.Parameters.Add(New ObjectParameter("PayDate", payDate))

Dim invoiceDisplay As String = "Vendor Name" & vbTab & vbTab & vbTab _
    & "Invoice No." & vbTab & "Balance Due" & vbCrLf
For Each invoice In invoicesDue
    invoiceDisplay &= invoice("Name").ToString & vbTab & vbTab _
                & IIf(invoice("Name").ToString.Length < 10, _
                        vbTab, "").ToString _
                & IIf(invoice("Name").ToString.Length < 20, _
                        vbTab, "").ToString _
                & invoice("InvoiceNumber").ToString & vbTab _
                & IIf(invoice("InvoiceNumber").ToString.Length < 8, _
                        vbTab, "").ToString _
                & FormatCurrency(CDec(invoice("BalanceDue"))) & vbCrLf
Next
MessageBox.Show(invoiceDisplay, "Vendor Invoice Relationship")
```

Description

- Instead of using joins to retrieve data from two or more tables when you use Entity SQL, you typically use the navigation properties defined by the Entity Data Model that identify the relationships between the entities.

- To refer to objects on the many side of a relationship, you can include the navigation property that identifies the collection in the From clause. Then, you can refer to properties of an object through the alias that's assigned to the collection.

Figure 19-7   How to query across relationships

How to load related objects

You can also load related objects in Entity SQL using techniques that are similar to the techniques you use in LINQ to Entities. These techniques are illustrated in figure 19-8.

The first example in this figure shows how to load related objects using a navigation property in the Select clause of a Select statement. In this case, the statement will retrieve the vendor name and the invoices for the vendor that's identified in the Where clause. Notice that because this statement retrieves a single vendor, the object query is executed using the First method. In addition, because the query returns an anonymous type, the result is stored in a DbDataRecord object. Then, you can retrieve the collection of invoices from this object as shown in the last statement in this example.

Another way to load related objects is to use the Include method with a *query path* that specifies which related objects to load. This works differently than it does for LINQ to Entities because you don't code the Include method in the Select statement. Instead, you code it on the statement that executes the query as shown in the second example in this figure. In this case, the Include method will cause the Invoices for the vendor that's returned by the query to be loaded.

You can also load related objects explicitly using the Load method. To load the collection of objects on the many side of a relationship, you use the Load method of the navigation property that refers to the collection. In the third example in this figure, the Load method is used to load the invoices for a vendor. Notice that before the invoices are loaded, the IsLoaded property is used to determine if they're already loaded. If so, they don't need to be loaded again.

The fourth example is similar except that it loads the object on the one side of a relationship. To do that, it uses the association property that's defined for the object on the many side of the relationship. In this case, the VendorReference property refers to the vendor that's related to an invoice.

An object query that uses a navigation property to load related objects

```
Dim selectStatement As String _
    = "SELECT Vendor.Name, Vendor.Invoices " _
    & "FROM Vendors AS Vendor " _
    & "WHERE Vendor.VendorID = @VendorID"
Dim vendorQuery As New ObjectQuery(Of DbDataRecord) _
    (selectStatement, payables, MergeOption.NoTracking)
vendorQuery.Parameters.Add(New ObjectParameter("VendorID", _
    CInt(txtVendorID.Text)))

Dim selectedVendor As DbDataRecord = vendorQuery.First
Dim invoiceList As List(Of Invoice) _
    = CType(selectedVendor("Invoices"), List(Of Invoice))
```

An object query that uses the Include method to load related objects

```
Dim selectStatement As String _
    = "SELECT VALUE Vendor " _
    & "FROM Vendors AS Vendor " _
    & "WHERE Vendor.VendorID = @VendorID"
Dim vendorQuery As New ObjectQuery(Of Vendor)(selectStatement, payables)
vendorQuery.Parameters.Add(New ObjectParameter("VendorID", _
    CInt(txtVendorID.Text)))

Dim selectedVendor As Vendor = vendorQuery.Include("Invoices").First
```

Code that explicitly loads the objects on the many side of a relationship

```
Dim selectedVendor As Vendor = vendorQuery.First
If Not selectedVendor.Invoices.IsLoaded Then
    selectedVendor.Invoices.Load()
End If
```

Code that explicitly loads the object on the one side of a relationship

```
Dim selectedInvoice As Invoice = invoiceQuery.First
If Not selectedInvoice.VendorReference.IsLoaded Then
    selectedInvoice.VendorReference.Load()
End If
```

Description

- To load entity objects that are related to another entity object, you can use a navigation property in the Entity SQL statement, you can use the Include method of the object query with a query path that specifies the related objects, or you can use the Load method to load the objects explicitly.

- To load the related objects on the many side of a relationship using the Load method, you use the navigation property for the object on the one side of the relationship. To load the related object on the one side of a relationship, you use the association property for the object on the many side of the relationship.

- You can use the IsLoaded property to check whether related objects are already loaded before loading them explicitly.

- To use the Include or Load method, the query must return an entity type.

Figure 19-8   How to load related objects

How to bind controls

Figure 19-9 shows four ways to bind controls to the results of a query. First, you can set the DataSource property of a control to the query results to complex-bind the control. In this example, the results of a query that retrieves vendor IDs and names is bound to a combo box. This technique also requires that you set the DisplayMember property of the combo box, and, in some cases, the ValueMember property.

Notice in this example that the Execute method is used to execute the object query. This method requires an argument that specifies a merge option. Because of that, it isn't necessary to specify a merge option on the constructor for the object query.

The second example is similar, but it assumes that the DataSource property of the combo box is set to a binding source that's generated from an object data source. Then, to display the results of the query in the combo box, the DataSource property of the binding source is set to the query results.

The third example shows how to simple-bind a control to an entity object. Here, the query retrieves a Vendor object with the specified ID. After this query is executed, the binding source for the controls that will be used to display the properties of the Vendor object is cleared. Then, the Vendor object is added to the list of bound objects for the bindings. That causes the properties of the Vendor object to be displayed in the bound controls.

The fourth example shows how to complex-bind a control so it displays the collection of objects related to another object. In this case, the Invoice objects related to a Vendor object are displayed. To do that, the invoices are loaded if necessary. Then, the DataSource property of the binding source for the control that displays the invoices is set to the Invoices navigation property of the Vendor object.

Code that binds a combo box to the results of a query

```
Dim selectStatement As String _
    = "SELECT Vendor.VendorID, Vendor.Name " _
    & "FROM Vendors AS Vendor " _
    & "ORDER BY Vendor.Name"

Dim vendors As New ObjectQuery(Of DbDataRecord)(selectStatement, payables)

NameComboBox.DataSource = vendors.Execute(MergeOption.NoTracking)
NameComboBox.DisplayMember = "Name"
NameComboBox.ValueMember = "VendorID"
```

A statement that binds a combo box using its binding source

```
VendorBindingSource.DataSource = vendors.Execute(MergeOption.NoTracking)
```

Code that binds text boxes to an entity object

```
Dim selectStatement As String _
    = "SELECT VALUE Vendor " _
    & "FROM Vendors AS Vendor " _
    & "WHERE Vendor.VendorID = @VendorID"

Dim vendorQuery As New ObjectQuery(Of Vendor) _
    (selectStatement, payables, MergeOption.OverwriteChanges)
vendorQuery.Parameters.Add(New ObjectParameter("VendorID", _
    CInt(NameComboBox.SelectedValue)))

Dim selectedVendor As Vendor = vendorQuery.First

VendorBindingSource.Clear()
VendorBindingSource.Add(selectedVendor)
```

Code that binds a control to related objects

```
If Not selectedVendor.Invoices.IsLoaded Then
    selectedVendor.Invoices.Load()
End If

InvoiceBindingSource.DataSource = selectedVendor.Invoices
```

Description

- You can complex-bind a control to the results of a query by setting the DataSource property of the control or the binding source associated with the control to the results. You can also complex-bind a control to an entity collection as shown in chapter 18.

- You can simple-bind controls that are created from an object data source to the properties of an entity object by clearing the binding source for the controls and then adding the object to the list of bound objects for the binding source.

- To display the objects on the many side of a one-to-many relationship, you can set the DataSource property of a control or the binding source associated with the control to the navigation property of the object on the one side. Before you do that, you must load the related objects.

Figure 19-9   How to bind controls

A Vendor Invoices application

Now that you've seen how to retrieve data using Entity SQL, you're ready to see how to use Entity SQL in an application. In the topics that follow, then, I'll present an application that displays vendor invoices.

The user interface

Figure 19-10 presents the user interface for the Vendor Invoices application. As you can see, the Vendor Invoices form includes a combo box that lets the user select a vendor. Then, the address information for that vendor is displayed in the text boxes on the form, and the invoices for that vendor are displayed in the DataGridView control.

The Entity Data Model

Figure 19-10 also presents the Entity Data Model for this application. It includes just Vendor and Invoice entities. Note that I changed the names of these entities as well as the name of the navigation property in the Invoice entity after the Entity Data Model was generated. I also changed the entity set names for the entities to Vendors and Invoices.

Although you can't tell from the user interface and object model, this application uses two object data sources for the Vendor and Invoice entities. I used the Vendor entity to generate the combo box and text boxes along with a Vendor binding source, and I used the Invoice entity to generate the DataGridView control along with an Invoice binding source. That way, I was able to set the DisplayMember and ValueMember properties of the combo box at design time, and I was able to format the DataGridView control so it looked the way I wanted it to. (Remember from chapter 4 that if you bind a combo box this way, you need to remove the binding from the Text property of the combo box. Otherwise, the combo box won't work correctly.)

The Vendor Invoices form

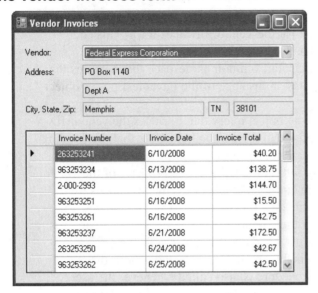

The Entity Data Model

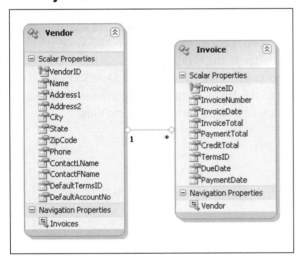

Description

- When the user selects a vendor from the combo box, the vendor address is displayed in the text boxes and the invoices for the vendor are displayed in the DataGridView control.

- The Entity Data Model for this application consists of just Vendor and Invoice entities. The entity and navigation property names have been modified as shown above. In addition, the entity set names have been changed to Vendors and Invoices.

- This application uses two object data sources that were created from the Vendor and Invoice entities. The Vendor entity is used to generate the combo box and text boxes on the form, and the Invoice entity is used to generate the DataGridView control.

Figure 19-10   The user interface and Entity Data Model for the Vendor Invoices application

The code for the Vendor Invoices form

Figure 19-11 presents the code for the Vendor Invoices form. This code starts by importing the System.Data.Objects namespace that contains the ObjectQuery class and the System.Data.Common namespace that contains the DbDataRecord class. Then, it creates an instance of the PayablesEntities object context.

When the form is first loaded, an object query that retrieves the vendor ID and names for all the vendors is bound to the combo box. Note that this binding is accomplished by setting the DataSource property of the combo box to the results of the query rather than by setting the DataSource property of the Vendor binding source to the results of the query. That's because the text boxes use the Vendor binding source to display the data for the selected vendor, so you don't want to use this binding source for the combo box.

After binding the combo box, the Load event handler calls the GetVendorInvoices procedure to display the invoices for the vendor that's selected in the combo box. This procedure is also called whenever the user selects a different vendor. It starts by getting the vendor ID of the selected vendor from the combo box. Then, it defines and executes a query that retrieves the vendor with that ID.

Next, this procedure uses the Load method to load the invoices for the selected vendor if they haven't already been loaded. Then, it clears the Vendor binding source and adds the selected vendor to the binding source so the vendor's address is displayed in the text boxes. Finally, it sets the DataSource property of the Invoice binding source to the Invoices property of the selected vendor so the invoices for that vendor are displayed in the DataGridView control.

The code for the Vendor Invoices form

```
Imports System.Data.Objects
Imports System.Data.Common

Public Class Form1

    Dim payables As New PayablesEntities

    Private Sub Form1_Load(ByVal sender As System.Object, _
            ByVal e As System.EventArgs) Handles MyBase.Load
        RemoveHandler NameComboBox.SelectedIndexChanged, _
            AddressOf NameComboBox_SelectedIndexChanged

        Dim selectStatement As String _
            = "SELECT Vendor.VendorID, Vendor.Name " _
            & "FROM Vendors AS Vendor " _
            & "ORDER BY Vendor.Name"
        Dim vendors As New ObjectQuery(Of DbDataRecord) _
            (selectStatement, payables)

        NameComboBox.DataSource = vendors.Execute(MergeOption.NoTracking)

        Me.GetVendorInvoices()
        AddHandler NameComboBox.SelectedIndexChanged, _
            AddressOf NameComboBox_SelectedIndexChanged
    End Sub

    Private Sub NameComboBox_SelectedIndexChanged( _
            ByVal sender As System.Object, ByVal e As System.EventArgs) _
            Handles NameComboBox.SelectedIndexChanged
        Me.GetVendorInvoices()
    End Sub

    Private Sub GetVendorInvoices()
        Try
            Dim vendorID As Integer = CInt(NameComboBox.SelectedValue)
            Dim selectStatement As String _
                = "SELECT VALUE Vendor " _
                & "FROM Vendors AS Vendor " _
                & "WHERE Vendor.VendorID = @VendorID"
            Dim vendorQuery As New ObjectQuery(Of Vendor) _
                (selectStatement, payables, MergeOption.NoTracking)
            vendorQuery.Parameters.Add(New ObjectParameter("VendorID", _
                vendorID))

            Dim selectedVendor As Vendor = vendorQuery.First
            If Not selectedVendor.Invoices.IsLoaded Then
                selectedVendor.Invoices.Load()
            End If
            VendorBindingSource.Clear()
            VendorBindingSource.Add(selectedVendor)
            InvoiceBindingSource.DataSource = selectedVendor.Invoices
        Catch ex As Exception
            MessageBox.Show(ex.Message, ex.GetType.ToString)
        End Try
    End Sub
End Class
```

Figure 19-11   The code for the Vendor Invoices form

Additional skills for using Entity SQL

Although you'll typically use the techniques you've already learned in this chapter to work with Entity SQL, you can also use two additional techniques. I'll introduce you to those techniques in the last two topics of this chapter.

How to work directly with the EntityClient data provider

When you execute an object query as shown earlier in this chapter, the query is first processed by Object Services and then passed to the EntityClient data provider. However, you can also bypass Object Services and work directly with the EntityClient data provider. To do that, you use connection, command, parameter, and data reader objects just like you do when you use the SQL Server data provider. Figure 19-12 illustrates how this works.

The table at the top of this figure lists the basic classes for working with the EntityClient data provider, and the example shows how to use three of these classes. To start, an EntityConnection object is created by naming a connection string that's stored in the App.Config file. You may recall from chapter 17 that you can store the connection string in this file when you use the Entity Data Model wizard to create an Entity Data Model. If you don't store the connection string in the App.Config file, you have to specify the actual connection settings when you create the EntityConnection object.

After the EntityConnection object is created, a string that contains the Select statement to be executed is declared. Notice that the From clause of this statement names the object context that contains the entity collection. Once the Select statement is declared, an EntityCommand object for that statement and the connection is created, and the connection is opened.

Next, an EntityDataReader object is created by executing the ExecuteReader method of the entity command. Note the command behavior that's specified on this method. As its name implies, it provides sequential access to the data that's returned by the query. This behavior is required when you create a data reader from an entity command.

After the data reader is created, the Read method is executed as the condition on a Do loop. Within the Do loop, each record is retrieved as an IExtendedDataRecord object. Then, the number of fields in the record is retrieved, and the name and value of each field is displayed. Finally, the connection is closed.

Common classes for working with the EntityClient data provider

Class	Description
EntityConnection	Establishes a connection to the underlying data source of an Entity Data Model.
EntityCommand	Represents an Entity SQL statement or a stored procedure that can be executed against an Entity Data Model.
EntityParameter	Identifies a variable used in the Entity SQL statement.
EntityDataReader	Provides read-only, forward-only access to the data in the underlying data source of an Entity Data Model.

Code that retrieves data using the EntityClient data provider

```
Dim entityConnection As New EntityConnection("name=PayablesEntities")

Dim selectStatement As String _
    = "SELECT Vendor.Name, Vendor.Address1, Vendor.Address2, " _
    & "        Vendor.City, Vendor.State, Vendor.ZipCode " _
    & "FROM PayablesEntities.Vendors AS Vendor " _
    & "ORDER BY Vendor.Name"
Dim entityCommand As New EntityCommand(selectStatement, entityConnection)
entityConnection.Open()

Dim reader As EntityDataReader = _
    entityCommand.ExecuteReader(CommandBehavior.SequentialAccess)
Do While reader.Read
    Dim vendorDisplay As String = ""
    Dim vendorRecord As IExtendedDataRecord _
        = CType(reader, IExtendedDataRecord)
    Dim fieldCount As Integer _
        = vendorRecord.DataRecordInfo.FieldMetadata.Count
    For fieldIndex As Integer = 0 To fieldCount - 1
        vendorDisplay &= vendorRecord.GetName(fieldIndex) & ": "
        If vendorRecord.IsDBNull(fieldIndex) = False Then
            vendorDisplay &= vendorRecord.GetValue(fieldIndex).ToString
        End If
        vendorDisplay &= vbCrLf
    Next
    MessageBox.Show(vendorDisplay, "Vendor Record")
Loop
entityConnection.Close()
```

Description

- Instead of using Object Services to execute queries against an Entity Data Model, you can work directly with the EntityClient data provider. To do that, you use the classes listed above. These classes are members of the System.Data.EntityClient namespace.

- To define a connection, you can specify the name of the object context for the Entity Data Model on the constructor of the EntityConnection class. You must also include the name of the object context on the entity set name in the From clause of the Select statement.

- The technique you use to retrieve data from the EntityDataReader object depends on the type of data that's returned. For more information, see the Visual Studio documentation.

Figure 19-12   How to work directly with the EntityClient data provider

How to use query builder methods

Another technique for querying an Entity Data Model is to use *query builder methods*. When you use this technique, you create an object query by executing methods that are equivalent to Entity SQL clauses. Figure 19-13 shows how this works.

The table at the top of this figure lists some of the Entity SQL clauses and the corresponding object builder methods. Then, the examples that follow show how to use some of these methods. As you review these examples, you should realize that each query builder method returns an ObjectQuery(Of T) object. Because of that, you can use the results of these methods in subsequent queries.

The first example in this figure shows how to code a separate query for each query builder method. The first query in this example retrieves the InvoiceNumber and InvoiceTotal properties from the Invoices collection of the PayablesEntities context. Here, the string *it* is an alias that represents the object of the current query. In this case, it refers to the invoices in the Invoices collection.

If you want to, you can change the name you use to refer to the query command. To do that, you set the Name property of the object query. Here, the name of the first object query, named invoices, is changed to Invoice.

The second query in this example uses the Where method to select only those invoices with invoice totals greater than $5000. Notice that the source of data for this query is the invoices query. Also notice that because I set the Name property of the invoices query to Invoice, I used that name instead of it to refer to the InvoiceTotal property. Then, I set the Name property of this object query, named largeInvoices, to LargeInvoice.

The third query is similar. It uses the OrderBy method to sort the results of the largeInvoices query by invoice total, and it uses the name LargeInvoice to refer to the InvoiceTotal property.

The second example in this figure shows how you can combine query builder methods in a single statement. This query retrieves the same data as the three queries in the first example. In most cases, this is the technique you'll use when you code queries using query builder methods.

The third example shows how to execute the query in the second example. Because this query returns DbDataRecord objects, you use the same technique shown earlier in this chapter for working with anonymous types.

You can also use this code to execute any of the queries in the first example by changing the query name in the For Each statement. Note that because the second query uses the results of the first query, the first query will be executed when you execute the second query. Similarly, the first and second queries will be executed when you execute the third query.

Query builder methods used to implement common Entity SQL clauses

Clause	Method
SELECT	Select, SelectValue
WHERE	Where
ORDER BY	OrderBy

A sequence of queries that use query builder methods

```
Dim payables As New PayablesEntities

Dim invoices As ObjectQuery(Of DbDataRecord) _
    = payables.Invoices.Select("it.InvoiceNumber, it.InvoiceTotal")
invoices.Name = "Invoice"

Dim largeInvoices As ObjectQuery(Of DbDataRecord) _
    = invoices.Where("Invoice.InvoiceTotal > 5000")
largeInvoices.Name = "LargeInvoice"

Dim sortedInvoices As ObjectQuery(Of DbDataRecord) _
    = largeInvoices.OrderBy("LargeInvoice.InvoiceTotal")
```

A query that combines the query builder methods

```
Dim payables As New PayablesEntities

Dim invoiceTotals As ObjectQuery(Of DbDataRecord) _
    = payables.Invoices.Select("it.InvoiceNumber, it.InvoiceTotal") _
                    .Where("it.InvoiceTotal > 5000") _
                    .OrderBy("it.InvoiceTotal")
```

Code that executes the query

```
Dim invoiceDisplay As String _
    = "Invoice No." & vbTab & "Invoice Total" & vbCrLf
For Each invoice In invoiceTotals
    invoiceDisplay &= invoice("InvoiceNumber").ToString & vbTab _
                & IIf(invoice("InvoiceNumber").ToString.Length <= 8, _
                    vbTab, "").ToString _
                & FormatCurrency(CDec(invoice("InvoiceTotal"))) & vbCrLf
Next
MessageBox.Show(invoiceDisplay, "Invoice Totals Over $5000")
```

Description

- *Query builder methods* provide a way to code an object query using a syntax that's similar to the syntax you use to code a LINQ query with extension methods.
- Each query builder method returns a new ObjectQuery(Of T) object. That means that you can combine the methods so that each method performs a query on the previous query results.
- The string *it* is an alias that represents the object of the current query. If you want to, you can set the Name property of an object query and then use that name instead of it in any subsequent queries.

Figure 19-13   How to use query builder methods

Perspective

As you've seen in this chapter, Entity SQL is more difficult to use than LINQ to Entities because you have to code the Select statements to be executed as strings. That means that you can't take advantage of IntelliSense, and the syntax of the Select statement isn't checked until runtime. Even so, the techniques presented in this chapter are good to know if you ever need to write a query that can't be written using LINQ to Entities.

Terms

Transact-SQL
object query
query builder method

Exercise 19-1   Develop the Vendor Invoices application

In this exercise, you'll develop the Vendor Invoices application presented in this chapter. That will show you how to build a simple application that uses Entity SQL.

Create the Entity Data Model for the application

1. Start a new application named VendorInvoices in your chapter 19 directory.

2. Use the Entity Data Model Wizard to create an Entity Data Model that includes the Vendors and Invoices tables from the Payables database. Change the entity and entity set names and navigation property names as described in figure 19-10.

Create and use the object data sources for the application

3. Use the Data Source Configuration Wizard as shown in the last chapter to create object data sources for the Vendor and Invoice entities in the Entity Data Model you just created.

4. In the Data Sources window, change the default control for the Vendor entity to Detail, and change the default control for the Name property to a combo box. Then, drag the vendor entity to the form and delete the navigation toolbar that's generated.

5. Set the binding properties for the combo box so the value of the Name property is displayed in the control and the value of the ID property is stored in the control. In addition, set the DropDownStyle property of the control to DropDownList, and remove the binding from the Text property of the control.

6. Drag the Invoice entity from the Data Sources window to the form to generate a DataGridView control.

7. Make the necessary adjustments to the form and its controls so the form looks like the one shown in figure 19-10.

Add code to load the combo box

8. Start an event handler for the Load event of the form. Then, create an instance of the Payables object context and store it in a variable that's declared at the class level.

9. Code a Select statement in the Load event handler that will retrieve the VendorID and Name columns from the Vendors table and sort the results by the Name column. Then, code an object query that uses the Select statement. This object query will return an anonymous type.

10. Code a statement that executes the query and assigns the results to the DataSource property of the combo box. Be sure to specify that no tracking is to be performed since the data won't be modified.

11. Run the application. At this point, the combo box list should include all the vendor names. However, the address and invoices for the selected vendor won't be displayed.

Add code to display the vendor and invoice data

12. Add a procedure named GetVendorInvoices that uses an object query to get the vendor that's selected in the combo box. To do that, you'll need to code an object query that uses a parameter to return a Vendor entity. This query should not use tracking. Bind the results of the query to the text boxes on the form.

13. Add code to the procedure that loads the invoices for the vendor if they're not already loaded and then binds those invoices to the DataGridView control. Call this procedure from the Load event handler and from the event handler for the SelectedIndexChanged event of the combo box.

14. Add a RemoveHandler statement at the beginning of the Load event handler that prevents the SelectedIndexChanged event of the combo box from firing as the combo box is loaded. Then, add an AddHandler statement to rewire this event at the end of the Load event handler.

15. Run the application again. This time, the address information should be displayed for the first vendor. In addition, if the vendor has any invoices, those invoices should be displayed in the DataGridView control.

16. Select a different vendor such as IBM to be sure that the correct invoices are displayed. When you're sure this is working correctly, end the application and close the solution.

20

How to use Entity data source controls with web applications

In the last three chapters, you learned how to create an Entity Data Model, use LINQ to Entities and Entity SQL to retrieve data using an Entity Data Model, and insert, update, and delete data using an Entity Data Model. Although the techniques presented in those chapters were for Windows application, you can use many of the same techniques in a web application.

To make it easy to work with an Entity Data Model, however, ASP.NET 3.5 provides an Entity data source control. You'll learn the basic skills for using Entity data source controls in this chapter.

Note that this chapter assumes that you already know how to develop web applications with Visual Studio and ASP.NET. It also assumes that you know how to work with data source controls such as the SQL Server data source control. If you don't have these skills, you can get them by reading our book, *Murach's ASP.NET 3.5 Web Programming with VB 2008*.

An introduction to the Entity data source control

When you use the Entity data source control, it uses Entity SQL in the form of query builder methods to work with an Entity Data Model. So before you create an Entity data source control, you need to define the Entity Data Model you want to work with as shown in chapter 17. Then, you can create an Entity data source control as shown in the topics that follow.

How the Entity data source control works

When you use an Entity data source control, you don't code queries directly. Instead, you assign values to the attributes of the control that identify the data you want to retrieve. This is illustrated in the example at the top of figure 20-1. Here, an Entity data source control provides the data for a drop-down list.

The ConnectionString attribute provides the connection string that's used to execute the query against the database. In most cases, this attribute just names the connection string that was stored in the web.config file when the Entity Data Model was created. Then, the DefaultContainerName attribute names the container class in the Entity Data Model that should be used to create the object context, and the EntitySetName attribute names the entity set whose data will be displayed in the control.

The EntityTypeFilter attribute comes into play only if your Entity Data Model uses inheritance. In that case, this attribute can name a specific derived type you want to work with.

The Select and OrderBy attributes are equivalent to the Select and OrderBy query builder methods. The Select attribute identifies the columns that will be included in the query results, and the OrderBy attribute indicates how the results are sorted. In this case, the VendorID and Name columns from the Vendors table will be included in the results, and the results will be sorted by the Name column.

In addition to these attributes, you can use the Where attribute to filter the rows that are retrieved, you can use the GroupBy attribute to group the rows that are retrieved, you can use the EnableInsert, EnableUpdate, and EnableDelete attributes to provide for inserting, updating, and deleting rows, and you can use the AutoPage and AutoSort attributes to provide for sorting and paging. You'll learn how to use some of these attributes later in this chapter.

A drop-down list that's bound to an Entity data source control

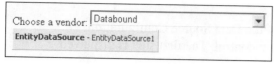

The code for the drop-down list and the Entity data source control

```
<asp:DropDownList ID="DropDownList1" runat="server"
    DataSourceID="EntityDataSource1" DataTextField="Name"
    DataValueField="VendorID" Width="250px">
</asp:DropDownList>
<asp:EntityDataSource ID="EntityDataSource1" runat="server"
    ConnectionString="name=PayablesEntities"
    DefaultContainerName="PayablesEntities" EntitySetName="Vendors"
    EntityTypeFilter="" OrderBy="it.[Name]"
    Select="it.[VendorID], it.[Name]">
</asp:EntityDataSource>
```

Basic attributes of the Entity data source control

Attribute	Description
ID	The ID of the control.
Runat	Must specify "server."
ConnectionString	The connection string used to execute the query.
DefaultContainerName	The name of the container class that defines the object context for the control.
EntitySetName	The name of the entity set that will be used by the control.
EntityTypeFilter	The name of the derived type that will be used by the control.
Select	Identifies the data to be included in the query results. If this attribute is omitted, all the columns in the data source are included in the query results.
Where	Specifies the conditions that must be met for a row to be retrieved from the data source. If this attribute is omitted, all the rows are retrieved.
OrderBy	Indicates how the elements that are retrieved by the query are sorted.
GroupBy	Indicates how the elements that are retrieved by the query are grouped.
EnableInsert	Indicates if the control provides for inserting data. The default is False.
EnableUpdate	Indicates if the control provides for updating data. The default is False.
EnableDelete	Indicates if the control provides for deleting data. The default is False.
AutoPage	Indicates if the control provides for paging. The default is True.
AutoSort	Indicates if the control provides for sorting. The default is True.

Description

- The Entity data source control uses Entity SQL to work with the data in an Entity Data Model.

- The Entity data source control names the container class that defines the object context and the entity set you want to work with, identifies the data to be retrieved, specifies how the data is sorted and grouped, and indicates whether the control will provide for insert, update, delete, paging, and sorting operations.

Figure 20-1   How the Entity data source control works

How to configure an Entity data source control

Figure 20-2 shows you the two steps of the Data Source Configuration Wizard for configuring an Entity data source control. The first step is displayed when you drag an EntityDataSource control from the Toolbox to a form and then select Configure Data Source from its smart tag menu. This step lets you configure the object context you want to use with the control by identifying the connection string and the container name. In most cases, you'll use a connection string that's stored in the web.config file by selecting its name from the drop-down list as shown here. However, you can also enter your own connection string settings.

The second step of the wizard lets you identify the data you want to retrieve. To start, you select an entity set from the first drop-down list. In addition, if the entity type has other types that are derived from it, you can select the entity type you want to retrieve from the EntityTypeFilter drop-down list. Then, all the scalar properties that are defined for the entity type are listed in the Select list, and you can select the ones you want to retrieve. In this example, I selected the InvoiceNumber, InvoiceDate, and InvoiceTotal properties. You can also retrieve all the columns by checking the Select All option, which is the default. Finally, you can set options that determine whether the control provides for inserts, updates, and deletes. You'll learn more about that later in this chapter.

By the way, you can also start the Data Source Configuration Wizard using the Choose Data Source command in the smart tag menu of a bindable control. Then, when the Choose a Data Source Type dialog box is displayed, you can select the Entity icon and click the OK button to display the first dialog box shown here.

The Data Source Configuration Wizard

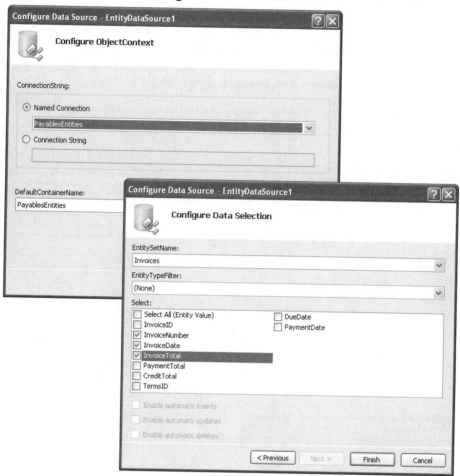

Description

- You can use the Data Source Configuration Wizard to configure an Entity data source control by choosing Configure Data Source from its smart tag menu.

- The Configure ObjectContext step of the wizard lets you select a named connection that's stored in the web.config file or enter the connection string settings. It also lets you select the container class in the Entity Data Model you want to use.

- The Configure Data Selection step of the wizard lets you select the entity set and properties you want to retrieve. By default, the Select All (Entity Value) check box is selected, which means that all the properties will be retrieved.

- The Enable Automatic Inserts, Enable Automatic Updates, and Enable Automatic Deletes check boxes are available only if the Select All check box is selected.

Figure 20-2   How to configure an Entity data source control

An Invoice Display application

Figure 20-3 presents an Invoice Display application that displays the list of invoices in a GridView control. This control is bound to an Entity data source control that uses an Entity Data Model that includes just an Invoice entity. The Entity data source control is configured as shown in figure 20-2.

The Invoice Display application

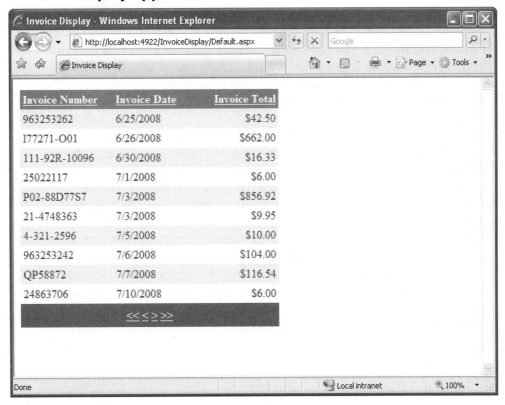

Description

- The Invoice Display application uses a GridView control that's bound to an Entity data source control. The Entity data source control retrieves selected columns from all the invoices in the Invoices table.

- Because the query returns a projection and paging is enabled, a sort expression must be specified. In this case, the invoices are sorted by invoice date.

- The Entity data source control uses an Entity Data Model that includes a single entity type named Invoice. The Invoice entity is mapped to the Invoices table of the Payables database.

Figure 20-3   An Invoice Display application

The aspx file for the Invoice Display application

Figure 20-4 presents the aspx code for the Invoice Display application. The first thing you should notice here is that the page includes a Register directive. This directive contains information about the Entity data source control, including its namespace, the assembly that contains the control, and the tag prefix that's used to refer to the namespace. This code is generated for you automatically.

The next thing you should notice is the definition of the Entity data source control. As you can see, it retrieves data using the Invoices entity set in the PayablesEntities container class. The Select attribute indicates that only the invoice number, invoice date, and invoice total will be retrieved, and the OrderBy attribute indicates that the rows that are returned will be sorted by invoice date.

Because no values are specified for the AutoPage and AutoSort attributes of the Entity data source control, the control provides for paging and sorting by default. If you look at the definition of the GridView control, you'll see that it provides for paging and sorting as well. Note, however, that because the query returns a projection, a sort expression must be specified on the OrderBy attribute for paging to work. That's why I sorted the invoices by invoice date.

The Default.aspx file

```
<%@ Page Language="VB" AutoEventWireup="false" CodeFile="Default.aspx.vb"
Inherits="_Default" %>

<%@ Register assembly="System.Web.Entity, Version=3.5.0.0, Culture=neutral,
PublicKeyToken=b77a5c561934e089" namespace="System.Web.UI.WebControls"
tagprefix="asp" %>

<!DOCTYPE html PUBLIC "-//W3C//DTD XHTML 1.0 Transitional//EN" "http://
www.w3.org/TR/xhtml1/DTD/xhtml1-transitional.dtd">

<html xmlns="http://www.w3.org/1999/xhtml">
<head runat="server">
    <title>Invoice Display</title>
</head>
<body>
    <form id="form1" runat="server">
    <div>
        <asp:GridView ID="GridView1" runat="server" AllowPaging="True"
            AllowSorting="True" AutoGenerateColumns="False" CellPadding="4"
            DataSourceID="EntityDataSource1" ForeColor="#333333"
            GridLines="None">
        <Columns>
            <asp:BoundField DataField="InvoiceNumber"
                HeaderText="Invoice Number" ReadOnly="True"
                SortExpression="InvoiceNumber" >
                <HeaderStyle HorizontalAlign="Left" Width="125px" />
            </asp:BoundField>
            <asp:BoundField DataField="InvoiceDate"
                HeaderText="Invoice Date" ReadOnly="True"
                SortExpression="InvoiceDate" DataFormatString="{0:d}" >
                <HeaderStyle HorizontalAlign="Left" Width="110px" />
            </asp:BoundField>
            <asp:BoundField DataField="InvoiceTotal"
                HeaderText="Invoice Total" SortExpression="InvoiceTotal"
                DataFormatString="{0:c}" ReadOnly="True" >
                <HeaderStyle HorizontalAlign="Right" Width="110px" />
                <ItemStyle HorizontalAlign="Right" />
            </asp:BoundField>
        </Columns>
        <HeaderStyle BackColor="#507CD1" Font-Bold="True"
         ForeColor="White" />
        <PagerSettings Mode="NextPreviousFirstLast" />
        <RowStyle BackColor="#EFF3FB" />
        <AlternatingRowStyle BackColor="White" />
        <PagerStyle BackColor="#2461BF" ForeColor="White"
         HorizontalAlign="Center" />
        </asp:GridView>
        <asp:EntityDataSource ID="EntityDataSource1" runat="server"
            ConnectionString="name=PayablesEntities"
            DefaultContainerName="PayablesEntities" EntitySetName="Invoices"
            OrderBy="it.[InvoiceDate]"
            Select="it.[InvoiceNumber], it.[InvoiceDate], it.[InvoiceTotal]">
        </asp:EntityDataSource>
    </div>
    </form>
</body>
</html>
```

Figure 20-4   The aspx file for the Invoice Display application

How to use the Expression Editor

Because the Data Source Configuration Wizard is limited in what it can do, you'll typically need to modify the Entity data source controls it generates. Although you can do that by setting the properties of the control in the Properties window or by editing the aspx code directly, it's easier to use the Expression Editor to enter more complex expressions. You'll see how to use this editor in the topics that follow.

How to filter the results of a query

Figure 20-5 shows how to use the Expression Editor to specify the filter condition for a query. To do that, you start by entering a Where expression like the one shown here. This expression consists of a compound condition that uses the And operator. The first condition checks the value of the VendorID property of the Vendor entity. To do that, it uses the Vendor navigation property of the Invoice entity, referred to in this expression as *it*. This property is compared to the value of a parameter named @VendorID to see if the two are equal. Then, the second condition checks that the invoice has a balance due.

Notice that the property names in this expression aren't enclosed in square brackets like the others you've seen in this chapter. When you use the Data Source Configuration Wizard to create an Entity data source control, it includes the brackets in the code it generates. When you enter your own expressions, though, you can usually omit the brackets.

If a Where expression uses parameters, you can use the controls in the bottom portion of the Expression Editor dialog box to define those parameters. To add a parameter, you click the Add Parameter button and then enter the name of the parameter in the name column of the Parameters box. Then, you select a value from the first drop-down list to indicate where the value of the parameter will come from. Some of the options are a control, a profile, and a query string. The remaining controls in the Expression Editor change depending on which option you choose.

In this example, I indicated that the source of data is a control. Then, I selected the control from the second drop-down list. Because the source control is a drop-down list, the value of the parameter was automatically set to the SelectedValue property of the control. If that's not what you want, you can click the Show Advanced Properties link to display all the properties for the parameter and then change the Value property. You may also need to select a value for the Type or DbType property to indicate the type of the parameter.

The aspx code that's generated for this Where expression is shown below the Expression Editor dialog box. Notice that in addition to the Where attribute, a ControlParameter element is defined within a WhereParameters element. This element defines the parameter that's used by the Where expression.

The Expression Editor for filtering the results of a query

The aspx code for the Where attribute and parameter

```
<asp:EntityDataSource ID="EntityDataSource2" runat="server"
    .
    .
    Where="it.Vendor.VendorID = @VendorID AND
            it.InvoiceTotal - it.PaymentTotal - it.CreditTotal &gt; 0">
    <WhereParameters>
        <asp:ControlParameter ControlID="ddlVendor" Name="VendorID"
            PropertyName="SelectedValue" Type="Int32" />
    </WhereParameters>
</asp:EntityDataSource>
```

Description

- To display the Expression Editor for filtering the results of a query, click the button with the ellipsis on it that appears when you select the Where property for the Entity data source control in the Properties window.

- To filter the results of a query, enter one or more conditions in the Where Expression text box.

- If an expression uses a parameter, click the Add Parameter button to add a parameter, enter a name for the parameter, and then define the parameter using the controls that appear to the right of the Parameters list.

- To set the type of a parameter, click the Show Advanced Properties link to display all the properties for the parameter and then set the Type or DbType property.

- If a parameter refers to a property of the entity type and has the same name as that property, you can select the Automatically Generate check box to have the Entity data source control generate the Where expression automatically.

Figure 20-5   How to filter the results of a query

Instead of entering a Where expression as shown here, you can let the Entity data source control generate it for you in some cases. That works if the Where expression simply checks that one or more properties of the entity type are equal to parameters with the same names. If you wanted to retrieve all the invoices for a given date, for example, you could just define a parameter named InvoiceDate. Then, you could select the check box at the top of the Expression Editor to have the Where expression generated based on that parameter.

How to sort the results of a query

Figure 20-6 shows the Expression Editor for sorting the results of a query. As you can see, it's almost identical to the Expression Editor you saw in the last figure for filtering the results of a query. To use it, you start by entering an OrderBy expression. Then, if the expression contains one or more parameters, you enter those parameters just as you do for a filter condition. You can also generate an OrderBy expression from the parameters you specify by selecting the check box at the top of the Expression Editor dialog box. In most cases, though, you won't use parameters in an OrderBy expression.

The OrderBy expression in this figure will sort the results by two properties: BalanceDue in descending sequence within DueDate. You can see the code that's generated for this expression in the example in this figure. It simply assigns the expression to the OrderBy attribute of the Entity data source control.

The Expression Editor for sorting the results of a query

The aspx code for the OrderBy attribute

```
<asp:EntityDataSource ID="EntityDataSource2" runat="server"
    .
    .
    OrderBy="it.DueDate, it.BalanceDue DESC"
    .
    .
</asp:EntityDataSource>
```

Description

- To display the Expression Editor for sorting the results of a query, click the button with the ellipsis on it that appears when you select the OrderBy property for the Entity data source control in the Properties window.

- To sort the results of a query, enter a sort expression in the OrderBy Expression text box.

- If an expression uses a parameter, click the Add Parameter button to add a parameter, enter a name for the parameter, and then define the parameter using the controls that appear to the right of the Parameters list.

- If a sort expression uses a parameter that refers to a property of the entity type and has the same name as that property, you can select the Automatically Generate check box to have the Entity data source control generate the OrderBy expression automatically.

Figure 20-6   How to sort the results of a query

How to select the data returned by a query

Figure 20-7 shows the Expression Editor you use to select the data you want a query to return. It lets you enter an expression and define parameters just like the Expression Editors for filtering and sorting data. Notice, however, that the Select expression can't be generated automatically.

The Select expression shown here retrieves four properties and a calculated value that's given the alias BalanceDue. This expression is assigned to the Select attribute of the Entity data source control as you can see in the code example. Then, when a control is bound to this data source control, it can display any of the items included in the Select expression, including the calculated value.

The Expression Editor for selecting the data returned by a query

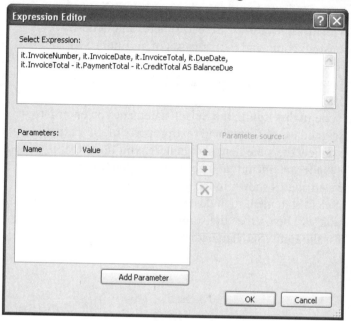

The aspx code for the Select attribute

```
<asp:EntityDataSource ID="EntityDataSource2" runat="server"
    .
    .
    Select="it.InvoiceNumber, it.InvoiceDate, it.InvoiceTotal,
           it.DueDate, it.InvoiceTotal - it.PaymentTotal
         - it.CreditTotal AS BalanceDue"
    .
    .
</asp:EntityDataSource>
```

Description

- To display the Expression Editor for selecting the data returned by a query, click the button with the ellipsis on it that appears when you select the Select property for the Entity data source control in the Properties window.
- To select the results of a query, enter an expression in the Select Expression text box.
- If an expression uses a parameter, click the Add Parameter button to add a parameter, enter a name for the parameter, and then define the parameter using the controls that appear to the right of the Parameters list.

Figure 20-7   How to select the data returned by a query

How to specify a custom command

Instead of coding individual values for the Select, Where, and OrderBy attributes, you can code a custom command that consists of an Entity SQL statement. To do that, you use the Expression Editor shown in figure 20-8. This Expression Editor lets you enter a Select statement and define any parameters used by that statement.

As you can see in the code in this figure, the Select statement you enter into the Expression Editor is assigned to the CommandText property of the Entity data source control. If you review the statement shown here, you'll see that it will retrieve the same data as the statement that's generated if you use the Select, Where, and OrderBy attributes shown in the previous figures. Note, however, that because the Select statement includes a From clause that specifies the name of the entity set that will be used as the source of data for the query, you don't specify a value for the EntitySetName attribute.

The Expression Editor for specifying a custom command

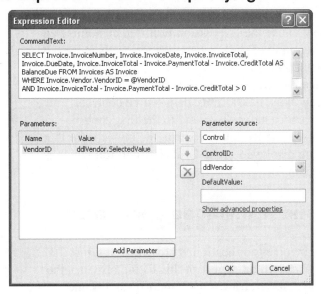

The code for the Entity data source control

```
<asp:EntityDataSource ID="EntityDataSource2" runat="server"
    ConnectionString="name=PayablesEntities"
    DefaultContainerName="PayablesEntities" AutoPage="False"
    CommandText="SELECT Invoice.InvoiceNumber, Invoice.InvoiceDate,
                    Invoice.InvoiceTotal, Invoice.DueDate,
                    Invoice.InvoiceTotal - Invoice.PaymentTotal
                 - Invoice.CreditTotal AS BalanceDue
            FROM Invoices AS Invoice
            WHERE Invoice.Vendor.VendorID = @VendorID
              AND Invoice.InvoiceTotal - Invoice.PaymentTotal
                 - Invoice.CreditTotal &gt; 0
            ORDER BY Invoice.DueDate, Invoice.InvoiceTotal
                    - Invoice.PaymentTotal - Invoice.CreditTotal DESC">
    <CommandParameters>
        <asp:ControlParameter ControlID="ddlVendor" DbType="Int32"
            Name="VendorID" PropertyName="SelectedValue" />
    </CommandParameters>
</asp:EntityDataSource>
```

Description

- To display the Expression Editor for entering a custom command, click the button with the ellipsis on it that appears when you select the CommandText property for the Entity data source control in the Properties window.

- To specify the custom command, enter it in the CommandText text box. If the command uses parameters, click the Add Parameter button for each parameter, enter a name for the parameter, and then define the parameter using the controls that appear to the right of the Parameters list.

- When you use a custom command, you must not specify a value for the EntitySetName attribute.

Figure 20-8   How to specify a custom command

A Vendor Invoices application

Now that you've learned how to use the Expression Editor to customize an Entity data source control, you're ready to study an application that's more complex than the Invoice Display application you saw earlier in this chapter. The user interface for this application, called Vendor Invoices, is in figure 20-9.

The Vendor Invoices application uses two Entity data source controls. The drop-down list that displays the vendor names is bound to the first control. When the user selects a different vendor from this control, the invoices for that vendor that have a balance due are displayed in the GridView control, which is bound to the second data source control.

The aspx file for the Vendor Invoices application

The aspx file for the Vendor Invoices application is presented in figure 20-10. The Entity data source control shown on page 1 of this listing provides the data for the drop-down list. To do that, it retrieves the VendorID and Name properties from the Vendors entity set defined by the PayablesEntities container class. It also sorts the results by the Name property.

The Entity data source control that provides the data for the GridView control is shown on page 2 of this listing. This data source control gets data from the Invoices entity set. To customize this control, I used the Expression Editors for the Where, OrderBy, and Select attributes as shown in figures 20-5, 20-6, and 20-7. Now that you can see all the code for this control, though, you should have a better idea of how it works. In particular, you can see that the value of the VendorID parameter that's used in the Where expression is retrieved from the SelectedValue property of the drop-down list that's shown on the first page of this listing. This works because the DataValueField property of the drop-down list, which identifies the value that's returned by the SelectedValue property, is set to VendorID.

The Vendor Invoices form

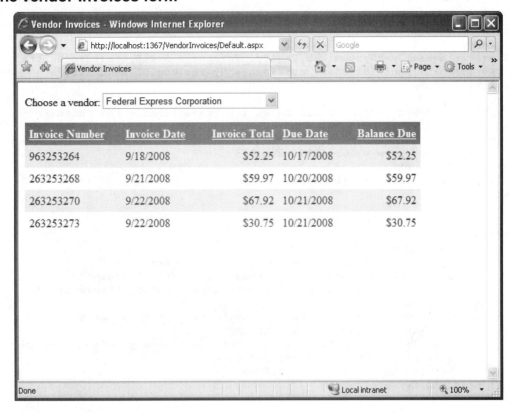

Description

- The Vendor Invoices application uses two Entity data source controls. These controls work with an Entity Data Model that contains Vendor and Invoice entities that are mapped to the Vendors and Invoices tables in the Payables database.

- The drop-down list displays the vendor names and is bound to the first Entity data source control.

- The GridView control display the invoices for the vendor that's selected in the drop-down list and is bound to the second Entity data source control.

Figure 20-9   A Vendor Invoices application

The Default.aspx file

```
<%@ Page Language="VB" AutoEventWireup="false" CodeFile="Default.aspx.vb"
Inherits="_Default" %>

<%@ Register assembly="System.Web.Entity, Version=3.5.0.0, Culture=neutral,
PublicKeyToken=b77a5c561934e089" namespace="System.Web.UI.WebControls"
tagprefix="asp" %>

<!DOCTYPE html PUBLIC "-//W3C//DTD XHTML 1.0 Transitional//EN" "http://
www.w3.org/TR/xhtml1/DTD/xhtml1-transitional.dtd">

<html xmlns="http://www.w3.org/1999/xhtml">
<head runat="server">
    <title>Vendor Invoices</title>
</head>
<body>
    <form id="form1" runat="server">
    <div>
        Choose a vendor:
        <asp:DropDownList ID="ddlVendor" runat="server"
            DataSourceID="EntityDataSource1" DataTextField="Name"
            DataValueField="VendorID" Width="250px" AutoPostBack="True">
        </asp:DropDownList>
        <asp:EntityDataSource ID="EntityDataSource1" runat="server"
            ConnectionString="name=PayablesEntities"
            DefaultContainerName="PayablesEntities" EntitySetName="Vendors"
            EntityTypeFilter="" OrderBy="it.Name"
            Select="it.[VendorID], it.[Name]">
        </asp:EntityDataSource>
        <br />
        <br />
        <asp:GridView ID="GridView1" runat="server" AllowPaging="True"
            AllowSorting="True" AutoGenerateColumns="False"
            DataSourceID="EntityDataSource2" CellPadding="6"
            ForeColor="#333333" GridLines="None">
            <Columns>
                <asp:BoundField DataField="InvoiceNumber"
                    HeaderText="Invoice Number" ReadOnly="True"
                    SortExpression="InvoiceNumber" >
                    <HeaderStyle HorizontalAlign="Left" Width="125px" />
                </asp:BoundField>
                <asp:BoundField DataField="InvoiceDate"
                    DataFormatString="{0:d}" HeaderText="Invoice Date"
                    ReadOnly="True" SortExpression="InvoiceDate" >
                    <HeaderStyle HorizontalAlign="Left" Width="100px" />
                </asp:BoundField>
                <asp:BoundField DataField="InvoiceTotal"
                    DataFormatString="{0:c}" HeaderText="Invoice Total"
                    ReadOnly="True" SortExpression="InvoiceTotal" >
                    <HeaderStyle HorizontalAlign="Right" Width="100px" />
                    <ItemStyle HorizontalAlign="Right" />
                </asp:BoundField>
```

Figure 20-10   The aspx file for the Vendor Invoices application (part 1 of 2)

The Default.aspx file   Page 2

```
            <asp:BoundField DataField="DueDate" DataFormatString="{0:d}"
                HeaderText="Due Date" ReadOnly="True"
                SortExpression="DueDate" >
                <HeaderStyle HorizontalAlign="Left" Width="80px" />
            </asp:BoundField>
            <asp:BoundField DataField="BalanceDue"
                DataFormatString="{0:c}" HeaderText="Balance Due"
                SortExpression="BalanceDue">
                <HeaderStyle HorizontalAlign="Right" Width="100px" />
                <ItemStyle HorizontalAlign="Right" />
            </asp:BoundField>
        </Columns>
        <HeaderStyle BackColor="#507CD1" Font-Bold="True"
         ForeColor="White" />
        <PagerSettings Mode="NextPreviousFirstLast" />
        <RowStyle BackColor="#EFF3FB" />
        <AlternatingRowStyle BackColor="White" />
        <PagerStyle BackColor="#2461BF" ForeColor="White"
         HorizontalAlign="Center" />
    </asp:GridView>
    <asp:EntityDataSource ID="EntityDataSource2" runat="server"
        ConnectionString="name=PayablesEntities"
        DefaultContainerName="PayablesEntities" EntitySetName="Invoices"
        EntityTypeFilter="" OrderBy="it.DueDate, it.BalanceDue DESC"
        Select="it.InvoiceNumber, it.InvoiceDate, it.InvoiceTotal,
                it.DueDate, it.InvoiceTotal - it.PaymentTotal
            - it.CreditTotal AS BalanceDue"
        Where="it.Vendor.VendorID = @VendorID AND
            it.InvoiceTotal - it.PaymentTotal - it.CreditTotal &gt; 0">
        <WhereParameters>
            <asp:ControlParameter ControlID="ddlVendor" Name="VendorID"
                PropertyName="SelectedValue" Type="Int32" />
        </WhereParameters>
    </asp:EntityDataSource>
    </div>
    </form>
</body>
</html>
```

Figure 20-10   The aspx file for the Vendor Invoices application (part 2 of 2)

How to update data

Before you can use an Entity data source control to update data, you need to set the appropriate attributes for enabling insert, update, and delete operations. In addition, you need to know how to provide for optimistic concurrency. That's what you'll learn in the topics that follow. Then, you'll see an application that provides for updating data.

How to configure an Entity data source control for updates

Figure 20-11 shows you how to use the Data Source Configuration Wizard to enable insert, update, and delete operations. To do that, you must select the Select All check box so that entire entity objects are returned by the query. Then, you simply select the check boxes at the bottom of the dialog box. This sets the EnableInsert, EnableUpdate, and EnableDelete attributes of the Entity data source control to True. You can also set these attributes from the Properties window or directly in the aspx code. If you do that, however, you need to be sure that a value isn't specified for the Select attribute.

Once you enable updating for the data source control, you can use it with any bound control that provides for updating. Then, when the data source control receives a request to perform an insert, update, or delete operation, it automatically creates the command needed to perform that operation. Because of that, you don't need to provide any additional aspx or Visual Basic code. However, you may want to respond to events of the control that's bound to the Entity data source control to perform processing before or after an insert, update, or delete operation. For example, you may want to use the before-action events to provide data validation. And you may want to use the after-action events to check that the operation completed successfully.

An Entity data source control that's being configured for insert, update, and delete operations

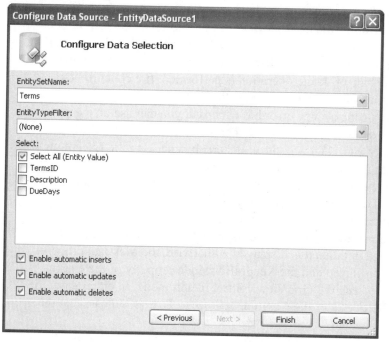

The aspx code for the control

```
<asp:EntityDataSource ID="EntityDataSource1" runat="server"
    ConnectionString="name=PayablesEntities"
    DefaultContainerName="PayablesEntities" EnableDelete="True"
    EnableInsert="True" EnableUpdate="True" EntitySetName="Terms">
</asp:EntityDataSource>
```

How to configure an Entity data source control for updates

- When you configure the Entity data source control, select the Enable Automatic Inserts, Enable Automatic Updates, and Enable Automatic Deletes options from the second step of the wizard. These options are available only if the Select All option in the Select list is selected.

- When you enable inserting, updating, or deleting for an Entity data source control, the control automatically generates the commands needed to perform these operations.

- You can use the events of a control that's bound to an Entity data source control to perform processing before or after an insert, update, or delete operation.

Figure 20-11   How to configure an Entity data source control for updates

How to provide for optimistic concurrency

The Entity data source control provides for optimistic concurrency by default. To do that, it stores the original values of any columns that can be changed in view state. Then, if the Concurrency Mode property of a column is set to Fixed, it compares the value of that column to the current value in the database when an update or delete operation is performed. If a concurrency error occurs, an OptimisticConcurrencyException is thrown.

To determine if a concurrency error has occurred, you can use an event handler like the one shown in figure 20-12. This event handler is for the RowUpdated event of a GridView control. It starts by checking the Exception property of the e argument to determine if any exception has occurred. If so, it uses the GetType method of that exception to get the exception type, and it uses the ToString method of the type to get the type name. Then, it compares this name to a string literal that contains the full name of an optimistic concurrency exception. If the names are the same, an error message that indicates that the row has been updated or deleted is displayed. Otherwise, the Message property of the exception is displayed and the KeepInEditMode property of the e argument is set to True to keep the GridView control in edit mode. In either case, the ExceptionHandled property of the e argument is set to True to indicate that the exception has been handled.

An event handler for the RowUpdated event of a GridView control

```
Protected Sub grdTerms_RowUpdated(ByVal sender As Object, _
        ByVal e As System.Web.UI.WebControls.GridViewUpdatedEventArgs) _
        Handles grdTerms.RowUpdated
    If e.Exception IsNot Nothing Then
        If e.Exception.GetType.ToString _
                = "System.Data.OptimisticConcurrencyException" Then
            lblError.Text = "Another user has updated or deleted " _
                & "those terms. Please try again."
        Else
            lblError.Text = "A database error has occurred. " _
                & e.Exception.Message
            e.KeepInEditMode = True
        End If
        e.ExceptionHandled = True
    End If
End Sub
```

Description

- By default, the Entity data source control provides for optimistic concurrency by storing the original values of the data in the Entity Data Model in view state. Then, when an update or delete operation is performed, the original values are compared to the values in the database. If the values have changed, an OptimisticConcurrencyException occurs.

- You can handle an OptimisticConcurrencyException in the event handlers for the control that the Entity data source control is bound to. For a GridView control, you use the RowUpdated and RowDeleted events. For a DetailsView, FormView, or ListView control, you use the ItemUpdated and ItemDeleted events.

- To determine the type of exception that was thrown from the event handler for a bound control, use the Exception property of the e argument to get the exception. Then, use the GetType method of the exception to get its type, and use the ToString property of the type to get the type name. To determine if the exception is for a concurrency error, check this name to see if it's System.Data.OptimisticConcurrencyException.

- If you handle an OptimisticConcurrencyException in the event handler for a bound control, you should set the ExceptionHandled property of the e argument to True to suppress the exception.

- If an OptimisticConcurrencyException occurs, you shouldn't set the KeepInEditMode property of the e argument to True. That's because the new values for the row aren't displayed until the row leaves edit mode.

- You can determine which column values are checked when an update or delete operation is performed by changing the Concurrency Mode property of the columns. For more information, see figure 18-8 in chapter 18.

- If you don't need to store the original values of the data in an object context in view state, you can set the StoreOriginalValuesInViewState property of the Entity data source control to False.

Figure 20-12   How to provide for optimistic concurrency

A Terms Maintenance application

To give you a better idea of how you can use an Entity data source control to update data, figure 20-13 presents a Terms Maintenance application that maintains the Terms table in the Payables database. This application uses an Entity Data Model that consists of just one entity class named Terms that is mapped to the Terms table. Then, a GridView control is used to display the rows in the Terms table along with Edit and Delete buttons. In this figure, the user has clicked the Edit button for the last row, placing that row in edit mode.

Beneath the GridView control, two text boxes let the user enter data for a new terms row. Then, if the user clicks the Add New Terms button, the data entered in these text boxes is used to add the row to the database. Although it isn't apparent from this figure, a required field validator is used for the Description text box, and required field and compare validators are used for the Due Days text box. (For simplicity, I didn't use validation controls for the Description and Due Days columns in the GridView control.) Also, there's a label control beneath the GridView control that's used to display error messages when an update, delete, or insert operation fails.

The aspx file for the Terms Maintenance application

Figure 20-14 shows the aspx code for this application. The only thing of interest here is the code for the Entity data source control that the GridView control is bound to. This data source control works with the Terms entity set defined by the PayablesEntities container class. Because this data source control doesn't include Where or Select attributes, all the rows and columns will be retrieved from the Terms table. In addition, the EnableDelete and EnableUpdate attributes indicate that this control will provide for delete and update operations.

At this point, you might be wondering why the Entity data source control doesn't provide for insert operations even though the application provides for inserting new rows. The answer is that this control can be used to insert data only if the control that's bound to it provides for inserting data. In this case, the GridView control doesn't provide for inserting data, so the Entity data source control doesn't need to provide for inserting data either. That doesn't mean that the application can't insert data, however. To do that, it uses code like the code you saw in chapter 18. You'll see that code in the next figure.

The Terms Maintenance application

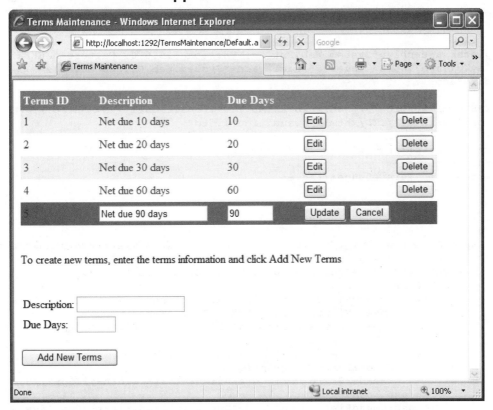

Description

- The Terms Maintenance application uses an Entity data source control to work with the Terms table in the Payables database. This control provides for retrieving, updating, and deleting the terms data.

- The GridView control is bound to the Entity data source control and provides for updating and deleting rows from the Terms table.

- To edit terms, the user clicks the Edit button. This places the GridView control into edit mode. The user can then change the Description and Due Days and click Update. Or, the user can click Cancel to leave edit mode.

- To delete terms, the user clicks the Delete button.

- To insert a new row, the user enters the description and due days into the text boxes on the form and then clicks the Add New Terms button. Then, the code for this button uses methods of the object context and Terms class to insert the row.

- If the user attempts to update or add a row with invalid data, an error message is displayed.

- The Concurrency Mode of the Description and DueDays properties of the Vendor entity has been changed to Fixed so that an OptimisticConcurrencyException will be thrown if a row being updated or deleted has been updated by another user.

Figure 20-13   A Terms Maintenance application

The default.aspx file

```
<%@ Page Language="VB" AutoEventWireup="false" CodeFile="Default.aspx.vb"
Inherits="_Default" %>

<%@ Register assembly="System.Web.Entity, Version=3.5.0.0, Culture=neutral,
PublicKeyToken=b77a5c561934e089" namespace="System.Web.UI.WebControls"
tagprefix="asp" %>

<!DOCTYPE html PUBLIC "-//W3C//DTD XHTML 1.0 Transitional//EN" "http://
www.w3.org/TR/xhtml1/DTD/xhtml1-transitional.dtd">

<html xmlns="http://www.w3.org/1999/xhtml">
<head runat="server">
    <title>Terms Maintenance</title>
</head>
<body>
    <form id="form1" runat="server">
    <div>
        <asp:GridView ID="grdTerms" runat="server" AutoGenerateColumns="False"
            DataKeyNames="TermsID" DataSourceID="EntityDataSource1"
            CellPadding="4"ForeColor="#333333" GridLines="None">
            <Columns>
                <asp:BoundField DataField="TermsID" HeaderText="Terms ID"
                    InsertVisible="False" ReadOnly="True">
                    <HeaderStyle HorizontalAlign="Left" Width="100px" />
                </asp:BoundField>
                <asp:BoundField DataField="Description"
                    HeaderText="Description">
                    <HeaderStyle HorizontalAlign="Left" Width="175px" />
                </asp:BoundField>
                <asp:BoundField DataField="DueDays" HeaderText="Due Days">
                    <HeaderStyle HorizontalAlign="Left" Width="100px" />
                </asp:BoundField>
                <asp:CommandField ButtonType="Button" ShowEditButton="True" />
                <asp:CommandField ButtonType="Button" CausesValidation="False"
                    ShowDeleteButton="True" />
            </Columns>
            <HeaderStyle BackColor="#507CD1" Font-Bold="True"
             ForeColor="White" />
            <RowStyle BackColor="#EFF3FB" />
            <AlternatingRowStyle BackColor="White" />
            <EditRowStyle BackColor="#2461BF" />
        </asp:GridView>
        <asp:EntityDataSource ID="EntityDataSource1" runat="server"
            ConnectionString="name=PayablesEntities"
            DefaultContainerName="PayablesEntities"
            EnableDelete="True" EnableUpdate="True"
            EntitySetName="Terms">
        </asp:EntityDataSource>
        <br /><br />
```

Figure 20-14   The aspx file for the Terms Maintenance application (part 1 of 2)

The default.aspx file

```
        To create new terms, enter the terms information
        and click Add New Terms<br />
        <asp:Label ID="lblError" runat="server" EnableViewState="False"
            ForeColor="Red">
        </asp:Label>
        <br /><br />
        <table>
            <tr>
                <td>
                    Description:</td>
                <td>
                    <asp:TextBox ID="txtDescription" runat="server">
                    </asp:TextBox>
                </td>
                <td>
                    <asp:RequiredFieldValidator ID="RequiredFieldValidator1"
                        runat="server" Display="Dynamic"
                        ControlToValidate="txtDescription"
                        ErrorMessage="Description is a required field."
                        ValidationGroup="Add">
                    </asp:RequiredFieldValidator>
                </td>
            </tr>
            <tr>
                <td>
                    Due Days:</td>
                <td>
                    <asp:TextBox ID="txtDueDays" runat="server" Width="50px">
                    </asp:TextBox>
                </td>
                <td>
                    <asp:RequiredFieldValidator ID="RequiredFieldValidator2"
                        runat="server" Display="Dynamic"
                        ControlToValidate="txtDueDays"
                        ErrorMessage="Due days is a required field."
                        ValidationGroup="Add">
                    </asp:RequiredFieldValidator>
                    <asp:CompareValidator ID="CompareValidator1"
                        runat="server" Display="Dynamic"
                        ControlToValidate="txtDueDays"
                        ErrorMessage="Due days must be an integer
                        greater than zero." Operator="GreaterThan"
                        Type="Integer" ValueToCompare="0"
                        ValidationGroup="Add">
                    </asp:CompareValidator>
                </td>
            </tr>
        </table>
        <br />
        <asp:Button ID="btnAdd" runat="server" Text="Add New Terms"
            ValidationGroup="Add" />
    </div>
    </form>
</body>
</html>
```

Figure 20-14   The aspx file for the Terms Maintenance application (part 2 of 2)

The Visual Basic code for the Terms Maintenance application

Figure 20-15 presents the Visual Basic code for the Terms Maintenance application. To start, you should notice the Imports statement at the beginning of this file. The namespace that's imported, PayablesModel, is the namespace that contains the PayablesEntities container class as well as the class that defines the Terms entity. This class is used by the event handler for the Click event of the Add button.

This Click event handler starts by creating an object context from the PayablesEntities class. Then, it uses the Create*ObjectName* and AddTo*EntitySetName* methods that you learned about in chapter 18 to create a new Terms object from the values the user enters and to add that object to the collection of Terms in the object context. Next, it executes the SaveChanges method of the object context to save the new terms to the database. Finally, it executes the DataBind method of the GridView control so that the new Terms are displayed in the control, and it clears the text boxes where the user entered the new values for the row.

The second event handler is called after each update operation. It starts by checking if an exception has occurred. If so, it checks whether an OptimisticConcurrencyException or some other exception occurred. In either case, an appropriate error message is displayed and the ExceptionHandled property of the e argument is set to True. In addition, if an error other than an OptimisticConcurrencyException occurred, the KeepInEditMode property of the e argument is set to True so the control remains in edit mode.

The third event handler is called after each delete operation. Like the event handler that's called after an update operation, this event handler checks if an exception occurred and, if so, if it was an OptimisticConcurrencyException. Notice that this event handler doesn't set the KeepInEditMode property, though, since the control isn't in edit mode when the Delete button is clicked.

The default.aspx.vb file

```
Imports PayablesModel

Partial Class _Default
    Inherits System.Web.UI.Page

    Protected Sub btnAdd_Click(ByVal sender As Object, _
            ByVal e As System.EventArgs) Handles btnAdd.Click
        Dim payables As New PayablesEntities
        Dim terms As Terms = terms.CreateTerms( _
            1, txtDescription.Text, CInt(txtDueDays.Text))
        payables.AddToTerms(terms)
        Try
            payables.SaveChanges()
            grdTerms.DataBind()
            txtDescription.Text = ""
            txtDueDays.Text = ""
        Catch ex As Exception
            lblError.Text = "An error has occurred. " & ex.Message
        End Try
    End Sub

    Protected Sub grdTerms_RowUpdated(ByVal sender As Object, _
            ByVal e As System.Web.UI.WebControls.GridViewUpdatedEventArgs) _
            Handles grdTerms.RowUpdated
        If e.Exception IsNot Nothing Then
            If e.Exception.GetType.ToString _
                    = "System.Data.OptimisticConcurrencyException" Then
                lblError.Text = "Another user has updated or deleted " _
                    & "those terms. Please try again."
            Else
                lblError.Text = "A database error has occurred. " _
                    & e.Exception.Message
                e.KeepInEditMode = True
            End If
            e.ExceptionHandled = True
        End If
    End Sub

    Protected Sub grdTerms_RowDeleted(ByVal sender As Object, _
            ByVal e As System.Web.UI.WebControls.GridViewDeletedEventArgs) _
            Handles grdTerms.RowDeleted
        If e.Exception IsNot Nothing Then
            If e.Exception.GetType.ToString _
                    = "System.Data.OptimisticConcurrencyException" Then
                lblError.Text = "Another user has updated or deleted " _
                    & "those terms. Please try again."
            Else
                lblError.Text = "A database error has occurred. " _
                    & e.Exception.Message
            End If
            e.ExceptionHandled = True
        End If
    End Sub

End Class
```

Figure 20-15   The Visual Basic code for the Terms Maintenance application

Perspective

The purpose of this chapter has been to present the basic skills for using the Entity data source control to work with an Entity Data Model. As you've seen, this control is easy to configure, particularly if you use the Configure Data Source wizard and the Expression Editor as shown in this chapter. It's also easy to use, whether you're displaying or maintaining data. Because of that, it's the preferred technique for working with an Entity Data Model in a web application.

In some cases, though, you may find that the Entity data source control won't provide the flexibility you need. In those cases, you should consider using code to work with the Entity Data Model as shown in chapters 18 and 19. Although these techniques require more work, they still let you use an Entity Data Model that provides the code for working with the database.

Appendix A

How to install and use the software and files for this book

To develop the Windows Forms applications presented in this book, you need to have Visual Studio 2008 or Visual Basic 2008 Express Edition installed on your system. To develop the web applications presented in this book, you need to have Visual Studio 2008 or Visual Web Developer 2008 Express Edition installed on your system.

In addition, if you're going to develop applications that use databases that are stored on your own PC rather than on a remote server, you need to install SQL Server on your PC. The easiest way to do that is to install SQL Server 2005 or 2008 Express Edition. SQL Server 2005 Express Edition is installed by default when you install most editions of Visual Studio 2008, but you can install SQL Server 2008 Express Edition separately if you prefer.

This appendix describes how to install Visual Studio 2008 or one of the Express Editions. In addition, it describes how to install SQL Server 2008 Express Edition and how to use it with our database. But first, it describes the files for this book that are available for download from our web site and shows you how to download, install, and use them.

How to use the downloadable files

Throughout this book, you'll see complete applications that illustrate the skills that are presented in each chapter. To help you understand how these applications work, you can download them from our web site. Then, you can open these applications in Visual Studio, view the source code, and run them.

These applications come in a single download that also includes the Payables database that they use. Figure A-1 describes how you can download, install, and use these files. When you download the single setup file and execute it, it will install all of the files for this book in the C:\Murach\ADO.NET 3.5 VB directory.

The Book Applications directory contains all of the applications that are presented in this book. If you like, you can use Visual Studio to open these applications as described in this figure. Then, you can view the source code for these applications, and you can run them to see how they work. Note that all of the web applications were developed as file-system applications, so you don't need IIS to run them. Also note that before you can run a web application, you must set the start page for the application.

The Exercise Starts directory contains all of the starting points for the exercises presented in this book. When you execute the setup file, the subdirectories of the Exercise Starts directory are copied to the C:\ADO.NET 3.5 VB directory. This makes it easy to locate the exercise starts as you work through the exercises. For example, you can find the exercise starts for chapter 6 in the C:\ADO.NET 3.5 VB\Chapter 06 directory. In addition, if you make a mistake and want to restore a file to its original state, you can do that by copying it from the directory where it was originally installed.

The Database and Database Backup directories contain the Payables database that's used throughout this book. In addition, the Database directory contains files that you can use to attach this database to a SQL Server Express database server, detach this database from the server, restore the original database from the Database Backup directory, and grant ASP.NET access to the database. Figure A-4 describes how to use these files.

If you run into any trouble using these files, you can read the Readme file that's included with this download. This file describes alternate techniques you can use to help you troubleshoot the cause of a problem.

What the downloadable files for this book contain

- All of the applications presented in this book including the source code
- The Payables database and the files that are used by the book applications and exercises
- The starting points for all of the exercises
- A Readme file that contains additional information about working with the SQL Server database and the applications

How to download and install the files for this book

- Go to www.murach.com, and go to the page for *Murach's ADO.NET 3.5, LINQ, and the Entity Framework with VB 2008*.
- Click the link for "FREE download of the book applications." Then, select the "All book files" link and respond to the resulting pages and dialog boxes. This will download a setup file named dvb8_allfiles.exe onto your hard drive.
- Use the Windows Explorer to find the setup file on your hard drive. Then, double-click this file and respond to the dialog boxes that follow. This installs the files in directories that start with C:\Murach\ADO.NET 3.5 VB.

How your system is prepared for doing the exercises

- Some of the exercises have you start from existing projects. The source code for these projects is in the C:\Murach\ADO.NET 3.5 VB\Exercise Starts directory. After the setup file installs the files in the download, it runs a batch file named exercise_starts_setup.bat that copies the applications you'll need to do the exercises to the C:\ADO.NET 3.5 VB directory. Then, you can find all of the starting points for the exercises in directories like C:\ADO.NET 3.5 VB\Chapter 06 and C:\ADO.NET 3.5 VB\Chapter 12.

How to view the source code for the applications

- The source code for the applications presented in this book can be found in the C:\Murach\ADO.NET 3.5 VB\Book Applications directory. You can view the source code for a Windows Forms application by using the File→Open Project command to open the project or solution in the appropriate directory. To view the source code for a web application, you can use the File→Open Web Site command to open the web site in the appropriate directory.

How to prepare your system for using the database

- To use the database that comes with this book on your PC, you need to make sure that SQL Server 2005 or 2008 Express is installed, and you need to attach the database to SQL Server Express. If you want to use the database from web applications as well as Windows Forms applications, you also need to grant ASP.NET access to the database. See figures A-3 and A-4 for more information.

Figure A-1   How to use the downloadable files for this book

How to install Visual Studio 2008

If you've installed Windows applications before, you shouldn't have any trouble installing Visual Studio 2008. You simply insert the DVD and the setup program starts automatically. This setup program will lead you through the steps for installing Visual Studio as summarized in figure A-2.

When you click the Install Visual Studio 2008 link, the setup program starts loading the installation components it needs. Then, after you click the Next button and accept the license agreement, the program lets you select the type of installation. In most cases, you'll perform a default installation so the most commonly used features are installed, including the .NET Framework, Visual Studio, Visual Basic, and SQL Server 2005 Express.

One reason you may not want to perform a default installation is if you want to use SQL Server 2008 Express instead of SQL Server 2005 Express. (SQL Server 2008 Express isn't included with Visual Studio 2008 because it didn't become available until several months after Visual Studio was released.) In that case, you need to perform a custom installation so you can omit SQL Server 2005 from the installation. To do that, you can remove the check mark from the SQL Server 2005 Express option when the list of items to be installed is displayed. Then, you can install SQL Server 2008 separately as described in the next figure.

After you install Visual Studio, you can install the documentation for Visual Studio and all of the products that come with it. To do that, just click the Install Product Documentation link.

If you're going to use the Visual Basic 2008 Express Edition and the Visual Web Developer 2008 Express Edition, you have to download and install these products and the documentation separately. But if you follow the directions on the Microsoft web site when you download these products, you shouldn't have any trouble installing them. Note that if you download the versions of these products that include Service Pack 1, you'll have the option of installing SQL Server 2008 Express as well. Otherwise, you'll need to download and install SQL Server 2008 Express separately.

The final setup step is to apply any updates that have become available since the product was released. In particular, you'll want to be sure that Service Pack 1 is installed so that you can use the Entity Framework as described in section 5 of this book. If you don't perform this step, though, you can check for updates from within Visual Studio by using the Help→Check for Updates command. In fact, you should use this command periodically to be sure that Visual Studio is up-to-date.

The Visual Studio 2008 setup program

How to install Visual Studio 2008

1. Insert the installation DVD. The setup program will start automatically.

2. Click the Install Visual Studio 2008 link and follow the instructions. When the Options page is displayed, you can accept the Default option unless you have special requirements.

3. To install the documentation for Visual Studio and the related products (Visual Basic, ASP.NET, etc.), click the Install Product Documentation link.

4. To install any updates that are available, click the Check for Service Releases link.

How to install the Express Editions

1. Go to the page on Microsoft's web site for the download of Visual Basic 2008 Express Edition or Visual Web Developer 2008 Express Edition and follow the directions to download the setup program.

2. Run the setup program. It works similarly to the setup program for Visual Studio 2008, but fewer options are available.

Description

- The Visual Studio 2008 Setup program installs not only Visual Studio, but also the .NET Framework, the development web server, and SQL Server 2005 Express. If you want to use SQL Server 2008 Express instead, you can select the Custom option from the setup program, remove the check mark from the SQL Server 2005 Express option, and then install SQL Server 2008 Express separately as described in figure A-3.

- The setup programs for Visual Basic 2008 Express and Visual Web Developer 2008 Express that include Service Pack 1 include an option to install SQL Server 2008 Express. If you don't download the programs with Service Pack 1, you'll need to download and install SQL Server 2008 Express Edition separately.

Figure A-2   How to install Visual Studio 2008

How to install and use SQL Server 2008 Express

SQL Server 2008 Express Edition is a free, lightweight version of SQL Server 2008 that you can install on your PC to test database applications. If you want to use SQL Server 2008 Express with Visual Studio 2008, you'll need to download and install it from Microsoft's web site as described in figure A-3. Note that before you can install SQL Server 2008 Express, you'll need to be sure you have some prerequisite components installed. These components are listed on the download page for SQL Server 2008 Express, and you can follow the instructions on that page to download and install them.

To download SQL Server 2008 Express, go to the main download page for this product on Microsoft's web site. On this page, you can choose from one of three editions to download. For this book, you only need the database engine, so you can choose the SQL Server 2008 Express (Runtime Only) edition. If you also want to install a graphical tool that you can use to work with the database, though, you can choose the SQL Server 2008 Express with Tools edition. Then, the SQL Server Management Studio Basic tool will be installed along with the database engine.

Before you install SQL Server 2008, you should realize that you don't have to have it to use this book. So if you already have SQL Server 2005 Express installed on your system, you can use it instead of SQL Server 2008. To accommodate that, we've provided the database for this book in 2005 format. That way, you can use it with either a 2005 or a 2008 database server.

You may also be able to upgrade an instance of SQL Server 2000 or 2005 to 2008. To do that, select the "Upgrade from SQL Server 2000 or 2005" option from the SQL Server Installation Center dialog box. Note that although this upgrades the database server to 2008, the existing databases will run as if they're running on 2000 or 2005.

If you can't upgrade the old instance of SQL Server, you can uninstall it before you install SQL Server 2008. Before you do that, you should detach any databases that are running on the older SQL Server instance and then copy the data (mdf) and log (ldf) files for the database to a safe location. Then, after you uninstall the old instance and install SQL Server 2008 Express, you can attach the databases to the new server. To detach and attach databases, you can use batch files like the ones provided for this book. See the next figure for details.

You can also install SQL Server 2008 alongside another instance of SQL Server. Each instance must have a different name, however. So if you have a 2005 instance named SQLEXPRESS, you'll need to give the 2008 instance another name like SQLEXPRESS2008. In that case, you'll need to modify the applications in this book to use this name since they assume you're using an instance named SQLEXPRESS.

After you install SQL Server Express, you can use the SQL Server Configuration Manager shown at the top of this figure to work with the server. In particular, you can use it to start, continue, pause, or stop the SQL Server engine. By default, SQL Server is started each time you start your PC. If that's not what you want, you can display the Properties dialog box for the server,

The SQL Server Configuration Manager

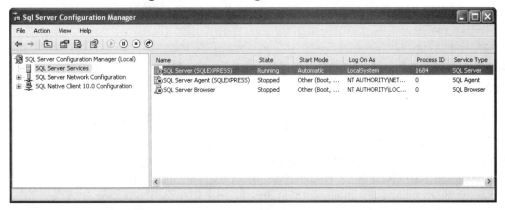

How to install SQL Server 2008 Express

- Download the setup program from Microsoft's web site. To install just the database engine, download SQL Server 2008 Express (Runtime Only). To install the database engine and the SQL Server Management Studio Basic tool, download SQL Server 2008 Express with Tools.

- Run the setup program. When the SQL Server Installation Center dialog box is displayed, select the Installation option, select the "New SQL Server standalone installation" option to start the SQL Server 2008 Setup wizard, and respond to the resulting dialog boxes.

- At the Feature Selection step, select all available features.

- At the Instance Configuration step, create a named instance with a name of SQLEXPRESS.

- At the Server Configuration step, select NT AUTHORITY/SYSTEM as the account name for the SQL Server Database Engine service to run SQL Server on your computer.

- At the Database Engine Configuration step, you can click the Add Current User button to add the current user as a SQL Server administrator.

How to use SQL Server Express

- After you install SQL Server Express, it will start automatically each time you start your PC. To start or stop this service or change its start mode, start the SQL Server Configuration Manager (Start→All Programs→Microsoft SQL Server 2008→Configuration Tools→SQL Server Configuration Manager), select the server in the right pane, and use the buttons in the toolbar.

- The setup program creates a copy of SQL Server with a name that consists of your computer name followed by a backslash and the name you enter in the Instance Configuration step of the wizard. You can use this name to define connections to the databases that you use with this server.

Figure A-3   How to install and use SQL Server 2008 Express

click the Services tab, and then select Manual for the Start Mode option. Then, you can start SQL Server whenever you need it using the Configuration Manager.

How to attach, detach, and restore the database for this book

If you want to use the Payables database presented in this book, you'll need to start by downloading and installing the book files as described in figure A-1. Then, you can run the batch file named db_attach.bat that's in the C:\Murach\ADO.NET 3.5 VB\Database directory. This batch file runs a SQL Server script named db_attach.sql that attaches the files for the database to the SQL Server Express database server that's running on your computer. Later, if you need to detach the database or restore the original database, you can do that using the db_detach.bat or db_restore.bat file in the Database directory.

Note, however, that if the database server on your system has a name other than the computer name appended with SQLEXPRESS, the batch files we provide won't work. But you can easily change them so they will work. To change a file, just open it in a text editor such as NotePad. If you open the db_attach.bat file, for example, you'll see this command:

```
sqlcmd -S localhost\SQLExpress -E /i db_attach.sql
```

Then, you can just change the server specification to the name of your server.

Another problem can arise if you try to run one of the batch files under Windows Vista. This is due to the fact that under Vista, you aren't automatically given administrator privileges even if you're logged on as an administrator, and you need to have administrator privileges to attach, detach, and restore the database. Normally, Vista will notify you when administrator privileges are required to perform a task, but this doesn't happen when you run a batch file.

To get around this problem, you can turn off a feature of Vista called User Account Control as described in this figure. Then, after you restart your system, you should be able to run the batch files without any problem. Be sure to turn User Account Control back on when you're done as it provides added security for your system.

How to grant ASP.NET access to the database

If you're using Windows XP and you're going to use the Payables database with ASP.NET applications, you'll also need to grant ASP.NET access to the database after you attach the database to the server. To do that, you can run the db_grant_access.bat file in the Database directory. But first, you must modify the db_grant_access.sql file that this batch file runs so it uses the name of your computer. To do that, open the file in a text editor, and replace each occurrence of [machineName] with the name of your computer. Then, save and close this file, and run the db_grant_access.bat file to grant ASP.NET access to the Payables database.

The dialog box for turning User Account Control on and off under Vista

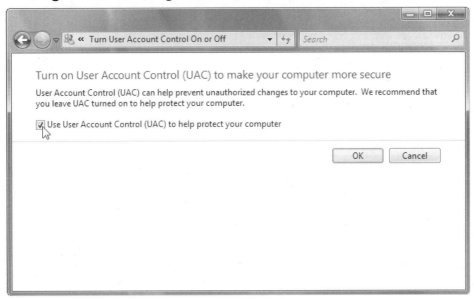

How to attach the database for this book to SQL Server Express

- If you're going to use the Payables database that's used by the applications throughout this book on your own PC, you need to attach it to SQL Server Express. To do that, you can use one of the batch files and SQL scripts that are downloaded and installed along with the other files for this book.
- To attach the database to SQL Server Express, run the db_attach.bat file. To do that, you can use the Windows Explorer to navigate to the C:\Murach\ADO.NET 3.5 VB\Database folder and double-click the db_attach.bat file.

How to detach the database and restore the original database

- To detach the database from the server, run the db_detach.bat file.
- To restore the original database, run the db_restore.bat file. This detaches the database, copies the original database files in the Database Backup directory over the current files in the Database directory, and reattaches the database.

How to work with the database under Windows Vista

- To use the batch files we provide to attach, detach, or restore the MMABooks database under Windows Vista, you will need to temporarily turn off a feature of Vista called User Account Control.
- To access User Account Control, display the Control Panel, switch to Classic View, double-click on User Accounts, and then click on the Turn User Account Control on or off link. Then, remove the check mark from the Use User Account Control option, click the OK button, and restart your system when instructed.

Figure A-4   How to attach, detach, and restore the database for this book

Index

D

Q

R

What software you need for this book

- To build Windows Forms applications, you need any full edition of Microsoft Visual Studio 2008 or the Express Editions of Microsoft Visual Basic 2008 and SQL Server 2008, which can be downloaded for free from Microsoft's website.

- If you want to build web applications as shown in chapters 15 and 20 of this book and you don't have a full edition of Microsoft Visual Studio 2008, you'll also need Microsoft's Visual Web Developer 2008 Express Edition, which can be downloaded for free from Microsoft's website.

- For information about downloading and installing these products, please see appendix A.

The downloadable files for this book

- All of the applications presented in this book including source code and data.

- The database files for the Payables database that's used by this book.

- A Readme file that contains additional information about working with the SQL Server database and the applications.

How to download the files for this book

- Go to www.murach.com, and go to the page for *Murach's ADO.NET 3.5, LINQ, and the Entity Framework with VB 2008*.

- Click the link for "FREE download of the book applications." Then, select the "All book files" link and respond to the resulting pages and dialog boxes. This will download a setup file named dvb8_allfiles.exe onto your hard drive.

- Use the Windows Explorer to find this exe file on your hard drive. Then, double-click this file and respond to the dialog boxes that follow. This installs the files in directories that start with C:\Murach\ADO.NET 3.5 VB, and then runs a batch file that copies the subdirectories of the C:\Murach\ADO.NET 3.5 VB\Excerise Starts directory to the C:\ADO.NET 3.5 VB directory.

How to prepare your system for this book

- If you want to attach the Payables database that's used by this book to a SQL Server Express database server that's running on your PC, use the Windows Explorer to navigate to the C:\Murach\ADO.NET 3.5 VB\Database folder and double-click on the db_attach.bat file.

- For more detailed instructions about preparing your system for this book, please see appendix A.

www.murach.com